Microsoft® Windows® XP Professional Administrator's Pocket Consultant, Second Edition

William R. Stanek

PUBLISHED BY
Microsoft Press
A Division of Microsoft Corporation
One Microsoft Way
Redmond, Washington 98052-6399

Library of Congress Control Number: 2004113976

Printed and bound in the United States of America.

1 2 3 4 5 6 7 8 9   QWE   8 7 6 5 4 3

Distributed in Canada by H.B. Fenn and Company Ltd.

Microsoft Press books are available through booksellers and distributors worldwide. For further informa-tion about international editions, contact your local Microsoft Corporation office or contact Microsoft Press International directly at fax (425) 936-7329. Visit our Web site at www.microsoft.com/mspress. Send comments to mspinput@microsoft.com.

Acquisitions Editor: Martin DelRe
Project Editor: Valerie Woolley
Technical Editor: Jim Johnson
Copy Editor: Roger LeBlanc
Indexer: William P. Meyers
Compositors: Kerri DeVault and Elizabeth Hansford
Development Editor: Devon Musgrave

Body Part No. X10-94979

Contents at a Glance

Part I   Windows XP Professional Essentials

1   Introduction to Windows XP Professional Administration..... 3
2   Configuring the Environment........................... 27
3   Configuring Hardware Devices and Drivers 65
4   Customizing Menus, the Windows Taskbar, and Toolbars 99
5   Optimizing the Desktop and Screen Appearance 117
6   Installing and Maintaining Programs 139

Part II   Windows XP Professional Core Administration

7   Managing User Access and Global Settings 159
8   Managing Laptops and Traveling Users 193
9   Configuring User and Computer Policies 209
10   Managing Disk Drives and File Systems 233
11   Managing File Security and Sharing 265
12   Configuring Offline Files, Disk Quotas, Shadow
      Copies, and More...................................... 295

Part III   Windows XP Professional Networking,
             Optimization, and Security

13   Configuring and Troubleshooting TCP/IP Networking...... 325
14   Managing Mobile Networking and Remote Access 347
15   Managing Advanced Internet Options 387
16   Optimizing Windows XP Professional 419
17   Troubleshooting Windows XP Professional 445
Appendix A   Working with Files and Folders 463

Table of Contents

Acknowledgments xvii

Introduction. xix

Part I   Windows XP Professional Essentials

1   Introduction to Windows XP Professional Administration 3

   Getting Started with Windows XP Professional 4
      Understanding Interface Changes 4
      Introducing New Mouse Tricks 7
      Introducing Security and Maintenance Changes. 8
      Improving the User Experience. 9
   Installing Administration Tools on Windows XP. 10
   Updating Group Policy Objects for Service Packs 11
   Introducing Support Services 12
   Working with the Automated Help System 14
      Using the Help And Support Center 14
      Introducing the Application Framework 16
      Monitoring System Health. 16
   Understanding and Using Error Reporting 18
      Error Reporting Basics 19
      Configuring Error Reporting 19
   Understanding and Using Automatic Updates. 21
      An Overview of Automatic Updates. 21
      Configuring Automatic Updates. 23
      Downloading and Installing Automatic Updates. 25
      Removing Automatic Updates to Recover from Problems. . 26
      Restoring Declined Updates 26

2   Configuring the Environment. 27

   Obtaining System Information 27
      Checking My Computer Information. 28
      Checking Advanced System Information 29
      Working with WMI Control 31
   Using System Support Tools 36
      Working with Standard Support Tools. 36
      Managing System Configuration, Startup, and Boot. 42

What do you think
    of this book?
We want to hear from you!

Microsoft is interested in hearing your feedback about this
publication so we can continually improve our books and learning
resources for you. To participate in a brief online survey, please visit:
www.microsoft.com/learning/booksurvey/

Managing System Properties 49
The General Tab 49
The Computer Name Tab 49
The Hardware Tab. 50
The Advanced Tab 50
The System Restore Tab 60
The Automatic Updates Tab 64
The Remote Tab 64

3   Configuring Hardware Devices and Drivers. 65
Installing and Maintaining Devices: The Basics 65
Accessing Device Utilities through Computer Management. . . . 67
Starting and using Computer Management 67
Managing Devices on Local and Remote Systems 68
Getting Started with Device Manager. 69
Using Device Drivers 70
Device Driver Essentials 70
Using Signed and Unsigned Device Drivers. 71
Configuring Device Drivers. 72
Tracking Driver Information 72
Installing and Updating Device Drivers. 73
Rolling Back Drivers 76
Removing Device Drivers for Removed Devices 77
Uninstalling Device Drivers. 77
Managing Hardware 78
Adding New Hardware 78
Enabling and Disabling Hardware 79
Troubleshooting Hardware 80
Customizing Hardware Device Settings 82
Configuring Keyboard Settings 83
Configuring Mouse Settings. 84
Configuring Sounds and Audio Devices. 85
Adjusting Regional Settings 91
Setting the Date and Time 92
Managing Internet Time 92
Internet Time Overview. 92
Configuring Internet Time in Workgroups. 97
Configuring Internet Time in Domains. 98

4   **Customizing Menus, the Windows Taskbar, and Toolbars** 99

   Optimizing Windows XP Menus 99
      Changing Between Classic and Simple Start Menu 99
      Customizing Classic Start Menu Options 100
      Customizing Simple Start Menu Settings 102
      Modifying Menus and Their Options 103
   Customizing the Taskbar 107
      Understanding the Taskbar 107
      Changing the Taskbar Size and Position 108
      Auto Hiding, Locking, and Controlling
      Taskbar Visibility 109
      Grouping Similar Taskbar Items 109
      Controlling Programs in the Notification Area 110
   Optimizing Toolbars 113
      Displaying Custom Toolbars 113
      Customizing the Quick Launch Toolbar 113
      Restoring the Show Desktop Button 114
      Creating Personal Toolbars 115
5   **Optimizing the Desktop and Screen Appearance** 117
   Using Keyboard Shortcuts to Master the Desktop 118
   Working with Desktop Themes 120
      Applying and Removing Themes 120
      Tailoring and Saving Themes 121
      Deleting Custom Themes 122
   Optimizing the Desktop Environment 122
      Setting the Desktop Background 122
      Controlling Default Desktop Icons 123
      Placing Custom Content on the Desktop 124
      Locking Custom Content on the Desktop 126
      Cleaning Up the Desktop 126
   Screen Saver Dos and Don'ts 127
      Configuring Screen Savers with Password Protection 128
      Reducing Screen Saver Resource Usage 129
      Setting Energy-Saving Settings for Monitors 129
   Modifying Display Appearance and Video Settings 131
      Configuring Display Appearance 131
      Configuring Video Settings 132
6   **Installing and Maintaining Programs** 139
   Program Installation: The Essentials 139
      Working with Autorun 140
      Program Setup and Compatibility 140
      Permissions Required for Installing Programs 141

Installing Programs Using Alternate Settings,
Permissions, and Configurations 142
Installing Programs without Autorun or Across
the Network 142
Making Programs Available to All or Selective Users 145
Running Setup Using Alternate Credentials 146
Special Installation Considerations for 16-Bit and
MS-DOS Programs 147
Forcing Program Compatibility 147
Managing Installed Programs 150
Uninstalling Programs 151
Resolving Failed Uninstalls 152
Working with the Windows Installer Clean Up Utility 152
Working with the Windows Installer Zapper 153
Removing Registry Settings for Failed Installations 154
Removing Partial or Damaged Registry Settings
for Individual Programs 155
Removing Adware, Spyware, and Other Rogue Programs 155

Part II   Windows XP Professional Core Administration

7   **Managing User Access and Global Settings 159**
Understanding User and Group Accounts 159
Local User Account Essentials 160
Group Account Essentials 162
Managing User Access to Workstations in Workgroups 164
Understanding User Access Levels in Workgroups 164
Creating Local User Accounts to Grant Access
to Workstations 165
Changing Access Levels for Users in Workgroups 166
Creating Workstation Passwords for User Accounts 167
Changing or Removing User Passwords 169
Recovering User Passwords 169
Controlling Logon: Welcome Screens and
Classic Logons 172
Configuring Fast User Switching 174
Logging On as Administrator 175
Managing User Access to Workstations in Domains 175
Understanding User Access Levels in Domains 175
Granting Access to Workstations 176
Changing Access Levels for Users 177
Changing and Resetting Workstation Passwords for
User Accounts 178

Requiring Secure Logon to Workstations 179
Denying Access to Workstations 179
Managing Stored Passwords 180
Adding Key Ring Entries. 180
Editing Key Ring Entries. 181
Removing Key Ring Entries 182
Using the .NET Passport Wizard to Create a Microsoft .NET
Passport 182
Managing Local User and Group Accounts 183
Creating Local User Accounts 183
Creating Local Groups for Workstations 185
Adding and Removing Local Group Members. 186
Enabling Local User Accounts. 187
Creating a Secure Guest Account. .187
Renaming Local User and Group Accounts 188
Deleting Local User and Group Accounts. 188
Managing Remote Access to Workstations. 189
Configuring Remote Assistance 189
Configuring Remote Desktop Access. 190
Making Remote Desktop Connections 191

8   Managing Laptops and Traveling Users 193
Configuring Power Management Settings 193
Using Power Schemes. 194
Using Alarms and Configuring Alarm Actions 197
Working with the Power Meter. 200
Configuring Advanced Behaviors and Power Buttons 202
Enabling or Disabling Hibernation. 202
Implementing Hardware Profiles 203
Configuring the Way Hardware Profiles Are Used. 203
Configuring Docked and Undocked Profiles 204
Copying, Renaming, and Deleting Hardware Profiles. 205
Configuring Networking for Laptops. 205
Configuring Dynamic IP Addresses 206
Configuring Alternate Private IP Addresses 207

9   Configuring User and Computer Policies 209
Group Policy Essentials. 209
Understanding Policy Application 210
Accessing and Using Local Group Policies 210
Accessing and Using Site, Domain, and Organizational
Unit Policies 211
Using the Group Policy Console. 212

Configuring Policies 212
    Viewing Policies and Templates 213
    Enabling, Disabling, and Configuring Policies 214
    Adding or Removing Templates. 214
Working with File and Data Management Policies 215
    Configuring Disk Quota Policies 215
    Configuring System Restore Policies 217
    Configuring Offline File Policies. 218
Working with Access and Connectivity Policies. 223
    Configuring Network Policies. 223
    Configuring Remote Assistance Policies 224
Working with Computer and User Script Policies 226
    Controlling Script Behavior through Policy 226
    Assigning Computer Startup and Shutdown Scripts. 228
    Assigning User Logon and Logoff Scripts. 229
Working with Logon and Startup Policies 230
    Hiding the Welcome Screen. 231
    Using Classic Logon vs. Simple Logon 231
    Setting Policy-Based Startup Programs 231
    Disabling Run Lists through Policy. 232

10   Managing Disk Drives and File Systems 233
Disk Management Essentials. 234
    Using My Computer. 234
    Using Disk Management. 235
    Using FSUtil and DiskPart 238
Working with Basic and Dynamic Disks 238
Using Basic and Dynamic Disks 240
    Understanding the Active, Boot, and System
    Designations 240
    Installing and Initializing New Physical Disks. 241
    Marking a Partition as Active 242
    Converting a Basic Disk to a Dynamic Disk and
    Vice Versa. 244
Working with Disks, Partitions, and Volumes. 245
Partitioning Disks and Preparing Them for Use. 247
    Creating Partitions and Logical Drives on Basic Disks 247
    Creating Simple, Spanned, and Striped Volumes on
    Dynamic Disks. 251
    Extending Volumes on Dynamic Disks 254
    Formatting Partitions and Volumes. 255
    Assigning, Changing, or Removing Drive Letters and
    Paths. 256

Assigning, Changing, or Deleting a Volume Label 257
Deleting Partitions, Volumes, and Logical Drives. 258
Converting a Volume to NTFS. 259
Recovering a Failed Simple, Spanned, or Striped Disk 261
Moving a Dynamic Disk to a New System. 261
Troubleshooting Common Disk Problems. 262

11   **Managing File Security and Sharing** **265**
File Security and Sharing Options. 265
Controlling Access to Files and Folders with
NTFS Permissions. 267
Understanding and Using the Basic Permissions 268
Assigning Special Permissions. 272
File Ownership and Permission Assignment. 276
Applying Permissions through Inheritance. 277
Determining the Effective Permissions and
Troubleshooting 281
Sharing Folders over the Network 282
Controlling Access to Network Shares. 282
Creating a Shared Folder 284
Using and Accessing Shared Folders 289
Using and Accessing Shared Folders for
Administration. 292

12   **Configuring Offline Files, Disk Quotas, Shadow Copies,**
and More **295**
Configuring Advanced Windows Explorer Options. 295
Setting Group Policy for Windows Explorer and
Folder Views. 296
Managing Drive Access in Windows Explorer 298
Managing File Type Associations 299
Configuring Offline Files 301
Understanding Offline Files. 301
Making Files or Folders Available Offline 301
Making Offline Files Unavailable 303
Configuring Computers to Use Offline Files. 304
Managing Offline Files on the User's Computer 305
Configuring Disk Quotas 310
Using Disk Quotas. 310
Enabling Disk Quotas on NTFS Volumes. 311
Viewing Disk Quota Entries. 313
Creating Disk Quota Entries 314
Updating and Customizing Disk Quota Entries 315

Deleting Disk Quota Entries 316

Exporting and Importing Disk Quota Settings 317

Disabling Disk Quotas 318

Using Shadow Copies and Recovering Shared Files 318

Configuring Shadow Copies on a Server 319

Viewing, Changing, and Restoring Shadow Copies 320

Part III   Windows XP Professional Networking, Optimization, and Security

13   **Configuring and Troubleshooting TCP/IP Networking** **325**

Installing Networking Components. 325

Installing Network Adapters. 326

Installing Networking Services (TCP/IP) 326

Configuring Local Area Connections. 327

Configuring Static IP Addresses 328

Configuring Dynamic IP Addresses and Alternate IP Addressing. 330

Configuring Multiple Gateways 331

Configuring DNS Resolution. 332

Configuring WINS Resolution. 334

Managing Local Area Connections 336

Enabling and Disabling Local Area Connections. 336

Checking the Status, Speed, and Activity for Local Area Connections 337

Viewing Network Configuration Information 338

Renaming Local Area Connections 339

Repairing Local Area Connections. 339

Troubleshooting and Testing Network Settings. 339

Performing Basic Network Tests. 340

Resolving IP Addressing Problems. 341

Releasing and Renewing DHCP Settings. 341

Registering and Flushing DNS 343

Performing Detailed Network Diagnostics. 344

14   **Managing Mobile Networking and Remote Access** **347**

Understanding Mobile Networking and Remote Access 347

Creating Connections for Remote Access. 349

Creating a Dial-Up Connection 350

Creating a Broadband Connection 357

Creating a VPN Connection 358

Configuring Connection Properties. 359

Configuring Automatic or Manual Connections 359

Configuring Proxy Settings for Mobile Connections 361

Configuring Connection Logon Information 363
Configuring Connection Attempts and Automatic
Disconnection 365
Configuring Redialing Options 366
Setting a Connection to Use Dialing Rules 366
Configuring Primary and Alternate Phone Numbers 367
Configuring Identity Validation 368
Configuring Networking Protocols and Components. 370
Enabling and Disabling the Windows Firewall for
Network Connections. 372
Establishing Connections. 373
Connecting with Dial-Up. 373
Connecting with Broadband. 376
Connecting with VPN. 376
Wireless Networking. 378
Wireless Network Devices and Technologies 378
Wireless Security 379
Installing and Configuring a Wireless Adapter. 381
Checking the Wireless Connection. 381
Connecting to and Configuring Available and
Preferred Wireless Networks. 383
Controlling Ad Hoc and Infrastructure Networking 385

15   **Managing Advanced Internet Options** 387
Customizing URLs. 388
Setting Home Page, Search, and Support URLs. 388
Customizing Favorites and Links. 389
Customizing the Browser User Interface 391
Creating Custom Titles. 391
Creating Custom Logos 392
Creating Custom Buttons for Internet Explorer 394
Setting Default Internet Programs 396
Managing Connection and Proxy Settings 398
Managing Connection Settings through Group Policy. . . .398
Enabling and Configuring Proxy Settings 400
Managing Browser Cookies and Other Temporary
Internet Files. 402
Secure Browsing and Local Machine Lockdown 404
Understanding the Browser Information Bar and
Browser Security Enhancements. 404
Using the Add-on Manager for Internet Explorer. 406
Configuring the Pop-up Blocker. 407

Managing Internet Explorer Security Zones 409
Understanding Security Zones 409
Controlling Security Zone Usage through
Group Policy 411
Configuring Security Zones through Group Policy 413
Configuring the Internet Security Zone 413
Configuring the Local Intranet Zone 414
Configuring the Trusted Sites Security Zone 415
Configuring the Restricted Sites Security Zone 416
Additional Policies That Might Be Useful for Managing
Internet Options 417

16   Optimizing Windows XP Professional 419
Improving Windows XP Performance 419
Optimizing Processor Scheduling 419
Optimizing Memory Management 420
Optimizing the Menu System 420
Optimizing Applications, Processes, and Services 421
Optimizing Disk Drives 422
Reducing Disk Space Usage 422
Checking for Disk Errors 423
Defragmenting Disks 424
Compressing Drives and Data 426
Encrypting Drives and Data 428
Enhancing Security 430
Using Security Center 430
Detecting and Resolving Windows XP Errors 437
Scheduling Maintenance Tasks 439
Understanding Task Scheduling 439
Viewing Tasks on Local and Remote Systems 439
Creating Tasks with the Scheduled Task Wizard 440
Changing Task Properties 442
Enabling and Disabling Tasks 443
Running Tasks Immediately 443
Copying and Moving Tasks from One System to Another . 443
Deleting Scheduled Tasks 444
Troubleshooting Scheduled Tasks 444

17   Troubleshooting Windows XP Professional 445
Using Remote Assistance to Resolve Problems 445
Understanding Remote Assistance 445
Creating Remote Assistance Invitations 447
Offering Remote Assistance 449

Responding To and Accepting Invitations. 450
Checking Invitation Status. 452
Expiring, Resending, and Deleting Invitations 453
Troubleshooting Startup and Shutdown .453
Resolving Startup Issues Using Safe Mode 453
Repairing Missing or Corrupted System Files. 454
Resolving Restart or Shutdown Issues 456
Repairing and Reinstalling Windows XP 456
Making Sense of Stop Errors 457
Using Restore Points. 459
Understanding System Restore. 459
Creating Manual Restore Points 461
Recovering from Restore Points 461

Appendix A Working with Files and Folders 463
Windows XP File Structures. 463
Working with FAT and NTFS Volumes 463
File Naming 465
Accessing Long File Names under MS-DOS 465
Exploring Files and Folders 466
Using Windows Explorer 467
Customizing Folder Views 470
Formatting Floppy Disks and Other Removable Disks 472
Copying Floppy Disks. 472
Managing Files 473
Selecting Files and Folders. 473
Copying Files and Folders by Dragging 473
Copying Files and Folders to Locations That
Aren't Displayed 474
Copying and Pasting Files 474
Moving Files by Cutting and Pasting. 474
Renaming Files and Folders. 475
Deleting Files and Folders 475
Creating Folders 475
Examining Drive Properties. 475
Examining File and Folder Properties 477

Index. 479

Acknowledgments

Writing *Microsoft Windows XP Professional Administrator's Pocket Consultant, Second Edition*, was a lot of fun—and a lot of work. Once you install Service Pack 2 or later on a computer running Windows XP, you'll find that many areas of the operating system are configured differently than before and that there is a major emphasis on security. Tracking down every security change from the minor to the major meant a lot of research and a lot of digging into the operating system internals. When all was said and done, I ended up with a book that was well over 800 pages in length and that just wasn't what a pocket consultant is meant to be. Pocket consultants are meant to be portable and readable—the kind of book you use to solve problems and get the job done wherever you might be. With that in mind, I had to go back in and carefully review the text, making sure I focused on the core of Windows XP administration. The result is the book you hold in your hand, which I hope you'll agree is one of the best practical, portable guides to Windows XP Professional.

It's gratifying to see techniques that I've used time and again to solve problems put into a printed book so that others might benefit from them. But no man is an island, and this book couldn't have been written without help from some very special people. As I've stated in all my previous books with Microsoft Press, the team at Microsoft Press is top-notch. Throughout the writing process, Valerie Woolley was instrumental in helping me stay on track and getting the tools I needed to write this book. Valerie did a fine job managing the editorial process. Lisa Pawlewicz was the copy editor for the book. She did a terrific job keeping everything consistent. Thanks also to Martin DelRe for believing in my work and shepherding it through production.

Unfortunately for the writer (but fortunately for readers), writing is only one part of the publishing process. Next came editing and author review. I must say, Microsoft Press has the most thorough editorial and technical review process I've seen anywhere—and I've written a lot of books for many different publishers. Special thanks to both Valerie and Lisa for helping me to meet review deadlines. Jim Johnson was the technical reviewer for the book. It was a great pleasure working with Jim. He watched the technical details very carefully and was always ready to help out if needed. Thank you, Jim—I hope we work together on many more books.

Last but not least, I want to thank my agents at Studio B, David Rogelberg and Neil Salkind. It has been a pleasure having you as my nonfiction agents over the past decade—hard to believe it's already been 10 years.

Hopefully, I haven't forgotten anyone—but if I have, it was an oversight. *Honest.* ;-)

Introduction

Microsoft Windows XP Professional Administrator's Pocket Consultant, Second Edition, is designed to be the perfect companion to the *Microsoft Windows Server 2003 Administrator's Pocket Consultant*. This book focuses on system and user issues for Windows XP Professional, featuring in-depth coverage of Windows XP Professional issues such as Windows desktop customization, mobile networking, and Group Policy. The book covers everything you need to know to perform core administration tasks for Windows XP Professional, and it has been updated to incorporate the latest service packs and changes. We added nearly 200 pages to bring you what we think is the best day-to-day administration guide to the Windows XP Professional operating system.

Because the focus is on giving you maximum value in a pocket-sized guide, you don't have to wade through hundreds of pages of extraneous information to find what you're looking for. Instead, you'll find exactly what you need to get the job done. In short, the book is designed to be the one resource you turn to whenever you have questions regarding Windows XP Professional administration. To this end, the book zeroes in on daily administration procedures, frequently used tasks, documented examples, and options that are representative while not necessarily being inclusive.

One of the goals is to keep the content concise enough so that the book remains compact and easy to navigate, but at the same time ensuring that the book is packed with as much information as possible—making it a valuable resource. Thus, instead of a hefty 1000-page tome or a lightweight 100-page quick reference, you get a valuable resource guide that can help you quickly and easily perform common tasks, solve problems, and implement everyday solutions for systems and users.

What Is This Book For?

Microsoft Windows XP Professional Administrator's Pocket Consultant, Second Edition, covers the Professional version of Windows XP. The book is designed for

- Current Windows system administrators
- Accomplished users who have some administrator responsibilities
- Administrators upgrading to Windows XP from previous versions
- Administrators transferring from other platforms

To pack in as much information as possible, I had to assume that you have basic networking skills and a basic understanding of the Windows XP operating system and that Windows XP is already installed on your system. With this in mind, I don't devote entire chapters to understanding Windows architecture, installing Windows XP, or startup and shutdown. I do, however, cover desktop customization, mobile networking, alternative TCP/IP configurations, user profiles, and system optimization.

I also assume that you are fairly familiar with Windows commands and procedures as well as the Windows user interface. If you need help learning Windows basics, you should read the Windows XP documentation.

How Is This Book Organized?

Microsoft Windows XP Professional Administrator's Pocket Consultant, Second Edition, is designed to be used in daily administration, and, as such, the book is organized by job-related tasks rather than by Windows XP features. The books in the *Pocket Consultants* family are the down-and-dirty, in-the-trenches books.

Speed and ease of reference are essential parts of this hands-on guide. The book has an expanded table of contents and an extensive index for finding answers to problems quickly. Many other quick-reference features have been added as well, including quick step-by-step instructions, lists, tables with fast facts, and extensive cross-references. The book is broken down into both parts and chapters. Each part contains an opening paragraph or two about the chapters contained in that part.

Part I, "Microsoft Windows XP Professional Essentials," covers the fundamental tasks you need for workstation administration. Chapter 1 introduces key administration tools, techniques, and concepts. Chapter 2 covers customizing system and environment settings. Chapter 3 explores hardware and device management. Chapters 4 and 5 focus on customizing the Windows desktop. You'll learn how to manage themes, color schemes, toolbars, and more. Finally, Chapter 6 discusses how to install, manage, and maintain programs.

In Part II, "Microsoft Windows XP Professional Core Administration," you'll find the essential tasks for managing access, permissions, and more. Chapter 7 discusses techniques you can use to manage user access to systems and configure global settings. Chapter 8 zeroes in on administration issues that are specific to laptops and traveling users. The chapter details considerations you should make when configuring laptops, such as power management, hardware profiles, and networking. Group Policy is the subject of Chapter 9. In this chapter, you'll find extensive lists that tell you exactly what policies you should use to manage permissions, rights, and capabilities. Chapter 10 discusses partitioning, monitoring, and optimizing drives. Chapter 11 explains how to configure shared folders and printers. Chapter 12 discusses additional file and folder options including offline files, shadow copies, and disk quotas.

Part III, "Microsoft Windows XP Professional Networking, Optimization, and Security," focuses on networking techniques and tasks, as well as on techniques you can use to improve performance and resolve problems. Networking is the subject of Chapter 13, which examines local area network settings. Here you'll find a complete discussion of installing and configuring TCP/IP networking. The chapter also covers troubleshooting networking and provides steps for performing detailed network diagnostics. Chapter 14 moves from corporate network environments to mobile environments, examining dial-up networking, wireless client connections, and remote access with virtual private networks (VPNs). Chapter 15 explains how to configure Internet options, such as default applications and trusted sites. You'll also learn how to customize Internet settings through Group Policy. In Chapter 16, you'll learn how to improve system performance, optimize drives, and enhance data security. You'll also learn how to resolve Windows XP errors and schedule routine maintenance tasks. In Chapter 17, you'll learn how to use Remote Assistance to remotely troubleshoot problems with devices, applications, and the Windows operating system itself. You'll also learn how to troubleshoot problems with startup and shutdown and how to create and use Restore Points. The hope is that after reading these chapters, you'll be able to improve the overall experience of your users and reduce downtime.

Conventions Used in This Book

I've used a variety of elements to help keep the text clear and easy to follow. You'll find code terms and listings in `monospace` type, except when I tell you to actually type a command. In that case, the command appears in **bold** type. When I introduce and define a new term, I put it in *italics*.

Other conventions include:

Note   To provide additional details on a particular point that needs emphasis

Best Practices   To examine the best technique to use when working with advanced configuration and administration concepts

Caution   To warn you when there are potential problems

Real World   To provide real-world advice when discussing advanced topics

Security   To point out important security issues

Tip   To offer helpful hints or additional information

I truly hope you find that *Microsoft Windows XP Professional Administrator's Pocket Consultant*, Second Edition, provides everything you need to perform the essential administrative tasks on Windows XP Professional systems as quickly and efficiently as possible. You are welcome to send your thoughts to me at williamstanek@aol.com. Thank you.

Support

Every effort has been made to ensure the accuracy of this book. Microsoft Press provides corrections for books through the World Wide Web at the following address:

http://www.microsoft.com/learning/support

If you have comments, questions, or ideas about this book, please send them to Microsoft Press using either of the following methods:

Postal Mail:

Microsoft Press
Attn: Editor, *Microsoft Windows XP Professional Administrator's Pocket
        Consultant, Second Edition*
One Microsoft Way
Redmond, WA 98052-6399

E-mail:

msinput@microsoft.com

Please note that product support isn't offered through these mail addresses. For support information about Windows XP Professional, you can call Windows Standard Support at (800) 936-4900 weekdays between 6 A.M. and 6 P.M. Pacific Time.

Part I
Windows XP Professional Essentials

The fundamental tasks you need for Microsoft Windows XP Professional administration are covered in Part I. Chapter 1 introduces key administration tools, techniques, and concepts. Chapter 2 covers configuring system and environment settings. You'll learn key techniques for obtaining system information, managing system support tools, and managing system configuration. Chapter 3 discusses techniques for configuring hardware devices and drivers. The chapter starts with a discussion on installing and maintaining devices and then goes on to detail how to configure device drivers, add new hardware, and customize hardware device settings. The next two chapters in this section focus on optimizing the user workspace. In Chapter 4, you'll learn how to optimize menus, the taskbar, and toolbars. In Chapter 5, you'll learn how to customize the desktop and optimize screen appearance. The emphasis is on improving the user experience and creating an enhanced operating environment. Chapter 6 rounds out the discussion of Windows XP Professional essentials by examining techniques for managing and maintaining programs.

Chapter 1

Introduction to Windows XP Professional Administration

In this chapter:

Getting Started with Windows XP Professional 4

Installing Administration Tools on Windows XP 10

Updating Group Policy Objects for Service Packs 11

Introducing Support Services 12

Working with the Automated Help System 14

Understanding and Using Error Reporting 18

Understanding and Using Automatic Updates. 21

Microsoft Windows XP Professional is designed primarily for workstations and network clients. The operating system is a direct replacement for Microsoft Windows NT 4 Workstation and Microsoft Windows 2000 Professional. A focus on client-related tasks sets Windows XP Professional apart from the server versions of the operating system, and, accordingly, Windows XP Professional supports a limited set of services while retaining excellent user support facilities. Beginning with Service Pack 2, Windows XP Professional has many security and maintenance enhancements that fundamentally change the way the operating system works in domains and workgroups. In this book, you'll learn about the many user support facilities built into Windows XP Professional, the administration of these systems, and the extensive changes to system security and maintenance implemented in Service Pack 2 and later. Although the focus of this book is on Windows XP Professional, the tips and techniques you learn can easily be applied to installations of Microsoft Windows Server 2003, especially if those server installations are being used by support staff rather than as actual servers with dedicated network roles. (In this book, "Windows XP" refers to Windows XP Professional unless otherwise indicated.)

Keep in mind that this book is meant to be used in conjunction with the *Microsoft Windows Server 2003 Administrator's Pocket Consultant* (Microsoft Press, 2003). In addition to coverage of broad administration tasks, the *Microsoft Windows Server 2003 Administrator's Pocket Consultant* examines directory services administration, data administration, and network administration. This book, on the other hand, zeroes in on user and system administration tasks. You'll find detailed coverage on the following topics:

- Customizing the operating system and Windows environment
- Configuring hardware and network devices
- Managing user access and global settings
- Configuring laptops and mobile networking
- Using remote management and remote assistance capabilities
- Troubleshooting system problems and much more

Getting Started with Windows XP Professional

If you are new to Windows XP administration or just getting started with Windows XP, you might be wondering what is new or different from previous versions of the Windows operating system. Let's start with the interface changes because they will make a big difference in your initial experience.

Understanding Interface Changes

Key interface changes involve the updated views and themes. Views provide different ways of looking at the Start menu and Control Panel. The Start menu views are as follows:

- **Classic Start Menu**   Shown in Figure 1-1, Classic Start Menu is the view used in previous versions of Windows. With this view, clicking Start displays a pop-up menu with direct access to common menus and menu items.

  With Classic Start Menu, you access administrative tools by clicking Start, clicking Programs, and then clicking Administrative Tools. Access Control Panel by clicking Start, pointing to Settings, and then clicking Control Panel.

 Note   With both the Classic Start Menu and the Simple Start Menu, the Administrative Tools menu is not displayed by default. You'll need to customize the Start Menu view to access this menu. See Chapter 4, "Customizing Menus, the Taskbar, and Toolbars," for details.

- **Simple Start Menu**   Shown in Figure 1-2, this view allows you to directly access commonly used programs and directly execute common tasks. You can, for example, click Start, click Log Off, and then select Log Off or press ENTER, rather than pressing CTRL+ALT+DELETE, clicking Log Off, and then selecting Log Off or pressing Enter as you would in Windows 2000.

  With Simple Start Menu, you access administrative tools by clicking Start, clicking All Programs, and then clicking Administrative Tools. Access Control Panel by clicking Start and then clicking Control Panel.

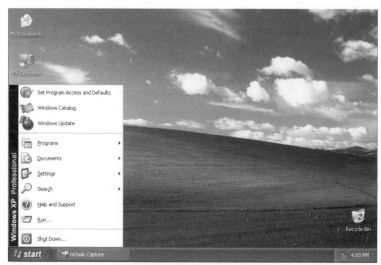

Figure 1-1 Classic Start Menu is the view used in previous versions of Windows.

Figure 1-2 Simple Start Menu is an updated view with direct access to commonly used programs and tasks.

Simple Start Menu is the default view. Complete details for customizing the Start menu are covered in Chapter 4, but for now you can use the following technique to change the Start menu view:

1. Right-click Start, and then select Properties. This displays the Taskbar And Start Menu Properties dialog box.
2. On the Start Menu tab, select the Start menu view you want to use and then click OK.

Control Panel has a similar set of views. These views are as follows:

- **Classic Control Panel**   The view used in previous versions of Windows, it displays a complete list of all Control Panel utilities with direct access to each.
- **Category Control Panel**   This organizes the Control Panel by category. Within categories, you can directly execute commonly used tasks or start a related Control Panel utility. Troubleshooting options are also provided for each category.

Category Control Panel is the default view. You can change the current view by clicking the Switch To link in the left pane of Control Panel. Figure 1-3 shows Category Control Panel with the Switch To link.

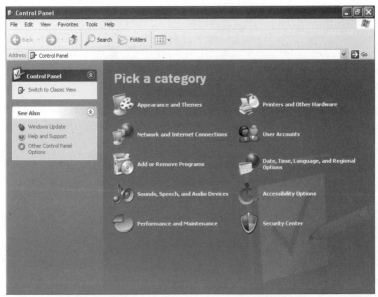

Figure 1-3   Category Control Panel, shown here, might be useful for beginners, but experienced administrators will prefer Classic Control Panel. Use the Switch To link to change the view.

Themes and your current display settings determine the look and feel of Windows XP in general. A theme is a predefined set of graphical elements, effects, and multimedia that is designed to enhance the look and feel of Windows XP. Themes are controlled using the Display utility found in Control Panel. If you are just getting started with Windows XP and want to use the default Windows 2000 theme while you are learning your way around the system, follow these steps:

1. Start the Display utility. The Themes tab should be selected by default, as shown in Figure 1-4.

2. Select Windows Classic from the Theme drop-down list box, and then click OK. You'll learn more about themes and personalizing the desktop in Chapter 4."

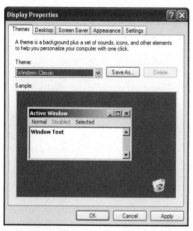

Figure 1-4   Use the Display utility to control the screen appearance of the Windows operating system.

Introducing New Mouse Tricks

Windows XP also has some mouse features that you might not have seen before. The following are some basic tips:

- **Double-click**   Double-clicking is the most common technique used for accessing folders and running programs. With a double-click, the first click selects an item and the second click opens or runs the item. In Windows XP you can also configure single-click open or run, meaning that moving the mouse pointer over an item selects it and a single click opens or runs the item.

  You can change the mouse click options with the Folder Options utility in Control Panel. Once you start the Folder Options utility, select the General tab, and then select Single-Click To Open An Item or Double-Click To Open An Item, as appropriate.

- **Right-click**   Most mouse devices have two buttons. In the default configuration, the left button is the primary button and the right button is the secondary button. The primary button selects or executes, and the secondary button brings up a shortcut menu for a specific item. Therefore, when someone says "right-click," that means you should push the secondary button while the mouse pointer is over a specific item.

You can change the primary and secondary buttons using the Mouse utility in Control Panel. Once you start the Mouse utility, select the Buttons tab and then select Switch Primary And Secondary Buttons as appropriate to configure the mouse for a left-handed user or clear this option to restore the default button settings for right-handed users.

Introducing Security and Maintenance Changes

Beginning with Service Pack 2, Microsoft introduced many fundamental changes in system security and maintenance. These changes affect just about every aspect of system administration, from network access to shared folders and beyond. Although the changes for computers in domains and workgroups are similar, the changes are much more noticeable in domains where many settings are locked down for administrator use only. In the default domain configuration, for example, you must be an administrator to install programs, to configure shared folders, and to change most local area connection properties. In a workgroup, on the other hand, standard accounts have administrator privileges by default so that these actions aren't restricted.

The security and maintenance changes cover four broad areas of the operating system.

- **Networking**   Changes to networking features are designed to lock down systems, making them more secure and less vulnerable to network-based attacks, such as viruses, worms, and cracking. With Service Pack 2 and later, the Internet Connection Firewall is reworked and renamed the Windows Firewall. There are significant changes to the Remote Procedure Call (RPC) service and the Distributed Component Object Model (DCOM). The changes affect the interaction of programs across networks and ensure that both RPC and DCOM work with the Windows Firewall. The Windows Firewall in turn is updated so that it is aware of RPC and DCOM. Another significant change is that Windows Firewall is enabled by default for all network connections on a computer using a single global configuration. For a detailed discussion of network protection technologies and the Windows Firewall, see the section of Chapter 16 entitled, "Enhancing Security".

- **Internet options**   Changes to Internet options affect the way Windows XP works with Internet browsing and e-mail messaging. There are significant changes to the standard Internet options and the browser configuration, which includes locking down the Local Machine zone to safeguard computers against malicious code, the addition of a pop-up blocker to prevent most pop-up windows from appearing, and additional advanced options to improve overall browser security. There are also changes to the configuration of Microsoft Outlook Express to prevent the execution of malicious code, which are similar to the changes implemented in Microsoft Office Outlook 2003. For a detailed discussion on Internet options, see Chapter 15, "Managing Advanced Internet Options."

- **Memory management**   Changes to memory management affect the core code of the operating system and are mostly behind the scenes. To better safeguard computers from memory-based vulnerabilities such as buffer overruns that allow too much data to be copied into areas of a computer's memory, the core components of the operating system were recompiled for Windows XP Service Pack 2. Core code was also updated to support hardware-enforced execution protection (referred to as a *no execute,* or *NX,* feature). Execution protection tells the CPU to mark all memory locations in an application as non-executable unless the location explicitly contains executable code. This prevents malicious code such as viruses from inserting itself into most areas of the memory because only specific areas of memory are marked as having executable code.

- **Computer maintenance** Changes for computer maintenance affect the way key features of the operating system work.The Add Or Remove Programs list is now filtered so that it doesn't display software updates by default—this makes it easier to find installed programs. Add Or Remove Programs can now be used to set program access and default programs for browsing, e-mail, and so on, and to control program accessibility. Windows Update Services and Automatic Updates have been changed in a number of ways—the biggest change is that the services are enabled by default to make automatic updates daily. The Windows installer has changed as well to include support for patch management, sequencing of update installation, and removal of support for some features that have potential vulnerabilities. A new feature, named Security Center, is also included to make it easier to manage security settings. These features are discussed as appropriate throughout this book.

Security   Windows XP Professional security has changed substantially. In domains, to perform most system modification tasks, you will need to use an account that is a member of the local machine's Administrators group. These changes are less noticeable—but no less extensive in workgroups—because most local user accounts created are members of the Administrators group by default.

Improving the User Experience

The XP in Windows XP stands for "experience," and as you might expect, Windows XP includes a number of features designed to improve the user experience, which means different things to different people.

To many users, a better experience means improved usability, manageability, and availability. Highly usable systems are easy to configure and customize. Highly manageable systems provide convenient, easy-to-use functions for local and remote management. Highly available systems are designed to have fewer problems and to recover quickly from problems that do arise.

Key features that directly support usability, manageability, and availability are as follows:

- **Support services** Provide the underlying architecture for key user support facilities.
- **Automated help** Provides a complete automated help system that can detect current and potential problems. You'll even find suggestions for resolving problems.

- **Error reporting**   Provides a mechanism for instantly submitting error reports to Microsoft.
- **Automatic updates**   Provide a mechanism for automatically updating the operating system and applications.

Each of these four features is discussed separately later in this chapter.

Installing Administration Tools on Windows XP

Many administrators use Windows XP as their desktop operating system. When you use Windows XP as your desktop you can remotely manage computers on the network in the same way as you do with Windows Server 2003 as long as you install the right tools. You'll find three sets of tools are essential in most environments:

- **Administrator Tools**   Include the tools you typically find on the Administrative Tools menu on a computer running a server version of the Windows operating system. Unlike a typical server configuration where only the tools related to services you've installed are available, the complete administrator tool set is available once you install the Administrator Tools. The Windows Server 2003 version of these tools can be installed on, and used with, all versions of Windows Server 2003 and Windows XP Professional. You can install these tools on a Windows XP system by completing the following steps:

1. Insert the Windows Server 2003 CD-ROM into the CD-ROM drive.
2. When the Autorun screen appears, click Perform Additional Tasks, and then click Browse This CD. This starts Windows Explorer.
3. Double-click I386 and then double-click Adminipak.msi. The complete set of Windows Server 2003 management tools are installed and can then be accessed from the Administrative Tools menu.

Note   The Windows 2000 administration tools are incompatible with Windows XP Professional and Windows Server 2003. If you upgraded to Windows XP Professional from Windows 2000 Professional, you'll need to re-install the Administrator Tools using the Windows Server 2003 version. The Windows Server 2003 tools are compatible with Windows 2000 Server, Windows XP Professional and Windows Server 2003.

- **Windows Support Tools**   Provide a set of utilities for performing common support and diagnostics tasks. handling everything from system diagnostics to network monitoring. The Windows Server 2003 version of these tools can be installed on, and used with, all versions of Windows Server 2003 and Windows XP Professional. You can install these tools on a Windows XP system by completing the following steps:

1. Exit any instances of the Help And Support console that you are running and then insert the Windows Server 2003 CD-ROM into the CD-ROM drive.
2. When the Autorun screen appears, click Perform Additional Tasks, and then click Browse This CD. This starts Windows Explorer.

3. Double-click Support and then double-click Tools. In the Tools folder, double-click Suptools.msi to start the Windows Support Tools Setup Wizard and follow the prompts.

4. After installation you can access the support tools through the Support Tools Help. Click Start, click Programs or All Programs as appropriate, click Windows Support Tools, and then select Support Tools Help.

■ **Windows Resource Kit Tools**   Provide an additional set of utilities as well as some third-party tools for administration. These tools are distributed on CD-ROM as part of the boxed resource kit set and also available as a free download from the Microsoft Windows Download Center. Use the Windows Server 2003 version of the Resource Kit to manage Windows XP and Windows Server 2003 computers. You can install the resource kit tools on a Windows XP system by completing the following steps:

1. Insert the Windows Server 2003 Resource Kit CD-ROM into the CD-ROM drive or double-click the executable file, Rktools.exe, that you downloaded from Microsoft.

2. When the Windows Resource Kit Tools Setup Wizard starts, click Next and follow the prompts.

3. When the installation is complete, you can access the resource kit tools through the Windows Resource Kit Tools Help. Click Start, click Programs or All Programs as appropriate, click Windows Resource Kit Tools, and then select Windows Resource Kit Tools Help

Updating Group Policy Objects for Service Packs

Most service packs support additional policies that can be used with computers running that service pack. Some of these additional policies can also be used with other operating systems as well as with later versions of the Windows operating system. On a Windows XP Professional computer with a particular service pack installed, you'll see the new policies as well as the standard policies if you examine the Local Computer policy. However, if you try to use the Windows XP Professional policies in a domain, you're going to have problems: the new policies won't be there. Don't worry, there's an easy way to fix this, and afterward you'll be able to set and enforce the new policies as appropriate throughout your domain.

New policies are implemented through a set of administrative templates. These templates contain the policy definitions for both the new policies and the standard policies. To push the policies out into the domain, you are going to need to update the appropriate Group Policy Objects (GPOs) in your domain. Once you make the update, compatible clients are able to take advantage of the enhanced policy set, and incompatible clients simply ignore the settings they don't support. Nothing else about how Group Policy is used has changed.

Note   You upgrade GPOs using a computer that has the latest service pack installed. Once you've performed the update and made any necessary changes, you can perform basic management, such as policy linking or blocking, using any computer. However, it is recommended that the actual policy editing be done on a computer with the latest service pack.

You update the domain GPO by following these steps:

1. Log on to a computer running Windows XP Professional and the latest service pack using an account with domain administrator privileges.

2. Click Start, and then click Run to open the Run dialog box. Afterward, type **mmc** in the Open field, and then click OK. This starts the Microsoft Management Console (MMC).

3. On the File menu, click Add/Remove Snap-In. This opens the Add/Remove Snap-In dialog box.

4. On the Standalone tab, click Add. In the Add Standalone Snap-In dialog box, click Group Policy Object Editor and then click Add.

5. In the Select Group Policy Object dialog box, click Browse, and select the default Group Policy Object for the site, domain, or organizational unit that you want to update, and then click OK.

6. Click Finish, click Close, and then click OK.

7. In the Group Policy snap-in, click the plus sign (+) next to Computer Configuration and then click the plus sign (+) next to User Configuration. When you expand these nodes, the current administrative templates are read in, and applied to, the GPO you've selected. Once Group Policy is refreshed, you can modify policy settings as necessary, and the changes will be updated as appropriate in the selected site, domain, or organizational unit.

Repeat this procedure to update the GPO for other sites, domains, or organizational units.

Introducing Support Services

Windows XP features built-in support services at several levels. If you access the Services node in the Computer Management administrative tool, you'll find a bundle of services dedicated to system support. These services include the following:

■ **Automatic Updates**   Responsible for performing automatic updates to the Windows XP operating system

■ **Background Intelligent Transfer Service**   Downloads data for programs when the computer is idle

■ **Help And Support**   Provides the application framework for automatic system monitoring

■ **MS Software Shadow Copy Provider**   Responsible for taking snapshots of the operating system and applications; works in conjunction with the Volume Shadow Copy service and is used primarily by the System Restore feature

■ **NetMeeting Remote Desktop Sharing**   Allows authorized users to remotely access a Windows desktop using Microsoft NetMeeting

■ **Remote Desktop Help Session Manager**   Manages and controls access to interactive help sessions

■ **System Restore Service**   Allows system files to be restored to a specific point in time, based on a snapshot

- **Volume Shadow Copy**   Creates shadow copies of disk volumes; primarily for the System Restore feature
- **Windows Installer**   Enables remote installation services to install, repair, and remove software
- **Windows Management Instrumentation**   Provides system management information
- **Windows Time**   Used to synchronize the system time with world time

These support services provide the foundation for the enhanced features in Windows XP. If they are not running or configured properly, you might have problems using certain support features. You can view these and other services in Computer Management by completing the following steps:

1. Click Start, point to Programs or All Programs as appropriate, then point to Administrative Tools, and finally select Computer Management. Alternatively, access Control Panel, double-click Administrative Tools, and then select Computer Management.

2. Right-click the Computer Management entry in the console tree and select Connect To Another Computer on the shortcut menu. You can now select the system whose services you want to view.

3. Expand the Services And Applications node by clicking the plus sign (+) next to it, and then select Services, as shown in Figure 1-5.

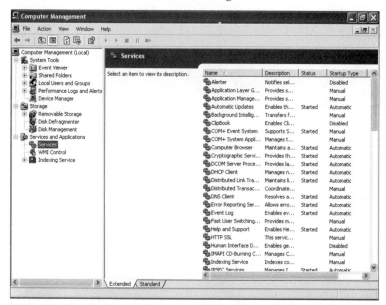

Figure 1-5   Use the Services view to manage services on Windows XP.

Working with the Automated Help System

The automated help system built into Windows XP is fairly complex. The system is designed to automatically monitor system health, perform preventative maintenance, and report problems so they can get resolved. The help system has the following three key components:

- A help center with integrated help facilities
- An application framework
- A monitor that gathers and logs state information

Using the Help And Support Center

The Help And Support Center is where you go to find system documentation and support services. You can start the Help And Support Center by clicking Start and then choosing Help And Support.

As you can see from Figure 1-6, the Help And Support Center is much different from the Help facilities built into previous versions of Windows. The Help And Support Center home page features links to online help documentation, support services, and recent news headlines. The Help And Support Center is designed to seamlessly integrate locally stored content and content made available through remote sites. Overall, the documentation is much more task-focused and solution-focused than previous versions.

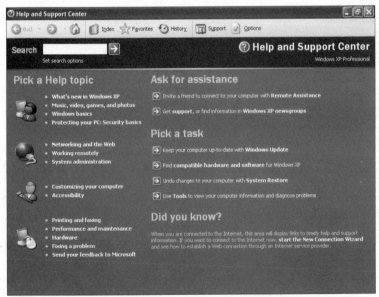

Figure 1-6   Use the Help And Support Center to find detailed technical information and to get support when you need it.

In the Ask For Assistance area of the Help And Support Center home page, you'll find a link labeled Get Support, Or Find Information In Windows XP Newsgroups. Click this link to access the integrated support utilities, including the following:

- **Ask A Friend To Help** Allows users to get live help from a technician. By clicking this link and sending a remote control invitation through an e-mail message, a user can get immediate help.

- **Get Help From Microsoft** Provides a list of online resources that you can use to contact Microsoft's Technical Support staff, to access support communities, and to get follow-up information, such as the status of a previously submitted support request.

- **Go To A Windows Web Site Forum** Allows users to access a help forum on the Web where they might be able to find answers to their questions.

The Ask A Friend To Help and Get Help From Microsoft options use the Remote Assistance feature (see Figure 1-7). Remote assistance is made possible through the Remote Desktop Help Session Manager service. If you are the technician receiving the remote control request, you see a control panel that allows you to view the user's desktop and to send chat messages to the user. You also have the option of taking control of the user's system, sending a file to the user's system, or exiting the session. If you take control of the user's system, you can configure the computer just as if you were sitting at the keyboard, and the user also sees these changes.

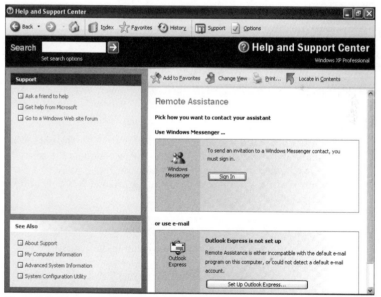

Figure 1-7 Remote Assistance is a useful tool when you want to troubleshoot users' problems. Not only can you directly access a user's desktop, but you can also chat with the user in real time.

Tip   In upcoming chapters, you'll learn more about the Help And Support Center and its features. In Chapter 2, "Configuring the Environment," you'll learn how to work with integrated utilities such as My Computer Information. In Chapter 17, "Troubleshooting Windows XP Professional," you'll learn more about assisted support and remote assistance.

Introducing the Application Framework

The Help And Support Center and the entire Windows XP help system are built on the application framework provided by the Windows service named Help And Support. As a Windows XP Professional administrator, you really don't need to understand the intricacies of the application framework. You should, however, know where the necessary files are stored so that you can check them if you must.

With this in mind, it is important to be aware that the Help And Support service runs under the SVCHOST.EXE process with the flags −K NETSVCS. When run in this mode, the SVCHOST.EXE process acts as a listener that monitors the health and well-being of the system on which it is running. The listener also periodically performs checkpoint operations that write system configuration information to the *%SystemRoot%*\Pchealth\Helpctr\Config\Checkpoint directory. In this directory, you'll find several files that are used as follows:

- **EDB.CHK**   A check file containing recovered file fragments
- **EDB.LOG**   A log file containing information useful in recovering the system configuration up to a point in time
- **RES1.LOG**   A reserved log file for the help system
- **RES2.LOG**   A reserved log file for the help system
- **TMP.EDB**   A temporary workspace for processing transactions

Once a checkpoint has been finalized, it is written to a database file in the *%System-Root%*\Pchealth\Helpctr\Database directory. This file is named HCDATA.EDB. The database also contains other types of help system information.

Note   Throughout this book you'll see references to *%SystemRoot%*. This is an environment variable used by Windows XP to designate the base directory for the Windows XP operating system, such as C:\Windows. For more information on environment variables, see Chapter 2, "Configuring the Environment."

Monitoring System Health

Status, a health monitor, is another key part of the Windows XP help system. Its goal is to collect system state information that can be used to identify current or potential system problems, such as an abnormal boot or a drive low on free space. The information can then be processed by the operating system and made available through the Help And Support Center console.

Status relies on a Windows service named Windows Management Instrumentation (WMI) to gather system information. If you examine this service, you'll find that it runs an executable named SVCHOST.EXE, which in turn uses WMIPRVSE.EXE to gather system information. The information gathered by the WMI provider service (WMIPRVSE) is obtained and displayed in Help And Support Center using separate executables. Help And Support Center runs under the HELPCTR.EXE executable, which provides the primary interface, and uses HELPHOST.EXE and HELPSVC.EXE to provide essential host listener and support services.

Viewing System Health Statistics

You can view the information gathered by Status by completing the following steps:

1. Click Start, and then select Help And Support for your Start menu view.
2. In the Pick A Task area of the Help And Support Center home page, you'll find a link labeled Use Tools To View Your Computer Information And Diagnose Problems. Click this link.
3. In the upper left pane, select My Computer Information. Then, in the right pane under My Computer Information, click View The Status Of My System Hardware And Software.
4. As shown in Figure 1-8, you'll see a summary of the system state. If there are any current or potential problems, they are identified, and you'll be given a link (if available) to a help document you can use to resolve the problem.

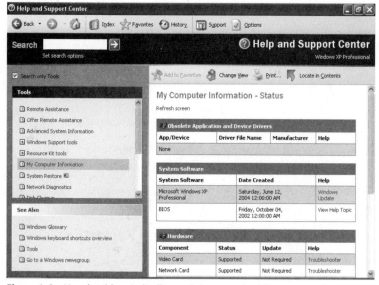

Figure 1-8   You should periodically monitor system health to ensure there are no current or potential problems on the system.

Note   Interestingly enough, system state information is gathered using the WMI service. WMI provides a set of interfaces that implement object classes for accessing the operating system and its components and representing their state values. One of these object classes is Win32_ComputerSystem, which has a property named BootupState. The bootup state indicates how the system was started. If the computer was started normally, the bootup state is set to Normal Boot. If the computer was started in Safe Mode, the bootup state is set to Fail-safe Boot. Property values gathered through WMI are reflected in the Help And Support Center under both My Computer Information and Advanced System Information.

Troubleshooting Problems with System Health Statistics

The Help And Support service must be running for Status to gather information. If the health statistics aren't accessible or are not being updated, you should ensure that the service is running and that it is configured properly. Services can be accessed from Computer Management or through the Services utility with either of the following techniques:

- With Classic Control Panel view, start Control Panel, click Administrative Tools, and then double-click Services.

- With Category Control Panel view, start Control Panel, click Performance And Maintenance, click Administrative Tools, and finally double-click Services.

You access Services on a remote system using Computer Management as discussed in the section of this chapter entitled "Using the Help And Support Center." Once you access Services, ensure that the Help And Support service is running. If it isn't, right-click the service and then select Start. The service should be configured to start up automatically. If it isn't, double-click the service, select Automatic as the Startup Type, and then click OK.

Another reason you might be experiencing problems obtaining system health information is if the system drive (the drive containing the Windows operating system) has no available space. The Help And Support service collects system health information and stores it in the data collection directory (*%SystemRoot%*\Pchealth\ Helpctr\Datacoll). State information collected by Status is stored in files formatted in Extensible Markup Language (XML), a markup language for structuring information. These files must be written properly so that they can be processed by the help subsystem. If the system drive is out of free space, you'll need to free some space so that system health information can be written to the drive.

Understanding and Using Error Reporting

Windows XP features a built-in error reporting system. The error reporting system allows you to send information about errors to Microsoft, and it is enabled by default for all Windows XP installations.

Error Reporting Basics

How an error is reported depends on where it originated. When a component or program error occurs, a dialog box appears asking if you want to report the problem. If you choose to report the problem, the error report is sent over the Internet to Microsoft. When an operating system error occurs, the system doesn't generate the error report until the next time you successfully boot and log on to the system. At this point, you again have the opportunity to report the problem.

Error reporting can be configured for the following specific areas:

■ **Windows Operating System**   Reports critical operating system errors that cause an error message to appear on a blue screen. The error report contains all the information that is displayed on the blue screen.

■ **Programs**   Reports illegal program operations and internal program errors that cause a program to stop working. With program errors, you can specify which programs should be monitored for errors and which shouldn't. By default, all program errors are presented to you for reporting, regardless of who the manufacturer is. You can change these settings to configure specific applications for which errors should or shouldn't be reported.

Note   When you configure error reporting, you can easily enable or disable error reporting for programs from Microsoft. There is no easy way, however, to specifically block the collection of non-Microsoft programs. They can be blocked only by naming them individually on the Do Not Report List.

The best news about error reporting is that if you report a problem for which there are possible solutions, you'll be able to get additional information that can help you troubleshoot. Possible solutions are shown in the Thank You dialog box that is displayed after you submit an error report.

Configuring Error Reporting

You can change error reporting settings by completing the following steps:

1. In Control Panel, start the System utility. Click the Advanced tab, and then click the Error Reporting button.

2. Select Enable Error Reporting, and then use the check box options to select areas to monitor. The options are Windows Operating System and Programs.

3. If you choose to report program errors, you can configure specific applications for which errors should or shouldn't be reported. Select Programs, and then click Choose Programs to specify the types of programs on which to report errors. (See Figure 1-9.)

Figure 1-9   Configuring error reporting for specific programs using the Choose Programs dialog box is a good idea. If you block errors from non-Microsoft programs, you can be certain that only errors for Microsoft components and applications are reported.

4. If you want to report errors for all programs, select All Programs.

5. If you want to report errors for specific programs, select All Programs In This List. You can now choose from the following options:

   Programs From Microsoft   Reports critical errors from Microsoft Programs, such as Microsoft Word, Excel, and PowerPoint. If your organization uses Microsoft Office and other Microsoft applications, you'll usually want to select this option to ensure that problems that you are experiencing get reported.

   Windows Components   Reports critical errors that cause component failure. The following are considered to be Windows components: Fax Services, Indexing Service, Management And Monitoring Tools, Internet Information Services, Message Queuing, Networking Services, Other Network File And Print Services, and Script Debugger.

6. To add more programs on which to report errors, click Add. This displays the Add Program dialog box. In this dialog box, type the complete file name (excluding the drive letter and path) of the program's executable, such as NOTEPAD.EXE, and then click OK. Repeat this step for each program that you want to add to the reporting list. If you make a mistake, select the program entry and then click Remove.

7. To ensure errors aren't reported on a program, click Add under Do Not Report Errors For These Programs. This displays the Add Program dialog box. In this dialog box, type the complete file name (excluding the drive letter and path) of the program's executable, such as NOTEPAD.EXE, and then click OK. Repeat this step for each program that you want to block from the reporting list.

8. Click OK.

To disable error reporting, complete the following steps:

1. In Control Panel, start the System utility. Click the Advanced tab, and then click the Error Reporting button.

2. Select Disable Error Reporting, and then click OK.

Understanding and Using Automatic Updates

The Automatic Updates feature helps you keep the Windows XP operating system up to date. It compares the programs, operating system components, and drivers installed on a system with a master list of items available and determines whether there are updates that should be installed.

An Overview of Automatic Updates

Automatic Updates is a client component that connects periodically to a designated server and checks for updates. Once it determines that updates are available, it can be configured to download and install the updates automatically or to notify users and administrators that updates are available. The server component to which Automatic Updates connects is either the Windows Update Web site hosted by Microsoft or a designated Windows Update Services server hosted by your organization.

Beginning with Service Pack 2 for Windows XP Professional, Automatic Updates has been modified to enhance system security. Automatic Updates now includes support for Microsoft Office, Microsoft SQL Server, and Microsoft Exchange and also provides for distribution of hardware drivers. This allows Automatic Updates to deliver changes for these applications and for hardware drivers, making the feature the central update mechanism for most system needs.

Unlike previous versions of Automatic Updates, which only distributed and installed critical updates, the Service Pack 2 and later versions supportsdistribution and installation of the following:

- **Critical updates**   Updates that are determined to be critical for the stability and safeguarding of a computer
- **Security updates**   Updates that are designed to make the system more secure
- **Update roll-ups**   Updates that include other updates
- **Service Packs**   Provides a comprehensive update to the operating system and its components, which typically include critical updates, security updates, and update roll-ups

A key part of the extended functionality allows Automatic Updates to prioritize downloads so that updates can be applied in order of criticality. This allows the most critical updates to be downloaded and installed before less critical updates. You can also control how a computer checks for new updates and how it installs them. The default polling interval used to check for new updates is 22 hours. Through Group Policy, you can change this interval. By default, computers install updates they've downloaded every day at 3:00 A.M. local time. You can modify the installation to require notification or change the install times if desired.

 Real World   Automatic Updates uses the Background Intelligent Transfer Service (BITS) to transfer files. BITS is a service that performs background transfers of files. Beginning with Service Pack 2 and later, BITS is updated to version 2.0. This new version improves the transfer mechanism so that bandwidth is used more efficiently, which in turn means less data is transferred with BITS 2.0 and the transfer is faster. Through Group Policy, BITS 2.0 can be configured to download updates only during specific times and to limit the amount of bandwidth used. You configure both settings using the Maximum Network Bandwidth That BITS Uses setting under Computer Configuration\Administrative Templates\Network\Background Intelligent Transfer Service in Group Policy. This policy is applicable only for computers using Windows XP Service Pack 2 and later or computers that have BITS 2.0 installed.

You can use Automatic Updates in several different ways. You can configure systems to do the following:

- **Automatically download recommended updates for my computer and install them**   With this option the operating system retrieves all updates at a configurable interval (22 hours by default) and then installs the updates at a scheduled time. This represents a major change in behavior because users are not required to accept updates before they are installed. Updates are instead downloaded automatically and then installed according to a specific schedule, which can be once a day at a particular time or once a week on a particular day and time.

- **Automatically download updates and notify the current user when they are ready to be installed**   With this option (the default), the operating system retrieves all updates as they become available and then prompts the user when they are ready to be installed. The user can then accept or reject the update. Accepted updates are installed. Rejected updates are not installed, but they remain on the system so that they can be installed later.

- **Notify the current user before downloading and installing any updates** With this option, the operating system notifies the user before retrieving any updates. If the user elects to download the update, she still has the opportunity to accept or reject the update. Accepted updates are installed. Rejected updates are not installed, but they remain on the system so that they can be installed later.

- **Disable automatic updates and allow updates only through a manual installation process**   When automatic updates are disabled, users are not notified about updates. You can, however, download updates manually from the Windows Update Web site (*http://windowsupdate.microsoft.com/*).

When Automatic Updates is configured for automatic update and install, users are not notified of update availability or installation. In a workgroup environment, an

Automatic Updates icon is placed in the notification area to provide an initial notification. This icon is a yellow shield with an exclamation point. Clicking this icon allows you to configure the initial update and installation schedule. Whenever there are notifications, the icon is displayed as well. In an Active Directory domain environment, an Automatic Updates icon is not placed in the notification area. It is assumed that in a domain administrators will configure Automatic Updates for users. Notifications are only displayed for users if you change the default configuration to require user interaction.

Automatic updates appear on the Install/Uninstall tab of the Add/Remove Programs dialog box, just like any other program you install. You can remove an automatic update from there the same way that you uninstall any other program. The only difference is that updates are not displayed by default. For details, see "Removing Automatic Updates to Recover from Problems," later in this chapter.

As part of the install process for Automatic Updates, computers might need to be restarted. With the introduction of Service Pack 1, several enhancements were made to reduce the number of restarts required and allow administrators to control whether and how restarts occur. You can control restart of a computer using Group Policy.

Configuring Automatic Updates

In an Active Directory domain, you can centrally configure and manage Automatic Updates using the policy settings under Computer Configuration\Administrative Templates\Windows Components\Windows Update and under User Configuration\Administrative Templates\Windows Components\Windows Update. Table 1-1 summarizes the key policies.

Table 1-1   Policies for Automatic Updates

Policy Setting	Description
Allow Automatic Updates Immediate Installation	When enabled, this setting allows Automatic Updates to immediately install updates that do not interrupt Windows services or require the computer to be restarted. These updates are installed immediately after they are downloaded and are ready to install.
Allow Non-Administrators To Receive Update Notifications	When enabled, this setting allows any user logged on to a computer to receive update notifications as appropriate for the Automatic Updates configuration. If disabled or not configured, only administrators receive update notifications.
Automatic Updates Detection Frequency	When enabled, this setting sets the interval to be used when checking for updates. By default, computers check approximately every 22 hours for updates. If you enable this policy and set a new interval, that interval will be used with a wildcard offset of up to 20 percent of the interval specified. This means that if you set an interval of 48 hours, the actual polling interval would be dependent on the computer and be between 38 and 48 hours.

Table 1-1   Policies for Automatic Updates

Policy Setting	Description
Configure Automatic Updates	When you enable this setting, you can configure how Automatic Updates works using similar options to those described later in this chapter. You can also schedule the installation.
Delay Restart For Scheduled Installations	By default, when a restart is required after an automatic update, the computer is restarted after a 5 minute delay. To use a different delay, enable this policy and then set the delay time.
Enable Client-side Targeting	When enabled, this setting allows an administrator to define a target group for the current Group Policy Object. Client-side targeting allows administrators to control which updates are installed on specified groups of computers. Before an update is deployed, it must be authorized for a particular target group.
No Auto-restart For Scheduled Automatic Updates Installations	When enabled, this setting specifies that the computer will not automatically restart after installing updates that require a restart if a user is currently logged on. Instead, Automatic Updates will notify the user that a restart is needed and wait until the computer is restarted. Restarting the computer enforces the updates.
Re-prompt for Restart With Scheduled Installations	When enabled and when Automatic Updates is configured for scheduled installation of updates, this setting ensures the logged-on user is prompted again after a set interval if a restart was previously postponed. If the setting is disabled or not configured, the default re-prompt interval of 10 minutes is used.
Remove Access To Use All Windows Update Features	When you enable this setting, all Windows Update features are removed. Users are blocked from accessing Windows Update, and automatic updating is completely disabled.
Reschedule Automatic Updates Scheduled Installations	When enabled, this setting specifies the amount of time for Automatic Updates to wait after system startup before proceeding with a scheduled installation that was previously missed.
Specify Intranet Microsoft Update Service Location	When enabled, this setting allows you to designate the fully qualified domain name of the Microsoft Update Services server hosted by your organization and of the related statistics server. Both services can be performed by one server.

You can configure automatic updates on a per computer basis by completing the following steps:

1. From Control Panel, double-click System. Then select the Automatic Updates tab in the System Properties dialog box, as shown in Figure 1-10.

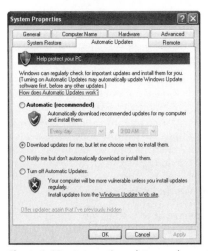

Figure 1-10 Automatic updates can be configured differently for different user groups. Select the option that makes the best sense for your environment.

2. Select one of the following update options:

   Automatic   This is the best option to use when you want the automatic update process to be seamless and occur behind the scenes. This option ensures updates are downloaded and installed in a specific way. If you select this option, you can also set an install schedule. Choose Every Day and an install time to install updates daily. Choose a specific day of the week and an install time to install updates once a week.

   Download Updates For Me, But Let Me Choose When To Install Them   This is the best option to use when you want to be sure users download updates, but you want users to be able to control whether updates are installed. However, this option doesn't ensure that updates will be installed.

   Notify Me But Don't Automatically Download Or Install Them   This option allows users to control whether downloads occur at all. Use this option for users who like more control over their environment.

   Turn Off Automatic Updating   This option turns off Automatic Updates completely.

3. Click OK.

Downloading and Installing Automatic Updates

When the Automatic Updates feature is enabled and configured to require notification, a bubble appears over the update icon announcing the availability of an update when it becomes available. Click the Automatic Updates icon to open the Automatic Updates window. From that window, click Install/Download if you have chosen to automatically download or if you have chosen to be notified before the download. This starts the Automatic Updates process. You can also click Remind Me Later to postpone the update. Once the updates are downloaded, you are again notified that the updates are ready to be installed. You are then able to choose which updates to install, or you can simply install all the updates.

If you want to see more information about the update or be able to selectively enable or disable update components, click the Details button. You then see descriptive information on each update. To disable an update for a specific component, clear the related check box to hide the update. When you are ready to proceed, you can begin the installation. Any updates that you've elected not to install (hidden) can be accessed again from the Automatic Updates tab in the System Properties dialog box by clicking the Offer Updates Again That I've Previously Hidden link. Keep in mind that only users who are members of the local administrators group can add or remove programs—this includes Automatic Updates.

 Caution   Some updates require that you restart the computer. If you are about to perform an update, have users save their work before you begin the process. If you have users perform updates themselves, make sure they know that they might have to restart.

Removing Automatic Updates to Recover from Problems

If an automatic update causes a problem on a system, don't worry. You can remove an automatic update in the same way that you uninstall any other program. Simply follow these steps:

1. In Control Panel, double-click Add Or Remove Programs. The Add Or Remove Programs dialog box is displayed with the Change Or Remove Programs button selected.

2. Updates are not displayed by default. To show updates that have been installed, click the Show Updates check box.

3. Select the update that you want to remove, and then click Remove. Repeat this step to remove other updates as desired.

4. Click Close. If the system needs to be restarted, you'll see a restart prompt.

Restoring Declined Updates

If a user declines an update that you want to install, you can restore the update so that it can be installed. To do this, complete the following steps:

1. From Control Panel, double-click System. Then select the Automatic Updates tab in the System Properties dialog box.

2. Click Offer Updates Again That I've Previously Hidden.

3. Windows XP will unhide the declined updates so that they can be reselected and installed. Click the Automatic Updates icon in the notification area, and then choose the updates that you want to install.

Chapter 2

Configuring the Environment

> **In this chapter:**
> Obtaining System Information 27
> Using System Support Tools 36
> Managing System Properties 49

Managing the operating system configuration is a key part of Microsoft Windows XP administration. (In this book, "Windows XP" refers to Windows XP Professional unless otherwise indicated.) In day-to-day operations, nothing affects your job more than the operating system environment. As a system administrator, you should know how to track key system information and monitor the status of system components. You should know how to manage system configuration files, such as BOOT.INI and WIN.INI. You should also know how to configure system properties with Control Panel's System utility. These and other tasks related to configuring the operating system environment are covered in this chapter.

Note Keep in mind that to configure system, hardware, and environment settings, the account you use must have the appropriate access permissions. In a domain, this typically means that the account must be a member of the Domain Administrators group. For a workgroup, this typically means the local machine account must have administrator privileges.

Obtaining System Information

In the Help And Support services toolkit, you'll find several tools for obtaining system information. These tools include the following:

- **My Computer Information** My Computer Information is a tool for obtaining summary information concerning system configuration and resource availability.
- **Status** Status is a tool for checking the overall health of a system. You can use Status to identify current or potential system problems, such as an abnormal boot or a drive low on free space.
- **Advanced System Information** Advanced System Information is a tool for obtaining detailed system statistics regarding configuration and resource availability. You can also use Advanced System Information to troubleshoot system problems.

My Computer Information, Status, and Advanced System Information gather most of their statistics using the Windows Management Instrumentation (WMI) service. If there are problems with the WMI service or its configuration, these utilities will not function properly. You manage the configuration settings for WMI using WMI Control. The following sections examine My Computer Information, Advanced System Information, and WMI Control. Status was covered in the section "Monitoring System Health" in Chapter 1, "Introduction to Windows XP Administration."

Checking My Computer Information

My Computer Information provides summary information regarding the system that you are currently logged on to. If you are logging on to a user's system for the first time and want to confirm the system configuration, this is a good resource to use. You can also direct users to this utility if they have questions about the system configuration. To access My Computer Information, follow these steps:

1. Click Start, and then select Help And Support.

2. On the Help And Support Center home page, under Pick A Task, click Use Tools.

3. In the left pane, under the Tools heading, click My Computer Information.

4. Under What Do You Want To Do? you now have the following options:

   ❑ **View General System Information About This Computer**   ❑Displays summary information about the computer, its hardware configuration, and operating system version.

   ❑ **View The Status Of My System Hardware And Software**   ❑Displays System Health statistics for hardware components, drivers, system software, hard disks, and random access memory (RAM) as discussed in Chapter 1 in the section entitled "Monitoring System Health."

   ❑ **Find Information About The Hardware Installed On This Computer**   Provides summary information about system hardware (such as local disk, display, video card, modem, sound card, USB controller, network card, and memory) that includes manufacturer, model, and drivers.

   ❑ **View A List Of Microsoft Software Installed On This Computer**   ❑Provides product identification, installation dates, and descriptions for Microsoft software installed on the computer. It also provides summary information for Dr. Watson that includes a date/time and a description of the problem that caused a crash.

The statistics for My Computer Information are gathered using the WMI service, which provides a set of interfaces for accessing the operating system and its components and representing their state values. As Figure 2-1 shows, the general information gathered includes the following:

- Computer model and basic input/output system (BIOS) version

- Operating system version, service pack, installation location, last update, and language

- Total physical memory as well as processor type, speed, and version

- Computer name, domain or workgroup, time zone, country/region, network role, proxy server, and Internet Protocol (IP) address
- Total hard disk capacity, total disk space available, and total disk space used

Figure 2-1   My Computer Information is useful to gather basic system information.

Tip   If you have problems obtaining computer information, check the credentials used by the WMI service, as discussed in the section "Working with WMI Control," later in this chapter. These credentials must be set properly.

Checking Advanced System Information

When you want to get detailed system information or check computer information on remote systems, use Advanced System Information. When you select View Detailed System Information or otherwise access MSINFO32.EXE, you can access the System Information tool. As shown in Figure 2-2, the System Information tool provides detailed information on several major areas of the operating system:

- **Hardware Resources**   Provides detailed information on input/output (I/O), interrupt requests (IRQs), memory, direct memory access (DMA), and Plug and Play devices. A key area you'll want to check if a system is having a device problem is the Conflicts/Sharing node. This area provides a summary of devices that are sharing resources or causing system conflicts.
- **Components**   Provides detailed information on installed components from audio codecs to input devices to universal serial bus (USB) ports. A key area you'll want to check if a system is having a component problem is the Problem Devices node. This area provides information on components that have errors.

■ **Software Environment**   Provides detailed information on the running config-uration of the operating system. When you are troubleshooting problems with a remote system, you'll find the Software Environment area to be extremely useful. In addition to drivers, environment variables, print jobs, and network connections, you can also check running tasks, services, program groups, and startup programs.

■ **Internet Settings**   Provides detailed information on the configuration of Internet options, primarily Microsoft Internet Explorer. You can check file ver-sions being used by Internet Explorer, connection configuration, security set-tings, caching, and content usage.

■ **Applications**   When available, provides detailed information on installed applications, such as Microsoft Word. Under the Microsoft Office Environ-ment node, you'll find information on open database connectivity (ODBC) drivers and object linking and embedding database (OLE DB) providers regis-tered and available for use with Microsoft Office applications.

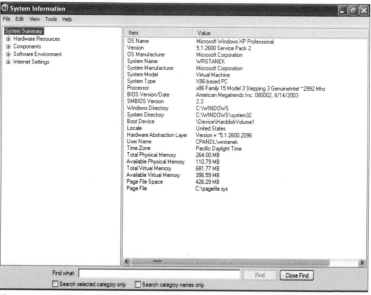

Figure 2-2   Advanced System Information can help you troubleshoot system configura-tion problems.

  Note   You can view system summaries by selecting the System Summary node in the System Information tool. The information is similar to that pro-vided by My Computer Information. As with My Computer Information, all configuration statistics provided are collected using the WMI service.

To access Advanced System Information, follow these steps:

1. Click Start, and then select Help And Support.
2. On the Help And Support Center home page, click Use Tools under Pick A Task.
3. In the left pane under the Tools heading, click Advanced System Information.
4. You now have the following options:

   ❑ **View Detailed System Information** ❑Runs MSINFO32.exe and provides very detailed information on the system. Use this tool to find hardware conflicts and component issues, and to determine environment settings.

   ❑ **View Running Services** ❑Provides an overview of services running on the system and is a quick way to find the executable path, status, and startup options for multiple services.

   ❑ **View Group Policy Settings Applied** ❑Provides detailed information on the policy that is applied to the current computer and the currently logged on user. You can use this information to double-check the application of Group Policy to individual computers and users in the domain.

   ❑ **View The Error Log** ❑Provides summary information on errors logged in the event logs. You can use this information to track down errors quickly without having to go through multiple event logs.

   ❑ **View Information For Another Computer** ❑Allows you to access My Computer and Advanced System information on remote computers.

If you want to browse configuration information for a remote computer, follow these steps:

1. Access Advanced System Information. Under What Do You Want To Do?, select View Information For Another Computer. This will display the View Remote Computer dialog box.
2. In the View Remote Computer dialog box, type the computer name in the field provided.
3. Click OK. The account you use must have the appropriate administrator access permissions for the domain or the local machine as appropriate. If you have other problems obtaining information from a remote system, check the credentials used by the WMI service, as discussed in the following section of this chapter.

Working with WMI Control

WMI is a key part of the Windows XP operating system. It is used to gather system statistics, monitor system health, and manage system components. To work properly, WMI relies on the WMI service. This service must be running and properly configured for the environment.

The sections that follow discuss how to access WMI Control and configure key properties, such as logon credentials, logging, and repository backups.

Accessing WMI Control on Local and Remote Systems

You control the configuration of the WMI service through WMI Control, which can be accessed on a local or remote system using the following steps:

1. Click Start, point to Programs or All Programs as appropriate, point to Administrative Tools, and then click Computer Management. Alternatively, access Control Panel, double-click Administrative Tools, and finally select Computer Management.

2. Right-click the Computer Management entry in the console tree, and select Connect To Another Computer on the shortcut menu. You can now choose the system whose services you want to manage.

3. Expand the Services And Applications node by clicking the plus sign (+) next to it. Next, click WMI control to select it (this is necessary so the control is read in). Right-click WMI Control, and then select Properties.

4. You can now use the WMI Control Properties dialog box to configure WMI.

As shown in Figure 2-3, the WMI Control Properties dialog box has the following tabs:

■ **General**   Fields on this tab provide summary information for the system and WMI. By default, WMI uses the credentials of the current user to obtain system information. You can set different credentials by clicking Change and updating the logon information.

■ **Logging**   WMI maintains error logs that can be used for troubleshooting problems with the WMI service. These logs are stored by default in *%System-Root%*\System32\Wbem\Logs. You can set a different logging level, size, and location using the fields on the Logging tab.

■ **Backup/Restore**   Statistics gathered by WMI are stored in a repository. By default, this repository is located in *%SystemRoot%*\System32\Wbem\Repository. These statistics are automatically backed up at regular intervals. You can back up or restore the repository manually using the fields on this tab.

■ **Security**   Security settings determine who has access to different levels of WMI statistics. By default, the Administrators group has full access to WMI and the interactive Everyone group has permissions to execute methods, enable accounts, and write gathered statistics.

■ **Advanced**   Advanced settings determine the default namespace for WMI. The default namespace is used in WMI scripting when a full namespace path isn't set for a WMI object. You can change the default setting by clicking Change, selecting a new default namespace, and then clicking OK.

 Note   WMI maintenance files, logs, and repositories can use up a considerable amount of disk space on a system. On average, these files used 40 MB on my test systems—the bulk of this (25–30 MB) being used to maintain repository backup files.

Figure 2-3   WMI Control is used to manage the configuration of the WMI service.

Setting WMI Logon Credentials

By default, WMI uses the credentials of the current user to obtain system information. You can set different credentials by completing the following steps:

1. Access the WMI Control Properties dialog box.
2. On the General tab, notice the logon credentials being used. These credentials are either <Currently Logged On User> or the name of a specific user.
3. Display the WMI Logon dialog box by clicking Change.
4. To have WMI log on as the current user, select Log On As Current User. Otherwise, clear this check box and set a specific user name and password for WMI logon.
5. Click OK, and then click OK again.

Configuring WMI Logging

WMI maintains log files that can be used for troubleshooting problems with the WMI service. These logs are stored by default in *%SystemRoot%*\System32\Wbem\Logs and include:

- **FRAMEWORK.LOG**   Contains logging information for the WMI application framework
- **MOFCOMP.LOG**   Contains logging information related to parsing Managed Object Format (MOF) files and creating framework objects
- **NTEVT.LOG**   Contains event logs for WMI, which can be used to track errors and warnings

> **Note**   MOF is part of the WMI system. MOF files tell the Common Information Model (CIM) repository what classes and class instances to add—they do so by describing the management interface of the hardware. MOFCOMP.LOG is the log file for the MOF Compiler, which is the tool that actually inserts the MOF data in the CIM repository.

- **REPLOG.LOG**   Contains logging information for the WMI repository and includes repository upgrade information

- **SETUP.LOG**   Contains logging information from the original installation of Web-Based Enterprise Management (WBEM)

- **WBEMCORE.LOG**   Contains information regarding core tasks performed by WMI and the WBEM framework, including queries and function calls

- **WBEMESS.LOG**   Contains information regarding the event system that WMI uses to manage event providers and event listeners (consumers)

- **WBEMPROX.LOG**   Contains error codes for logon and Distributed Component Object Model (DCOM) connections to objects

- **WBEMSNMP.LOG**   Contains log information generated by Simple Network Management Protocol (SNMP) that is used in conjunction with WMI

- **WINMGMT.LOG**   Contains log information generated by WMI management tasks, such as the stopping of a ResyncTask that has timed out

- **WMIADAP.LOG**   Contains log information for WMI adapters

- **WMIPROV.LOG**   Contains log information for WMI providers

By default, the WMI logs contain errors only and are restricted to 65 KB in size. You can change these settings by completing the following steps:

1. Access the WMI Control Properties dialog box, and then click the Logging tab, shown in Figure 2-4.

Figure 2-4   Logs are useful in troubleshooting problems with WMI but aren't otherwise essential.

2. On the Logging tab, notice the current logging configuration.

3. To change the level of logging, select one of the following options:

   ❏ **Disabled**   Turns WMI logging off, which can provide a slight performance boost for WMI.

❑ **Errors Only**   Sets logging so that only errors are logged. This is the default setting.

❑ **Verbose**   Turns on detailed logging, which can be used for troubleshooting WMI problems. Because verbose logging uses additional system resources and can slow the performance of WMI, don't use this option unless it's necessary to resolve problems.

4. Optionally, enter a new value for Maximum Size. This setting controls the byte size of log files. The default is 65,536 bytes (65 KB).

5. By default, WMI log files are stored in *%SystemRoot%*\System32\Wbem\Logs. If you want to set a new folder location, click Browse and use the Browse For Folder dialog box to select a new logging location. Then click OK to close that dialog box.

6. Click OK.

Backing Up and Restoring the WMI Repository

Information gathered by WMI is stored in a collection of system files called a *repository*. By default, the repository files are stored under *%SystemRoot%*\System32\Wbem\ Repository. The repository is the heart of WMI and the Help And Support services framework. Information is moved through the repository using a staging file. If repository data or the staging file becomes corrupt, WMI might not function properly. This condition is usually temporary, but you can safeguard against it by backing up the repository file manually.

To back up the WMI repository manually, complete the following steps:

1. Access the WMI Control Properties dialog box, and click the Backup/Restore tab.

2. Click Back Up Now. Next, use the Specify A Name dialog box to set the file location and name of the WMI backup file, and then click Open.

3. The Backup In Progress dialog box is displayed while the recovery file is being created. The recovery file is saved with an .rec extension, and its size depends on how much information is being stored. Usually this file is between 6 and 15 MB in size.

If you later need to restore the WMI repository from a backup file, complete these steps:

1. Access the WMI Control Properties dialog box, and click the Backup/Restore tab.

2. Click Restore Now. Next, use the Specify A Backup File To Restore dialog box to set the location and name of the existing recovery file, and then click Open.

3. The Restore In Progress dialog box is displayed temporarily, and then you'll see a warning prompt. Click OK.

4. Your connection to WMI Control is broken. Once the restore operation is complete, you can reconnect to the computer. To do this, close and reopen the WMI Control Properties dialog box. This forces WMI Control to reconnect to the local or remote computer but you can only do this if the restore is complete.

Note If the connection fails, it usually means that WMI Control isn't finished restoring the repository. Wait for another 30 to 60 seconds, and then try again.

Using System Support Tools

The Help And Support Center provides access to tools you can use to manage and maintain Windows XP systems via the Tools console. You'll also find a standard set of tools on the Tools menu of the System Information utility (MSINFO32.EXE).

Working with Standard Support Tools

The Tools console provides quick access to key system support tools. Once you access Help And Support Center, under Pick A Task, click Use Tools to display a list of available tools. Tools that are available include the following:

- **Backup (NTBACKUP.EXE)** Runs Backup, which you can use to back up and recover the Windows XP system as described in Chapter 15 of *Microsoft Windows Server 2003 Administrator's Pocket Consultant* (Microsoft Press, 2003).

- **Disk Cleanup (CLEANMGR.EXE)** Runs the Disk Cleanup utility, which examines disk drives for files that aren't needed or can be compressed. By default, Disk Cleanup examines temporary files, the Recycle Bin, and catalogs used by the Content Indexer to see whether there are files that can be deleted. Disk Cleanup also examines files that haven't been used in a while and recommends that they be compressed, which can save a considerable amount of disk space.

- **Disk Defragmenter (DFRG.MSC)** Runs the Disk Defragmenter utility, which examines disk drives for fragmentation and can then be used to defragment the drive. A drive with many fragmented files can reduce the system's performance. See Chapter 16, "Optimizing Microsoft Windows XP Professional," for more information about this utility.

- **Network Diagnostics** Scans the system, examining hardware and software configurations for networking problems. This can be used to troubleshoot connectivity issues with Transmission Control Protocol/Internet Protocol (TCP/IP) and Domain Name System (DNS) as well as issues with modems, network adapters, and network clients. See Chapter 13, "Configuring and Troubleshooting TCP/IP Networking," for details on using this utility.

- **Remote Assistance** Allows you to create a remote assistance invitation that can be used to get remote help from a technician. Remote Assistance is discussed in detail in Chapter 18, "Troubleshooting Windows XP Professional."

- **Offer Remote Assistance** Allows you to offer remote assistance to a user. If the user accepts the offer, you can troubleshoot problems on his system as discussed in Chapter 18.

- **System Configuration Utility (MSCONFIG.EXE)** Allows you to manage system configuration information. You can configure normal, diagnostic, and selective startup as well.

The System Information utility (MSINFO32.EXE) also provides access to helpful tools. To use this utility, click Start, and then select Help And Support. On the Help And Support Center home page, click Use Tools under Pick A Task. In the left pane under the Tools heading, click Advanced System Information and then click View Detailed System Information (Msinfo32.exe).

Once you access System Information, click the Tools menu to display the following list of available tools:

- **DirectX Diagnostic Tool (DXDIAG.EXE)**   Runs a diagnostic tool that you can use to troubleshoot problems with DirectX. DirectX is used to speed up the performance of applications, provided the system hardware supports this feature.

- **Dr. Watson (DRWTSN32.EXE)**   Runs the Dr. Watson properties editor, which is used to configure how Dr. Watson creates crash dumps and diagnostic logs regarding program errors for the currently selected system. By default, crash dumps and logs are saved to the Documents And Settings\All Users\Application Data\Microsoft\Dr Watson folder. Any setting changes are made available to all users of the system and are stored in the Windows Registry under the key \\HKEY_LOCAL_MACHINE\SOFTWARE\Microsoft\DrWatson.

- **File Signature Verification Utility (SIGVERIF.EXE)**   Used to check operating system files that have been digitally signed. Any files that aren't digitally signed are displayed in a results list. The complete list of system files checked is available in a log file stored in *%SystemRoot%*\SIGVERIF.TXT.

- **Net Diagnostics**   Accesses the Network Diagnostics console, which scans the system, examining hardware and software configurations for networking problems. This can be used to troubleshoot connectivity issues with TCP/IP and DNS as well as issues with modems, network adapters, and network clients.

- **System Restore (RSTRUI.EXE)**   Accesses the System Restore utility, which can be used to create restore points or to roll back a system to a specific restore point. The System Restore utility is discussed in Chapter 18.

The tools you might want to take a closer look at include Disk Cleanup, Dr. Watson, File Signature Verification, and System Configuration.

Working with Disk Cleanup

Disk Cleanup checks disk drives for files that aren't needed or can be compressed. You can start to work with Disk Cleanup by completing the following steps:

1. Click Start, Programs or All Programs, Accessories, System Tools, and then select Disk Cleanup.

   Note   The executable for Disk Cleanup is CLEANMGR.EXE. To run Disk Cleanup directly, click Start and select Run. In the Open field of the Run dialog box, type **CLEANMGR.EXE** and then click OK.

2. If the system has multiple hard disk drives, the Select Drive dialog box is displayed. Use the Drives drop-down list to choose the drive you want to clean up, and then click OK.

3. Disk Cleanup then examines the selected drive, looking for temporary files that can be deleted and files that are candidates for compression. The more files on the drive, the longer the search process takes.

4. When Disk Cleanup finishes, you'll see a report similar to the one shown in Figure 2-5. File categories that you might see in the report include the following:

   ❑ **Downloaded Program Files** Contains programs downloaded for use by your browser, such as ActiveX controls and Java applets. These files are temporary and can be deleted.

   ❑ **Temporary Internet Files** Contains Web pages stored to support browser caching of pages. These files are temporary and can be deleted.

   ❑ **Office Setup Files** Contains the office setup files that are created when you install Microsoft Office 2003 or later and related applications. The setup files contain the data necessary for installation of Office components that are installed on first use. They are also used to help track the components installed so that Office can check for component updates and for using the detect and repair feature.

 Real World When you install Microsoft Office 2003 applications, Office installation files are copied to disk as part of the standard installation unless you choose to delete these files at the end of the installation when prompted. These installation files are used to install Office components as they are needed and to aid in the update, detect, and repair process for Microsoft Office. If you do not specify a location for these installation files, they are stored to the disk drive with the most available space in most cases, which could be a drive other than that used by the base installation of Microsoft Office itself. You can configure the drive used by selecting the LOCALCACHEDRIVE option, if you run Microsoft Office Setup from the command line. For more information, see Microsoft Knowledge Base Article 826530 (*http://support.microsoft.com/default.aspx?scid=kb;en-us;826530*). Also remember that the only way to delete these files after installation without causing errors and problems with the Office installation is to delete the installation cache files using Disk Cleanup.

   ❑ **Recycle Bin** Contains files that have been deleted from the computer but not yet purged. Emptying the Recycle Bin permanently removes the files.

   ❑ **Temporary Files** Contains information stored in the Temp folder. These files are primarily temporary data or work files for applications.

   ❑ **Web Client/Publisher Temporary Files** Contains local copies of network files that you've specifically designated for use offline. If you delete these files without reconfiguring for online access only, the files are copied back to this folder the next time you connect to the network.

   ❑ **Temporary Offline Files** Contains temporary data and work files for recently used network files. These files are stored to enable working and can be deleted.

❑ **Offline Files**   Contains local copies of recently used network files. These files are stored to enable offline access to files and can be deleted.

❑ **Compress Old Files**   Contains a list of files that haven't been accessed in a while and thus are candidates for compression. By default, files are marked for possible compression when they haven't been used in 50 days. You can change the waiting period by selecting Compress Old Files in the list and then clicking Options. Then enter a new Compress After duration, and click OK.

❑ **Catalog Files For The Content Indexer**   Contains old catalogs that are no longer needed by the Content Indexer. These files can be deleted.

Figure 2-5   Use Disk Cleanup to help you find files that can be deleted or compressed.

5. Use the check boxes provided in the Files To Delete list to choose the files that you want to clean up, and then click OK. When prompted to confirm the action, click Yes.

Configuring Dr. Watson

Dr. Watson creates crash dumps and diagnostic logs regarding program errors. By default, when an error occurs, Dr. Watson does the following:

■ Displays an error prompt, indicating that an error occurred

■ Writes debugging information to a crash dump file named USER.DMP that is written to the Documents And Settings\All Users\Application Data\Microsoft\Dr Watson folder

- Records diagnostic information to a log file named DRWTSN32.LOG that is written to the Documents And Settings\All Users\Application Data\Microsoft\Dr Watson folder

You can change the default behavior using the Dr. Watson properties editor. To access the editor and make property changes, complete the following steps:

1. From the Tools menu of the System Information utility (MSINFO32.EXE), select Dr. Watson. This displays the Dr. Watson properties editor, as shown in Figure 2-6.

 Note   The executable for Dr. Watson is DRWTSN32.EXE. To run Dr. Watson directly, click Start and select Run. In the Open field of the Run dialog box, type **DRWTSN32.EXE** and then click OK.

Figure 2-6   Use the Dr. Watson properties editor to configure error handling for programs.

2. Use the properties editor to change the default behavior of Dr. Watson. The following options are available:

   ❑ **Log File Path**   Sets the folder path for diagnostic logs. If you change the folder location, make sure the interactive Everyone group has access to the new folder location. Otherwise, Dr. Watson won't be able to write to the log file and will prompt the user for a new file path.

   ❑ **Crash Dump**   Sets the folder path for the crash dump file. As before, if you change the folder location, make sure the interactive Everyone group has access to the new folder location. Otherwise, Dr. Watson won't be able to write to the dump file and will prompt the user for a new file path.

   ❑ **Wave File**   If you select Sound Notification and have a sound card, you can use this field to specify the path to a sound file in Microsoft .wav file format. This file is then played whenever a program error occurs. Note that this option is grayed out if the computer doesn't have a sound card configured.

❏ **Number Of Instructions**   Sets the number of instructions before and after the current memory location that Dr. Watson will disassemble and write to the crash dump file.

❏ **Number Of Errors To Save**   Sets the maximum number of errors that Dr. Watson will write to the diagnostic log. Dr. Watson also writes an event to the Application log.

❏ **Crash Dump Type**   Sets the type of the crash dump. The options are Full for a complete dump, Mini for a partial dump with key information only, and NT 4 Compatible Full for a crash dump file that uses a Windows NT 4 crash dump file. The only time you'll use NT 4 Compatible Full is when you need to generate crash dump files for a program that reads crash files generated only by Windows NT 4.

❏ **Dump Symbol Table**   Specifies whether Dr. Watson dumps the symbol table for each module when an error occurs. If you select this option, the dump file can grow very large.

❏ **Dump All Thread Contexts**   Specifies whether Dr. Watson logs the state of all threads or only the state of the thread that caused the program error.

❏ **Append To Existing Log File**   Specifies whether Dr. Watson appends new error data to the existing log file or overwrites the log file each time an error occurs. If you select this option, the log file can grow very large.

❏ **Visual Notification**   Specifies whether Dr. Watson displays an error dialog box when an error occurs, but does not control whether Dr. Watson writes error information. If this option is not selected, Dr. Watson continues to log error information as appropriate.

❏ **Sound Notification**   Specifies whether Dr. Watson plays a sound when an error is detected. The default sound is to play two beeps. If the computer contains a sound card, you can use the Wave File field to set a sound file to play.

❏ **Create Crash Dump File**   Specifies whether Dr. Watson writes a crash dump file. If this option is selected, Dr. Watson writes debugging information to the crash dump file. Otherwise, no debugging information is recorded.

Note   Property changes are made available to all users of the system and are stored in the Windows Registry under the key \\HKEY_LOCAL_MACHINE\SOFTWARE\Microsoft\DrWatson.

3. Click OK when you are finished.

Note   If you select the Dump All Thread Contexts option, Dr. Watson writes dump information for each thread according to the Number Of Instructions and Number Of Errors To Save properties. Otherwise, Dr. Watson only writes this information for the thread that causes the program error.

Verifying System Files Using File Signature Verification

Critical files used by the operating system are digitally signed. Digital signatures help to prove the authenticity of these files and ensure that it is easy to track changes that might cause problems on a system. When you are having problems that cannot easily be explained, such as happens when a system becomes unstable after an application installation, it is a good idea to verify that critical system files haven't been changed. You can do this using the File Signature Verification Utility.

You can start and work with the File Signature Verification Utility by completing the following steps:

1. From the Tools menu of the System Information utility (MSINFO32.EXE), select File Signature Verification Utility.

 Note The executable for File Signature Verification Utility is SIGVERIF.EXE. To run this utility directly, click Start and select Run. In the Open field of the Run dialog box, type **SIGVERIF.EXE** and then click OK.

2. Click Start to run the File Signature Verification Utility using the default configuration. By default, the File Signature Verification Utility displays a list of system files that aren't digitally signed and writes verification results to *%SystemRoot%*\SIGVERIF.TXT.

3. Notice the list of files displayed in the File Signature Verification Utility report. These files don't have digital signatures and could have been maliciously replaced by other programs of the same name. Review event logs and other error reports to see if these files show up in the error reports.

4. Use Microsoft Notepad to access the verification log located in *%SystemRoot%*\SIGVERIF.TXT. Check the log to see if there are files that have been altered since they were installed. Files are listed by status as Signed, Unsigned, Not Scanned, etc. Any files that have been changed will be marked as such.

Managing System Configuration, Startup, and Boot

Whether you want to update system configuration files or troubleshoot startup problems, your tool of choice should be the System Configuration Utility. System Configuration is an integrated tool for managing system configuration information. Using this utility, you can manage the following elements:

- Operating system startup options
- System configuration files: SYSTEM.INI, WIN.INI, and BOOT.INI
- Startup applications
- Service-startup options

The following sections examine key tasks that you can perform with the System Configuration Utility. You access the utility through Help And Support Center. After you start Help And Support Center, under Pick A Task, click Use Tools and then select System Configuration Utility.

Understanding Startup Modes and Troubleshooting System Startup

You can use the System Configuration Utility to select the startup mode for a computer. The following three startup modes are available:

- **Normal Startup**   Normal startup is used for normal system operations. In this mode, the operating system loads all system configuration files and device drivers and also runs all startup applications and enabled services.

- **Diagnostic Startup**   Diagnostic startup is used to troubleshoot system problems. In diagnostic mode, the system loads only basic device drivers and essential services. Once you start the system in diagnostic mode, you can modify system settings to resolve configuration problems.

- **Selective Startup**   Selective startup is used to pinpoint problem areas in the configuration. Here, you can selectively enable and disable configuration files, system services, and startup items. If you add startup options incrementally, you can identify the settings that are causing system problems and correct them as necessary.

Normal is the default startup mode. If you are experiencing problems with a system and want to use a different startup mode, complete the following steps:

1. Start Help And Support Center. Under Pick A Task, click Use Tools and then select System Configuration Utility. In the right pane, click Open System Configuration Utility to display the System Configuration Utility dialog box shown in Figure 2-7.

    Note   The executable for the System Configuration Utility is MSCON-FIG.EXE. To run this utility directly, click Start and select Run. In the Open field of the Run dialog box, type **MSCONFIG.EXE** and then click OK.

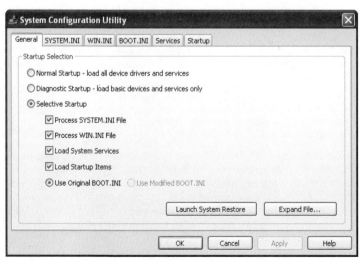

Figure 2-7   Use the System Configuration Utility's General tab to control system startup.

2. On the General tab, select either Diagnostic Startup or Selective Startup. If you choose selective startup, you can use the following options to select the items that you want the system to use:

    ❑ **Process SYSTEM.INI File**   Tells the system to process the SYSTEM.INI file on startup. If you select this option, use the settings on the SYSTEM.INI tab to control how the SYSTEM.INI file is used.

    ❑ **Process WIN.INI File**   Tells the system to process the WIN.INI file on startup. If you select this option, use the settings on the WIN.INI tab to control how the WIN.INI file is used.

    ❑ **Load System Services**   Tells the system to load Windows services on startup. If you select this option, use the settings on the Services tab to specify which services are started.

    ❑ **Load Startup Items**   Tells the system to run applications designated for startup at boot time. If you select this option, you can enable and disable startup applications using the option on the Startup tab.

    ❑ **Use Original BOOT.INI**   Tells the system to process the original BOOT.INI file on startup instead of one you've created by modifying the Boot.ini settings using the System Configuration Utility.

    ❑ **Use Modified BOOT.INI**   You can change settings on the BOOT.INI tab to control how the BOOT.INI file is used and to set additional boot flags. If you make changes on the BOOT.INI tab, the Selective Startup and Use Modified BOOT.INI options are automatically selected on the General tab.

3. When you are ready to continue, click OK and then reboot the system. If you have problems rebooting the system, restart the system in Safe Mode and then repeat this procedure. Safe Mode appears automatically as an option after a failed boot.

Changing System Configuration Files

System configuration files control the loading of device drivers, extensions, and operating system components. System configuration files you might want to examine include the following:

- AUTOEXEC.BAT
- CONFIG.SYS
- SYSTEM.INI
- WIN.INI

AUTOEXEC.BAT and CONFIG.SYS are located on drive C and are used for hardware and system configuration. In Windows XP, these files are usually empty, but they might contain remnants from installations of previous versions of Windows. SYSTEM.INI and WIN.INI are located in the *%SystemRoot%* folder and control system initialization for drivers, devices, and components. SYSTEM.INI and WIN.INI are the key configuration files necessary for Windows XP startup.

You can edit the configuration files in several different ways. If you want to selectively enable or disable entries in the configuration files, the best tool to use is the System Configuration Utility. Start the System Configuration Utility, and then use the check boxes in the SYSTEM.INI and WIN.INI tabs to enable or disable initialization options. After you make changes, restart the computer to test the changes.

If you need to edit the files directly, you can do so in Notepad. However, it is easier to use the SysEdit utility, which opens all the configuration files at once for simultaneous viewing and editing. To use this utility, follow these steps:

1. Click Start, and then select Run.
2. Type **sysedit** and then click OK.
3. Edit the system configuration files as necessary, and then close the editor window.
4. When prompted to save the changes, click Yes and then restart the computer.

Changing Boot Options

Another critical system file that you might want to examine is BOOT.INI. BOOT.INI identifies boot partitions and determines the boot method used by the operating system. Although BOOT.INI is formatted using ASCII text and can be edited in Notepad, you should rarely edit the file directly. Instead use the System Configuration Utility to make the necessary changes to BOOT.INI, and then restart the system.

As shown in Figure 2-8, when you start the System Configuration Utility and click the BOOT.INI tab, the contents of the BOOT.INI file are displayed in a preview window. Beneath the preview window, you have the following options for manipulating the contents of the BOOT.INI file:

- **Check All Boot Paths**   Tells Windows XP to check boot paths to ensure they are correct.
- **Set As Default**   Sets the currently selected boot partition as the default partition. The default partition is selected automatically if you don't choose an option before the timeout interval.
- **Move Up**   Moves the currently selected boot partition up in the display order.
- **Move Down**   Moves the currently selected boot partition down in the display order.
- **Timeout**   Sets the amount of time the computer waits before using the default boot partition.

Note   On a computer with a single operating system, the Set As Default, Move Up, and Move Down buttons are grayed out. The reason for this is that there is no other operating system to switch to or from.

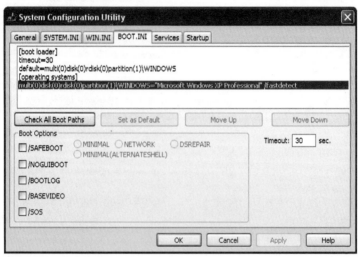

Figure 2-8 BOOT.INI identifies boot partitions and determines the boot method used by the operating system.

You can also set the following boot options:

- **/SAFEBOOT**   Starts the computer in Safe Mode with additional flags for minimal, network, and alternate shell minimal boots as well as the directory service repair state (dsrepair). Once you successfully boot a system in Safe Mode, you can modify system settings to resolve configuration problems.

- **/NOGUIBOOT**   Boots the computer to the Windows prompt and doesn't load the graphical components of the operating system. Booting to the prompt is useful when you are having problems with the graphical components of Windows XP.

- **/BOOTLOG**   Turns on boot logging so that key startup events are written to a log.

- **/BASEVIDEO**   Forces the computer to use Video Graphics Adapter (VGA) display settings. Use this mode when you are trying to resolve display settings, such as when the display mode is set to a size that the monitor cannot display.

- **/SOS**   Starts the computer using verbose output so that you can view the details of startup activities prior to the loading of Windows graphical components.

Enabling and Disabling Startup Applications for Troubleshooting

If you suspect that an application loaded at startup is causing problems with the system, there is an easy way to diagnose this. Disable the program from starting automatically, and then reboot the system. If the problem no longer appears, you might have pinpointed the problem and might remedy it by permanently disabling automatic startup of this program. If the problem still occurs, you might want to repeat this process with other startup applications.

To disable startup applications, follow these steps:

1. Start Help And Support Center. Under Pick A Task, click Use Tools and then select System Configuration Utility. In the right pane, click Open System Configuration Utility.
2. Click the Startup tab. As shown in Figure 2-9, this tab displays a list of programs that currently load at startup.

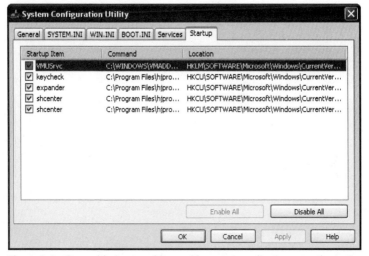

Figure 2-9 To troubleshoot problems with startup applications, use the options on the Startup tab.

3. Clear the check box next to any application that you do not want to load at startup.

Caution   Disable only those programs that you've identified as potential problems and only if you know how they are used by the operating system. If you don't know what a program does, don't disable it. Sometimes you can learn more about a startup program by following its command path and then examining its base installation folder.

4. Click OK. You need to reboot the system to check the changes, so if you are prompted to restart the system, click Yes. Otherwise, reboot manually.
5. Repeat this procedure as necessary to pinpoint the program causing the system problems. If you can't identify an application as the cause of the problem, the trouble might be with a Windows component, service, or device driver.

Enabling and Disabling Services for Troubleshooting

Just as automatically started applications can cause problems on a system, so can automatically started services. To help troubleshoot service problems, you can temporarily disable services using the System Configuration Utility and then reboot to see if the problem goes away. If the problem no longer appears, you might have pinpointed it. You can then permanently disable the service or check with the service vendor to see if an updated executable is available for the service.

To temporarily disable services, follow these steps:

1. Start Help And Support Center. Under Pick A Task, click Use Tools and then select System Configuration Utility. In the right pane, click Open System Configuration Utility.

2. Click the Services tab. As shown in Figure 2-10, this tab displays a list of all services installed on the computer and includes flags that identify the state of the service, such as running or stopped, and whether the service is essential to the proper operation of the system.

Figure 2-10   To troubleshoot problems with Windows services, use the options on the Services tab.

3. Clear the check box next to any service that you do not want to run at startup.

 Caution   Disable only those services that you've identified as potential problems and only if you know how they are used by the operating system. If you don't know what a service does, don't disable it. You can learn the specific purpose of a service using the Services utility in the Administrative Tools menu. Select the service to view its description on the Extended tab or double-click the service to read its description on the General tab of the related properties dialog box.

4. Click OK. You need to reboot the system to check the changes, so if you are prompted to restart the system, click Yes. Otherwise, reboot the system manually.

5. Repeat this procedure as necessary to pinpoint the service causing the system problems. If you can't identify a service as the cause of the problem, the trouble might be caused by a Windows component, a startup application, or a device driver.

Managing System Properties

You use the System utility to manage system properties. To access the System utility, double-click System on Control Panel. The following sections examine key configuration areas of the System utility.

The General Tab

General system information is available for any Windows XP system through the System utility's General tab, which is shown in Figure 2-11. The information provided on the General tab includes the following:

- Operating system version
- Registered owner
- Windows serial number
- Processor type
- Total system RAM

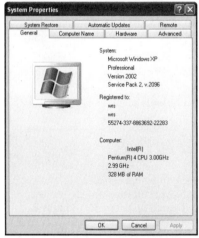

Figure 2-11 Use the System utility to manage system environment variables, profiles, and properties.

Note Original Equipment Manufacturers (OEMs), such as Dell and Compaq, can also provide information on this tab—usually support or contact information.

The Computer Name Tab

The computer's network identification can be displayed and modified with the System utility's Computer Name tab, shown in Figure 2-12. As the figure shows, the tab displays the full computer name of the system and the domain membership. The full computer name is essentially the DNS name of the computer, which also identifies the computer's place within the Active Directory hierarchy.

Figure 2-12 Use the Computer Name tab to display and configure system identification.

To access the Network Identification tab, start the System utility by double-clicking the System icon in Control Panel. Click the Computer Name tab. You can now perform the following actions:

- Click Network ID to start the Network Identification Wizard, which guides you through modifying network access information for the computer.
- Click Change to change the computer name and the domain or workgroup associated with the computer.

The Hardware Tab

The Hardware tab provides access to several important system utilities, including Device Manager and Hardware Wizard. These utilities are discussed in Chapter 3, "Configuring Hardware Devices and Drivers." The Hardware tab also provides access to hardware profiles that might be configured on the system. Hardware profiles are most useful for mobile computers, such as laptops. For details on using hardware profiles, see Chapter 7, "Managing User Access and Global Settings."

The Advanced Tab

The System utility's Advanced tab, shown in Figure 2-13, controls many of the key features of the Windows operating system, including application performance, virtual memory usage, user profile, environment variables, and startup and recovery. To access the Advanced tab, start the System utility by double-clicking the System icon in Control Panel. Click the Advanced tab.

Note User profiles contain global user settings and configuration information. They are created the first time a user logs on to a local computer or domain and are different for local and domain accounts. A user's profile maintains the desktop environment so that it is the same each time the user logs on. You'll find an extensive discussion on user profiles under "Managing User Profiles" in Chapter 10 of the *Windows Server 2003 Administrator's Pocket Consultant*.

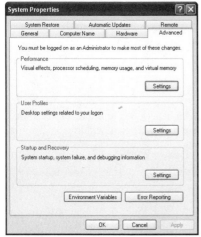

Figure 2-13   The Advanced tab lets you configure advanced features, including performance options, environment variables, and startup and recovery.

Setting Windows Performance

Many graphics enhancements have been added to the Windows XP interface. These enhancements include many visual effects for menus, toolbars, windows, and the taskbar. You can configure Windows performance by completing the following steps:

1. Click the Advanced tab in the System utility, and then click Settings on the Performance panel to display the Performance Options dialog box.

2. The Visual Effects tab should be selected by default. You have the following options for controlling visual effects:

   ❑ **Let Windows Choose What's Best For My Computer**   Allows the operating system to choose the performance options based on the hardware configuration. For a newer computer, this option will probably be identical to the Adjust For Best Appearance option. The key distinction, however, is that this option is chosen by Windows based on the available hardware and its performance capabilities.

❑ **Adjust For Best Appearance** When you optimize Windows for best appearance, you enable all visual effects for all graphical interfaces. Menus and the taskbar use transitions and shadows. Screen fonts have smooth edges. List boxes have smooth scrolling. Folders use Web views and more.

❑ **Adjust For Best Performance** When you optimize Windows for best performance, you turn off the resource-intensive visual effects, such as slide transitions and smooth edges for fonts, while maintaining a basic set of visual effects.

❑ **Custom** You can customize the visual effects as well. To do this, select or clear the visual effects options in the Performance Options dialog box. If you clear all options, Windows does not use visual effects.

3. When you are finished changing visual effects, click Apply. Click OK twice to close the open dialog boxes.

Setting Application Performance

Application performance is related to processor scheduling and memory caching options that you set for the Windows XP system. Processor scheduling determines the responsiveness of the current active application (as opposed to background applications that might be running on the system). Memory caching determines whether physical memory is optimized for applications or the system cache.

You control application performance by completing the following steps:

1. Click the Advanced tab in the System utility, and then click Settings on the Performance panel to display the Performance Options dialog box.

2. The Performance Options dialog box has several tabs. Click the Advanced tab.

3. In the Processor Scheduling panel, you have the following options:

❑ **Programs** To give the active application the best response time and the greatest share of available resources, select Programs. Generally, you'll want to use this option for all Windows XP workstations.

❑ **Background Services** To give background applications a better response time than the active application, select Background Services. Generally, you'll want to use this option for Windows XP computers running as servers (meaning they have server-like roles and are not being used as Windows XP workstations). For example, a Windows XP computer may be the print server for the department.

4. In the Memory Usage panel, you have the following options:

❑ **Programs** Choose this option to optimize physical memory usage for applications. Generally, you'll want to use this option for all Windows XP workstations.

❑ **System Cache** Choose this option to optimize physical memory usage for the system cache. Generally, you'll want to use this option for servers (not for Windows XP workstations).

5. Click OK.

Tip   Remember that a Windows XP workstation could be configured as a "server" to perform certain tasks, such as acting as a print server or sharing files on the network. If a Windows XP system provides service functions rather than acting as a desktop, the System Cache setting might be a good choice.

Configuring Virtual Memory

Virtual memory allows you to use disk space to extend the amount of available RAM on a system. This feature of processors using Intel 386 and later writes RAM to disks using a process called *paging*. With paging, a set amount of RAM, such as 32 MB, is written to the disk as a paging file, where it can be accessed from the disk when needed.

An initial paging file is created automatically for the drive containing the operating system. By default, other drives don't have paging files, so you must create these paging files manually if you want them. When you create a paging file, you set an initial size and a maximum size. Paging files are written to the volume as a file named PAGEFILE.SYS.

Best Practices   Microsoft recommends that you create a paging file for each physical volume on the system. On most systems, multiple paging files can improve the performance of virtual memory. Thus, instead of a single large paging file, it's better to have several small ones. Keep in mind that removable drives don't need paging files.

You can configure virtual memory by completing the following steps:

1. Start the System utility, and click the Advanced tab.
2. Click Settings in the Performance section to display the Performance Options dialog box. Click the Advanced tab, and then click Change to display the Virtual Memory dialog box shown in Figure 2-14. The following information is provided:

    ❑ **Drive [Volume Label] and Paging File Size (MB)**   Shows how virtual memory is currently configured on the system. Each volume is listed with its associated paging file (if any). The paging file range shows the initial and maximum size values set for the paging file.

    ❑ **Paging File Size For Selected Drive**   Provides information on the currently selected drive and allows you to set its paging file size. Space Available indicates how much space is available on the drive.

    ❑ **Total Paging File Size For All Drives**   Provides a recommended size for virtual RAM on the system and tells you the amount currently allocated. If this is the first time you're configuring virtual RAM, notice that the recommended amount has already been given to the system drive (in most instances).

Figure 2-14 Virtual memory extends the amount of RAM on a system.

Tip Although Windows XP can expand paging files incrementally as needed, this can result in fragmented files, which slow system performance. For optimal system performance, set the initial size and the maximum size to the same value. This ensures that the paging file is consistent and can be written to a single contiguous file (if possible, given the amount of space on the volume). In most cases, I recommend setting the total paging file size so that it's twice the physical RAM size on the system. For instance, on a computer with 256 MB RAM, you would ensure that the Total Paging File Size For All Drives setting is at least 512 MB.

3. In the Drive list box, select the volume you want to work with.
4. Use the Paging File Size For Selected Drive area to configure the paging file for the drive. Select Custom Size, and then enter an initial size and a maximum size. Click Set to save the changes.
5. Repeat steps 3 and 4 for each volume you want to configure.
6. Click OK, and if prompted to overwrite an existing PAGEFILE.SYS file, click Yes.
7. Close the System utility.

Note   If you updated the settings for a paging file that is currently in use, you'll see a prompt explaining that you need to restart the system for the changes to take effect. Click OK. When you close the System utility, you'll see a prompt asking if you want to restart the system. Click Yes.

Configuring Data Execution Prevention

Data Execution Prevention (DEP) is a memory protection technology enabled with Service Pack 2 or later. DEP tells the computer's processor to mark all memory locations in an application as non-executable unless the location explicitly contains executable code. If code is executed from a memory page marked as non-executable, the processor can raise an exception and prevent it from executing. This prevents malicious code such as a virus from inserting itself into most areas of memory because only specific areas of memory are marked as having executable code.

Note   32-bit versions of Windows support DEP as implemented by those AMD processors that provide the no-execute page-protection (NX) processor feature. Such processors support the related instructions and must be running in Physical Address Extension (PAE) mode. 64-bit versions of Windows also support the NX processor feature.

You can determine whether a computer supports DEP by using the System utility. If a computer supports DEP, you can also configure it by completing the following steps:

1. Click the Advanced tab in the System utility, and then on the Performance panel click Settings to display the Performance Options dialog box.

2. The Performance Options dialog box has several tabs. Click the Data Execution Prevention tab. The text at the bottom of this tab specifies whether the computer supports execution protection.

3. If a computer supports execution protection and is configured appropriately, you can configure DEP by using the following options:

    ❑ **Turn On DEP For All Programs**   Enables DEP. This is the default and recommended option for computers that support execution protection and are configured appropriately.

    ❑ **Turn Off DEP**   Disables DEP. This option is not recommended for computers that support execution protection.

    ❑ **Help Protect All Programs Except**   Configures DEP. Select this option, and then click Add to specify programs that should run without execution protection. In this way, execution protection will work for all programs except those you have listed here.

4. Click OK.

Real World   To be compatible with this feature, applications must be able to explicitly mark memory with Execute permission. Applications that cannot do this will not be compatible with the NX processor feature. If you are experiencing memory-related problems running applications, you should determine the applications that are having problems and configure them as exceptions rather than completely disabling execution protection. In this way, you still get the benefits of memory protection and can selectively disable memory protection for programs that aren't running properly with the NX processor feature.

Execution protection is applied to both user-mode and kernel-mode programs. A user-mode execution protection exception results in a STATUS_ACCESS_VIOLATION exception. In most processes, this exception will be an unhandled exception and will result in termination of the process. This is the desired behavior because most programs violating these rules will be malicious in nature, such as a virus or worm.

Unlike applications, execution protection for kernel-mode device drivers cannot be selectively disabled or enabled. Furthermore, on compliant 32-bit systems, execution protection is applied by default to the memory stack. On compliant 64-bit systems, execution protection is applied by default to the memory stack, the paged pool, and the session pool. A kernel-mode execution protection access violation for a device driver results in an ATTEMPTED_EXECUTE_OF_NOEXECUTE_MEMORY exception.

Configuring System and User Environment Variables

System and user environment variables are configured by means of the Environment Variables dialog box, shown in Figure 2-15. To access this dialog box, start the System utility, click the Advanced tab, and select Environment Variables.

Creating an environment variable   You can create environment variables by completing the following steps:

1. Click New under System Variables or User Variables, whichever is appropriate. This opens the New System Variable dialog box or the New User Variable dialog box, respectively.

2. In the Variable Name field, type the variable name. Then in the Variable Value field, type the variable value.

3. Click OK.

Figure 2-15   The Environment Variables dialog box lets you configure system and user environment variables.

Editing an environment variable   You can edit an existing environment variable by completing the following steps:

1. Select the variable in the System Variables or User Variables list box.

2. Click Edit under System Variables or User Variables, whichever is appropriate. The Edit System Variable dialog box or the Edit User Variable dialog box will open.

3. Type a new value in the Variable Value field, and click OK.

Deleting an environment variable   You can delete an environment variable by selecting it and clicking Delete.

Note   When you create or modify system environment variables, the changes take effect when you restart the computer. When you create or modify user environment variables, the changes take effect the next time the user logs on to the system.

Configuring System Startup and Recovery

System startup and recovery properties are configured by means of the Startup And Recovery dialog box, shown in Figure 2-16. To access this dialog box, start the System utility, click the Advanced tab, and then, under Startup And Recovery, click Settings.

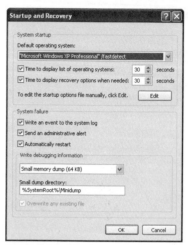

Figure 2-16   The Startup And Recovery dialog box lets you configure system startup and recovery procedures.

Setting startup options   The System Startup area of the Startup And Recovery dialog box controls system startup. In a computer with multiple bootable operating systems, to set the default operating system, select one of the operating systems listed in the Default Operating System field. These options are obtained from the operating system section of the computer's BOOT.INI file.

At startup of a computer with multiple bootable operating systems, Windows XP displays the startup configuration menu for 30 seconds by default. You can affect this by either of the following actions:

- Boot immediately to the default operating system by clearing the Time To Display List Of Operating Systems check box.

- Display the available options for a specific amount of time by selecting the Time To Display List Of Operating Systems check box and then setting a time delay in seconds.

Generally, on most systems you'll want to use a value of 3 to 5 seconds. This is long enough to be able to make a selection, yet short enough to expedite the system startup process.

When the system is in a recovery mode and booting, a list of recovery options might be displayed. As with the standard startup options, you can configure recovery startup options in one of two ways. You can set the computer to boot immediately using the default recovery option by clearing the Time To Display Recovery Options When Needed check box, or you can display the available options for a specific amount of time by selecting Time To Display Recovery Options When Needed and then setting a time delay in seconds.

Setting recovery options   The System Failure and Write Debugging Information areas of the Startup And Recovery dialog box control system recovery. Recovery options allow administrators to control precisely what happens when the system encounters a fatal system error (also known as a STOP error). The available options for the System Failure area are as follows:

- **Write An Event To The System Log**   Logs the error in the system log, which allows administrators to review the error later using the Event Viewer.

- **Send An Administrative Alert**   Sends an alert to the recipients specified in the Alert dialog box.

- **Automatically Restart**   Check this option to have the system attempt to reboot when a fatal system error occurs.

Note   Configuring automatic reboots isn't always a good thing. Sometimes you might want the system to halt rather than reboot to ensure that the system gets proper attention. Otherwise, you would know that the system rebooted only when you viewed the system logs or if you happened to be in front of the system's monitor when it rebooted.

The Write Debugging Information selection menu allows you to choose the type of debugging information that you want to write to a dump file. The dump file can in turn be used to diagnose system failures. The options are as follows:

- **None**   Use this option if you don't want to write debugging information.

- **Small Memory Dump**   Use this option to dump the physical memory segment in which the error occurred. This dump is 64 KB in size.

- **Kernel Memory Dump**   Use this option to dump the physical memory area being used by the Windows kernel. The dump file size depends on the size of the Windows kernel.

- **Complete Memory Dump**   Use this option to dump all physical memory being used at the time of the failure. The maximum dump file size is the same as the total physical memory size.

If you elect to write a dump file, you must also set a location for it. The default dump locations are *%SystemRoot%*\Minidump for small memory dumps and *%SystemRoot%*\MEMORY.DMP for all other memory dumps. You'll usually want to select Overwrite Any Existing File as well. This option ensures that any existing dump files are overwritten if a new STOP error occurs.

Best Practices   The dump file can be created only if the system is properly configured. The system drive must have a sufficiently large memory-paging file (as set for virtual memory on the Advanced tab), and the drive where the dump file is written must have sufficient free space as well. For example, my system has 128 MB of RAM and requires a paging file on the system drive of the same size—128 MB. Because the same drive is used for the dump file, the drive must have at least 256 MB of free space to create a complete dump of debugging information correctly (that's 128 MB for the paging file and 128 MB for the dump file).

Enabling and Disabling Error Reporting

Windows XP features built-in system and program error reporting. Error reporting sends information about errors to Microsoft. Error reporting is enabled by default for all Windows XP installations and can be configured to monitor these specific areas:

- **Windows Operating System**   Reports critical operating system errors that cause a blue screen crash. The error report contains all the information that is displayed on the blue screen.

- **Programs**   Reports illegal operations and internal errors that cause a program to stop working. With program errors, you can specify which programs should be monitored for errors and which shouldn't.

How an error is reported depends on where it originated. When a component or program error occurs, a dialog box appears asking if you want to report the problem. If you choose to report the problem, the error report is sent over the Internet to Microsoft and a Thank You dialog box is displayed with additional information that might be helpful in resolving the problem. When an operating system error occurs, the system doesn't generate the error report until the next time you successfully boot and log on to the system.

You can enable and configure error reporting by completing the following steps:

1. Start the System utility. Click the Advanced tab, and then click the Error Reporting button.

2. Select Enable Error Reporting, and then select areas to monitor.

 Tip   By default, all program errors are reported, regardless of who the manufacturer is. If you choose to report program errors, you can change the default configuration. To do this, select Programs, click Choose Programs, and then use the Choose Programs dialog box to specify the types of programs on which to report errors.

3. Click OK.

You can disable error reporting by completing these steps:

1. Start the System utility. Click the Advanced tab, and then click the Error Reporting button.

2. Select Disable Error Reporting and then click OK.

The System Restore Tab

System Restore is a new feature of Windows XP. With System Restore enabled, a computer makes periodic snapshots of the system configuration. These snapshots include Windows settings, lists of programs that have been installed, and so on. If the computer has problems starting or isn't working properly because of a system configuration change, you can use a snapshot to restore the system configuration to the point at which the snapshot was made. For example, suppose your system is working fine and then you install a new service pack release for Microsoft Office.

Afterward, the computer generates errors and Office applications won't run. You try to uninstall the update, but that doesn't work, so you decide to run System Restore. Using System Restore, you could restore the system using a snapshot taken prior to the update.

System Restore can provide several different types of snapshots. One type, System Checkpoint, is scheduled by the operating system and occurs at regular intervals. Another type of snapshot, Installation Restore Point, is created automatically based on events that are triggered by the operating system when you install applications. Other snapshots, known as Manual Restore Points, are created manually by users. You should recommend that users create Manual Restore Points prior to performing an operation that might cause problems on the system.

System Restore manages restore points on a per-drive basis. Each drive with critical applications and system files should be monitored for configuration changes. By default, System Restore is enabled for all drives on a system. This means each drive has disk space made available to System Restore. You can turn off monitoring of all configuration changes for all drives or individual drives as needed. If a drive isn't configured for System Restore monitoring, configuration changes are not tracked and the disk cannot be recovered if problems occur.

You control how System Restore works using the System Restore tab of the System utility, as discussed in the sections that follow. For complete details on creating restore points and restoring systems using System Restore, see Chapter 18.

Tip   The system process responsible for monitoring configuration and application changes is the System Restore Service. This service is configured for automatic startup and runs under the Local System account. The System Restore process won't work if this service isn't running or configured properly.

Changing Disk Usage for System Restore

System Restore monitors all available drives on a system and saves system checkpoint information to these drives. The amount of disk space available to System Restore determines the number of restore points that can be created. When System Restore runs out of available space, the operating system overwrites previously created restore points. On disks with 1-GB to 2-GB capacity, the maximum amount of disk space available to System Restore is between 100 and 200 MB. On disks with 9-GB to 18-GB capacity, it is between 1 and 2 GB.

To view or change the disk space usage settings for a particular drive, follow these steps:

1. Start the System utility by double-clicking the System icon in Control Panel, and then click the System Restore tab.
2. As Figure 2-17 shows, the Drive Settings panel shows a list of available drives on the system. If a drive is configured for System Restore, the drive status shows Monitoring. If a drive isn't configured for System Restore, the drive status shows Turned Off.

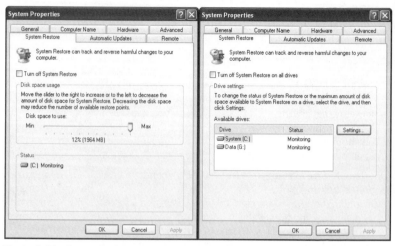

Figure 2-17   System Restore manages restore points on a per-drive basis. Each drive containing critical applications and system files should be monitored.

3. If a computer has a single drive, disk space usage is configured on the System Restore tab. If a computer has multiple drives, you can change the maximum amount of disk space available on a monitored drive by selecting the drive in the Available Drives list and then clicking Settings.

4. As shown in Figure 2-18, the Disk Space To Use slider controls the amount of disk space for System Restore. Disk space available to System Restore is expressed as a percentage of total disk space and an actual size in megabytes, such as 12 percent (960 MB) in this example. You can adjust the slider as follows:

   ❑ Moving the slider to the right increases the amount of disk space available to System Restore.

   ❑ Moving the slider to the left decreases the amount of disk space available to System Restore.

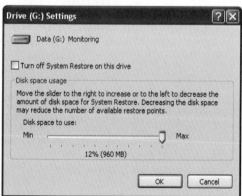

Figure 2-18   Move the Disk Space To Use slider left or right to control the maximum amount of space available to System Restore.

5. Click OK when you are finished. Repeat this process for other monitored drives as necessary.

Enabling or Disabling System Restore

System Restore manages configuration changes on a per-drive basis. This allows you to enable or disable configuration tracking for all drives on a system or individual drives. As you look at which drives should use System Restore, keep in mind that each drive containing critical applications and system files should be monitored for configuration changes. On the other hand, drives with saved documents, e-mail, or temporary application data do not need to be monitored because System Restore doesn't track changes to these types of data; these types of changes must be managed in the applications themselves.

By default, System Restore tracks all drives on a system, which can place an additional workload on system resources. To reduce the resource burden, you might want to remove tracking for noncritical drives. For example, if a computer has the operating system and application program files on drive C and document files on drive D, you might want to remove monitoring for drive D.

The configuration of System Restore for computers varies somewhat depending on whether the computer has a single drive or multiple drives. Complete the following steps to manage System Restore monitoring of a computer with a single drive:

1. Start the System utility by double-clicking the System icon in Control Panel, and then click the System Restore tab.
2. System Restore can be enabled or disabled using the Turn Off System Restore check box in the following ways:
    - ❏ Clear Turn Off System Restore to enable system configuration tracking for the computer. This enables configuration tracking for the drive.
    - ❏ Select Turn Off System Restore to disable system configuration tracking for the computer. This disables configuration tracking for the drive.
3. When you are finished making configuration changes, click OK.

Complete the following sequence to manage System Restore monitoring of a computer with multiple drives:

1. Start the System utility by double-clicking the System icon in Control Panel, and then click the System Restore tab.
2. System Restore can be enabled or disabled for all drives on a system using the Turn Off System Restore On All Drives check box in the following ways:
    - ❏ Clear Turn Off System Restore On All Drives to enable system configuration tracking for all drives on a computer.
    - ❏ Select Turn Off System Restore On All Drives to disable system configuration tracking for all drives on a computer.
3. The Drive Settings panel shows a list of available drives on the system. If a drive is configured for System Restore, the drive status shows Monitoring. If a drive isn't configured for System Restore, the drive status shows Turned Off.

4. To enable or disable monitoring for individual drives, select the drive in the Available Drives list and then click Settings. Next, select or clear Turn Off System Restore On This Drive, and then click OK.

5. When you are finished making configuration changes, click OK.

 Note   The system drive contains the operating system files for Windows XP. You cannot disable System Restore on a system drive without disabling it on all drives. To do this, in the Drive Settings dialog box, click OK or Cancel to close the Drive Settings dialog box, and then disable all drives by selecting Turn Off System Restore On All Drives on the System Restore tab.

The Automatic Updates Tab

Automatic Updates are configured using the System utility. To access the Automatic Updates configuration, start the System utility by double-clicking the System icon in Control Panel and then click the Automatic Updates tab. When enabled, the Automatic Updates service compares programs, operating system components, and drivers installed on a system with a master list of items available at the Microsoft Web site and determines whether there are updates that should be installed. For more information, see the section of Chapter 1 entitled "Understanding and Using Automatic Updates."

The Remote Tab

The Remote tab of the System utility controls Remote Assistance invitations and Remote Desktop connections. These options are discussed in Chapter 7 in the section entitled "Managing Remote Access to Workstations."

Chapter 3

Configuring Hardware Devices and Drivers

In this chapter:

Installing and Maintaining Devices: The Basics 65
Accessing Device Utilities through Computer Management 67
Getting Started with Device Manager 69
Using Device Drivers. 70
Configuring Device Drivers 72
Managing Hardware. 78
Customizing Hardware Device Settings. 82
Managing Internet Time 92

In this chapter, you'll learn how to configure hardware devices and drivers. Microsoft Windows XP provides three key tools for configuring hardware devices and drivers. (In this book, "Windows XP" refers to Windows XP Professional unless otherwise indicated.) The three tools are the following:

- Device Manager
- Add Hardware Wizard
- Hardware Troubleshooter

You'll use these tools whenever you install, uninstall, or troubleshoot hardware devices and drivers. Other tools are available for managing specific types of hardware devices, such as keyboards and sound cards.

Installing and Maintaining Devices: The Basics

You can add many different types of devices to systems. The following are the key device types:

- **Cards/Adapters**   Circuit cards and adapters are plugged into expansion slots on the motherboard inside the computer case or, in the case of a laptop, into expansion slots available directly on the side of the system. Most cards and adapters have a connector on them into which you can plug other devices.

- **Drives**   Many different types of drives can be installed, from CD-ROM to DVD to Zip drives, floppy disks, and hard disks. Drives usually have two types of cables. One cable attaches to the motherboard, to other drives, or to interface cards. The other cable attaches to the computer's power supply.

- **External devices**   External devices plug into ports on the computer. The port can be a standard one, such as LPT1 or COM1, a port that you added with a circuit card, or a high-speed serial port such as a universal serial bus (USB) port or an IEEE-1394 port (commonly called a FireWire port). Printers, scanners, USB flash-drives, and most digital cameras are external devices.

- **Memory**   Memory chips are used to expand the total amount of physical memory on the computer. Memory can be added to the motherboard or to a particular device, such as a video card. The most commonly used type of memory is random access memory (RAM).

Most available new devices are Plug and Play compatible. This means that you should be able to easily install new devices. Simply shut down the computer, insert the device into the appropriate slot or connect it to the computer, restart the computer, and then let Windows XP automatically detect the new device. Well, that's the idea, but it doesn't always work out that way.

Depending on the device, one of several things might happen when you turn the computer back on:

- Windows XP might automatically detect the new device and install a built-in driver to support it. If this happens, the device should run immediately without any problems.

- Windows XP might automatically detect the new device and prompt you to insert a driver disk. New devices should have a driver disk. If you don't have one, download the driver from the manufacturer's Web site or use one of the drivers from the Windows XP installation disk.

- Windows XP might act as if it has detected the device and installed the driver, but the device doesn't work. This usually means that you need to run a special setup program that came with the new device. Once you run the setup program, the device should operate normally. In some cases, however, failure of this type might mean that there's a resource conflict on the system and you'll need to resolve it before the device will be available.

 Real World   Installing Personal Digital Assistant (PDA) devices, such as the Palm and the Treo, can sometimes cause resource conflicts of this nature. Typically, the PDA defaults to COM1 and holds it so that other devices can't use it. This can cause conflicts with modems and other devices that might be using COM1. For tips on resolving resource conflicts, see the section of this chapter entitled "Troubleshooting Hardware."

- Windows doesn't detect the device automatically at all and you must use the Add New Hardware Wizard to install the device manually. For details on manually installing devices, see the section of this chapter entitled "Managing Hardware."

Once you've successfully installed a device, you'll need to perform maintenance tasks for the device and its drivers periodically. When new drivers for a device are released, you might want to test them in a development or support environment to see if the drivers resolve problems that users have been experiencing. If the drivers install without problems and resolve outstanding issues, you might then want to install the updated drivers on computers that use this device. The driver update procedure should be implemented as follows:

- Check the device and driver information on each system prior to installing the new driver. Note the location, version, and file name of the existing driver.

- Create a System Restore point as discussed in Chapter 17, "Troubleshooting Microsoft Windows XP Professional."

- Install the updated driver, and reboot the computer. If the computer and the device function normally after the reboot, the update can be considered a success.

- If the computer or the device malfunctions after the driver installation, roll back to the previously installed driver using the standard Device Manager utilities. If the computer cannot be restarted and the driver cannot be restored, restore the system to the System Restore point you created previously.

Note Beginning with Windows XP Service Pack 2, there are two important changes for device drivers. The first change affects the driver update process. Device drivers can be updated automatically through a Windows Update Services server. If your organization has deployed its own update servers, you can configure the management and distribution of updates for the operating system, the applications, and the device drivers. The second change affects device driver memory usage when the execution protection feature of an AMD processor is enabled. For detailed information on this issue, see the section entitled "Configuring Data Execution Prevention" in Chapter 2, "Configuring the Environment."

Accessing Device Utilities through Computer Management

Most device management utilities are accessed through the Computer Management console. You'll spend a lot of time working with this tool, so you should get to know it before working with devices.

Starting and Using Computer Management

The Computer Management console is designed to handle core system administration tasks on local and remote systems. You can start the Computer Management console with either of the following techniques:

- **With Category view in Control Panel** In Control Panel, click Performance And Maintenance, click Administrative Tools, and then double-click Computer Management.

- **With Classic view in Control Panel** In Control Panel, double-click Administrative Tools, and then double-click Computer Management.

As Figure 3-1 shows, the main window has a two-pane view similar to Windows Explorer. You use the console tree in the left pane for navigation and tool selection. Tools are divided into three broad categories:

- **System Tools** General-purpose tools for managing systems and viewing system information
- **Storage** Displays information on removable and logical drives and provides access to drive management tools
- **Services And Applications** View and manage the properties of services and applications installed on the server

You'll find device management utilities within the System Tools area.

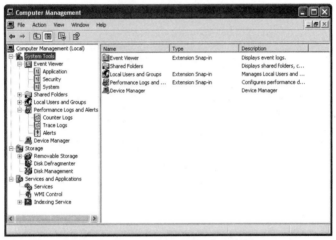

Figure 3-1 Use the Computer Management console to manage network computers and resources.

Managing Devices on Local and Remote Systems

The Computer Management console is designed to be used with local and remote systems. You can select a remote computer to manage by completing the following steps:

1. Right-click the Computer Management entry in the console tree, and then select Connect To Another Computer on the shortcut menu. This opens the Select Computer dialog box.

2. Select Another Computer, and then type the fully qualified name of the computer you want to work with, such as *wk1.technology.microsoft.com* (where *wk1* is the computer name and *technology.microsoft.com* is the domain name). You can also click Browse to search for the computer you want to work with.

3. Click OK.

Getting Started with Device Manager

You view and configure hardware devices using Device Manager. To access Device Manager and obtain a detailed list of all the hardware devices installed on a system, complete the following steps:

1. Start Computer Management. In the Computer Management console, click the plus sign (+) next to the System Tools node. This expands the node to display its tools.

2. Select Device Manager. As shown in Figure 3-2, you should now see a complete list of devices installed on the system. By default, this list is organized by device type.

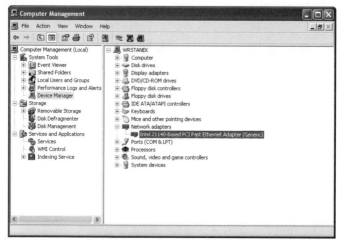

Figure 3-2   Use Device Manager to work with hardware devices.

3. Click the plus sign (+) next to a device type to see a list of the specific instances of that device type.

Once you access Device Manager, you can work with any of the installed devices. If you right-click a device entry, a shortcut menu is displayed. The options available depend on the type of device, but they include the following:

- **Properties**   Displays the Properties dialog box for the device
- **Uninstall**   Uninstalls the device and its drivers
- **Disable**   Disables the device but doesn't uninstall it
- **Enable**   Enables a device if it's disabled
- **Update Driver**   Starts the Hardware Update Wizard, which you can use to update the device driver
- **Scan For Hardware Changes**   Tells Windows XP to check the hardware configuration and determine if there are any changes

Tip The device list shows warning symbols if there are problems with a device. A yellow warning symbol with an exclamation point indicates a problem with a device. A red X indicates a device that was improperly installed or disabled by the user or the administrator for some reason.

You can use the options on the View menu in the Computer Management console to change the defaults for which types of devices are displayed and how the devices are listed. The options are as follows:

- **Devices By Type** Displays devices by the type of device installed, such as disk drive or printer. The connection name is listed below the type. This is the default view.
- **Devices By Connection** Displays devices by connection type, such as audio and video codecs.
- **Resources By Type** Displays the status of allocated resources by type of device using the resource. Resource types are direct memory access (DMA) channels, input/output (I/O) ports, interrupt requests (IRQ), and memory addresses.
- **Resources By Connection** Displays the status of all allocated resources by connection type rather than device type.
- **Show Hidden Devices** Displays non–Plug and Play devices as well as devices that have been physically removed from the computer but haven't had their drivers uninstalled.

Using Device Drivers

For each hardware component installed on a computer, there is an associated device driver. The job of the device driver is to handle the low-level communications tasks between the operating system and a hardware component. By installing a hardware component through the operating system, you are telling the operating system about the device driver it uses, and from then on the device driver loads automatically and runs as part of the operating system.

Device Driver Essentials

Windows XP Professional includes an extensive library of device drivers. In the base installation of the operating system, these drivers are maintained in a compressed file named Driver.cab. Some service packs you install will also include a compression file containing updates to the driver library. For example, with Service Pack 2 many drivers had to be recompiled to support the new security features, and the new drivers are stored in a compressed file named Sp2.cab. These files are collectively referred to as the *driver cache*. You can find the driver cache files in a subfolder of the *%SystemRoot%*\Driver Cache folder. If your system is based on the Intel i386 architecture, the subfolder is i386 (*%SystemRoot%*\Driver Cache\I386).

Every device driver in the driver cache is certified to be fully compatible with Windows XP Professional and also digitally signed by Microsoft to assure you of its authenticity. When you install a new Plug and Play–compatible device, Windows XP checks the driver cache for a compatible device driver. If one is found, the operating system automatically installs the device.

Every device driver has an associated Setup Information file. This file ends with the .inf extension and is a text file containing detailed configuration information about the device being installed. These files are stored in the *%SystemRoot%*\Inf folder for all the driver cache devices and any additional devices that are installed on a system. When you install a new device driver, the driver is written to *%SystemRoot%*\System32\Drivers and configuration settings are stored in the Registry. The driver's .inf file is used to control the installation and write the registry settings. If the driver doesn't already exist in the driver cache, it does not already have an .inf file on the system. In this case, a copy of the driver's .inf file is written to the *%SystemRoot%*\Inf folder when you install the device.

Using Signed and Unsigned Device Drivers

Every device driver in the driver cache is digitally signed, which authenticates the drive as having passed extensive testing by the Windows Hardware Quality Lab. A device driver with a digital signature should not cause your system to crash or become unstable. The presence of a digital signature also ensures that the device driver hasn't been tampered with. If a device driver doesn't have a digital signature, it hasn't been approved for use through testing or its files might have been modified from the original installation by another program. This means unsigned drivers are much more likely to cause the operating system to freeze or the computer to crash than any other program you've installed.

To prevent problems with unsigned drivers, Windows XP Professional warns you when you try to install an unsigned device driver by default. Windows can also be configured to eliminate this warning or to prevent unsigned drivers from being installed altogether. To manage device driver settings for computers throughout the organization, you can use Group Policy. When you do this, Group Policy specifies the least secure setting using one of three configuration settings. These settings are:

- **Ignore**   Use this setting to allow users to install any unsigned driver without having to see and respond to a warning prompt.
- **Warn**   Use this setting to prompt users each time either to continue with the installation of an unsigned driver or to stop the installation.
- **Block**   Use this setting to prevent users from installing unsigned driver software.

Note   When Group Policy is set to Ignore or Warn, unsigned drivers can be installed. When Group Policy is set to Block, unsigned device drivers can't be installed without first overriding Group Policy.

You can configure device driver–signing settings on a per user basis using the Code Signing For Device Drivers policy. This policy is located in User Configuration\Administrative Templates\System. When you enable this policy, you can specify the action to take as Ignore, Warn, or Block. Once enabled, the system doesn't implement any setting less secure than the established setting.

Tip   If you're trying to install a device and find that you can't install an unsigned driver, you should first check the System utility settings for driver signing. If you find that the settings are set to Block and you can't change the setting, the Code Signing For Device Drivers policy has been enabled and set to Block in Group Policy. You must override Group Policy to install the unsigned device driver.

You can configure device driver–signing settings for an individual computer by completing the following steps:

1. Start the System utility. In the Hardware tab, click Driver Signing. This displays the Driver Signing Options dialog box.

2. Choose the action you want the Windows operating system to take whenever someone tries to install an unsigned device driver as Ignore, Warn, or Block.

3. To apply these options to only the current user, clear the Make This Action The System Default option. Otherwise, select this option to make this the default for all users of this computer.

4. Click OK twice to apply the changes.

Configuring Device Drivers

Device drivers are required for devices, such as sound cards and display adapters, to work properly. Windows XP provides comprehensive management tools for maintaining and updating device drivers. These tools allow you to perform the following tasks:

- Track driver information
- Install and update driver versions
- Roll back to a previously installed driver
- Uninstall device drivers

Tracking Driver Information

Each driver being used on a system has a driver file associated with it. You can view the location of the driver file and related details by completing the following steps:

1. Start Computer Management. In the Computer Management console, click the plus sign (+) next to the System Tools node. This expands the node to display its tools.

2. Select Device Manager. You should now see a complete list of devices installed on the system. By default, this list is organized by device type.

3. Right-click the device you want to manage, and then select Properties from the shortcut menu. This opens the Properties dialog box for that device.

4. In the Driver Tab, click Driver Details to display the Driver File Details dialog box. As shown in Figure 3-3, the information displayed includes the following:

   ❑ **Driver Files**   Displays the full file path to locations where the driver exists
   ❑ **Provider**   The creator of the driver
   ❑ **File Version**   The version of the file

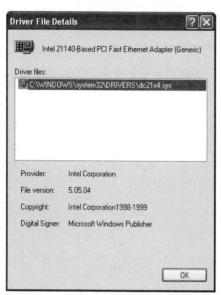

Figure 3-3   The Driver File Details dialog box displays information on the driver file locations, the provider, and the file versions.

Installing and Updating Device Drivers

To keep devices operating smoothly, it's essential that you keep the device drivers current. You install and update drivers using the Hardware Update Wizard. By default, this wizard can search for updated device drivers in the following locations:

- On the local computer
- On a hardware installation CD
- On the Windows Update site or your organization's Windows Update server

In Group Policy, several policies control the search possibilities.

- **Turn Off Access To All Windows Update Features under Computer Configuration\Administrative Templates\System\Internet Communication Management\Internet Communication Settings**   If this policy setting is enabled, all Windows Update features are blocked and not available to users. Users will also be unable to access the Windows Update Web Site.

- **Turn Off Windows Update Device Driver Searching under Computer Configuration\Administrative Templates\System\Internet Communication Management\Internet Communication Settings**   By default, Windows Update searching is optional when installing a device. If you enable this setting, Windows Update will not be searched when a new device is installed. If you disable this setting, Windows Update will always be searched when a new device is installed, if no local drivers are present.

■ **Turn Off Windows Update Device Driver Search Prompt under Computer Configuration\Administrative Templates\System**   If you disable, or do not configure, Turn Off Windows Update Device Driver Searching, this policy setting affects whether a search prompt is displayed for Windows Update of device drivers. If this policy setting is enabled, administrators aren't prompted to search Windows Update and the search will or will not take place automatically based on the Turn Off Windows Update Device Driver Searching setting. Otherwise, administrators will be prompted before Windows Update is searched.

You can install and update device drivers by completing the following steps:

1. Start Computer Management. In the Computer Management console, click the plus sign (+) next to the System Tools node. This expands the node to display its tools.

2. Select Device Manager in the Computer Management console. You should now see a complete list of devices installed on the system. By default, this list is organized by device type.

3. Right-click the device you want to manage, and then select Update Driver from the shortcut menu. This starts the Hardware Update Wizard.

 Best Practices   Updated drivers can add functionality to a device, improve performance, and resolve device problems. However, you should rarely install the latest drivers on a user's computer without first testing them in a test environment. Test first, then install.

4. If the Group Policy configuration allows administrators to be prompted to determine whether Windows Update should be searched, the first Wizard page has the options shown in Figure 3-4. These options are used as follows:

   ❑ **Yes, This Time Only**   Windows Update will be searched for this driver install only.

   ❑ **Yes, Now And Every Time I Connect A Device**   Windows Update will be searched automatically for driver updates. This setting applies to the installation of this driver and every time Driver Update is run.

   ❑ **No, Not This Time**   Windows Update will not be searched for this driver install only.

Figure 3-4   If allowed by Group Policy, administrators are prompted to determine whether Windows Update should be searched.

5. Click Next. You can specify whether you want to install the drivers automatically or manually by selecting the driver from a list or specific location.

6. If you elect to install the driver automatically, Windows XP looks for a more recent version of the device driver and installs the driver if found. If a more recent version of the driver is not found, Windows XP keeps the current driver. In either case, click Finish to complete the process and then skip the remaining steps.

7. If you chose to install the driver manually, you'll have the opportunity to select one of the following options:

   ❑ **Search For The Best Driver In These Locations**   If you search for drivers, the Wizard checks for drivers on the driver database on the system and any of the optional locations you specify, such as a floppy disk or a CD-ROM. Any matching drivers found are displayed, and you can select a driver.

   ❑ **Don't Search. I Will Choose The Driver To Install**   If you decide to install drivers yourself, the next Wizard window shows a list of compatible hardware and a recommended list of drivers for this hardware, as seen in Figure 3-5. If a correct driver is listed, all you need to do is to select it. If a correct driver isn't listed, clear the Show Compatible Hardware check box. You can now view a list of manufacturers to find the manufacturer of the device. Once you find the manufacturer, select the appropriate device driver in the right pane.

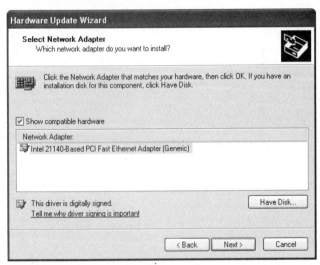

Figure 3-5   Select the appropriate device driver for the device you're adding.

Note   If the manufacturer or device you want to use isn't listed, insert your device driver disk into the floppy drive or CD-ROM drive, and then click the Have Disk button. Follow the prompts. Afterward, select the appropriate device.

8. After selecting a device driver through a search or a manual selection, continue through the installation process by clicking Next. Click Finish when the driver installation is completed. Keep in mind that in some cases you'll need to reboot the system to activate the newly installed or updated device driver.

Rolling Back Drivers

Sometimes you'll find that a device driver that you've installed causes device failure or other critical problems on a system. Don't worry, because you can recover the system to the previously installed device driver. To do this, follow these steps:

1. If you are having problems starting the system, you will need to boot the system in Safe Mode as discussed in Chapter 17 under "Troubleshooting Startup and Shutdown."

2. Start Computer Management. In the Computer Management console, click the plus sign (+) next to the System Tools node. This expands the node to display its tools.

3. Select Device Manager in the Computer Management console. You should now see a complete list of devices installed on the system. By default, this list is organized by device type.

4. Right-click the device you want to manage, and then select Properties from the shortcut menu. This opens the Properties dialog box for the device.

5. Click the Driver tab, and then click Roll Back Driver. When prompted to confirm the action, click Yes.

6. Click OK.

Note   If the driver file hasn't been updated, a backup drive file won't be available. Instead of being able to roll back the driver, you'll see a prompt that tells you no driver files have been backed up for this device. If you are having problems with the device, click Yes to start the Troubleshooter. Otherwise, click No to quit the operation.

Removing Device Drivers for Removed Devices

Usually when you remove a device from a system, Windows XP detects this fact and removes the drivers for that device automatically. However, sometimes when you remove a device, Windows XP doesn't detect the change and you must remove the drivers manually. You can remove device drivers by completing the following steps:

1. Start Computer Management. In the Computer Management console, click the plus sign (+) next to the System Tools node. This expands the node to display its tools.

2. Select Device Manager in the Computer Management console.

3. Right-click the device you want to remove, and then select Uninstall from the shortcut menu.

4. When prompted to confirm the action, click OK.

Uninstalling Device Drivers

Uninstalling a device driver uninstalls the related device. When a device isn't working properly, sometimes you can completely uninstall the device, restart the system, and then reinstall the device driver to restore normal operations. You can uninstall and then reinstall a device by completing the following steps:

1. Start Computer Management. In the Computer Management console, click the plus sign (+) next to the System Tools node. This expands the node to display its tools.

2. Select Device Manager in the Computer Management console. You should now see a complete list of devices installed on the system. By default, this list is organized by device type.

3. Right-click the device you want to manage, and then select Uninstall from the shortcut menu.

4. When prompted to confirm the action, click OK.

5. Reboot the system. Windows XP should detect the presence of the device and automatically reinstall the necessary device driver. If the device isn't automatically reinstalled, reinstall manually as discussed in the section of this chapter entitled "Adding New Hardware."

Note   To prevent a device from being reinstalled automatically, disable the device instead of uninstalling it. You disable a device by right-clicking it in Device Manager and then selecting Disable from the shortcut menu.

Managing Hardware

Windows Plug and Play technology does a good job of detecting and automatically configuring new hardware. However, if the hardware doesn't support Plug and Play or it isn't automatically detected, you'll need to enter information about the new hardware into the Windows XP system. You do this by installing the hardware device and its related drivers on the system using the Add Hardware Wizard. You can also use this wizard to troubleshoot problems with existing hardware.

Adding New Hardware

You can install new hardware using the Add Hardware Wizard by completing the following steps:

1. In Control Panel, double-click Add Hardware. This starts the Add Hardware Wizard. If the wizard recognizes the device, it will attempt to install the device and its driver. If successful, the device will be completely installed automatically and you do not need to complete the remaining steps.

2. At this point, you have two options:

   ❑ If you've already connected the new hardware, select Yes, I Have Already Connected The Hardware and click Next to continue. The Add Hardware Wizard page shown in Figure 3-6 should be displayed. Go on to step 3.

   ❑ If you haven't connected the hardware, click No, I Have Not Added The Hardware Yet and then click Next. The only option you have now is to click Finish. You'll need to connect the hardware (which may require shutting down the computer) and then restart the Add Hardware Wizard. Skip the remaining steps.

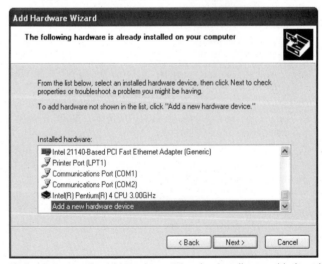

Figure 3-6   Use the Add Hardware Wizard to install or troubleshoot hardware devices.

3. To add new hardware, select Add A New Hardware Device from the Installed Hardware list box and then click Next. This option is located at the very bottom of the Installed Hardware list. In the Find New Hardware dialog box, determine whether the Wizard should search for new hardware or whether you want to select the hardware from a list.

   ❏ If you choose the search option, the Wizard searches for and automatically detects new hardware. The process takes a few minutes to go through all the device types and options. When the search is completed, any new devices found are displayed, and you can select a device.

   ❏ If you choose the manual option, or if no new devices are found in the automatic search, you'll have to select the hardware type yourself. Select the type of hardware, such as Modem or Network Adapter, and then click Next. Scroll through the list of manufacturers to find the manufacturer of the device, and then choose the appropriate device in the right pane.

   Tip If the device type you're trying to install isn't listed, select Show All Devices. This expands the device list to include all the possible types of devices that can be installed.

4. Once you complete the selection and installation process, click Next and then click Finish. The new hardware should now be available.

Enabling and Disabling Hardware

When a device isn't working properly, sometimes you'll want to uninstall or disable it. Uninstalling a device removes the driver association for the device so that it temporarily appears that the device has been removed from the system. The next time you restart the system, Windows XP might try to reinstall the device. Typically, Windows XP reinstalls Plug and Play devices automatically, but not non-Plug and Play devices.

Disabling a device turns it off and prevents Windows XP from using it. Because a disabled device doesn't use system resources, you can be sure that it isn't causing a conflict on the system.

You can uninstall or disable a device by completing the following steps:

1. Start Computer Management. In the Computer Management console, click the plus sign (+) next to the System Tools node. This expands the node to display its tools.

2. Select Device Manager in the Computer Management console. You should now see a complete list of devices installed on the system. By default, this list is organized by device type.

3. Right-click the device you want to manage, and then select one of the following options:

   ❏ Enable to enable the device
   ❏ Uninstall to uninstall the device
   ❏ Disable to disable the device

4. If prompted to confirm the action, click Yes or OK as appropriate.

Troubleshooting Hardware

You can use the Add Hardware Wizard to troubleshoot hardware problems as well. The basic steps are as follows:

1. In Control Panel, double-click Add Hardware. This starts the Add Hardware Wizard.

2. At this point, assuming the Wizard finds no new hardware to be installed, you have two options:

   ❏ If you've already connected the hardware that you want to examine, select Yes, I Have Already Connected The Hardware and click Next to display the Installed Hardware list box. Go on to step 3.

   ❏ If you haven't connected the hardware, click No, I Have Not Added The Hardware Yet and then click Next. The only option you have now is to click Finish. You'll need to connect the hardware (which may require shutting down the computer) and then restart the Add Hardware Wizard. Skip the next step.

3. Select the hardware device that you want to troubleshoot from the Installed Hardware list, and then click Next. The final Wizard dialog box provides a device status. When you click Finish, the Wizard does one of two things:

   ❏ If an error code is shown with the device status, the Wizard accesses the error code in the online help documentation—if it's available and installed. The help documentation should include a proposed technique to resolve the issue.

   ❏ Otherwise, the Wizard starts the device-specific hardware troubleshooter, which attempts to solve the hardware problem using your responses to the questions it asks. Follow the advice of the hardware troubleshooter to resolve the hardware problem.

You can also access the hardware troubleshooter directly. To do that, complete the following steps:

1. In the Computer Management console, access Device Manager.

2. Right-click the device you want to troubleshoot, and then select Properties on the shortcut menu.

3. In the General tab, click Troubleshoot.

Whenever a device is installed incorrectly or has another problem, Device Manager displays a warning icon indicating the device has a problem. If you double-click the device, an error code is displayed. As Table 3-1 shows, this error code can be helpful when trying to solve device problems as well. Most of the actions assume you have the device's Properties dialog box open to the General tab.

Table 3-1   Common Device Errors and Techniques to Resolve Them

Error Message	Correction Action
This device is not configured correctly. (Code 1)	Obtain a compatible driver for the device, and click Update Driver to start the Hardware Update Wizard.
The driver for this device might be corrupted, or your system may be running low on memory or other resources. (Code 3)	Run the Hardware Update Wizard by clicking the Update Driver button on the Driver tab. You may see an "Out of Memory" message at startup because of this.
This device cannot start. (Code 10)	Run the Hardware Update Wizard by clicking the Update Driver button on the Driver tab. Don't try to automatically find a driver. Instead, choose the manual install option, and select the device yourself.
This device cannot find enough free resources that it can use. (Code 12)	Resources assigned to this device conflict with another device, or the BIOS is incorrectly configured.
	Check the BIOS. Check for resource conflicts using the Resources tab of the device's Properties dialog box.
This device cannot work properly until you restart your computer. (Code 14)	Typically, the driver is installed correctly, but will not be started until you restart the computer.
Windows cannot identify all the resources this device uses. (Code 16)	Check to see if a signed driver is available for the device. If one is available and you've already installed it, you might need to manage the resources for the device. Check the Resources tab of the device's Properties dialog box.
This device is asking for an unknown resource type. (Code 17)	Reinstall or update the driver using a valid, signed driver.
Reinstall the drivers for this device. (Code 18)	After an upgrade, you might need to log on as an administrator to complete the device installation. If this is not the case, click Update Driver on the Driver tab to reinstall the driver.
Your registry might be corrupted. (Code 19)	Remove and reinstall the device. This should clear out the incorrect or conflicting registry settings.
Windows is removing this device. (Code 21)	The system will remove the device. The registry might be corrupted. If the device continues to display this message, restart the computer.
This device is disabled. (Code 22)	This device has been disabled using Device Manager. To enable it, select Use This Device (Enable) under Device Usage on the General tab of the device's Properties dialog box.
This device is not present, is not working properly, or does not have all its drivers installed. (Code 24)	Typically from a bad device or bad hardware. Can also occur with legacy ISA devices; upgrade the driver.
The drivers for this device are not installed. (Code 28)	Obtain a compatible driver for the device, and then click Update Driver to start the Hardware Update Wizard.
This device is disabled because the firmware of the device did not give it the required resources. (Code 29)	Check the device documentation on how to assign resources. You might need to enable the device in the system BIOS or upgrade the BIOS.

Table 3-1   Common Device Errors and Techniques to Resolve Them

Error Message	Correction Action
This device is not working properly because Windows cannot load the drivers required for this device. (Code 31)	The device driver might be incompatible with Windows XP Professional. Obtain a compatible driver for the device, and click Update Driver to start the Hardware Update Wizard.
A driver for this device was not required and has been disabled. (Code 32)	A dependent service for this device has been set to Disabled. Check the event logs to determine which services should be enabled and started.
Windows cannot determine which resources are required for this device. (Code 33)	Typically from a bad device or bad hardware. Can also occur with legacy ISA devices; upgrade the driver and/or refer to the device documentation on how to set resource usage.
Windows cannot determine the settings for this device. (Code 34)	The legacy device must be manually configured. Verify the device jumpers or BIOS settings, and then configure the device resource usage using the Resources tab of the device's Properties dialog box.
Your computer's system firmware does not include enough information to properly configure and use this device. (Code 35)	This error occurs on multiprocessor systems. Update the BIOS; check for a BIOS option to use MPS 1.1 or MPS 1.4. Usually you want MPS 1.4.
This device is requesting a PCI interrupt but is configured for an ISA interrupt (or vice versa). (Code 36)	ISA interrupts are non-shareable. If a device is in a PCI slot but the slot is configured in BIOS as "reserved for ISA," the error might display. Change the BIOS settings.
Windows cannot initialize the device driver for this hardware. (Code 37)	Run the Hardware Update Wizard by clicking the Update Driver button on the Driver tab.
Windows cannot load the device driver for this hardware because a previous instance of the device driver is still in memory. (Code 38)	A device driver in memory is causing a conflict. Restart the computer.
Windows cannot load the device driver for this hardware. The driver may be corrupted or missing. (Code 39)	Check to ensure the hardware device is properly installed and connected and that it has power. If it is properly installed and connected, look for an updated driver or reinstall the current driver.
Windows cannot access this hardware because its service key information in the registry is missing or recorded incorrectly. (Code 40)	The registry entry for the device driver is invalid. Reinstall the driver.
Windows has stopped this device because it has reported problems. (Code 43)	The device was stopped by the operating system. You might need to uninstall and then reinstall the device. The device might have problems with the no-execute processor feature. In this case, check for a new driver.
An application or service has shut down this hardware device. (Code 44)	The device was stopped by an application or service. Restart the computer. The device might have problems with the no-execute processor feature. In this case, check for a new driver.

Customizing Hardware Device Settings

Few system settings have more impact on the user experience than the settings for hardware devices such as the keyboard and mouse. Although these devices may seem to have straightforward uses, you can control several settings for them.

Configuring Keyboard Settings

Keyboard settings are controlled with the Keyboard utility in Control Panel. Double-click Keyboard to display the dialog box shown in Figure 3-7. You can now use the settings on the Speed tab to update the basic keyboard configuration. These settings are as follows:

- **Repeat Delay**   Controls the delay for repeating characters when you hold down a key. The default repeat delay is fairly short. For novice typists or children, you may want to set a longer delay rate.
- **Repeat Rate**   Controls how quickly characters repeat when you hold down a key. The default repeat rate is fast. You'll rarely want to change this setting.
- **Cursor Blink Rate**   Controls the rate at which the cursor blinks. If you find the blinking cursor annoying, set Cursor Blink Rate to None. With this setting, the cursor doesn't blink.

Figure 3-7   Keyboard controls can help you optimize settings for individual users. For example, you can get rid of a blinking cursor by setting Cursor Blink Rate to None.

Keyboards also have device drivers that can be managed like any other device driver. You can view driver details, update drivers, and uninstall drivers. You can also roll back drivers if necessary. One way to access the device drivers for a keyboard is to follow these steps:

1. Double-click Keyboard in Control Panel. This displays the Keyboard Properties dialog box shown in Figure 3-7.
2. On the Hardware tab, click Properties and then in the Keyboard Properties dialog box, click the Driver tab.

Configuring Mouse Settings

Mouse settings are controlled with the Mouse utility in Control Panel. Double-click Mouse to display the Mouse Properties dialog box shown in Figure 3-8. Here are some tips for optimizing mouse behavior for different users:

- On the Buttons tab, select Switch Primary And Secondary Buttons to configure the mouse buttons for left-handed users.

- On the Buttons tab, select Turn On ClickLock to select or drag without having to hold down the mouse button.

- Customize the display of the mouse pointer by using schemes. In the Pointers tab, use the options in the Scheme list to set a pointer scheme.

- If you have problems double-clicking, in the Buttons tab, change the Double-Click Speed rate to match your clicking speed.

- If the pointer distracts you when you are typing, in the Pointer Options tab, select Hide Pointer While Typing.

- If you need a better visual cue as to the location of the pointer when you move it, in the Pointer Options tab, select Display Pointer Trails.

Figure 3-8   Optimize the mouse settings to enhance the user experience and customize the environment.

As with keyboards, mouse devices also have device drivers. One way to access the device drivers for a mouse is to follow these steps:

1. Double-click Mouse in Control Panel. This displays the Mouse Properties dialog box shown in Figure 3-8.

2. On the Hardware tab, click Properties, and then in the Mouse Properties dialog box, click the Driver tab.

Configuring Sounds and Audio Devices

Most computers have sound cards, audio input devices (such as microphones), and audio output devices (such as built-in speakers or attached stereo speakers). To control these devices, you'll use the Sounds And Audio Devices utility in Control Panel.

Controlling Sound Volume

Sound volume is a key audio setting that you'll want to control. To set the sound volume for the default device, follow these steps:

1. Double-click Sounds And Audio Devices in Control Panel. This displays the Sounds And Audio Devices Properties dialog box shown in Figure 3-9.

Figure 3-9 Use the Volume tab to control the master device volume or to mute all devices.

2. Click the Volume tab if it isn't already selected.

3. The slider in the Device Volume area is the master volume control for the system. Move the slider to the left to lower the sound level. Move the slider to the right to increase the sound level.

4. If you want to turn off sound completely, click Mute.

To configure sound volume for individual devices, you'll need to access the advanced volume controls by doing the following:

1. Double-click Sounds And Audio Devices in Control Panel. This displays the Sounds And Audio Devices Properties dialog box.

2. Click the Volume tab if it isn't already selected.

3. In the Device Volume area of the Volume tab, click Advanced. This displays the Volume Control dialog box, whose contents will be similar to that shown in Figure 3-10.

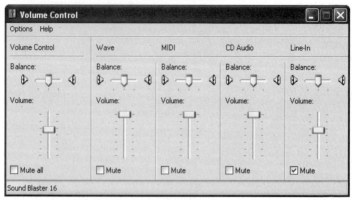

Figure 3-10 Use the Volume Control dialog box to manage the master volume and to set the volume of individual audio devices.

4. By default, the dialog box is configured to manage audio playback devices. Depending on the system setup, you might see controls for CD Audio, MIDI, Wave, PC Speaker, and Phone. You can work with the main controls as follows:

❑ Each device can be adjusted separately by dragging its Volume slider up or down.

❑ You can also adjust speaker balance by dragging the Balance slider left or right.

❑ You can mute a device's audio output by selecting Mute.

Other volume control tasks that you may want to perform are examined in the following sections.

Displaying a Shortcut to Volume Control   To display a shortcut to Volume Control, follow these steps:

1. Double-click Sounds And Audio Devices in Control Panel. The Volume tab should be selected.

2. Select Place Volume Icon In The Taskbar, and then click OK.

3. A volume shortcut is now displayed in the taskbar notification area. Simply double-click the shortcut to access Volume Control.

If you want to remove the shortcut, right-click the icon in the taskbar notification area and then select Adjust Audio Properties from the shortcut menu. Next clear the Place Volume Icon In The Taskbar check box, and then click OK.

Controlling Which Devices Have Volume Controls   You have complete control over which devices have volume controls in the Volume Control dialog box. To change the current settings, follow these steps:

1. Double-click Sounds And Audio Devices in Control Panel. This displays the Sounds And Audio Devices Properties dialog box.

2. Click the Volume tab if it isn't already selected.

3. Click Advanced in the Device Volume area. This displays the Volume Control dialog box.

4. In the Volume Control dialog box, select Properties from the Options menu. This displays the Properties dialog box.

5. Next select items in the Show The Following Volume Controls list, and then click OK.

Configuring Audio Settings for Recording Devices

You can configure audio settings for recording devices by completing the following steps:

1. Double-click Sounds And Audio Devices in Control Panel. This displays the Sounds And Audio Devices Properties dialog box.

2. Click the Volume tab if it isn't already selected.

3. Click Advanced in the Device Volume area. This displays the Volume Control dialog box.

4. In the Volume Control dialog box, select Properties from the Options menu. This displays the Properties dialog box.

5. Under Adjust Volume For, select Recording, and then select the recording items you want to manage using the Show The Following Volume Controls list.

6. When you click OK, you'll see the Recording Control dialog box shown in Figure 3-11. Use this dialog box to set the master recording volume for the system as well as the recording volume for individual recording devices.

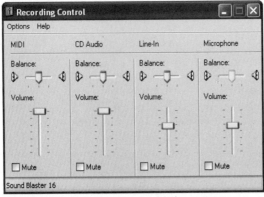

Figure 3-11   Use Recording Control to manage the master recording volume and to set the recording volume of individual audio devices.

Configuring Speakers and Audio Playback

The Sounds And Audio Devices utility can be used to configure speakers and to set hardware options for audio playback. Related tasks that you might want to perform are examined in the following sections.

Configuring Speakers and Headphones   Using Sounds And Audio Devices, you can configure systems so that they send audio output to a variety of devices including stereo headphones, desktop speakers, monitor speakers, and keyboard speakers. To do this, complete the following steps:

1. Double-click Sounds And Audio Devices in Control Panel. This displays the Sounds And Audio Devices Properties dialog box.
2. Click the Volume tab if it isn't already selected.
3. In the Speaker Settings area, click Advanced. This displays the Advanced Audio Properties dialog box.
4. In the Speakers tab, use the Speaker Setup list to specify the output device that should be used. When you are finished, click OK and then click OK again.

 Tip   You can also configure systems so that external speakers aren't used. To do this, select No Speakers from the Speaker Setup list.

Setting the Volume of External Speakers and Headphones   After you configure the type of speakers or headphones that you want to use, you might want to set the speaker volume. Speaker volume can be set separately for the left and right audio channels, or the volume can be set to the same level for both channels. To set speaker volume, follow these steps:

1. Double-click Sounds And Audio Devices in Control Panel. This displays the Sounds And Audio Devices Properties dialog box.
2. Click the Volume tab if it isn't already selected.
3. In the Speaker Settings area, click Speaker Volume. This displays the Speaker Volume dialog box.
4. Use the Left slider to set the volume for the left speaker. Use the Right slider to set the volume for the right speaker.
5. When you are finished configuring speaker volume, click OK and then click OK again.

Setting Hardware Performance and Playback Quality   Audio performance options control how Windows XP plays audio. Two parameters can be configured:

- **Hardware acceleration**   Controls the level of hardware acceleration used to play back audio and the compatibility of the audio mode with different types of hardware
- **Sample rate conversion quality**   Controls the playback quality of audio and the amount of system resources used to manage audio playback

You can set hardware acceleration and sample rate conversion quality by completing the following steps:

1. Double-click Sounds And Audio Devices in Control Panel. This displays the Sounds And Audio Devices Properties dialog box.
2. Click the Volume tab if it isn't already selected. In the Speaker Settings area, click Advanced. This displays the Advanced Audio Properties dialog box.

3. Click the Performance tab, shown in Figure 3-12.

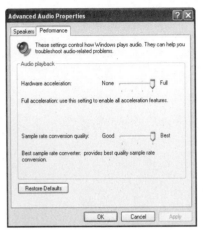

Figure 3-12 Configure acceleration, playback quality, and compatibility using the options in the Performance tab.

4. Use the Hardware Acceleration slider to control hardware acceleration features and the compatibility mode of the audio hardware. The slider has four settings. From left to right, they are the following:

   ❑ **Emulation Only** With no acceleration, the system operates in emulation mode. You should use this option if the system has problems with other acceleration levels.

   ❑ **Basic** With basic acceleration, Windows XP enables only the required acceleration features.

   ❑ **Standard** With standard acceleration, Windows XP enables Direct-Sound acceleration.

   ❑ **Full** With full acceleration, Windows XP enables DirectMusic and DirectShow acceleration for audio.

5. Use the Sample Rate Conversion Quality slider to control the playback quality of audio and the amount of system resources used for audio conversion. The slider has three settings. From left to right, they are the following:

   ❑ **Good** Standard sample rate conversion provides good quality and fast performance.

   ❑ **Improved** Improved sample rate conversion provides higher quality, but it requires more system resources and processing.

   ❑ **Best** Best sample rate conversion provides the highest quality audio playback, which requires a high level of processing and additional system resources.

6. When you are finished setting performance options, click OK and then click OK again.

Configuring System Sound Effects

System sound effects allow you to play audio files when certain program events occur. You can choose sounds for each event individually, or you can use a Windows XP sound scheme to apply sound settings automatically. Several sound schemes are available. Windows XP desktop themes can also have sound schemes associated with them. This means that if you change your desktop theme, the system's sound scheme might also change.

You can configure sound effects and schemes by completing the following steps:

1. Double-click Sounds And Audio Devices in Control Panel. This displays the Sounds And Audio Devices Properties dialog box.
2. Click the Sounds tab, which is shown in Figure 3-13.

Figure 3-13   Sound effects can be applied to individual program events or through schemes that contain multiple sound effects already applied to program events.

3. To choose a sound scheme, use the Sound Scheme list box.
4. To preview a sound for a particular event, select the event in the Program Events list and then click the play button (the button with the right-pointing triangle).
5. To change the sound for an event, select the event in the Program Events list and then use the Sounds list to choose an available sound. You can also click Browse to select other sounds available on the system. The sound files must be in Microsoft .wav format.
6. To save a changed sound scheme, click Save As, type a name for the scheme in the field provided, and then click OK.
7. Click OK to close the Sounds And Audio Devices Properties window.

Configuring Multimedia Audio and Voice Settings

If a system has multiple input or output audio devices, you may want to specify which device is used for a particular task. To do this, complete the following steps:

1. Double-click Sounds And Audio Devices in Control Panel. This displays the Sounds And Audio Devices Properties dialog box.

2. Use the options on the Audio tab to configure audio playback and recording devices. As shown in Figure 3-14, each device has a Default Device list that you can use to choose the preferred device.

3. Use the options on the Voice tab to configure voice playback and recording devices. As with audio devices, each voice device has a Default Device list that you can use to choose the preferred device.

4. Click OK when you are finished.

Figure 3-14   Use the Audio tab to select audio playback and recording devices. The Voice tab has similar options for selecting voice playback and recording devices.

Adjusting Regional Settings

Regional settings are used to set country-specific standards and formats. In different countries, the unit of measurement, currency, and date formatting can be different. By choosing a region, you choose all the appropriate settings for it. To configure regional settings, double-click Regional And Language Options in Control Panel and then select a country or region in the Standards And Formats area. The Samples pane should now display the formatting standards for the region. To customize these settings, click Customize and then use the Customize Regional Options dialog box to modify the basic number, currency, time, and date settings for the region.

Regional settings are also used to specify your present location for the purposes of presenting local information in dialog boxes and within Help And Support Services windows. To set the system location, double-click Regional And Language Options in Control Panel and then select a country or a region in the Location area.

Setting the Date and Time

System time can be set in several different ways. Typically, you'll use the Date And Time utility from Control Panel. To adjust the system time, in Control Panel, double-click Date And Time, set the date and time as needed, and then click OK when finished. In the Date And Time Properties dialog box, you can set a time zone as well. To choose a time zone, click the Time Zone tab and then use the list provided.

Some time zones within the United States and abroad use Daylight Saving Time. If you select a time zone where this is applicable, you'll see the Automatically Adjust Clock For Daylight Saving Changes check box. Daylight Saving Time is used by default wherever applicable. If you don't want to use Daylight Saving Time, clear this check box.

Note   To keep system time in close synchronization with world time, you'll want to use Internet time. See the two sections of this chapter entitled "Configuring Internet Time in Workgroups" and "Configuring Internet Time in Domains."

Notice also that the lithium battery that maintains the complementary metal-oxide semiconductor (CMOS) memory on the motherboard also maintains the PC clock within a computer when the system is shut off. This battery is designed to last several years but it does need to be replaced periodically. If a computer consistently loses time, that battery could be to blame, and you might want to consider replacing it.

Managing Internet Time

System time has an increasingly important role as the Windows operating system matures, particularly with regard to Kerberos security, which is the default Windows XP authentication mechanism. With Kerberos security, the network depends on system clocks being in close synchronization. If the clocks on different systems aren't closely synchronized, authentication tickets can become invalid before they reach a destination host, which can prevent logon and authentication.

Internet Time Overview

Keeping the system synchronized with the actual time isn't easy. System clocks can lose time, users can accidentally set the system clock to the wrong time, and other things can also go wrong. To help resolve problems with system time and time synchronization, Windows XP uses Windows Time service to set a consistent Internet time based on the time at an Internet time server. Windows Time service allows synchronization within 100 milliseconds of world time. Here's a basic overview of how Windows Time service works:

- Windows XP systems are configured to synchronize with an Internet time server automatically. This time server is referred to as the *authoritative time server*. The default time servers are time.microsoft.com and time.nist.gov. Administrators can specify either of these servers or type in the name of another time server.

Real World   In most cases, you'll want Windows XP workstations to sync with a local time server (one located in your domain, for instance) and then have the local time server synchronize with an authoritative time server, such as time.nist.gov. This reduces network traffic and can improve performance for time synchronization.

- The Windows Time service uses the Simple Network Time Protocol (SNTP) to poll the authoritative time server. The global settings MinPollInterval and Max-PollInterval control the exact rates.

- If there are differences in time between the time server and the system, the Windows Time service slowly corrects the time. The global settings UpdateInterval and FrequencyCorrectRate control the exact correction rate.

Note   SNTP defaults to using User Datagram Protocol (UDP) port 123. If this port is not open to the Internet, you can't synchronize the system with an Internet time server.

You can configure the Windows Time service via the Registry or Group Policy. Table 3-2 provides detailed information on the most used time service settings. The related Group Policy settings are under Computer Configuration\Administrative Templates\System\Windows Time Service\Global Configuration Settings. If the Global Configuration Settings policy is enabled, its settings take precedence over local Registry settings. The related Registry settings are under HKLM\SYSTEM\CurrentControlSet\Services\W32Time\Config. If you change Registry values for time services, you can apply them by typing the following command at the command prompt:

```
w32tm /config /update
```

Table 3-2   Global Configuration Settings for Windows Time Services

Setting	Description	Accepted Values/Flags
Announce-Flags	Default value: 10 (8+2). Sets the time server classification. A computer must be classified first as a time server to be subsequently classified as a reliable time server. This is why the default flag is 10 (meaning flags 2 and 8 are applied). This setting is only used by domain controllers and determines how the time service is advertised by the Netlogon service.	10 (default with 8+2 flags) 0; the domain controller does not advertise time services. 1; the domain controller always advertises time service. 2; the domain controller is a time server and automatically determines whether it should advertise time service. 4; the domain controller will always advertise reliable time service. 8; the domain controller is a reliable time server and automatically determines whether it should advertise reliable time service.

Table 3-2   Global Configuration Settings for Windows Time Services

Setting	Description	Accepted Values/Flags
EventLog-Flags	Determines the types of events that the time service logs. Default value: 2.	1; logs when the time service must make a discontinuous change to the clock. 2; logs when the time service chooses a new source of time information. 3; logs when the time service has not acquired time samples for a period that is 1.5 times the maximum poll interval and no longer trusts the local clock to be accurate.
Frequency-CorrectRate	Modifies the rate at which the time service corrects (synchronizes) the system clock. The value used is multiplied by the number of clock ticks in 64 seconds to come up with the base gain used to correct the system time. Generally, the smaller the value, the more responsive the system is to time changes. However, if the value is too small, the system time can change too frequently to be stable. A value of 3–5 is generally a stable range.	4 (default)
HoldPeriod	Determines the number of seconds the last consistently read time sample is held. It is essentially designed to prevent frequent time changes due to inconsistent time samples. During this period, time synchronization (as determined by the FrequencyCorrectRate) and spike detection (for consistent time samples) are switched off to allow for faster time correction (convergence).	5 (default)
LargePhase-Offset	Determines the time offset in milliseconds that triggers direct setting of the system clock. If the system clock is off by more than this amount, system time is set directly to the appropriate time rather than using time correction (convergence). Set the offset to a higher value to make it less likely that the system time will be set directly. However, if you do this, it is more likely that bad time samples will be considered to be good.	128,000 (default)

Table 3-2   Global Configuration Settings for Windows Time Services

Setting	Description	Accepted Values/Flags
LocalClock-Dispersion	Indicates the relative reliability of the local CMOS clock when it is used as a time source for other computers but is not synchronized with another network time source. The dispersion value is the number of seconds by which the time service should consider the local CMOS clock will be off from the estimated true time at any given time. The higher the reliability by which the local CMOS should be considered, the lower the dispersion value should be set. If the clock is synchronized from a network time source, the dispersion applies to that time source.	10 (default)
MaxAllowed-PhaseOffset	Specified the maximum time correction allowed when convergence is used (rather than direct time setting). If the system clock is off by more than this number of seconds, the time is corrected over multiple convergence intervals. This value is designed to prevent large sudden changes in time.	300 (default for DCs) 1 (default for other computers)
Max-NegPhase-Correction	Specifies the largest negative time correction the time service is allowed to make. If the time is off by more than this amount, the required change is logged rather than corrected. For example, if the clock is set to 5:00 PM but it is really 1:59 AM of that same day (an earlier time), the required time change would be logged rather than corrected. An administrator would then need to set the time manually. A smaller value is considered more secure as it could prevent malicious time servers from changing system times erroneously.	54,000 (default)
Max-PollInterval	Determines the longest time interval to be used for checking the time. The value is set in units of 2^n seconds where n is the value for this setting. The default value is 2^{15} (32,768 seconds). The Windows Time Service will consider itself to be in an unsynchronized state when 1.5 times the MaxPollInterval has elapsed and it is unable to obtain a time reading from a reliable time server. This value is also referred to as the maximum clock age and in the Network Time Protocol, the maximum clock age allowed is 86,400 seconds. Thus, if you set MaxPollInterval to a value greater than 15, the time server may be ignored completely by peers.	15 (default)

Table 3-2   Global Configuration Settings for Windows Time Services

Setting	Description	Accepted Values/Flags
MaxPosPhas eCorrection	Specifies the largest positive time correction the time service is allowed to make. If the time is off by more than this amount, the required change is logged rather than corrected. For example, if the clock is set to 1:59 AM but it is really 5:00 PM of that same day (a later time), the required time change would be logged rather than corrected. An administrator would then need to set the time manually. A smaller value is considered more secure as it could prevent malicious time servers from changing system times erroneously.	54,000 (default)
MinPol-lInterval	Determines the shortest time interval to be used for checking the time. The value is set in units of 2^n seconds where n is the value for this setting. The default value for DCs is 2^6 (64 seconds) because time synchronization is more important and 2^10 (1024 seconds) for other computers to reduce the number of network accesses. Windows XP and Windows Server 2003 won't poll more frequently than once every 16 seconds regardless of the Min-PollInterval used.	6 (default for DCs) 10 (default for other computers)
Phase-Correction-Rate	Specifies the time correction interval in seconds. This is the interval for time correction when convergence is used. With the default value the time can be corrected once every second.	1 (default)
PollAdjust-Factor	Sets an adjustment interval for polling the time. The value is set in units of 2^n seconds where n is the value for this setting.	5 (default)
SpikeWatch-Period	Sets the period in seconds during which suspicious time changes are watched before they are accepted as valid. If you lower this value, you allow the time server to correct time spikes (sudden changes in time) more quickly but also make it more likely that bad time samples will be considered as good.	90 (default)
Update-Interval	Determines the interval used for phase correction adjustments. The lower the value the more accurate the time. The higher the more efficient the time sampling. Thus there is a trade to be made between accuracy and efficiency. On DCs, you want more accuracy and can use more system resources to maintain the system clock as clock accuracy is very important. On other computers, you balance the need for efficiency against the need for accuracy.	100 (domain controllers), 30,000 (member servers), 360,000 (standalone computers)

Configuring Internet Time in Workgroups

Most organizations will want to use Internet time so that computers can easily synchronize with external time servers. As enabling Internet time is the default setting for Windows XP, the real challenge lies in opening UDP port 123 on your firewall to allow the flow of Windows Time service traffic. Once you open this port on your firewall, the time service should operate normally.

You can enable or disable Internet time for individual systems in a workgroup by completing the following steps:

1. In Control Panel, double-click Date And Time and then click the Internet Time tab.

2. To enable Internet time, select Automatically Synchronize With An Internet Time Server and then select the time server you want to use. You should also ensure that the Windows Time service is running in the Services utility.

3. To disable Internet time, clear the Automatically Synchronize With An Internet Time Server check box.

4. Use the Server field to specify the Internet time server to use. Two default time servers are listed: time.windows.com and time.nist.gov. You can select one of these or type in the fully qualified domain name of another time server to use.

5. Click OK.

When you use Internet time, keep in mind that on large networks, it's much more efficient to set up a local time server. With a local time server, SNTP messages from workstations and servers are broadcast locally and don't go out to the Internet. The messages sent between the local time server and the external time server are the only external time traffic.

If a computer isn't set to the correct time, network access is usually the problem. Computers must have access to the network to access a local time server. They must have access to the Internet to access an Internet time server, which also requires that UDP port 123 be open to the computer on the organization's firewall or proxy server.

You can check on the status of time synchronization at any time, and you can force a computer to update the time immediately as well. If you suspect that time synchronization is failing, you can check the status of the last synchronization by following these steps:

1. In Control Panel, double-click Date And Time and then click the Internet Time tab.

2. Any error encountered during the last synchronization attempt will be displayed.

Once you've accessed the Internet Time tab, you can troubleshoot the configuration as follows:

1. Ensure that the time server is set correctly. If necessary, retype the value.

2. Click Update Now to force Windows XP to attempt to synchronize with the specified time server.

3. If an error occurs, check the network connectivity as well as the status of the Windows Time service. Again, the computer must have appropriate network or Internet access, and the Windows Time service must be running for this feature to work properly.

Configuring Internet Time in Domains

In Active Directory domains, a domain controller is chosen automatically as the reliable time source for the domain, and other computers in the domain synchronize time with this server. Should this server be unavailable to provide time services, another domain controller takes over. You cannot, however, change the Windows Time configuration. If you want to manage Windows Time in a different way, you must first enable and configure Internet Time through Group Policy. The related policies are found under Computer Configuration\Administrative Templates\System\Windows Time Service\Time Providers and include the following settings:

- **Enable Windows NTP Client**   When this setting is enabled, this computer can synchronize its clock with designated NTP servers.

- **Enable Windows NTP Server**   When this setting is enabled, this computer can service NTP requests from other computers.

- **Configure Windows NTP Client**   When you enable this setting, you are able to set the Internet time configuration options, including the name of the time server to use.

You can also configure global time services options using Global Configuration Settings under Computer Configuration\Administrative Templates\System\Windows Time Service.

With this in mind, you configure Internet Time in a domain by completing the following steps:

1. Access local policy on a server that is a member of the appropriate domain, site, or organizational unit.

2. Expand Computer Configuration, Administrative Templates, System, Windows Time Service, Time Providers.

3. Double-click Enable Windows NTP Server, select Enabled, and then click OK.

4. Access the appropriate domain, site, or organizational unit Group Policy Object in the Group Policy Object Editor.

5. Expand Computer Configuration, Administrative Templates, System, Windows Time Service, Time Providers.

6. Double-click Enable Windows NTP Client, select Enabled, and then click OK.

7. Double-click Configure Windows NTP Client, and then select Enabled. Use the fields available to set the default NTP settings, including the name of the time server to use. Click OK when you are finished.

Chapter 4

Customizing Menus, the Windows Taskbar, and Toolbars

In this chapter:

Optimizing Windows XP Menus 99
Customizing the Taskbar 107
Optimizing Toolbars 113

As an administrator, you'll often be asked to help users customize their workspaces. You might even be asked to create a default workspace for new users that closely maps to the corporate standard or core user preferences. One way to create a default workspace is to create a default user account, log on as that user, set up the workspace as necessary, and then use the account and its associated profile as the starting point for new accounts. In this chapter, you'll learn how to customize Windows XP menus, the taskbar, and toolbars. (Unless otherwise indicated, "Windows XP" in this book refers to Windows XP Professional.) In Chapter 5, "Optimizing the Desktop and Screen Appearance," you'll learn how to customize the screen and desktop appearance.

Optimizing Windows XP Menus

The Start menu and its related menus are designed to provide easy access to applications and utilities installed on a system. Unfortunately, the more applications and utilities you install, the more cluttered the menu system becomes. To help users escape the clutter and better use the menu system, this section focuses on techniques you can use to optimize menus.

Changing Between Classic and Simple Start Menu

As discussed in Chapter 1, "Introduction to Windows XP Professional Administration," Windows XP provides two views of the Start menu: classic and simple. The Classic Start menu provides the traditional view of the menu system as found in previous versions of the Windows operating system. The Simple Start menu provides a streamlined view of the menu system that's better organized than its more traditional predecessor. Many hardcore Windows users and administrators are apt to hate the Simple Start menu when they first see it, but they grow to love it once they customize it.

You can change between the Classic Start and the Simple Start menus at any time by following these steps:

1. Right-click Start on the taskbar, and then select Properties on the shortcut menu.
2. Select Start Menu to use the Simple view, or select Classic Start Menu to use the classic view.
3. Click OK. If you've already customized settings for the menu view, these custom settings are restored automatically.

Customizing Classic Start Menu Options

If you choose the Classic Start menu, Windows XP provides excellent control over the Start menu. You can choose which commands appear on the Start menu and in what arrangement. You can add menus for Control Panel, Network Connections, Printers And Faxes, and other key tools. You can also enable or disable personalized menus on the Programs menu.

To change the Start menu options, follow these steps:

1. Right-click Start on the taskbar, and then select Properties on the shortcut menu.
2. Verify that Classic Start Menu is selected, and click Customize to the right of the Classic Start Menu option. This displays the Customize Classic Start Menu dialog box, shown in Figure 4-1.

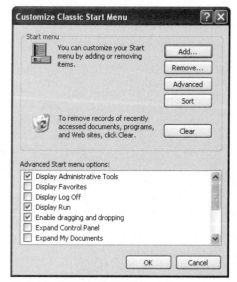

Figure 4-1   Customize the Classic Start menu using this dialog box.

3. Select or clear any of the check boxes in the Advanced Start Menu Options list box.

4. Click OK.

5. Click OK to close the Taskbar And Start Menu Properties dialog box.

Table 4-1 provides a list of the Classic Start menu options. As the table shows, most of the options control user actions or determine whether various selections are available directly from the Start menu or through separate windows.

Table 4-1   Classic Start Menu Options

Setting	Purpose
Display Administrative Tools	Adds or removes the Administrative Tools menu. When selected, the menu is available from the Programs menu.
Display Favorites	Adds or removes the Favorites menu. When selected, the menu is available from the Start menu. Enable this option if a user uses the Favorites list frequently.
Display Log Off	Adds or removes the Log Off command. When selected, the Log Off command is available on the Start menu. If you don't select this option, users must press Ctrl+Alt+Del to access the Log Off command.
Display Run	Adds or removes the Run command. When selected, the Run command is available on the Start menu.
Enable Dragging And Dropping	Controls whether users can use drag-and-drop to manage the contents and order of the Start menu. Typically you'll want to enable this option unless there is a specific security reason to disable it.
Expand Control Panel	When enabled, the Control Panel options appear as a submenu of the Settings, Control Panel command. Otherwise, Control Panel appears as a separate option that opens the Control Panel window.
Expand My Documents	Same as Expand Control Panel, except it applies to the Documents, My Documents submenu.
Expand My Pictures	Same as Expand Control Panel, except it applies to the Documents, My Pictures submenu.
Expand Network Connections	Same as Expand Control Panel, except it applies to the Settings, Network Connections submenu.
Expand Printers	Same as Expand Control Panel, except it applies to the Settings, Printers And Faxes submenu.
Scroll Programs	Controls whether the Programs menu displays all options or allows for horizontal scrolling. Depending on the screen display size, this option is only used when there are more than 29 or more than 38 items.
Show Small Icons In Start Menu	When selected, this option reduces the size of icons used on menus.
Use Personalized Menus	When selected, this option prompts Windows XP to track the menu options that you use as you work. It displays only a partial list when you open menus, hiding infrequently used options until you click the down pointing arrow at the bottom of the menu.

Tip   The Scroll Programs and Use Personalized Menus options can be
somewhat annoying to users (and to you). I recommend disabling these
features. You'll have happier users and fewer questions about disappearing
options.

Customizing Simple Start Menu Settings

The Simple Start menu has all the options of the Classic Start menu, plus a few
additional options that aren't available otherwise. Because of this, you can customize the Simple Start menu in many more ways than you can the Classic Start menu.

To change the Start menu options, follow these steps:

1. Right-click Start on the taskbar, and then select Properties on the shortcut
    menu.

2. Ensure the Start Menu option is selected, and click Customize to the right of
    the Start Menu option. This displays the Customize Start Menu dialog box
    shown in Figure 4-2.

3. Use the options on the General tab to control the general appearance of the
    Start menu. The areas of the tab are as follows:

    ❑ **Select An Icon Size For Programs**   Controls the size of icons for menu
    options. To reduce the size of icons used on menus, select Small Icons.
    Otherwise, select Large Icons to display standard-size icons on menus.

    ❑ **Programs**   Controls the number of shortcuts to recently used programs
    that appear on the most-frequently used list on the Start menu. Use the
    selection menu to assign a value from 0 to 30. The actual number of
    programs listed in this most-frequently used list will depend on the
    screen resolution as well as the number of items in the pinned items list,
    which is above the most-frequently used list. Click Clear List to reset the
    usage tracking for recently used programs.

    ❑ **Show On Start Menu**   Controls shortcuts to Internet browsers and e-
    mail applications. If you want these items to appear on the Start menu,
    select the appropriate check boxes and then choose the application to use.

4. Options available on the Advanced tab tailor the behavior of the menu and its
    options. The available options on this tab are as follows:

    ❑ **Open Submenus When I Pause On Them With My Mouse**   Controls the
    behavior of menus. When this option is selected, menus open when you
    point to them. Otherwise, menus open only when you click them.

    ❑ **Highlight Newly Installed Programs**   When this option is selected,
    menus for recently installed applications are highlighted, as are the menu
    options.

    ❑ **Start Menu Items**   Controls which commands appear on the Start menu
    and in what arrangement. Some items have suboptions of Display As A
    Link, Display As A Menu, and Don't Display This Item. Display As A Link
    specifies that an item, such as Control Panel, will appear as a separate
    option that opens a window when selected. Display As A Menu specifies

that an item will provide access to a submenu that allows you to choose its related options. Don't Display This Item removes the item from the Start menu.

❑ **List My Most Recently Opened Documents**   Controls tracking of recently used documents. When selected, a Recent Documents item is displayed, providing quick access to recently used documents. Click Clear List to reset the usage tracking for recently used documents.

5. When you are finished customizing the Start menu, click OK.
6. Click OK to close the Taskbar And Start Menu Properties dialog box.

Figure 4-2   Set general and advanced options for the Simple Start menu using the Customize Start Menu dialog box.

Modifying Menus and Their Options

In the Windows XP file system, the Start menu is represented by a pair of folders, each with the name Start Menu. Programs that are to be made available only to the currently logged on user are placed in the Start Menu folder that is located within the profile data for that user (*%UserProfile%*\Start Menu), and programs that are to be available to any user that logs on to the computer are placed in the Start Menu folder for All Users (*%SystemDrive%*\Documents And Settings\All Users\Start Menu). During system startup, Windows XP merges the contents of both Start Menu folders to create the single Start menu, accessible when you click the Start button. In each case, below the Start Menu folder, you'll find a Programs folder. The structure for these Programs menus and their related menus is determined by the folders and shortcuts stored in them. Each folder within the Programs folders represents a menu. Shortcuts within folders represent menu options and act as pointers to the programs you want to launch. If you want to modify menus and their options, you have several choices. You can work directly with the appropriate file system representation of the Start menu, or you can work with the menu system itself.

Rearranging Items on the Start Menu

The easiest way to rearrange items on the Start menu is to use the menu system. You can change the position of menus and options within menus. The technique you use is as follows:

1. Click Start, and point to Programs or All Programs as appropriate.
2. Point to the item that you want to manipulate.
3. Press and hold the left mouse button.
4. Drag the item to a new location on any menu or submenu; simply point to a submenu to open it. A horizontal line shows where the selected item is going.
5. Release the mouse button when the menu or item is in the desired location.

In the Classic Start menu, you can drag items to the upper-left corner of the Start menu where they will remain displayed. When you have the mouse pointer in the proper location, you'll see the horizontal position line that highlights where the item will be placed when you release the mouse button.

With the Simple Start menu, there are some other techniques for adding and removing items from this upper-left area of the Start menu, known in the Simple Start menu as the *pinned items* list.

- To add items to the pinned items area, right-click the item and then select Pin To Start Menu.
- To remove items from the pinned items area, right-click the item on the menu and then select Remove From This List. There is also an Unpin From Start Menu command on this shortcut menu, which will delete the entry from the pinned items list, but, if the item has been recently used, it may then appear in the most frequently used list. Using the Remove From This List command ensures that will not happen.

Reorganizing Menu Options

The Program menu's contents are normally sorted with submenus at the top and menu options below. Within each of those two categories, the menu contents are initially listed alphabetically. As you install applications and move items around on the Programs menu, however, it is easy for items to become disorganized, largely because menus and menu options for new programs are placed at the bottom of the Programs menu. You can resolve this problem by re-alphabetizing the entire Programs menu—and users who have a lot of programs installed will love you for it.

To re-alphabetize the entire Programs menu, follow these steps:

1. Click Start, and then select Programs or All Programs, depending on your choice of Start menu.

2. Right-click on any entry in the Programs list, and select Sort By Name from the shortcut menu.

Adding, Modifying, and Deleting Menus

As mentioned earlier, the Start menu is represented on the file system as a folder that can be accessed through the profile data for a particular user as well as a folder that can be accessed through the profile data for All Users. To access the Start Menu folder for the current user, right-click Start and then select Explore. This opens Windows Explorer with the *%UserProfile%*\Start Menu folder selected. To access the Start Menu folder for All Users, right-click Start and then select Explore All Users. This opens Windows Explorer with the *%SystemDrive%*\Documents And Settings\All Users\Start Menu folder selected. Once you open a Start Menu folder, you can perform all the normal folder operations to update the Start menu, including the following:

- Add new menus to the Start menu by creating folders within the Programs folder or any subfolder of the Programs folder (except Startup).

- Modify menus by moving folders or shortcuts to new locations within the Programs folder.

- Rename folders or shortcuts to update their names on the Start menu. Another way to rename items is through the menu system. With the Start menu active, right-click the item you want to rename and select Rename. Type a new name for the item, and then click OK.

- Delete any unwanted folders or shortcuts to remove the related menus or menu options from the Start menu. Another way to delete items is through the menu system. With the Start menu active, right-click the item you want to delete and then select Delete.

Caution   Don't rename or remove the Startup folder. This folder holds shortcuts for programs that should load automatically at startup. If you alter this folder, Windows XP might not be able to use it. Additionally, you shouldn't rename or remove the Administrative tools menu. The availability of the Administrative Tools menu is controlled through Taskbar And Start Menu Properties.

Adding Menu Options to the Start Menu

Menu options are represented as shortcuts in the Windows XP file system. This means you can create menu options simply by adding shortcuts to the Programs folder or its subfolders. After you create a shortcut, you can update its properties to include comments that are displayed when someone points to the option on the Start menu. The complete steps to create a menu option, unique to the currently logged on user, are as follows:

1. Right-click Start, and then select Explore from the shortcut menu. This opens Windows Explorer with the *%UserProfile%*\Start Menu folder selected.

2. In the left pane of Windows Explorer, select the folder to which you want to add the menu option.

3. In the Contents or View pane, right-click an open area, point to New on the shortcut menu, and then select Shortcut. This starts the Create Shortcut Wizard.

4. In the field provided, type the file path to the program or file you want to associate with the shortcut. If you don't know the file path, click Browse and then use the Browse For Folder dialog box to locate the item you want to use.

5. Click Next, and then type a name for the shortcut. The value you enter is the name that will appear on the Start menu.

6. Click Finish. If you want to enter comments for the shortcut, right-click the shortcut and then select Properties. Enter the comments in the Comment field, and then click OK.

Displaying the Administrative Tools Menu

The Administrative Tools menu is not displayed by default in Windows XP. If you want to display this menu on your computer or for a user with Administrator privileges, you'll need to customize the Start menu.

With the Classic Start menu, you add the Administrative Tools menu to the Programs submenu of the Start menu by completing the following steps:

1. Right-click Start, and then select Properties from the shortcut menu.

2. If Classic Start Menu isn't selected, select this option and then click the related Customize button. This displays the Customize Classic Start Menu dialog box.

3. Select Display Administrative Tools in the Advanced Start Menu Options list box.

4. Click OK twice.

 Tip   You might want to click Sort before you click OK. This forces Windows to re-alphabetize the Programs menus and menu options. If you don't sort the menus, the Administrative Tools menu is displayed at the bottom of the Programs menu.

With the Simple Start menu, there are several different ways you can add the Administrative Tools menu to the Start Menu. To get started, follow these steps:

1. Right-click Start, and then select Properties from the shortcut menu.

2. If the Simple Start menu isn't selected, select Start Menu and then click the related Customize button. This displays the Customize Start Menu dialog box.

3. Select the Advanced tab, and then scroll down the Start Menu Items list until you can see the System Administrative Tools heading.

4. At this point, you have two options:
   - ❑ If you want to display the Administrative Tools menu as a submenu of the All Programs menu, select Display On The All Programs Menu.
   - ❑ If you want to display the Administrative Tools menu directly on the Start menu and as a submenu of the All Programs menu, select Display On The All Programs Menu And The Start Menu.
5. Click OK twice.

   You might want to sort the All Programs menu to move the Administrative Tools menu into the correct alphabetic sequence of folder names.

Enabling and Disabling Personalized Menus

The Classic Start menu offers personalized menus, and when they are enabled, Windows XP tracks the Start menu options you use as you work. It then displays only a partial list when you open menus, hiding infrequently used options until you click the down-pointing arrow at the bottom of the menu. However, many users don't like this behavior because they have difficulty finding options they want to use. Therefore, you might want to change the default setting for personalized menus and disable this feature. If a few users like this feature, you can enable it on a per user basis as necessary.

To enable or disable personalized menus, follow these steps:

1. Right-click Start, and then select Properties from the shortcut menu.
2. If Classic Start Menu isn't currently selected, select this option and then click the related Customize button. This displays the Customize Classic Start Menu dialog box.
3. Select or clear the Use Personalized Menus item in the Advanced Start Menu Options list box, and then click OK twice.

Customizing the Taskbar

The taskbar provides quick access to frequently needed information and active applications. You can change the taskbar's behavior and properties in many ways. This section explores key techniques you can use to do this.

Understanding the Taskbar

The taskbar is one of the least appreciated areas of the Windows desktop. Users and administrators tend to pay very little attention to its configuration, yet we use it day in and day out, relying on it for quick access to just about everything we do with the Windows operating system. If you find that users are having frequent problems accessing Windows features or running applications, you can help them by tailoring the taskbar to their needs. The Windows taskbar can contain several toolbars that can assist the user in different ways, several of which are shown in Figure 4-3.

Sometimes, you can provide tremendous productivity increases simply by adding a frequently used item to the taskbar. For example, most people spend a lot of time finding and reading documents. They browse the Web or the corporate intranet to find the latest information. They open documents in Microsoft Word, Excel, Power-Point, or other applications, finding documents individually and starting applications to read those documents as well. By adding an Address bar to the taskbar, users can access documents directly and launch the appropriate application automatically. They just need to type the document path and click Go. As time passes, the history feature of the Address bar tracks more and more of the user's previously accessed documents, making it easier to find the needed information.

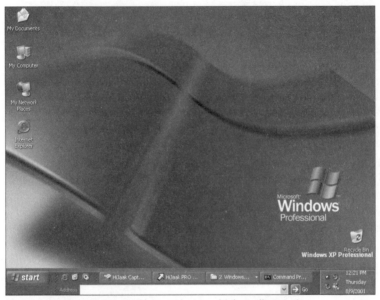

Figure 4-3   The Windows taskbar can have multiple toolbars active.

Changing the Taskbar Size and Position

By default, the taskbar appears at the bottom of the screen and is sized so that one row of options is visible. As long as the taskbar position isn't locked, you can dock it to any edge of the Windows desktop and resize it as necessary. To move the taskbar, simply click it and drag it to a different edge of the desktop. You won't see the taskbar move as you drag, but when you release the mouse button, the taskbar appears in the new location. To resize the taskbar, move the mouse pointer over the taskbar edge and then drag it up or down.

Real World   New users seem to have the most problems with the task-bar. Sometimes you might even be told that the taskbar has vanished. In most cases, the user accidentally resized the taskbar so that it isn't visible. If you've selected the Windows Classic theme on the Display Properties dialog box, look along the desktop edge for a thin gray bar. If you've selected the Windows XP theme on the Display Properties dialog box, look along the desktop edge for a thin blue bar. Move the mouse pointer to it, and then drag it toward the center of the screen so that the bar expands to its normal size. Alternatively, on keyboards with a Windows key, press this key, which makes the Start menu pop out from the edge of the screen that has the minimized taskbar. You can then instruct the user to slide the cursor toward that edge until the pointer changes and drag the bar out. If the user has locked the taskbar, instruct him to right-click when the pointer changes and choose Properties. Then in the Taskbar And Start Menu Properties dialog box, clear Lock The Taskbar.

Auto Hiding, Locking, and Controlling Taskbar Visibility

When you want to control the visibility of the taskbar, you have several options. You can enable the Auto Hide feature to hide the taskbar from view when it is not in use. You can lock the taskbar so that it can't be resized or repositioned. You can also make the taskbar appear on top of other windows when you point to it. Once the taskbar is positioned and sized the way a user wants it, you should enable all three of these options. In this way, the taskbar has a fixed location so users don't have to hunt for it, and the taskbar is visible when it is pointed to so that it isn't hidden behind other windows.

To enable these options, follow these steps:

1. Right-click the taskbar, and then select Properties from the shortcut menu.
2. Select the Taskbar tab in the Taskbar And Start Menu Properties dialog box if it isn't already selected.
3. Select Lock The Taskbar, Auto-Hide The Taskbar, and Keep The Taskbar On Top Of Other Windows.
4. Click OK.

Tip   Locking the taskbar is one of the most useful taskbar options. If you lock the taskbar once it is optimized, users will have fewer problems caused by accidentally altering taskbar options. Locking the taskbar doesn't pre-vent users from changing the taskbar on purpose. If users really want to change the taskbar, all they need to do is right-click the taskbar, select Properties, and then clear Lock The Taskbar.

Grouping Similar Taskbar Items

The option of grouping taskbar items, a new feature in Windows XP, is designed to remove some of the clutter from the taskbar by grouping related items into a menu. For example, if a user opens multiple folders in Windows Explorer and the taskbar needs additional room for other items, these folders are grouped under a single menu heading. As shown in Figure 4-4, individual instances of Windows Explorer are then accessible by clicking the menu heading and selecting the item the user wants to use. For novice users, this behavior can be confusing, so you might want to turn it off. But most experienced users will find this feature beneficial.

You can enable or disable grouping of similar items on the taskbar by completing these steps:

1. Right-click the taskbar, and then select Properties from the shortcut menu.
2. Select the Taskbar tab in the Taskbar And Start Menu Properties dialog box if it isn't already selected.
3. Select Group Similar Taskbar Buttons.
4. Click OK.

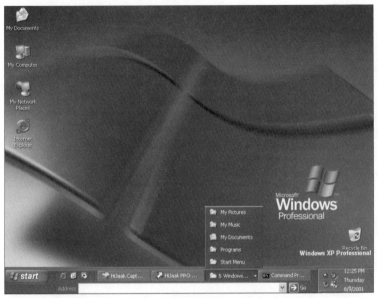

Figure 4-4   Similar items can be automatically grouped to clear up the taskbar.

Controlling Programs in the Notification Area

The notification area or system tray is the area on the far right side of the taskbar that shows the system clock and applications that were loaded automatically by the operating system at startup and are running in the background. When you point to icons in the notification area, a ScreenTip provides information on the running application. To control an application in this area, right-click the application icon to display a menu of available options. Each application has a different menu of options, most of which provide quick access to routine tasks.

You can optimize the notification area for users in several ways. One way is to add or remove startup programs. Another is to set properties of the notification area that control whether the clock is displayed and whether icons are displayed or hidden.

Adding or Removing Startup Programs

Administrator-installed or user-installed applications that run in the background can be managed through the Startup folder. The Startup folder is configured at two levels. Under the All Users folder, there is a Startup folder for all users of a given system. Any application referenced in the All Users folder runs in the background regardless of which user logs on. Within the user's profile data, there is a Startup folder specific to that user's logon. Applications referenced in a user's personal Startup folder are run only when that user logs on.

To add or remove startup programs for all users, follow these steps:

1. Right-click Start, and then select Explore All Users from the shortcut menu. This opens Windows Explorer with the Documents And Settings\All Users\Start Menu folder selected.

2. In the left pane, click the Programs folder under Start Menu and then click Startup.

3. You can now add or remove startup programs for all users. To add startup programs, create a shortcut to the program that you want to run. To remove a startup program, delete its shortcut from the Startup folder.

To add or remove startup programs for a specific user, follow these steps:

1. Log on as the user whose startup applications you want to manage. Right-click Start and then select Explore from the shortcut menu. This opens Windows Explorer with the *%UserProfile%*\Start Menu folder selected.

2. In the left pane, click the Programs folder under Start Menu and then click Startup.

3. You can now add or remove startup programs for this user. To add startup programs, create a shortcut to the program that you want to run. To remove a startup program, delete its shortcut from the Startup folder.

Note Technically, you don't need to log on as the user to manage that user's startup applications—it's just easier if you do. If you can't log on as the user, access the Documents And Settings folder on the system drive and work your way down through the user's profile data folders. These are listed by account name.

Controlling Icon Display in the Notification Area

Icons for applications appear in the notification area for several reasons. Some programs, such as Windows Update, are managed by Windows itself and appear periodically when there are pending notifications. For example, Windows Update runs periodically to check for updates to the operating system. When an update is detected, the user can be notified and given the opportunity to apply the update.

Other types of programs are configured to run in the background at startup, such as an antivirus program. You can typically enable or disable the display of icons through setup options in the related applications, but Windows XP provides a common interface for controlling icon display in the notification area. You can specify whether and how icons are displayed on a per application basis.

To control the display of icons in the notification area, follow these steps:

1. Right-click the taskbar, and then select Properties from the shortcut menu.

2. If you want all icons to be displayed, clear the Hide Inactive Icons check box and then click OK. Skip the remaining steps.

3. If you want to customize the appearance of icons, click the Hide Inactive Icons check box and then click Customize. This displays the Customize Notifications dialog box shown in Figure 4-5.

Figure 4-5   Specify the notification behavior for background applications in the Customize Notifications dialog box.

4. You can now optimize the notification behavior for current items displayed in the notification area as well as items that were displayed in the past but aren't currently active. The Name column shows the name of the application. The Behavior column shows the currently selected notification behavior. Each entry in the Behavior column can be clicked to display a selection menu with the following options:

   ❑ Hide When Inactive
   ❑ Always Hide
   ❑ Always Show

5. When you are finished updating the notification entries, click OK twice.

Note   You can directly access the Customize Notifications dialog box when the Hide Inactive Icons option is selected in the Taskbar And Start Menu Properties dialog box. Right-click the notification area, and then select Customize Notifications.

Optimizing Toolbars

Several custom toolbars are available for the taskbar. The toolbar that most users are familiar with is the Quick Launch toolbar, which provides quick access to commonly used programs and the Windows desktop. The taskbar can display other toolbars that come with Windows XP, and users can create their own toolbars as well.

Displaying Custom Toolbars

Four custom toolbars are available for the taskbar:

- **Address**   Provides an Address box into which you can type Uniform Resource Locators (URLs) and other addresses that you want to access, either on the Web, on the local network, or on the local computer. When full file paths are specified, the default application for the file is launched automatically to display the specified file.

- **Links**   Provides access to the Links folder on the Favorites menu of Microsoft Internet Explorer. To add links to files, Web pages, or other resources, drag shortcuts onto the Links toolbar. To remove links, right-click the link and select Delete. When prompted, confirm the action by clicking Yes.

- **Desktop**   Provides access to all the shortcuts on the local desktop so that you don't have to minimize Windows or click Show Desktop on the Quick Launch toolbar to access them.

- **Quick Launch**   Provides quick access to commonly used applications. By default, this is the only toolbar displayed on the taskbar.

To display or hide individual toolbars, follow these steps:

1. Right-click the taskbar to display the shortcut menu.
2. Point to Toolbars, and then select the toolbar name in the list provided. This toggles the toolbar on and off.

Tip   By default, a name label is displayed for all toolbars except Quick Launch. You can turn off the name label by right-clicking the toolbar and then choosing Show Title to deselect that command.

Customizing the Quick Launch Toolbar

The Quick Launch toolbar is featured in Figure 4-6. By default, this toolbar includes buttons that provide quick access to the Windows Desktop, the default Web browser, and the default mail program. If your organization has custom applications or a preferred suite of applications, you can add buttons for these applications on the Quick Launch toolbar. If an application that has an icon on the Quick

Launch toolbar is no longer used, you can remove the button to prevent users from accidentally starting the application. For example, when you install Microsoft Office, a shortcut for Microsoft Outlook is added to the toolbar, but the Microsoft Outlook Express shortcut remains. Because you really don't want both e-mail applications to be used, you should remove the Outlook Express button.

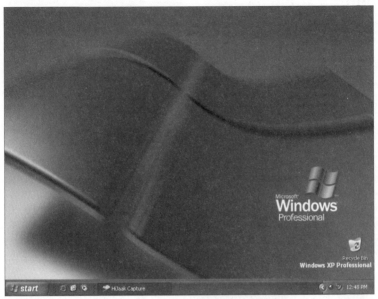

Figure 4-6   The Quick Launch toolbar on the Windows taskbar provides a handy way to access frequently used applications.

To add a button to the Quick Launch toolbar, follow these steps:

1. Select the item or existing shortcut that you want to place on the toolbar.

2. Drag the item or shortcut and drop it on the Quick Launch toolbar in the location where you want it.

To remove a button from the Quick Launch toolbar, follow these steps:

1. Right-click the button on the toolbar, and then select Delete from the shortcut menu.

2. When prompted to confirm the action, click Yes.

Restoring the Show Desktop Button

The most useful button on the Quick Launch toolbar is Show Desktop. The first time you click this button, the operating system brings the Windows desktop to the foreground in front of all open windows. The second time you click this button, the operating system restores the original view, sending the desktop to the background.

Users often start deleting buttons and accidentally delete the Show Desktop button—one of the most common problems encountered with the Quick Launch toolbar. Users might not tell you that they've removed this button accidentally (indeed, they might not even know that they did it), and they might get frustrated when they can't get to the desktop quickly. Fixing this problem is easy, but it requires a few steps.

As with other aspects of the menu system, the Quick Launch toolbar options have a representation in the file system. You'll find Quick Launch options in the *%UserProfile%*\Application Data\Microsoft\Internet Explorer\Quick Launch folder. Unlike other buttons on the toolbar, which are created through shortcuts, the Show Desktop button is created using a Windows command file called SHOW DESKTOP.SCF.

Note Application Data is a hidden folder. To view this folder, you'll need to select the advanced folder option Show Hidden Files And Folders. In Windows Explorer, select Folder Options from the Tools menu and then select the View tab. On the View tab, select Show Hidden Files And Folders and then click OK.

To restore the button to the toolbar, you have several options. You can copy SHOW DESKTOP.SCF from another user's profile data, or you can recreate the file. To recreate the file, follow these steps:

1. Start Microsoft Notepad, and then add the following lines of text:

   ```
   [Shell]
   Command=2
   IconFile=explorer.exe,3
   [Taskbar]
   Command=ToggleDesktop
   ```

2. From the File menu, select Save As and then save the file in the *%UserProfile%*\Application Data\Microsoft\Internet Explorer\Quick Launch folder. Use the file name SHOW DESKTOP.SCF.

   Note If you don't know the actual value for the *%UserProfile%* environment variable, open a command prompt and type **set userprofile**. The command prompt then displays the variable value, such as D:\Documents and Settings\Wrstanek.

Creating Personal Toolbars

You can create personal toolbars for users as well. Personal toolbars are based on existing folders, and their buttons are based on the folder contents. The most common toolbars you might create are ones that point to shared folders on the network. For example, if all users have access to a CorpData shared folder in which corporate information is stored and a UserData folder in which personal information is stored, you could add toolbars to the taskbar that point to these resources. When users want to access one of the folders, they could simply click the corresponding toolbar button.

You can create personal toolbars by completing these steps:

1. Right-click the taskbar to display the shortcut menu. Point to Toolbars, and then click New Toolbar. This displays the New Toolbar dialog box.

2. Use the Choose A Folder list box to select the folder you want to make into a toolbar.

3. When you click OK, the folder is displayed as a new toolbar on the taskbar. If you add shortcuts to the toolbar, the shortcuts are added to the folder. Similarly, if you delete items from the toolbar view, the items are removed from the folder.

 Note   When it comes to personal toolbars, there's good news and bad news. The good news is that most users find them valuable. The bad news is that if a user decides to close the toolbar, it must be recreated before it can be viewed on the taskbar again.

Chapter 5

Optimizing the Desktop and Screen Appearance

In this chapter:

Using Keyboard Shortcuts to Master the Desktop.................118

Working with Desktop Themes....................................120

Optimizing the Desktop Environment..........................122

Screen Saver Dos and Don'ts....................................127

Modifying Display Appearance and Video Settings 131

Microsoft Windows XP provides a whole new level of desktop and screen customization options. (In this book, "Windows XP" refers to Windows XP Professional unless otherwise indicated.) Although these options are useful, they can cause problems that you, as an administrator, might be asked to help resolve. You might also see users struggling to fix these issues on their own, so you might want to lend a hand. This chapter focuses on the configuration and troubleshooting of the following areas:

- Keyboard shortcuts to the desktop
- Desktop themes
- Desktop backgrounds
- Desktop cleanup
- Screen saver dos and don'ts
- Display appearance and settings

Using Keyboard Shortcuts to Master the Desktop

Commonly used keyboard shortcuts are summarized in Table 5-1. Keyboard shortcuts are a handy way to get around the desktop and the menu system. As an administrator, you'll find these shortcuts to be invaluable, particularly if you ever have to navigate the desktop, menus, or dialog boxes without a mouse.

Table 5-1   Commonly Used Keyboard Shortcuts

Task to Perform	Keyboard Shortcut
Activate menu bar in current program	F10
Cancel the current task	Esc
Close or quit the active item	Alt+F4
Close the active document	Ctrl+F4
Copy	Ctrl+C
Copy selected item	Ctrl while dragging an item
Create shortcut to selected item	Ctrl+Shift while dragging an item
Cut	Ctrl+X
Cycle through items in order opened	Alt+Esc
Cycle through screen elements in a window	F6
Delete	Delete
Delete selected item permanently	Shift+Delete
Display properties for a selected item	Alt+Enter
Display shortcut menu for selected item	Shift+F10
Display the System menu for active window	Alt+Spacebar
Display the Address bar list in My Computer or Windows Explorer	F4
Display the corresponding menu	Alt+underlined letter in menu name
Display the Start menu	Ctrl+Esc
Execute command	Select the underlined letter in a command
Highlight a block of text	Ctrl+Shift with any arrow key
Move insertion point to beginning of previous word	Ctrl+Left Arrow
Move insertion point to beginning of next paragraph	Ctrl+Down Arrow
Move insertion point to beginning of next word	Ctrl+Right Arrow
Move insertion point to beginning of previous paragraph	Ctrl+Up Arrow
Open next menu to left, or close submenu	Left Arrow
Open next menu to right, or open submenu	Right Arrow
Paste	Ctrl+V
Prevent CD from automatically playing when you insert it	Shift
Refresh active window	F5
Rename selected item	F2
Search for a file or folder	F3 (This feature doesn't work if the Start Menu is open and you've selected a submenu.)
Select all	Ctrl+A

Table 5-1   Commonly Used Keyboard Shortcuts

Task to Perform	Keyboard Shortcut
Select multiple items in a window	Shift with any arrow key
Switch between open items	Alt+Tab
Undo	Ctrl+Z
View folder one level up in My Computer or Windows Explorer	Backspace

Another type of graphical element that you might need to navigate without a mouse is a dialog box. Table 5-2 provides a summary of shortcut keys for navigating dialog boxes.

Table 5-2   Shortcuts for Dialog Boxes

Task to Perform	Keyboard Shortcut
Display Help for an item	F1
Display items in a selection list	F4
Execute command for active option	Enter
Execute command or select an option	Alt+Underlined letter
Move backward through options	Shift+Tab
Move backward through tabs	Ctrl+Shift+Tab
Move forward through options	Tab
Move forward through tabs	Ctrl+Tab
Open a folder one level up if a folder is selected in the Save As or Open dialog box	Backspace
Select a button option or an option in a drop-down list	Arrow keys
Select or clear a check box	Spacebar

On Microsoft Natural Keyboards or other keyboards that have a Windows key, there are additional keyboard shortcuts that are useful. These keyboard shortcuts are summarized in Table 5-3.

Table 5-3   Shortcuts for the Windows Key

Task to Perform	Keyboard Shortcut
Cycle through buttons on the taskbar	Windows+Tab
Display Help And Support	Windows+F1
Display Search For Computers	Ctrl+Windows+F
Display Search For Files Or Folders	Windows+F
Display the Run dialog box	Windows+R
Display the Start menu	Windows
Display the System Properties dialog box	Windows+Break
Display the Utility Manager	Windows+U
Lock the keyboard	Windows+L
Minimize Windows	Windows+M
Open My Computer	Windows+E
Restore minimized windows	Shift+Windows+M
Show the Desktop	Windows+D

Working with Desktop Themes

Desktop themes are combinations of backgrounds plus sets of sounds, icons, and other elements that help personalize the desktop and the operating environment. Administrators tend to hate themes; users tend to love them. In this section, you'll learn how to apply themes, how to tailor individual theme options, and how to delete themes.

Applying and Removing Themes

Several types of themes are available. Some themes are installed with the operating system. To apply a theme, follow these steps:

1. Right-click an open area of the desktop, and then select Properties. This opens the Display Properties dialog box shown in Figure 5-1.

Figure 5-1   Select the theme to use in the Display Properties dialog box.

2. Select the Themes tab and use the Theme list to select the theme you want to use. If you want to obtain a theme from the Plus! For Windows XP Web site, select More Themes Online. This launches Microsoft Internet Explorer, which you can use to purchase and download the Plus! Software package. The necessary Uniform Resource Locator (URL) is automatically accessed.

3. The Sample pane provides an overview of the theme's appearance. If the theme appears as you expected, click OK. Otherwise, select a different theme and then click OK.

To restore the original desktop theme, follow these steps:

1. Right-click an open area of the desktop, and then select Properties.

2. On the Themes tab of the Display Properties dialog box, select Windows XP as the theme and then click OK.

Tailoring and Saving Themes

When you apply a theme to the Windows desktop, many different system settings can be affected. Typically, users might like a theme but dislike a specific aspect of it, such as the sounds. To fix this, you can change the system setting the user doesn't like and then save the updated theme so that he or she can restore it in the future.

The primary settings that themes affect are as follows:

- **Screen savers**   To change the screen saver, right-click the desktop and then select Properties. In the Screen Saver tab, select a new screen saver and then click OK. Select None to remove the screen saver.
- **Program event sounds**   To change program event sounds, access Sounds And Audio Devices in Control Panel and then use the Sound Scheme list box on the Sounds tab to select a different set of program event sounds. To restore the default, select Windows Default. To turn off program event sounds, select No Sounds.
- **Mouse pointers**   To change mouse pointers, access the Mouse utility in Control Panel and then use the Scheme list box on the Pointers tab to select a different set of pointers. Select either None or Windows Default to restore the default pointer set.
- **Windows and buttons**   To change the appearance of dialog boxes and buttons, right-click the desktop and then select Properties. In the Appearance tab, use the Windows And Buttons list box to select a new style. Select Windows Classic to restore the traditional window and button style.
- **Color schemes**   To change color schemes, right-click the desktop and then select Properties. In the Appearance tab, use the Color Scheme list box to select a new style. Select Default (Blue) to restore the standard Windows XP color scheme. Select Windows Standard to restore the default Windows Classic color scheme. Keep in mind that the Windows And Buttons selection determines which color schemes are available as options.

Once you've modified the system settings and are satisfied, you can save the settings as a new theme by following these steps:

1. Right-click an open area of the desktop, and then select Properties. This opens the Display Properties dialog box, shown previously in Figure 5-1.
2. In the Themes tab, click Save As and then use the Save As dialog box to save the theme. Theme definition files end with the .theme file extension.
3. Unless deleted in the future, the custom theme will appear as an option in the Theme list box.

Note   Program event sounds and pointer schemes are not saved with the theme definition. If you want to restore these with a custom theme, you'll need to do so individually.

Deleting Custom Themes

Themes that users install from other locations, such as the Plus! For Windows XP Web site, can take up a lot of space on the hard disk. To delete a theme and remove the theme-related files, follow these steps:

1. Right-click an open area of the desktop, and then select Properties.
2. In the Themes tab, select the name of the theme to be deleted and click Delete. Windows removes that theme's definition file and the theme-related media files.

 Tip   Themes installed by Windows are located in the *%WinDir%*\ Resources\Themes folder, and themes installed by the user are stored in the *%UserProfile%*\Application Data\Microsoft\Windows\Themes folder. If you want to see the total space used by themes, check the space used by these folders and their subdirectories. You shouldn't delete files from these folders manually. Use the technique just outlined instead.

Optimizing the Desktop Environment

Windows XP provides many different ways to optimize the desktop environment. One of the most basic techniques is to add a background containing a corporate logo or other symbol to the standard desktop build. This is particularly useful with loaner laptops; for example, you can create a logo with a message such as "Technology Department Loaner." Another technique is to add custom content directly to the desktop. This allows you to provide direct access to the corporate intranet or other corporate resources from the desktop. If you then lock the desktop, you prevent users from altering the desktop and removing the quick access content you've provided.

Setting the Desktop Background

To set the background for the desktop, follow these steps:

1. Right-click an open area of the desktop, and then select Properties. Click the Desktop tab, shown in Figure 5-2.
2. If you want to display a custom background, use the Background list to select a background image. If the background you want to use isn't listed, click Browse to search for the background on the file system or network.

 Tip   Background images are stored in the *%WinDir%* and *%WinDir%*\Web\Wallpaper folders. If you add .bmp, .gif, or .jpeg images to either folder, they'll be available from the Background selection list. Images in a user's My Pictures folder are available from the Background selection list as well. If you want to make background images available only for a particular user, copy the images to the user's My Pictures folder.

Figure 5-2   Configure desktop backgrounds and colors by using the Desktop tab of the Display Properties dialog box.

3. Use the Position list box to select a display option for the background. You have three display position options:

   ❏ **Center**   Centers the image on the desktop background. Any area that the image doesn't fill uses the current desktop color.

   ❏ **Stretch**   Stretches the image to fill the desktop background. This is a good option for photos and large images.

   ❏ **Tile**   Repeats the image so that it covers the entire screen. This is a good option for small images and icons.

4. If you want to set a color for the background, use the Color selector to assign one of the 16 predefined colors or select Other to specify a custom color. This color is used to fill out the desktop when Position is set to Center for a background image and, under some conditions, will also be used as the background color for text used to name desktop icons.

5. When you are finished updating the background, click OK.

Controlling Default Desktop Icons

With the Classic Start menu, several icons are added to the desktop automatically: My Documents, My Network Places, My Computer, Internet Explorer, and Recycle Bin. With the Simple Start menu, only the Recycle Bin is added to the desktop by default. Users have very little control over the display of these icons. This section provides techniques for adding and removing them from the desktop (the right way) and recovering them if they've been deleted accidentally.

Adding and Removing Default Desktop Icons

On the desktop, My Documents, My Network Places, My Computer, Internet Explorer, and Recycle Bin are special desktop icons. Although you can create shortcuts for these items by dragging the related item to the desktop from Windows Explorer, the best way to add or remove these desktop icons is to follow these steps:

1. Right-click an open area of the desktop, and then select Properties. Click the Desktop tab.
2. Click Customize Desktop.
3. The Desktop Icons panel has check boxes for each of the default icons except for the Recycle Bin. Clear the corresponding check box to remove an icon. Select the check box to add an icon.
4. Click OK twice.

Restoring Icons to the Desktop

In previous editions of Windows, users could accidentally delete desktop icons in such a way that recreating them was difficult. In Windows XP, this problem has been eliminated. Users can now drag icons to the Recycle Bin or right-click icons and select Delete to remove them from the desktop if they wish. While this isn't the best way to remove icons, it no longer causes problems and you can recreate and display the icons through the Customize Desktop options by following these steps:

1. Right-click an open area of the desktop, and then select Properties. Click the Desktop tab.
2. Click Customize Desktop.
3. Select the check box for each icon that you want to display.
4. Click OK twice.

Placing Custom Content on the Desktop

Using custom content, you can add an embedded browser window to the desktop background. The content for this window can come from the Internet, a corporate intranet, or any network resource. Once added to the desktop background, there are several options for making the content available offline and synchronizing the content to keep it fresh. You can also keep the content online so that each time the user logs on and accesses the desktop, the content is downloaded.

Adding Custom Content

Custom content can be easily added to the desktop to enable quick access to an essential resource. Once the embedded browser is added to the desktop, a user can control it much like any other window. A control bar is available at the top of the window. Simply point to the top of the window to display it. In the left corner, a button with a down arrow provides access to a shortcut menu. In the right corner are buttons for resizing the window to cover the desktop, to split the desktop between the window and existing icons, and to close the window.

To add custom content to the desktop, follow these steps:

1. Right-click an open area of the desktop, and then select Properties. Click the Desktop tab.

2. Click Customize Desktop, and then click the Web tab in the Desktop Items dialog box, as shown in Figure 5-3.

Figure 5-3 You can add custom content to the desktop using the options on the Web tab of the Desktop Items dialog box.

3. The Web Pages list box shows content that has been configured previously. To use previously defined content, simply select the associated check box and then click OK. Skip the remaining steps.

4. To specify a new source of content, click New. You can now choose to add content from the Desktop Gallery at the Microsoft Web site or from a specified location in the following ways:

    ❑ To add content from the Desktop Gallery at the Microsoft Web site, click Visit Gallery. After Internet Explorer starts, select the gallery item that you want to download and then confirm the action by clicking Yes or OK. In some cases, you'll also need to confirm the download and installation of control components that are needed for the gallery item to operate.

    ❑ To specify a URL or file location, type the URL or file path in the Location field or click Browse to look for the item. In most cases, you'll want to specify a top-level directory or Web site or a specific page on a Web site that provides access to other pages. For example, if you want to ensure users have quick access to the corporate intranet, you could enter the top-level intranet URL, such as *intranet.yourorganization.com*.

5. After you select the resource you want to add, the Add Item To Desktop dialog box is displayed. This dialog box shows the name and URL that will be used for the resource. If you want to modify these and other default settings, click Customize. Otherwise, click OK. Windows XP will then begin synchronizing the content from the resource.

Tip   Custom content is stored in the *%WinDir%*\Offline Web Pages folder. You can view the contents of this folder to determine how much space is being used by custom content and other offline Web pages. Once accessed, you can manage the content by right-clicking it and selecting options from the shortcut menu. For example, to delete the content, right-click the item and then select Delete. There are, of course, other ways of managing the custom content.

Removing Custom Content

To remove custom content from the desktop, point to the top of the embedded window and click Close. You can also click the button with the down arrow and then select Close. To remove the custom content and all its related files permanently, follow these steps:

1. Point to the top of the embedded window to reveal the control bar.
2. Access the shortcut menu by clicking the down arrow in the left corner of the control bar, and then select Customize My Desktop. This opens the Desktop Items dialog box.
3. In the Web tab, select the item in the Web Pages list.
4. Click Delete. When prompted, confirm the action by clicking Yes.
5. Click OK twice.

Locking Custom Content on the Desktop

To prevent users from accidentally making changes to custom content once you've set it up, you can lock the desktop. Once this option is enabled, users must specifically elect to remove the lock before they can make changes to custom content. You can lock custom content on the desktop by following these steps:

1. Right-click an open area of the desktop to display the shortcut menu.
2. Point to Arrange Icons By, and then select Lock Web Items On Desktop.

Cleaning Up the Desktop

Over time, the desktop can become cluttered with shortcuts and other resources that are never used. Keeping the desktop clean can improve productivity, but who wants to (or has time to) focus on maintaining the desktop? To better manage clutter and clean up resources that aren't used, you can schedule the Desktop Cleanup Wizard to run periodically. You also can run the wizard manually.

To schedule the Desktop Cleanup Wizard to run periodically, follow these steps:

1. Right-click an open area of the desktop and then select Properties. Click the Desktop tab.
2. Click Customize Desktop. In the Desktop Items dialog box, select Run Desktop Cleanup Wizard Every 60 Days.
3. Click OK twice.

Note The wizard cleans up the desktop by moving unused shortcuts to a desktop folder named Unused Desktop Shortcuts. The wizard doesn't modify any programs, and you can restore the shortcuts by moving them out of the Unused Desktop Shortcuts folder and back onto the desktop.

To run the Desktop Cleanup Wizard manually, follow these steps:

1. Right-click an open area of the desktop to display the shortcut menu.
2. Point to Arrange Icons By, and then select Run Desktop Cleanup Wizard.
3. Once the Desktop Cleanup Wizard starts, click Next. The Shortcuts Wizard page is displayed, as shown in Figure 5-4.

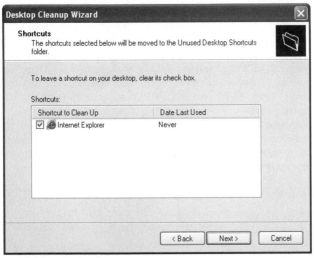

Figure 5-4 Select unused shortcuts to remove from the desktop and then click Next.

4. Any shortcuts selected in this window haven't been used recently and will be moved to the Unused Desktop Shortcuts folder. If you want to keep a shortcut on the desktop, clear the appropriate check box.
5. When you are ready to continue, click Next and then click Finish.

Screen Saver Dos and Don'ts

Screen savers are designed to turn on when a computer has been idle for a specified period of time. The original job of the screen saver was to prevent image burn-in on monitors by displaying a continuously changing image. With today's monitors, burn-in is no longer a problem, but screen savers are still around. The primary benefit they offer today is the ability to password-lock computers automatically when the screen saver turns on.

Configuring Screen Savers with Password Protection

Password-protecting the screen saver deters unauthorized users from accessing a computer, which can protect both the personal data of the user and the intellectual property of the organization. As an administrator, you should ensure that the computers you deploy have password-protected screen savers enabled.

You can password protect the screen saver by doing the following:

1. Right-click an open area of the desktop, and then select Properties. Click the Screen Saver tab, as shown in Figure 5-5.

2. Use the Screen Saver list box to select a screen saver. To disable the screen saver, select None and skip the remaining steps.

 Real World   Unfortunately, screen savers can use up a lot of the computer's resources, increasing both the energy usage of the computer (which otherwise would be idle) and its memory and processor usage. Some screen savers, particularly the three-dimensional ones such as 3D FlowerBox and 3D Pipes, cause the processor to run at a steady 99 to 100 percent utilization. The reason for this is the 3D designs are very complex and the computer must make a lot of computations to maintain and update the screen saver image. For tips on reducing resource usage when screen savers turn on, see the next two sections of this chapter, entitled "Reducing Screen Saver Resource Usage" and "Setting Energy-Saving Settings for Monitors."

3. Select On Resume, Password Protect.

4. Use the Wait box to specify how long the computer must be idle before the screen saver is activated. A reasonable value is between 10 and 15 minutes.

5. Click OK.

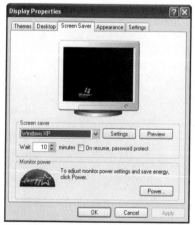

Figure 5-5   Set a screen saver with password protection for user and organization security.

Reducing Screen Saver Resource Usage

A computer running Windows XP that performs background tasks or network duties, such as print services, should not be configured to use a complex screen saver, such as 3D FlowerBox or 3D Pipes. Instead, the computer should be configured with a basic screen saver, such as the Blank screen saver. You can also modify the settings for advanced screen savers to reduce resource usage. Typically, you do this by reducing the redraw and refresh rates of the advanced screen saver.

To reduce screen saver resource usage, follow these steps:

1. Right-click an open area of the desktop, and then select Properties. Click the Screen Saver tab.

2. If you want to use a screen saver that uses fewer resources without making configuration changes, use the Screen Saver list box to select a basic screen saver, such as Blank or Windows XP.

3. If you want to use a more advanced screen saver but reduce its resource usage, select that screen saver and then click Settings. Afterward, use the Setup dialog box to reduce the Complexity, Speed, or similar field values that affect the drawing or refreshing of the screen saver. In the example shown in Figure 5-6, the Complexity slider was originally set at Max, but the value has been reduced to Min.

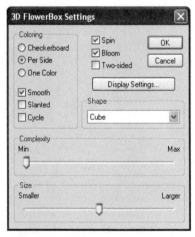

Figure 5-6   Advanced screen savers have settings that you can use to reduce resource usage.

4. Click OK once or twice as necessary to close the open dialog boxes.

Setting Energy-Saving Settings for Monitors

Many newer cathode ray tube (CRT) monitors have energy-saving features that let them shut themselves off after a certain period of inactivity. Enabling this feature can reduce the organization's electricity bill because CRT monitors typically use a lot of electricity to stay powered up. On some systems, this feature might have been automatically enabled by the operating system during installation. This depends, however, on the operating system properly detecting the monitor and installing any necessary drivers.

On a portable laptop computer running on batteries, saving energy is especially important. By configuring the monitor to shut off when the computer is idle, you can save the battery life and extend the battery availability time when the laptop is unplugged.

To manage a monitor's energy settings, follow these steps:

1. Right-click an open area of the desktop, and then select Properties. Click the Screen Saver tab.

2. Click Power. The Power Options Properties dialog box is displayed, as shown in Figure 5-7.

Figure 5-7   Energy-saving CRT monitors, as well as monitors on laptops and portables, can be configured to turn off automatically after a certain amount of idle time.

 Note   If the computer is connected to a monitor that doesn't support this feature, some power options may be grayed out or unavailable. If you are configuring the computer in a build area and are using a different monitor than the one the user will have, you might want to obtain the user's monitor model and repeat this process.

3. For a laptop or portable computer, even though you have not selected the Portable/Laptop power scheme, you'll find Turn Off Monitor list boxes for when the computer is Plugged In and for when the computer is Running On Batteries. Set both of these selection lists to an appropriate value. For a desktop computer, simply set the Turn Off Monitor value.

Real World   Typically, you'll want this feature to turn off the monitor after 15 to 30 minutes of idle time. On my office computer, I turn on the screen saver in 7 minutes and then turn off the monitor after 15 minutes of idle time. On my laptop, I use settings of 5 minutes and 10 minutes, respectively.

4. Click OK twice.

Modifying Display Appearance and Video Settings

The display appearance and video settings have a major impact on the look and feel of the Windows XP desktop and its graphical elements. Appearance options control window, button, color, and font settings. Video settings control screen resolution, color quality, refresh frequency, hardware acceleration, and color management.

Configuring Display Appearance

Three key areas of the display appearance can be optimized: graphical elements (windows and buttons), color schemes, and fonts. Through advanced properties, you can customize Windows elements based on the current graphical style and color scheme.

To configure display options, follow these steps:

1. Right-click an open area of the desktop, and then select Properties. Click the Appearance tab.

2. Use the Windows And Buttons list box to set the style for dialog boxes, buttons, and the taskbar. Windows Classic Style is the traditional style used in previous versions of Windows.

3. Use the Color Scheme list box to select a color scheme for all graphical elements, including the desktop, dialog boxes, buttons, menus, and the taskbar. Windows Classic and Windows XP (the standard scheme for Windows XP) provide a style consistent with current and previous versions of Windows. Be sure to choose a color scheme that is easy to read. The best color schemes have good contrast between backgrounds and text, such as a light background with dark text or a dark background with light text.

4. If you want to override default settings for individual elements, such as the desktop or message boxes, click Advanced. Then use the Item list to select the items you want to modify, and set the size, color, and font options (not all of these options will be available for some items). Changes you make are recorded when you make them, allowing you to configure multiple elements before clicking OK to apply the changes.

5. Use the Font Size list box to select the relative size for text used in windows, dialog boxes, and other graphical elements. Keep in mind that the previous options you've chosen might have altered the options that are now available. Typical font sizes available include Normal, Large, and Extra Large. In most cases, you'll find that extra large fonts are too big and that the normal or large settings work best.

Note   With some system and monitor configurations, you may see specific numeric point sizes. In that case, choose a font size that works best for you.

6. Click OK to close the Advanced Appearance dialog box, and then click Apply when you are finished. If you want to save the changes along with other settings for the display, select Save As in the Themes tab. Specify a name for the custom theme, and then click OK.

Configuring Video Settings

Video settings control screen resolution, color quality, refresh rate, hardware acceleration, and color management. The focus of this section is on making sure Windows XP has correctly identified the video card and monitor and on optimizing various video settings.

Checking the Current Video Adapter and Monitor

Proper display is dependent on accurate information about the video adapter and the monitor being used by a computer. Depending on which video adapter and monitor models Windows XP thinks you have, different driver files are installed. These drivers are extremely important in determining which display resolutions, color depths, and refresh rates are available and appropriate for the system. If the adapter and monitor aren't detected and configured properly, Windows XP won't be able to take advantage of their capabilities.

Current settings for the video adapter or monitor can be wrong for many reasons. Sometimes, Plug and Play doesn't detect the device and a generic device driver is used. At other times, Windows XP detects the wrong type of device, such as a different model. In this case, the device will probably work, but some features won't be available.

To check the current video adapter and monitor configured for a computer, follow these steps:

1. Right-click an open area of the desktop, and then select Properties. Click the Settings tab.

2. Under Display, you'll find the currently configured monitor and video card. The format of the entry under Display is <*Monitor Type*> on <*Video Adapter*> driver. In the example shown in Figure 5-8, the computer has configurations for multiple monitors stored and the video card driver is NeoMagic MagicGraph256AV. Check the information shown in the dialog box as follows:

    ❑ If the correct video adapter isn't displayed or you want to examine the driver settings further, see the next section, entitled "Changing the Video Driver."

    ❑ If the correct monitor isn't displayed or you want to examine the monitor settings further, see the section entitled "Changing the Monitor," later in this chapter.

3. Click OK to close the Display Properties dialog box.

Figure 5-8 If you're having display problems, check the monitor and video driver being used.

Changing the Video Driver

If the video driver shown in the Display Properties dialog box does not match the make and model installed on the computer, you might want to try to install a different driver. For example, if the computer has a generic S3 video driver configured and you are sure the computer has an nVidia GeForce2 video adapter, you'll want to change the video driver.

To determine whether the video card make and model are correct, you'll need to know how the system is configured. The system documentation can tell you which video adapter is installed on the computer. Other administrators are also useful resources. Typically, someone else on the technology team will know immediately what video adapter is installed with a particular type of computer. If you can't figure out the make and model of the video adapter, you have several options. If the current settings are working, you can leave the display settings alone. You can also try the following techniques to determine the video adapter make and model:

- Shut down the computer, and then power it back on—don't do a restart. Watch the screen when the computer is first turned on. The name of the video card might appear briefly before Windows XP begins loading.

- Shut down the computer, and then remove the computer cover. Locate the name and model number on the video adapter itself. If the monitor is still attached to the rear of the computer, the video adapter is the card to which the monitor cable is connected.

- If the video adapter is built into the computer's motherboard (meaning there isn't a separate card), check the motherboard to see whether you can find a chip that lists the video information on it or write down the motherboard model number and visit the manufacturer's Web site to see whether the information is available.

Once you determine the video adapter make and model, see if you can locate the necessary drivers on the manufacturer's Web site. Some video adapters come with installation disks. On the disk, you might find a setup program (SETUP.EXE). Run this program to install the video driver. If the installation disk contains the drivers but no setup program, you'll need to install the drivers manually.

When you are ready to install the video adapter driver, follow these steps:

1. Right-click an open area of the desktop, and then select Properties. Click the Settings tab.

2. Click Advanced. This displays the monitor and video driver properties dialog box.

3. Click the Adapter tab. Note the current information in the Adapter Type and Adapter Information panel. Click Properties.

4. In the Driver tab, click Update Driver. This starts the Hardware Update Wizard.

5. Select Install From A List Or Specific Location, and then click Next.

6. Select Don't Search. I Will Choose The Driver To Install, and then click Next.

7. The next wizard page shows a list of compatible hardware and a recommended list of drivers for this hardware.

   ❏ If a correct driver is listed, all you need to do is to select it.

   ❏ If a correct driver isn't listed, clear the Show Compatible Hardware check box. You can now view an extended list of adapters with related model numbers. Select a manufacturer, and then select the appropriate adapter in the Model pane.

   ❏ If the model you want to use isn't listed, insert your device driver disk into the drive and then click Have Disk. Follow the prompts. Then select the appropriate device.

8. After selecting a device driver, continue through the installation process by clicking Next. Click Finish when the driver installation is completed. Keep in mind that in some cases you'll need to reboot the system to activate the newly installed or updated device driver.

Changing the Monitor

The overall display quality is controlled by the combined capabilities of a computer's monitor and video adapter. If a computer has a Plug and Play monitor, Windows XP might have detected it and installed it properly, or it might have installed a similar driver but not the one that exactly matches the monitor make and model. For the best quality, Windows XP should use the driver designed for the applicable monitor. Otherwise, the display mode, color depth, refresh rate, and color-matching options might not be appropriate for the monitor.

To change the monitor setup, follow these steps:

1. Right-click an open area of the desktop, and then select Properties. Click the Settings tab.

2. Click Advanced. This displays the monitor and video driver properties dialog box.

3. Click the Monitor tab. Use the Monitor Type list box to select the monitor type that you want to work with and then click Properties.

4. In the Driver tab, click Update Driver. This starts the Hardware Update Wizard. When prompted to connect to Windows Update to search for software, select No, Not At This Time.

5. Select Install From A List Or Specific Location, and then click Next.

6. Select Don't Search. I Will Choose The Driver To Install, and then click Next.

7. The next wizard page shows a list of compatible monitors. You then have the following options:

   ❏ If a correct monitor is listed, all you need to do is to select it.

   ❏ If a correct monitor isn't listed, clear the Show Compatible Hardware check box. You can now view a list of manufacturers to find the manufacturer of the monitor. Once you find the manufacturer, select an appropriate monitor in the Model pane.

   ❏ If the manufacturer or model you want to use isn't listed, insert your monitor disk into the drive and then click Have Disk. Follow the prompts. Then select the appropriate device.

8. After selecting a monitor, continue through the installation process by clicking Next. Click Finish when the monitor installation is completed.

Changing the Screen Resolution and Color Quality

Screen resolution and color quality are key factors affecting display appearance. Screen resolution is the number of pixels that make up the display. Color quality is the number of colors that can be displayed simultaneously on the screen.

A typical monitor has resolutions of 640 × 480, 800 × 600, and 1024 × 768. High-end monitors have additional resolutions of 1280 × 1024, 1600 × 1200, 2048 × 1536, and sometimes even higher. The best resolution to use depends on what the user plans to do with the computer and the size of the monitor. Designers and developers who need a large screen area will appreciate a higher resolution, such as 1280 × 1024. They can then see more of what they're working with on the screen. Users who spend most of their time reading e-mail or working with Microsoft Word documents might prefer a lower resolution such as 800 × 600. At that resolution screen elements are easier to see and users will have less eyestrain.

Color quality depends greatly on screen resolution settings. Color quality can range from 16 colors for standard Video Graphics Adapter (VGA) monitors to 16 million colors (24-bit) for high-end monitors. Most video cards display fewer colors the higher you set the screen resolution. This means that a computer might be able to use 16-bit, 24-bit, or 32-bit color, but the screen resolution must be decreased to achieve this color quality. In most cases, the higher the color quality you can set, the better. Keep in mind that the amount of memory required to maintain the video display is determined by multiplying the number of pixels on the screen (based on screen resolution) by the number of bits per pixel (determined by color quality).

Furthermore, the maximum resolution and color quality combination allowed is a function of the video memory on the video adapter. For example, a video card with 32 MB of memory might use a screen resolution of 1024 × 768 with 32-bit color, 1280 × 1024 with 24-bit color, and 1600 × 1200 with 16-bit color.

You can set the screen resolution and color quality by completing the following steps:

1. Right-click an open area of the desktop, and then select Properties. Click the Settings tab.
2. Use the Screen Resolution slider to set the display size, such as 1024 × 768 pixels.
3. Use the Color Quality list box to select a color quality, such as High (24-bit).
4. Click OK. If you changed the screen resolution, a dialog box is displayed telling you that Windows XP will now change the display. Click OK. Once Windows XP resizes the display, another dialog box appears, asking whether you want to keep the settings. If the settings look good, click Yes. Otherwise, click No to restore the original settings.

 Note   Step 4 describes the default behavior when changing the screen resolution or the color quality. Advanced options can modify this behavior to force a restart of the computer or additional prompting. To change these options, click the Advanced button on the Settings tab and then use the Compatibility options to reconfigure the compatibility mode. The key reason you might want to force a computer to restart after changing display settings is that some programs might not operate properly after the modification. If your organization uses applications that exhibit this behavior, you might want to configure the Restart option.

Changing the Display Refresh Rate

The *refresh rate* is the rate at which the screen is repainted. The higher the refresh rate, the less flicker in the display. If you've ever seen video footage of a computer system with a monitor that seemed to be scrolling or blinking, this was because the computer's refresh rate was out of sync with the video recording speed. Your eyes don't notice the flicker as much, but a low refresh rate (under 72 Hz) can make your eyes tired if you look at the display too long.

When you set the refresh rate, you have several options. You can use the default setting of the video card by selecting Adapter Default. You can use the highest or optimal setting available by choosing Optimal Setting. You can also choose a specific setting. Keep in mind that if the refresh rate exceeds the capabilities of the monitor or the video card, the screen can become distorted. Running the computer at a higher refresh rate than it supports can also damage the monitor and video adapter.

To set the display refresh rate, follow these steps:

1. Right-click an open area of the desktop, and then select Properties. Click the Settings tab.

2. Click Advanced. This displays the monitor and video driver properties dialog box.

3. Click the Monitor tab, shown in Figure 5-9. If multiple monitors are configured, select the monitor you are currently working with and then use the Screen Refresh Rate list box to set the refresh rate.

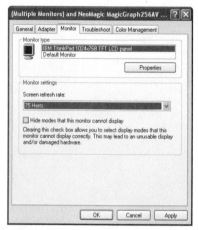

Figure 5-9   Set the refresh rate for the selected monitor. To prevent eyestrain, use the highest refresh rate setting that the monitor and graphics card support.

4. When you click OK, a dialog box tells you that Windows XP will now change the display settings. Click OK. Once Windows XP resets the refresh rate, another dialog box appears, asking if you want to keep the settings. If the settings look good, click Yes. Otherwise, click No to restore the original settings.

Setting Color Matching for Graphics Design

Color matching is extremely important to graphics design and the proper display of colors on the screen. Without appropriate color matching, colors on the screen can look irregular in hue (color tone), saturation (color strength or purity), and luminosity (color brightness). Of greater importance to graphic designers, if color matching is not set correctly, the colors on the screen won't match the colors that print out on paper.

After working with graphic designers who spend a great deal of time with Pantone color wheels and color charts, I came to appreciate the exact science of color, and you can, too. On-screen colors and in-print colors can vary greatly. Green can appear blue, brown can appear orange, yellow can appear green, and much more can and will go wrong without color matching. The good news is that color profiles are becoming increasingly available for monitors, and they are also distributed with graphic design applications.

To configure color matching, you assign a color profile to the computer based on the monitor and the color mappings available. Follow these steps:

1. Right-click an open area of the desktop, and then select Properties. Click the Settings tab.

2. Click Advanced. This displays the monitor and video driver properties dialog box.

3. Click the Color Management tab. The Color Profiles list box shows any color profiles that have been previously associated with the current monitor and video adapter.

4. Color profiles installed with the monitor or video adapter are stored in the %WinDir%\System32\Spool\Drivers\Color folder. You can now add, remove, and configure default color profiles using the following methods:

   ❏ To add a color profile, click Add and then use the Add Profile Association dialog box to choose a profile from this folder or another location.

   ❏ To remove a profile, select it and then click Remove.

   ❏ To set a profile as the default for the computer, select it and then click Set As Default.

5. Click OK twice.

Chapter 6

Installing and Maintaining Programs

In this chapter:

Program Installation: The Essentials............................139

Installing Programs Using Alternate Settings, Permissions,
and Configurations...142

Managing Installed Programs...................................150

Uninstalling Programs 151

Resolving Failed Uninstalls.....................................152

Removing Adware, Spyware, and Other Rogue Programs 155

Often it is the responsibility of administrators and support staff to install and configure the applications that will be used on desktops. As users install additional
applications, you might also be called on to help troubleshoot installation problems
or to help uninstall programs. Most program installation problems are fairly easy to
solve if you know what to look for. Others problems are fairly difficult to resolve
and require more work than you might expect to clear up. In this chapter, you'll
learn techniques for installing, uninstalling, and maintaining programs. You'll also
learn troubleshooting techniques.

Program Installation: The Essentials

The process of installing programs is fairly straightforward. What isn't so straightforward is troubleshooting the many things that can go wrong and fixing problems
so that programs run properly. To solve problems that might occur, you first need
to understand the installation process. In many cases, the typical installation process starts when Autorun is triggered and Autorun in turn invokes a setup program.
Once the setup program gets started, the installation process can begin. Part of the
installation process involves checking the user's credentials to ensure she has the
appropriate permissions to install the program.

Working with Autorun

When you insert an application CD or DVD into a CD or DVD drive, Microsoft Windows XP checks for a program named AUTORUN.INF. If present, AUTORUN.INF specifies the action that the operating system should take and can also define other installation parameters. AUTORUN.INF is a text-based file that can be opened in any standard text editor. If you were to examine the contents, you'd see something similar to the following code:

```
[autorun]
OPEN=SETUP.EXE AUTORUN=1
ICON=SETUP.EXE,4
SHELL=OPEN
DisplayName=Microsoft Digital Image Suite 9
ShortName=PIS
PISETUP=PIP\pisetup.exe
```

This AUTORUN.INF file specifies that the action to take when the CD or DVD is inserted into the CD or DVD drive is to open a file named SETUP.EXE. Because the file is an actual program, this program is invoked. The AUTORUN.INF file also specifies an icon to use, the status of the shell, the program display name, the program's short name, and an additional parameter, which in this case is the location of another setup program to run.

The file specified to open won't always be a program. Consider the following example:

```
[autorun]
OPEN=Autorun\ShelExec default.htm
```

This AUTORUN.INF file specifies that the action to take when the CD or DVD is inserted into the CD or DVD drive is to execute the shell and open a file named DEFAULT.HTM. As a result, when AUTORUN.INF is triggered, DEFAULT.HTM is opened in the computer's Web browser. It's important to note that even in this case the Web document opened contains links that point to a setup program.

 Tip   With an application CD or DVD in a CD or DVD drive, you can restart the Autorun process at any time. In Windows Explorer, expand My Computer, right-click the CD or DVD drive node, and then select AutoPlay from the shortcut menu. If you are using Windows Explorer and the Folders view is not displayed, you must first click the Folders button on the toolbar.

Program Setup and Compatibility

Most programs have a setup program that uses InstallShield, Wise Install, or Microsoft's Windows Installer. When you start the setup program, the installer helps track the installation process and should also make it possible to easily uninstall the program. If you are installing an older application, the setup program might use an older version of one of these installers, and this might mean the uninstall process won't completely uninstall the program.

Even if you are absolutely certain a program has a current installer, you should consider the possibility that you will need to recover the system if something goes wrong with the installation. To help ensure that you can recover your system, you should create a System Restore checkpoint before installing the program, as discussed in Chapter 18, "Troubleshooting Windows XP Professional," in the section "Using Restore Points." Then if you run into problems, you can try to uninstall the program and use System Restore to recover the system to the state it was in prior to installing the program.

Before you install any application, you should check to see if it is compatible with Windows XP. To determine compatibility, you can perform the following check:

- Check the software packaging, which should specify whether the program is compatible.
- Check the software developer's Web site for a list of compatible operating systems.
- Start Help and Support, and click the Find Compatible Hardware And Software For Windows XP link to see whether the program is listed in the compatible application database.

As part of the compatibility check, you might also want to check for updates or patches for the program. If available, you will usually want to install updates or patches after installing the program.

Permissions Required for Installing Programs

To install most programs under Windows XP, you must use an account with administrator permissions. If you use an account with administrator permissions, you will be able to install any program that is compatible with Windows XP. You will also be able to perform maintenance and uninstallation tasks such as modifying, repairing, or removing programs.

If you use a limited user account or a standard domain account, you will not be able to install most programs. Although users with limited user accounts will be able to start the setup program for an application, setup usually will stop before completing successfully. In most cases, no error will be given—the installation will simply stop. Some newer programs might report that you must be an administrator to install the application. Some older, legacy applications might report inappropriate error messages, such as the inability to copy programs or the failure to modify the registry.

The only programs users with limited user accounts can install are those that

- Copy files only to the user's profile.
- Modify registry settings only in the HKEY_CURRENT_USER hive.
- Install program shortcuts only for the currently logged on user.

Security   Under Windows XP, there are two types of local machine accounts: limited user and computer administrator. If you have administrator permissions on the local machine, you can use the User Accounts utility in Control Panel to view or change a user's account type. If a computer was upgraded to Windows XP from Windows 2000, some user accounts might be members of the Power Users group. As members of the Power Users group, these user accounts have additional permissions and should be able to install most applications. However, an application installation might also fail for members of the Power Users group, especially if the setup program writes to sensitive areas of the registry or areas of the file system that are accessible only to administrators. In a domain, the Power Users group is on the list of default groups in Windows XP. To check group membership on the local machine, in Administrative Tools, start Computer Management, expand System Tools, expand Local Users And Groups, and then select Groups. You will then see a list of available groups. Double-click Power Users. You'll learn more about working with user and group accounts in Chapter 7, "Managing User Access and Global Settings."

Any time a setup program performs additional tasks, setup will fail unless the user has administrator permissions.

Installing Programs Using Alternate Settings, Permissions, and Configurations

Autorun-initiated installation works best when a user with administrator permissions is logged on to the computer on which you want to install the program. The administrator logs on to the computer and inserts the application CD or DVD into the CD or DVD drive, and Autorun begins the installation process. Program installation isn't always so easy or straightforward, however.

Often you might need to use alternate settings, permissions, or configurations. A user might, for example, need to install a program that has been made available over the network. Not all programs are made available to all users of a computer. As a result, you might need to run an application's setup program using alternate credentials. When you want to install 16-bit or MS-DOS programs, there are special considerations you might need to make. Additionally, there are times when you might need to adjust compatibility options for older programs to get them to run. Techniques for handling these situations are discussed in the sections that follow.

Installing Programs without Autorun or Across the Network

The Add Or Remove Programs utility in Control Panel is helpful when you are installing programs with alternate settings or configurations. By using Add Or Remove Programs, you ensure that Windows XP finds the right setup program to use and that you can install programs from locations other than the local drives.

When you start Add Or Remove Programs by double-clicking its icon in Control Panel and you click Add New Programs as shown in Figure 6-1, you have several options, as follows:

- **Add A Program From CD-ROM Or Floppy Disk**   To install a program and have Windows XP search for the appropriate setup program on all available removable media, click the CD Or Floppy button to start the Install Program From Floppy Disk Or CD-ROM wizard. When prompted, insert the program's installation disk and then click Next. Windows XP will search for the appropriate setup program to use and run it automatically if possible. If Windows XP cannot locate the setup program automatically, click the Browse button on the Run Installation Program page to manually search for the setup program.

- **Add Programs From Microsoft**   To add new Windows features, drivers, or system updates over the Internet, click the Windows Update button to manually start the Windows Update process.

- **Add Programs From Your Network**   When a computer is a member of a domain, you have an additional option for adding programs from the corporate network. If a network administrator has made programs available over the network and the currently logged on user is a member of an authorized group or is authorized specifically to install an application, it will be listed as available.

Figure 6-1   Use Add Or Remove Programs to help install programs with alternate settings or configurations.

You make applications available to users over the network through Group Policy. When you use Group Policy to deploy applications, administrators have two distribution options.

- The first option is to *assign* the application to users or computers. When an application is assigned to a computer, it is completely installed the next time the computer is restarted and becomes available to all users of that computer the next time they log on. When an application is assigned to a user, it is completely installed the next time the user logs on to the network.

■ The second option is to *publish* the application and make it available for installation. When you publish an application, authorized users see the program on the list of available applications in Add Or Remove Programs. Published applications can also be made available through extension activation. With extension activation configured, the program is installed when a user tries to open any file with an extension specific to the application. For example, if a user double-clicks a file with a .doc extension, Microsoft Word could be installed automatically using an extension activation configuration.

You deploy applications for computers using a Microsoft Windows Installer Package (.msi file) and Computer Configuration\Software Settings\Software Installation policy. You deploy applications for users using a Windows Installer Package (.msi file) and User Configuration\Software Settings\Software Installation policy. The basic steps required to deploy applications through Group Policy are as follows:

1. For clients to access it, the Windows Installer Package must be located on a network share. As necessary, copy the Windows Installer Package (.msi file) to a network share that will be accessible to the appropriate users.

2. Access the Group Policy Object (GPO) from which you want to deploy the application in the Group Policy Object Editor. Once deployed, the application will be made available to all clients for which the GPO is applicable. This means the application will be available to computers and users in the related domain, site, or organizational unit.

3. Expand Computer Configuration\Software Settings or User Configuration\Software Settings as appropriate, right-click Software Installation, point to New, and then select Package.

4. Use the Open dialog box to locate the Windows Installer Package (.msi file) for the application and then click Open. As shown in Figure 6-2, you are then given the choice to select the deployment method as Published, Assigned, or Advanced.

Figure 6-2   Choose a deployment option for the program.

5. To publish or assign the program, choose Published or Assigned as appropriate and then click OK. If you are configuring computer policy, the program is available the next time a computer affected by the GPO is restarted. If you are configuring user policy, the program is available to users in the domain, site, or organizational unit the next time they log on. Currently logged on users will need to log off and then log on.

6. To configure additional deployment options for the program using the properties sheet, select Advanced and then click OK. You can then set additional deployment options as necessary.

Making Programs Available to All or Selective Users

Usually when you install a program from an administrator's account, the program is made available to all users on a computer. This occurs because the program's shortcuts are placed in the *%AllUsersProfile%*\Start Menu\Programs folder so that any user who logs on to a system has access to the program. Some programs prompt you during installation as to whether you want to install the program for all users or only for the currently logged on user. Other programs simply install themselves only for the current user.

If setup installs a program so that it is only available for the currently logged on user and you want other users to have access to the program, you'll need to take one of the following actions:

■ Log on to the computer using each user account that should have access to the program and rerun setup. In this way, you can selectively make the program available to the appropriate users. You will also need to remember to run setup again each time a new user account is added to the computer and that user needs access to the program.

■ For programs that don't require per user settings to be added to the registry before running, you can in some cases make the program available to all users on a computer by adding the appropriate shortcuts to the *%AllUsersProfile%*\Start Menu\Programs folder. Copy or move the program shortcuts from the currently logged on user's profile to the *%AllUsersProfile%*\Start Menu\Programs folder.

If you want to make a program available to all users on a computer, you can copy or move a program's shortcuts by completing the following steps:

1. Right-click the Start button, and select Explore. This starts Windows Explorer with the currently logged on user's Start Menu folder selected.

2. Expand Programs, right-click the folder for the program group or the shortcut you want to work with, and choose Copy or Cut from the shortcut menu.

3. Right-click the Start button, and select Explore All Users. This starts Windows Explorer with the *%AllUsersProfile%*\Start Menu folder selected.

4. Right-click Program, and then select Paste. The program group or shortcut should now be available to all users of the computer.

If you want to make a program available only to the currently logged on user rather than all users on a computer, you can move a program's shortcuts by completing the following steps:

1. Right-click the Start button, and select Explore All Users. This starts Windows Explorer with the *%AllUsersProfile%*\Start Menu folder selected.

2. Select Program, right-click the folder for the program group or the shortcut you want to work with, and choose Cut from the shortcut menu.

3. Right-click the Start button, and select Explore. This starts Windows Explorer with the currently logged on user's Start Menu folder selected.

4. Right-click Programs, and then select Paste. The program group or shortcut should now be available only to the currently logged on user.

 Note Moving the program group or shortcut serves to hide the fact the program is available on the computer—it doesn't prevent other users from running the program. Other users on a computer will still be able to run the program. They would be able to do this using the Run dialog or from Windows Explorer.

Running Setup Using Alternate Credentials

You can run setup (and any other program for that matter) using alternate credentials. This allows a user with a limited account to be logged on while you install a program for them. Right-click the setup program icon, and then choose Run As from the shortcut menu. In the Run As dialog box shown in Figure 6-3, choose The Following User. Next select a user account in the User Name combo box or type the name of the account to use in *DOMAINNAME\UserName* or *MACHINE-NAME\UserName* format such as WRSTANEK\Administrator. In the Password field, type the password for the account and then click OK. This option installs the program using the permissions of the designated user account, which should be an account with computer administrator permissions on the local computer.

 Note The account you are using cannot have a blank password or policy-based restrictions. If it does, logon will fail.

Figure 6-3 You can use alternate credentials to install a program.

Special Installation Considerations for 16-Bit and MS-DOS Programs

You'll find that many 16-bit and MS-DOS programs will install and run on Windows XP without any problems. However, most 16-bit and MS-DOS programs do not support long file names. To help ensure compatibility, Windows XP maps between long and short file names as necessary. This ensures long file names are protected when they are modified by a 16-bit or MS-DOS program. Additionally, it is important to note that some 16-bit and MS-DOS programs require 16-bit drivers, which are not supported on Windows XP and as a result, these programs won't run.

Most existing 16-bit and MS-DOS programs were originally written for Windows 3.0 or Windows 3.1. Windows XP runs these older programs using a virtual machine that mimics the 386-enhanced mode used by Windows 3.0 or Windows 3.1. By default, each 16-bit and MS-DOS application runs as a thread within a single virtual machine. This means if you run multiple 16-bit and MS-DOS applications, they all share a common memory space. Unfortunately, if one of these applications hangs or crashes, it usually means the others will as well.

You can help prevent one 16-bit or MS-DOS application from causing others to hang or crash by running it in a separate memory space. To do this, follow these steps.

1. Right-click the program's shortcut icon, and then choose Properties. If the program doesn't have a shortcut, create one and then display the shortcut's Properties dialog box.
2. On the Shortcut tab, click the Advanced Button. This displays the Advanced Properties dialog box.
3. Select the Run In Separate Memory Space check box.
4. Click OK twice to close all open dialog boxes and save the changes.

Note   Running a program in a separate memory space uses additional memory. However, you'll usually find that the program is more responsive. Another added benefit is that you'll be able to run multiple instances of the program—as long as all the instances are running in separate memory spaces.

Tip   The Windows XP command prompt (CMD.EXE) is a 32-bit command prompt. If you want to invoke a 16-bit MS-DOS command prompt, you can use COMMAND.COM. Type **command** in the Run dialog box.

Forcing Program Compatibility

Some programs won't install or run on Windows XP even if they worked on previous versions of the Windows operating system. If you try to install a program that has known compatibility problems, Windows XP should display a warning prompt telling you about the compatibility issue. In most cases, you won't want to continue installing or running a program with known compatibility problems, especially if the program is a system utility such as an antivirus program or a disk partitioning program, because running an incompatible system utility can cause serious problems. Running other types of incompatible programs can also cause problems, especially if they write to disk.

That said, if a program will not install or run on Windows XP, you might be able to run the program by adjusting its compatibility settings. Windows XP provides two mechanisms for managing compatibility settings. You can use the Program Compatibility Wizard, or you can edit the program's compatibility settings directly using the program's Properties dialog box. Both techniques work the same way. However, the Program Compatibility Wizard is the only way you can change compatibility settings for programs that are on shared network drives, CD or DVD drives, or other types of removable media drives. As a result, you can sometimes use the Program Compatibility Wizard to install and run programs that would not otherwise install and run.

Using the Program Compatibility Wizard

To set program compatibility using the Program Compatibility Wizard, follow these steps.

1. Click Start, Programs or All Programs as appropriate, Accessories, and then select Program Compatibility Wizard.

2. When the wizard starts, click Next. As shown in Figure 6-4, you now need to specify how you want to locate the program. You can chose from a list of programs, use the program in the CD-ROM (or other removable media drive), or locate the program by browsing files and folders.

Figure 6-4   Decide how you want to locate the program.

3. Click Next. Choose the operating system for which the program was designed. As shown in Figure 6-5, the choices are Windows 95, Windows NT 4.0 with Service Pack 5, Windows 98/Windows Me, or Windows 2000. Your choice sets the compatibility mode. When running the program, Windows XP will simulate the environment for the chosen operating system.

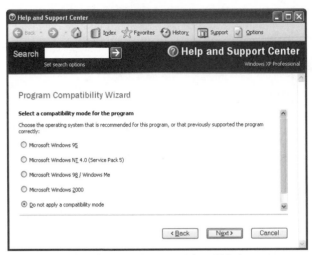

Figure 6-5   Select the operating system for which the program was originally designed.

4. Click Next. If you are trying to run a game, an educational program, or any other program that requires specific display settings, you can select the required display settings. By selecting 256 Colors, 640 × 480 Screen Resolution, or both, you are restricting the video display. This can help with programs that have problems running at higher screen resolutions and color depths.

5. Click Next twice. The wizard will then run the program with the chosen compatibility settings. When you are finished testing the program, return to the wizard and complete the configuration process.

Setting Compatibility Options Directly

If you've already installed the program but it won't run correctly, you might want to edit the compatibility settings directly rather than through the wizard. To do this, follow these steps.

1. Right-click the program's shortcut icon, and then choose Properties.

2. On the Compatibility tab shown in Figure 6-6, choose the compatibility settings you want Windows XP to use. Programs that are part of the Windows XP operating system cannot be run in compatibility mode. Because of this, the options on the Compatibility tab are grayed out (unavailable) for built-in programs.

3. Select the Run This Program In Compatibility Mode For check box and then use the selection menu to choose the operating system for which the program is designed.

4. If necessary, use the options in the Display Settings panel to restrict the video display settings for the program. Select 256 colors, 640 × 480 screen resolution, or both, as required.

5. Click OK. Double-click the shortcut to run the program and test the compatibility settings. If you still have problems running the program, you might need to modify the compatibility settings again.

Figure 6-6 You can also configure compatibility directly.

Managing Installed Programs

You manage a computer's installed programs using the Add Or Remove Programs utility, which is in Control Panel. To see a list of currently installed programs on a computer, use the utility's default view, which shows the currently installed programs sorted by Name. As Figure 6-7 shows, the list of currently installed programs can be adjusted in two ways.

- **Show Updates** Using the Show Updates check box, you can show or hide updates that have been applied to the computer through Windows Update or by the manual installation of services packs, hot fixes, and patches.

- **Sort By** Using the Sort By list, you can sort the installed programs by Name, Size, Frequency Of Use, or Date Last Used. If you want to clean up programs that aren't being used, sort by Frequency Of Use. With this option, Windows XP checks the number of times the program has been used in the past 30 days and sorts the list by usage frequency. The most frequently used programs are at the top of the list; the less frequently used programs are at the bottom of the list. If you want to clean up disk space, sort the list by Size. Here, the programs that use the most space are listed at the top of the list.

When you select a program in the Currently Installed Programs list, you'll find a button or buttons that you can use to manage the program. For programs with multiple setup options, you'll find separate Change and Remove buttons. Clicking Change allows you to rerun setup and change the installation configuration. Typically, you do this by adding new components, selecting different options, or removing installed components.

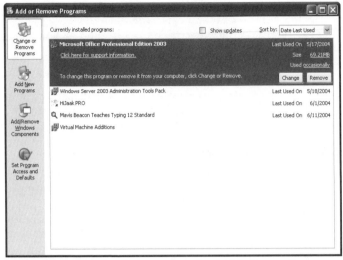

Figure 6-7   Manage installed programs using Add Or Remove Programs.

Tip   You might also see a support link. Clicking the support link in most cases will give you a Repair option, which you can click to have Windows Installer reinstall the program. A reinstall should fix any problems with program components and registry settings because these are all completely refreshed. This is different from a Repair option that you might find in a program. For example, the Detect And Repair option on the Help menu in Microsoft Office is used to detect damaged or missing components and then repair them without the need to reinstall the entire program.

Uninstalling Programs

Before you remove a program, you should confirm that the program isn't in use. If other users are logged on to the computer, you should log them off to ensure that they aren't using the program. To remove a program, start the Add Or Remove Program utility in Control Panel. Select the program in the Currently Installed Programs list, and then click the Change/Remove or Remove button. This starts the uninstall process.

Caution   Programs that use InstallShield, Wise Install, or Microsoft Windows Installer should have an uninstaller. In some cases, you'll be given an opportunity to confirm that you want to uninstall the program before the uninstaller removes the program. In other cases, the uninstaller will simply start and remove the program without any warning or prompting.

Most uninstallers don't completely uninstall a program. Typically, you'll find that folders and data files that were used by the program will remain, especially if the data files have custom user settings or stored results, such as with educational programs or games. You'll need to track down and delete these additional folders and files as necessary.

Keep in mind that you can only use Add Or Remove Programs to uninstall programs that were installed using an installer of some type. If the program copied its files directly to a folder on disk, you'll need to manually uninstall the program by removing its files and shortcuts.

Resolving Failed Uninstalls

Most programs include an uninstaller that attempts to remove the program, its data, and its registry settings. Sometimes, however, programs either do not include an uninstall utility or for one reason or another do not fully remove their registry settings. In addition to unnecessarily cluttering the registry, the leftover registry settings can sometimes prevent you from successfully reinstalling the program or from installing other programs. For programs that were installed with Windows Installer, Windows Support Tools (which must be installed from the \Support\Tools folder on the Windows XP product CD) provides two utilities that help you maintain the registry.

- Windows Installer Clean Up (MSICUU.EXE)
- Windows Installer Zapper (MSIZAP.EXE)

Both tools are designed to work with programs installed using Windows Installer and must be run using an account with Administrator permissions. In addition to being able to clear out registry settings for programs you've installed then uninstalled, you can also use these utilities to recover the registry to the state it was in prior to a failed or inadvertently terminated program installation. This works as long as the application used Windows Installer.

Working with the Windows Installer Clean Up Utility

The Windows Installer Clean Up utility removes registry settings for programs that were installed using Windows Installer. The utility is most useful for cleaning up registry remnants of applications that were partially uninstalled or whose uninstall failed. It is also useful for cleaning up applications that can't be uninstalled or reinstalled because of partial or damaged settings in the registry.

 Caution   Don't use Windows Installer Clean Up as an uninstaller. You should first attempt to remove a program using the normal uninstall process. This is necessary because this utility cleans up only registry entries. It won't clean up the program's files or shortcuts, which will make it necessary to reinstall the application to use it again. Also keep in mind that the profile of the current user is part of the registry. Because of this, Windows Installer Clean Up will remove user-specific installation data from the profile of the currently logged on user. It won't, however, remove this information from other profiles.

If you've already installed the Support Tools, you can run this utility by typing
msicuu at the command line. When the Windows Installer Clean Up dialog box is
displayed, as shown in Figure 6-8, select the program or programs to clean up, and
then click Remove. Windows Installer Clean Up keeps a log file to record the programs that users delete in this manner. The log is stored in the *%UserProfile%*\Local
Settings\Temp directory and is named MSICU.LOG.

Figure 6-8   Select the program or programs to clean up.

Note   Windows Installer Clean Up is a GUI for the Windows Installer Zapper discussed in the next section. When you use the Windows Installer
Clean Up utility, it runs the Windows Installer Zapper with the T parameter
to delete an application's registry entries. The Windows Installer Clean Up
utility has an added benefit because it creates a log file, which is not used
with Windows Installer Zapper.

Working with the Windows Installer Zapper

Another way to resolve uninstall problems is to use the Windows Installer Zapper
(MSIZAP.EXE). This command-line utility removes registry settings for applications
that were installed using the Windows Installer. Like Windows Installer Clean Up,
it can be used to clean up registry settings for applications that were partially uninstalled or for which the uninstall failed, as well as applications that can't be uninstalled or reinstalled because of partial or damaged settings in the registry. This
utility can be used to remove registry settings related to failed installations or failed
rollbacks of installations. It can also be used to correct failures related to multiple
instances of a setup program running simultaneously and in cases when a setup
program won't run.

The complete syntax for the Windows Installer Zapper is as follows:

```
msizap [*] [!] [A] [P] [S] [W] [T] [G] [AppToZap]
```

where

- *AppToZap*   Specifies an application's product code or the file path to the application's Windows Installer (.msi) program
- *   Deletes all Windows Installer configuration information on the computer, including information stored in the registry and on disk. Must be used with the ALLPRODUCTS flag
- !   Turns off any warning prompts that would ask you to confirm your actions
- **A**   Gives administrators Full Control permissions on the applicable Windows Installer data so that it can be deleted even if the administrator doesn't have specific access to the data
- **P**   Deletes registry information related to in-progress installations
- **S**   Deletes registry information saved for rollback to the previous state
- **W**   Examines all user profiles, instead of just the current user's profile, for data that should be deleted
- **T**   Used when you are choosing a specific application to clean up
- **G**   Removes orphaned Windows Installer files that have been cached; for all users

 Caution   As with Windows Installer Clean Up, don't use Windows Installer Zapper as an uninstaller. You should first attempt to remove a program using the normal uninstall process.

Removing Registry Settings for Failed Installations

Program installations can fail during installation or after installation. When programs are being installed, an InProgress key is created in the registry under the HKLM\SOFTWARE\Microsoft\Windows\CurrentVersion\Installer subkey. In cases when installation fails, the system might not be able to edit or remove this key, which could cause the setup to fail the next time you try to run it. Running Windows Installer Zapper with the P parameter clears out the InProgress key, which should allow you to run setup.

After installation, programs rely on their registry settings to configure themselves properly. If these settings become damaged or the installation becomes damaged, the program won't run. Some programs have a repair utility that can be accessed simply by rerunning the installation. During the repair process, the Windows Installer might attempt to write changes to the registry to repair the installation or roll it back to get back to the original state. If this process fails for any reason, the registry can contain unwanted settings for the program. Running Windows Installer Zapper with the S parameter clears out the rollback data for the active installation. Rollback data is stored in the HKLM\SOFTWARE\Microsoft\Windows\CurrentVersion\Installer\Rollback key.

Tip Any running installation also has rollback data, so you typically use the P and S parameters together. This means you would type **msizap ps** at the command line.

Removing Partial or Damaged Registry Settings for Individual Programs

When a program can't be successfully uninstalled you can attempt to clean up its settings from the registry using the Windows Installer Zapper. To do this, you need to know the product code for the program or the full path to the Windows Installer file used to install the program. The installer file ends with the .msi extension and usually is found in one of the program's installation directories.

You then type **msizap t** followed by the product code or .msi file path. For example, if the installer file path is C:\MyApps\Mobile\Mobile.msi, you would type **msizap t c:\myapps\mobile\mobile.msi** at the command line to clear out the application's settings.

Tip Because the current user's profile is a part of the registry, user-specific settings for the program will be removed from this profile. If you want to clear out these settings for all user profiles on the system, add the W parameter, such as **msizap wt c:\myapps\mobile\mobile.msi**. Additionally, if you use Run As, you can delete installer data and settings for a specific user rather than the current user or all users.

Removing Adware, Spyware, and Other Rogue Programs

Lately, I've had a real problem with rogue programs installed when users browse Web sites—and you might have as well. It seems that despite many security precautions and the use of antivirus programs, rogue programs such as adware or spyware invariably find a way to install themselves. One of the easiest ways to determine if adware or spyware has been installed is to browse the Web. If you browse sites and notice many pop ups, especially ones that generate other pop ups when you try to close them, the computer probably has been infected by a rogue program.

Most rogue programs are difficult to remove because they not only install themselves in a program folder, but they also copy their DLLs to the *%SystemRoot%* or *%SystemRoot%*\System32 folder. To make matters worse, rogue programs don't usually have an uninstaller, or if they do, the uninstaller might only serve to more deeply embed the program on the computer.

Real World   Although a good antivirus program might be able to detect or block rogue programs, most aren't 100 percent effective. One antivirus program that I was using at the time of this writing did an excellent job of detecting the presence of rogue programs. Unfortunately, it detected these programs after they were already installed, and although its cleanup process was generally effective, I still needed to manually clear out some rogue programs. Another antivirus program that I was using at the time of this writing did an excellent job of blocking rogue programs so that they couldn't install themselves. This worked best with the Pop-up Blocker enabled. However, the antivirus program was unable to detect rogue programs that were already installed and didn't provide any means to detect them, either. The best way to ensure rogue programs cannot be installed from the Web is to set the Internet zone security to High or to use custom settings that disable scripts, applets, and ActiveX controls. Windows XP Service Pack 2 also includes a built-in Pop-up Blocker. See Chapter 15, "Managing Advanced Internet Explorer Options," for more information.

You can track down and remove most rogue programs by following these steps:

1. In Windows Explorer, examine the *%SystemDrive%* and look for folders created on or after the date you suspect the computer was infected by the rogue program. Usually, these folders aren't created in the *%SystemDrive%*\Program Files folder, but they can be there, so look carefully. Make a note of any folders that you don't recognize, and then check the folders for unknown executables and other files. The rogue programs I've seen have mostly been created directly under the *%SystemDrive%* folder.

2. Go to the Web site for the antivirus program your organization uses. If you search for the executables or DLLs you uncovered, you might find them listed as belonging to adware, spyware, or other rogue programs. In this case, follow the advice posted on the site for removing the program or complete the remaining steps in this process.

3. Press Ctrl+Alt+Delete, and then select Task Manager. Use the Processes tab in Task Manager to look for instances of the executables that are running. If you've determined an executable is from a rogue program, right-click the process and select End Process Tree.

4. Search the *%SystemDrive%* for other instances of the executables or DLLs that you found in the folder for the rogue program. Usually, you will want to remove all instances that you find. If you are unable to remove executables or DLLs, it means they are in use and you will need to stop the related process or processes in Task Manager and then try to delete the executables or DLLs again.

5. You should now be able to remove the program folder and files for the rogue program in Windows Explorer. If you are unable to, try renaming the folder and then restarting the computer. When the computer restarts, you should be able to delete the renamed folder.

6. Check Task Manager one more time. No instances of the rogue program's executables should be running on the computer. If they are, you haven't tracked down and removed every instance of the program.

Part II
Windows XP Professional Core Administration

In this part, you'll find tips and techniques for performing core administration tasks. Chapter 7 discusses techniques for managing user access to Microsoft Windows XP systems. You'll find detailed coverage for working with local user and group accounts as well as managing access to systems. The chapter also covers remote access. Chapter 8 explores administration tasks you might need to perform for laptops and traveling users. You'll also find discussions on power management, hardware profiles, and configuring networking for laptops.

Chapter 9 is the first of several chapters that closely examine group policies. After providing an overview of how group policies are used and applied, the chapter provides guidance on configuring policies, data management, and working with administrative templates. Chapter 10 details file system and drive management. The chapter discusses drive partitioning and formatting and also covers drive optimization, compression, and encryption. Chapter 11 examines file security and sharing. Chapter 12 completes the discussion of core Windows XP administration with a discussion on configuring folder options, offline files, and quotas.

Chapter 7
Managing User Access and Global Settings

In this chapter:

Understanding User and Group Accounts. 159

Managing User Access to Workstations in Workgroups. 164

Managing User Access to Workstations in Domains 175

Managing Stored Passwords 180

Using the .NET Passport Wizard to Create a Microsoft .NET Passport 182

Managing Local User and Group Accounts. 183

Managing Remote Access to Workstations. 189

Microsoft Windows XP workstations can be configured as members of a work-group or members of a domain. (In this book, "Windows XP" refers to Windows XP Professional unless otherwise indicated.) When a workstation is configured as a member of a workgroup, user access and global settings are configured on the workstation itself. When a workstation is configured as a member of a domain, user access and global settings are configured at two levels: the local system level and the domain level. User access can be configured at the local system level for a specific machine and at the domain level for multiple systems or resources in the domain. In this chapter, you'll learn how to manage local system access and local accounts. For a discussion on configuring domain access and permissions, see Chapters 6 through 10 in the *Microsoft Windows Server 2003 Administrator's Pocket Consultant*. Keep in mind that every task examined in this chapter can be performed through a local logon or a remote desktop connection.

Understanding User and Group Accounts

Windows XP provides user accounts and group accounts (of which users can be members). User accounts are designed for individuals. Group accounts, usually referred to as *groups*, are designed to simplify the administration of multiple users. You can log on to user accounts, but you can't log on to a group account.

Local User Account Essentials

Two types of user accounts are defined in Windows XP:

- **Local user accounts**   User accounts defined on a local computer are called *local user accounts*. These accounts have access to the local computer only, and they must authenticate themselves before they can access network resources. You create local user accounts with the Administrative Tools, Computer Management, System Tools, Local Users And Groups utility.

- **Domain user accounts**   User accounts defined in the Active Directory directory service are called *domain user accounts*. Through Single Sign-On, these accounts can access resources throughout a domain. When a computer is a member of an Active Directory domain, you can create domain user accounts using Active Directory Users And Computers. This Microsoft Management Console (MMC) tool is available on the Administrative Tools menu when you install the Windows Server 2003 Administrator Tools (ADMINPAK.MSI) on your Windows XP computer.

All user accounts are identified with a logon name. In Windows XP, this logon name has two parts:

- **User name**   The text label for the account
- **User workgroup or domain**   The workgroup or domain in which the user account exists

For the user WRSTANEK, whose account is created in the MICROSOFT workgroup, the full logon name for Windows XP is MICROSOFT\wrstanek. With a workgroup account, WRSTANEK could log on to his local workstation but would need to authenticate himself in the domain to access domain resources.

When working with domains, the full logon name includes the user account name and the domain name separated by the @ symbol. For example, the full logon name for WRSTANEK in the technology.microsoft.com domain would be WRSTANEK@technology.microsoft.com.

Although Windows XP displays user names to describe privileges and permissions, the key identifiers for accounts are security identifiers (SIDs). SIDs are unique identifiers generated when accounts are created. Each consists of a workgroup or domain security ID prefix combined with a unique relative ID for the user. Windows XP uses these identifiers to track accounts independently from user names. SIDs serve many purposes, but the two most important ones are to allow you to easily change user names and delete accounts without worrying that someone might gain access to resources simply by recreating an account.

When you change a user name, you tell Windows XP to map a particular SID to a new name. When you delete an account, you tell Windows XP that a particular SID is no longer valid. Even if you create an account with the same user name later, the new account won't have the same privileges and permissions as the previous one because the new account will have a new SID.

User accounts can also have passwords and public certificates associated with them. *Passwords* are authentication strings for an account. *Public certificates* combine a public and private key to identify a user. You log on with a password interactively, whereas you log on with a public certificate using a smart card and a smart card reader.

When you install Windows XP, the operating system installs default user accounts. You'll find several built-in accounts, which have purposes similar to those of accounts created in Windows domains. The key accounts you'll see are the following:

- **Administrator**   Administrator is a predefined account that provides complete access to files, directories, services, and other facilities. You can't delete or disable this account. In Active Directory, the Administrator account has domain-wide access and privileges. On a local workstation, the Administrator account generally has access only to the local system.

- **Guest**   Guest is designed for users who need one-time or occasional access. Although guests have only limited system privileges, you should be very careful about using this account because using it opens the system up to potential security problems. The risk is so great that the account is initially disabled when you install Windows XP.

- **HelpAssistant**   Windows XP interactive support is built on an application framework that allows users to initiate Remote Assistance sessions. Technicians responding to Remote Assistance requests log on to the user's system using the HelpAssistant account. This account has limited system capabilities, which are designed to allow HelpAssistant to use Terminal Services to log on locally to systems.

- **Support**   The Support account is used by the built-in Help And Support service. The account is a member of the HelpServicesGroup and has the right to log on as a batch job. This user rights assignment allows the Support account to execute batch updates. The format for the account name is Support_<*id*>, where <id> is a placeholder for an actual value, such as Support_388945a0.

Before you modify any of the built-in accounts, you should note the property settings and group membership. By default, some of these accounts are members of various groups. This membership grants or limits the user access to specific system resources. For example, the Support account is a member of the HelpServices-Group. Being a member of this group makes it possible for the account to be used for Help And Support services.

In addition to the built-in accounts, Windows XP has several pseudo-accounts that are used to perform specific types of system actions. The pseudo-accounts are available only on the local system. You can't change the settings for these accounts with the user administration tools. Users can't log on to a computer with these accounts either. The pseudo-accounts available include the following:

- **LocalSystem**   LocalSystem is a pseudo-account for running system processes and handling system-level tasks. This account grants the logon right Log On As A Service. Most services run under the LocalSystem account. In some cases, these services have privileges to interact with the desktop. Services that need additional privileges or logon rights run under the LocalService or Network-Service accounts. Services that run as LocalSystem include Automatic Updates, Computer Browser, DHCP Client, Event Log, Help And Support, Messenger, Net Logon, and Uninterruptible Power Supply.

- **LocalService**   LocalService is a pseudo-account for running services that need additional privileges and logon rights on a local system. Services that run under this account are granted the right to Log On As A Service and the privileges Adjust Memory Quotas For A Process, Generate Security Audits, and Replace A Process Level Token by default. Services that run as LocalService include Alerter, Remote Registry, Smart Card, Smart Card Helper, SSDP Discovery Service, TCP/IP NetBIOS Helper, and WebClient.

- **NetworkService**   NetworkService is a pseudo-account for running services that need additional privileges and logon rights on a local system and the network. As with LocalService, services that run under the NetworkService account are granted the right to Log On As A Service and the privileges Adjust Memory Quotas For A Process, Generate Security Audits, and Replace A Process Level Token by default. Services that run as NetworkService include Distributed Transaction Coordinator, DNS Client, Performance Logs And Alerts, and Remote Procedure Call (RPC) Locator.

Group Account Essentials

Windows XP also provides groups, which you use to grant permissions to similar types of users and to simplify account administration. If a user is a member of a group that can access a resource, that particular user can access the same resource. Thus, you can give a user access to various work-related resources just by making the user a member of the correct group. Note that although you can log on to a computer with a user account, you can't log on to a computer with a group account. Because different Active Directory domains or workgroups might have groups with the same name, groups are often referred to by *Domain\GroupName* or *Workgroup\GroupName*, such as Technology\GMarketing for the GMarketing group in the Technology domain or workgroup.

Windows XP uses the following three types of groups:

- **Local groups**   Defined on a local computer and used on the local computer only. You create local groups with the Local Users And Groups utility.

- **Security groups**   Can have security descriptors associated with them. You use a Windows server to define security groups in domains, using Active Directory Users And Computers.

- **Distribution groups**   Used as e-mail distribution lists. They can't have security descriptors associated with them. You define distribution groups in domains using Active Directory Users And Computers.

As with user accounts, group accounts are tracked using unique SIDs. This means that you can't delete a group account, recreate it, and expect all the permissions and privileges to remain the same. The new group will have a new SID and all the permissions and privileges of the old group will be lost.

When you assign user access levels, you have the opportunity to make the user a member of the following built-in or predefined groups:

- **Administrators** Members of this group are local administrators and have complete access to the workstation. They can create accounts, modify group membership, install printers, manage shared resources, and more. Because this account has complete access, you should be very careful about adding users to this group.

- **Backup Operators** Members of this group can back up and restore files and directories on the workstation. They can log on to the local computer, back up or restore files, and shut down the computer. Because of how the account is set up, they can back up files regardless of whether they have read/write access to the files. However, they can't change access permissions of the files or perform other administrative tasks.

Note Operators have privileges to perform very specific administrative tasks, such as backing up file systems. By default, no other group or user accounts are members of the operator groups. This feature exists primarily to make sure that you grant explicit access to these accounts.

- **Guests** Guests are users with very limited privileges. Members of this group can access the system and its resources remotely, but they can't perform most other tasks.

- **Network Configuration Operators** Members of this group can manage network settings on the workstation. They can also configure Transmission Control Protocol/Internet Protocol (TCP/IP) settings and perform other general network configuration tasks.

- **Power Users** Members of this group have all the privileges of the Users group, as well as a few additional privileges, such as the capability to modify computer settings and install programs. If you want to give users of a Windows XP workstation extra control, Microsoft recommends that you make them members of this group, which allows them to perform limited administration tasks on their workstations.

- **Remote Desktop Users** Members of this group can log on to the workstation remotely using Terminal Services And Remote Desktop. Their permissions on the workstation once they are logged on are determined by the additional groups of which each user is a member. A user that is a member of the Administrators group is granted this privilege automatically (however, remote logons must be enabled before an administrator can remotely log on to a workstation).

- **Replicator**   Members of this group can manage the replication of files for the local machine. File replication is primarily used with Active Directory domains and Microsoft Windows Server 2003.

- **Users**   Users are people who do most of their work on a single Windows XP workstation. Because of this, members of the Users group have more restrictions than privileges. Members of this group can log on to a Windows XP workstation locally, keep a local profile, lock the workstation, and shut down the workstation.

In most cases, you'll configure user access using the Users, Power Users, or Administrators groups. You can configure User and Administrator access levels by setting the Limited or the Computer Administrator access level, respectively. To make a user a member of the Power Users group or another group, you need to create or modify the account using the Local Users And Groups node of Computer Management.

Managing User Access to Workstations in Workgroups

When a computer is a member of a workgroup instead of a domain, user account management is very different. As part of a workgroup, users can take advantage of features that allow them to quickly switch between users and to create password reset disks. Workgroup user accounts can also be configured without password protection. In this configuration, anyone can log on to an account.

Understanding User Access Levels in Workgroups

In workgroups, Windows XP provides the following two default user account types:

- **Computer Administrator**   These users are configured as members of the local Administrators group. By default, the Administrators group includes the Administrator account and any accounts that you create during setup of the operating system. Computer administrators have full control over the local computer. This allows them to perform all tasks, including installing applications, installing or removing hardware, changing system settings, creating or managing local users and groups, accessing files, taking ownership of files, and logging on in Safe Mode.

- **Limited**   Limited users are members of the standard Users group. This allows them to log on to the computer, but it doesn't allow them to perform advanced tasks, such as installing applications or changing system settings. However, limited users can manage the password, picture, and Microsoft .NET Passport associated with their accounts. They can also run programs that have been installed on the computer, manage files in their folders, and view files in shared folders (as appropriate for the permissions assigned).

When you are choosing between computer administrator and limited access levels, keep in mind that the limited level is the most secure. The limited level allows users to log on and run programs. It doesn't allow them to perform most other tasks. A user can be made a member of any built-in or predefined group that exists on the local system. For example, if you make a user a member of the local Administrators group, the user has full privileges on the local system. The user does not, however, have administrator privileges in the domain. Most workstation users will want to have at least Power User privileges on their personal systems, which will allow them to install and uninstall applications and to manage system settings, such as system time and the Display utility. Power Users do have some restrictions. Thus, if you are configuring access levels for the primary system owner, you'll probably want to create the account as a limited user and then make the user a member of the Power Users group.

Security   Using a limited account also provides fewer opportunities for malicious hackers to gain access to the system. If the user can't install programs, a program created by a malicious hacker likely won't be able to install itself either. Administrators should also consider using a limited account as their main account. If you do so, you would then use Run As to access a program as an administrator. Right-click the program icon and then choose Run As from the shortcut menu. In the Run As dialog box, choose The Following User. Then select a user account in the User Name combo box or type the name of the account to use in *DOMAINNAME\UserName* or *MACHINENAME\UserName* format, such as WRSTANEK\Administrator. In the Password field, type the password for the account, and then click OK. You can also use Run As from the command line. Type **runas /user:USERNAME@DOMAINNAME** cmd where *cmd* is the command you want to run as the specified user.

Creating Local User Accounts to Grant Access to Workstations

You grant access to workstations using the User Account utility. Follow these steps:

1. In Control Panel, double-click User Accounts. This displays the User Accounts Wizard shown in Figure 7-1.

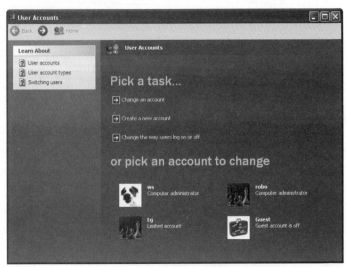

Figure 7-1   Use the User Accounts utility to manage user access to a workstation.

2. Click Create A New Account. This displays the Name The New Account page.

3. Type the name of the local account. This name is displayed on the Welcome screen and Start Menu. Click Next.

4. On the Pick An Account Type page, set the level of access for the user as either Computer Administrator or Limited. To give the user full permissions on the local computer, select Computer Administrator.

5. Click Create Account. If you need to set other permissions or add the user to other local groups, you'll need to access the account in Local Users And Groups and then make the necessary changes. Follow the steps specified in the section of this chapter entitled "Managing Local User and Group Accounts."

Changing Access Levels for Users in Workgroups

The User Accounts utility provides an easy way to change access levels for users in workgroups. You can quickly set one of the two default access levels for users. For more advanced control, however, you'll need to use Local Users And Groups to assign group membership individually. (See the section of this chapter entitled "Adding and Removing Local Group Members.")

To change the access level for a user, follow these steps:

1. In Control Panel, double-click User Accounts.

2. In the User Accounts Wizard, click the account you want to change and then click Change The Account Type.

3. On the Pick An Account Type page, set the level of access for the user as either Computer Administrator or Limited and then click Change Account Type.

Note You can also customize access by creating an account directly in Local Users And Groups. See the section of this chapter entitled "Managing Local User and Group Accounts."

Creating Workstation Passwords for User Accounts

Accounts created in a workgroup are created without passwords by default. This means that, by default, users can log on simply by clicking their account name on the Welcome screen, or clicking OK on the classic Log On To Windows screen. To improve security, all local accounts should have passwords.

For the easiest management of accounts in a workgroup environment, you should log on to each account that should have a password and then assign a password to the account using the User Accounts Wizard. If you are logged on as the user when you create the password, you don't have to worry about losing encrypted data. If you don't log on as the user and create the password, the user will lose access to his or her encrypted files, encrypted e-mail, and stored passwords. This occurs because the user's master key, which is needed to access his or her personal encryption certificate and unlock this data, is encrypted with a hash that is based on an empty password. So when you create a password, the hash doesn't match, and there's no way to unlock the encrypted data. The only way to resolve this is to remove the password from the account to restore the original settings. The user will then be able to access his or her encrypted files. Again, this issue is only related to local user accounts for computers and not to domain user accounts.

Tip Only the User Accounts Wizard allows you to assign a password hint that can be helpful in recovering a forgotten or lost password. Another technique for recovering a forgotten or lost password is a password reset disk. Before assigning passwords, it is important to note that these are the only techniques you should use to recover passwords for users unless you want to risk data loss. Why? Although you can create, change, or remove a password from a user account, doing so deletes any personal certificates and stored passwords associated with this account. As a result, the user will no longer be able to access his or her encrypted files or private e-mail messages that have been encrypted with his or her personal key and will lose stored passwords for Web sites and network resources. It is also important to note that this issue is only for local user accounts. Administrators can change or reset passwords for domain user accounts without affecting access to encrypted data.

You can create a password for an account in a workgroup by completing the following steps:

1. Log on as the user whose password you want to create. In Control Panel, double-click User Accounts or type **control userpasswords** at a command prompt.

Note If the account is a Computer Administrator, all user accounts available on the machine are shown, and you'll need to click the account you want to work with—to prevent possible data loss this should be the same as the account under which you are currently logged on. Any account that has a current password is listed as Password Protected. Any account without this label doesn't have a password.

2. In the User Accounts Wizard, click Create A Password.
3. As shown in Figure 7-2, type a password and then confirm it. Afterward, type a unique password hint. The password hint is a word or phrase that can be used to obtain the password if it is lost. This hint is visible to anyone who uses the computer.
4. Click Create Password. If you are using simple file sharing as opposed to standard file sharing, you'll have the option to make your personal files and folders private, which prevents users with limited accounts from accessing them. Click Yes, Make Private, or No as appropriate.

 Tip If you have set up the User Accounts Wizard to use the Welcome page, then from now on, when you click the user account on the Welcome page, you'll see a Type Your Password prompt. Type the password, and then press Enter or click the right arrow button. Notice also the question mark button after the prompt. Clicking this button displays the password hint. The classic logon screen does not provide the question mark button or a password hint.

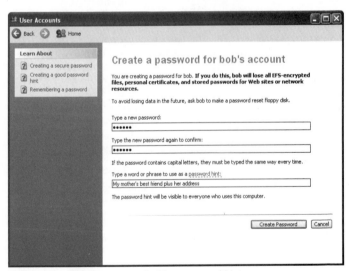

Figure 7-2 Create a password with a password hint.

Changing or Removing User Passwords

For the easiest management of accounts in a workgroup environment, you should log on to each account for which you want to change or remove a password in turn and then modify the account password as necessary using the User Accounts Wizard. If you are logged on as the user when you change or remove the password, you don't have to worry about losing encrypted data. If you don't log on as the user to change or remove the password, the user will lose access to his or her encrypted files, encrypted e-mail, and stored passwords. This occurs because the user's master key, which is needed to access his or her personal encryption certificate and unlock this data, is encrypted with a hash of his or her password. So when you change the password, the hash doesn't match and there's no way to unlock the encrypted data. The only way to resolve this is to change the password back to the old password or to use the original password reset disk to change the password. Again, this issue is only related to local user accounts for computers and not domain user accounts.

You can change or remove a password from a user account by completing the following steps:

1. If possible, log on as the user whose password you want to change or remove. In Control Panel, double-click User Accounts or type **control userpasswords** at a command prompt.

    Note If the account is a Computer Administrator, all user accounts available on the machine are shown, and you'll need to click the account you want to work with—to prevent possible data loss this should be the same as the account under which you are currently logged on. Any account that has a current password is listed as Password Protected. Any account without this label doesn't have a password.

2. In the User Accounts Wizard, click Change The Password or Remove The Password as appropriate.

3. If you elected to change the password, type the password and then confirm it. Afterward, type a unique password hint. Click Change Password.

4. If you elected to remove the password, confirm the action by clicking Remove Password.

Recovering User Passwords

As discussed previously, it is preferable to try to recover a user password than to change or remove the password. By recovering the password rather than changing or removing it, you can preserve access to any encrypted data and stored passwords that the user might have.

Windows XP provides two ways to recover user passwords.

- **Password Hint**   The hint can be accessed on the Welcome screen. Ordinarily, the Welcome screen is displayed when the computer is started and no one is logged on. If someone is logged on to the workstation, have him log off. Click the user's name to display the Type Your Password prompt, and then click the blue question mark button to display the password hint. Hopefully, the password hint will help the user remember the password. If it doesn't, you'll need to use the password reset disk.

- **Password Reset Disk**   Password reset disks can be created for any user account with a password. They allow anyone to change the password of the related account without needing to know the old password. Because anyone with access to these disks can change account passwords, you should store password reset disks in a secure location. If users are allowed to create their own password reset disks, be sure they know how important the disks are as well.

In a workgroup, you can create a password reset disk for a local user account by completing the following steps:

1. Log on to the computer using the user account for which you want to create the password reset disk.
2. In Control Panel, double-click User Accounts.
3. In the User Accounts Wizard, click the account you are logged in as.
4. In the upper-left corner of the wizard page you'll see a box labeled Related Tasks. Click Prevent A Forgotten Password. This starts the Forgotten Password Wizard as shown in Figure 7-3.
5. Click Next. When prompted, insert a blank, formatted disk in drive A and then click Next.
6. Type the current user account password, and then click Next. The wizard will then create the password reset disk. Click Next again, and then click Finish.

Figure 7-3   Use the Forgotten Password Wizard to create a password reset disk.

To use a password reset disk to recover a forgotten or lost password, follow these steps:

1. On the Welcome screen or the classic logon prompt, whichever is applicable, try to log on by typing a password and pressing Enter or clicking the right arrow.

2. When you fail to log on, a prompt is displayed with a Use Your Password Reset Disk link. If you aren't using a Welcome screen, you see a Reset button. Click either the link or the button to start the Password Reset Wizard.

3. Click Next. When prompted, insert the password reset disk in drive A and then click Next. Click Finish.

4. On the Reset The User Account Password page, type a password and then confirm it. Afterward, type a unique password hint that will help you remember the password. Click Next.

5. Back on the Welcome screen or the classic logon prompt, whichever is applicable, log on.

Real World   Password reset disks can be created for local user accounts for computers in domains as well. To create the disk, press Ctrl+Alt+Del to display the Windows Security dialog box. Click Change Password, and then click Backup to start the Forgotten Password Wizard. Then at the logon screen, if you fail to log on, you'll be able to click Reset and then insert the password reset disk. Afterward, follow the prompts to change the password. You will then be able to log on with the new password. Keep in mind you do not need to create a new password reset disk. The current disk has the necessary data for recovering the password in the future.

Controlling Logon: Welcome Screens and Classic Logons

By default, Windows XP displays a Welcome screen and allows fast user switching—except in domains. The Welcome screen is displayed when no one is logged on or when the screen saver is activated and you attempt to log back in. The Welcome screen is handy because it displays a list of available accounts and allows you to log on by clicking on an account name. To enhance security, you can use the classic logon prompt instead of the Welcome screen—as is the case for Windows XP computers in domains. Using the classic logon prompt requires users to type a logon name rather than selecting from a list of available accounts.

With the Welcome screen, you will see a list of accounts on the computer. To log on with one of those accounts, you click the account and type a password if required. Contrary to what most people think, the Welcome screen doesn't display all the accounts that are created on the computer. Some accounts, such as Administrator, are hidden from view automatically. Others are hidden using the special accounts user list. You can control which accounts are hidden and which are displayed using the special accounts user list at HKLM\SOFTWARE\Microsoft\Windows NT\CurrentVersion\Winlogon\SpecialAccounts\UserList key in the registry. As Figure 7-4 shows, you can access this key in Registry Editor, and the list of accounts hidden from view using the special accounts user list is quite long. You can add a user account to the list and thus prevent it from being displayed on the Welcome screen by creating a new DWORD value with the name set to the user name of the account you want to hide and the value set to 0.

 Tip Accounts on the special accounts user list aren't displayed on the Welcome screen and therefore aren't available for fast user switching either. However, you can log on to these hidden accounts from the Welcome screen, providing no other user is logged on. To do this, press Ctrl+Alt+Del two times to display the Log On To Windows dialog box. Type the account name in the User Name field, type the password as required, and then click OK.

With classic logon, you use the Log On To Windows dialog box for logon. This dialog box has several features you can control.

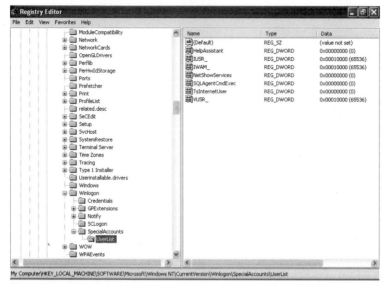

Figure 7-4   The special accounts user list is used to prevent accounts from being displayed on the Welcome screen.

By default, the name of the last user to log on is displayed in the User Name field of the Log On To Windows dialog box. Hiding the user name of the last user to log on can improve security by requiring users to know a valid account name for the computer. To do this, start the Local Security Policy tool in the Administrative Tools menu or type **secpol.msc** at the command prompt. Then under Local Policies\Security Options, double-click Interactive Logon: Do Not Display Last User Name. Click Enabled, and then click OK.

By default, you cannot bypass the requirement to press Ctrl+Alt+Del to access the Log On To Windows dialog box. If you want to allow for faster logon you can eliminate this requirement. In the Local Security Policy tool, expand Local Policies\Security Options and then double-click Interactive Logon: Do Not Require Ctrl+Alt+Del. Click Enabled, and then click OK.

You can configure whether the Welcome screen is used by completing the following steps:

1. If multiple users are currently logged on, you should have the other users log off before you change the Welcome screen settings.

2. Double-click User Accounts in Control Panel. Under Pick A Task, click Change The Way Users Log On Or Off. This displays the Select Logon And Logoff Options page as shown in Figure 7-5.

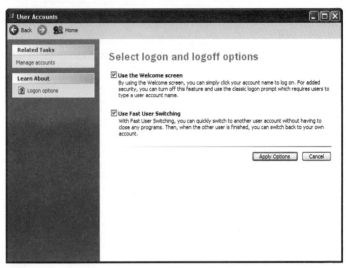

Figure 7-5   You can control logon options using the User Accounts Wizard.

3. If you want to use the classic logon prompt, clear Use The Welcome Screen, which also disables fast user switching. Otherwise, select Use The Welcome Screen to enable the Welcome screen.

4. Click Apply Options.

Real World   If you can't change the Welcome screen options, you might be restricted from doing so in the registry or in Group Policy. In the registry, the LogonType value for the HKLM\SOFTWARE\Microsoft\WindowsNT\CurrentVersion\WinLogon key controls the Welcome screen. You can set the value to 0 to use the classic logon or set the value to 1 to use the Welcome screen. In Group Policy, the Always Use Classic Logon policy under Computer Configuration\Administrative Templates\System\Logon controls the Welcome screen and overrides any setting you make in the User Accounts Wizard and in the registry. Enable the policy to use classic logon. Disable the policy to use the Welcome screen. Or use Not Configured to use the setting in the User Accounts Wizard or registry.

Configuring Fast User Switching

With the Welcome screen enabled, Fast User Switching is available as an option in a workgroup. Fast user switching allows multiple users to be logged on to the computer at the same time and to quickly change between the logged on users. To switch to another user, press the Windows logo key+L to display the Welcome screen. The next user can then log on by clicking his or her name and typing a password if required. Another way to use this feature is to click Start, Log Off and then in the Log Off Windows dialog box, click Switch User.

Note   For fast user switching to work, Use The Welcome Screen and Use Fast User Switching must be enabled in the User Accounts Wizard, the computer must not be a member of a domain, and offline files must be disabled. Additionally, it is important to note that multiple user logons use more system resources than a single user logon. With this in mind, a system might need extra memory and a faster processor to accommodate fast user switching, particularly if the logged on users run multiple applications.

To configure fast user switching, follow these steps:

1. Double-click User Accounts in Control Panel. Under Pick A Task, click Change The Way Users Log On Or Off. This displays the Select Logon And Logoff Options page shown previously in Figure 7-5.

    Tip   If a warning prompt is displayed stating fast user switching cannot be used because Offline Files is enabled, click OK to open the Offline File Settings dialog box. Clear Enable Offline Files, and then click OK. You will then need to click Change The Way Users Log On Or Off in the User Accounts Wizard again.

2. If you want to use fast user switching, you must select Use The Welcome Screen and then select Use Fast User Switching.
3. Click Apply Options.

Logging On as Administrator

In a workgroup, the Administrator account is listed on the Welcome screen only in certain situations, such as when no other computer administrator account is available, when you start the computer in Safe Mode, or when you're already logged on as the Administrator. Otherwise, the Administrator account is hidden from view. As discussed previously, you can log on to hidden accounts including Administrator. Press Ctrl+Alt+Del two times to display the Log On To Windows dialog box. Type the account name in the User Name field, type a password as required, and then click OK.

Managing User Access to Workstations in Domains

In this section, you'll learn how to manage access to local workstations running Windows XP in a domain environment. The focus is on using the User Accounts utility in Control Panel to manage access permissions, stored passwords, passports, and secure logon settings.

Understanding User Access Levels in Domains

All administrators in the domain have access to resources on local workstations unless they are specifically denied access to a resource. Users, on the other hand, aren't granted access to local workstations other than the one they normally log on to. If a user needs access to a local workstation, you can grant access using the User

Accounts utility on the workstation. You can also use this utility to restrict or deny access to a user.

Local access to workstations can be controlled through Windows XP, which provides the following three default levels of user access:

- **Standard**   Standard users are configured as members of the Power Users group. This allows them to perform most tasks, including installing applications and changing system settings. However, standard users can't create or manage local users and groups.

- **Restricted**   Restricted users are members of the Users group. This allows them to log on to the computer, but it doesn't allow them to perform advanced tasks, such as installing applications or changing system settings.

- **Other**   The Other level allows you to specify the group membership for the account. A user can be made a member of any built-in or predefined group that exists on the local system. For example, if you make a user a member of the local Administrators group, the user has full privileges on the local system. The user does not, however, have administrator privileges in the domain.

 Note   When you are choosing between Standard User and Restricted User access levels, keep in mind that the most secure level is restricted. The restricted level allows users to log on and run programs. It doesn't allow them to perform most other tasks. Remember, most workstation users will want to have Power User privileges on their personal systems, which will allow them to install and uninstall applications and to manage system settings, such as system time and the Display utility. Thus, if you are configuring access levels for the primary system owner, you'll probably want to use the standard level.

Granting Access to Workstations

You grant access to workstations using the User Account utility. The user account to which you grant access can be a domain account or an existing local account on another machine. If the user account doesn't exist, however, you can't grant access to the workstation in this manner.

To grant access to a workstation, follow these steps:

1. In Control Panel, double-click User Accounts. This displays the User Accounts dialog box shown in Figure 7-6.

Figure 7-6   Use the User Accounts utility to manage user access to a workstation.

2. Click Add. This displays the Add New User dialog box.

3. In the User Name and Domain fields, type the name and domain of the account to which you want to grant access. If you don't know the name and domain information, click Browse to find the account you want to use. Click Next when you are ready to continue.

4. Set the level of access: Standard User, Restricted User, or Other. If you select Other, you must also select a local group to which the user should be added as a member. Select an appropriate group that grants the necessary level of permissions. To give the user full permissions on the local computer, select Administrators.

5. Click Finish. If you need to set other permissions or add the user to other local groups, you'll need to access the account in Local Users And Groups and then make the necessary changes. Follow the steps specified in the section of this chapter entitled "Managing Local User and Group Accounts."

Changing Access Levels for Users

The User Accounts utility provides an easy way to change access levels for workstations. You can quickly set one of the three default access levels for users. For more advanced control, however, you'll need to use Local Users And Groups to assign group membership individually. (See the section of this chapter entitled "Adding and Removing Local Group Members.")

To change the access level for a user, follow these steps:

1. In Control Panel, double-click User Accounts.

2. In the Users For This Computer list box, select the account you want to configure and then click Properties.

3. In the Properties dialog box, click the Group Membership tab and then select the new access level that you want to grant to the user. The options are Standard User, Restricted User, and Other.

4. Click OK.

 Note You can also customize access by creating an account directly in Local Users And Groups. See the section of this chapter entitled "Managing Local User and Group Accounts."

Changing and Resetting Workstation Passwords for User Accounts

For the easiest management of accounts in a domain environment, you should have users change their own passwords whenever possible. Users can change their password at any time by pressing Ctrl+Alt+Del and then clicking Change Password in the Windows Security dialog box. When users change their own passwords, you don't have to worry about losing encrypted data.

Administrators can change user passwords with the User Accounts dialog box or the Local Users Or Groups node in Computer Management. However, when you do this, the user will no longer have access to his or her encrypted files, encrypted e-mail messages, and stored passwords. This occurs because the user's master key, which is needed to access the personal encryption certificate and unlock this data, is encrypted with a hash of the password. So when you change the password, the hash doesn't match and there's no way to unlock the encrypted data. The only way to resolve this is to change the password back to the old password or to use the original password reset disk to change the password.

To prevent problems with passwords, you can create a Password Reset Disk for local user accounts. If you need help creating a Password Reset Disk or recovering a user's password, see the section of this chapter entitled "Recovering User Passwords." Be sure to read the Real World sidebar discussing recovery of local user account password for computers that are members of domains.

If it's absolutely necessary, you can change or reset a user's password by completing the following steps:

1. In Control Panel, double-click User Accounts.
2. In the Users For This Computer list box, select the account for which you want to reset the password. Click Reset Password.

 Note If you are trying to change the password for the account under which you are currently logged on, the Reset Password button is grayed out (unavailable) and you are instead instructed to press Ctrl+Alt+Del and then click Change Password. This requirement is designed to prevent an administrator from accidentally changing his or her own local account password and losing access to encrypted data.

3. In the Reset Password dialog box, type a new password for the local account and then confirm it by retyping the password again. Click OK.

You can also change or reset passwords for local user accounts by completing these steps:

1. Access Local Users And Groups and then select the Users folder. Right-click the account name, and then select Reset Password or Set Password, as appropriate.

2. Type a new password for the user and confirm it. The password should conform to the password policy set for the computer.

3. Double-click the account name, and then clear Account Is Disabled, Account Is Locked Out, or both as necessary.

Requiring Secure Logon to Workstations

By default, you must press Ctrl+Alt+Del to access the Windows XP logon screen. This feature is designed to enhance system security and prevent malicious coders from creating look-alike logon screens that could be used to capture your logon information. In most organizations, this feature, named Secure Logon, should be enabled. If a user isn't required to press Ctrl+Alt+Del before logging on, you might want to ensure that this feature is turned on.

To verify that secure logons are enabled or to modify this feature, follow these steps:

1. In Control Panel, double-click User Accounts. Then click the Advanced tab in the User Accounts dialog box.

2. The Secure Logon feature is enabled when the Require Users To Press Ctrl+Alt+Del check box is selected. To disable this feature, clear this check box.

Denying Access to Workstations

Domain administrators are automatically granted access to local resources on workstations. Other users have access to the workstation only if it is specifically granted. As workstations are moved around the enterprise, you might find that previous owners of a workstation still have access to its resources or that users who were granted temporary access to a workstation were never removed from the access list.

To remove a user from a workstation's access list and effectively deny access, follow these steps:

1. In Control Panel, double-click User Accounts.

2. In the Users For This Computer list box, select the account you want to deny access to, and then click Remove.

3. When prompted to confirm the action, click Yes. The user will automatically be removed from the account list. Keep in mind that if the user is a member of a group that has special privileges, such as Administrators, she could still be able to gain access to the workstation.

Managing Stored Passwords

Windows XP can store essential network and Web site passwords for the current user. These passwords are stored in an electronic key ring that provides easy logon to essential resources wherever they might be located. If you find that a user frequently has problems logging on to password-protected resources, such as the company intranet or an external Internet site, you can create a key ring for that user. To do this, you create a logon session for each resource that includes the resource location, logon account name, and password.

 Real World   The techniques discussed for working with stored passwords are for Windows XP co mputers in domains. The procedures are identical for Windows XP computers in workgroups except for how you get to the Stored User Names And Passwords dialog box. The fastest way to do this in either a domain or a workgroup is to type **control userpasswords2** at the command prompt to start the User Accounts dialog box, and then on the Advanced tab to click Manage Passwords.

The following sections examine techniques for adding, editing, and removing key ring entries.

Adding Key Ring Entries

Each user account has a unique key ring. Entries in the key ring are stored in the user's profile settings and contain information needed to log on to password-protected resources. If you are logged on to a domain account when you create a key ring entry and the account has a roaming profile (instead of a local or mandatory profile), the information stored in the key ring entry is available when you log on to any computer in the domain. Otherwise, the information in the key ring entry is only available on the specific computer on which you create the entry.

To add an entry to the current logged-on user's key ring, follow these steps:

1. In Control Panel, double-click User Accounts. This displays the User Accounts dialog box.

2. On the Advanced tab, click Manage Passwords. The Stored User Names And Passwords dialog box appears, and you'll see a list of current entries if there are any.

3. Click Add and then use the Logon Information Properties dialog box to configure the resource location, logon account name, and password. (See Figure 7-7.) The fields available are as follows:

   ❏ **Server**   The network or Internet resource for which you are configuring the key ring entry. This can be an actual server name, such as technology.microsoft.com, or it can be an address containing a wildcard, such as *.microsoft.com. When you use a fully qualified domain name, the entry is used for accessing a specific server or service. When you use a wildcard, the entry is used for any server in the domain. For example, the entry *.microsoft.com could be used to access www.microsoft.com, ftp.microsoft.com, smtp.microsoft.com, and extranet.microsoft.com.

❑ **User Name**   The user name required by the server, including any necessary domain qualifiers. For a Windows domain, type the full domain account name such as Technology\WRSTANEK. For an Internet service, type the full service account name, such as WRSTANEK@msn.com.

❑ **Password**   The password required by the server. One of the things most users forget is that whenever they change their password on the server or service, they must also change their password on their key ring. If a user forgets to change the password on the key ring, repeated attempts to log on or connect to the server or service might result in the account being locked.

Figure 7-7   Create the key ring entry by setting the necessary logon information.

Note   Remind users that Windows XP provides an easier way to maintain service and key ring passwords. To update the key ring and the service password at the same time, use the Change feature of the Logon Information Properties dialog box. See the next section of this chapter for details.

4. Click OK.

Editing Key Ring Entries

You can edit key ring entries at any time, but keep in mind that local key ring entries are visible only on the computer on which they were created. This means that if you want to modify an entry, you must log on to the local workstation where it was created. The only exception is for users with roaming profiles. When a user has a roaming profile, key ring entries can be edited from any computer where the user is logged on.

Use the following steps to edit a user's key ring:

1. In Control Panel, double-click User Accounts. This displays the User Accounts dialog box.

2. On the Advanced tab, click Manage Passwords. The Stored User Names And Passwords dialog box appears.

3. In the Stored User Names And Passwords dialog box, you'll see a list of current entries. Select the entry you want to modify, and then click Properties.

4. Change the resource location and logon account name as necessary. If you need to change the password associated with the entry, retype it in the Password field.

Tip   If you want to change your password for a service and update the logon information to use the new password, click Change. Type your current password in the Old Password field. Then specify and confirm your new password using the fields provided. Complete the process by clicking OK. If there are multiple entries for this same account in the current domain, the other entries are automatically updated as well. This means you don't have to change the password associated with these entries.

Removing Key Ring Entries

When a user no longer needs a key ring entry, you should remove it. To remove a user's key ring entry, follow these steps:

1. In Control Panel, double-click User Accounts. This displays the User Accounts dialog box.

2. On the Advanced tab, click Manage Passwords. The Stored User Names And Passwords dialog box appears.

3. In the Stored User Names And Passwords dialog box, you'll see a list of current entries. Select the entry you want to delete, and then click Remove. When prompted to confirm the action, click OK.

As stated previously, local key ring entries can be removed only on the computer on which they were created. When a user has a roaming profile, key ring entries, on the other hand, can be deleted from any computer where the user is logged on.

Using the .NET Passport Wizard to Create a Microsoft .NET Passport

Typically, users will communicate with other users with an instant messenger client such as MSN Messenger Service. If this is part of your organization's culture, you might want to walk users through the process of creating a Microsoft .NET Passport, which can give them personalized access to MSN, MSN Messenger Service, related Web sites, and other .NET Passport–enabled services. The primary advantage of a .NET Passport is that a user will have only one account for all compliant sites and services. Users can also store essential information in their .NET Passports so that they don't have to retype it each time they fill out forms at Passport-enabled sites or services.

Creating a .NET Passport is a process that you'll usually want users to perform themselves because their .NET Passports might contain sensitive information that others shouldn't see. To help the currently logged on user create a .NET Passport, direct him or her to the .NET Passport Wizard, which is accessed by completing these steps:

1. Click Start, and then select Run.

2. In the Run dialog box, type **control userpasswords2**. This opens the User Accounts dialog box.

3. On the Advanced tab, click .NET Passport Wizard. This starts the .NET Passport Wizard.

Tip The previously described technique works for both computers in a domain and in a workgroup. The alternative is to double-click User Accounts in Control Panel. However, the dialog box they will see depends on whether the computer is a member of a domain or a workgroup. In a domain, they'll see the User Accounts dialog box and be able to select the Advanced tab. In a workgroup, they'll see the User Accounts Wizard. They'll then have to click their account under Pick An Account To Change. Afterward, under What Do You Want To Change About Your Account, they'll have to click Set Up My Account To Use A .NET Passport.

When a user creates a .NET Passport, it is associated with the domain account and becomes that user's default .NET Passport for use on any computer attached to the domain. If the user needs to change the default .NET Passport, this can be done by restarting the .NET Passport Wizard and specifying new account information. Do not use this process, however, if the user wants to associate the same e-mail address with an existing .NET Passport. The user will need to log on to MSN and manage the .NET Passport properties already in place.

Managing Local User and Group Accounts

Local user and group accounts are managed much like domain accounts. You can create accounts, manage their properties, reset accounts when they are locked or disabled, and so on. These and other tasks are examined in this section.

Creating Local User Accounts

You create local user accounts with Local Users And Groups. You can access this utility and create an account by completing the following steps:

1. Click Start, point to Programs or All Programs as appropriate, then Administrative Tools, and finally select Computer Management. Alternatively, access Control Panel, double-click Administrative Tools, and finally select Computer Management.

2. Right-click the Computer Management entry in the console tree and select Connect To Another Computer on the shortcut menu. You can now select the Windows XP workstation whose local accounts you want to manage; domain controllers do not have local users or groups.

3. Expand the System Tools node by clicking the plus sign (+) next to it, and then select Local Users And Groups.

4. Right-click Users and then select New User. This opens the New User dialog box shown in Figure 7-8. The fields in the dialog box are used as follows:

   ❑ **User Name**   The logon name for the user account. This name should follow the conventions for the local user name policy.

   ❑ **Full Name**   The full name of the user, such as William R. Stanek.

   ❑ **Description**   A description of the user. Normally you'd type the user's job title, such as Webmaster. You could also type the user's job title and department.

   ❑ **Password**   The password for the account. This password should follow the conventions of your password policy.

   ❑ **Confirm Password**   A field to ensure that you assign the account password correctly. Simply retype the password to confirm it.

   ❑ **User Must Change Password At Next Logon**   If this check box is selected, the user must change the password upon logon.

   ❑ **User Cannot Change Password**   If this check box is selected, the user can't change the password.

   ❑ **Password Never Expires**   If this check box is selected, the password for this account never expires. This setting overrides the local account policy.

   ❑ **Account Is Disabled**   If this check box is selected, the account is disabled and can't be used. Use this field to temporarily prevent anyone from using an account.

5. Click Create when you're finished configuring the new account.

Figure 7-8   Configure new workstation accounts using the New User dialog box in Local Users And Groups.

Creating Local Groups for Workstations

You create local groups with Local Users And Groups. You can access this utility and create a group by completing the following steps:

1. Click Start, point to Programs or All Programs as appropriate, then Administrative Tools, and finally select Computer Management. Alternatively, access Control Panel, double-click Administrative Tools, and finally select Computer Management.

2. Right-click the Computer Management entry in the console tree, and select Connect To Another Computer on the shortcut menu. You can now select the system whose local accounts you want to manage. Domain controllers don't have local users and groups.

3. Expand the System Tools node by clicking the plus sign (+) next to it, and then select Local Users And Groups.

4. Right-click Groups, and then select New Group. This opens the New Group dialog box shown in Figure 7-9.

Figure 7-9   The New Group dialog box allows you to add a new local group to a Windows XP workstation.

5. After you type a name and description for the group, use the Add button to add names to the group. This opens the Select Users dialog box.

6. In the Select Users dialog box, type the name of a user you want to use in the Enter The Object Names To Select field and then click Check Names. If matches are found, select the account you want to use, and then click OK. If no matches are found, update the name you entered and try searching again. Repeat this step as necessary and click OK when finished.

7. The New Group dialog box is updated to reflect your selections. If you made a mistake, select a name and remove it by clicking Remove.

8. Click Create when you're finished adding or removing group members.

Adding and Removing Local Group Members

You add or remove local group members using Local Users And Groups. Complete the following steps:

1. Access Local Users And Groups in Computer Management, and then select the Groups folder. Double-click the group you want to work with.

2. Use the Add button to add user accounts to the group. This opens the Select Users dialog box. In the Select Users dialog box, type the name of a user you want to use in the Enter The Object Names To Select field and then click Check Names. If matches are found, select the account you want to use, and then click OK. If no matches are found, update the name you entered and try searching again. Repeat this step as necessary and click OK when finished.

3. Use the Remove button to remove user accounts from the group. Simply select the user account you want to remove from the group and then click Remove.

4. Click OK when you are finished.

Enabling Local User Accounts

Local user accounts can become disabled for several reasons. If a user forgets the password and tries to guess it, he might exceed the account policy for bad logon attempts. Another administrator could have disabled the account while a user was on vacation. When an account is disabled or locked out, you can enable it using the methods described here.

When an account is disabled, complete the following steps:

1. Access Local Users And Groups in Computer Management, and then select the Users folder.
2. Double-click the user's account name, and then clear the Account Is Disabled check box.
3. Click OK.

When an account is locked out, complete the following steps:

1. In Local Users And Groups, select the Users folder.
2. Double-click the user's account name, and then clear the Account Is Locked Out check box.
3. Click OK.

Creating a Secure Guest Account

In some environments, you might need to set up a guest account that can be used by visitors. Most of the time, you'll want to configure the guest account for use on a specific computer or computers and carefully control how the account can be used. To create a secure guest account, I recommend that you perform the following:

- **Enable the guest account for use**   By default, the guest account is disabled so you must first enable it to make it available. To do this, access Local Users And Groups in Computer Management and then select the Users folder. Double-click Guest, and then clear the Account Is Disabled check box. Click OK.

- **Set a secure password on the guest account**   By default, the guest account has a blank password. To improve security on the computer, you should set one. In Local Users And Groups, right-click Guest and then select Set Password. Click Proceed at the warning prompt. Type and then confirm the new password. Click OK.

- **Rename the guest account**   Like Administrator, the guest account is a widely known account. To improve security, you should consider renaming the account to something fewer people know or can guess. To do this, start the Local Security Policy tool in the Administrative Tools menu or type **secpol.msc** at the command prompt. Then under Local Policies\Security Options, double-click Accounts: Rename Guest Account. Type the name to use for the guest account, and then click OK.

- **Ensure that the guest account cannot be used over the network**   The guest account shouldn't be accessible from other computers. If it is, users at another computer could log on over the network as a guest. To prevent this, start the Local Security Policy tool in the Administrative Tools menu or type **secpol.msc** at the command prompt. Then under Local Policies\User Rights Assignment, ensure the Deny Access To This Computer From The Network policy lists Guest as a restricted account.

- **Prevent the guest account from shutting down the computer**   When a computer is shutting down or starting up, there is a possibility that a guest user (or anyone with local access) might be able to gain unauthorized access to the computer. To help deter this, you should ensure the guest account doesn't have the Shut Down The System user right. In Local Security Policy tool, expand Local Policies\User Rights Assignment and ensure the Shut Down The System policy doesn't list the Guest account.

- **Prevent the guest account from viewing event logs**   To help maintain the security of the system, the guest account shouldn't be allowed to view the event logs. To ensure this is the case, start the Registry Editor by typing **regedit** at the command prompt and then access the HKLM\SYSTEM\CurrentControlSet\Services\Eventlog key. Here you'll find three subkeys: Application, Security, and System. Make sure each of these subkeys has a DWORD value named RestrictGuestAccess with a value of 1.

Renaming Local User and Group Accounts

When you rename an account, you give it a new label. Because the SID for the account remains the same, the permissions and properties associated with the account don't change. To rename an account, complete the following steps:

1. In Local Users And Groups, select the Users or Groups folder as appropriate.
2. Right-click the account name, and then select Rename. Type the new account name and then click a different entry.

Deleting Local User and Group Accounts

Deleting an account permanently removes it. Once you delete an account, you can't create another account with the same name to automatically get the same permissions because the SID for the new account won't match the SID for the old account.

Because deleting built-in accounts can have far-reaching effects on the workstation, Windows XP doesn't let you delete built-in user accounts or group accounts. You *can* remove other types of accounts by selecting them and pressing the Del key or by right-clicking and selecting Delete from the shortcut menu. When prompted, click Yes.

 Note   When you delete a user account, Windows XP doesn't delete the user's profile, personal files, or home directory. If you want to delete these files and directories, you'll have to do it manually.

Managing Remote Access to Workstations

As discussed in Chapters 1 and 2, Windows XP has several remote connectivity features. With Remote Assistance, invitations can be sent to support technicians, allowing them to service a computer remotely. With Remote Desktop, users can connect remotely to a computer and access its resources. In this section, you learn how to configure Remote Assistance and Remote Desktop. By default, only the Remote Assistance feature is enabled. You must enable the Remote Desktop feature manually.

Configuring Remote Assistance

Remote Assistance is a useful feature for help desks, whether in-house or outsourced. A user can allow support personnel to both view and take control of her desktop. This feature can be used to walk users through a complex process or to manage system settings while they watch the progress of the changes. The key to Remote Assistance is in the access levels you grant.

By default, Remote Assistance is configured to allow support personnel to view and control computers. Because users can send assistance invitations to internal and external resources, this could present a security concern for organizations. To reduce potential security problems, you might want to allow support staff to view but not control computers.

Another key aspect of Remote Assistance you can control is the time limit for invitations. The default maximum time limit is 30 days. Although the intent is to give support personnel a time window in which to respond to requests, it also means that they could use an invitation to access a computer over a period of 30 days. For instance, suppose you send an invitation with a 30-day time limit to a support person who resolves the problem the first day. That person would then still have access to the computer for another 29 days, which wouldn't be desirable for security reasons. To reduce the risk to your systems, you'll usually want to reduce the default maximum time limit considerably—say, to 1 hour. If the problem were not solved in the allotted time period, you can issue another invitation.

To configure Remote Assistance, follow these steps:

1. Double-click the System utility in Control Panel, and then click the Remote tab.
2. To disable Remote Assistance, clear the Allow Remote Assistance Invitations check box, and then click OK. Skip the remaining steps.
3. To enable Remote Assistance, select Allow Remote Assistance Invitations. Afterward, click Advanced. This displays the Remote Assistance Settings dialog box shown in Figure 7-10.

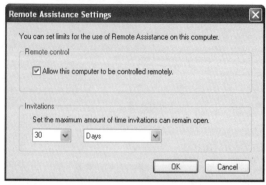

Figure 7-10   The Remote Assistance Settings dialog box is used to set limits for Remote Assistance.

4. The Allow This Computer To Be Controlled Remotely option sets limits for Remote Assistance. When selected, this setting allows assistants to view and control the computer. To provide view-only access to the computer, clear this check box.

5. The Invitations options control the maximum time window for invitations. You can set a value in minutes, hours, or days, up to a maximum of 99 days. If you set a maximum limit value of 10 days, for example, a user can create an invitation with a time limit up to but not more than 10 days. The default maximum expiration limit is 30 days.

6. Click OK twice when you are finished configuring Remote Assistance options.

Configuring Remote Desktop Access

Unlike Remote Assistance, which provides a view of the current user's desktop, Remote Desktop provides several levels of access:

- If a user is currently logged on to the desktop locally and then tries to log on remotely, the local desktop locks automatically and the user can access all of the currently running applications just as if he were sitting at the keyboard. This feature is useful for users who want to work from home or other locations outside the office, allowing them to continue to work on applications and documents that they might have been using prior to leaving the office.

- If a user is listed on the workstation's Remote Access list and is not logged on otherwise, she can initiate a new Windows session. The Windows session behaves just as if the user were sitting at the keyboard. It can even be used when other users are also logged on to the computer. In this way, multiple users can share a single workstation and use its resources.

Remote Desktop is not enabled by default. You must specifically enable it, thereby allowing remote access to the workstation. When it is enabled, any members of the Administrators group can connect to the workstation. Other users must be specifically placed on a remote access list to gain access to the workstation. To configure remote access, follow these steps:

1. Double-click the System utility in Control Panel, and then click the Remote tab.

2. To disable Remote Desktop, clear the Allow Users To Connect Remotely check box, and then click OK. Skip the remaining steps.

3. To enable Remote Desktop, select Allow Users To Connect Remotely. Afterward, click Select Remote Users.

4. To grant Remote Desktop access to a user, click Add. This opens the Select Users dialog box. In this dialog box, type the name of a user you want to use in the Enter The Object Names To Select field and then click Check Names. If matches are found, select the account you want to use, and then click OK. If no matches are found, update the name you entered and try searching again. Repeat this step as necessary and click OK when finished.

5. To revoke remote access permissions for a user account, select the account and then click Remove.

6. Click OK twice when you are finished.

Making Remote Desktop Connections

As an administrator, you can make Remote Desktop connections to Windows servers and workstations. With Microsoft Windows 2000 Server, Remote Desktop connections are enabled by installing Terminal Services and then configuring Terminal Services in remote access mode. With Microsoft Windows Server 2003 and Windows XP, Remote Desktop is installed automatically but not enabled until you specifically do so as discussed in the previous section of this chapter. Once remote access is enabled on a computer, all administrators have remote access to that computer. Other users can be granted remote access as well.

To make a Remote Desktop connection to a server or workstation, follow these steps:

1. At a command prompt, type **mstsc** or click Start, point to Programs or All Programs as appropriate, then Accessories, then Communications, and finally select Remote Desktop Connection. This displays the Remote Desktop Connection dialog box shown in Figure 7-11.

Figure 7-11   Type the name of the computer to which you want to connect, and then click Connect in the Remote Desktop Connection dialog box.

2. In the Computer field, type the name of the computer to which you want to connect. If you don't know the name of the computer, use the drop-down list provided to choose an available computer, or select Browse For More on the drop-down list to display a list of domains and computers in those domains.

3. By default, Windows XP uses your current user name, domain, and password to log on to the remote computer. If you want to use different account information, click Options and then enter values in the related User Name, Password, and Domain fields.

4. Click Connect. Type your account password if prompted, and then click OK. If the connection is successful, you'll see the Remote Desktop window on the selected computer and you'll be able to work with resources on the computer. In the case of a failed connection, check the information you provided and then try to connect again.

Note   Clicking Options in the Remote Desktop Connection dialog box displays additional options for creating and saving connections. These advanced options allow you to change display size for the Remote Desktop; manage connections to local resources, such as printers, serial ports, and disk drives; run programs automatically on connection; and enable or disable local caching and data compression.

Chapter 8

Managing Laptops and Traveling Users

In this chapter:

Configuring Power Management Settings 193

Implementing Hardware Profiles 203

Configuring Networking for Laptops. 205

Laptop administration might also extend to maintaining offline files and configuring additional network connections. You'll find a discussion on offline files in Chapter 12, "Configuring Offline Files, Disk Quotas, Shadow Copies, and More." You'll find coverage of Transmission Control Protocol/Internet Protocol (TCP/IP) networking in Chapter 13, "Configuring and Troubleshooting TCP/IP Networking."

Configuring Power Management Settings

Power management settings control the behavior of a laptop in different power use situations, such as when it is plugged in or running on a battery. When it comes to configuration options, the following five different areas can be managed:

- **Power schemes**   Power schemes are collections of power management settings that control power usage and consumption. A laptop can have multiple power schemes, but only one can be active at any given time.

- **Alarms**   Alarms determine whether the laptop sounds an alarm or displays a warning message when its battery reaches a certain level. Two levels can be set: low and critical. An alarm action associated with each alarm allows you to specify what specific actions the operating system should take when an alarm level is reached.

- **Power meters**   Power meters provide a graphical representation of the remaining power in a particular battery and also provide access to detailed information on the battery make and model.

- **Behaviors**   Behaviors control advanced options and power button actions. Most laptops have preset behaviors for when the laptop is closed, for when the power button is pressed, and for when the sleep button is pressed. You can customize this behavior to meet the needs of individual users or groups of users.

■ **Hibernation**   Hibernation settings control whether the computer goes into a hibernation state. Not all laptops support this feature.

These power management features are discussed in the following sections.

Tip   As you work through the techniques discussed in this chapter, keep in mind that some of them apply to desktop computers as well. For example, desktop computers can be configured with basic power management settings, and they can be configured to go into standby and hibernation modes.

Using Power Schemes

Using power schemes, you control when a laptop goes into power conservation modes. The following four conservation modes are available:

■ **Turn off monitor**   Determines whether the computer turns off the monitor and if so, specifies the period of inactivity that must elapse before the monitor is turned off

■ **Turn off hard disks**   Determines whether the computer turns off hard disks and if so, specifies the period of inactivity that must elapse before the hard disks are turned off

■ **System standby**   Determines whether the computer goes into standby mode and if so, specifies the period of inactivity that must elapse before standby mode is activated

■ **System hibernates**   Determines whether the computer goes into hibernation and if so, specifies the period of inactivity that must elapse before the hibernation mode is activated (The listing of this mode is controlled by the Enable Hibernation option on the Hibernate tab of the Power Options Properties dialog box.)

Turning off the monitor and hard disks separately allows a computer to progressively go into standby mode. When a computer is fully in standby mode (also known as sleep mode), the monitor and hard disks are switched off so that the laptop uses less power. When the computer is brought out of standby mode, the monitor and hard disks are turned back on, restoring the user workspace. You should configure standby mode so that when a laptop is running on batteries, it goes into power conservation mode when the user is away from the laptop for a short period of time, such as 20 or 30 minutes.

In contrast, the hibernation mode is designed for cases when users do not use their laptops for a long time, such as 45 minutes or 1 hour. When a computer goes into hibernation, a snapshot of the user workspace and the current operating environment is taken by writing the current memory to disk. When the computer is turned back on, the user workspace and operating environment are restored by reading the memory from disk. This aspect is the key difference between the standby and hibernation modes; as a result, only the hibernation mode can protect the user's work in case of power failure.

Because a computer can have multiple power schemes, they can be optimized for the way the laptop is used at a particular time. You can configure multiple power schemes for different situations. At home or in the office, laptops might need different power management configurations than they do when users are giving presentations. In one case, you might want to configure the laptop to quickly conserve energy when running on batteries. In another case, you might want to ensure that the laptop never turns off the monitor, thus halting a presentation.

Six power schemes are configured by default on most laptops. The standard schemes for laptops with Windows XP Service Pack 2 or later are listed, followed by the original/desktop scheme name in parentheses:

- **Long Life (Home/Office Desk)**   This scheme is designed for desktops or laptops in a docking station. In the default configuration, when the computer is plugged into such a station, the scheme turns off the monitor after 20 minutes but performs no other power conservation. When the computer is running on battery, the scheme uses a full array of power conservation techniques.

- **Normal (Portable Laptop)**   In this scheme, designed for portables and laptops, computers use most conservation techniques when plugged in or running on batteries. However, hibernation mode is not turned on for several hours, which is a long time whether the computer is plugged in or running on batteries.

- **High Power (Presentation)**   This scheme is designed to be used when a user gives a presentation. In this scheme, a computer never uses power conservation when plugged in and never turns off the monitor when running on batteries.

> **Tip**   The High Power scheme is extremely useful. The key to success with this scheme is educating users and showing them how to switch to this scheme prior to giving a presentation and making sure they know to switch back to their standard scheme afterward.

- **Full Power (Always On)**   This scheme is designed so that a computer never goes into standby or hibernation mode, whether plugged in or running on batteries. When running on batteries, however, the computer will turn off the monitor and hard disks after a certain duration, effectively entering standby mode.

- **Minimal Power Management**   This scheme is designed for laptops running on batteries. The goal is to turn off only the monitor to conserve power when the laptop is plugged in but to allow the computer to go into standby/hibernate when it is running on batteries. By default, the scheme is configured to turn off the monitor and go into standby mode after 5 minutes, which is a pretty short length of time.

- **Max Battery** This scheme is designed to provide maximum conservation when the computer is running on battery. When plugged in, the computer will enter standby and hibernation mode after 20 minutes and 45 minutes, respectively. When running on batteries, however, the computer quickly turns off the monitor and hard disks and enters standby mode within 2 minutes.

Creating or Optimizing Power Schemes

Although laptops can have multiple power schemes, only one of them can be active at any given time. To create or optimize a power scheme, follow these steps:

1. In Control Panel, double-click Power Options. This displays the Power Options Properties dialog box shown in Figure 8-1.

Figure 8-1 Use the Power Options Properties dialog box to work with power schemes.

2. Use the Power Schemes selection list to select the scheme you want to work with or on which to base your new scheme.

3. Under When Computer Is Plugged In, specify whether or when the computer goes into the available power conservation modes when plugged into AC power. If you select Never, the option will not be used.

4. Under When Computer Is Running On Batteries, specify whether or when the computer goes into the conservation mode when running on batteries. Typically, you'll want a computer to enter conservation mode sooner when running on batteries. For example, if you set the monitor to turn off after 15 minutes when plugged in, you might want the computer to turn off the monitor after 10 minutes when running on batteries.

5. Once you've made the necessary changes to the scheme, click Save As. Next, enter a name for the scheme, and then click OK. If you use the same name as an existing power scheme, the current settings replace the settings on that power scheme. If you enter a new name, the power scheme appears as an option in the selection list from then on.

Caution   Microsoft Windows XP doesn't warn you when it's about to overwrite an existing power scheme. If you make changes to a power scheme and save it using the current scheme name, the changes are applied immediately, and there is no way to undo them.

Deleting Power Schemes

You can delete a user's power scheme by following these steps:

1. In Control Panel, double-click Power Options. This displays the Power Options Properties dialog box.

2. Use the Power Schemes drop-down list to select the power scheme that you want to delete, and then click Delete.

3. When prompted to confirm the action, click Yes. Remember, the deleted power scheme affects only the current user and might still be available to other users of this computer.

Using Alarms and Configuring Alarm Actions

Alarms determine whether the laptop sounds an alarm or displays a warning message when its battery reaches a certain level. You can configure two levels of alarms for laptops: Low Battery Alarm and Critical Battery Alarm. The Low Battery Alarm is meant to alert the user when the battery power level is nearly depleted. Typically, the low-power state is activated when the battery has 10 percent or less power remaining. The Critical Battery Alarm is meant to alert the user when the batteries are about to fail. Typically, the critical-power state is activated when the battery has 5 percent or less power remaining. On a battery with a 3-hour life, 5 percentage points is about 9 minutes of usage.

An alarm action associated with each alarm allows you to dictate what specific actions the operating system should take when an alarm level is reached. The computer can also be configured to run a program when an alarm occurs. This is useful if you need to run a cleanup script or another program that helps maintain the system and the user's data. Because there are different considerations for configuring the alert levels, I'll examine each separately.

Configuring Low Battery Alarms

As stated previously, the low battery alarm is intended to give the user a warning that the system is getting low on power. Typically, when entering the low-power state, the system notifies the user with either a text prompt alone or a text prompt and an audible alarm. In some cases, you might want to configure the computer to go a step further by entering standby mode instead of giving a warning. In this instance, the computer immediately goes into power conservation mode by turning off the monitor and hard disks.

To configure the low battery alarm, follow these steps:

1. In Control Panel, double-click Power Options, and then click the Alarms tab shown in Figure 8-2.

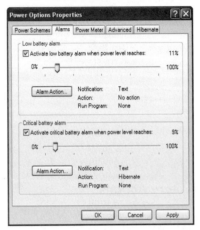

Figure 8-2   Use the Alarms tab to set the low and critical battery alarms.

2. To enable the low battery alarm, select Activate Low Battery Alarm When Power Level Reaches, and then use the power level slider to select the appropriate alarm level. Next, click Alarm Action to set the action as specified in the section of this chapter entitled "Configuring Alarm Actions."

 Tip   The default low battery alarm level is based on the total battery life and typically is 10 to 11 percent. On most systems this is an appropriate value. I've found that on some systems, especially those with poor batteries, this isn't enough, and then I increase the level to between 12 and 15 percent. In contrast, on energy-efficient systems or those with two batteries, the default value is often too much. Here, I adjust the level so that the user is notified when there is about 20 minutes of battery power remaining.

3. To disable the low battery alarm, clear the Activate Low Battery Alarm When Power Level Reaches check box.
4. Click OK.

Configuring Critical Battery Alarms

Critical battery alarms are designed to ensure that systems enter an appropriate mode prior to running out of power. Typically, when entering a critical-power state, the system notifies the user and then enters standby mode. In standby mode, the monitor and hard disks are shut off to conserve power. I often configure the low-power alarm so that it enters standby mode. I then configure the critical-power alarm to enter hibernation mode or shut down the computer. This takes power management to the next level and helps ensure the system state is preserved before power is completely exhausted.

To configure the critical battery alarm, follow these steps:

1. In Control Panel, double-click Power Options, and then click the Alarms tab.

2. To enable critical battery alarms, select Activate Critical Battery Alarm When Power Level Reaches, and then use the power level slider to select the appropriate alarm level. Next, click Alarm Action to set the alarm action as specified in the following section of this chapter, entitled "Configuring Alarm Actions."

Tip   The default critical alarm level is based on the total battery life and is usually between 6 and 8 percent. In most cases, this value is appropriate. However, if you plan to have the computer go into hibernation or shut down, you might want to reduce this value. You also want to take into account the battery life. If a computer has a long battery life, the default typically is too high, but if a computer has a short battery life, it might not be high enough. I usually set the critical power alarm so that the alarm action is triggered when there is 6 to 8 minutes of power remaining.

3. To disable the critical battery alarm, clear the Activate Critical Battery Alarm When Power Level Reaches check box.

4. Click OK.

Configuring Alarm Actions

The low and critical battery alarms can have alarm actions associated with them. You set the alarm action by following these steps:

1. In Control Panel, double-click Power Options, and then click the Alarms tab.

2. Each alarm has a separate control panel. Click Alarm Action for the alarm you want to configure. This displays a dialog box similar to the one shown in Figure 8-3.

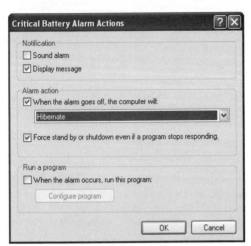

Figure 8-3   Use the Critical Battery Alarm Actions dialog box to set actions that the operating system should take when a critical battery alarm is triggered.

3. Under Notification, you have two options for notifying users of the alarm state: You can sound an alarm, and you can display a warning prompt. Select Sound Alarm, Display Message, or both, as appropriate.

4. Under Alarm Action, you'll find the options for enabling power conservation modes. If you want the computer to go into a power conservation state or shut down, select When The Alarm Goes Off, The Computer Will and then use the selection list to select an action: Stand By, Hibernate, or Shut Down.

5. If you set a power level action, you can also force the computer to enter the power conservation or shutdown mode when programs do not respond by selecting Force Stand By Or Shutdown Even If A Program Stops Responding. Keep in mind that this might cause the user to lose data because the application state might not be able to be preserved or current documents might not be saved.

6. Under Run A Program, you'll find options for running a program when an alarm occurs. To enable this feature, select the related check box, and then click Configure Program. You can then configure a scheduled task to run when the alarm is triggered. As with all scheduled tasks, you can run a script, a batch file, or an application.

7. Click OK twice when you are finished.

Working with the Power Meter

The power meter provides a graphical representation of the remaining battery power on the Windows taskbar and on the Power Meter tab of the Power Options Properties dialog box. Usually the power meter appears on the taskbar only when the computer is running on batteries. While running on batteries, the taskbar icon is a battery; if you move the pointer over the icon, you'll see the time and battery power remaining. Conversely, while running on AC power, the taskbar icon is an AC electrical plug, and passing the pointer over that icon will display On AC Power.

You can control the power meter in several different ways. When the icon is displayed on the taskbar, you can double-click it to display a dialog box similar to the one shown in Figure 8-4. The dialog box gives you several options for controlling the icon display and its detail.

- If you want the icon to always be displayed on the taskbar, select Always Show Icon On The Taskbar. Otherwise, the icon is only displayed when the computer is running on batteries.

- If the computer has multiple batteries and you want to see details for each battery separately, select Show Details For Each Battery. Otherwise, the statistics for both batteries are combined to provide the values for total battery power remaining and time remaining.

- To view additional details for a battery, click the battery icon in the Power Meter dialog box. Each battery has an icon that, when clicked, displays a dialog box containing the battery name, type (chemistry), power state, and a unique ID which typically identifies the manufacturer. The normal states for batteries are Discharging; On Line; or On Line, Charging.

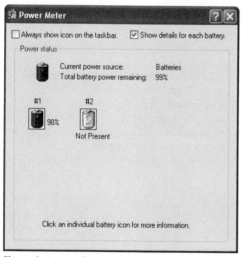

Figure 8-4   Use the Power Meter dialog box to configure display and details for the power meter icon.

Note   Another way to view the same information is to go through the Power Options utility. Start the utility, and then click the Power Meter tab. The only difference is that you do not have the option to always display a taskbar icon. To display the power meter icon on the taskbar, click the Advanced tab, and then select Always Show Icon On The Taskbar.

Configuring Advanced Behaviors and Power Buttons

Most laptops have preset behaviors for when the laptop is closed, for when the power button is pressed, and for when the sleep button is pressed. You can customize these by completing the following steps:

1. In Control Panel, double-click Power Options. This displays the Power Options Properties dialog box.

2. On the Advanced tab, you'll find options for controlling the behavior of a portable computer's power buttons as well as an option to prompt for a password when a computer resumes from standby (or hibernation). It is a good idea to prompt for a password to help ensure the security of the system.

3. Most laptops enter standby mode by default when you close them. Some users might prefer a different result. To change the result, use the selection list labeled When I Close The Lid Of My Portable Computer. The options are Do Nothing, Stand By, and Hibernate. To disable this feature entirely, select the Do Nothing option.

4. The default action for the power button is to shut down the computer. To change the action, use the selection list labeled When I Press The Power Button On My Computer. The options are Do Nothing, Ask Me What To Do, Stand By, Hibernate, and Shut Down.

 Tip   The Ask Me What To Do option is useful for users who accidentally power off their systems. In this case, instead of shutting down and losing valuable work, a laptop set up for connecting to a domain—or a laptop set up for connecting to a workgroup that uses the classic logon screen—will display the Shut Down Windows prompt that allows users to make the laptop log off, shut down, restart, enter standby, or hibernate. Users of a laptop set up for a workgroup connection that uses the Welcome screen will see the Turn Off Computer prompt, which allows the user to choose among log off, shut down, and restart. In all cases, the user can also click Cancel to abort the action.

5. By default, the sleep button causes the computer to enter standby mode. To change this action, use the selection list labeled When I Press The Sleep Button On My Computer. The options are Do Nothing, Ask Me What To Do, Stand By, Hibernate, and Shut Down.

6. Click OK when you are finished making changes.

Enabling or Disabling Hibernation

When a computer goes into hibernation, a snapshot is taken of the user workspace and the current operating environment. This snapshot is then written from memory to disk. When the computer is turned back on, the user workspace and operating environment are restored by reading the memory from disk. To enable or disable hibernation, access the Power Options Properties dialog box, and then click the Hibernate tab. Next, select Enable Hibernation to turn this feature on, or clear the check box to turn this feature off.

Note The disk space used by this feature is equal to the total system RAM. If a system, for example, has 512 MB of RAM, the disk space required to hibernate is 512 MB. Remember, not all laptops support hibernation. Laptop manufacturers must design the machines to take advantage of this feature.

Implementing Hardware Profiles

Windows XP workstations can use multiple hardware profiles, which are most useful for mobile computers, such as laptops. (In this book, "Windows XP" refers to Windows XP Professional unless otherwise indicated.) Using hardware profiles, you can configure one profile for when the computer is connected to the network (*docked*) and one for when the computer is mobile (*undocked*). You can then enable and disable devices as appropriate for these profiles. Once this is done, the user doesn't have to wait while the operating system updates the configuration for various states and doesn't have to respond to hardware device detection prompts that might be displayed otherwise.

Keep the following points about hardware profiles in mind:

- Any hardware profiles configured on a system are available to all users of that system. This means that you can create a hardware profile that will be available to any user who logs on to a computer.

- Hardware profiles can only be configured by an administrator or members of the Administrators group. Because of this, you might need to log on as an administrator to create a hardware profile for a user.

The following sections provide tips and techniques for working with hardware profiles.

Configuring the Way Hardware Profiles Are Used

To configure hardware profiles, access the System utility's Hardware tab, and then click Hardware Profiles. This opens the Hardware Profiles dialog box shown in Figure 8-5. You can configure the way hardware profiles are used, as follows:

- Set a default profile by changing the profile's position in the Available Hardware Profiles list. The top profile is the default profile.

- Have the system wait indefinitely for user input at startup by selecting Wait Until I Select A Hardware Profile.

- Determine how long the system displays the startup hardware profile menu by setting a value using the field Select The First Profile Listed If I Don't Select A Profile In. The default value is 30 seconds.

Figure 8-5   Multiple hardware profiles can be configured for any Windows XP system and are particularly useful for laptops.

Configuring Docked and Undocked Profiles

To configure a computer for docked and undocked profiles, complete the following steps:

1. Access the System utility's Hardware tab, and then click Hardware Profiles.
2. In the Available Hardware Profiles list, select the default profile, and click Copy.
3. In the Copy Profile dialog box, type a name for the docked profile in the To field, and click OK.
4. Select the new profile, and then click Properties.
5. Select the This Is A Portable Computer check box, and then select The Computer Is Docked.
6. Select Always Include This Profile As An Option When Windows Starts, and then click OK.
7. Select the default profile in the Available Hardware Profiles list, and click Copy.
8. In the Copy Profile dialog box, type a name for the undocked profile in the To field, and click OK.
9. Select the new profile, and then click Properties.
10. Select the This Is A Portable Computer check box, and then select The Computer Is Undocked.
11. Select Always Include This Profile As An Option When Windows Starts, and then click OK.

12. Now set the default hardware profile for the computer's current state as either docked or undocked, as appropriate. Click OK.

When the system is booted, the hardware profiles are displayed and the user can select the appropriate profile. To get the most out of this feature, you'll need to configure hardware as appropriate for the docked and undocked modes. Use the Device Manager utility to enable and disable devices in a profile. When you disable a device in a hardware profile, the device drivers are not loaded when the computer is started and the user doesn't see the pop-up dialog boxes looking for hardware.

Copying, Renaming, and Deleting Hardware Profiles

To copy, rename, or delete a hardware profile, complete the following steps:

1. Access the System utility's Hardware tab, and then click Hardware Profiles.

2. The Available Hardware Profiles list box shows the currently available hardware profiles. The default profile is the profile at the top of the list marked with (Current). You can use the buttons under the list box to manage profiles. The options are the following:

- ❑ **Properties**   Displays the properties of the currently selected profile.
- ❑ **Copy**   Copies a selected profile, allowing you to create a new profile based on an existing profile.
- ❑ **Rename**   Renames a profile so that you can assign a new name to an existing profile.
- ❑ **Delete**   Deletes a profile from the system. This affects all users of the system.

Note   You cannot delete the default profile. To remove this profile, move another profile to the top of the selection list, making it the default profile. Afterward, you can delete the unwanted profile.

3. Click OK twice.

Configuring Networking for Laptops

Most laptops need several different network configurations: one for the office and one for home (and maybe another for when the user is traveling). At the office the laptop uses a dynamic Internet Protocol (IP) address and network settings that are assigned by a Dynamic Host Configuration Protocol (DHCP) server. At home, the laptop uses a static IP address and different network settings to communicate on a network and access a shared printer and broadband Internet device. In some cases, a laptop might need to be configured to make a Wi-Fi connection using a Wi-Fi PCMCIA card with a static IP configuration when the user is away from his or her desk and a DHCP configuration when the laptop is physically connected to the network, or vice versa. Previous versions of Windows couldn't handle these situations very well, and users were left to reconfigure their machines manually in many cases.

Fortunately, Windows XP resolves this long-standing problem. When a system uses DHCP to obtain its primary network settings, you can configure alternate network settings for those times when a DHCP server isn't available, such as when the user is traveling or at home. Systems can use alternate configurations in one of two ways: either automatically or user-configured.

Configuring Dynamic IP Addresses

DHCP gives you centralized control over IP addressing and TCP/IP default settings. If the network has a DHCP server, you can assign a dynamic IP address to any of the network adapter cards on a computer. Afterward, you rely on the DHCP server to supply the basic information necessary for TCP/IP networking. To configure dynamic IP addressing, complete these steps:

1. Click Start, point to Programs or All Programs as appropriate, then to Accessories, then to Communications, and finally select Network Connections. Next double-click the connection you want to work with.

2. Click Properties, and then open the Internet Protocol (TCP/IP) Properties dialog box by double-clicking Internet Protocol (TCP/IP). You can also select Internet Protocol (TCP/IP) and then click Properties. This displays the Internet Protocol (TCP/IP) Properties dialog box shown in Figure 8-6.

Figure 8-6 To use DHCP, configure the computer to obtain an IP address automatically.

3. Select Obtain An IP Address Automatically. If desired, select Obtain DNS Server Address Automatically, or select Use The Following DNS Server Addresses, and then type a preferred and alternate Domain Name System (DNS) server address in the fields provided.

4. When you're finished, click OK. Afterward, configure alternate private IP addressing and Windows Internet Naming Service (WINS) as necessary.

Configuring Alternate Private IP Addresses

When you use DHCP, an alternate IP address is assigned automatically when the DHCP server can't be reached during startup or when the current IP address lease expires. By default, the alternate IP address is in the range from 169.254.0.1 to 169.254.255.254 with a subnet mask of 255.255.0.0. Because the automatic private IP address (APIPA) configuration does not include a default gateway, DNS, or WINS server settings, a computer using the alternate IP addressing is essentially isolated on its own network segment.

If you want to ensure that a computer uses specific IP address and network configuration settings when no DHCP server is available, you need to specify an alternate configuration manually. One of the key reasons for using an alternate configuration is to accommodate laptop users who take their computers home. In this way, the user's laptop could be configured to use a dynamically assigned IP address at work and an alternate IP address configuration at home. Before you get started, you might want to ask the users for their home networking settings, including the IP address, gateway, and DNS server addresses required by their service provider.

To configure alternate private IP addressing, complete the following steps:

1. Click Start, point to Programs or All Programs as appropriate, then Accessories, then Communications, and then finally select Network Connections. Next, double-click the connection you want to work with.

2. Click Properties, and then open the Internet Protocol (TCP/IP) Properties dialog box by double-clicking Internet Protocol (TCP/IP). You could also select Internet Protocol (TCP/IP) and then click Properties.

3. Provided you've already configured the adapter to obtain an IP address automatically, you should be able to click the Alternate Configuration tab shown in Figure 8-7.

Figure 8-7   Use the Alternate Configuration tab to configure private IP addressing for the computer.

4. On the Alternate Configuration tab, select the User Configured option, and then type the IP address you want to use in the IP Address field. The IP address you assign to the computer should be a private IP address, and it must not be in use anywhere else at the time the settings are applied. Private IP addresses normally used by computers are in the ranges 10.0.0.1 to 10.255.255.254, 172.16.0.1 to 172.31.255.254, and 192.168.0.1 to 192.168.255.254.

5. The Subnet Mask field ensures that the computer communicates over the network properly. Windows XP should insert a default value for the subnet mask into this field. If the network doesn't use subnets, the default value should suffice. However, if it does use subnets, you'll need to change this value as appropriate for the target network.

6. If the computer needs to access other TCP/IP networks, the Internet, or other subnets, you must specify a default gateway. Type the IP address of the network's default router in the Default Gateway field.

7. DNS servers are needed for domain name resolution. Type a preferred and alternate DNS server address in the fields provided.

8. If WINS is used on the network for backward compatibility with previous versions of Windows, configure a preferred and alternate WINS server using the fields provided.

9. When you're finished, click OK twice, and then click Close.

Chapter 9

Configuring User and Computer Policies

In this chapter:

Group Policy Essentials. 209

Configuring Policies 212

Working with File and Data Management Policies 215

Working with Access and Connectivity Policies. 223

Working with Computer and User Script Policies 226

Working with Logon and Startup Policies. 230

Group policies simplify administration by giving administrators central control over privileges, permissions, and capabilities of both users and computers. You can think of a group policy as a set of rules that helps you manage users and computers. Group policies can be applied to multiple domains, to individual domains, to sub-groups within a domain, or to individual systems. Policies that apply to individual systems are referred to as *local group policies* and are stored on the local system only. Other group policies are linked as objects in the Active Directory directory service.

In this chapter, you'll learn how to manage group policy settings. The chapter examines policies that you might want to configure in the domain and on local computers. These policies are organized by topic area, such as file and data management. Group policies apply only to systems running Microsoft Windows 2000, Windows XP, Windows Server 2003, or any combination of these. (In this book, "Windows XP" refers to Windows XP Professional unless otherwise indicated.)

Group Policy Essentials

Careful management of policies is essential to proper operations. Policy settings are divided into two broad categories: those that apply to computers and those that apply to users. Computer policies are normally applied during system startup, and user policies are normally applied during logon.

Understanding Policy Application

During startup and logon, policies are applied in an exact sequence, which is often important in troubleshooting system behavior.

When multiple policies are in place, they are applied in the following order:

1. Microsoft Windows NT 4 policies (NTCONFIG.POL)
2. Local group policies
3. Site group policies
4. Domain group policies
5. Organizational unit (OU) group policies
6. Child OU group policies

If there are conflicts among the policy settings, settings applied later take precedence and overwrite previous policy settings. For example, OU policies take precedence over domain group policies. As you might expect, there are exceptions to the precedence rule that allow administrators to block, oversee, and disable policies.

The events that take place during startup and logon are as follows:

1. The network starts, and then Windows XP applies computer policies. By default, the computer policies are applied one at a time in the previously specified order. No user interface is displayed while computer policies are being processed.
2. Windows XP runs startup scripts. By default, startup scripts are executed one at a time, with each completing or timing out before the next starts. Script execution isn't displayed to the user unless specified.
3. A user logs on. After the user is validated, Windows XP loads the user profile.
4. Windows XP applies user policies. By default, the policies are applied one at a time in the previously specified order. The user interface is displayed while user policies are being processed.
5. Windows XP runs logon scripts. Group policy logon scripts are executed simultaneously by default. Script execution isn't displayed to the user unless specified. Scripts in the Netlogon share are run last in a normal command-shell window.
6. Windows XP displays the start shell interface configured in Group Policy.

Accessing and Using Local Group Policies

Each computer running Windows XP has one local group policy stored in its *%SystemRoot%*\System32\GroupPolicy folder. You shouldn't edit these folders and files directly. Instead, you should use the appropriate features of the Group Policy console.

You access and use local policies on a computer by completing the following steps:

1. Open the Run dialog box by clicking Start and then clicking Run.
2. Type **mmc** in the Open field, and then click OK. This opens the Microsoft Management Console (MMC).

3. In MMC, click File, and then click Add/Remove Snap-In. This opens the Add/Remove Snap-In dialog box.

4. Click the Standalone tab, and then click Add.

5. In the Add Standalone Snap-In dialog box, select Group Policy Object Editor, and then click Add. This opens the Select Group Policy Object dialog box.

6. Select Local Computer to edit the local policy on your computer, or browse to find the local policy on another computer.

7. Click Finish, and then click Close.

8. Click OK. You can now manage the local policy on the selected computer. For more details, see the section of the chapter entitled "Configuring Policies."

Accessing and Using Site, Domain, and Organizational Unit Policies

Each site, domain, and OU can have one or more group policies. Policies displayed higher in the Group Policy list have a higher precedence than policies lower in the list. Group policies set at this level are associated with Active Directory. This ensures that site policies get applied appropriately throughout the related domains and OUs. Site, domain, and OU group policies are stored in the *%SystemRoot%*\Sysvol\sysvol*DomainName*\Policies folder on domain controllers, where Domain-Name is the DNS name of the domain. In this folder, you'll find one subfolder for each policy you've defined on the domain controller. You shouldn't edit these folders and files directly. Instead, you should use the appropriate features of the Group Policy console.

You access and use site, domain, and OU policies by completing the following steps:

1. For sites, open the Active Directory Sites and Services console to create a Group Policy object that is linked to the site. For domains and OUs, open the Active Directory Users and Computers console to create a Group Policy object that is linked to the domain or OU.

2. In the left pane of the appropriate Active Directory window, right-click the site, the domain, or the OU for which you want to create or manage a group policy. Then select Properties on the shortcut menu, which opens the Properties dialog box.

3. In the Properties dialog box, click the Group Policy tab. You can now:
   - ❏ **Create a new policy**   To create a new policy, click New. Enter a name for the policy and press Enter. Then click Edit to configure the new policy.
   - ❏ **Edit an existing policy**   To edit an existing policy, select the policy and then click Edit. Then you can edit the policy. For more details, see the section of this chapter entitled "Configuring Policies."
   - ❏ **Change the priority of a policy**   To change the priority of a policy, use the Up or Down buttons to change its position in the Group Policy Object Links list.

Using the Group Policy Console

Once you've selected a policy for editing or created a new policy, you use the Group Policy console (Group Policy Object Editor in Windows Server 2003) to work with group policies. As Figure 9-1 shows, the Group Policy console has two main nodes:

- **Computer Configuration**   Allows you to set policies that should be applied to computers, regardless of who logs on
- **User Configuration**   Allows you to set policies that should be applied to users, regardless of which computer they log on to

    Note   Keep in mind that user configuration options set through local group policies apply only to computers on which the options are configured. If you want the options to apply to all computers the user might use, you must use domain, site, or OU group policies.

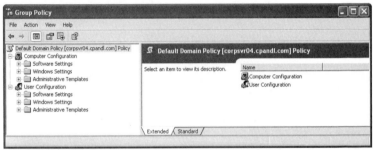

Figure 9-1   Group Policy options depend on the type of policy you're creating and the add-ons installed.

The exact configuration of Computer Configuration and User Configuration depends on the add-ons installed and which type of policy you're creating. You'll usually find that both nodes have subnodes for the following:

- **Software Settings**   Sets policies for software settings and software installation. When you install software, subnodes may be added to Software Settings.
- **Windows Settings**   Sets policies for folder redirection, scripts, and security.
- **Administrative Templates**   Sets policies for the operating system, Windows components, and programs. These policies, examined later in this chapter, apply specifically to users and computers.

Configuring Policies

When you want to manage users and computers, you'll want to configure the administrative template policies. These policies provide easy access to registry-based policy settings that control the operating system, Windows components, and programs.

Viewing Policies and Templates

As shown in Figure 9-2, you can view the currently configured templates in the Group Policy console's Administrative Templates node, which contains policies that can be configured for local systems, OUs, domains, and sites. Different sets of templates are found under Computer Configuration and User Configuration. You can add additional templates containing new policies, both manually in the Group Policy console and when you install new Windows components.

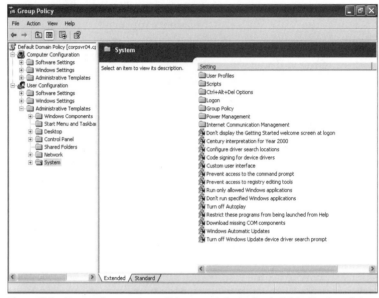

Figure 9-2   User and computer policies are set through administrative templates.

Any changes you make to policies available through the administrative templates are saved in the registry. Computer configurations are saved in HKEY_LOCAL_MACHINE and user configurations are saved in HKEY_CURRENT_USER. The best way to get to know what administrative template policies are available is to browse the Administrative Templates node in the Group Policy console. As you browse the templates, you'll find that policies are in one of three states:

- **Not Configured**   The policy isn't used, and no settings for it are saved in the registry.
- **Enabled**   The policy is actively being enforced, and its settings are saved in the registry.
- **Disabled**   The policy is turned off and isn't enforced unless overridden. This setting is saved in the registry.

Enabling, Disabling, and Configuring Policies

In the Group Policy console, you'll find administrative templates in two nodes: Computer Configuration and User Configuration. In most cases, the policies in these areas don't overlap and don't cause conflict. If there is a conflict, however, computer policies have precedence, which means that the computer policy is the one that is enforced. Later in this chapter, you'll find details on commonly used policies and how you can employ them.

You can enable, disable, and configure policies by completing the following steps:

1. Access the Group Policy console for the resource you want to work with. Then in the Computer Configuration or User Configuration node, whichever is appropriate for the type of policy you want to set, access the Administrative Templates folder.

2. In the left pane, click the subfolder containing the policies you want to work with. The related policies are then displayed in the right pane.

3. Double-click or right-click a policy and select Properties to display its related Properties dialog box.

4. Click the Explain tab to see a description of the policy, if one is available.

5. To set the policy's state, click the Setting tab, and then use the following buttons to change the state of the policy:

   ❑ **Not Configured**   The policy is not configured.

   ❑ **Enabled**   The policy is enabled.

   ❑ **Disabled**   The policy is disabled.

6. If you enabled the policy, set any additional parameters specified on the Setting tab, and then click Apply.

7. Use the Previous Setting and Next Setting buttons to manage other policies in the current folder. Then configure them in the same way.

8. Click OK when you're finished managing policies.

Adding or Removing Templates

You can add or remove template folders in the Group Policy console. To do this, complete the following steps:

1. Access the Group Policy console for the site, the domain, or the OU you want to work with.

2. In the Computer Configuration or User Configuration node, whichever is appropriate for the type of template you want to add or remove, right-click the Administrative Templates folder and select Add/Remove Templates. This displays the Add/Remove Templates dialog box shown in Figure 9-3.

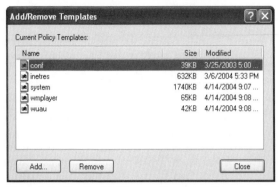

Figure 9-3   Use the Add/Remove Templates dialog box to add more templates or remove existing ones.

3. To add new templates, click Add. Then, in the Policy Templates dialog box, select the template you want to add and click Open.

4. To remove an existing template, select the template to remove, and then click Remove.

5. When you're finished adding and removing templates, click Close.

Working with File and Data Management Policies

Every system administrator should be familiar with file and data management policies, which affect the amount of data a user can store on systems, how offline files are used, and whether the System Restore feature is enabled.

Configuring Disk Quota Policies

Policies that control disk quotas are applied at the system level. You access these policies through Computer Configuration\Administrative Templates\System\Disk Quotas. The available policies are summarized in Table 9-1.

Table 9-1   Disk Quota Policies

Policy Name	Description
Apply Policy To Removable Media	Determines whether to extend quota policies to NTFS volumes on removable media. If you do not enable this policy, quota limits only apply to fixed media drives.
Default Quota Limit And Warning Level	Sets a default quota limit and warning level for all users. This setting overrides other settings and only affects new users of a volume.
Enable Disk Quotas	Turns disk quotas on or off for all NT file system (NTFS) volumes of the computer and prevents users from changing the setting.
Enforce Disk Quota Limit	Specifies whether quota limits are enforced. If quotas are enforced, users are denied disk space if they exceed the quota. This overrides settings on the Quota tab on the NTFS volume.

Table 9-1   Disk Quota Policies

Policy Name	Description
Log Event When Quota Limit Exceeded	Determines whether an event is logged when users reach their limit and prevents users from changing their logging option.
Log Event When Quota Warning Level Exceeded	Determines whether an event is logged when users reach the warning level.

Whenever you work with quota limits, you'll want to use a standard set of policies on all systems. Typically, you won't want to enable all of the policies. Instead, selectively enable policies and then use the standard NTFS features to control quotas on various volumes. If you want to enable quota limits, use the following technique:

1. Access Group Policy for the system you want to work with, such as a file server. Next, access the Disk Quotas node through Computer Configuration\Administrative Templates\System\Disk Quotas.

2. Double-click Enable Disk Quotas. On the Setting tab, select Enabled and then click Next Setting. This displays the Enforce Disk Quota Limit Properties dialog box.

3. If you want to enforce disk quotas on all NTFS volumes residing on this computer, select Enabled. Otherwise, select Disabled and then set specific limits on a per-volume basis as discussed in Chapter 12, "Configuring Folder Options, Offline Files, and Quotas."

4. Click Next Setting. This displays the Default Quota Limit And Warning Level Properties dialog box shown in Figure 9-4. Select Enabled.

Figure 9-4   Use the Default Quota Limit And Warning Level Properties dialog box to establish disk quota values.

5. Under Default Quota Limit, set a default limit that is applied to new users when they first write to the quota-enabled volume. The limit does not apply to current users and doesn't affect current limits. On a corporate share, such as a

share used by all members of a team, a good limit is between 500 and 1000 MB. Of course, this depends on the size of the data files the users routinely work with. Graphic designers and data engineers, for example, might need much more disk space.

6. If you scroll down in the subwindow provided on the Setting tab, you'll be able to set a warning limit as well. A good warning limit is about 90 percent of the default quota limit, meaning if you set the default quota limit to 1000 MB, you'd set the warning limit to 900 MB.

7. Click Next Setting. This displays the Log Event When Quota Limit Exceeded Properties dialog box. Select Enabled so that limit events are recorded in the application log.

8. Click Next Setting. This displays the Log Event When Quota Warning Exceeded Properties dialog box. Select Enabled so that warning events are recorded in the application log.

9. Click Next Setting. This displays the Apply Policy To Removable Media Properties dialog box. Select Disabled so that the quota limits only apply to fixed media volumes on the computer.

10. Click OK.

Configuring System Restore Policies

System Restore is designed to save the state of system volumes and enable users to restore a system in the event of a problem. It is a helpful feature for the average user, but it can use a tremendous amount of disk space. As you learned in Chapter 2, "Configuring the Environment," you can turn System Restore off for individual drives or for all drives on a computer.

In the Group Policy console, you'll find the System Restore policies under Computer Configuration\Administrative Templates\System\System Restore. Through System Restore policies, you can override and disable management of this feature. The following policies are available:

- **Turn Off System Restore**   If you enable this policy, System Restore is turned off and can't be managed using the System utility or the System Restore Wizard. If you disable this policy, System Restore is enforced and cannot be turned off.

- **Turn Off Configuration**   If you enable this policy, you prevent configuration of the System Restore feature. Users can't access the Settings dialog box but can still turn off System Restore. If you disable this policy, users can access the Settings dialog box but can't manipulate it, and they can still turn off System Restore.

To configure System Restore policies, follow these steps:

1. Access Group Policy for the system you want to work with. Next, access the System Restore node by expanding Computer Configuration\Administrative Templates\System\System Restore.

2. To enable or disable System Restore, double-click Turn Off System Restore. On the Setting tab, select either Enabled or Disabled as appropriate. Click OK.

3. To enable or disable configuration of System Restore, double-click Turn Off Configuration. On the Setting tab, select either Enabled or Disabled as appropriate. Click OK.

Configuring Offline File Policies

Offline file policies are set at both the computer and the user level, and there are identically named policies at each level. If you work with identically named policies at both levels, keep in mind that computer policies override user policies and that these policies may be applied at different times.

The primary policies you'll want to use are summarized in Table 9-2. As the table shows, most offline policies affect access, synchronization, caching, and encryption. You'll find Offline File policies under Computer Configuration\Administrative Templates\Network\Offline Files and User Configuration\Administrative Templates\Network\Offline Files.

Table 9-2   Offline File Policies

Policy Type	Policy Name	Description
Computer	Allow Or Disallow Use Of The Offline Files Feature	Forces enabling or disabling of the Offline Files feature and prevents overriding by users. In this way, you can administratively control Offline File settings for a system.
Computer	At Logoff, Delete Local Copy Of User's Offline Files	Cleans up the offline file cache on the local computer at logoff.
Computer	Default Cache Size	Limits size of automatically cached offline files and prevents users from changing related options. If you enable this option, you can set a cache size. If you disable this option, the limit is 10 percent of drive space.
Computer	Encrypt The Offline Files Cache	Determines whether offline files are encrypted to improve security.
Computer	Files Not Cached	Lists types of files that cannot be used offline by file extension.
Computer	Subfolders Always Available Offline	Makes subfolders available offline when a parent folder is available offline.
Computer\User	Action On Server Disconnect	Specifies how the system responds when a server becomes unavailable. The Work Offline action ensures offline files are available.
Computer\User	Administratively Assigned Offline Files	Specifies files and folders that are always available offline by Universal Naming Convention (UNC) path.
Computer\User	Event Logging Level	Ensures offline file events are logged in the application log.
Computer\User	Prevent Use Of Offline Files Folder	Prevents users from accessing the Offline Files folder. Users can't view or open copies of cached files, but they can work offline.

Table 9-2   Offline File Policies

Policy Type	Policy Name	Description
Computer\User	Prohibit "Make Available Offline" For These Files And Folders	Prohibits users from making specific files and folders available offline. Enter UNC paths to resources.
Computer\User	Prohibit User Configuration Of Offline Files	Prevents users from enabling, disabling, and configuring Offline Files. This locks down the default settings for Offline Files.
Computer\User	Remove "Make Available Offline"	Prevents users from making files available offline.
Computer\User	Synchronize All Offline Files Before Logging Off	Forces full synchronization before users log off and prevents them from changing synchronization timing.
Computer\User	Synchronize All Offline Files When Logging On	Forces full synchronization when users log on and prevents them from changing synchronization timing.
Computer\User	Synchronize Offline Files Before Suspend	Forces synchronization before a computer goes into standby or hibernate mode. You can specify quick or full synchronization.
User	Do Not Automatically Make Redirected Folders Available Offline	By default, if Folder Redirection is configured, these folders are available offline automatically. If you enable this policy, you turn off automatic redirection. Users can, however, enable offline use of the redirected folders.

Setting Offline File Configuration Policies

Offline file configuration can be easily controlled through policy. You can allow users to specify which files and folders should be available offline, prevent them from configuring offline file features on their own, and allow them to work offline but not access other cached resources. Follow these steps to set offline file configuration policies:

1. Access Group Policy for the system you want to work with. Most offline file policies can be configured in either computer or user policy (with user policies having precedence by default) using the Offline Files node. This means you can access the policies for offline files either by expanding Computer Configuration\Administrative Templates\Network\Offline Files or User Configuration\Administrative Templates\Network\Offline Files unless specifically noted otherwise.

2. To control the availability of offline files, in Computer Configuration\Administrative Templates\Network\Offline Files, double-click Allow Or Disallow Use Of The Offline Files Feature. On the Setting tab select either Enabled or Disabled as appropriate. Click OK. Users are now able to select specific files and folders that they want to have available when working offline. To prevent this user selection of files, but to assign specific offline files folders, you'll need to prohibit this feature and administratively assign offline files.

3. To prevent users from changing offline file configuration settings, double-click Prohibit User Configuration Of Offline Files. On the Setting tab, select Enabled. Once this policy is set, users can't configure offline file options.

4. To prevent users from accessing the offline files folder but still allow them to work offline, double-click Prevent Use Of Offline Files Folder. On the Setting tab, select Enabled. Once you select this option, users cannot view or open copies of cached files. They can, however, save current work and continue to use active files when offline.

Administratively Controlling Offline Files and Subfolders

You can administratively control which files and folders are available for offline use. Typically, you'll want to do this on file servers or other systems sharing resources on the network. You can use several different techniques to administratively control which resources are available offline.

You can prevent users from making files available offline and, instead, assign specific offline resources by following these steps:

1. Access Group Policy for the system you want to work with. Next, access the Offline Files node by expanding Computer Configuration\Administrative Templates\Network\Offline Files or User Configuration\Administrative Templates\Network\Offline Files.

2. To prevent users from making files available offline, double-click Remove "Make Available Offline." On the Setting tab, select Enabled. Click OK. Once this policy is enforced, users are unable to specify files that should be used offline.

3. To assign resources that are available offline automatically, double-click Administratively Assigned Offline Files. On the Setting tab, select Enabled. Next, click Show, and then, in the Show Contents dialog box, specify resources according to their UNC path, such as \\corpserver\data. Figure 9-5 shows a list of resources that have been added to the Show Contents list.

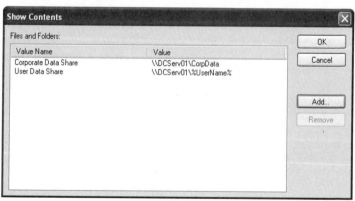

Figure 9-5   Use the Show Contents dialog box to specify resources according to their UNC path.

Caution   You should carefully consider which resources are made available offline automatically. The more resources you assign through this technique, the more network traffic is generated to maintain offline file caches. You can slow down an entire network by assigning too many resources to be available automatically.

You can make specific files automatically available, and prevent others from being used offline, by following these steps:

1. Access Group Policy for the system that you want to work with. Next, access the Offline Files node by expanding Computer Configuration\Administrative Templates\Network\Offline Files or User Configuration\Administrative Templates\Network\Offline Files.

2. To assign resources that are available offline automatically, double-click Administratively Assigned Offline Files. On the Setting tab, select Enabled. Next, click Show, and then, in the Show Contents dialog box, specify resources according to their UNC path, such as \\corpserver\data.

3. To specify resources that users shouldn't be able to make available offline, double-click Prohibit "Make Available Offline" For These Files And Folders. On the Setting tab, select Enabled. Next, click Show, and then, in the Show Contents dialog box, specify resources according to their UNC path, such as \\corpserver\data. This setting doesn't prevent automatic caching of resources assigned through step 2.

4. Click OK until all open dialog boxes are closed.

Setting Offline File Synchronization Policies

Offline file synchronization is normally controlled using the Synchronization Manager, accessed by selecting Start, All Programs or Programs, Accessories, Synchronize. However, you can set specific synchronization timing and techniques through policies. Normally, resources are either fully synchronized—meaning that all files are checked to ensure they are complete and current—or quickly synchronized—meaning files are checked to ensure they are complete, but file contents are not examined for currency.

Several events can trigger automatic synchronization, such as logon, logoff, standby, and hibernate. Again, the Synchronization Manager normally determines which events are used. Using policies, you can override this behavior. In most circumstances, you'll want to synchronize files only when a user logs on. The advantage to synchronizing when users log on is that they'll always have the freshest copies of files. The disadvantage is that the logon process might take longer. The notable exception for synchronizing at logon is for laptop users. Here, you might want to synchronize at logoff to ensure that users have the freshest copy of files when they go home and use their laptop offline.

To configure synchronization policies, follow these steps:

1. Access Group Policy for the system you want to work with. Next, access the Offline Files node by expanding Computer Configuration\Administrative Templates\Network\Offline Files or User Configuration\Administrative Templates\Network\Offline Files.

2. The policies that control synchronization are Synchronize All Offline Files When Logging On, Synchronize All Offline Files Before Logging Off, and Synchronize Offline Files Before Suspend. Double-click the policy related to the synchronization technique that you want to use for this computer. On the Setting tab, select Enabled. For the Synchronize Offline Files Before Suspend policy, ensure that the appropriate Action is selected; choose either Full or Quick.

 Tip   A full synchronization ensures the latest version of the user's offline files are stored prior to the suspend operation. A quick synchronize ensures all the offline files are available but not necessarily in the most current version.

3. Click OK.

Setting Offline File Cache Policies

Careful configuration of the offline file cache is essential to managing the system and network overhead generated by offline file usage. You can specify a maximum file cache size, whether the cache is encrypted for security, and which file types should never be cached. To configure policies for the offline file cache, follow these steps:

1. Access Group Policy for the system you want to work with. Next, access the Offline Files node by expanding Computer Configuration\Administrative Templates\Network\Offline Files or User Configuration\Administrative Templates\Network\Offline Files.

2. To set the maximum cache size, double-click Default Cache Size. On the Setting tab, select Enabled. Afterward, use the Default Cache Size Properties dialog box, shown in Figure 9-6, to set the default cache size. The value entered is the percentage of disk space used times 10,000, meaning that if you enter 15,000 the cache can use up to 15 percent of the free space on the system drive.

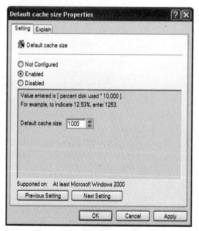

Figure 9-6   Set a default cache size for offline files in the Default Cache Size Properties dialog box.

Note   If you don't configure the Default Cache Size policy or disable it, the cache size limit is 10 percent of the free space on the system drive.

3. To specify file types that are not cached, double-click Files Not Cached and then select Enabled. Next, in the Extensions field, type a semicolon-separated list of file extensions to exclude. Each extension must be preceded by an asterisk and a period. You could enter *.**wbk**; *.**tmp**; *.**lnk**; *.**ndx** to block caching of many temporary types of files.

4. To encrypt the cache, double-click Encrypt The Offline Files Cache, and then select Enabled. Once enabled, all existing and new files in the cache are encrypted and users cannot unencrypt the offline files.

Working with Access and Connectivity Policies

Access and connectivity policies control network connections, dial-up connections, and Remote Assistance configurations. These policies affect a system's connectivity to the network as well as remote access to the system.

Configuring Network Policies

Many network policies are available. Network policies that control Internet Connection Sharing, Internet Connection Firewall, Windows Firewall, and Network Bridge are configured at the computer level. Network policies that control local area network (LAN) connections, Transmission Control Protocol/Internet Protocol (TCP/IP) configuration, and remote access are configured at the user level. The primary policies that you'll want to use are summarized in Table 9-3. You'll find Network policies under Computer Configuration\Administrative Templates\Network\Network Connections and User Configuration\Administrative Templates\Network\Network Connections.

Note   Under Network Connections, there's a new subfolder for Windows Firewall when Windows XP Service Pack 2 or later policies are available.

Table 9-3   Network Policies

Policy Type	Policy Name	Description
Computer	Prohibit Installation And Configuration Of Network Bridge On Your DNS Domain Network	Determines whether users can install and configure network bridges. This policy only applies to the domain in which it is assigned.
Computer	Prohibit Use Of Internet Connection Firewall On Your DNS Domain Network	Determines whether users can enable the Internet Connection Firewall. This policy only applies to the domain in which it is assigned.
Computer	Prohibit Use Of Internet Connection Sharing On Your DNS Domain Network	Determines whether administrators can enable and configure connection sharing. This policy only applies to the domain in which it is assigned.

Table 9-3   Network Policies

Policy Type	Policy Name	Description
User	Ability To Change Properties Of An All User Remote Access Connection	Determines whether users can view and modify the properties of remote access connections available to all users of the computer.
User	Ability To Delete All User Remote Access Connections	Determines whether users can delete remote access connections available to all users of the computer.
User	Ability To Enable/Disable A LAN Connection	Determines whether users can enable or disable LAN connections.
User	Prohibit Access To Properties Of A LAN Connection	Determines whether users can change the properties of LAN connections.
User	Prohibit Access To Properties Of Components Of A Remote Access Connection	Determines whether users can access and change properties of remote access connections.
User	Prohibit Deletion Of Remote Access Connections	Determines whether users can delete remote access connections.
User	Prohibit TCP/IP Advanced Configuration	Determines whether users can access advanced TCP/IP settings.

As shown in the table, network policies for computers are designed to restrict actions on the organization's network. When you enforce these restrictions, users are prohibited from using features such as Internet Connection Sharing in the applicable domain. This is designed to protect the integrity of corporate networks, but it doesn't prevent users with laptops, for example, from taking their computers home and using these features on their own networks. To enable or disable these restrictions, follow these steps:

1. Access Group Policy for the resource you want to work with. Next, access the Network Connections node by expanding Computer Configuration\Administrative Templates\Network\Network Connections.

2. Double-click the policy that you want to configure. On the Setting tab, select Enabled or Disabled as appropriate. Click OK.

User policies for network connections usually prevent access to certain configuration features, such as the advanced TCP/IP property settings. To configure these policies, follow these steps:

1. Access Group Policy for the resource you want to work with. Next, access User Configuration\Administrative Templates\Network\Network Connections.

2. Double-click the policy that you want to configure. On the Setting tab, select Enabled or Disabled as appropriate. Click OK.

Configuring Remote Assistance Policies

Remote Assistance policies can be used to prevent or permit use of remote assistance on computers. Typically, when you set Remote Assistance policies, you'll want to prevent unsolicited offers for remote assistance while allowing requested offers.

You can also force a specific expiration time limit for invitations through policy rather than setting this through the System utility.

To configure policy in this manner, follow these steps:

1. Access Group Policy for the computer you want to work with. Next, access Computer Configuration\Administrative Templates\System\Remote Assistance.

2. Double-click Solicited Remote Assistance. On the Setting tab, select Enabled. When enabled, this policy allows authorized users to respond to remote assistance invitations.

3. You can now specify the level of access for assistants. The Permit Remote Control Of This Computer selection list has two options:

   ❑ **Allow Helpers To Remotely Control This Computer**   Permits viewing and remote control of the computer.

   ❑ **Allow Helpers To Only View This Computer**   Permits only viewing; assistants cannot take control to make changes.

4. Next, as shown in Figure 9-7, use the Maximum Ticket Time (Value) and Maximum Ticket Time (Units) fields to set the maximum time limit for remote assistance invitations. The default maximum time limit is 1 hour.

Real World   The method for sending e-mail invitations is set to Mailto by default. This is a browser-based mail submission technique in which the invitation recipient connects through an Internet link. You can also select Simple MAPI to use MAPI for sending the e-mail invitation, in which the invitation is sent as an attachment to the invitation e-mail message. As long as computers can establish a connection with each other over port 80 and you're using a standard e-mail program, such as Microsoft Outlook or Outlook Express, you'll probably want to use Mailto.

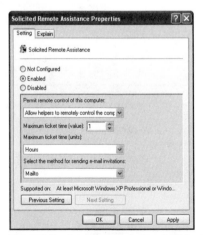

Figure 9-7   Set a time expiration limit for Remote Assistance invitations.

5. Click Previous Setting or Next Setting as appropriate. In the Offer Remote Assistance Properties dialog box, select Disabled. Disabling this policy prevents unsolicited assistance offers.

6. Click OK.

To prevent remote assistance and remote control of computers entirely, follow these steps:

1. Access Group Policy for the computer you want to work with. Next, access Computer Configuration\Administrative Templates\System\Remote Assistance.

2. Double-click Solicited Remote Assistance. On the Setting tab, select Disabled, and then click Previous Setting or Next Setting as appropriate.

3. In the Offer Remote Assistance dialog box, select Disabled, and then click OK.

Working with Computer and User Script Policies

Script policies control the behavior and assignment of computer and user scripts. Four types of scripts can be configured:

- **Computer startup**   Executed during startup
- **Computer shutdown**   Executed prior to shutdown
- **User logon**   Executed when a user logs on
- **User logoff**   Executed when a user logs off

You can write these scripts as command-shell batch or Windows scripts. Batch scripts use the shell command language. Windows scripts use Windows Script Host (WSH) and are written in a scripting language, such as VBScript or JScript.

Controlling Script Behavior through Policy

Through policy you can control the behavior of startup, shutdown, logon, and logoff scripts. The key policies that you'll use are described in Table 9-4. As you'll see, there are quite a few options for configuring script behavior.

Table 9-4   Computer and User Script Policies

Policy Type	Policy Name	Description
Computer	Maximum Wait Time For Group Policy Scripts	Sets the maximum time to wait for scripts to finish running. The default value is 600 seconds (10 minutes).
Computer	Run Shutdown Scripts Visible	Displays shutdown scripts and their instructions as they execute.
Computer	Run Startup Scripts Asynchronously	Allows the system to run startup scripts simultaneously rather than one at a time.
Computer	Run Startup Scripts Visible	Displays startup scripts and their instructions as they execute.
Computer/ User	Run Logon Scripts Synchronously	Ensures the system waits for logon scripts to finish before displaying the Windows interface.

Table 9-4   Computer and User Script Policies

Policy Type	Policy Name	Description
User	Run Legacy Logon Scripts Hidden	Hides logon scripts configured through System Policy Editor in Windows NT 4.
User	Run Logoff Scripts Visible	Displays logoff scripts and their instructions as they execute.
User	Run Logon Scripts Visible	Displays logon scripts and their instructions as they execute.

Although there are many ways to control script behavior and many different combinations, you'll usually want scripts to behave as follows:

- Logon and startup scripts should run simultaneously (in most cases).
- All scripts should be hidden rather than visible.
- The system should wait no more than 1 minute for a script to complete (in most cases).

To enforce this behavior, follow these steps:

1. Access Group Policy for the computer you want to work with. Next, access Computer Configuration\Administrative Templates\System\Scripts.

2. Double-click Run Logon Scripts Synchronously. On the Setting tab, select Disabled.

3. Double-click Run Startup Scripts Asynchronously. On the Setting tab, select Enabled.

4. Double-click Run Startup Scripts Visible. On the Setting tab, select Disabled.

5. Double-click Run Shutdown Scripts Visible. On the Setting tab, select Disabled.

6. Double-click Maximum Wait Time For Group Policy Scripts. On the Setting tab, select Enabled, and then enter a value of 60 for the wait time in the Seconds field, as shown in Figure 9-8. Click OK.

Figure 9-8   Set the maximum wait time for scripts.

7. Access User Configuration\Administrative Templates\System\Scripts.

8. Double-click Run Legacy Logon Scripts Hidden. On the Setting tab, select Enabled.

9. Double-click Run Logon Scripts Visible. On the Setting tab, select Disabled.

10. Double-click Run Logoff Scripts Visible. On the Setting tab, select Disabled, and then click OK to complete the configuration process for scripts.

Assigning Computer Startup and Shutdown Scripts

Computer startup and shutdown scripts can be assigned as part of a group policy. In this way, a computer and all its users—or all computers that are members of the site, domain, or OU—execute scripts automatically when they're booted or shut down.

To assign computer scripts, follow these steps:

1. For easy management, copy the scripts you want to use to the Scripts\Startup or Scripts\Shutdown folder for the related policy. Scripts are stored in the *%SystemRoot%*\Sysvol\Sysvol*%UserDnsDomain%*\Policies*GUID*\Machine folder on domain controllers and *%SystemRoot%*\System32\GroupPolicy\Machine on Windows XP workstations.

2. Access the Group Policy console for the resource you want to work with. Then access Computer Configuration\Windows Settings\Scripts.

3. To work with startup scripts, right-click Startup and then select Properties. To work with shutdown scripts, right-click Shutdown and then select Properties. This opens a dialog box similar to the one shown in Figure 9-9.

Figure 9-9   Manage computer startup scripts using the Startup Properties dialog box.

4. Click Show Files. If you copied the computer script to the correct location, you should see the script.

5. Click Add to assign a script. This opens the Add A Script dialog box. In the Script Name field, type the name of the script you copied to the Scripts\Startup or the Scripts\Shutdown folder for the related policy. In the Script Parameters field, enter any command-line arguments to pass to the command-line script or parameters to pass to the scripting host for a WSH script. Repeat this step to add other scripts.

6. During startup or shutdown, scripts are executed in the order in which they're listed in the Properties dialog box. Click Up or Down to reposition scripts as necessary.

7. If you want to edit the script name or parameters later, select the script in the Script For list, and then click Edit.

8. To delete a script, select the script in the Script For list and then click Remove.

Assigning User Logon and Logoff Scripts

User scripts can be assigned as part of a group policy. In this way, all users who access a computer or are members of the site, domain, or OU execute scripts automatically when they log on or log off.

To assign user scripts, complete the following steps:

1. For easy management, copy the scripts you want to use to the Scripts\Logon or the Scripts\Logoff folder for the related policy. User scripts are stored in the *%SystemRoot%*\Sysvol\Sysvol*%UserDnsDomain%*\Policies*GUID*\User folder on domain controllers and *%WinDirSystemRoot%*\System32\GroupPolicy\User on Windows XP workstations.

2. Access the Group Policy console for the resource you want to work with. Then access User Configuration\Windows Settings\Scripts.

3. To work with logon scripts, right-click Logon, and then select Properties. To work with logoff scripts, right-click Logoff, and then select Properties. This opens a dialog box similar to the one shown in Figure 9-10.

4. Click Show Files. If you copied the user script to the correct location, you should see the script.

5. Click Add to assign a script. This opens the Add A Script dialog box. In the Script Name field, type the name of the script you copied to the Scripts\Logon or the Scripts\Logoff folder for the related policy. In the Script Parameter field, enter any command-line arguments to pass to the command-line script or parameters to pass to the scripting host for a WSH script. Repeat this step to add other scripts.

6. During logon or logoff, scripts are executed in the order in which they're listed in the Properties dialog box. Click Up or Down to reposition scripts as necessary.

7. If you want to edit the script name or parameters later, select the script in the Script For list, and then click Edit.

8. To delete a script, select the script in the Script For list and then click Remove.

Figure 9-10   Manage user logon scripts using the Logon Properties dialog box.

Working with Logon and Startup Policies

Windows XP provides a set of policies to control the logon process, some of which allow you to configure the way programs run at logon. This makes them similar to logon scripts, in that you can execute specific tasks at logon. Other policies change the view in the welcome and logon screens. The main logon and startup policies that you'll use are available at Administrative Templates\System\Logon and are summarized in Table 9-5.

Table 9-5   Logon and Startup Policies

Policy Type	Policy Name	Description
Computer	Always Use Classic Logon	This overrides the default simple logon screen and uses the logon screen from previous versions of Windows.
Computer	Always Wait For The Network At Computer Startup And Logon	Requires the computer to wait for the network to be fully initialized. At startup, this Group Policy is fully applied rather than using a background refresh. At logon, this means the user cannot log on using cached credentials and must be fully authenticated.
Computer	Don't Display The Getting Started Welcome Screen At Logon	Hides the welcome screen that is displayed when new users log on. This only applies to Windows XP and not to servers.
Computer/User	Do Not Process The Legacy Run List	Disables running startup applications other than those set through System Policy Editor in Windows NT 4.

Table 9-5   Logon and Startup Policies

Policy Type	Policy Name	Description
Computer/User	Do Not Process The Run-Once List	Forces the system to ignore customized run-once lists.
Computer/User	Run These Programs At User Logon	Sets programs that all users should run at logon. Use the full file path (unless program is in *%SystemRoot%*).

Hiding the Welcome Screen

Experienced users often find the welcome screen annoying, particularly because it is displayed automatically every time they log on to a new computer. To hide the welcome screen at logon, follow these steps:

1. Access Group Policy for the computer you want to work with. Next, access Computer Configuration\Administrative Templates\System\Logon.

2. Double-click Don't Display The Getting Started Welcome Screen At Logon. On the Setting tab, select Enabled, and then click OK.

Using Classic Logon vs. Simple Logon

The simple logon window is new in Windows XP. It is the default authentication, and although that view can be useful, some users might prefer to see only the classic logon window. To use classic logon rather than simple logon, follow these steps:

1. Access Group Policy for the computer you want to work with. Next, access Computer Configuration\Administrative Templates\System\Logon.

2. Double-click Always Use Classic Logon. On the Setting tab, select Enabled, and then click OK.

Setting Policy-Based Startup Programs

Although users can configure their startup applications separately, it usually makes more sense to handle this through policy, especially in an enterprise in which the same applications should be started by groups of users. To specify programs that should start at logon, follow these steps:

1. Access Group Policy for the computer you want to work with. Next, access Computer Configuration\Administrative Templates\System\Logon.

2. Double-click Run These Programs At User Logon. On the Setting tab, select Enabled.

3. To assign startup applications through policy, click Show. In the Show Contents dialog box that appears, specify applications according to their full file or UNC path, such as D:\Program Files\Internet Explorer\IEXPLORE.EXE or \\DCServ01\Apps\STATS.EXE.

4. Close all open dialog boxes.

Disabling Run Lists through Policy

Using policy, you can disable legacy run lists as well as run-once lists. Legacy run lists are stored in the registry in

```
HKEY_LOCAL_MACHINE
 \SOFTWARE
  \Microsoft
   \Windows
    \CurrentVersion
     \Run
```

and

```
HKEY_CURRENT_USER
 \Software
  \Microsoft
   \Windows
    \CurrentVersion
     \Run
```

Run-once lists can be created by administrators to specify programs that should run the next time the system starts but not on subsequent restarts. Run-once lists are stored in the registry under

```
HKEY_LOCAL_MACHINE
 \SOFTWARE
  \Microsoft
   \Windows
    \CurrentVersion
     \RunOnce
```

To disable run lists, follow these steps:

1. Access Group Policy for the computer you want to work with. Next, access Computer Configuration\Administrative Templates\System\Logon or User Configuration\Administrative Templates\System\Logon.

2. Double-click Do Not Process The Run Once List. On the Setting tab, select Enabled.

3. Double-click Do Not Process The Legacy Run List. On the Setting tab, select Enabled and then click OK.

Chapter 10

Managing Disk Drives and File Systems

In this chapter:

Disk Management Essentials 234

Working with Basic and Dynamic Disks. 238

Using Basic and Dynamic Disks. 240

Working with Disks, Partitions, and Volumes. 245

Partitioning Disks and Preparing Them for Use. 247

Moving a Dynamic Disk to a New System. 261

Troubleshooting Common Disk Problems 262

Most computers have several types of drives, including physical drives and removable media drives. A hard disk drive is the typical primary storage device. The first hard disk drive installed is designated as Disk 0 in most cases. If there are additional hard disk drives installed, they are designated as Disk 1, Disk 2, and so on. Microsoft Windows XP allows you to designate a physical drive as either a basic disk or a dynamic disk:

- **Basic disks** Are the historically available disk type. A basic disk can be divided into one or more partitions. A partition is a logical section of a disk that operates as if it is a physically separate disk. Computers can support primary and extended partitions on basic disks. A primary partition is used to start the operating system. You access a primary partition directly by its drive designator. You cannot subdivide a primary partition. An extended partition, on the other hand, is accessed indirectly. After you create an extended partition, you must divide it into one or more logical drives. You can then access the logical drives independently of each other. To use a partition or a logical drive, you must format it for a particular file system (FAT, FAT32, or NTFS) and assign a drive designator. The formatted partition or logical drive is then referred to as a *basic volume*, and you can access it as a local disk on the computer.

- **Dynamic disks**   Were introduced with Microsoft Windows 2000 and allow you to perform most common disk maintenance tasks without having to restart the computer. Like a basic disk, a dynamic disk can be divided. Dynamic disks are divided into volumes rather than partitions, however. A volume is very similar to a partition. The most commonly used type of volume is a *simple volume*, which can be used to start the operating system and for general data storage. Other types of volumes can be used as well, including those that allow you to extend a single volume across several disks (a *spanned volume*). As with a partition or a logical drive, you must format a volume on a dynamic disk and assign it a drive designator before you can use it. The formatted volume is referred to as a *dynamic volume*, and you can access it as a local disk on the computer. When a dynamic volume combines space from multiple physical drives, it will still appear as a single local disk, accessed by a single drive designator.

The tools and techniques you can use to manage disk drives and file systems are discussed in this chapter. You'll learn how to partition, format, and convert disks from one disk type to the other.

Disk Management Essentials

Windows XP provides several tools for working with a computer's disks. The first and most often overlooked is My Computer. Other tools include Disk Management, FSUtil, and DiskPart.

Using My Computer

To access My Computer, click Start and select My Computer. Using My Computer, you can quickly determine the available storage devices on a computer. As Figure 10-1 shows, My Computer provides the following details:

- **Files Stored On This Computer**   Provides access to the My Documents folders of each local user. Any shared files, such as shared music or pictures, can be accessed via Shared Documents. This Shared Documents option is available only for computers that are members of workgroups.

- **Hard Disk Drives**   Lists the local disks available on the computer. Right-click a disk to display available management options, including Explore, which opens the disk in Windows Explorer with a complete Folders view and is much handier than Open, which opens the disk in Windows Explorer but doesn't display a complete Folders view.

- **Devices With Removable Storage**   Lists the removable storage devices on the computer, including CD, DVD, and floppy disk drives. Right-click a device to display available management options, including Eject, which is handy for ejecting current media so that new media can be inserted.

Tip   USB flash drives and FireWire/USB-attached external hard drives are being used more and more in place of floppies and other types of removable media. If a computer has a USB or FireWire port, you can easily connect or disconnect a drive. Before you disconnect a USB or FireWire drive, you should ensure that it is in a safe state. The Eject option provides one way to do this. Right-click the disk designator in Windows Explorer or any related views, such as the Devices With Removable Storage list, and then select Eject. As long as files on the drive are not in use, you should then be able to safely disconnect the drive.

■ **Network Drives**   Lists any available network drives. A network drive provides access to a shared folder or a disk on another computer. You can connect network drives using the Map Network Drive feature of Windows Explorer.

Figure 10-1   My Computer provides easy access to a computer's storage devices.

Using Disk Management

When you want to configure drives, the tool of choice is Disk Management. Disk Management provides the tools you need to manage disks, partitions, volumes, logical drives, and their related file systems. Disk Management is a Microsoft Management Console (MMC) snap-in that can be accessed through a preconfigured console or added to any custom console you've created. Using Disk Management, you'll be able to perform the following tasks:

- Determine the capacity, free space, status, and other properties of disks
- Create partitions and logical drives on basic disks
- Create volumes on dynamic disks
- Extend volumes to increase their size or to span multiple disks
- Format volumes and specify the file system to use as FAT, FAT32, or NTFS
- Assign drive letters and paths to volumes
- Convert basic disks to dynamic disks and vice versa

You can start Disk Management at a command prompt by typing **diskmgmt.msc**. Alternatively, right-click My Computer on the Start menu, choose Manage to start Computer Management, and then select Disk Management in the left pane of the Computer Management window.

When you start Disk Management, you're automatically connected to the local computer. To examine drives on another computer, right-click the Computer Management entry in the console tree and select Connect To Another Computer on the shortcut menu. You can now choose the system whose drives you want to examine. From the command line, you can connect to another computer when starting Computer Management by typing **compmgmt.msc /computer=**ComputerName, where ComputerName is the name of the remote computer to which you want to connect.

In the default configuration, as shown in Figure 10-2, Disk Management displays the Volume List view in its upper-right corner and the Graphical view in its lower-right corner. Although only two views can be shown at any one time, there are three views available all together.

- **Volume List** Provides a detailed summary of all the drives on the computer. Clicking a column label, such as Name, allows you to sort the disk information based on that column.

- **Graphical View** Provides a graphical overview of all the physical and logical drives available. Summary information for the physical disk devices includes the disk number and device type, such as basic, removable, or CD-ROM; the disk capacity; and the status of the disk device, such as online or offline. Additional details are also provided for each local disk on the physical disk that includes the drive letter and text label for the associated partition or volume; the file system type, such as FAT, FAT32, or NTFS; the size of the drive section in megabytes (MB); and the local disk status, such as healthy or unhealthy.

- **Disk List** Provides summary information about physical drives. This information includes the disk number and device type, such as basic, removable, or CD-ROM; the disk capacity; the size of unallocated space on the disk (if any); the status of the disk device, such as online or offline; and the device interface type, such as Integrated Device Electronics (IDE), Small Computer System Interface (SCSI), Universal Serial Bus (USB), or FireWire (1394).

You can change the view for the top or bottom pane using the options of the View menu. To change the top view, select View, choose Top, and then select the view you want to use. To change the bottom view, select View, choose Bottom, and then select the view you want to use.

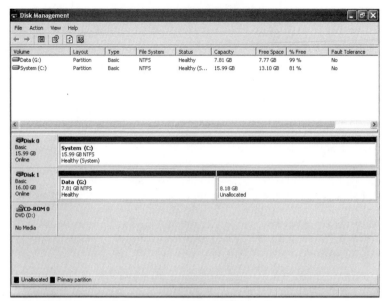

Figure 10-2   Use Disk Management to manage disk configurations.

As you can see, the available views provide summaries and overviews of available disks. To get more detailed information on a local disk, right-click it in any of Disk Management's views, and then select Properties from the shortcut menu. When you do this, you'll see a dialog box much like the one shown in Figure 10-3. This is the same dialog box that you can access from Windows Explorer (by right-clicking the top-level icon for the drive and then choosing Properties from the shortcut menu).

Figure 10-3   Examine detailed information for a drive using its Properties dialog box.

Using FSUtil and DiskPart

Windows XP provides several command-line tools for working with disks, including the following:

- **FSUtil**   Meant to be used by support professionals who need to manage disks at a fairly low level. Using FSUtil, you can examine and work with meta-information related to disks and the information they contain, including update sequence number (USN) change journals, reparse points, and hard links. You can also obtain detailed sector and cluster information, such as the number of free or reserved sectors on a disk. To learn more about FSUtil, type **fsutil help** at a command prompt.

- **DiskPart**   A text-mode command interpreter that you can use to manage disks, partitions, and volumes from the command prompt. Not only can Disk-Part perform many of the same operations as Disk Management, but it can also be used with scripts to automate disk management processes. You start DiskPart by typing **diskpart** at a command prompt. You will then be at the DISKPART> prompt. If you type **help** and press Enter, you will see a list of available commands along with a description of their usage.

 Note   Unlike Disk Management, which provides a friendly interface and is fairly easy to use, FSUtil and DiskPart are very complex tools and meant for advanced administrators. Their use is covered in detail in Chapters 8, 9, and 10 of the *Microsoft Windows Command-Line Administrator's Pocket Consultant* (Microsoft Press, 2004), and you'll find a detailed example using DiskPart in the section of this chapter entitled "Marking a Partition as Active."

Working with Basic and Dynamic Disks

Not that long ago, all Windows computers shipped with basic disks. Now computers are increasingly being shipped with dynamic disks. This is happening because people want larger or more robust disks, and computer manufacturers have responded by shipping computers with dynamic disks. Instead of having a single 90 GB drive, a new computer might have a spanned disk with 270 GB, where three 90 GB drives act as a single local disk. In this scenario, disk spanning is used to make multiple disks appear to be a single disk, and the primary way to implement this on Windows XP is to use dynamic disks. In other words, it means that you can no longer take it for granted that a new computer (or any computer, for that matter) has a basic disk. The only way to be sure of the disk type is to check Disk Management; all the views show the disk type.

As more and more computers are shipped with dynamic disks, you might wonder whether your existing computers should be using basic disks or whether they should be converted to dynamic disks. In some cases, the need for standardization might prompt your decision. For example, you might want all desktops in a particular department to have the same configuration for better manageability. In other cases, IT management might direct the change, as the conversion from basic disks to dynamic disks can be considered an upgrade process, that is, you are moving computers from an older disk type to a newer disk type. However, before you decide to move from one disk type to another, you should understand what is involved, what features are supported, and what features are not supported.

A basic disk is a physical disk that has one or more basic volumes that can be configured as primary partitions, extended partitions, and logical drives. A primary partition is a drive section that you can access directly for file storage. Each physical drive can have up to four primary partitions. You make a primary partition accessible to users by creating a file system on it. In the place of one of the four permitted primary partitions, you can create an extended partition (meaning the basic disk could have up to three primary partitions and one extended partition). Unlike primary partitions, you can't access extended partitions directly. Instead, you can configure extended partitions with one or more logical drives that are used to store files. Being able to divide extended partitions into logical drives allows you to divide a physical drive into more than four sections. For example, you could create logical drives F, G, and H in a single extended partition.

A dynamic disk is a physical disk that has one or more dynamic volumes that can be configured as simple, spanned, or striped volumes. Unlike a basic disk, a dynamic disk can have an unlimited number of volumes—any one of which can be extended or used as a system volume. Although basic disks can be used with any Windows-based operating system, dynamic disks can be used only with Windows 2000 or later and are incompatible with earlier versions of Windows. As an example, this means that if Disk 0 is a dynamic disk, you would not be able to boot that disk to Windows 98.

A key advantage of dynamic disks is the capability to combine physical disks using the spanning or striping feature of Windows XP. When you span or stripe drives, you create a single dynamic volume that extends from one disk to other disks, using all or part of each disk in the set. The difference between spanning and striping is in how data is written. With spanning, Windows XP writes data to the underlying disks that make up the volume as the disks fill. With striping, Windows XP writes a portion of the data to each of the underlying disks that make up the volume. In most cases, striping gives you faster read/write access to data because data is read from and written to multiple disks.

Caution   Technically, disk striping is RAID level 0 (RAID-0). Neither disk striping nor spanning provides fault tolerance, however, and the failure of any disk in the set causes the volume to fail.

You can't create spanned or striped drives using the basic disk type. You would need to upgrade to dynamic disks and then create volumes that use either spanning or striping as appropriate. These features and the ability to modify disks without having to restart the computer are the key capabilities that distinguish basic and dynamic disks. Other features available on a disk depend on the disk formatting, such as whether you are using FAT, FAT32, or NTFS.

Although you can use both basic and dynamic disks on the same computer, the disks that make up a volume must use the same disk type. For example, if you have striped Disk 0 and Disk 1, which were created under Microsoft Windows NT 4.0, you can use these drives under Windows XP. If you want to upgrade Disk 0 to the dynamic disk type, you must also upgrade Disk 1. Converting from basic to dynamic and vice versa is covered in the section later in this chapter entitled "Converting a Basic Disk to a Dynamic Disk and Vice Versa." It is important to note that although you can convert the disk type from basic to dynamic and preserve the data on the disk, you must delete any existing partitioning on a dynamic disk before you can convert from dynamic to basic. Deleting the partitioning destroys any data on the associated disks.

Finally, dynamic disks cannot be created on any removable-media drives (Zip, Jazz, CD-ROM, etc.) or any disk on portable computers. This means laptops, tablet PCs, and other types of portable computers can have only basic disks. Although this limits your options for portable computer disk configuration, most portable computers don't have multiple internal physical disks anyway, so spanning configurations are a moot point.

 Caution   Be careful when working with laptops. Some laptop configurations might make Disk Management think that you can convert a basic disk to a dynamic disk. This can occur on computers that do not support Advanced Power Management (APM) or Advanced Configuration and Power Interface (ACPI) and are not listed in the BIOS information file (*%SystemRoot%*\Inf\Biosinfo.inf). Although support for dynamic disks might seem to be enabled, this is an error, and trying to convert a basic disk to a dynamic disk on one of these laptops could corrupt the entire disk.

 Note   External hard drives attached via FireWire or USB can in some cases be converted to dynamic disks. Microsoft Knowledge Base article 299598, "HOW TO: Convert an IEEE 1394 Disk Drive to a Dynamic Disk Drive in Windows XP," provides the details of how this can be done. However, this article doesn't provide enough cautions. The external hard drive must only be used with a single computer. If you think you will need to move the drive to another computer in the future, you shouldn't convert it to a dynamic disk. Further, before you attempt to convert any external hard drive attached via FireWire or USB, you should back up the data. If possible, perform the conversion on an identical but nonessential drive in a development or testing environment, and then test the drive operation.

Using Basic and Dynamic Disks

That's it, essentially, when it comes to the hows and whys of basic and dynamic disks. When it comes to using basic and dynamic disks there are several related tasks you'll perform, such as initializing new disks, setting a drive as active, or changing the drive type. Before you perform these tasks, however, you should have a firm understanding of what the active, boot, and system designations mean.

Understanding the Active, Boot, and System Designations

Regardless of whether you are working with basic or dynamic disks, there are three special types of drive sections you should pay particular attention to.

- **Active** The active partition or volume is the drive section from which an x86-based computer starts. When the computer uses multiple operating systems, the active drive section must contain the startup files for the operating system you want to start and it must be a primary partition on a basic disk. If you use Microsoft Windows NT, Windows 95, Windows 98, Windows Me, or MS-DOS, the active drive section should be the primary partition on Disk 0. If you use Windows 2000 or later, the active drive section can be a primary partition on a basic disk or a simple volume on a dynamic disk. The active partition is not normally marked as such in Disk Management. In most cases, it is the primary partition or the first simple volume on Disk 0. However, if you change the default configuration, you will see an Active label.

> **Caution** With removable media disks, you might see an Active status, which shouldn't be confused with the Active label associated with an active partition. Specifically, USB and FireWire card readers that use compact flash or other types of cards are displayed as having an Active status when media is inserted and the related drive is online. It is also important to note that in some cases, a removable media drive might be listed as Disk 0. In this case, you will need to look for the active partition on the first physical hard disk according to its disk number. For example, if the computer has Disk 0, Disk 1, and Disk 2 and the first physical disk in sequence is Disk 1, the active partition is most likely to be on the first primary partition on Disk 1.

- **System** The system partition or volume contains the hardware-specific (boot-strap) files needed to load the operating system. The system partition or volume can't be part of a striped or spanned volume. The system partition is labeled as such in the Status field of Disk Management's Volume List and Graphical View.

- **Boot** The boot partition or volume contains the operating system and its support files. On most systems, system and boot are the same partition or volume. Although it seems the boot and system partitions are named backward, this convention has been used since Windows NT was first introduced and has remained unchanged. Like the active partition, the boot partition is not normally marked as such in Disk Management. In most cases, it is the primary partition or the first simple volume on Disk 0. However, if the operating system is installed on a different partition or volume, you might see a Boot label.

Installing and Initializing New Physical Disks

Windows XP makes it much easier to add new physical disks to a computer. After you install the disks following the disk manufacturer's instructions, you need to log on and start Disk Management. If the new disks have already been initialized, meaning they already have disk signatures allowing them to be read and written, they should be brought online automatically if you select Rescan Disks from the Action menu. If you are working with new disks that have not been initialized, meaning they don't have disk signatures, Disk Management will start the Initialize And Convert Disk Wizard as soon it starts up and detects the new disks.

You can use the Initialize And Convert Disk Wizard to initialize the disks by completing the following steps:

1. Click Next to exit the Welcome page. On the Select Disks To Initialize page, the disks you added are selected for initialization automatically, but if you don't want to initialize a particular disk, you can clear the related option.

2. Click Next to display the Select Disks To Convert page. This page lists any non-system or boot disks that can be converted to dynamic disks as well as the new disks. The new disks aren't selected by default. If you want to convert the disks, select them and then click Next.

3. The final page shows you the options you've selected and the actions that will be performed on each disk. If the options are correct, click Finish. The wizard then performs the designated actions. If you've elected to initialize a disk, the wizard writes a disk signature to the disk. If you've elected to convert a disk, the wizard converts the disk to a dynamic disk after writing the disk signature.

If you don't want to use the wizard, you can close it and use Disk Management instead to view and work with the disk. In the Disk List view, the disk will be marked with a red icon that has an exclamation point, and the disk's status will be listed as Not Initialized. You can then right-click the disk's icon and then select Initialize Disk from the shortcut menu. Confirm the selection (or add to the selection if more than one disk is available for initializing), and then click OK to start the initialization of the disk. Conversion to a dynamic disk would then be as discussed under "Converting a Basic Disk to a Dynamic Disk and Vice Versa."

Marking a Partition as Active

You don't normally need to change a partition's designation. If you are using only Windows XP or if you are multibooting to Windows XP and any other Windows-based operating system, you do not have to change the active partition. On an x86-based computer, the active partition typically is the primary partition or the first simple volume on Disk 0. If you install Windows XP on drive C and Windows 2000 or later on a different partition, such as drive D, you don't need to change the active partition to boot Windows XP or the other operating system either. However, if you want to boot a non-Windows operating system, such as Linux, you typically must mark its operating system partition as active and then reboot to use this operating system.

 Note   Only primary partitions can be marked as active. You can't mark logical drives as active. You can't mark volumes as active. When you upgrade a basic disk containing the active partition to a dynamic disk, this partition becomes a simple volume that's active automatically.

To mark a partition as active, complete the following steps:

1. Make sure that the necessary startup files are on the primary partition that you want to make the active partition. For Windows NT, Windows 2000, and Windows XP, these files are BOOT.INI, NTDETECT.COM, NTLDR, and BOOT-SECT.DOS. You might also need NTBOOTDD.SYS.

2. Start Disk Management by typing **diskmgmt.msc** at a command prompt.

3. Right-click the primary partition you want to mark as active, and then select
    Mark Partition As Active.

Caution If you mark a partition or volume as active, Disk Management
might not let you change the designation. As a result, if you restart the
computer, the operating system might fail to load. The only workaround
I've found is to use DiskPart to make the appropriate changes either before
rebooting or using the recovery console after a failed start.

Listing 10-1 shows a sample DiskPart session for setting the active partition. As you
can see, when you first start DiskPart it shows the DiskPart program name and the
version you are using, as well as the name of the computer. You then select the disk
you want to work with and list its partitions. In this example, you select disk 0 to
work with, list its partitions, and then select partition 1. Once you've selected a disk
and a partition on that disk, you can work with that partition. Simply typing the
ACTIVE command at this point and pressing Enter sets the partition as active.
When you are finished, you quit DiskPart using the EXIT command.

Note This example uses disk 0. On your system, disk 0 might not be the
one you want to work with. You can use the **list disk** command to list the
available disks and then use the information provided to determine which
disk you want to work with.

Listing 10-1 Using DiskPart to Set the Active Partition
```
C:>diskpart

Microsoft DiskPart version 5.1.3565

Copyright (C) 1999-2003 Microsoft Corporation.
On computer: CORPWSTN05

DISKPART> select disk 0

Disk 0 is now the selected disk.
DISKPART> list partition

  Partition ###  Type              Size     Offset
  -------------  ----------------  -------  -------
  Partition 1    Primary            16 GB    32 KB

DISKPART> select partition 1

Partition 1 is now the selected partition.

DISKPART> active

DiskPart marked the current partition as active.

DISKPART> exit
```

Converting a Basic Disk to a Dynamic Disk and Vice Versa

The easiest way to convert a basic disk to a dynamic disk and vice versa is to use Disk Management. When you upgrade to a dynamic disk, partitions are changed to volumes of the appropriate type automatically. Any volume sets created under Windows NT are created as spanned or striped volumes as appropriate. Any primary partitions will become simple volumes. Any logical drives in an extended partition will become simple volumes. Any unused (free) space in an extended partition will be marked as Unallocated. You can't change these volumes back to partitions. Instead, you must delete the volumes on the dynamic disk and then change the disk back to a basic disk. Deleting the volumes destroys all the information on the disk.

Before you convert a basic disk to a dynamic disk, there are several important considerations. You should ensure that you don't need to boot the computer to a previous version of Windows. You should also ensure that the disk has 1 MB of free space at the end of the disk. Although Disk Management reserves this free space when creating partitions and volumes, disk management tools on other operating systems might not; as a result, the conversion will fail. It is also important to point out the following restrictions:

- You can't convert drives that use sector sizes larger than 512 bytes. If the drive has large sector sizes, you'll need to reformat before upgrading.

- You can't convert removable media to dynamic disks. You can configure removable media drives only as basic drives with primary partitions.

- You can't convert a disk if the system or the boot partition is part of a spanned or striped volume. You'll need to stop the spanning or striping before you perform the conversion.

 Note You can convert disks with other types of partitions that are part of spanned or striped volumes. These volumes become dynamic volumes of the same type. However, you must convert all drives in the set together.

To convert a basic disk to a dynamic disk, complete the following steps:

1. In Disk Management, right-click a basic disk that you want to convert, either in the Disk List view or in the left pane of the Graphical view. Then select Convert To Dynamic Disk.

2. In the Convert To Dynamic Disk dialog box, select the check boxes for the disks you want to convert, as shown in Figure 10-4. If you're upgrading a striped volume originally created on Windows NT, be sure to select all the basic disks in this set. You must convert the set together. Click OK when you're ready to continue.

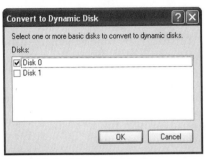

Figure 10-4   Select the basic disk to convert.

3. The Disks To Convert dialog box shows the disks you're converting. Notice the value in the Will Convert column, which should be Yes as long as the disk meets the conversion criteria, and then click Details to see the volumes on the selected drive. Click OK to close the Convert Details dialog box when you are ready to continue.

4. To begin the conversion, click Convert. Disk Management warns you that once you convert the disk, you won't be able to boot previous versions of Windows from volumes on the selected disks. Click Yes to continue.

5. Next you are warned that file systems on the disks to be converted will be dismounted, meaning they will be taken offline and be inaccessible temporarily. Click Yes to continue. If a selected drive contains the boot partition, the system partition, or a partition in use, Disk Management will need to restart the computer and you will see another prompt.

To convert a dynamic disk to a basic disk, complete the following steps:

1. Before you can change a dynamic disk back to a basic disk, you must delete all dynamic volumes on the disk. Because this destroys all the data on the volumes, you should back up the volumes and then verify the backups before doing this.

2. When you are ready to start the conversion process, start Disk Management. In Disk Management, right-click the disk you want to convert and select Convert To Basic Disk. This changes the dynamic disk to a basic disk, and you can then create new partitions and logical drives on the disk.

Working with Disks, Partitions, and Volumes

Before you can store data on a physical disk, you must prepare the disk for use by partitioning its space, assigning a drive designator, and formatting the resulting partitions or volumes. Although basic disks can have up to four primary partitions—or three primary partitions and one extended partition, with one or more logical drives in the extended partition—dynamic disks can have an unlimited number of volumes.

After you partition a disk, you must assign each partition or volume a drive designator. The drive designator can be a letter or a path. You use drive letters to access file systems in various partitions on physical drives. Generally speaking, the drive letters A through Z are available. However, the drive letter A is usually assigned to the system's floppy drive. If the system has a second floppy drive or other removable media drive, such as a Zip drive, the letter B is usually assigned to it (or unassigned otherwise). The drive letter C is usually assigned to the first partition or volume created on Disk 0. The drive letter D is usually assigned to the first CD-ROM or DVD-ROM. Thus, on most systems, the drive letters E through Z are available. If you need additional volumes, you can create them using drive paths.

A drive path is set as a folder location on an existing local disk. For example, you could mount additional drives as C:\Docs1, C:\Docs2, and C:\Docs3. Drive paths can be used with basic and dynamic disks. The only restriction for drive paths is that you mount them on empty folders that are on NTFS-formatted local disks.

Formatting a partition or a volume sets the file system that will be used and creates the necessary file structures. Generally speaking, you can format a partition or a volume as FAT, FAT32, or NTFS. There are restrictions and requirements for the use of each, however.

FAT is a 16-bit file system designed to be used with volume sizes of up to 4 GB and is also referred to as FAT16. FAT uses a boot sector that stores information about the disk type, the starting and ending sectors, and the active partition. FAT gets its name from the file allocation table it uses to track the cluster locations of files and folders. There is a primary table and a duplicate table. The duplicate is used to restore the primary table if it becomes corrupted. FAT also has the capability to mark clusters (sections of disk containing data) as unused, in use, bad, or reserved. This helps to make FAT a fairly robust file system. FAT is best with volumes of 2 GB or less and has a maximum file size of 2 GB as well. FAT can be used with floppy disks and removable disks.

FAT32 is a 32-bit version of FAT16, with some additional features and capabilities. Like FAT16, FAT32 uses a primary and a duplicate file allocation table. FAT32 can also mark clusters as unused, in use, bad, or reserved. FAT32 can also be used with floppy disks and removable disks. Unlike FAT16, FAT32 has a minimum volume size of 33 MB, a maximum volume size of 32 GB, and a maximum file size of 4 GB. This means FAT32 can be used with considerably larger partitions and volumes than FAT16.

 Note It is important to note that the 4-GB maximum file size limitation for FAT32 is specific to Windows 2000 and later versions of the Windows operating system. Using FAT32, some earlier versions of Windows can create volumes of larger size, as can other operating systems.

NTFS is very different from FAT16 and FAT32. Instead of using a file allocation table, NTFS uses a relational database to store information about files and folders. This database is called the Master File Table (MFT), and it stores a record of each file and folder on a volume as well as additional information that helps to maintain the volume. Overall, the MFT makes NTFS much more reliable and recoverable than either FAT16 or FAT32. This means that NTFS can recover from disk errors more readily than FAT16 and FAT32, and that NTFS generally has fewer disk problems.

NTFS has a maximum volume size of 2 TB (terabytes, or trillion bytes) or higher (dependent on disk configuration) and a maximum file size that is limited only by the volume size. Although you can't use NTFS with floppy disks, you can use NTFS with removable disks. Additionally, unlike FAT16 and FAT32, which have limited security features (namely that you can mark a file only as read-only, hidden, or system), NTFS has very advanced security (meaning that you can set very specific file and folder access by using permissions). NTFS supports many other advanced features as well, including compression, encryption, and disk quotas.

Note   Several versions of NTFS have been implemented. NTFS 4 was first available with Windows NT. NTFS 5 was first available with Windows 2000. NTFS 5.1 was first available with Windows XP. Because most current computers have NTFS 5 or later, I focus on NTFS 5 and later in this book. It is also worth noting that if you upgrade a system with a version older than the current version, you are given the opportunity to convert existing NTFS volumes to the latest version during installation. In most cases, you want to do this because this ensures support for the latest NTFS features.

Partitioning Disks and Preparing Them for Use

Disk Management is the primary tool that you'll use to partition disks and prepare them for use. Using Disk Management, you can partition, assign drive designators to, and format both partitions and volumes. Disk Management's command-line counterparts include DiskPart for partitioning and drive designator assignment and Format for formatting.

Creating Partitions and Logical Drives on Basic Disks

In Disk Management you create partitions and logical drives by completing the following steps:

1. In Disk Management's Graphical View, right-click an unallocated or free area, and then choose New Partition. This starts the New Partition Wizard. Read the Welcome page, and then click Next.

2. On the Select Partition Type page, choose a partition type as shown in Figure 10-5, and then click Next. The available options are used as follows:

    ❏ Select Primary Partition to create a primary partition. Each physical drive can have up to four primary partitions. A primary partition can fill an entire disk or be sized as appropriate for the workstation or server you're configuring.

    ❏ Select Extended Partition to create an extended partition. Each physical drive can have one extended partition. This extended partition can contain one or more logical drives, which are simply sections of the partition with their own file system.

    ❏ Select Logical Drive if you want to create a logical drive within an existing extended partition. If a drive already contains an extended partition, the Extended Partition option won't be available, but this option will be available instead. This occurs because each basic disk can have only one extended partition.

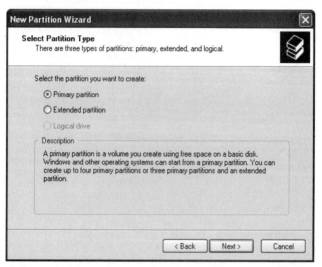

Figure 10-5   Choose the type of partition.

3. You should see the Specify Partition Size page, shown in Figure 10-6. This page specifies the minimum and maximum size for the partition in megabytes and lets you size the partition within these limits. Size the partition using the Partition Size In MB field, and then click Next.

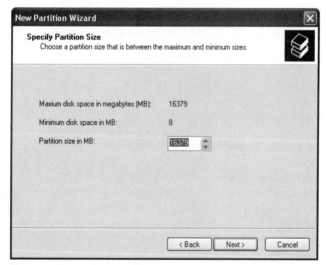

Figure 10-6   Set the size of the partition.

4. If you are creating a primary partition or logical drive, specify whether you want to assign a drive letter or path. These options are used as follows:

   □ **Assign The Following Drive Letter**   Choose this option to assign a drive letter, and then select an available drive letter in the selection list provided, shown in Figure 10-7. By default, Windows XP selects the lowest available drive letter and excludes reserved drive letters as well as those assigned to local disks or network drives.

   □ **Mount In The Following Empty NTFS Folder**   Choose this option to mount the partition in an empty NTFS folder. You must then type the path to an existing folder or click Browse to search for or create a folder to use.

   □ **Do Not Assign**   Choose this option if you want to create the partition without assigning a drive letter or path. If you later want the partition to be available for storage, you can assign a drive letter or path at that time.

Note   Partitions don't have to be assigned a drive letter or a path. A partition with no designators is considered to be unmounted and is for the most part unusable. An unmounted partition can be mounted by assigning a drive letter or a path at a later date. See "Assigning, Changing, or Removing Drive Letters and Paths" later in this chapter.

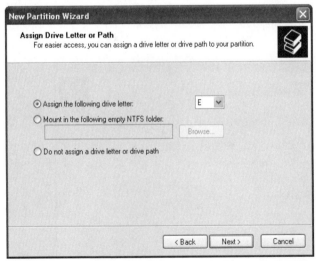

Figure 10-7   Assign the drive designator or choose to wait until later.

5. If you are creating a primary partition or logical drive, determine whether the partition should be formatted using the Format Partition page, shown in Figure 10-8. If you want to format the partition, choose Format This Partition With The Following Settings and then configure the following options:

   □ **File System**   Sets the file system type as FAT, FAT32, or NTFS. NTFS is selected by default in most cases. If you create a file system as FAT or FAT32, you can later convert it to NTFS by using the Convert utility. You can't, however, convert NTFS partitions to FAT or FAT32.

❏ **Allocation Unit Size** Sets the cluster size for the file system. This is the basic unit in which disk space is allocated. The default allocation unit size is based on the size of the volume and, by default, is set dynamically prior to formatting. To override this feature, you can set the allocation unit size to a specific value. If you use lots of small files, you might want to use a smaller cluster size, such as 512 or 1024 bytes. With these settings, small files use less disk space.

❏ **Volume Label** Sets a text label for the partition. This label is the partition's volume name and by default is set to New Volume. You can change the volume label at any time by right-clicking the volume in Windows Explorer, choosing Properties, and typing a new value in the Label field provided on the General tab.

❏ **Perform A Quick Format** Tells Windows XP to format without checking the partition for errors. With large partitions, this option can save you a few minutes. However, it's usually better to check for errors, which allows Disk Management to mark bad sectors on the disk and lock them out.

❏ **Enable File And Folder Compression** Turns on compression for the disk. Built-in compression is available only for NTFS. Under NTFS, compression is transparent to users and compressed files can be accessed just like regular files. If you select this option, files and directories on this drive are compressed automatically. For more information on compressing drives, files, and directories, see the section entitled "Compressing Drives and Data" in Chapter 16, "Optimizing Windows XP Professional."

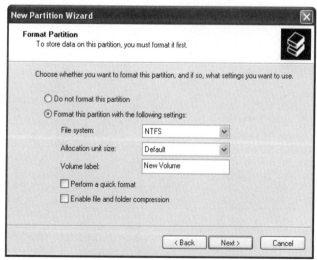

Figure 10-8 Set the formatting options for the partition.

6. Click Next, confirm your options, and then click Finish.

Creating Simple, Spanned, and Striped Volumes on Dynamic Disks

In Disk Management you create simple volumes on dynamic disks by completing the following steps:

1. In Disk Management's Graphical View, right-click an unallocated area, and then choose New Volume. This starts the New Volume Wizard. Read the Welcome page, and then click Next.

2. On the Select Volume Type page, choose a volume type as shown in Figure 10-9, and then click Next. The available options are used as follows:

   ❑ Select Simple to create a volume that uses free space on a single dynamic disk. If you later need more space, you can extend the volume by adding free space on the same disk or another disk.

   ❑ Select Spanned to create a volume that uses free space on multiple dynamic disks. If you have unallocated space on two or more dynamic disks, you can combine this space to create a spanned volume. A spanned volume has no fault tolerance and has average read/write performance. Files are written first to one disk and then the next as space is used. If any of the disks fail, the entire volume will fail as well, and all data will be lost.

   ❑ Select Striped to create a volume that uses free space on multiple disks and stripes the data as it is written. Striping gives you faster read/write access to data because data is read from and written to multiple disks. For example, with a three-disk striped volume, data from a file may be written to Disk 1, then to Disk 2, and then to Disk 3. Like a spanned volume, a striped volume has no fault tolerance, so if any of the disks fail, the entire volume will fail as well, and all data will be lost.

   Note If you have only one dynamic disk available, Simple will be your only option. If you have multiple dynamic disks, you will also be able to choose Spanned or Striped. You'll find more information on spanned and striped disks in the section of this chapter entitled "Extending Volumes on Dynamic Disks."

   Caution Simple and spanned volumes can be extended to increase their volume size. Striped volumes, however, cannot be extended. So when you create a striped volume, you should be very certain that the volume size is what you want to use. Otherwise, you might have to delete and then re-create the striped volume.

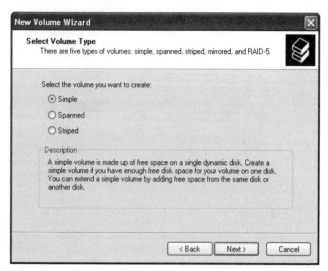

Figure 10-9   Select the volume type.

3. You should see the Select Disks page, shown in Figure 10-10. Use this page to select dynamic disks that are to be a part of the volume and to size the volume segments on those disks.

4. Available dynamic disks are shown in the Available list box. Select a disk in this list box, and then click Add to add the disk to the Selected list box. If you make a mistake, you can remove disks from the Selected list box by selecting the disk and then clicking Remove.

5. Specify the space that you want to use on each disk by selecting each disk in the Selected list box and then using the Select The Amount Of Space In MB list box to specify the amount of space to use on the selected disk. Keep in mind that the Maximum field shows you the largest area of free space available on the selected disk and the Total Volume Size field shows you the total disk space currently allocated to the volume. Click Next.

 Tip   There's a quick way to use the same amount of space on all selected disks. To do this, highlight each disk by pressing Shift and then clicking the first disk and the last disk in the Selected list box. Now when you set the amount of space to use, you'll set the amount for all selected disks.

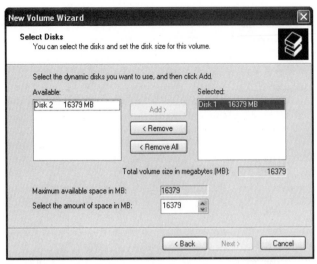

Figure 10-10 Specify the amount of space to use for each volume.

6. On the Assign Drive Letter Or Path page, specify whether you want to assign a drive letter or path and then click Next. The available options are used as follows:

❑ **Assign The Following Drive Letter** Choose this option to assign a drive letter, and then select an available drive letter in the selection list provided. By default, Windows XP selects the lowest available driver letter and excludes reserved drive letters as well as those assigned to local disks or network drives.

❑ **Mount In The Following Empty NTFS Folder** Choose this option to mount the partition in an empty NTFS folder. You must then type the path to an existing folder or click Browse to search for or create a folder to use.

❑ **Do Not Assign** Choose this option if you want to create the partition without assigning a drive letter or path. If you later want the partition to be available for storage, you can assign a drive letter or path at that time.

Note Partitions don't have to be assigned a drive letter or a path. A partition with no designators is considered to be unmounted and is for the most part unusable. An unmounted partition can be mounted by assigning a drive letter or a path at a later date. See "Assigning, Changing, or Removing Drive Letters and Paths" later in this chapter.

7. On the Format Volume page, set the formatting for the volume, and then click Next. Although simple volumes can be formatted using FAT, FAT32, or NTFS as appropriate for their sizes, spanned and striped volumes can be formatted only using NTFS. If you want to format the partition, choose Format This Par-

tition With The Following Settings, and then configure the following options:

- ❏ **File System**   Sets the file system type as FAT, FAT32, or NTFS. NTFS is selected by default in most cases. If you create a file system as FAT or FAT32, you can later convert it to NTFS by using the Convert utility. You can't, however, convert NTFS partitions to FAT or FAT32.

- ❏ **Allocation Unit Size**   Sets the cluster size for the file system. This is the basic unit in which disk space is allocated. The default allocation unit size is based on the size of the volume and, by default, is set dynamically prior to formatting. To override this feature, you can set the allocation unit size to a specific value. If you use lots of small files, you might want to use a smaller cluster size, such as 512 or 1024 bytes. With these settings, small files use less disk space.

- ❏ **Volume Label**   Sets a text label for the partition. This label is the partition's volume name and by default is set to New Volume. You can change the volume label at any time by right-clicking the volume in Windows Explorer, choosing Properties, and typing a new value in the Label field provided on the General tab.

- ❏ **Perform A Quick Format**   Tells Windows XP to format without checking the partition for errors. With large partitions, this option can save you a few minutes. However, it's usually better to check for errors, which allows Disk Management to mark bad sectors on the disk and lock them out.

- ❏ **Enable File And Folder Compression**   Turns on compression for the disk. Built-in compression is available only for NTFS. Under NTFS, compression is transparent to users and compressed files can be accessed just like regular files. If you select this option, files and directories on this drive are compressed automatically. For more information on compressing drives, files, and directories, see the section entitled "Compressing Drives and Data" in Chapter 16. Click Next, confirm your options, and then click Finish.

Extending Volumes on Dynamic Disks

With dynamic disks, you can extend any simple or spanned volume to increase its volume size. In extending a volume, you convert areas of unallocated space and add them to the existing simple or spanned volume. The space can come from any available dynamic disk and not only those on which the volume was originally created. This means you can combine areas of free space on multiple dynamic disks and use those areas to increase the size of an existing volume.

 Caution   Before you try to extend a volume, there are several limitations you should know about. First, simple and spanned volumes can be extended only if they are formatted and the file system is NTFS. You can't extend striped volumes. You can't extend volumes that aren't formatted or that are formatted with FAT or FAT32. Additionally, you can't extend a system or boot volume, regardless of its configuration.

You can extend a simple volume or a spanned volume by completing the following steps:

1. In Disk Management, right-click the volume that you want to extend and then select Extend Volume. This option is available only if the volume meets the previously discussed criteria and there is free space available on one or more of the system's dynamic disks.

2. In the Extend Volume Wizard, click Next to exit the Welcome page.

3. On the Select Disks page, shown previously in Figure 10-10, select the disk or disks from which you want to allocate free space. Any disks currently being used by the volume will automatically be selected. By default, all remaining free space on those disks will be selected for use.

4. Specify the additional space that you want to use on each disk by selecting each disk in the Selected list box and then using the Select The Amount Of Space In MB list box to specify the amount of unallocated space to use on the selected disk. For example, if you wanted to use 1000 additional megabytes of space on Disk 1, you would select Disk 1 and then type **1000** in the Select The Amount Of Space In MB list box. The Total Volume Size field shows you the total disk space currently allocated to the volume plus the free space you've just specified.

5. Click Next, confirm your options, and then click Finish.

Formatting Partitions and Volumes

When you format a partition or a volume, you create a file system that can be used to store data and permanently deletes any existing data in the associate section of the physical disk. This is a high-level formatting that creates the file system structure rather than a low-level formatting that initializes a drive for use. To format a partition or a volume, right-click it in Disk Management, and then choose Format. This opens the Format dialog box shown in Figure 10-11. If you compare Figure 10-8 and Figure 10-11, you'll see that the available fields are essentially the same.

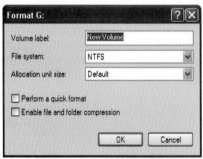

Figure 10-11 Use the Format dialog box to format a partition or a volume by specifying its file system type and volume label.

After you've selected the appropriate options, click OK to proceed. Because formatting a partition destroys any existing data, Disk Management gives you one last chance to abort the procedure. Click OK to start formatting the partition. Disk Management then changes the status of the drive to reflect the formatting and, unless you are using the Perform A Quick Format option, the percentage of completion. When formatting is complete, the drive status will change to reflect this.

Assigning, Changing, or Removing Drive Letters and Paths

Each primary partition, logical drive, or volume on a computer can be assigned one driver letter and one or more drive paths, provided the drive paths are mounted on empty NTFS folders. Once assigned, the drive letter or path remains constant every time you start the computer. At any time, you can change the drive letter or path assignment except on partitions or volumes that are designated as system or boot. You can also remove a drive letter or path assignment except on partitions or volumes that are designated as system or boot.

 Note   The drive letter or path assignment for the system or boot volume can be changed only by editing the Registry. The procedure for Windows 2000 is described in Microsoft Knowledge Base article 223188. The procedure for Windows XP is the same. However, it is important to be aware that if anything goes wrong during this procedure, you will likely be unable to boot the system and might have to recover the computer from backups.

To manage a partition's or a volume's drive letters or paths, right-click the partition or volume you want to configure in Disk Management, and then choose Change Drive Letter And Paths. This opens the dialog box shown in Figure 10-12. You can now perform the following actions:

- **Add a drive path**   Click Add, select Mount In The Following Empty NTFS Folder, and then type the path to an existing folder, or click Browse to search for or create a folder.
- **Remove a drive path**   Select the drive path to remove, click Remove, and then click Yes.
- **Assign a drive letter**   Click Add, select Assign The Following Drive Letter, and then choose an available letter to assign to the drive.
- **Change the drive letter**   Select the current drive letter, and then click Change. Select Assign The Following Drive Letter, and then choose a different letter to assign to the drive.
- **Remove a drive letter**   Select the current drive letter, click Remove, and then click Yes.

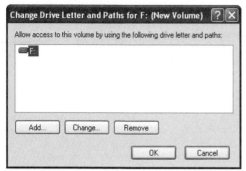

Figure 10-12   Use this dialog box to change or remove the drive letter and path assignment.

Note   If you try to change the letter of a drive that's in use, Windows XP displays a warning. You'll need to exit programs that are using the drive and try again or allow Disk Management to force the change by clicking Yes when prompted.

Real World   If the drive letter you want to use isn't available, it means it is in use or reserved for another purpose. You can clear up this problem in some cases by swapping drive letters. For example, if drive letter D is being used by the CD-ROM and drive letter E is a local disk, you might want to swap these letters so that D is used by the local disk and E is used by the CD-ROM. To do this, you must remove the drive letter assigned to the CD-ROM and free drive letter D for use. Next change the driver letter assignment for the local disk so that it is set to D. This frees up E, which you can assign to the CD-ROM. Keep in mind that changing the letter of a drive can have unintended consequences. For example, the path to an application might be stored in the Registry with the drive letter. This path would no longer be valid if you change the drive letter. Shortcuts to files or programs on the drive would be affected by the drive letter change as well and would need to be modified or re-created.

Assigning, Changing, or Deleting a Volume Label

A volume label is a text descriptor for a partition or a volume. The volume label is displayed when the drive is accessed in various Windows XP utilities, such as Windows Explorer and My Computer, and is designed to provide additional descriptive information about the contents of a drive.

Note   With FAT and FAT32, the volume label can be up to 11 characters in length and can include spaces. With NTFS, the volume label can be up to 32 characters in length. Additionally, although FAT and FAT32 don't allow you to use some special characters, including * / \ [ ] : ; | = , . + " ? < >, NTFS does allow you to use these special characters.

You can assign, change, or delete a volume label using either Disk Management or Windows Explorer. In Disk Management you can assign, change, or delete a label by completing the following steps:

1. Right-click the partition or volume you want to work with, and then choose Properties.

2. On the General tab of the Properties dialog box, use the Label field to type a new label or to delete the existing label. Click OK.

In Windows Explorer you can assign, change, or delete a label by completing these steps:

1. Right-click the drive icon, and then choose Properties. If the drive icon isn't available, select the Folders button on the toolbar.

2. On the General tab of the Properties dialog box, use the Label field to type a new label for the volume or to delete the existing label. Click OK.

Deleting Partitions, Volumes, and Logical Drives

To change the configuration of an existing drive that's fully allocated, you might need to delete existing partitions, logical drives, or volumes. Because this deletion is irreversible, you should always back up and verify any important files and folders before deleting a partition, a logical drive, or a volume. If a computer has spanned or striped volumes, be careful when deleting volumes. Deleting any volume in a set erases the entire volume set, meaning the entire volume and all its data will be lost.

 Caution   Deleting a partition, a logical drive, or a volume is a drastic step that cannot be reversed. It removes the associated file system, and all data in the file system is lost.

 Note   To protect the integrity of the system, you can't delete the system or boot partition. However, Windows XP will let you delete the active partition or volume if it is not designated as boot or system. As discussed previously, the active partition has the files needed to start the operating system, which can include BOOT.INI, NTDETECT.COM, NTLDR, and BOOTSECT.DOS. Always check to ensure the partition or volume that you are deleting doesn't contain these files.

You can delete a primary partition, a volume, or a logical drive by completing the following steps:

1. In Disk Management, right-click the partition, volume, or drive you want to delete, and then choose Explore. Using Windows Explorer, move all the data to another volume or verify an existing backup to ensure the data was properly saved.

2. In Disk Management, right-click the partition, volume, or drive again and select Delete Partition, Delete Volume, or Delete Logical Drive, as appropriate.

3. Confirm that you want to delete the selected item by clicking Yes.

Deleting an extended partition is a bit different from deleting a primary partition or a logical drive. To delete an extended partition, you must first delete all the logical drives on the partition by following the steps outlined in the preceding list. You will then be able to select the extended partition area itself and delete it.

Converting a Volume to NTFS

Windows XP provides a command-line utility for converting FAT or FAT32 volumes to NTFS. This utility, named Convert (CONVERT.EXE), is located in the *%System-Root%*\System32 folder. When you convert a volume using this tool, the file and directory structure is preserved and no data is lost.

Caution   Windows XP doesn't provide a utility for converting NTFS to FAT or FAT32. The only way to go from NTFS to FAT or FAT32 is to delete the partition by following the steps outlined in the previous section and then to re-create the partition as a FAT or FAT32 volume.

If you want to convert a drive, use the following syntax at a command prompt:

```
convert volume /FS:NTFS
```

where volume is the drive letter followed by a colon (:), a drive path, or a volume name. For example, if you wanted to convert drive D to NTFS, you would use the following command:

```
convert D: /FS:NTFS
```

The complete syntax for the CONVERT command is:

```
CONVERT volume /FS:NTFS [/V] [/X] [/CvtArea:filename] [/NoSecurity]
```

These options and switches are used as follows:

- **volume**   Sets the volume to work with and must include the full drive designator (the drive letter followed by colon).
- **/FS:NTFS**   Converts the designated volume to NTFS. This is the only file system option.
- **/V**   Sets verbose mode, which provides more detail in the output.
- **/X**   Forces the volume to dismount before the conversion (if necessary).
- **/CvtArea:***filename*   Specifies a contiguous file in the root directory to be the placeholder for the NTFS system files stored on the MFT. If you omit a file name, CONVERT uses the default configuration and reserves 12.5 percent of the partition or volume size. This helps to prevent fragmentation of the MFT.
- **/NoSecurity**   Sets the NTFS security settings on all files and folders so that the group Everyone can access them. This effectively makes the entire file system accessible to anyone that can access the system locally or remotely.

The CONVERT command checks to see if the drive has enough free space to perform the conversion before starting. Generally, CONVERT needs a block of free space that's roughly equal to 25 percent of the total space used on the drive. For example, if the drive stores 100 MB of data, CONVERT needs about 25 MB of free space. If there isn't enough free space, CONVERT aborts and tells you that you need to free up some space. On the other hand, if there is enough free space, CONVERT initiates the conversion. Be patient. The conversion process takes several minutes (longer for large drives). Don't access files or applications on the drive while the conversion is in progress.

Note   Before you use the Convert utility, double-check to see if the partition is being used as the active boot partition or a system partition containing the operating system. With Intel x86 systems, you can convert the active boot partition to NTFS. Doing so requires that the system gain exclusive access to this partition, which can be obtained only during startup. Thus, if you try to convert the active boot partition to NTFS, Windows XP displays a prompt asking if you want to schedule the drive to be converted the next time the system starts. If you click Yes, you can restart the system to begin the conversion process. Often it'll take several restarts of a system to completely convert the active boot partition. Don't panic. Let the system proceed with the conversion.

Real World   You can improve performance on the volume using the /CvtArea option so that space for the MFT is reserved. This option helps to prevent fragmentation of the MFT. How? Over time, the MFT might grow larger than the space allocated to it. The operating system must then expand the MFT into other areas of the disk. Although the Windows XP Disk Defragmenter utility can defragment the MFT, it cannot move the first section of the MFT, and it is very unlikely there will be space after the MFT because this will be filled by file data.

To help prevent fragmentation in some cases, you might want to reserve more space than the default (12.5 percent of the partition or volume size). For example, you might want to increase the MFT size if the volume will have many small or average-sized files rather than a few large files. To specify the amount of space to reserve, you can use FSUtil to create a placeholder file equal in size to that of the MFT you want to create. You can then convert the volume to NTFS and specify the name of the placeholder file to use with the /CvtArea option.

In this example, you use FSUtil to create a 1.5 GB (1,500,000,000 bytes) placeholder file named TEMP.TXT:

fsutil file createnew c:\temp.txt 1500000000
To use this placeholder file for the MFT when converting drive C to NTFS, you would then type the command:

convert c: /fs:ntfs /cvtarea:temp.txt
Notice that the placeholder file is created on the partition or volume that is being converted. During the conversion process, the file will be overwritten with NTFS metadata and any unused space in the file will be reserved for future use by the MFT.

Recovering a Failed Simple, Spanned, or Striped Disk

Simple disks are fairly easy to troubleshoot and recover because there is only one disk involved. Spanned or striped disks, on the other hand, might have multiple disks, and the failure of any one disk makes the entire volume unusable. The drive status might show it is Missing, Failed, Online (Errors), Offline, or Unreadable.

You might see the Missing (and sometimes Offline) status if drives have been disconnected or powered off. If the drives are part of an external storage device, check the storage device to ensure it is connected properly and has power. Reconnecting the storage device or turning on the power should make it so the drives can be accessed. You then must start Disk Management and rescan the missing drive. Right-click the missing drive, and choose Rescan Disks. When Disk Management finishes, right-click the drive, and then choose Reactivate.

You might see the Failed, Online (Errors), and Unreadable statuses if a drive has input/output (I/O) problems. As before, try rescanning the drive, and then try to reactivate the drive. If the drive doesn't come back to the Healthy state, you might need to replace it.

Tip   Sometimes you might need to reboot the computer to get a disk back online. If this still doesn't resolve the problem, check for problems with the drive, its controller, and the cables. Also, make sure that the drive has power and is connected properly.

Moving a Dynamic Disk to a New System

An important advantage of dynamic disks over basic disks is that you can easily move them from one computer to another. For example, if after setting up a computer, you decide that you don't really need an additional hard disk, you could move it to another computer where it could be better used. Before you move disks, you should complete the following steps:

1. Access Disk Management on the computer where the dynamic disks are currently installed and check their status. The status should be Healthy. If it isn't, you should fix any problems before moving the disks.

2. Check the hard disk subsystems on the original computer and the computer to which you want to transfer the disk. Both computers should have identical hard disk subsystems. If they don't, the Plug and Play ID on the system disk from the original computer won't match what the destination computer is expecting. As a result, the destination computer won't be able to load the right drivers and boot might fail.

3. Check to see whether any dynamic disks that you want to move are part of a spanned, extended, or striped set. If they are, you should make a note of which disks are part of which set and plan on moving all disks in a set together. If you are moving only part of a disk set, you should be aware of the consequences. For spanned, extended, or striped volumes, moving only part of the set will make the related volumes unusable on the current computer and on the computer to which you are planning to move the disks.

When you are ready to move the disks, complete the following tasks:

1. On the original computer, start Computer Management. Then, in the left pane, select Device Manager. In the Device List, expand Disk Drives. This shows a list of all the physical disk drives on the computer. Right-click each disk that you want to move, and then select Uninstall. If you are unsure which disks to uninstall, right-click each disk and select Properties. In the Properties dialog box, select the Volumes tab, and then choose Populate. This shows you the volumes on the selected disk.

2. Next, select the Disk Management node in Computer Management on the original computer. Right-click each disk that you want to move, and then select Remove Disk.

3. Once you perform these procedures, you can move the dynamic disks. If the disks are hot swappable and this feature is supported on both computers, remove the disks from the original computer and then install them on the destination computer. Otherwise, turn off both computers, remove the drives from the original computer, and then install them on the destination computer. When you're finished, restart the computers.

4. On the destination computer, access Disk Management, and then select Rescan Disks from the Action menu. When Disk Management finishes scanning the disks, right-click any disk marked Foreign, and click Import. You should now be able to access the disks and their volumes on the destination computer.

 Note The volumes on the dynamic disks should retain the drive letters that they had on the original computer. If a drive letter is already used on the destination computer, a volume receives the next available drive letter. If a dynamic volume previously did not have a drive letter, it does not receive a drive letter when moved to another computer. Additionally, if automounting is disabled, the volumes aren't automatically mounted and you must manually mount volumes and assign drive letters.

Troubleshooting Common Disk Problems

Using Disk Management, you can determine the status of disks and the volumes they contain. Disk status is displayed in Graphical View below the physical disk number and in the Disk List view in the Status field. Volume status is displayed as part of the volume information in Graphical View and in the Status column in Volume List view.

Table 10-1 lists status message you might see for disks. You'll also find a diagnosis and suggested corrective action in the Resolution column.

Table 10-1 Understanding and Resolving Disk Status Issues

Status	Description	Resolution
Online	The normal disk status. It means the disk is accessible and doesn't have problems. Both dynamic disks and basic disks display this status.	The drive doesn't have any known problems. You don't need to take any corrective action.
Online (Errors)	I/O errors have been detected on a dynamic disk.	You can try to correct temporary errors by right-clicking the disk and choosing Reactivate Disk. If this doesn't work, the disk might have physical damage or you might need to run a thorough CHKDSK.
Offline	The disk isn't accessible and might be corrupted or temporarily unavailable. If the disk name changes to Missing, the disk can no longer be located or identified on the system.	Check for problems with the drive, its controller, and cables. Make sure that the drive has power and is connected properly. Use the REACTIVATE DISK command to bring the disk back online (if possible).
Foreign	The disk has been moved to your computer but hasn't been imported for use. A failed drive brought back online might sometimes be listed as Foreign.	Right-click the disk, and choose Import Foreign Disks to add the disk to the system.
Unreadable	The disk isn't accessible currently, which can occur when rescanning disks. Both dynamic and basic disks display this status.	With FireWire/USB card readers, you might see this status if the card is unformatted or improperly formatted. You might also see this status after the card is removed from the reader. Otherwise, if the drives aren't being scanned, the drive might be corrupted or have I/O errors. Right-click the disk, and choose Rescan Disk (on the Action menu) to try to correct the problem. You might also want to reboot the system.
Unrecognized	The disk is of an unknown type and can't be used on the system. A drive from a non-Windows system might display this status.	If the disk is from another operating system, don't do anything. You can't use the drive on the computer, so try a different drive.
Not Initialized	The disk doesn't have a valid signature. A drive from a non-Windows system might display this status.	If the disk is from another operating system, don't do anything. You can't use the drive on the computer, so try a different drive. To prepare the disk for use on Windows XP, right-click the disk and choose Initialize Disk.
No Media	No media has been inserted into the CD-ROM or removable drive, or the media has been removed. Only CD-ROM and removable disk types display this status.	Insert a CD-ROM, a floppy disk, or a removable disk to bring the disk online. With FireWire/USB card readers, this status is usually but not always displayed when the card is removed.

Table 10-2 lists status messages you might see for volumes. You'll also find a diagnosis and suggested corrective action in the Resolution column.

Table 10-2 Understanding and Resolving Volume Status Issues

Status	Description	Resolution
Failed	An error disk status. The disk is inaccessible or damaged.	Ensure that the related dynamic disk is online, and, as necessary, right-click the disk and choose Reactivate Disk. Right-click the volume and choose Reactivate Volume. For a basic disk, you might need to check the disk for a faulty connection.
Formatting	A temporary status that indicates the volume is being formatted.	The progress of the formatting is indicated as the percent complete, unless the Perform A Quick Format option was chosen.
Healthy	The normal volume status.	The volume doesn't have any known problems. You don't need to take any corrective action.
Healthy (At Risk)	Windows had problems reading from or writing to the physical disk on which the dynamic volume is located. This status appears anytime Windows encounters errors.	Right-click the disk and choose Reactivate Disk. If the disk continues to have this status or has this status periodically, the disk might be failing and you should back up all data on the disk.
Healthy (Unknown Partition)	Windows does not recognize the partition. This can occur because the partition is from a different operating system or is a manufacturer-created partition used to store system files.	No corrective action is necessary.
Initializing	A temporary status that indicates disk is being initialized.	The drive status should change after a few seconds.
Unknown	The volume cannot be accessed. It might have a corrupted boot sector.	The volume might have a boot sector virus. Check it with an up-to-date antivirus program. If no virus is found, boot from the Windows XP CD-ROM and use the Recovery Console FIXMBR command to fix the master boot record.

Chapter 11

Managing File Security and Sharing

In this chapter:

File Security and Sharing Options. 265

Controlling Access to Files and Folders with NTFS Permissions 267

Sharing Folders over the Network 282

Whether you are using Microsoft Windows XP in a domain or a workgroup, few areas of the operating system are more important than file security and sharing. File security and file sharing are so interconnected that it is hard to talk about one without talking about the other. File security protects important data on your systems by restricting access as appropriate. File sharing allows you to share data so that it can be accessed over the network by other users.

File Security and Sharing Options

For all computers running Windows XP Professional, two factors control your file security and sharing options: disk format and account settings. The format of the local disk that you are working with determines the file security options that are available. Local disks can be formatted as FAT (FAT16/FAT32) or NTFS. The security options on FAT and NTFS volumes differ greatly.

- **FAT**   With FAT, you have very limited control over file access. Files can be marked only as read-only, hidden, or system. Although these flags can be set on files and folders, anyone with access to the FAT volume can override or change these settings. This means there are no safeguards for file access or deletion. Any user can access or delete any file without restriction.

- **NTFS**   With NTFS, you can control access to files and folders by assigning permissions that specifically allow or deny access. Permissions can be set for individual users and for groups of users. This gives you very granular control over file and folder access. For example, you could specify that users in the Sales Managers group have full control over a folder and its files, but users in the Sales Reps group have no access to the folder whatsoever.

The account settings on a computer determine the way files can be shared. Windows XP supports two very different file-sharing models.

- **Simple File Sharing**   Designed primarily for the home-user market, this file-sharing model allows you to share folders with everyone in a workgroup without needing to set specific file and folder access permissions for users and groups. Simple file sharing is enabled by default in a workgroup environment and is not available in a domain environment. When enabled, anyone with access to the network or the computer can access the shared data on a computer using a folder called Shared Documents. The advantage of the Shared Documents folder is that anything placed in this folder is shared automatically. The Guest account is used for all network logons, and you can't control access permissions for different users.

     Security   With simple file sharing, all the files in a user's profile, including the My Documents folder, Desktop, and Favorites, are available to anyone who logs on locally and has an account with administrator privileges (rather than a limited account). You access this locally shared data using My Computer. You can override the default public setting for user profile data by making a folder private. Your private folders, and the related files and subfolders, are then only accessible to you. To make a folder private, right-click it, choose Sharing And Security on the shortcut menu, and then choose Make This Folder Private.

- **Standard File Sharing**   This file sharing allows you to configure very specific file-sharing permissions. Remote users are granted access to a shared folder only if they are given specific permission to do so or if they are a member of a group that has access. When you share a folder, no one is automatically allowed access to the shared data. You must set specific sharing and file permissions to enable access. The top-level share permissions set the maximum level of access for users who access the shared data over the network. Permissions set on individual files and folders serve to further control access to data.

     Security   With standard file sharing, local users don't have automatic access to any data stored on a computer. Local access to files and folders is fully controlled by the security settings on the local disk. If a local disk is formatted with FAT, you can use the read-only, system, or hidden flags to help protect files and folders, but you cannot restrict access. If a local disk is formatted with NTFS, you can carefully control access by allowing or denying access to individual users and groups of users.

Although it is tempting to use simple file sharing, most organizations—even small businesses—should use standard file sharing. Simply put, standard file sharing offers more security, better protection, and, rather than opening the floodgates to your organization's data, closes the doors and battens down the hatches. Increasing security is essential to protecting one of the most valuable assets of any organization—its data.

In many ways, file security and standard file-sharing settings are like wrappers around your data. File security settings, the first wrapper, protect your data with regard to local access. If a user logs on to a system locally, file security settings can allow or deny access to files and folders. File-sharing settings, the second wrapper, are used when you want to allow remote access. If a user accesses data remotely, file-sharing settings allow or deny initial access, but because your data is also wrapped in a file security blanket, the user must also successfully pass the file security settings before working with files and folders.

File security and standard sharing settings are referred to as permissions and can either be complementary or increasingly limiting. In a complementary example, the Engineering Group has full access permissions to the EngData share on a computer, and because the local file security settings don't override or modify this, members of this group can open, change, and delete files in this folder. In a limiting (restrictive) example, the user BobJ has access to the EngData share on a computer but is prevented by file security settings from reading, changing, or deleting files in the associated local folder. In either case, you have very precise control over data access and can implement a very strong protection plan for your data.

You can change the file-sharing model a computer uses by completing the following steps:

1. Using an account with local administrator privileges, access the Folder Options dialog box by selecting Folder Options from the Tools menu in Windows Explorer or typing **control folders** at the command prompt.

2. Select the View tab. Clear the Use Simple File Sharing option to use standard file sharing, or select Use Simple File Sharing to use simple file sharing.

3. Click OK.

Controlling Access to Files and Folders with NTFS Permissions

When you use the standard file-sharing model, you control access to files and folders using NTFS permissions. These permissions provide the innermost layer of security and are used whenever files and folders are accessed locally. When files and folders are accessed over the network, the file-sharing permissions are checked first to either allow initial access or to deny access immediately. If a user is allowed initial access, a maximum permission level is set according to the file-sharing permissions and the local NTFS permissions are then used to further restrict the permitted actions (if any) with regard to data in the shared folder.

NTFS permissions are fairly complex, and to understand their management, you need to understand the following:

- **Basic permissions** What the basic permissions are and how they are used
- **Special permissions** What the special permissions are and how they are used
- **Ownership** What is meant by file ownership and how file ownership is used
- **Inheritance** What is meant by inheritance and how inheritance is used
- **Effective permissions** How to determine the effective permissions on files

Understanding and Using the Basic Permissions

In Windows XP, the owner of a file or a folder has the right to allow or deny access to that resource, as do members of the Administrators group and other authorized users. Using Windows Explorer, you can view the currently assigned basic permissions by right-clicking a file or a folder, selecting Properties on the shortcut menu, and then selecting the Security tab in the Properties dialog box.

 Security If the Security tab is not available in the Properties dialog box, Simple File Sharing is enabled. You must disable Simple File Sharing before you can assign permissions. Access the Folder Options dialog box in Windows Explorer, and then on the View tab clear the Use Simple File Sharing option.

As shown in Figure 11-1, the Group Or User Names list shows all the users and groups with permissions set for the selected resource. If you select a user or a group in this list, the assigned permissions are shown in the Permissions For list. If permissions are shaded (unavailable) as shown in the figure, it means they have been inherited from a parent folder. Inheritance is covered in detail in the section of this chapter entitled "Applying Permissions through Inheritance."

Figure 11-1 The Security tab shows the currently assigned basic permissions.

Working with and Setting Basic Permissions

All permissions are stored in the file system as part of the access control list (ACL) assigned to a file or a folder. As described in Table 11-1, six basic permissions are used with folders and five with files. Although some permissions are inherited based on permissions of a parent folder, all permissions are defined explicitly at some level of the file system hierarchy.

Table 11-1   Basic File and Folder Permissions

Permission	Description
Full Control	Grants the user or group full control over the selected file or folder and permits reading, writing, changing, and deleting files and subfolders. A user with Full Control over a folder can delete files in the folder regardless of the permission on the files and can also take ownership of a folder or a file. Selecting this permission selects all the other permissions as well.
Modify	Allows the user or group to read, write, change, and delete files. A user with Modify permission can also create files and subfolders but cannot take ownership of files. Selecting this permission selects all the permissions below it.
Read & Execute	Permits viewing and listing files and subfolders as well as executing files. If applied to a folder, this permission is inherited by all files and subfolders within the folder. Selecting this permission selects the List Folder Contents and Read permissions as well.
List Folder Contents (folders only)	Very similar to Read & Execute permission but available only for folders. Permits viewing and listing files and subfolders as well as executing files. Unlike Read & Execute, this permission is inherited only by subfolders but not by files within the folder or subfolders.
Read	Allows the user or group to view and list the contents of a folder. A user with this permission can view file attributes, read permissions, and synchronize files. Read is the only permission needed to run scripts. Read access is required to access a shortcut and its target.
Write	Allows the user or group to create new files and write data to existing files. A user with this permission can also view file attributes, read permissions, and synchronize files. Giving a user permission to write to but not delete a file or a folder doesn't prevent the user from deleting the folder or file's contents.

Equally as important as the basic permissions themselves are the users and groups to which you assign permissions. If a user or a group whose permissions you want to assign is already selected in the Group Or User Names list on the Security tab, you can modify the assigned permissions using the Allow and Deny columns in the Permissions For list. Select check boxes in the Allow column to add permissions, or clear check boxes to remove permissions.

To expressly forbid a user or a group from using a permission, select the appropriate check boxes in the Deny column. Because denied permissions have precedence over other permissions, Deny is useful in several specific scenarios:

- If a user is a member of a group that has been granted a permission and you (a) don't want the user to have the permission and (b) don't want to or can't remove the user from the group, you can override the inherited permission by denying that specific user the right to use the permission.

- If a permission is inherited from a parent folder and you'd rather a user or a group not have the inherited permission, you can override the allowed permissions (in most cases) by expressly denying the user or group the use of the permissions.

If a user or a group whose permissions you want to assign isn't already available in the Group Or User Names list on the Security tab, you can easily add it.

To set basic permissions for users or groups not already listed on a file or a folder's Security tab, follow these steps:

1. On the Security tab, click Add to display the Select Users, Computers, Or Groups dialog box, shown in Figure 11-2.

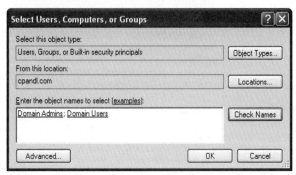

Figure 11-2 Use Select Users, Computers, Or Groups to specify the groups whose permissions you want to configure.

 Tip Always double-check the value of the From This Location field. Generally speaking, in workgroups it is set to the local computer you are working with, and in domains it is set to the default (logon) domain of the currently logged on user. If this isn't the location you want to use for selecting user and group accounts to work with, click Locations to see a list of locations you can search, including the current domain, trusted domains, and other resources that you can access.

2. Type the name of a user or a group account in the selected or default domain. Be sure to reference the user account name rather than a user's full name. When entering multiple names, separate them with semicolons.

3. Click Check Names. If a single match is found for each of your entries, the dialog box is automatically updated as appropriate and the entry is underlined. Otherwise, you'll see an additional dialog box. When no matches are found, you've either entered an incorrect name part or you're working with an incorrect location. Modify the name in the Name Not Found dialog box and try again, or click Locations to select a new location. When multiple matches are found, select the name(s) you want to use in the Multiple Names Found dialog box, and then click OK.

4. When you click OK, the users and groups are added to the Name list. You can then configure permissions for each user and group added by selecting an account name and then allowing or denying access permissions as appropriate.

Special Identities and Best Practices for Assigning Permissions

When you work with basic permissions, it is important to understand not only how the permissions are used but also how special identities can be used to help you assign permissions. The special identities you'll see the most are Creator Owner and Users, but others are used occasionally as well, as described in Table 11-2.

Table 11-2   Special Identities Used When Setting Permissions

Special Identity	Description
Anonymous Logon	Includes any network logons for which credentials are not provided. This special identity is used to allow anonymous access to resources, such as those available on a Web server.
Authenticated Users	Includes users who log on with a user name and password; does not include users who log on as Guest, even if the Guest account has been assigned a password.
Creator Owner	The special identity for the person who created a file or a folder. Windows XP uses this group to automatically grant access permissions to the creator of a file or a folder.
Dialup	Includes any user who accesses the computer with a dial-up connection. This identity is used to distinguish dial-up users from other types of users.
Everyone	Includes all interactive, dial-up, and authenticated users. Although this group includes Guests, it does not include Anonymous logons. In previous versions of Windows, Everyone was used to give wide access to a system resource.
Interactive	Includes any user logged on locally or through a Remote Desktop connection.
Network	Includes any user who logs on over the network. This identity is used to allow remote users to access a resource and does not include Interactive logons that use Remote Desktop Connections.
Users	Includes Authenticated Users and Domain Users only. In Windows XP, the built-in Users group is preferred over Everyone.

Having a solid understanding of these special identities can help you more effectively configure permissions on NTFS volumes. Additionally, whenever you work with permissions you should keep the following guidelines in mind:

- **Follow the file system hierarchy**   Inheritance plays a big part in how permissions are set. By default, permissions you set on a folder apply to all files and subfolders within that folder. With this in mind, start at the root folder of a local disk or a user's profile folder (both of which act as top-level folders) when you start configuring permissions.

- **Have a plan**   Don't set permissions without a clear plan. If permissions get out of sync on folders, and you are looking for a way to start over so that you have some continuity, you might want to configure the permissions as they should be in a parent folder and then reset the permissions on all subfolders and files in that folder using the technique discussed in the section of this chapter entitled "Restoring Inherited Permissions."

- **Grant access only as necessary** An important aspect of the file access controls built into NTFS is that permissions must be explicitly assigned. If you don't grant a permission to a user and that user isn't a member of a group that has a permission, the user doesn't have that permission—it's that simple. When you are assigning permissions, it is important to keep this rule in mind especially because it's tempting just to give users full control rather than the specific permissions they really need.

- **Use groups to manage permissions more efficiently** Whenever possible you should make users members of the appropriate groups and then assign permissions to those groups whenever possible rather than assigning permissions to individual users. In this way, you can grant permissions to new users by making them members of the appropriate groups and then, when a user leaves or goes to another group, you can change the group membership as appropriate. For example, when Sarah joins the Sales team, you can add her to the SalesUS and SalesCan groups so that she can access those groups' shared data. If she later leaves the Sales team and joins the Marketing team, you can remove her from the SalesUS and SalesCan groups and add her to the MarketingUS and MarketingCan groups. This is much more efficient than editing the properties for every folder Sarah will need access to and assigning permissions.

Assigning Special Permissions

Windows XP uses special permissions to very carefully control the permissions of users and groups. Behind the scenes whenever you work with basic permissions, Windows XP manages a set of related special permissions that specify exactly the permitted actions. The special permissions that are applied for each of the basic permissions are as follows:

- Read
    1. List Folder/Read Data
    2. Read Attributes
    3. Read Extended Attributes
    4. Read Permissions
- Read & Execute or List Folder Contents
    1. All special permissions for Read listed previously
    2. Traverse Folder/Execute File
- Write
    1. Create Files/Write Data
    2. Create Folders/Append Data
    3. Write Attributes
    4. Write Extended Attributes
- Modify
    1. All special permissions for Read listed previously
    2. All special permissions for Write listed previously
    3. Delete

- Full Control
    1. All special permissions listed previously
    2. Delete Subfolders And Files
    3. Change Permissions
    4. Take Ownership

Table 11-3 describes how Windows XP uses each of the special permissions.

Table 11-3   Special Permissions for Files and Folders

Special Permission	Description
Traverse Folder/Execute File	Traverse Folder allows direct accessing of a folder in order to reach subfolders, even if you don't have explicit access to read the data it contains. Execute File allows you to run an executable file.
List Folder/Read Data	List Folder lets you view file and folder names. Read Data allows you to view the contents of a file.
Read Attributes	Allows you to read the basic attributes of a file or a folder. These attributes include Read-Only, Hidden, System, and Archive.
Read Extended Attributes	Allows you to view the extended attributes (named data streams) associated with a file.
Create Files/Write Data	Create Files allows you to put new files in a folder. Write Data allows you to overwrite existing data in a file (but not add new data to an existing file because this is covered by Append Data).
Create Folders/Append Data	Create Folders allows you to create subfolders within folders. Append Data allows you to add data to the end of an existing file (but not to overwrite existing data because this is covered by Write Data).
Write Attributes	Allows you to change the basic attributes of a file or a folder. These attributes include Read-Only, Hidden, System, and Archive.
Write Extended Attributes	Allows you to change the extended attributes (named data streams) associated with a file.
Delete Subfolders and Files	Allows you to delete the contents of a folder. If you have this permission, you can delete the subfolders and files in a folder even if you don't specifically have Delete permission on the subfolder or the file.
Delete	Allows you to delete a file or a folder. If a folder isn't empty and you don't have Delete permission for one of its files or subfolders, you won't be able to delete it. You can delete a folder that contains other items only if you have Delete Subfolders And Files permission.
Read Permissions	Allows you to read all basic and special permissions assigned to a file or a folder.
Change Permissions	Allows you to change basic and special permissions assigned to a file or a folder.
Take Ownership	Allows you to take ownership of a file or a folder. By default, administrators can always take ownership of a file or a folder and can also grant this permission to others.

In Windows Explorer, you can view special permissions for a file or a folder by right-clicking the file or the folder you want to work with and then selecting Properties on the shortcut menu. In the Properties dialog box, select the Security tab and then click Advanced to display the Advanced Security Settings dialog box, as shown in Figure 11-3. In this dialog box, the permissions are presented much as they are on the Security tab. The key differences are that you see individual allow or deny permission sets along with whether and how the permissions are inherited, as well as the resources to which the permissions will apply.

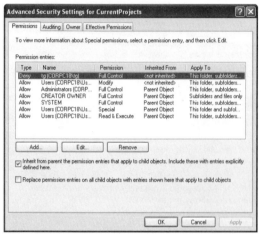

Figure 11-3   Use the Advanced Security Settings dialog box to configure special permissions.

Once you've accessed the Advanced Security Settings dialog box, you can set special permissions using the Add, Edit, and Remove buttons. To add a user or a group and then set special permissions for that user or group, follow these steps:

1. Click Add on the Permissions tab of the Advanced Security Settings dialog box. This displays the Select User Or Group dialog box.

2. Type the name of a user or a group account in the selected or default domain. Be sure to reference the user account name rather than a user's full name. Only one name can be entered at a time.

3. When you click OK, the Permission Entry For dialog box shown in Figure 11-4 is displayed.

Figure 11-4   Configure the special permissions that should be allowed or denied.

4. Allow or deny special permissions as appropriate. If any permissions are grayed out (unavailable), they are being inherited from a parent folder. You can override the inherited permission if necessary by selecting the opposite permission, such as Deny rather than Allow.

5. If the options on the Apply Onto list are available, choose the appropriate options to ensure the permissions are properly inherited. The options include the following:

   ❏ **This folder only**   The permissions will apply only to the currently selected folder.

   ❏ **This folder, subfolders and files**   The permissions will apply to this folder, any subfolders of this folder, and any files in any of these folders.

   ❏ **This folder and subfolders**   The permissions will apply to this folder and any subfolders of this folder. They will not apply to any files in any of these folders.

   ❏ **This folder and files**   The permissions will apply to this folder and any files in this folder. They will not apply to any subfolders of this folder.

   ❏ **Subfolders and files only**   The permissions will apply to any subfolders of this folder and any files in any of these folders. They will not apply to this folder itself.

   ❏ **Subfolders only**   The permissions will apply to any subfolders of this folder but will not apply to the folder itself or any files in any of these folders.

   ❏ **Files only**   The permissions will apply to any files in any of these folders and any files in subfolders of this folder. They will not apply to this folder itself or to subfolders.

6. When you are finished configuring permissions, click OK.

File Ownership and Permission Assignment

The owner of a file or a folder has the right to allow or deny access to that resource. Although members of the Administrators group and other authorized users also have the right to allow or deny access, the owner has the authority to lock out these other users—even members of the Administrators group—and then the only way to regain access to the resource is to take ownership of it. This makes the file or folder owner very important in terms of what permissions are allowed or denied with respect to a given resource.

The default owner of a file or a folder is the person who created the resource. Ownership can be taken or transferred in several different ways. A current owner of a file or a folder can transfer ownership to another user at any time. A member of the Administrators group can take ownership of a file or a folder or transfer ownership to the Administrators group at any time—even if they are locked out of the resource according to the permissions. Any user with the Take Ownership permission on the file or the folder can take ownership, as can any member of the Backup Operators group (or anyone else with the Backup Files And Directories user right, for that matter).

Taking Ownership of Files and Folders

If you are an administrator, an authorized user, or a Backup Operator, you can take ownership of a file or a folder by completing the following steps:

1. In Windows Explorer, access the file or folder's Properties dialog box by right-clicking the file or folder and then selecting Properties.

2. On the Security tab of the Properties dialog box, click Advanced to display the Advanced Security Settings dialog box and then select the Owner tab, as shown in Figure 11-5.

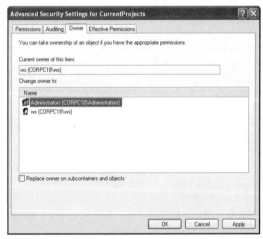

Figure 11-5   Use the Owner tab to take ownership of a file or a folder.

3. In the Change Owner To list box, select the new owner. If you're taking ownership of a folder, you can take ownership of all subfolders and files within the folder by selecting the Replace Owner On Subcontainers And Objects option.

4. Click OK twice when you are finished.

Granting the Take Ownership Right

If you are an administrator or the current owner of a file, you can grant someone the right to take ownership of a file or a folder by completing these steps:

1. In Windows Explorer, access the file or folder's Properties dialog box by right-clicking the file or folder and then selecting Properties.

2. On the Security tab of the Properties dialog box, click Advanced to display the Advanced Security Settings dialog box.

3. On the Permissions tab, click Add to display the Select User Or Group dialog box.

4. Type the name of a user or a group, and click Check Names. If multiple names match the value you entered, you'll see a list of names and will be able to choose the one you want to use. Otherwise, the name will be filled in for you, and you can click OK to close the Select User Or Group dialog box.

5. The Permission Entry For dialog box is displayed. Select the permissions the user should have, including the Take Ownership permission.

6. Click OK three times to close all open dialog boxes when you are finished.

Applying Permissions through Inheritance

In the file and folder hierarchy used by Windows XP, the root folder of a local disk and the *%UserProfile%* folder are the parent folders of all the files and folders they contain by default. Any time you add a resource, it inherits the permissions of the local disk's root folder or the user's profile folder. You can change this behavior by modifying a folder's inheritance settings so that it no longer inherits permissions from its parent folder. This would create a new parent folder, and any subfolders or files you added would then inherit the permissions of this folder.

Inheritance Essentials

Inheritance is automatic, and inherited permissions are assigned when a file or a folder is created. If you do not want a file or a folder to have the same permissions as a parent, you have several choices. You can

- Stop inheriting permissions from the parent folder and then copy or remove existing permissions as appropriate.

- Access the parent folder and configure the permissions you want all included files and folders to have.

- Try to override an inherited permission by selecting the opposite permission. In most cases, Deny overrides Allow.

Inherited permissions are grayed out on the Security tab of a file or a folder's properties dialog box. It is also important to point out that when you assign new permissions to a folder, the permissions propagate down to the subfolders and files contained in that folder and either supplement or replace existing permissions. This propagation lets you allow additional users and groups to access a folder's resources or to further restrict access to a folder's resources independently of a parent folder.

To better understand inheritance, consider the following examples:

- On drive C, you create a folder named Data and then create a subfolder named CurrentProjects. By default, Data inherits the permissions of the C:\ folder, and these permissions are in turn inherited by the CurrentProjects folder. Any files you add to the C:\, C:\Data, and C:\Data\CurrentProjects folders will have the same permissions—those inherited from the C:\ folder.

- On drive C, you create a folder named Docs and then create a subfolder named Working. You stop inheritance on the Working folder by removing the inherited permissions of the parent. Any files you add to the C:\Docs\Working folder inherit the permissions of the C:\Docs folder and no other.

- On drive C, you create a folder named Backup and then create a subfolder named Sales. You add permissions to the Sales folder that grant access to members of the Sales group. Any files added to the C:\Backup\Sales folder inherit the permissions of the C:\ folder and also have additional access permissions for members of the Sales group.

 Real World   Many new administrators wonder what the advantage of inheritance is and why it is used. Although it occasionally seems inheritance is more trouble than it's worth, inheritance allows you to very efficiently manage permissions. Without inheritance, you'd have to configure permissions on every file and folder you created. If you wanted to change permissions later, you'd have to go through all your files and folders again. With inheritance, all new files and folders automatically inherit a set of permissions. If you need to change permissions, you can make the changes in a top-level or parent folder and the changes can be automatically applied to all subfolders and files in that folder. In this way, a single permission set can be applied to many files and folders without the need to edit the security of individual files and folders.

Viewing the Inherited Permissions

To view the inherited permissions on a file or a folder, right-click the file or the folder in Windows Explorer and then select Properties. On the Security tab of the Properties dialog box, click Advanced to display the Advanced Security Settings dialog box, shown in Figure 11-6. The Permission column lists the current permissions assigned to the resource. If the permission is inherited, the Inherited From column shows the parent folder from which the permission has been inherited. If the permission will be in turn inherited by other resources, the Apply To column shows the types of resources that will inherit the permission.

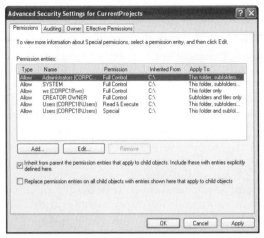

Figure 11-6   The Permissions tab shows the permissions on a file or a folder and how they apply.

Stopping Inheritance

If you want a file or a folder to stop inheriting permissions from a parent folder, follow these steps:

1. In Windows Explorer, right-click the file or folder and then select Properties. On the Security tab of the Properties dialog box, click Advanced to display the Advanced Security Settings dialog box, shown previously in Figure 11-6.

2. Clear Inherit From Parent The Permission Entries That Apply To Child Objects.

3. As shown in Figure 11-7, you now have the opportunity to copy over the permissions that were previously applied or remove the inherited permission and apply only the permissions that you explicitly set on the folder or file. Click Copy or Remove as appropriate. Assign additional permissions as necessary.

Tip   If you remove the inherited permissions and there are no other permissions assigned, everyone but the owner of the resource will be denied access. This effectively locks everyone except the owner out of a folder or file. However, administrators still have the right to take ownership of the resource regardless of the permissions. Thus, if an administrator were locked out of a file or a folder and truly needed access, she could take ownership and then have unrestricted access.

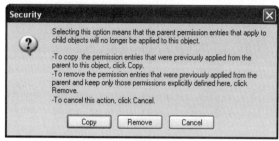

Figure 11-7   Copy or remove the inherited permissions.

Restoring Inherited Permissions

Over time, the permissions on files and subfolders can get so far out of whack from those of a parent folder that it is nearly impossible to manage access effectively. To help make it easier to manage file and folder access, you might want to take the drastic step of restoring the inherited permissions to all resources contained in a parent folder. In this way, subfolders and files get all inheritable permissions from the parent folder and all other explicitly defined permissions on the individual subfolders and files are removed.

To restore the inherited permissions of a parent folder, follow these steps:

1. In Windows Explorer, right-click the folder and then select Properties.
2. On the Security tab of the Properties dialog box, click Advanced to display the Advanced Security Settings dialog box, shown previously in Figure 11-6.
3. Select Replace Permission Entries On All Child Objects With Entries Shown Here, and click OK.
4. As shown in Figure 11-8, you will see a prompt explaining that this action will remove all explicitly defined permissions and enable propagation of inheritable permissions. Click Yes.

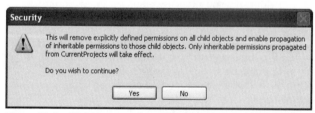

Figure 11-8   Click Yes to confirm that you want to replace the existing permissions.

Determining the Effective Permissions and Troubleshooting

NTFS permissions are complex and can be difficult to manage. Sometimes a change—even a very minor one—can have unintended consequences. Users might suddenly find they are denied access to files they could previously access, or they might suddenly find they have access to files where such access should never have been granted. In either scenario, you have a problem. Something has gone wrong with permissions, and you need to fix it.

If you have these or other problems with permissions, you should start your trouble-shooting by determining the effective permissions for the files or the folders in question. As the name implies, the effective permissions tell you exactly which permissions are in effect with regard to a particular user or group. The effective permissions are important because they allow you to quickly determine the cumulative set of permissions that apply.

For a user, the effective permissions are based on all the permissions the user has been allowed or denied, no matter if they were applied explicitly or obtained from groups of which the user is a member. For example, if JimB is a member of the Users, Sales, Marketing, SpecTeam, and Managers groups, the effective permissions on a file or a folder would be the cumulative set of the permissions JimB has been explicitly assigned and those permissions assigned to the Users, Sales, Marketing, SpecTeam, and Managers groups.

To determine the effective permissions for a user or a group with regard to a file or a folder, complete the following steps:

1. In Windows Explorer, right-click the file or folder you want to work with, and select Properties. In the Properties dialog box, select the Security tab and then click Advanced to display the Advanced Security Settings dialog box.

2. To determine effective permissions that are applied to a user or a group, click the Effective Permissions tab, click Select, type the name of the user or group, and then click OK.

3. The Effective Permissions for the specified user or group are displayed using the complete set of special permissions. If a user has full control over the selected resource, he or she will have the permissions, as shown in Figure 11-9. Otherwise, you'll see a subset of permissions selected and you'll have to very carefully consider whether the user or group has the appropriate permissions. Use Table 11-3 to help you interpret the permissions.

Note   You must have appropriate permissions to view the effective permissions of any user or group. It is also important to remember that you cannot determine the effective permissions for implicit groups or special identities, such as Authenticated Users or Everyone. Furthermore, the effective permissions do not take into account those permissions granted to a user because he or she is the Creator Owner.

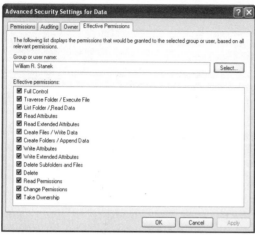

Figure 11-9   Any checked permissions have been granted to the specified user or group.

Sharing Folders over the Network

Windows XP supports two folder-sharing models: Simple folder sharing and standard folder sharing. Because security is so important in a domain, Windows XP supports only the standard folder-sharing model in Active Directory domains. Although computers configured as part of a workgroup can use either model, the model most organizations will want to use is standard folder sharing because this allows you to use a standard set of permissions to control folder access and improves the overall security of your network. Using an account with local administrator privileges, you can enable standard folder sharing on a computer by selecting Folder Options from the Tools menu in Windows Explorer, clearing Use Simple File Sharing on the View tab of the Folder Options dialog box, and clicking OK.

Controlling Access to Network Shares

When a user is accessing a folder over the network and standard folder sharing is enabled, two levels of permissions are used, and together they determine the actions a user can perform with regard to files or other folders in a shared folder. The first level of permissions comprises those set on the share itself. They define the maximum level of access. A user or a group can never have more permissions than those granted by the share. The second level of permissions are those permissions set on the files and folders themselves. These permissions serve to further restrict the permitted actions.

Three share permissions are available.

- **Full Control**   Users allowed this permission have Read and Change permissions, as well as the additional capabilities to change file and folder permissions and take ownership of files and folders. If you have Full Control, you have full access to the shared folder.

- **Change**   Users allowed this permission have Read permissions and the additional capability to create files and subfolders, modify files, change attributes on files and subfolders, and delete files and subfolders. If you have Change permissions on a share, the most you can do is perform read operations and change operations.

- **Read**   Users with this permission can view file and subfolder names, access the subfolders of the share, read file data and attributes, and run program files. If you have Read permissions on a share, the most you can do is perform read operations.

Permissions assigned to groups work like this: If a user is a member of a group that is granted share permissions, the user also has those permissions. If a user is a member of multiple groups, the permissions are cumulative. For example, if one group of which the user is a member has Read access and another has Change access, the user will have Change access. If one group of which the user is a member has Read access and another has Full Control access, the user will have Full Control access.

You can override this behavior by specifically denying an access permission. Denying permission takes precedence and overrides permissions that have been granted. If you don't want a user or a group to have a permission, configure the share permissions so the user or the group is denied that permission. For example, if a user is a member of a group that has been granted Full Control over a share, but the user should have only Change permissions, configure the share to deny Full Control to that user.

Security   Whenever creating or working with shares on Windows XP, you should consider several security issues. If you shared folders (other than the default folders and profiles that were shared) under simple folder sharing and then switch to standard folder sharing, the folders will continue to be shared. The permissions on these shares will give the implicit group Everyone access to the folder. This access is set at both the share permission level and the file system level. When users are granted the permission to make changes, the Everyone group will have Change access on the share and Modify, Read & Execute, List Folder Contents, and Read permissions at the file level. When users are not granted the permission to make changes, the Everyone group will have Read access on the share and Read & Execute, List Folder Contents, and Read permissions at the file level.

Giving Everyone access to a folder means all interactive, dial-up, and authenticated users, including Guests, have some level of access to the shared folder and its contents. To improve security, you should consider changing access so that the Users group has the appropriate access permissions and then removing the access permissions for the Everyone group. When you create new shared folders using standard folder sharing, Everyone is also given access permissions to the share by default. However, unlike simple file sharing, Windows does not modify the existing permissions at the file level.

Creating a Shared Folder

Folders can be shared in both workgroups and domains. In a workgroup, you must be a member of the Administrators or Power Users group on the local computer to share a folder. In a domain, you must be a member of the Domain Admins or Power Users group to share a folder.

You can create shares using several different tools, including the following:

- **Windows Explorer**   Use Windows Explorer when you want to share folders on the computer to which you are logged on.
- **Computer Management**   Use Computer Management when you want to share folders on any computer to which you can connect.
- **NET SHARE**   Use NET SHARE from the command line when you want to use a script to share folders. Type **net share /?** at the command prompt for the syntax of the command.

Creating a shared folder is a multipart process. First you share the folder so that it can be accessed, then you set the share permissions. Afterward, you should check and modify as necessary the file-system permissions as well. This section examines sharing a folder and setting its permissions using Windows Explorer and Computer Management. For details on working with file-system permissions, see the section of this chapter entitled "Controlling Access to Files and Folders with NTFS Permissions."

Sharing a Folder and Setting Share Permissions in Windows Explorer

To share a folder and set its permissions using Windows Explorer, follow these steps:

1. In Windows Explorer, right-click the folder you want to share and select Sharing And Security. This displays the folder's Properties dialog box with the Sharing tab selected.
2. Select Share This Folder, as shown in Figure 11-10. In the Share Name field, type a name for the share. This is the name users will use to connect to the folder.

 Tip   Share names must be unique for each system. They can be up to 80 characters in length and can contain spaces. If you want to provide support for Windows 98, Windows Me, or Windows NT, you should limit the share name to 12 characters or fewer.

Shares are visible to all users with network access to a computer by default. If you want to hide the share from users (which means that they won't be able to see the shared resource when they try to browse to it in Windows Explorer or at the command line), type $ as the last character of the share name. This hides the share from normal users but not from administrators. Administrators will still be able to get a list of the shares on the computer using Computer Management or the NET SHARE command.

Figure 11-10 Set the share name and description.

3. Type a description of the share's contents in the Comment field. Users will see the description when they view shares in My Network Places and other Windows dialog boxes.

4. Click Permissions to view and set the share permissions. By default, the implicit group Everyone is given Read access to the share, as shown in Figure 11-11. If you want to change this, select Everyone in the Group Or User Names list and then allow or deny permissions as appropriate.

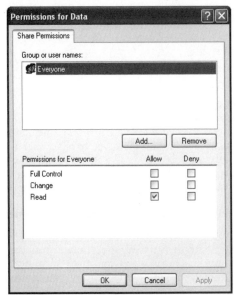

Figure 11-11 After you set the share information, set the share permissions to configure access.

5. On the Share Permissions tab, choose Add. This opens the Select Users Or Groups dialog box.

 Tip   Be sure to check the value of the From This Location field. Generally speaking, in workgroups it is set to the local computer you are working with and in domains it is set to the default (logon) domain of the currently logged on user. If this isn't the location you want to use for selecting user and group accounts to work with, click Locations to see a list of locations you can search, including the current domain, trusted domains, and other resources that you can access.

6. In the Enter The Object Names To Select field, type the name of a user or a group account previously defined in the selected or default domain. Be sure to reference the user account name rather than a user's full name. When entering multiple names, separate them with semicolons.

7. Click Check Names. If a single match is found for each of your entries, the dialog box is automatically updated as appropriate and the entry is underlined. Otherwise, you'll see an additional dialog box. When no matches are found, you've either entered an incorrect name part or you're working with an incorrect location. Modify the name in the Name Not Found dialog box and try again, or click Locations to select a new location. When multiple matches are found, select the name(s) you want to use in the Multiple Names Found dialog box, and then click OK.

8. When you click OK, the users and groups are added to the Name list. You can then configure permissions for each user and group added by selecting an account name and then allowing or denying share access permissions as appropriate.

9. Finally, click OK to create the share. The share is immediately available for use. In Windows Explorer, you should see that the folder icon now includes a hand to indicate it is a share.

 Note   If you access the folder's Sharing tab again, you'll see a new button, labeled New Share, at the bottom of the tab. This button allows you to share the folder again using a different name and a different set of access permissions. When you create multiple shares, the Share Name box of the Sharing tab becomes a selection list that allows you to select a share to work with and configure. Once you've selected a share to work with, the options on the Sharing tab apply to that share only. You'll also have a Remove Share option, which you can use to remove the additional share.

Sharing a Folder and Setting Share Permissions in Computer Management

Using Computer Management, you can share a folder on any computer to which you have administrator access. By connecting remotely to the computer rather than logging on locally, you typically save time because you don't need to access the computer or leave your desk. Follow these steps to use Computer Management to share a folder:

1. Click Start, right-click My Computer, and choose Manage to start Computer Management. By default, Computer Management connects to the local computer, and the root node of the console tree has the label: Computer Management (Local).

   Tip If you want to share a folder on a local computer using the Create A Shared Folder Wizard, you can start the wizard directly and skip steps 1 through 4. Simply type **shrpubw** at a command prompt, and then click Next when the wizard starts.

2. Right-click Computer Management in the console tree, and then select Connect To Another Computer. In the Select Computer dialog box, the Another Computer option is selected by default. Type the fully qualified domain name of the computer you want to work with, such as **engpc08.microsoft.com**, where engpc08 is the computer name and microsoft.com is the domain name. If you don't know the computer name, click Browse to search for the computer you want to work with.

3. Next expand System Tools and Shared Folders, and then select Shares to display the current shares on the system you are working with, as shown in Figure 11-12.

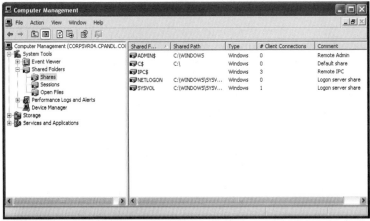

Figure 11-12 All available shares on the computer are listed on the Shares node.

4. Right-click Shares, and then select New File Share to start the Create A Shared Folder Wizard. Click Next to display the Set Up A Shared Folder page, shown in Figure 11-13.

5. In the Folder To Share field, type the full path to the folder that you want to share, such as **C:\Data**. If you don't know the full path, click Browse and then use the Browse For Folder dialog box to find the folder you want to share. The Browse For Folder dialog box will also let you create a new folder that you can then share.

6. In the Share Name field, type a name for the share. Share names must be unique for each system. They can be up to 80 characters in length and can contain spaces. If you want to provide support for Windows 98, Windows Me, or Windows NT, you should limit the share name to 12 characters or fewer.

7. Type a description of the share's contents in the Share Description field. Users will see the description when they view shares in My Network Places and other Windows dialog boxes.

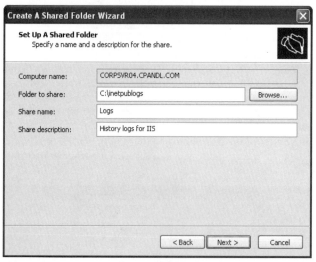

Figure 11-13   Use the Create A Shared Folder Wizard to configure the share settings and permissions.

8. When you are ready to continue, click Next to display the Shared Folder Permissions page, shown in Figure 11-14. The available options are as follows:

   ❏ **All Users Have Read-Only Access**   Default option. Gives users the right to view files and read data but restricts them from creating, modifying, or deleting files and folders.

   ❏ **Administrators Have Full Access; Other Users Have Read-Only Access**   Gives administrators full access to the share and gives other users read-only access. This allows administrators to create, modify, and delete files and folders. On NTFS, it also gives administrators the right to change permissions and to take ownership of files and folders. Other users can only view files and read data. They can't create, modify, or delete files and folders.

   ❏ **Administrators Have Full Access; Other Users Have No Access**   Gives only administrators full access to the share.

   ❏ **Customize Permissions**   Allows you to configure access for specific users and groups, which is usually the best technique to use. To use this option, select Customize Permissions, click Custom, and then follow steps 4 through 8 under "Sharing a Folder and Setting Share Permissions in Windows Explorer." When you click OK to close the Customize Permissions dialog box, you'll be back in the Create A Shared Folder Wizard.

Figure 11-14   Configure the access permissions for the share.

9. After you set up permissions on the share, click Next and then click Finish to share the folder.

Using and Accessing Shared Folders

Once you create a shared folder, users can connect to it as a network resource or map to it by using a driver letter on their machines. Shares can be accessed and mapped using a variety of tools, including the following:

- **My Network Places**   My Network Places is designed to be *the* tool you use when you want to work with network resources, including shared folders. You can use it to quickly access shortcuts to any network resources that are available, to view network connections, to search Active Directory, and to browse the network. If your Start Menu doesn't already have a My Network Places option, you can open this tool through My Computer. Start My Computer, and then under Other Places, click My Network Places.

- **Windows Explorer**   Windows Explorer is the standard tool for working with files and folders. Any shared folders that have previously been mapped and are still connected are available as network drives. You can map new network drives for shared folders as well. To quickly access Windows Explorer, click Start, right-click My Computer, and then select Explore.

Using My Network Places to Access Shared Folders

By default, Windows XP periodically searches the network for shared folders and shared printers. Any shared folders or shared printers that are found are listed as network locations in My Network Places.

 Note   Automatic discovery of network places is controlled by an option in Windows Explorer. This option must be enabled for automatic discovery to work. Choose Tools, Folder Options in Windows Explorer, and then select the View tab. To enable automatic discovery, select the Automatically Search For Network Folders And Printers option. To disable automatic discovery, clear the Automatically Search For Network Folders And Printers option.

You can create network places manually as well. To do this, follow these steps:

1. In the My Network Places task pane, click Add A Network Place under Network Tasks. This starts the Add Network Place Wizard. Click Next.

 Tip   If the Explorer Bar is displayed, you must close it before you can access the task pane in My Computer. Do this by clearing any selected option on the View, Explorer Bar list.

2. On the Where Do You Want To Create This Network Place? page, select Choose Another Network Location and then click Next.

3. On the What Is The Address Of This Network Place? page, click Browse. In the Browse For Folder dialog box, expand Entire Network\Microsoft Windows Network and then expand the name of the workgroup or domain you want to work with, as shown in Figure 11-15.

Figure 11-15   Browse the network until you find the share you want to use.

4. When you expand the name of a computer in a workgroup or domain, you'll see a list of shared folders. Select the shared folder you want to work with, and then click OK.

5. Click Next. Type a descriptive name for the network location. Click Next, and then click Finish.

6. You can now access the network location at any time by double-clicking it in My Network Places. If the account you are logged on with has appropriate permissions, you will be given immediate access. Otherwise, you'll be prompted to enter your user name and password—you can avoid this by creating a key ring entry, as discussed in Chapter 7, "Managing User Access and Stored Settings."

Tip The network place also appears as an option under My Network Places in the Open and Save dialog boxes of most applications. For example, in Microsoft Word, you would choose File, Open, and then in the Open dialog box, you would click My Network Places to see the available network locations.

Using Windows Explorer to Create Network Drives and Access Shared Folders

The quickest and easiest way to access shared folders in Windows Explorer is to use network drives. Once a network drive is mapped, users can access it just as they would a local drive on their computer. All they have to know to map to the shared folder is the name of the server on which the folder is located and the share name.

You can map a network drive to a shared folder by completing the following steps:

1. In Windows Explorer, select Map Network Drive from the Tools menu. This displays the Map Network Drive dialog box, shown in Figure 11-16.

Figure 11-16   Map the share you want to use to a network drive.

2. Use the Drive field to select a free drive letter to use, and then click the Browse button to the right of the Folder field. In the Browse For Folder dialog box, expand Entire Network\Microsoft Windows Network and then expand the name of the workgroup or the domain you want to work with.

3. When you expand the name of a computer in a workgroup or a domain, you'll see a list of shared folders. Select the shared folder you want to work with, and then click OK.

4. Select Reconnect At Logon if you want Windows XP to connect to the shared folder automatically at the start of each session.

5. If your current logon doesn't have appropriate access permissions for the share, click the Different User Name link. You can then enter the user name and password of the account with which you want to connect to the shared folder. Typically, this feature is used by administrators who log on to their computers with a limited account and also have an administrator account for managing the network.

6. Click Finish. If you later decide you don't want to map the network drive, right-click the network drive icon in Windows Explorer and choose Disconnect.

Using and Accessing Shared Folders for Administration

In Windows XP, you'll find several special shares are created automatically and are intended for use by administrators or the operating system. Most of the special shares are hidden from users because of a dollar sign ($) that has been added to the end of the share name. As an administrator, you occasionally might need to create your own hidden shares or work with the already available special shares.

Creating a hidden share is fairly easy. All you need to do is add a dollar sign ($) to the end of the share name. For example, if you want to share the C:\Reports folder but don't want it to be displayed in the normal file share lists, you could name it Reports$ rather than Reports. That's all it would take to hide the share. Hiding a share doesn't control access to the share, however. Access to shares is controlled using permissions regardless of whether a share is a normal share or a hidden share.

Which special shares are available on a system depends on its configuration. This means some computers might have more special shares than others. The most commonly found special shares are listed in Table 11-4.

Table 11-4   Special and Administrative Shares

Share Name	Description
C$, D$, E$, and Other Local Disk Shares	A special share to the root of a drive. All local disks, including CD/DVD-ROM drives and their shares, are known as C$, D$, E$, and so on. These shares allow members of the Administrators and Backup Operators groups to connect to the root folder of a local disk and perform administrative tasks. For example, if you map to C$, you are connecting to C:\ and have full access to this local disk.
ADMIN$	An administrative share for accessing the *%SystemRoot%* folder in which the operating system files reside. This share is meant to be used for remote administration. For administrators working remotely with systems, ADMIN$ provides a handy shortcut for directly accessing the operating system folder.

Table 11-4   Special and Administrative Shares

Share Name	Description
IPC$	An administrative share used to support named pipes that programs used for interprocess (or process-to-process) communications. Because named pipes can be redirected over the network to connect local and remote systems, they also enable remote administration.
PRINT$	Supports printer sharing by providing access to printer drivers. Any time you share a printer, the system puts the printer drivers in this share so that other computers can access them as needed.

The best tools to use when you want to work with any special or otherwise hidden shares are the NET SHARE command and Computer Management. To see a list of all shares on the local computer, including special shares for administrators, simply type **net share** at a command prompt. You can see a list of all shares available on any computer on the network by completing the following steps:

1. Click Start, right-click My Computer, and choose Manage to start Computer Management. By default, Computer Management connects to the local computer, and the root node of the console tree has the label Computer Management (Local).

2. Right-click Computer Management in the console tree, and then select Connect To Another Computer. In the Select Computer dialog box, the Another Computer option is selected by default. Type the fully qualified domain name of the computer you want to work with, such as **engpc08.microsoft.com**, where engpc08 is the computer name and microsoft.com is the domain name. If you don't know the computer name, click Browse to search for the computer you want to work with.

3. Next expand System Tools and Shared Folders, and then select Shares to display a list of the shares on the system you are working with.

Sometimes when you are managing folders or files, you might not want users to be connected to a shared folder. For example, if you need to move files to a new location, before you move the files you might want to ensure no one is using them. One way to see who is working with shared folders and their related files is to examine user sessions and open files.

Every user who connects to a shared folder creates a user session. To determine who is currently connected, click Sessions under Shared Folders in the console tree. The current users are listed in the right pane. To disconnect a user and end his or her session, right-click the session entry in the right pane, select Close Session, and then click OK to confirm the action. To disconnect all user sessions, right-click Sessions in the console tree, select Disconnect All Sessions, and then click OK to confirm the action.

Every shared file that is being accessed is listed as an open file. To determine which files are open, click Open Files under Shared Folders in the console tree. The currently open files are listed in the right pane. To close an open file, right-click the related entry in the right pane, select Close Open File, and then click OK to confirm the action. To close all open files, right-click Open Files in the console tree, select Disconnect All Open Files, and then click OK to confirm the action.

Chapter 12

Configuring Offline Files, Disk Quotas, Shadow Copies, and More

In this chapter:

Configuring Advanced Windows Explorer Options. 295

Configuring Offline Files 301

Configuring Disk Quotas 310

Using Shadow Copies and Recovering Shared Files. 318

Folder management is a key part of user and system administration. When you look beyond standard file and folder management, the key tasks you'll perform frequently include configuring Windows Explorer options, managing offline file settings, working with disk quotas, and using shadow copies to restore files. Through Windows Explorer options, you control the available file and folder management features as well as the available file types. Offline file settings control the availability of files and folders when users are working offline. Quotas help you limit the amount of disk space available to users. Shadow Copies are point-in-time replicas of shared files that can be used for recovery purposes.

Configuring Advanced Windows Explorer Options

Both users and administrators spend a lot of time working with Windows Explorer or one of the related views, such as My Computer and My Network Places. As an administrator, you'll often want to be able to do a bit more with Windows Explorer. You might want to

- Deploy computers that have certain Windows Explorer features blocked out. For example, you might not want users to be able to access the Hardware tab, which would prevent users from viewing or changing hardware on a computer.

- Hide or restrict access to local disks. For example, you might not want users to be able to access the floppy disk drives on the computers that you deploy.

- Configure file type associations so that a specific program is started when a file is opened. For example, Windows Picture And Fax Viewer might be the default program for .jpg files, and you might want files of this type to open in Adobe Photoshop instead.

These and other advanced configuration options for computers are discussed in this section.

Setting Group Policy for Windows Explorer and Folder Views

As with many other Windows XP features, Group Policy can be used to control the options available in Windows Explorer. Because many of these options extend to folder views and settings, they are useful to examine. Table 12-1 provides an overview of policies that you might want to implement and how those policies are used when they are enabled. These policies are located in User Configuration\Administrative Templates\Windows Components\Windows Explorer.

Table 12-1   Policies for Windows Explorer

Policy Name	Policy Description
Allow Only Per User Or Approved Shell Extensions	Permits a computer to run only shell extensions that have been approved by an administrator or that don't affect other users on that computer. Approved shell extensions must have a Registry entry in HKLM\SOFTWARE\ Microsoft\Windows \CurrentVersion\Shell Extensions\Approved.
Display Confirmation Dialog When Deleting Files	Displays a confirmation dialog box whenever you delete files or move files to the Recycle Bin.
Hide These Specified Drives In My Computer	Hides icons representing selected hard drives from My Computer and Windows Explorer. Users can still gain access to drives through other methods.
Hide The Manage Item On The Windows Explorer Context Menu	Removes the Manage item on the shortcut menu in Windows Explorer, My Computer and the Start menu. This shortcut-menu option is used to open Computer Management.
Maximum Number Of Recent Documents	Specifies the maximum number of document shortcuts that My Recent Documents displays. The default is 15. Note that you must select List My Recently Opened Documents on the Advanced tab of the Customize Start Menu dialog box in order for this list to be available.
No "Computers Near Me" In My Network Places	Removes computers in the user's workgroup or domain from the list of network resources in Windows Explorer and My Network Places.
No "Entire Network" In My Network Places	Removes network resources for all computers outside the user's workgroup or local domain from the list of network resources in Windows Explorer and My Network Places. The "Entire Network" option is removed from Windows Explorer and My Network Places.
Prevent Access To Drives From My Computer	Prevents users from accessing files on selected drives in My Computer and Windows Explorer. Users also can't access files on these drives using Run or Map Network Drive.
Remove "Map Network Drive" And "Disconnect Network Drive"	Prevents users from mapping or disconnecting network drives using Windows Explorer or My Network Places. This doesn't prevent other techniques, such as using the command prompt.

Table 12-1   Policies for Windows Explorer

Policy Name	Policy Description
Remove CD Burning Features	Removes CD creation and modification features from Windows Explorer. Users are not prevented from using other CD burning programs.
Remove DFS Tab	Removes the DFS tab from Windows Explorer and Windows Explorer–based windows, preventing users from using the tab to view or change distributed file system (DFS) settings. Note that the DFS tab is only available when DFS is configured in the workgroup or domain.
Remove File Menu From Windows Explorer	Removes the File menu from Windows Explorer and My Computer, but doesn't prevent users from performing tasks that are available on this menu through other means.
Remove Hardware Tab	Removes the Hardware tab from all dialog boxes, preventing users from using the tab to view, change, or troubleshoot hardware devices.
Remove Search Button From Windows Explorer	Removes the Search button from Windows Explorer and other Windows Explorer–based windows, such as My Computer. This doesn't affect Microsoft Internet Explorer.
Remove Security Tab	Removes the Security tab in the Properties dialog boxes of files, folders, shortcuts, and drives. This prevents users from changing or viewing the related file and folder permissions.
Remove Windows Explorer's Default Context Menu	Prevents users from right-clicking and displaying shortcut menus on the desktop and in Windows Explorer.
Remove The Folder Options Menu Item From The Tools Menu	Prevents users from accessing the Folder Options dialog box and as a result, users can't change folder views, file types, or offline file settings.
Request Credentials For Network Installations	Requires user to enter a user name and a password prior to installing applications over the network. If not enabled, users are only prompted for credentials when installing applications from local disks.
Turn On Classic Shell	Removes Active Desktop and related views, including Web and thumbnail views. This also prevents opening items by single-clicking.

As detailed in Table 12-1, many Windows Explorer policies control the availability of options, such as menu items and tabs in dialog boxes. To configure these options for all users of a computer, follow these steps:

1. Access Group Policy for the system you want to work with. Next, access the Windows Explorer node by expanding User Configuration\Administrative Templates\Windows Components\Windows Explorer.

2. Double-click the policy you want to configure. This displays the Properties dialog box, as shown in Figure 12-1. Select one of the following options:

   ❑ **Enabled**   Enables the policy and updates the registry

   ❑ **Disabled**   Disables the policy and updates the registry

   ❑ **Not Configured**   Specifies that no changes will be made to the registry for this policy

3. Click OK.

Figure 12-1   Configure Windows Explorer options by enabling or disabling the related policies.

Note   You'll find detailed coverage of some of these policies in later sections of this chapter. In particular, be sure to read the next section, "Managing Drive Access in Windows Explorer," which covers hiding or preventing access to drives in Windows Explorer.

Managing Drive Access in Windows Explorer

You might want to block access to files on certain drives or even hide certain drives on a system. You manage this through Group Policy. The policies you use are Hide These Specified Drives In My Computer and Prevent Access To Drives From My Computer.

Hiding drives prevents users from accessing them in My Computer and Windows Explorer, but it doesn't prevent them from accessing the drives using other techniques. In contrast, blocking access to drives prevents users from accessing any files on them and ensures that these files cannot be accessed using My Computer, Windows Explorer, Run or Map Network Drive. It doesn't, however, hide drive icons or the folder structure in My Computer or Windows Explorer.

To hide selected drives or to prevent access to files on selected drives, follow these steps:

1. Access Group Policy for the system you want to work with. Next, access the Windows Explorer node by expanding User Configuration\Administrative Templates\Windows Components\Windows Explorer.

2. To hide drives, double-click Hide These Specified Drives In My Computer and then select Enabled. Next specify which drives you are hiding and then click OK. Key options are the following:

❑ Select Restrict All Drives to restrict access to all internal hard drives and floppy drives.

❑ Select Restrict A And B Drives Only to restrict access to floppy drives.

❑ Select Restrict A, B And C Drives Only to restrict access to floppy drives and drive C.

❑ Select Do Not Restrict Drives to remove other restrictions that would otherwise apply.

3. Click OK.

4. To block access to files on specific drives, double-click Prevent Access To Drives From My Computer and select Enabled. Next select the drives you want to restrict access to.

5. Click OK.

Note In most cases, if you block access to files, you'll also want to hide the drives. This ensures that users cannot view or access files on those drives.

Managing File Type Associations

File type associations determine which programs are started when users double-click to open a file. You can view and manage file type associations using the File Types tab of the Folder Options dialog box, shown in Figure 12-2.

Figure 12-2 Manage file type associations using the File Types tab of the Folder Options dialog box.

Viewing File Type Associations

When programs are installed, they often create file type associations for specific types of files. For example, when you install a drawing application, image file types such as .gif, and .jpg might be associated with the program. You can view the file associations for a program by following these steps:

1. In Windows Explorer, select Folder Options from the Tools menu. This displays the Folder Options dialog box.

2. On the File Types tab, you'll see a list of file extensions and the associated file types. If you click the heading for the File Types column, you can sort entries so that files of the same type are listed together. This can often help you find multiple file types associated with the same program.

3. When you find a file type that you want to examine, select it. In the Details For <file extension> Extension panel, you'll see the name of the application or executable that is launched when files of this type are accessed.

Changing File Type Associations

Sometimes, you'll find that programs have file types associated with them that users would rather have associated with other files. If this happens, you can change the file type association by completing these steps:

1. In Windows Explorer, select Folder Options from the Tools menu. Click the File Types tab.

2. You must change each file extension associated with the file type you want to modify. Select the first file extension that you want to reconfigure and then click Change. This displays the Open With dialog box.

3. Under Programs, you'll see a list of recommended programs and other programs that might be able to use this file extension. Select the program to use and then click OK.

4. As necessary, repeat steps 2 and 3 for other file extensions associated with this file type.

 Tip   If you make a mistake and want to change the settings back to the default application, select a file extension and then click Restore. This restores the original default settings for the file extension.

Deleting File Extensions

Each file type configured on a computer can have multiple file extensions associated with it. Each file extension in turn can be associated with a default application so that when you double-click a file with the extension, the file is opened in the default application. If you want to prevent automatic association with any installed program, you can do this by deleting the file type extension. To do this, follow these steps:

1. In Windows Explorer, select Folder Options from the Tools menu. Click the File Types tab.

2. Select the file extension that you want to remove and then click Delete.

3. When prompted to confirm the action, click Yes.

 Note   The Delete option is only available if there is a default application associated with the file extension. Otherwise, the Delete option is shaded and cannot be selected.

Configuring Offline Files

Configuring offline files is a multistep process that begins with setting appropriate group policies, continues through configuration of specific offline folders, and ends with setting user options for working offline. The primary users who work offline use laptops, which they take home or to other locations. Configuring group policy for offline files was discussed in Chapter 9, "Configuring User and Computer Policies." This section provides a more detailed overview of offline files and provides specific steps for their configuration.

Understanding Offline Files

Using offline files, users can store network files on their computer so that they are available when the users are not connected to the network. When working offline, users can work with network files in the same way that they do when they are connected to the network. They have the same privileges when working offline, meaning if they only had read access to a file they'll still only be able to read and not modify the file. Users know they are working offline when they see a red X over Network Drives or in the notification area of the taskbar.

When users reconnect to the network, their changes are automatically updated on the network. The way changes are applied depends on how they were made. If multiple users make changes to a particular offline file, they'll have the opportunity to save their version of the file over the existing version, keep the other version, or save both versions on the network. If a user deletes an offline file, the file is also deleted on the network, except when someone modifies the file on the network so that it has a more recent date and time stamp. In this case, the file is deleted from the user's computer and not from the network. If users change an offline file that someone else deletes from the network, they can choose to save their version to the network or delete it from their computer.

Both users and administrators have control over when offline files are synchronized. Manual synchronization is controlled through the Synchronization Manager. Automatic synchronization can be triggered by user logon and logoff and by computers entering the standby or hibernate modes. The exact settings for automatic synchronization depend on Group Policy and user settings. For details on configuring offline files through Group Policy, see the section of Chapter 9 entitled "Configuring Offline File Policies."

Making Files or Folders Available Offline

Shared network folders can be made available for use offline. By default, all subfolders and files within the shared folders are also available offline. If necessary, you can change the availability of individual files and subfolders. To do this, you'll need to change the availability of each individual file or subfolder. Keep in mind that new files added to a shared folder that is designated for offline use are not automatically distributed to users working offline. The offline folder must be synchronized to obtain the updates.

You can configure offline files using Windows Explorer or the Computer Management console. Because Computer Management allows you to work with and manage offline files on any of your network computers, it's usually the best tool to use. To configure offline files on a server running Microsoft Windows 2000 or Windows Server 2003, you must be a member of the Administrators or the Server Operators group. To configure offline files on a Windows XP workstation, you must be a member of the Administrators or the Power Users group.

Step 1: Share Folders

In the Computer Management console, you make a folder available for sharing by completing the following steps:

1. Right-click Computer Management in the console tree, and then select Connect To Another Computer. Use the Select Computer dialog box to choose the computer you want to work with.

2. In the console tree, expand System Tools and Shared Folders, and then select Shares. The current shares on the system are displayed in the details pane.

3. Right-click Shares, and then select New File Share. This starts the Create Shared Folder Wizard, which can be used to share folders as discussed in Chapter 11, "Managing File Security and Sharing," under "Sharing a Folder and Setting Share Permissions in Computer Management."

Step 2: Make Folders Available for Offline Use

In the Computer Management console, you make a shared folder available for offline use by completing these steps:

1. Right-click Computer Management in the console tree, and then select Connect To Another Computer. Use the Select Computer dialog box to choose the computer you want to work with.

2. In the console tree, expand System Tools and Shared Folders, and then select Shares.

3. Current shared folders are displayed in the details pane. Double-click the share you want to configure for offline use. On the General tab, click Caching.

4. In the Caching Settings dialog box, shown in Figure 12-3, select Allow Caching Of Files In This Shared Folder. Next, select one of the following options:

   ❑ **Automatic Caching Of Documents** Use this setting for folders containing user data. Opened files are automatically downloaded and made available for offline use. If an older version of a document was cached previously, the older version is deleted. When using a file online, the server version always reflects that the file is in use.

   ❑ **Automatic Caching Of Programs And Documents** Use this setting for folders containing read-only data files and program executables that can be run from the network. Opened files are retrieved first from the local cache if available, bypassing the network server, which provides improved performance but also introduces a risk if data is manipulated locally because there are no locks on the server to show that a file is in use.

Caution   If you use this setting, be sure that all files in the folder are read-only and cannot be changed by users. Otherwise, users might alter data locally that could cause conflicts with updates made by other users if saved to the server.

❑ **Manual Caching Of Documents**   Use this setting when you want users to manually specify any files that they want available when working offline. This is the default option and is best used when multiple users want to modify the same files within a folder. Once configured for manual caching, files are automatically downloaded and made available for offline use. If an older version of a document was cached previously, the older version is deleted. When using a file online, the server version always reflects that the file is in use.

5. Click OK twice.

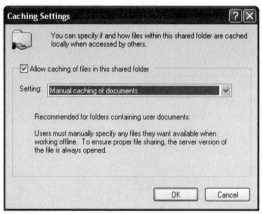

Figure 12-3   Configure caching options for offline files in the Caching Settings dialog box.

Making Offline Files Unavailable

As an administrator, you can specify files that should not be available for offline use. Typically, you'll do this when a shared folder contains specific files that users shouldn't manipulate. To make a file unavailable for offline use, you should set a specific exclusion policy as described in Chapter 9 in the section entitled "Administratively Controlling Offline Files and Subfolders."

You can also make files from certain computers unavailable for offline processing. This is done when a specific user doesn't want or shouldn't use offline files for shared folders on the computer. To make files unavailable to a specific user and computer for offline processing, follow these steps:

1. In Windows Explorer, select Folder Options from the Tools menu. This displays the Folder Options dialog box.

2. On the Offline Files tab, click Advanced. This displays the Offline Files–Advanced Settings dialog box shown in Figure 12-4.

Figure 12-4   Configure advanced options for offline files, including notification, restriction, and exception lists, in the Offline Files–Advanced Settings dialog box.

3. Under Exception List, click Add. This displays the Offline Files–Add Custom Action dialog box.

4. Click Browse, and then use the Browse For Computer dialog box to select the computer that you want to work with. The computer name should now be in the Computer field.

5. Under When A Network Connection Is Lost, select Never Allow My Computer To Go Offline. Click OK.

6. You should now see the computer listed on the Exception List with the custom behavior. If you want to add other computers to the list, repeat this process. You can also edit the properties for existing exceptions to allow offline files for a specific computer to be used offline. To do this, select Notify Me And Begin Working Offline.

Configuring Computers to Use Offline Files

By default, most computers are set up to use offline files. In some cases, this setting might have been changed to prevent offline file usage. If there isn't a Group Policy preventing offline file usage, you can enable offline files on a per user basis by completing these steps:

1. In Windows Explorer, select Folder Options from the Tools menu.

2. On the Offline Files tab, select Enable Offline Files.

3. Optionally, select a synchronization technique. Files can be fully synchronized at logon by selecting Synchronize All Offline Files When Logging On, at logoff by selecting Synchronize All Offline Files Before Logging Off, or both by selecting both options. If you don't select an option, a quick synchronization still takes place at logon, logoff, or both.

Note Synchronization can be performed in one of two modes: quick or full. In quick mode, a quick check is performed on files to ensure the contents are complete. File dates are not checked, however, which means that users might have complete copies of offline files but not necessarily the most current versions of the files. In full mode, the file contents and the file date are checked to determine whether files should be synchronized. This ensures the most current and complete copies of files are available offline.

4. Click Advanced. This displays the Offline Files–Advanced Settings dialog box shown previously in Figure 12-4.
5. Select Notify Me And Begin Working Offline and then click OK.
6. Click OK again to close the Folder Options dialog box.

To prevent a computer from using offline files, follow these steps:

1. In Windows Explorer, select Folder Options from the Tools menu.
2. On the Offline Files tab, clear the Enable Offline Files check box and then click OK.

Managing Offline Files on the User's Computer

Users can manage offline files on their local computer as well, and they can perform many tasks similar to those that an administrator performs to implement and maintain offline files. As an administrator, you can perform these techniques on users' computers to help them configure and maintain offline files.

Viewing Offline Files

On a user's computer, you can use the Offline Files folder to view files that are currently available offline and to determine the amount of space being used by offline files. To do this, follow these steps:

1. In Windows Explorer, select Folder Options from the Tools menu.
2. On the Offline Files tab, click View Files. This displays the Offline Files folder (as long as there is no policy that restricts access to this folder).
3. To determine how much space is being used by Offline Files, select all the files by pressing Ctrl+A and then choose Properties from the File menu.

Making Folders Available Offline Manually

If a folder isn't made available for offline use administratively, you can make the folder available to individual users by completing these steps:

1. In Windows Explorer, in the right-hand pane, select the file or folder that you want to make available offline. The folder must be a shared network folder, and the user's computer must be configured to use offline files.

2. From the File menu, select Make Available Offline. If you want to reverse this action later, simply select the file or folder, and then clear the Make Available Offline option on the File menu.

Making Web Pages Available Offline Manually

Like other types of resources, Web resources can be made available offline. You have much more control over the availability of Web resources than over other types of data. You can make individual pages, folders, or collections of folders available for offline use. You can also specify the number of levels below the current page level to cache. This tells the browser to follow links and cache the related resources.

To make Web pages available offline, follow these steps:

1. In Internet Explorer, access the page that you want to cache. Remember that you can cache several levels of pages below the current page.

2. From the Favorites menu, select Add To Favorites. This displays the Add Favorite dialog box.

3. Select Make Available Offline and then click Customize. This starts the Offline Favorite Wizard. If the introduction screen is shown, click Next.

4. Under Set Up The Following Page, select Yes as shown in Figure 12-5. You can now specify the depth of link levels to cache. In most cases you'll only want to cache one or two link levels, which provides sufficient access to most of the related documents.

Figure 12-5   Specify whether links to other pages should be followed and how many levels of linked pages should be cached.

5. Click Next, and then specify how you would like to synchronize the page. You can synchronize manually by selecting Only When I Choose Synchronize From The Tools Menu, or you can create a synchronization schedule that allows automatic synchronization on a periodic basis by selecting I Would Like To Create A New Schedule.

   If you opt to schedule synchronization, use the Every field and the Days At field to set the time interval and start time, such as Every 5 Days At 7:00 PM. Then specify a name for the scheduled task. As Figure 12-6 shows, you can also force the computer to make a connection as needed for synchronization. This option is useful for laptop users who have dial-up connections at home.

Figure 12-6 Set an optional synchronization schedule using the Offline Favorite Wizard.

6. Click Next and, if the site requires a logon password, select Yes, My User Name And Password Are and then enter the necessary account information.

7. Click Finish to complete the process. In the Add Favorite dialog box, check the name for the favorite you are creating. In most cases the default name is just fine. If this is the case, click OK. Otherwise update the Name field and then click OK.

Note Depending on the synchronization options, synchronization might begin immediately. In this case you'll see the Synchronization dialog box. If you want to skip synchronization at this time, click Stop. Otherwise the synchronization continues until it is completed.

To make Web pages unavailable offline or reconfigure file caching, follow these steps:

1. In Internet Explorer, select Synchronize from the Tools menu. This displays the Items To Synchronize dialog box shown in Figure 12-7.

Figure 12-7 Configure synchronization of offline Web pages and check their status in the Items To Synchronize dialog box.

2. In the Name column, you'll see a list of offline Web pages. To change the way a resource is synchronized, select it and then click Properties. This displays a Properties dialog box.

3. To stop using the page offline, on the Web Document tab, clear the Make This Page Available Offline check box.

4. To change the current offline Web file settings rather than stopping use, use the options on the Schedule and Download tabs. The Schedule tab is used to change the synchronization schedule or enable manual synchronization. The Download tab is used to configure the level of links to follow as well as additional options not available originally, including the following:

   ❑ **Follow Links Outside Of This Page's Web Site** Specifies that links to external pages should be cached along with other pages. This is useful when users want to be able to track related sets of resources without going online.

   ❑ **Limit Hard Disk Usage For This Page To** Allows you to limit the amount of disk space used for caching of the page and related links. The default setting is 500 KB.

   ❑ **When This Page Changes Send E-Mail To** Allows users to receive notification when a page changes. Enter an e-mail address and a mail server to use for notification.

5. When you are finished configuring offline files, click Close.

Configuring Automatic Synchronization of Offline Resources

Both offline files and offline Web files can be synchronized automatically. Although the techniques are slightly different, the concepts are the same. To configure automatic synchronization of offline files, follow these steps:

1. In Windows Explorer, select Folder Options from the Tools menu. Click the Offline Files tab.
2. To fully synchronize files at logon, select Synchronize All Offline Files When Logging On. If you clear this option, quick synchronization is used at logon.
3. To fully synchronize files at logoff, select Synchronize All Offline Files Before Logging Off. If you clear this option, quick synchronization is used at logoff.
4. Click OK.

To configure automatic synchronization of offline Web files, follow these steps:

1. In Windows Explorer or Internet Explorer, select Synchronize from the Tools menu. This displays the Items To Synchronize dialog box.
2. Click Setup. You can now use the Synchronization Settings dialog box to configure when offline Web pages are used. Items can be synchronized at logon or logoff, when the computer is idle, or at scheduled intervals.

Synchronizing Offline Resources Manually

You can synchronize offline resources (both offline files and offline Web files) manually for users at any time by following these steps:

1. In Windows Explorer, select Synchronize from the Tools menu.
2. The Items To Synchronize dialog box shows a list of items to synchronize. By default, most of the options should be selected, meaning they'll be synchronized. If you would rather not synchronize a particular item at this time, in the Name column, clear the related check box.
3. When you are ready to begin synchronization, click Synchronize. In the Synchronizing dialog box, you'll see the current item being synchronized and a progress bar for the item. If, for some reason, you need to stop synchronization abruptly, click Stop. Otherwise the synchronization continues until it is completed.

Configuring Offline File Disk Space Usage and Caching

All offline files share a common cache and the total space available for this cache can be limited by Group Policy or by specific user settings. To manage disk space usage and caching through Group Policy, see the section of Chapter 9 entitled "Setting Offline File Cache Policies." To manage these features for individual users, follow these steps:

1. In Windows Explorer, select Folder Options from the Tools menu. Click the Offline Files tab.
2. The disk space usage for offline files is set as a percentage of disk space on the system drive. Use the Amount Of Disk Space slider to change the maximum amount of disk space that can be used by the offline file cache.

3. To clear out the cache and delete all local copies of offline files, click Delete
   Files. This displays the Confirm File Delete dialog box.

4. To delete only temporary offline versions of files, select Delete Only The Temporary Offline Versions.

5. To delete all offline file versions, including those configured to be always available, select Delete Both The Temporary Offline Versions And The Versions
   That Are Always Available Offline.

6. Click Close.

Configuring Disk Quotas

The following sections discuss how to use and manage disk quotas. Disk quotas
allow you to manage disk space usage, and they are configured on a per volume
basis. Only NTFS volumes can have quotas, so you can't create them for file allocation table (FAT16 or FAT32) volumes. The first step in configuring quotas is to
enable disk quota policies as described in Chapter 9 in the section entitled "Configuring Disk Quota Policies." Once you configure the necessary policies, you can set
up quotas for specific volumes on a system.

Using Disk Quotas

Administrators use disk quotas to manage disk space usage for critical volumes,
such as those that provide corporate or user data shares. When you enable disk
quotas, you set a disk quota limit and a disk quota warning. The disk quota limit
sets the upper boundary for space usage, which prevents users from writing additional information to a volume, logs events regarding the user exceeding the limit,
or both. You use the disk quota warning to warn users and to log warning events
when users are getting close to their disk quota limits.

 Real World Although most administrators configure quotas that are
enforced, you *can* set disk quotas that are not. You might be wondering
why you would do this. Sometimes you might want to track disk space
usage on a per user basis and know when users have exceeded some predefined limit. Instead of denying the users additional disk space, however,
you can record an event in the application log to track the overage.

Disk quotas apply only to end users, not to administrators. Administrators can't be
denied disk space even if they exceed enforced disk quota limits. Disk quota limits
and warnings can be set in kilobytes (KB), megabytes (MB), gigabytes (GB), terabytes (TB), petabytes (PB), and exabytes (EB). In a typical environment, you'll
restrict disk space usage in megabytes or gigabytes. For example, on a corporate
data share that is used by multiple users in a department, you might want to limit
disk space usage to between 20 and 100 GB. For a user data share, you might want
to set the level much lower, such as 5 to 20 GB, which would restrict the user from
creating large amounts of personal data. Often you'll set the disk quota warning as
a percentage of the disk quota limit. For example, you could set the warning at 90
to 95 percent of the disk quota limit.

Because disk quotas are tracked on a per-volume, per user basis, disk space used by one user does not affect the disk quotas for other users. Thus, if one user runs over his limit, any restrictions applied to this user don't apply to other users. For example, if a user exceeds a 5 GB disk quota limit and the volume is configured to prevent writing over the limit, the user can no longer write data to the volume. However, he can remove files and folders from the volume to free up disk space. The user could also move files and folders to a compressed area on the volume, which can free up space, or the user could elect to compress the files. Moving files to a different location on the volume doesn't affect the quota restriction. The amount of file space is the same unless the user is moving uncompressed files and folders to a folder with compression. In any case, the restriction on a single user does not affect other users' ability to write to the volume (as long as there is free space on the volume).

You can enable disk quotas on local volumes and on remote volumes. To manage disk quotas on local volumes, you work with the local disk itself. To manage disk quotas on remote volumes, you must share the root directory for the volume and then set the disk quota on the volume. Keep in mind that when you enable disk quotas on a local volume, the Windows XP system files are included in the volume usage for the user who installed those files. In some cases this might cause the user go over the disk quota limit. To prevent this you can set a higher limit on a local workstation volume.

Only members of the domain Administrators group or the local system Administrators group can configure disk quotas. Through local group policy, you can enable disk quotas for an individual computer. Through site, domain, or organizational unit policies, you can enable disk quotas for groups of users and computers. Keeping track of disk quotas does cause some overhead on computers, which is a function of the number of disk quotas being enforced, the total size of volumes and their data, and the number of users to which the disk quotas apply.

Although on the face of it disk quotas are tracked per user, behind the scenes Windows XP manages disk quotas according to security identifiers (SIDs). Because disk quotas are tracked by SIDs, you can safely modify user names without affecting the disk quota configuration. Tracking by SIDs does cause some additional overhead when viewing disk quota statistics for users because Windows XP must correlate SIDs to user account names so that the account names can be displayed in dialogs. This means contacting the local user manager or the Active Directory domain controller as necessary. Once names are looked up, they are cached to a local file so that they are available immediately the next time they are needed. The query cache is infrequently updated, so if you notice a discrepancy between what is displayed and what is configured, you'll need to refresh the information. Usually, this means selecting Refresh or pressing F5 in the current window.

Enabling Disk Quotas on NTFS Volumes

Disk quotas are set on a per-volume basis, and only NTFS volumes can have disk quotas. Disk quotas must first be configured through Group Policy, as discussed in Chapter 9. Once the appropriate group policies are configured, you can set disk quotas for local and remote volumes using the Computer Management console.

To enable disk quotas on an NTFS volume, follow these steps:

1. Start Computer Management. You are connected to the local computer by default. If you want to configure disk quotas on a remote computer, right-click Computer Management in the console tree and then select Connect To Another Computer. In the Select Computer dialog box, select the computer you want to work with.

2. In the console tree, expand Storage and then select Disk Management. The volumes configured on the selected computer are displayed in the details pane.

3. Using the Volume List or Graphical View, right-click the volume you want to work with and then select Properties.

4. Click the Quota tab, shown in Figure 12-8, and then select the Enable Quota Management check box.

Figure 12-8   Once you enable quota management, you can configure a quota limit and quota warning for all users.

5. To set a default disk quota limit for all users, select Limit Disk Space To and then use the fields provided to set a limit in KB, MB, GB, TB, PB, or EB. Next, use the Set Warning Level To fields to set the default warning limit. You'll usually want the disk quota warning limit to be 90 to 95 percent of the disk quota limit.

Note   Although the default quota limit and warning apply to all users, you can configure different levels for individual users through the Quota Entries dialog box. If you create many unique quota entries and don't want to re-create them on a volume with similar characteristics and usage, you can export the quota entries and import them on a different volume.

6. To enforce the disk quota limit and prevent users from going over the limit, select the Deny Disk Space To Users Exceeding Quota Limit check box. Keep in mind that this creates an actual physical limitation for users, but not administrators.

7. To configure logging when users exceed a warning limit or the quota limit, use the Log Event check boxes.

8. If the quota system isn't currently enabled, you'll see a prompt asking you to enable the quota system. Click OK to allow Windows XP to rescan the volume and update disk usage statistics. Actions can be taken against users that exceed the current limit or warning levels, which can include preventing additional writing to the volume, notifying users the next time they access the volume, and logging applicable events in the application log.

Viewing Disk Quota Entries

Disk space usage is tracked on a per user basis. When disk quotas are enabled, each user storing data on a volume has an entry in the disk quota file. This entry is updated periodically to show the current disk space used, the applicable quota limit, the applicable warning level, and the percentage of allowable space being used. As an administrator you can modify disk quota entries to set different limits and warning levels for particular users. You can also create disk quota entries for users who have not yet saved data on a volume. By creating entries, you ensure that when a user does make use of a volume, she has an appropriate limit and warning level.

To view the current disk quota entries for a volume, follow these steps:

1. Start Computer Management. You are connected to the local computer by default. If you want to view disk quotas on a remote computer, right-click Computer Management in the console tree and then select Connect To Another Computer. In the Select Computer dialog box, select the computer you want to work with.

2. In the console tree, expand Storage and then select Disk Management. The volumes configured on the selected computer are displayed in the details pane.

3. Using the Volume List or Graphical View, right-click the volume you want to work with and then select Properties.

4. On the Quota tab, click Quota Entries. This displays the Quota Entries dialog box shown in Figure 12-9. As you can see from the figure, each quota entry is listed according to a status. The status is meant to quickly depict whether a user has gone over her limit. A status of OK means the user is working within the quota boundaries. Any other status usually means the user has reached the warning level or the quota limit.

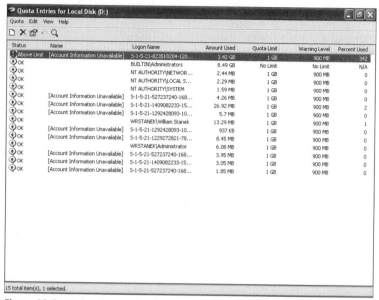

Figure 12-9   Disk quota entries show current disk space usage on a particular volume as well as applicable quota limits and warning levels.

Creating Disk Quota Entries

You can create disk quota entries for users who have not yet saved data on a volume as well as for users who have already saved data on a volume. This allows you to set custom limits and warning levels for any user as necessary. Usually you'll use this feature when one user frequently stores more information than others. For example, a graphic designer might have much higher storage needs than a customer-support person. The good news about custom quota entries is that you can export them to other volumes, which allows you to apply the same set of rules to multiple volumes quickly.

To create a quota entry on a volume, follow these steps:

1. In Computer Management, expand Storage and then select Disk Management. Using the Volume List or Graphical View, right-click the volume you want to work with and then select Properties.

2. On the Quota tab, click Quota Entries. Current quota entries for all users are listed. To refresh the listing, press F5 or select Refresh from the View menu.

3. If the user doesn't have an existing entry on the volume, you can create one from the Quota menu by selecting New Quota Entry. This opens the Select Users dialog box.

4. In the Select Users dialog box, type the name of a user in the Enter The Object Names To Select field and then click Check Names. If multiple matches are found, select the desired account and then click OK. If no matches are found, update the name you entered and try again. Repeat this step as necessary and click OK when finished.

5. Once you've selected a name, the Add New Quota Entry dialog box is displayed, as shown in Figure 12-10. You have several options. You can remove all quota restrictions for this user by selecting Do Not Limit Disk Usage. In addition, you can set a specific limit and warning level by selecting Limit Disk Space To and then entering the appropriate values in the fields provided.

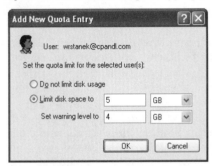

Figure 12-10   You can customize the user's quota limit and warning level or remove all quota restrictions using the Add New Quota Entry dialog box.

6. Click OK. Close the Quota Entries dialog box. Click OK on the Properties dialog box.

Updating and Customizing Disk Quota Entries

You can modify and customize disk quota entries for individual users at any time by following these steps:

1. In Computer Management, expand Storage and then select Disk Management. Using the Volume List or Graphical View, right-click the volume you want to work with and then select Properties.

2. On the Quota tab, click Quota Entries. Current quota entries for all users are listed. To refresh the listing, press F5 or select Refresh from the View menu.

3. Double-click the quota entry for the user. This displays the Quota Settings For dialog box, which is similar to the dialog box shown previously in Figure 12-10.

4. To remove all quota restrictions for this user, select Do Not Limit Disk Usage.

5. To modify the current limit and warning level, select Limit Disk Space To and then enter the appropriate values in the fields provided.

6. Click OK.

Deleting Disk Quota Entries

When you've created disk quota entries on a volume and a user no longer needs to use the volume, you can delete the associated disk quota entry. When you delete a disk quota entry, all files owned by the user are collected and displayed in a dialog box so that you can permanently delete the files, take ownership of the files, or move the files to a folder on a different volume.

To delete a disk quota entry for a user and manage the remaining files on the volume, follow these steps:

1. In Computer Management, expand Storage and then select Disk Management. Using the Volume List or Graphical View, right-click the volume you want to work with and then select Properties.

2. On the Quota tab, click Quota Entries. Current quota entries for all users are listed. To refresh the listing, press F5 or select Refresh from the View menu.

3. Select the disk quota entry that you want to delete and then press Del or select Delete Quota Entry from the Quota menu. You can select multiple entries using the Shift or Ctrl key.

4. When prompted to confirm the action, click Yes. This displays the Disk Quota dialog box with a list of current files owned by the selected user or users.

5. As shown in Figure 12-11, use the List Files Owned By selection list to display files for the user whose quota entry you are deleting. You must then specify how the files for the user are to be handled. Each file can be handled separately by selecting individual files and then choosing an appropriate option. Multiple files can be selected using the Shift or Ctrl key. The following options are available:

   ❑ **Show Folders Only**   Changes the view to show only folders that the user has files in. In this way, you can delete, move, or take ownership of all the user's files in a particular folder.

   ❑ **Show Files Only**   Shows all files that the user owns according to the folder in which they are created. This is the default view.

   ❑ **Permanently Delete Files**   Select the files to delete and then press Del. When prompted to confirm the action, click Yes.

   ❑ **Take Ownership Of Files**   Select the files that you want to take ownership of and then click Take Ownership.

   ❑ **Move Files To**   Select the files that you want to move and then enter the path to a folder on a different volume in the field provided. If you don't know the path that you want to use, click Browse to display the Browse For Folder dialog box, which you can use to find the folder. Once you find the folder, click Move.

6. Click Close when you are finished managing the files. Provided that you've appropriately handled all user files, the disk quota entries are deleted.

Figure 12-11   For each user's disk quota entry that you are deleting, you must specify how the user's files will be handled.

Exporting and Importing Disk Quota Settings

Rather than recreating custom disk quota entries on individual volumes, you can export the settings from a source volume and import them to another volume. Both volumes must be formatted using NTFS. To export and then import disk quota entries, perform the following steps:

1. Start Computer Management. You are connected to the local computer by default. If you want to work with disk quotas on a remote computer, right-click Computer Management in the console tree and then select Connect To Another Computer. In the Select Computer dialog box, select the computer you want to work with.

2. In the console tree, expand Storage and then select Disk Management. The volumes configured on the selected computer are displayed in the details pane.

3. Using the Volume List or Graphical View, right-click the source volume and then select Properties.

4. On the Quota tab, click Quota Entries. This displays the Quota Entries dialog box.

5. From the Quota menu, select Export. This displays the Export Quota Settings dialog box. Use the Save In selection list to choose the save location for the file containing the quota settings and then set a name for the file using the File Name field. Next, click Save.

Tip   If you save the settings file to a mapped drive on the target volume, you'll have an easier time importing the settings. Quota files are usually fairly small so you won't need to worry about disk space usage.

6. From the Quota menu, select Close to exit the Quota Entries dialog box. Click OK to close the Properties dialog box.

7. Right-click Computer Management in the console tree. From the shortcut menu, select Connect To Another Computer. In the Select Computer dialog box, select the computer containing the target volume on which you want to use the exported settings.

8. Expand Storage and then select Disk Management. Using the Volume List or Graphical View, right-click the target volume and then select Properties.

9. Click the Quota tab, ensure that Enable Quota Management is selected, and then click Quota Entries. This displays the Quota Entries dialog box for the target volume.

10. From the Quota menu, select Import. In the Import Quota Settings dialog box, select the quota settings file that you saved previously. Click Open.

11. If the volume had previous quota entries, you'll have the opportunity to replace or keep existing entries. When prompted about a conflict, click Yes to replace an existing entry or click No to keep the existing entry. The option to replace or keep existing entries can be applied to all entries on the volume by selecting Do This For All Quota Entries prior to clicking Yes or No.

Disabling Disk Quotas

You can disable quotas for individual users or all users on a volume. When you disable quotas for a particular user, that user is no longer subject to the quota restrictions, but disk quotas are still tracked for other users. When you disable quotas on a volume, quota tracking and management are completely removed. To disable quotas for a particular user, follow the technique outlined in the section of this chapter entitled "Updating and Customizing Disk Quota Entries." To disable quota tracking and management on a volume, follow these steps:

1. Start Computer Management. You are connected to the local computer by default. If you want to disable disk quotas on a remote computer, right-click Computer Management in the console tree and then select Connect To Another Computer. In the Select Computer dialog box, select the computer you want to work with.

2. In the console tree, expand Storage and then select Disk Management. The volumes configured on the selected computer are displayed in the details pane.

3. Using the Volume List or Graphical View, right-click the volume and then select Properties.

4. On the Quota tab, clear the Enable Quota Management check box. Click OK. When prompted to confirm, click OK.

Using Shadow Copies and Recovering Shared Files

The Volume Shadow Copy service, which is available on computers running Windows Server 2003, allows you to configure volumes so that copies of files in shared folders are automatically created at specific intervals during the day. These point-in-time copies of shared files are referred to as *shadow copies,* and they allow you to go back and look at earlier versions of files stored in shared folders. Not only can you use these earlier copies of files to recover accidentally deleted, incorrectly modified, or inadvertently overwritten files, you can also compare versions of files to determine what changes have been made over time. Up to 64 versions of shared files can be maintained, provided there is adequate disk space available.

On Windows Server 2003, you enable and configure shadow copies on a per-volume basis using Disk Management. Once shadow copies are configured, users working with other versions of Windows can access the shadow copies using one of the available clients. The sections that follow detail how to configure shadow copies on a server and how to manage shadow copies.

Note   Before users can access shadow copies of shared files, a client software module must be installed on their computers. Two clients are available: Previous Versions Client and Shadow Copy Client. Previous Versions Client is installed by default on Windows Server 2003 and is included when you install Windows XP Service Pack 2. Thus any computer running Windows XP Service Pack 2 or later will have the Previous Versions Client, and you don't need to install any other client.

Configuring Shadow Copies on a Server

You can configure shadow copies on a server from your Windows XP desktop. To do this, start Computer Management and then follow these steps:

1. Start Computer Management. You are connected to the local computer by default. If you want to configure shadow copies on a remote computer, right-click Computer Management in the console tree and then select Connect To Another Computer. In the Select Computer dialog box, select the computer you want to work with. Remember, only computers running a Windows Server 2003 or later server version of the Windows operating system can use the Volume Shadow Copy service to create shadow copies.

2. In the console tree, expand Storage and select Disk Management.

3. In the Disk Management Volume List or Graphical View, right-click the NTFS volume containing the shared folders for which you want to create shadow copies, and then select Properties.

4. In the Properties dialog box, select the Shadow Copies tab. Select the volume for which you want to configure shadow copies, and then click Settings.

5. Use the Located On This Volume selection list to specify where the shadow copies should be created. Shadow copies can be created on the volume that you are configuring or on any other volume available on the computer. Keep in mind that the initial shadow copy of a volume requires at least 100 MB of free space to create and that, by default, the Volume Shadow Copy service will reserve 10 percent of the free space on the designated volume for shadow copies.

Tip   On a heavily used volume, a volume with many files, or a volume with less than 10 percent free space, you will probably want to use a separate volume for storing shadow copies. Otherwise, use the same volume for storing the shadow copies. If you are unsure of the amount of space on the selected volume, click Details to see the free space and total available disk space, and then click OK.

6. As necessary, use the Maximum Size options to set the maximum size that shadow copies for this volume can use. Once set, the maximum size is fixed and the Volume Shadow Copy service will not reevaluate storage needs. Because of this, you should do a bit of planning before setting the maximum size. In most cases, you'll want to set a maximum size value that is at least 25 percent of the total space used by shared folders on the volume or at least 10 percent of the total free space on the volume.

7. As necessary, click Schedule to set the times and days when shadow copies are created. By default, shadow copies are created each weekday (Monday through Friday) at 7:00 A.M. and 12:00 P.M. You might want to modify the replica-creation schedule if these times represent high-usage times for the server, there are conflicts with other running services such as backups, or your organization has a work schedule other than Monday through Friday.

8. Click OK to close the Settings dialog box.

9. On the Shadow Copies tab of the Properties dialog box, select the volume on which you want to enable shadow copies and click Enable. When prompted, click Yes to confirm the action. Windows will then create an initial shadow copy snapshot of the volume.

10. Click OK to close the Properties dialog box.

Viewing, Changing, and Restoring Shadow Copies

You can access shadow copies using Windows Explorer or My Network Places:

- Use Windows Explorer when you want to access shadow copies on a volume you've already mapped as a network drive. In Windows Explorer, right-click the network drive that has the shadow copies you want to work with, choose Properties, and then click the Previous Versions tab.

- Use My Network Places to access shadow copies in other locations. In My Network Places, expand Entire Network and Microsoft Windows Network to display the available domains and then expand the domain node to display servers on the network. When you expand a server node, any publicly shared resources on that server are listed. Right-click the share that has the shadow copies you want to work with, choose Properties, and then click the Previous Versions tab.

Real World   When you work with shadow copies, it is important to note if a server has volumes mounted to empty NTFS folders (mount points). If a volume is a mount point, you must share the mount point and access the full mount point path separately to access its shadow copies. For example, if you have the folder D:\CorpDocs\FY2004 and the FY2004 folder is a mount point for volume H, you could share D:\CorpDocs as \\DataSvr01\Docs and users would be able to access both D:\CorpDocs and D:\CorpDocs\FY2004. However, if you later configured shadow copies on volume D, D:\Corp-Docs\FY2004 would not have shadow copies. To correct this, you would need to create a share for volume H and then configure shadow copies on H. Then, if users needed to access shadow copies for volume H, they would do so via the share you created.

Once you've used Windows Explorer or My Network Places to access the Previous Versions tab of a shared folder, select the folder version that you want to work with. Each folder has a date and time stamp that indicates when the replica was created. You would then click the button corresponding to the action you want to perform. Three options are available.

- **View**   Click View to open the shadow copy replica of the selected folder in Windows Explorer. You can then work with the files it contains, much like a normal folder. Although you can copy files to other locations, you won't be able to delete or save files in the shadow copy folder.

- **Copy**   Click Copy to display the Copy Items dialog box, which lets you copy the replica of the folder to a location you specify. This is a convenient way to restore multiple files without affecting existing files or to create a copy of a folder replica so that you can work with the files.

- **Restore**   Click Restore to roll back the shared folder to its state as of the replica that you selected. Be very careful of using this option because it will most likely result in losing any changes subsequent to the date and time of the replica that you've selected. If, for example, a user accidentally deleted multiple files or altered many files incorrectly, you might want to use this option to restore the entire folder to a previous point in time. Otherwise, you'll probably want to view or copy the folder so that you can work with individual files.

Tip   In the *Microsoft Windows Server 2003 Resource Kit* tools, you'll find a handy command-line tool for working with shadow copies, VolRest. You can use this tool to search for a file on a server and list its available versions as well as to locate previous versions of a file and restore those versions to a designated folder. You can download the resource kit tools package for free from the Microsoft Download Center Web site (search for RKTOOLS.EXE) and install it on any Windows XP Professional or Windows Server 2003 computer. Afterward, type **volrest /?** at the command prompt to see the command's syntax and review the VolRest articles in the Help And Command Center to learn how to use the command.

Part III

Windows XP Professional Networking, Optimization, and Security

This part of the book covers the interrelated topics of networking and security. Chapter 13 covers techniques you can use to configure TCP/IP networking and local area connections. The chapter also provides tips for troubleshooting network problems. Chapter 14 explores mobile networking and remote access. In addition to learning how to configure dial-up, broadband, wireless, and virtual private networking, you'll learn how to troubleshoot these types of connections.

Chapter 15 starts by explaining how to customize the Microsoft Internet Explorer interface for your organization and then explores dozens of ways that you can optimize Internet settings for programs, proxies, connections, and security zones to make your environment more secure and easier to work with.

In Chapter 16, you'll find tips and techniques for correcting disk errors, defragmenting volumes, enhancing performance, and scheduling maintenance tasks. Chapter 17 starts with a discussion on remote assistance and troubleshooting and then goes on to discuss creating restore points and recovering systems from restore points.

Chapter 13

Configuring and Troubleshooting TCP/IP Networking

In this chapter:

Installing Networking Components...............................325

Configuring Local Area Connections 327

Managing Local Area Connections...............................336

Troubleshooting and Testing Network Settings..................339

This chapter focuses on managing local area connections, which are used to communicate on a network. For local area networking to work properly, you must install networking components and configure network communications using Dynamic Host Configuration Protocol (DHCP), Domain Name System (DNS), and Windows Internet Naming Service (WINS). DHCP is used for dynamic configuration of networking and Internet Protocol (IP) address settings. Both DNS and WINS provide name resolution services, with DNS being the preferred service and WINS being maintained for backward compatibility with previous versions of the Microsoft Windows operating system.

Installing Networking Components

If you want to install networking on a computer, you must install Transmission Control Protocol/Internet Protocol (TCP/IP) networking and a network adapter. Microsoft Windows XP uses TCP/IP as the default wide area network (WAN) protocol. (In this book, "Windows XP" refers to Windows XP Professional unless otherwise indicated.) Together these protocols make it possible for computers to communicate across various networks and the Internet using network adapters, whether network interface cards, universal serial bus (USB)–attachable network adapters, Personal Computer Memory Card International Association (PCMCIA)–attachable network adapters, or built-in adapters on the motherboard.

Installing Network Adapters

Network adapters are hardware devices that are used to communicate on networks. You can install and configure network adapters by completing the following steps:

1. Configure the network adapter following the manufacturer's instructions. For example, you might need to modify the Interrupt setting or the Port setting of the adapter using the software provided by the manufacturer.

2. If installing a network interface card, disconnect the computer, unplug it, and install the adapter card in the appropriate slot on the computer. When you're finished, boot the system.

3. Windows XP should detect the new adapter during startup. If you have a separate driver disk for the adapter, you should insert it now. Otherwise, you might be prompted to insert a driver disk.

4. If Windows XP doesn't detect the adapter automatically, follow the installation instructions in the sections of Chapter 3 entitled "Configuring Device Drivers" and "Managing Hardware."

5. If networking services aren't installed on the system, install them as described in the next section.

Installing Networking Services (TCP/IP)

Networking is normally installed during Windows XP installation. You can also install TCP/IP networking through Network Connections. If you're installing TCP/IP after installing Windows XP, log on to the computer using an account with Administrator privileges and then follow these steps:

1. Access Network Connections. (Click Start, then point to Programs or All Programs as appropriate, then to Accessories, then to Communications, and finally to Network Connections. Alternatively, type **control netconnections** at a command prompt.)

2. Double-click the connection you want to work with. In the Local Area Connection Status dialog box, click Properties. This displays the Local Area Connection Properties dialog box shown in Figure 13-1. If Internet Protocol (TCP/IP) isn't shown in the list of installed components, you'll need to install it. Click Install. Click Protocol, and then click Add. In the Select Network Protocol dialog box, select Internet Protocol (TCP/IP), and then click OK.

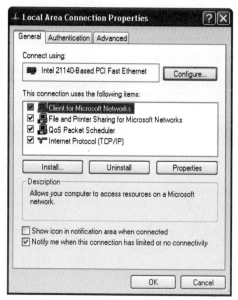

Figure 13-1   Use the Local Area Connection Properties dialog box to install and configure TCP/IP.

3. In the Local Area Connection Properties dialog box, make sure that the Internet Protocol (TCP/IP) check box is selected, and then click OK.

4. As necessary, follow the instructions in the next section for configuring local area connections for the computer.

Configuring Local Area Connections

A local area connection is created automatically if a computer has a network adapter and is connected to a network. If a computer has multiple network adapters and is connected to a network, you'll see one local area connection for each adapter. If no network connection is available, you should connect the computer to the network or create a different type of connection, as explained in the section of this chapter entitled "Managing Local Area Connections."

Computers use IP addresses to communicate over TCP/IP. Windows XP provides the following ways to configure IP addressing:

- **Manually**   IP addresses that are assigned manually are called static IP addresses. Static IP addresses are fixed and don't change unless you change them. You'll usually assign static IP addresses to Windows servers, and when you do this, you'll need to configure additional information to help the server navigate the network.

- **Dynamically**   A DHCP server (if one is installed on the network) assigns dynamic IP addresses at startup, and the addresses might change over time. Dynamic IP addressing is the default configuration.

- **Alternatively**   When a computer is configured to use DHCP and no DHCP server is available, Windows XP assigns an alternate private IP address automatically. By default, the alternate IP address is in the range from 169.254.0.1 to 169.254.255.254 with a subnet mask of 255.255.0.0. You can also specify a user-configured alternate IP address, which is particularly useful for laptop users.

Configuring Static IP Addresses

When you assign a static IP address, you need to tell the computer the IP address you want to use, the subnet mask for this IP address, and, if necessary, the default gateway to use for internetwork communications. An IP address is a numeric identifier for a computer. IP addressing schemes vary according to how your network is configured, but they're normally assigned from a range of addresses for a particular network segment. For example, if you're working with a computer on the network segment 10.0.10.0 with a subnet mask of 255.255.255.0, the address range you have available for computers is from 10.0.10.1 to 10.0.10.254. In this range, the address 10.0.10.255 is reserved for network broadcasts.

If you're on a private network that is indirectly connected to the Internet, you should use private IP addresses. Private network addresses are summarized in Table 13-1.

Table 13-1   Private Network Addresses

Private Network ID	Subnet Mask	Network Address Range
10.0.0.0	255.0.0.0	10.0.0.0–10.255.255.255
172.16.0.0	255.240.0.0	172.16.0.0–172.31.255.255
192.168.0.0	255.255.0.0	192.168.0.0–192.168.255.255

All other network addresses are public and must be leased or purchased. If the network is connected directly to the Internet and you've obtained a range of IP addresses from your Internet Service Provider, you can use the IP addresses you've been assigned.

Using the PING Command to Check an Address

Before you assign a static IP address, you should make sure that the address isn't already in use or reserved for use with DHCP. You can check to see if an address is in use with the PING command. Open a command prompt and type **ping**, followed by the IP address you want to check. To test the IP address 10.0.10.12, you would use the following command:

```
ping 10.0.10.12
```

If you receive a successful reply from the PING test, the IP address is in use and you should try another one. If the request times out for all four PING attempts, the IP address isn't active on the network at this time and probably isn't in use. Your company's network administrator would be able to confirm this for you as well.

Configuring Static IP Addresses

To configure static IP addresses, complete the following steps:

1. Access Network Connections. (Click Start, point to Programs or All Programs as appropriate, then to Accessories, then to Communications, and finally to Network Connections. Alternatively, type **control netconnections** at a command prompt.)

   Note   One local area network (LAN) connection is shown for each network adapter installed. These connections are created automatically.

2. Double-click the connection that you want to work with. Click Properties and then double-click Internet Protocol (TCP/IP) to open the Internet Protocol (TCP/IP) Properties dialog box shown in Figure 13-2, or you can select Internet Protocol (TCP/IP) and then click Properties.

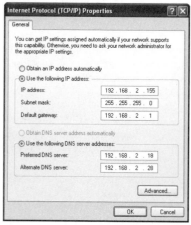

Figure 13-2   Use the Internet Protocol (TCP/IP) Properties dialog box to configure dynamic or static IP addressing.

3. Click Use The Following IP Address, then type the IP address in the IP Address text box. The IP address you assign to the computer must not be used anywhere else on the network.

4. Press the Tab key. The Subnet Mask field ensures that the computer communicates over the network properly. Windows XP should insert a default value for the subnet mask into the Subnet Mask text box. If the network doesn't use subnets, the default value should suffice, but if it does use subnets, you'll need to change this value as appropriate for your network.

5. If the computer needs to access other TCP/IP networks, the Internet, or other subnets, you must specify a default gateway. Type the IP address of the network's default router in the Default Gateway text box.

6. DNS is needed for domain name resolution. Type a preferred and alternate DNS server address in the text boxes provided.

7. When you're finished, click OK, and then click Close. Repeat this process for other network adapters you want to configure. Keep in mind that each network adapter must have a unique IP address.

8. Configure WINS as necessary, following the technique outlined in the section of this chapter entitled "Configuring WINS Resolution."

Configuring Dynamic IP Addresses and Alternate IP Addressing

Although static IP addresses can be used with workstations, most workstations use dynamic and alternative IP addressing. You configure dynamic and alternative addressing by completing the following steps:

1. Access Network Connections. (Click Start, point to Programs or All Programs as appropriate, then to Accessories, then to Communications, and finally to Network Connections. Alternatively, type **control netconnections** at a command prompt.)

 Note One LAN connection is shown for each network adapter installed. These connections are created automatically. If you don't see a LAN connection for an installed adapter, check the driver for the adapter. It might be installed incorrectly.

2. Double-click the connection that you want to work with. Click Properties and then double-click Internet Protocol (TCP/IP) to open the Internet Protocol (TCP/IP) Properties dialog box, or you can select Internet Protocol (TCP/IP) and then click Properties.

3. Select Obtain An IP Address Automatically. If desired, select Obtain DNS Server Address Automatically. Or select Use The Following DNS Server Addresses and then type a preferred and alternate DNS server address in the text boxes provided.

4. When you use dynamic addressing with desktop computers, you should configure an automatic alternative address. To use this configuration, on the Alternate Configuration tab, select Automatic Private IP Address. Click OK, click Close, and then skip the remaining steps.

5. When you use dynamic addressing with mobile computers, you'll usually want to configure the alternative address manually. To use this configuration, on the Alternate Configuration tab, select User Configured and then type the IP address you want to use in the IP Address text box. The IP address that you assign to the computer should be a private IP address, as shown in Table 13-1, and it must not be in use anywhere else when the settings are applied.

6. Complete the alternate configuration by entering a subnet mask, default gateway, DNS, and WINS settings. When you're finished, click OK, and then click Close.

Note   You'll find more detailed information on configuring laptops in the section entitled "Configuring Networking for Laptops," in Chapter 8, "Managing Laptops and Traveling Users."

Configuring Multiple Gateways

To provide fault tolerance in case of a router outage, you can choose to configure Windows XP computers so that they use multiple default gateways. When multiple gateways are assigned, Windows XP uses the gateway metric to determine which gateway is used and at what time. The gateway metric indicates the routing cost of using a gateway. The gateway with the lowest routing cost, or metric, is used first. If the computer can't communicate with this gateway, Windows XP tries to use the gateway with the next lowest metric.

The best way to configure multiple gateways depends on the configuration of your network. If computers use DHCP, you'll probably want to configure the additional gateways through settings on the DHCP server. If computers use static IP addresses or you want to set gateways specifically, assign them by completing the following steps:

1. Access Network Connections. (Click Start, point to Programs or All Programs as appropriate, then to Accessories, then to Communications, and finally to Network Connections. Alternatively, type **control netconnections** at a command prompt.)

2. Double-click the connection that you want to work with. Click Properties and then double-click Internet Protocol (TCP/IP) to open the Internet Protocol (TCP/IP) Properties dialog box, or you can select Internet Protocol (TCP/IP) and then click Properties.

3. Click Advanced to open the Advanced TCP/IP Settings dialog box shown in Figure 13-3.

Figure 13-3   Use the Advanced TCP/IP Settings dialog box to configure multiple IP addresses and gateways.

4. The Default Gateways panel shows the current gateways that have been manually configured (if any). You can enter additional default gateways, as necessary. Click Add, and then type the gateway address in the Gateway text box.

5. By default, Windows XP automatically assigns a metric to the gateway. You can also assign the metric manually. To do this, clear the Automatic Metric check box and then enter a metric in the text box provided.

6. Click Add and then repeat steps 4–6 for each gateway you want to add.

7. Click OK twice, and then click Close.

Configuring DNS Resolution

DNS is a host name resolution service that you can use to determine the IP address of a computer from its host name. This allows users to work with host names, such as *http://www.msn.com* or *http://www.microsoft.com*, rather than an IP address, such as 192.168.5.102 or 192.168.12.68. DNS is the primary name service for Windows XP and the Internet.

As with gateways, the best way to configure DNS depends on the configuration of your network. If computers use DHCP, you'll probably want to configure DNS through settings on the DHCP server. If computers use static IP addresses or you want to specifically configure DNS for an individual user or system, you'll want to configure DNS manually.

Basic DNS Settings

You can configure basic DNS settings by completing the following steps:

1. Access Network Connections. (Click Start, point to Programs or All Programs as appropriate, then to Accessories, then to Communications, and finally to Network Connections. Alternatively, type **control netconnections** at a command prompt.)

2. Double-click the connection that you want to work with. Click Properties and then double-click Internet Protocol (TCP/IP) to open the Internet Protocol (TCP/IP) Properties dialog box, or you can select Internet Protocol (TCP/IP) and then click Properties.

3. If the computer is using DHCP and you want DHCP to specify the DNS server address, select Obtain DNS Server Address Automatically. Otherwise, select Use The Following DNS Server Addresses and then type primary and alternate DNS server addresses in the text boxes provided.

Advanced DNS Settings

You configure advanced DNS settings using the DNS tab of the Advanced TCP/IP Settings dialog box shown in Figure 13-4. You use the fields of the DNS tab as follows:

- **DNS Server Addresses, In Order Of Use**   Use this area to specify the IP address of each DNS server that is used for domain name resolution. Click Add if you wish to add a server IP address to the list. Click Remove to remove a selected server address from the list. Click Edit to edit the selected entry. You can specify multiple servers for DNS resolution. Their priority is determined by the order. If the first server isn't available to respond to a host name resolution request, the next DNS server on the list is accessed, and so on. To change the position of a server in the list box, select it and then use the Up or Down arrow button.

- **Append Primary And Connection Specific DNS Suffixes**   Normally, this option is selected by default. Select this option to resolve unqualified computer names in the primary domain. For example, if the computer name Gandolf is used and the parent domain is microsoft.com, the computer name would resolve to gandolf.microsoft.com. If the fully qualified computer name doesn't exist in the parent domain, the query fails. The parent domain used is the one set in the System Properties dialog box on the Computer Name tab. (Double-click System in Control Panel and then click the Computer Name tab to check the settings.)

- **Append Parent Suffixes Of The Primary DNS Suffix**   This option is selected by default. Select this option to resolve unqualified computer names using the parent-child domain hierarchy. If a query fails in the immediate parent domain, the suffix for the parent of the parent domain is used to try to resolve the query. This process continues until the top of the DNS domain hierarchy is reached. For example, if the computer name Gandolf is used in the dev.microsoft.com domain, DNS would attempt to resolve the computer name to gandolf.dev.microsoft.com. If this didn't work, DNS would attempt to resolve the computer name to gandolf.microsoft.com.

- **Append These DNS Suffixes (In Order)**   Select this option to set specific DNS suffixes to use rather than resolving through the parent domain. Click Add if you want to add a domain suffix to the list. Click Remove to remove a selected domain suffix from the list. Click Edit to edit the selected entry. You can specify multiple domain suffixes, which are used in order. If the first suffix doesn't resolve properly, DNS attempts to use the next suffix in the list. If this fails, the next suffix is used, and so on. To change the order of the domain suffixes, select the suffix, and then use the Up or Down arrow button to change its position.

- **DNS Suffix For This Connection**   This option sets a specific DNS suffix for the connection that overrides DNS names already configured for use on this connection. Instead, you'll usually set the DNS domain name through the System Properties dialog box on the Computer Name tab.

- **Register This Connection's Addresses In DNS**   Select this option if you want all IP addresses for this connection to be registered in DNS under the computer's fully qualified domain name. This option is selected by default.

Note   Dynamic DNS updates are used in conjunction with DHCP to allow a client to update its A (Host Address) record if its IP address changes and to allow the DHCP server to update the PTR (Pointer) record for the client on the DNS server. DHCP servers can also be configured to update both the A and PTR records on the client's behalf. Dynamic DNS updates are only supported by Microsoft Windows 2000 Server and Microsoft Windows Server 2003. Microsoft Windows NT Server 4 doesn't support this feature.

■ **Use This Connection's DNS Suffix In DNS Registration**   Select this option if you want all IP addresses for this connection to be registered in DNS under the parent domain.

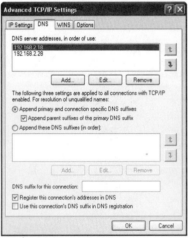

Figure 13-4   Use the DNS tab of the Advanced TCP/IP Settings dialog box to configure advanced DNS settings.

Configuring WINS Resolution

You use WINS to resolve NetBIOS computer names to IP addresses. You can use WINS to help computers on a network determine the address of other computers on the network. If a WINS server is installed on the network, you can use the server to resolve computer names. Although WINS is supported on all versions of Windows, Windows XP primarily uses WINS for backward compatibility.

You can also configure Windows XP computers to use the local file LMHOSTS to resolve NetBIOS computer names. However, LMHOSTS is consulted only if normal name resolution methods fail. In a properly configured network, these files are rarely used. Thus, the preferred method of NetBIOS computer name resolution is WINS in conjunction with a WINS server.

As with gateways and DNS, the best way to configure WINS depends on the configuration of your network. If computers use DHCP, you'll probably want to configure WINS through settings on the DHCP server. If computers use static IP addresses or you want to configure WINS specifically for an individual user or system, you'll want to configure WINS manually.

You can configure WINS by completing the following steps:

1. Access the Advanced TCP/IP Settings dialog box and click the WINS tab. This displays the window shown in Figure 13-5.

Figure 13-5 Use the WINS tab of the Advanced TCP/IP Settings dialog box to configure WINS resolution for NetBIOS computer names.

2. The panel named WINS Addresses, In Order Of Use allows you to specify the IP addresses of each WINS server that is used for NetBIOS name resolution. Click Add if you want to add a server IP address to the list. Click Remove to remove a selected server from the list. Click Edit to edit the selected entry.

3. You can specify multiple servers, which are used in order, for WINS resolution. If the first server isn't available to respond to a NetBIOS name resolution request, the next WINS server on the list is accessed, and so on. To change the position of a server in the list box, select it and then use the Up or Down arrow button.

4. To enable LMHOSTS lookups, select the Enable LMHOSTS Lookup check box. If you want the computer to use an existing LMHOSTS file defined somewhere on the network, retrieve this file by clicking Import LMHOSTS. You generally will use LMHOSTS only when other name resolution methods fail.

5. NetBIOS Over TCP/IP services are required for WINS name resolution. Select one of the following options to configure WINS name resolution using NetBIOS:

❏ If you use DHCP and dynamic addressing, you can get the NetBIOS setting from the DHCP server. Select Default: Use NetBIOS Setting From The DHCP Server.

❏ If you use a static IP address or the DHCP server does not provide NetBIOS settings, select Enable NetBIOS Over TCP/IP.

❏ If WINS and NetBIOS are not used on the network, select Disable NetBIOS Over TCP/IP. This eliminates the NetBIOS broadcasts that would otherwise be sent by the computer.

6. Repeat this process for other network adapters, as necessary.

 Best Practices   LMHOSTS files are maintained locally on a computer-by-computer basis, which can eventually make them unreliable. Rather than relying on LMHOSTS, ensure that your DNS and WINS servers are configured properly and are accessible to the network for centralized administration of name resolution services.

Managing Local Area Connections

Local area connections make it possible for computers to access resources on the network and the Internet. One local area connection is created automatically for each network adapter installed on a computer. This section examines techniques you can use to manage these connections.

Enabling and Disabling Local Area Connections

Local area connections are created and connected automatically. If you want to disconnect from the network or start another connection, complete the following steps:

1. Access Network Connections. (Click Start, point to Programs or All Programs as appropriate, then to Accessories, then to Communications, and finally to Network Connections. Alternatively, type **control netconnections** at a command prompt.)

2. Right-click the connection that you want to disable, and then select Disconnect or Disable to deactivate the connection. Typically, dial-up connections have a Disconnect option, and most other types of connections have a Disable option.

3. Later, if you want to activate the connection, you can right-click it and select Connect or Enable. Typically, dial-up connections have a Connect option, and most other types of connections have an Enable option.

Checking the Status, Speed, and Activity for Local Area Connections

To check the status of a local area connection, right-click the connection and then select Status. This displays the Local Area Connection Status dialog box. If the connection is disabled or the media is unplugged, you won't be able to access this dialog box. Enable the connection or connect the network cable to resolve the problem and then try to display the status dialog box again.

The General tab of this dialog box, shown in Figure 13-6, provides useful information regarding the following:

- **Status**   The current connection state. You'll typically see the status as Connected because if the state should change, Windows XP usually closes the status dialog box.

- **Duration**   The amount of time the connection has been established. If the duration is fairly short, the user either recently connected to the network or the connection was reset recently.

- **Speed**   The speed of the connection. This should read 10.0 Mbps for 10 Mbps connections and 100.0 Mbps for 100 Mbps connections. An incorrect setting can affect the user's performance.

- **Packets**   The number of TCP/IP packets sent and the number received by the connection. As the computer sends or receives packets, you'll see the computer icons light up to indicate the flow of traffic.

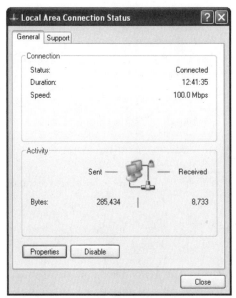

Figure 13-6   The General tab of the Local Area Connection Status dialog box provides access to summary information regarding connections, properties, and support.

Viewing Network Configuration Information

In Windows XP you can view the current configuration for network adapters in several ways. To view configuration settings using the Local Area Connection Status dialog box, follow these steps:

1. Access Network Connections. (Click Start, point to Programs or All Programs as appropriate, then to Accessories, then to Communications, and finally to Network Connections. Alternatively, type **control netconnections** at a command prompt.)

2. Right-click the connection that you want to examine and then select Status.

3. Click the Support tab, shown in Figure 13-7. The fields of the Internet Protocol (TCP/IP) panel provide basic information about the connection, including address type (Static, Assigned By DHCP, or Autoconfigured), IP address, subnet mask, and default gateway.

Figure 13-7 Use the Support tab to obtain information on the current configuration of a local area connection.

4. For more detailed information, click Details. This displays the Network Connection Details dialog box in which you'll find both the basic information fields and additional information, including:

   ❏ **Physical Address** The machine or Media Access Control (MAC) address of the network adapter. This address is unique for each network adapter.

   ❏ **IP Address** The IP address assigned to the network connection.

   ❏ **Subnet Mask** The subnet mask assigned to the network connection.

❏ **Default Gateway**   The IP address of the default gateway used by the network connection.

❏ **DHCP Server**   The IP address of the DHCP server from which the current lease was obtained (DHCP only).

❏ **Lease Obtained**   A date and time stamp for when the DHCP lease was obtained (DHCP only).

❏ **Lease Expires**   A date and time stamp for when the DHCP lease expires (DHCP only).

❏ **DNS Servers**   DNS server IP addresses.

❏ **WINS Servers**   WINS server IP addresses.

You can also use the IPCONFIG command to view advanced configuration settings. To do so, follow these steps:

1. Click Start and select Run. In the Run dialog box, type **cmd** in the Open text box and then click OK. This starts a command prompt.

2. At the command line, type **ipconfig /all** to see detailed configuration information for all network adapters configured on the computer.

Renaming Local Area Connections

Windows XP assigns default names for local area connections initially. You can rename the connections at any time by right-clicking the connection, selecting Rename, and then typing a new connection name. If a computer has multiple local area connections, proper naming can help you and others better understand what a particular connection is used for.

Repairing Local Area Connections

Occasionally network cables can get unplugged or the network adapter might experience a problem that temporarily prevents it from working. After you plug the cable back in, or solve the adapter problem, the connection should automatically reconnect. If it doesn't, right-click the connection and select Repair. Repairing the connection can sometimes resolve connection issues. With connections that use DHCP, the repair operation will also attempt to release and then renew the DHCP lease, as discussed in "Releasing and Renewing DHCP Settings."

Note   If the repair operation doesn't work, see the following section.

Troubleshooting and Testing Network Settings

Windows XP includes many tools for troubleshooting and testing TCP/IP connectivity. This section looks at a few basic tests that you should perform whenever you install or modify a computer's network settings. It then examines techniques for resolving difficult networking problems involving DHCP and DNS. The final section shows you how to perform detailed network diagnostics testing.

Performing Basic Network Tests

Whenever you install a new computer or make configuration changes to the computer's network settings, you should test the configuration. The most basic TCP/IP test is to use the PING command to test the computer's connection to the network. PING is a command-line command, and to use it, type **ping <host>** at the command prompt, where <host> is either the computer name or the IP address of the host computer you're trying to reach.

With Windows XP, you can use the following methods to test the configuration using PING:

- **Try to PING IP addresses** If the computer is configured correctly and the host you're trying to reach is accessible to the network, PING should receive a reply. If it can't reach the host, PING times out.

- **On domains that use WINS, try to PING NetBIOS computer names** If NetBIOS computer names are resolved correctly by PING, the NetBIOS facilities, such as WINS, are correctly configured for the computer.

- **On domains that use DNS, try to PING DNS host names** If fully qualified DNS host names are resolved correctly by PING, DNS name resolution is configured properly.

You might also want to test network browsing for the computer. If the computer is a member of a Windows XP domain and computer browsing is enabled throughout the domain, log on to the computer and then use Windows Explorer or My Network Places to browse other computers in the domain. Afterward, log on to a different computer in the domain and try to browse the computer you just configured. These tests tell you if the DNS resolution is being handled properly in the local environment. If you can't browse, check the configuration of the DNS services and protocols.

 Real World Access to network resources in My Network Places is dependent on the Computer Browser service. This service is responsible for maintaining a list of computers on a network. If the service is stopped or isn't working properly, a computer won't see available resources in My Network Places. You can check the status of the Computer Browser service in Computer Management. Expand Services And Applications, and then select Services in the left pane. The status of the Computer Browser service should be Started. If the status is blank, the service isn't running and should be started.

In some cases, the Computer Browser service might be running normally, but there might not be an update-to-date list of resources in My Network Places. This can happen because the service performs periodic updates of the resource list rather than checking continuously for updates. If a resource you want to use isn't listed, you can either wait for it to become available (which should take less than 15 minutes in most cases), or you can connect to the resource directly using the UNC name or IP address of the resource as discussed in Chapter 11 in the section "Using and Accessing Shared Folders."

Resolving IP Addressing Problems

The current IP address settings of a computer can be obtained as discussed earlier in this chapter in the section "Viewing Network Configuration Information." If a computer is having problems accessing network resources or communicating with other computers, there might be an IP addressing problem. Take a close look at the IP address currently assigned, as well as other IP address settings, and use these pointers to help in your troubleshooting:

- If the IP address currently assigned to the computer is in the range 169.254.0.1 to 169.254.255.254, the computer is using Automatic Private IP Addressing (APIPA). An automatic private IP address is assigned to a computer when it is configured to use DHCP and its DHCP client cannot reach a DHCP server. When using APIPA, Windows XP will automatically check for a DHCP server to become available periodically. If a computer doesn't eventually obtain a dynamic IP address, it usually means there is a problem with the network connection. Check the network cable, and if necessary trace the cable back to the switch or hub into which it connects.

- If the IP address and the subnet mask of the computer are currently set as 0.0.0.0, the network is either disconnected or someone attempted to use a static IP address that duplicated another IP address already in use on the network. In this case, you should access Network Connections and determine the state of the connection. If the connection is disabled or disconnected, this should be shown. Right-click the connection, and select Enable or Repair as appropriate. If the connection is already enabled, you will need to modify the IP address settings for the connection.

- If the IP address is dynamically assigned, check to make sure that another computer on the network isn't using the same IP address. You can do this by disconnecting the network cable for the computer that you are working with and pinging the IP address in question. If you receive a response from the PING test, you know that another computer is using the IP address. This computer probably has an improper static IP address or a reservation that isn't set up properly.

- If the IP address appears to be set correctly, check the network mask, gateway DNS, and WINS settings by comparing the network settings of the computer you are troubleshooting with those of a computer that is known to have a good network configuration. One of the biggest problem areas is the network mask. When subnetting is used, the network mask used in one area of the network might look very similar to that of another area of the network. For example, the network mask in one area might be 255.255.255.240 and in another area it might be 255.255.255.248.

Releasing and Renewing DHCP Settings

DHCP servers can assign many network configuration settings automatically. These include IP addresses, default gateways, primary and secondary DNS servers, primary and secondary WINS servers, and more. When computers use dynamic addressing, they are assigned a lease on a specific IP address. This lease is good for a specific time period and must be renewed periodically. When the lease needs to be renewed, the computer contacts the DHCP server that provided the lease. If the server is available, the lease is renewed and a new lease period is granted. You can also renew leases manually as necessary on individual computers or by using the DHCP server itself.

Problems can occur during the lease assignment and renewal process that prevent network communications. If the server isn't available and cannot be reached before a lease expires, the IP address can become invalid. If this happens, the computer might use the alternate IP address configuration to set an alternate address, which in most cases has settings that are inappropriate and prevent proper communications. To resolve this problem, you'll need to release and then renew the DHCP lease.

Another type of problem occurs when users move around to various offices and subnets within the organization. While moving from location to location, their computers might obtain DHCP settings from the wrong server. When the users return to their offices, the computer might seem sluggish or perform incorrectly due to the settings assigned by the DHCP server at another location. If this happens, you'll need to release and then renew the DHCP lease.

You can release and renew DHCP leases using the graphical interface by completing the following tasks:

1. Click Start, then point to Programs or All Programs as appropriate, then to Accessories, then to Communications, and finally to Network Connections.

2. Right-click the connection you want to examine and then select Status. This displays the Local Area Connection Status dialog box.

3. Click the Support tab. You can now attempt to update the current DHCP lease by clicking Repair. The repair operation will first try to renew the lease. If this isn't possible, it will release the lease and then try to obtain a new one.

4. At the end of the repair operation, the Repair Local Area Connection dialog box tells you it is completed. Click Close.

 Real World   The release and renewal process takes a bit longer than simply renewing a lease, and it can be more problematic. In some cases, the settings might be set incorrectly to the alternate IP address configuration. If this happens, it is usually because the computer couldn't communicate with the DHCP server. Other times, the prompt tells you the process was successful, but a check of the Lease Obtained and Lease Expires values shows you that a new lease wasn't really obtained. You'll know this because both values are set to the date and time you attempted to release and renew the settings. (To view the Lease Obtained and Lease Expires values, click Details on the Support tab of the Local Area Connection Status dialog box.)

You can also use the IPCONFIG command to renew and release settings by following these steps:

1. Click Start and select Run. Type **cmd** in the Open text box of the Run dialog box and then click OK. This starts a command prompt.

2. To release the current settings for all network adapters, type **ipconfig /release** at the command line. Then renew the lease by typing **ipconfig /renew**.

3. To only renew a DHCP lease for all network adapters, type **ipconfig /renew** at the command line.

4. You can check the updated settings by typing **ipconfig /all** at the command line.

> **Real World**   If a computer has multiple network adapters and
> you only want to work with one or a subset of the adapters, you can
> do this by specifying all or part of the connection name after the
> **ipconfig /renew** or **ipconfig /release** command. Use the asterisk as a
> wildcard to match any characters in a connection's name. For example,
> if you wanted to renew the lease for all connections with names starting
> with "Loc," you could type the command **ipconfig /renew Loc***. If you
> wanted to release the settings for all connections containing the word
> "Network," you could type the command **ipconfig /release *Network***.

Registering and Flushing DNS

The DNS resolver cache maintains a history of DNS lookups that have been performed when a user accesses network resources using TCP/IP. This cache contains forward lookups, which provide host name to IP address resolution, and reverse lookups, which provide IP address to host name resolution. Once a DNS entry is stored in the resolver cache for a particular DNS host, the local computer no longer has to query external servers for DNS information on that host. This allows the computer to resolve DNS requests locally, which provides a quicker response.

How long entries are stored in the resolver cache depends on the Time to Live (TTL) value assigned to the record by the originating server. To view current records and see the remaining TTL value for each record, at the command line type **ipconfig /displaydns**. These values are given as the number of seconds that a particular record can remain in the cache before it expires. These values are continually being counted down by the local computer. When the TTL value reaches zero, the record expires and is removed from the resolver cache.

Occasionally, you'll find that the resolver cache needs to be cleared out to remove old entries and allow computers to check for updated DNS entries before the normal expiration and purging process takes place. Typically, this happens because server IP addresses have changed and the current entries in the resolver cache point to the old addresses rather than the new ones. Sometimes the resolver cache itself can get out of sync, particularly when DHCP has been misconfigured.

Real World Skilled administrators know that they should start to decrease the TTL values for DNS records that are going to be changed several weeks in advance of the actual change. Typically, this means reducing the TTL from a number of days (or weeks) to a number of hours, which allows for quicker propagation of the changes to computers that have cached the related DNS records. Once the change is completed, administrators should restore the original TTL value to reduce renewal requests.

In most cases, you can resolve problems with the DNS resolver cache by either flushing the cache or reregistering DNS. When you flush the resolver cache, all DNS entries are cleared out of the cache and new entries are not created until the next time the computer performs a DNS lookup on a particular host or IP address. When you reregister DNS, Windows XP attempts to refresh all current DHCP leases and then performs a lookup on each DNS entry in the resolver cache. By looking up each host or IP address again, the entries are renewed and reregistered in the resolver cache. You'll generally want to flush the cache completely and allow the computer to perform lookups as needed. Reregister DNS only when you suspect that there are problems with DHCP and the DNS resolver cache.

You can use the IPCONFIG command to flush and reregister entries in the DNS resolver cache by following these steps:

1. Click Start and select Run. Type **cmd** in the Open text box of the Run dialog box and then click OK. This starts a command prompt.

2. To clear out the resolver cache, type **ipconfig /flushdns** at the command line.

3. To renew DHCP leases and reregister DNS entries, type **ipconfig /registerdns** at the command line.

4. When the tasks are complete, you can check your work by typing **ipconfig /displaydns** at the command line.

Performing Detailed Network Diagnostics

Because there are so many interdependencies between services, protocols, and configuration settings, troubleshooting network problems can be difficult. Fortunately, Windows XP includes a powerful network diagnostics toolkit for pinpointing problems that relate to the following:

- General network connectivity problems
- Internet service settings for e-mail, newsgroups, and proxies
- Settings for modems, network clients, and network adapters
- DNS, DHCP, and WINS configuration
- Default gateways and IP addresses

You can, for example, use the toolkit to find out that another computer is using the IP address you've configured for the current system. To run the diagnostics tests using the default setup, follow these steps:

1. Click Start and then select Help And Support. This displays the Help And Support Center.

2. Under Pick A Task, select Use Tools To View Your Computer Information And Diagnose Problems.

3. In the Tools console, select Network Diagnostics and then in the right pane, click Scan Your System. This starts the diagnostic testing.

During testing, the Help And Support Services console is displayed with a progress bar showing the status of the diagnostics tests. Default tests include PING tests to determine if the network is reachable; connectivity tests over the configured modems and network adapters; and Internet service tests for e-mail, newsgroups, and proxies. The tests also return information about the computer system, operating system configuration, and operating system version.

When complete, you'll see the results of the testing, as shown in Figure 13-8. As you examine the results, look for items that are labeled Not Configured or Failed because these might point to problem areas. If you see items with these or other labels that indicate problems, click the plus sign (+) to the left of the entry to examine the related diagnostics information. Continue to navigate through the information provided until you find the problem area.

Real World   On a test system I was working with, the DNS server entries were misconfigured and the servers were unreachable. The failure to PING the DNS servers showed up as a failure of the primary network adapter. When I expanded the adapter entry, the DNSServerSearchOrder entry was flagged as Failed. By continuing to expand the entries, I found that the computer was unable to send packets to the DNS servers because the primary and secondary DNS server IP addresses were set incorrectly on the DHCP server. After I updated the settings on the DHCP server and renewed the DHCP lease, the computer was again able to resolve DNS properly.

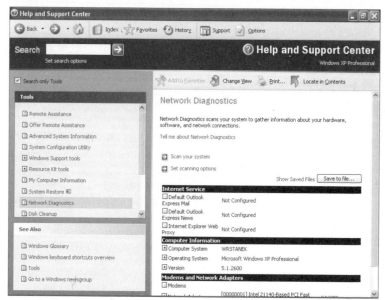

Figure 13-8   Use network diagnostics to pinpoint network configuration problems.

If you want to conduct more extensive testing, follow these steps:

1. Scroll back to the top of this Network Diagnostics pane and click Set Scanning Options. This displays an Options page.

2. Under Actions, select actions that should be performed by selecting or clearing the related check boxes. To get more details, select Verbose.

3. Under Categories, select the types of tests that should be performed by selecting or clearing the related check boxes. Additional tests that you might want to perform include the following:

   ❏ **Domain Name System (DNS)**   Performs thorough DNS testing
   ❏ **Dynamic Host Configuration Protocol (DHCP)**   Analyzes the DHCP configuration and checks the current lease
   ❏ **Default Gateways**   Ensures that all the specified gateways are available

4. To save the setting changes, click Save Options.

5. Rerun the diagnostics tests by clicking Scan Your System at the top of this Network Diagnostics pane. Note any problems, and resolve them following the techniques discussed earlier in this chapter.

Chapter 14
Managing Mobile Networking and Remote Access

In this chapter:

Understanding Mobile Networking and Remote Access 347

Creating Connections for Remote Access 349

Configuring Connection Properties 359

Establishing Connections 373

Wireless Networking 378

Users often want to connect to their organization's network from an off-site computer. To do so, they need a dial-up, broadband, or virtual private network (VPN) connection. Dial-up networking allows users to connect off-site computers to their organization's network using a modem and a standard telephone line. Broadband allows users to connect off-site computers to their organization's network using high-speed Digital Subscriber Line (DSL) routers or cable modems. VPN uses encryption to provide secure connectivity over an existing connection, which can be a local area, dial-up, or broadband connection. Increasingly, wireless connections are being used as well. With a wireless connection, computers establish connections using a network adapter that has an antenna that allows it to communicate with similar wireless devices.

Understanding Mobile Networking and Remote Access

Although the underlying technologies are fundamentally different, both dial-up and broadband connections make it possible for users to access your organization's network remotely. With a typical dial-up network configuration, off-site users use their computer's modem and a standard telephone line to connect to a modem pool located at the office. A Microsoft Windows 2000 Server or Microsoft Windows Server 2003 server managing the modem pool and running Routing And Remote Access authenticates the logon ID and password and authorizes the user to connect to the internal network. The user can then access network resources just as she does when working on-site. As long as the user doesn't have another type of connection open, dial-up connections are fairly secure because the user is connecting directly to the office network.

Figure 14-1 provides a representation of dial-up connections using modem pools. Analog modems use dedicated telephone lines to connect users to the internal network at speeds up to 33.6 kilobits per second (Kbps). Digital modems use channels of a T1 line to connect users to the internal network at speeds up to 56 Kbps. In a standard configuration, you might have 8, 12, or 16 modems configured in the pool, each with its own line (or channel). Typically, the modem pool has a lead number that users can call. This number connects to the first modem in the pool. When the lead number is busy, the line rolls over to the next number, which connects to the next modem in the pool, and so on, allowing users to dial a single number to gain access to all modems in the pool.

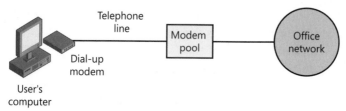

Figure 14-1   Use dial-up to access an office network through a modem pool.

Unlike dial-up connections, which can be made directly to the office network, broadband connections are made through an Internet service provider's (ISP's) network. The user's DSL router or cable modem establishes a connection to the ISP, which in turn connects the user to the public Internet. To connect to the office network, broadband users must establish a VPN between the user's computer and the office network. Figure 14-2 provides a representation of how VPN works.

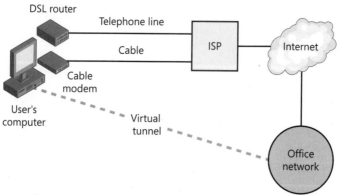

Figure 14-2   Use broadband and VPN to access an office network.

A VPN is an extension of a private network across the public Internet. Once connected, it appears to users that they are directly connected to the office network and they can access network resources just as they do when working on-site. These seamless connections are possible because a virtual tunnel is established between the user's computer and the office network where the VPN technology takes care of routing information over the public Internet. One of two VPN technologies is typically used: Point-to-Point Tunneling Protocol (PPTP) or Layer 2 Tunneling Protocol (L2TP).

Both L2TP and PPTP offer encryption and protection from attacks, but only L2TP uses IP Security (IPSec) for advanced encryption, making it the more secure of the two technologies. Unfortunately, L2TP is also more difficult to configure. When you use L2TP, you'll need to use Microsoft Certificate Services to create a root authority certificate for the organization and then issue individual certificates for each system that will connect to the network using L2TP.

You can also use VPN with dial-up connections. Figure 14-3 shows a typical implementation for using dial-up and VPN together. In this configuration, users go through their ISP to establish a connection to the public Internet and later establish a private connection to the office network. When this configuration becomes standard procedure for dial-up users, your organization won't need dedicated private lines like those reserved for a modem pool.

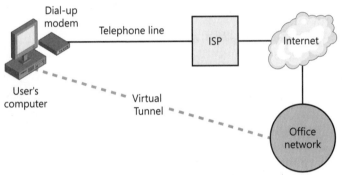

Figure 14-3   Use VPN with dial-up connections to establish secure connections to the office network.

Creating Connections for Remote Access

As discussed previously, you can create both dial-up and broadband connections for remote access. If you want additional security, you can also configure these connections to use VPN. Microsoft Windows XP provides a wizard for creating these connections. (In this book, "Windows XP" refers to Windows XP Professional unless otherwise indicated.) In most cases, you'll want to access this wizard through the Communications folder. Click Start, point to Programs or All Programs as appropriate, then to Accessories, then to Communications, and then finally select New Connection Wizard. You can then create dial-up, broadband, and VPN connections.

Note   The New Connection Wizard can also be accessed in Network Connections. Click the Create A New Connection link under New Tasks.

Real World   Consider whether Group Policy can help you reduce your workload. If you want to use the same connection settings on multiple computers, you could import the settings into Group Policy, and they would then be available to all computers in the related Group Policy object. You can use this technique to deploy new connection configurations, to update existing configurations when you need to make changes, and to delete existing configurations and replace them with new ones. See the section of Chapter 15 entitled "Managing Connection and Proxy Settings" for more information.

Creating a Dial-Up Connection

Windows XP provides two options for making dial-up connections. You can create a dial-up connection to an ISP or a dial-up connection to the workplace. Although the connections are created using a slightly different technique, the settings for the connection options are the same, with the following exceptions:

- A dial-up connection to an ISP doesn't use the Client For Microsoft Networks component, and redials if the line is dropped by default.

- A dial-up connection to the workplace uses the Client For Microsoft Networks component, and doesn't redial if the line is dropped by default.

The networking component Client For Microsoft Networks allows Windows XP systems to communicate in a Windows domain or workgroup. Because most workplaces use Windows domains or workgroups and some ISPs don't, the component is configured for workplace environments and not for ISPs.

Creating dial-up connections is a two-part process. Before you create a dial-up connection, you should check the current phone and modem options, which set dialing rules. Once the dialing rules are configured, you can create the dial-up connection.

Working with Dialing Rules and Locations

Dialing rules are used with modems to determine how phone lines are accessed, what the caller's area code is, and what additional features should be used when dialing connections. Sets of dialing rules are saved as dialing locations in the Phone And Modem Options tool.

Viewing and Setting the Default Dialing Location   To view and set the default dialing location, follow these steps:

1. Access Phone And Modem Options in the Control Panel. The first time you start this tool, you'll see the Location Information dialog box, as shown in Figure 14-4.

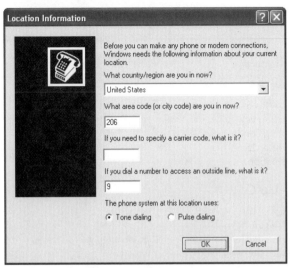

Figure 14-4   The first time you use Phone And Modem Options, you must configure the initial location, which is called My Location.

2. Answer the following questions to configure the default location (My Location):

❑ **What Country/Region Are You In Now?**   Select the country or region you are in, such as United States.

❑ **What Area Code (Or City Code) Are You In Now?**   Type the area or city code as appropriate, such as 212.

❑ **If You Need To Specify A Carrier Code, What Is It?**   You can specify the telephone carrier to use when dialing and establishing connections by entering its carrier code. A carrier code might be necessary if you are making long distance or international calls.

❑ **If You Dial A Number To Access An Outside Line, What Is It?**   Type the number you need to access an outside line, if any. An access code might be necessary to bypass a switch panel within a company or when dialing from a hotel.

❑ **The Phone System At This Location Uses**   Select either Tone Dialing or Pulse Dialing, as appropriate. Most areas of the United States and Canada use tone dialing.

3. Once you configure an initial location and click OK, you'll see the dialog box shown in Figure 14-5. From now on when you access Phone And Modem Options, you'll see this dialog box.

Figure 14-5 Check dialing rules to ensure they are configured properly.

4. Locations configured for the computer are shown in the Locations list by name and area code. The location from which you are currently dialing is selected and highlighted in bold.

5. Initially, the default location is set as My Location. By selecting a different location, you can make it the current or default location. I recommend editing the default location (My Location) and renaming it so that the name used includes the city or office location. To view the configuration of a selected location, click Edit. Then, to rename the location, type a new value in the Location Name field on the General tab and then click OK.

 Note Of all the available dialing rules, the area code is the one you'll work with the most. During installation of the operating system, a default location might have been created with the area code set by the person who installed the computer. In many cases, the default area code is not the one the user needs to use when dialing another location from home.

Creating Dialing Locations You can create dialing locations to set unique rules for each area code from which the user will make dial-up connections. To create a dialing location, follow these steps:

1. Access Phone And Modem Options in the Control Panel. In the Phone And Modem Options dialog box, click New on the Dialing Rules tab. This displays the New Location dialog box shown in Figure 14-6.

Figure 14-6   You can create dialing locations to specify unique sets of dialing rules on a per-area-code basis.

2. The New Location dialog box has three tabs:

    ❑ **General**   Sets the location name, country/region, and area code. On this tab, you can also set access numbers for outside lines when dialing local or long-distance calls, disable call waiting, and specify whether tone or pulse dialing is used. Be sure to use an appropriate location name. Typically, this is the name of the city or metro area from which the user is dialing.

    ❑ **Area Code Rules**   Sets rules that determine how phone numbers are dialed from the location's area code to other area codes and within the location's area code. These rules are useful when multiple area codes that are not long distance are used in the same location. They are also useful when calls within the area code might be local or long-distance calls based on number prefixes.

    ❑ **Calling Card**   Sets a calling card to use when dialing from this location. Calling card information for major carriers is provided and you can also create calling card records.

3. When you are finished creating the location, check that the default location in the Phone And Modem Options dialog box is correct. You might need to select a different entry. Click OK when you are finished.

Deleting Dialing Locations   To delete a dialing location, follow these steps:

1. Access Phone And Modem Options in the Control Panel.

2. In the Phone And Modem Options dialog box, select the location you want to permanently remove and then click Delete. If prompted to confirm the action, click Yes.

3. Select the dialing location that you want to use as the default and then click OK.

Creating a Dial-Up Internet Connection to an ISP

You can create dial-up connections in the following ways:

- If users are dialing up through an ISP that has point of presence (POP) locations throughout the United States and the world, you'll usually want to configure dialing rules and connections for specific locations. Here, you could create a dial-up location called Seattle and a dial-up connection called Connect To ISP In Seattle. In this configuration, you would set the area code for Seattle as well as any special dialing rules and then configure the connection to use the ISP's access numbers for Seattle. You'd also need to show users how to change their current locations when they travel from place to place.

- If users are dialing an 800 number or long distance to access the office modem pool or a special out-of-area access number for an ISP, you'll usually want to configure separate connections rather than separate locations. Here, you would create a connection that dials long distance to establish the connection and a connection that is used when the user is in the local area. You would then need only one dialing location.

To create a dial-up Internet connection, follow these steps:

1. Before you create a dial-up connection, you should check the current phone and modem options as discussed earlier in the section entitled "Working with Dialing Rules and Locations."

 Note If you use dialing rules with a connection and then set area and country codes, you are making it possible for the connection to be used for long-distance calls, which can sometimes be very expensive. If this isn't what you want, you might want to reconsider these selections.

2. To start the New Connection Wizard, click Start, point to Programs or All Programs as appropriate, then to Accessories, then to Communications, and finally select New Connection Wizard.

3. Click Next to display the New Connection Type page shown in Figure 14-7. To make a dial-up connection to an ISP, select Connect To The Internet, click Next, select Set Up My Connection Manually, and click Next again.

4. In the next window, select Connect Using A Dial-up Modem and then click Next. In the ISP Name field, enter the name for the connection, such as Service Provider. Keep in mind that the name should be short (50 characters or fewer) but descriptive.

5. Click Next. You can now set the phone number to dial for this connection using the Phone Number text box.

6. In a domain, the next window allows you to make connections available on a per-machine or per user basis. If you want the connection to be available only to the current user, select My Use Only. If you want the connection to be available to all users of the computer, select Anyone's Use. The Anyone's Use option is best when you plan to assign the connection through Group Policy. Click Next.

Figure 14-7   Select a network connection type, and then click Next.

7. In the next window, shown in Figure 14-8, you are given the opportunity to set account information for the connection. Enter the user name in the field provided and then enter and confirm the password.

8. In most cases, you'll want only the currently logged-on user to be able to use the user name and password you previously specified for this connection. If this is the case, and the option is available, clear Use This Account Name And Password When Anyone Connects To The Internet From This Computer. Clearing this option will force other users to enter their own account information as appropriate.

Figure 14-8   Specify the account information and final settings for the connection.

9. In most cases, you won't want a dial-up connection to be the default, as users will connect primarily to the corporate network through their local area connection. If this is the case, clear Make This My Default Internet Connection.

Security   With Windows XP Service Pack 2 and later, Windows Firewall is enabled for all connections automatically. This is a change from earlier releases for which you had to enable the firewall on each connection specifically. With connections to ISPs, you'll want the Windows Firewall to be on to guard the connection from attacks. However, when you connect directly to the office modem pool *and* no other connections are active at the same time, you don't need the Windows Firewall.

10. Click Next. To add a desktop shortcut, a feature that makes it quick and easy to establish connections, select Add A Shortcut To This Connection To My Desktop.

11. Click Finish to complete the connection creation process. To test the connection settings, follow the steps outlined later in this chapter in the section entitled "Establishing Connections."

Real World   Most organizations use digital phone systems, which don't allow you to make an analog connection to an outside line. If this is the case at your office, you'll need to access an analog line before you can test the connection. Some digital phones can be equipped with digital-to-analog converters that you can use for testing dial-up connections. You might find these converters used with conference phones or fax machines, or you might find that conference phones or fax machines are already connected to analog phone lines.

Creating a Dial-Up Connection to the Workplace

To create a dial-up connection to the workplace, follow these steps:

1. Before you create a dial-up connection, you should check the current phone and modem options, as discussed earlier in the section entitled "Working with Dialing Rules and Locations."

Note   If you use dialing rules with a connection and then set area and country codes, you are making it possible for the connection to be used for long-distance calls, which can sometimes be very expensive. If this isn't what you want, you might want to reconsider these selections.

2. To start the New Connection Wizard, click Start, point to Programs or All Programs as appropriate, then to Accessories, then to Communications, and finally select New Connection Wizard.

3. Click Next to display the New Connection Type page, and then select Connect To The Network At My Workplace.

4. Click Next. Select Dial-Up Connection, and then click Next again. In the Company Name field, type the name for the connection, such as Corporate Office or Seattle Office. Keep in mind that the name should be short (50 characters or fewer) but descriptive.

5. Click Next. You can now set the phone number to dial for this connection using the Phone Number text box.

6. In a domain, the next window allows you to make connections available on a per-machine or per user basis. If you want the connection to be available only to the current user, select My Use Only. If you want the connection to be available to all users of the computer, select Anyone's Use. The Anyone's Use option is best when you plan to assign the connection through Group Policy. Click Next.

7. To add a desktop shortcut, a feature that makes it quick and easy to establish connections, select Add A Shortcut To This Connection To My Desktop.

8. Click Finish to complete the connection creation process. To test the connection settings, follow the steps outlined later in this chapter in the section entitled "Establishing Connections."

9. With a workplace connection, you are prompted by default for your name and password when you make a connection. In many cases, you'll also have to provide a logon domain. If this is the case with your network, access Network Connections and then double-click the connection. On the Options tab, select Include Windows Logon domain and then click OK.

Creating a Broadband Connection

In many respects, broadband connections are much easier to configure than dial-up connections. When you work with broadband, you don't need to set up dial-up rules or locations. You don't need to worry about calling cards, ISP access numbers, or redialing preferences either, making broadband much easier to work with.

Most broadband providers give users a router or modem, which users need to connect to the service provider. Each user must also have a network adapter on her computer, connected to a DSL router or cable modem. In this configuration, the necessary connection is established over the local area network (LAN) rather than a specific broadband connection. Therefore, it is the local area connection that must be properly configured to gain access to the Internet. You won't need to create a broadband connection.

You can, however, create a specific broadband connection if needed. In some cases, you need to do this to set specific configuration options required by the ISP, such as secure authentication, or you might want to use this technique to set the user name and password required by the broadband provider. You create a broadband connection by following these steps:

1. To start the New Connection Wizard, click Start, point to Programs or All Programs as appropriate, then to Accessories, then to Communications, and finally select New Connection Wizard.

2. Click Next to display the New Connection Type page. Select Connect To The Internet, click Next, select Set Up My Connection Manually, and click Next again.

3. If you are creating a connection that is always active and doesn't require you to sign on, select Connect Using A Broadband Connection That Is Always On. Afterward, click Next and then Click Finish. Skip the remaining steps.

4. If you are creating a broadband connection that requires authentication, select Connect Using A Broadband Connection That Requires A User Name And Password.

5. Click Next and then enter a name for the connection, such as Broadband, in the ISP Name text box. Keep in mind that the name should be short (50 characters or fewer) but descriptive.

6. To complete the configuration, follow steps 7 through 11 of the procedure given earlier for creating a dial-up Internet connection.

 Tip You need a DSL router or cable modem to test the connection. Be sure to configure any special settings required by the ISP, as detailed later in this chapter in the section entitled "Configuring Connection Properties."

Creating a VPN Connection

VPNs are used to establish secure communications channels over an existing dial-up or broadband connection. You must know the IP address or host name of the Routing And Remote Access server to which you are connecting. If you know the necessary connection is available and you know the host information, you can create the connection by following these steps:

1. To start the New Connection Wizard, click Start, point to Programs or All Programs as appropriate, then to Accessories, then to Communications, and finally select New Connection Wizard.

2. Click Next and then select Connect To The Network At My Workplace.

3. Click Next, select Virtual Private Network Connection, and then click Next.

4. Type a name for the connection in the Company Name field and then click Next.

5. To specify that an existing connection should always be used to establish the tunnel, select Do Not Dial The Initial Connection. In this configuration, the user will need to establish a connection—either dial-up or broadband—before attempting to use the VPN.

6. To have the computer automatically initialize the connection over dial-up or broadband prior to using VPN, select Automatically Dial This Initial Connection and then select the default connection you want to use.

7. Next, type the IP address or fully qualified host name of the computer to which you are connecting, such as 192.168.10.50 or *external.microsoft.com*. In most cases, this is the Routing And Remote Access server you've configured for the office network.

8. In a domain, the next window allows you to make connections available on a per-machine or per user basis. If you want the connection to be available only to the current user, select My Use Only. If you want the connection to be available to all users of the computer, select Anyone's Use. The Anyone's Use option is best when you plan to assign the connection through Group Policy.

9. Click Next. To add a desktop shortcut, a feature that makes it quick and easy to establish connections, select Add A Shortcut To This Connection To My Desktop.

10. Click Finish to complete the connection creation process. To test the connection settings, follow the steps outlined later in this chapter in the section entitled "Establishing Connections."

Configuring Connection Properties

Whether you are working with dial-up, broadband, or VPN, you'll often need to set additional properties after creating a connection. The key properties that you'll work with are examined in this section.

Note   As you work with connection properties, keep in mind that VPN connections are on top of existing connections and that the configuration of each connection is separate. With VPN the primary connection is established first using the settings assigned to this connection and then the VPN connection is attempted using the VPN connection settings. With this in mind, you should configure the primary connection first and then configure the options for VPN. You should change this approach only when you are troubleshooting problems with VPN. In this case, you should start with the VPN configuration and work your way back to the settings for the primary connection.

Configuring Automatic or Manual Connections

Windows XP can be configured to establish dial-up, broadband, or VPN connections automatically when users access programs that need to connect to the Internet, such as Microsoft Internet Explorer. Automatic connections work in ways that depend on settings in the Internet Options tool. The options include the following:

- **Never Dial A Connection**   Users must manually establish connections.

- **Dial Whenever A Network Connection Is Not Present**   The connection is established automatically when needed but only when the local area connection isn't working.

- **Always Dial My Default Connection**   The default connection is always established when an Internet connection is needed (even if other connections are already established).

Tip   The way you configure automatic connections really depends on the way your organization works. Contrary to what most adminis-trators think, laptop users are usually happier (and less frustrated) when their computers are set to never dial a connection. This is because laptop users might not have access to a dial-up connection while out of the office and having the computer attempt to dial a con-nection when visiting customers or giving a presentation can be dis-ruptive. On the other hand, if you are configuring dial-up networking for users with desktops at a remote or home office, they'll probably want to use automatic connections.

To configure computers to connect manually, follow these steps:

1. Double-click the Internet Options tool in the Control Panel, and then, in the Internet Properties dialog box, click the Connections tab, shown in Figure 14-9.

2. Select Never Dial A Connection, and then click OK.

Figure 14-9   Configure manual or automatic connections by using the Connections tab.

You can configure automatic connections by following these steps:

1. Double-click the Internet Options tool in the Control Panel and then, in the Internet Properties dialog box, click the Connections tab.

2. Select Dial Whenever A Network Connection Is Not Present to establish con-nections automatically if a local area connection isn't working. Select Always Dial My Default Connection to always attempt to establish connections.

3. The Dial-Up And Virtual Private Network Settings list shows the dial-up, broadband, and VPN connections that are currently configured. Select the connection you want to use as the default when establishing connections and then click Set Default.

4. Click OK twice.

Configuring Proxy Settings for Mobile Connections

As with the connections themselves, proxy server settings can be set manually or automatically. With manual configuration, you'll need to configure each property, step by step. With automatic configuration, the computer can attempt to detect proxy server settings and then configure the appropriate options, or the computer can read a configuration script to use in configuring the proxy.

Note   Proxy settings can be configured for multiple systems through Group Policy as discussed in the section of Chapter 15 entitled "Managing Connection and Proxy Settings." If you elect not to configure proxy settings through Group Policy, you can configure them on a per-connection basis as discussed in this section.

Configuration scripts can be stored in a file on the local computer or at an Internet address. Using configuration scripts can save you a lot of time, especially when you consider that each connection you create is configured separately. Further, as VPN connections are established on top of an existing setting, the proxy settings for the VPN can be different from those set in the original connection.

To use automatic proxy configuration for a connection, complete the following steps:

1. Double-click the Internet Options tool in the Control Panel and then, in the Internet Properties dialog box, click the Connections tab.

2. Select the connection you want to configure in the Dial-Up And Virtual Private Network Settings list box and then click Settings. This displays a Settings dialog box similar to the one shown in Figure 14-10.

Figure 14-10   Proxy settings can be automatically configured through detection or scripts.

3. To attempt to automatically detect proxy settings when establishing the connection, select Automatically Detect Settings.

4. To use a configuration script, select Use Automatic Configuration Script and then type the file path or Uniform Resource Locator (URL) of the script. With file paths, you can use environment variables, such as *%UserProfile%* PROXY.VBS. With URLs, be sure to type the computer URL, such as *http://proxy.microsoft.com/proxy.vbs*.

5. To ensure that only automatic settings are used, clear the Use A Proxy Server For This Connection check box.

6. Click OK twice.

To use manual proxy configuration, complete the following steps:

1. Double-click the Internet Options tool in the Control Panel and then, in the Internet Properties dialog box, click the Connections tab.

2. Select the connection you want to configure in the Dial-Up And Virtual Private Network Settings list box and then click Settings. This displays a Settings dialog box similar to the one shown in Figure 14-10.

3. Clear the Automatically Detect Settings and Use Automatic Configuration Script check boxes if they were selected.

4. Select Use A Proxy Server. The Bypass Proxy Server For Local Addresses check box is not selected by default. In most cases, however, you won't want to use a proxy for requests made to servers on the same network segment, so you'll want to select Bypass Proxy Server For Local Addresses as well. It is important to note that if Bypass Proxy Server For Local Addresses is not selected, users might need additional permissions to access intranet servers through your proxy servers.

5. Click Advanced to display the Proxy Settings dialog box shown in Figure 14-11.

Figure 14-11   You can use the same proxy for all services, or you can configure multiple proxies.

6. Set the IP address for proxies using the text boxes in the Servers panel. You'll find the following two columns of text boxes:

   ❏ **Proxy Address To Use**   Sets the IP address of the related proxy server or servers. Enter the IP address for each service. If multiple proxies are configured for a particular service, type the IP addresses for each proxy server in the order in which you want the Web client to attempt to use them. Each address must be separated by a semicolon. If a proxy isn't configured for a service, do not fill in the related text box.

   ❏ **Port**   Sets the port number on which the proxy server responds to requests. Most proxies respond to port 80 for all requests. That said, however, the standard ports are port 80 for Hypertext Transfer Protocol (HTTP), port 443 for Secure Sockets Layer (SSL; listed as Secure), port 21 for File Transfer Protocol (FTP), port 70 for Gopher, and port 1081 for Socks. Check with your organization's Web administrator for the proper settings.

7. By default, the Use The Same Proxy Server For All Protocols check box is selected. This setting allows you to use the same IP address and port settings for the HTTP, SSL, FTP, Gopher, and Socks services. You have the following options:

   ❏ If your organization has proxy servers that handle all requests, type the IP address or addresses that you want to use and the port number on which the server or servers respond.

   ❏ If you want to use a unique proxy server or servers for each type of service, clear the Use The Same Proxy Server For All Protocols check box and then enter the necessary IP addresses and port numbers in the text boxes provided.

8. If your network has multiple segments or there are specific servers that shouldn't use proxies, enter the appropriate IP addresses or IP address ranges in the Exceptions list. Each entry must be separated with a semicolon. The asterisk (*) character can be used as a wildcard to specify an address range of 0 through 255, such as 192.*.*.*, 192.168.*.*, or 192.168.10.*.

9. Click OK three times.

Configuring Connection Logon Information

Each connection you create has separate settings for logon information. You can set a user name, password, and domain by performing the following steps:

1. Double-click the Internet Options tool in the Control Panel and then, in the Internet Properties dialog box, click the Connections tab.

2. Select the connection you want to configure in the Dial-Up And Virtual Private Network Settings list box and then click Settings. This displays a Settings dialog box similar to the one shown in Figure 14-10.

3. Type the user name and password for the connection in the User Name and Password text boxes, respectively.

4. If a domain name is required, enter the domain name in the Domain text box.

5. Click OK twice.

Setting a connection to use the appropriate logon information isn't the last step in ensuring a proper configuration. You should also set options that determine whether users are prompted for logon information or a phone number. If a logon domain is required to establish a connection, you should ensure that the logon domain is passed with the other logon information. By default, the domain name is not included.

To configure additional options, follow these steps:

1. Double-click the Internet Options tool in the Control Panel and then, in the Internet Properties dialog box, click the Connections tab.

2. Select the connection you want to configure in the Dial-Up And Virtual Private Network Settings list box and then click Settings.

3. In the Settings dialog box, click Properties. This displays a properties dialog box.

4. Click the Options tab, shown in Figure 14-12. You can now configure the following additional options:

   ❑ To display status messages while connecting, select Display Progress While Connecting.

   ❑ To ensure users are prompted for logon information if necessary, select Prompt For Name And Password, Certificate, Etc.

   ❑ To ensure the logon domain is included when requested, select Include Windows Logon Domain.

   ❑ To prompt for a phone number when needed, select Prompt For Phone Number.

   ❑ Click OK three times.

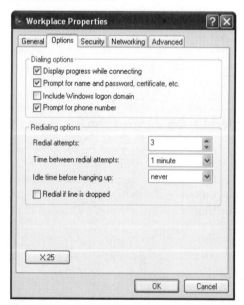

Figure 14-12 You might need to set additional options on a per-connection basis.

Configuring Connection Attempts and Automatic Disconnection

By default, Windows XP attempts to make a connection 10 times before giving up, and it won't disconnect idle connections automatically. You can use advanced options to change the way connection attempts and disconnection are handled by following these steps:

1. Double-click the Internet Options tool in the Control Panel and then, in the Internet Properties dialog box, click the Connections tab.

2. Select the connection you want to configure in the Dial-Up And Virtual Private Network Settings list box and then click Settings.

3. In the Settings dialog box, click Advanced. This displays the Advanced Dial-Up dialog box shown in Figure 14-13.

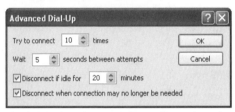

Figure 14-13   When users have advanced needs, you can configure the way Windows XP attempts to make connections as well as how automatic disconnection is handled.

4. You can now configure the following options:

   ❑ **Try To Connect ... Times**   Sets the number of times Windows XP attempts to make a connection. The minimum value is 1.

   ❑ **Wait ... Seconds Between Attempts**   Sets the number of seconds to wait between connection attempts. The minimum value is 5.

   ❑ **Disconnect If Idle For ... Minutes**   Specifies whether Windows XP disconnects connections that haven't been actively used for the specified time. The minimum value is 3 minutes. Typically, you should set this value to between 20 and 30 minutes, or longer if the user transfers large files using protocols that might not update their state during the transfer, such as FTP.

   ❑ **Disconnect When Connection May No Longer Be Needed**   Specifies whether Windows XP disconnects when a user quits all Internet programs that would otherwise use the connection.

5. Click OK three times when you are finished.

Tip   If users complain about getting disconnected during dial-up sessions, the Disconnect settings can be the problem. Talk with the users about how they use the Internet and then determine if you should change the settings to better meet their needs. Another reason for disconnection is if the Idle Time Before Hanging Up option is used with redialing settings.

Configuring Redialing Options

With dial-up connections, you can set dialing options that allow connections to be automatically redialed when lines are busy and when the connection is dropped. To configure redialing options, follow these steps:

1. Double-click the Internet Options tool in the Control Panel and then, in the Internet Properties dialog box, click the Connections tab.

2. Select the connection you want to configure in the Dial-Up And Virtual Private Network Settings list box and then click Settings.

3. In the Settings dialog box, click Properties. This displays a properties dialog box.

4. Click the Options tab. Use the following settings in the Redialing Options panel to configure redialing:

   ❑ **Redial Attempts**   Sets the number of times to redial the phone number automatically. To disable redialing, enter 0 as the redial value.

   ❑ **Time Between Redial Attempts**   Sets the time to wait before redial attempts. The available values are 1 second, 3 seconds, 5 seconds, 10 seconds, 30 seconds, 1 minute, 2 minutes, 5 minutes, and 10 minutes.

   ❑ **Idle Time Before Hanging Up**   Specifies whether Windows XP disconnects the phone line when the connection hasn't been actively used for a specified time. The available values are Never (the standard default), 1 minute, 5 minutes, 10 minutes, 30 minutes, 1 hour, 2 hours, 4 hours, 8 hours, and 24 hours.

   ❑ **Redial If Line Is Dropped**   Specifies whether Windows XP attempts to redial the connection if the line is dropped. With connections to the workplace, this option is usually cleared by default. In most cases, however, you'll want to select it.

5. Click OK three times.

Setting a Connection to Use Dialing Rules

Dial-up connections can be configured with or without dialing rules. If you don't use dialing rules with a connection, the seven-digit phone number assigned to the connection is dialed at all times. When you assign dialing rules, the current dialing location determines whether the connection is attempted as a local or long-distance phone call.

To view or set the dialing rules for a connection, follow these steps:

1. Double-click the Internet Options tool in the Control Panel and then, in the Internet Properties dialog box, click the Connections tab.

2. Select the connection you want to configure in the Dial-Up And Virtual Private Network Settings list box and then click Settings.

3. In the Settings dialog box, click Properties. This displays a properties dialog box.

4. To ensure the connection uses the appropriate dialog rules, on the General tab select Use Dialing Rules and then type an area code and select a country/region code as shown in Figure 14-14.

Figure 14-14   Dialing rules are useful when you want to ensure numbers are dialed as either local or long-distance calls based on the current dialing location.

5. If you don't want to use dialing rules, clear the Use Dialing Rules check box.

6. Click OK three times.

Configuring Primary and Alternate Phone Numbers

With dial-up connections, you can configure two types of phone numbers: the primary number to dial whenever a connection is attempted, and alternate phone numbers to try if a primary number fails. To configure phone numbers, follow these steps:

1. Double-click the Internet Options tool in the Control Panel and then, in the Internet Properties dialog box, click the Connections tab.

2. Select the connection you want to configure in the Dial-Up And Virtual Private Network Settings list box and then click Settings.

3. In the Settings dialog box, click Properties. This displays a properties dialog box.

4. As shown in Figure 14-14, the primary phone number is listed in the Phone Number text box. Type a new number as necessary.

5. Click Alternates. This displays the Alternate Phone Numbers dialog box shown in Figure 14-15. You can now manage primary and alternate phone numbers using the following techniques:

   ❑ To add a phone number, click Add to display the Add Alternate Phone Number dialog box. Next, enter the seven-digit number used to dial the alternate number locally in the Phone Number text box. You can use a dash if desired, such as 555-1234. If you want to set dialing rules, select Use Dialing Rules and then type an area code and select a country/region code. Click OK.

❑ To change the order in which numbers are dialed, select a number and then use the Up or Down arrow to change its position in the Phone Numbers list. The top number in the list becomes the primary number.

❑ To edit existing numbers, select the number in the Phone Numbers list and then click Edit. Afterward, use the Edit Alternate Phone Number dialog box to change the number settings.

❑ To remove a number, select the number in the Phone Numbers list and then click Delete.

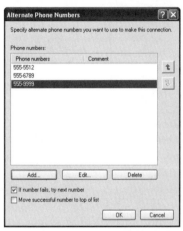

Figure 14-15   Configure alternate phone numbers to use if a primary number fails.

6. If you want to automatically use alternate numbers, select If Number Fails, Try Next Number. You can also move successful numbers to the top of the list (making them the primary number) if Windows XP is able to successfully dial them after a previous number fails. To do this, select Move Successful Number To Top Of List.

7. Click OK four times.

Configuring Identity Validation

Proper identity validation is essential to maintaining the integrity of your network. When users dial in to the office, you should ensure that identities are validated securely if at all possible. This isn't the default setting for standard dial-up connections, however. With most connections, the user's logon information for connections can be validated using the following options:

- **Allow Unsecured Password**   Allows the user logon information to be passed in clear text over the connection. You can think of this as basic authentication.

- **Require Secured Password**   Forces Windows XP to attempt to pass logon information using a secure technique, such as Windows Authentication, rather than clear text.

- **Use Smart Card**   Tells Windows XP to validate the logon using a smart card.

With dial-up and broadband connections, you can use any of these options. With VPN, you can only use the secure techniques. When you require a secured password, you can also automatically pass the Windows logon name, password, and domain specified in the configuration. Passing the Windows logon information automatically is useful when users connect to the office and must be authenticated in the Windows domain. With both secure validation techniques, you can require data encryption and force Windows XP to disconnect if encryption cannot be used. Data encryption is automatically used with Windows Authentication for both secured passwords and smart cards.

To configure identity validation, follow these steps:

1. Double-click the Internet Options tool in the Control Panel and then, in the Internet Properties dialog box, click the Connections tab.

2. Select the connection you want to configure in the Dial-Up And Virtual Private Network Settings list box and then click Settings.

3. In the Settings dialog box, click Properties. This displays a properties dialog box.

4. Click the Security tab shown in Figure 14-16.

Figure 14-16   Proper identity validation techniques are essential, especially when dialing in to the office.

5. In the Security Options panel, you can select Typical (Recommended Settings) or Advanced (Custom Settings). The Typical options are Allow Unsecured Password, Require Secure Password, and Use Smart Card.

6. If you require secure passwords, you can also set automatic logon and require data encryption. Both options are useful when logging on to a Windows domain. The settings must be supported, however; if they aren't, users won't be able to validate their logons and connections won't be completed.

7. If you use smart cards, you should also require data encryption. Data encryption is essential to ensuring the integrity and security of the data passed between the smart card and the authenticating computer.

8. Click OK three times.

Configuring Networking Protocols and Components

The way in which networking protocols and components are configured depends on the type of connection. As Table 14-1 describes, dial-up connections can use either Point-to-Point Protocol (PPP) or Serial Line Internet Protocol (SLIP) as the connection protocol. Broadband connections use Point-to-Point Protocol over Ethernet (PPPoE). VPN connection use either PPTP or L2TP.

Table 14-1   Connection Protocol Availability by Connection Type

Connection Type	Connection Protocol	Description
Dial-up	PPP	Used to establish connections to Window servers over dial-up.
	SLIP	Used to establish connections to UNIX servers over dial-up.
Broadband	PPPoE	Used to establish a point-to-point broadband connection over Ethernet.
VPN	Automatic	Used to automatically detect which VPN protocol is available and establish a virtual tunnel using this protocol.
	PPTP VPN	Sets the PPTP for VPN. PPTP is an extension of PPP.
	L2TP IPSec VPN	Sets the L2TP for VPN. L2TP is a more secure extension of PPTP that uses IPSec.

Four network components are used with mobile networking: Internet Protocol (TCP/IP), QoS Packet Scheduler, File And Printer Sharing For Microsoft Networks, and Client For Microsoft Networks. As Table 14-2 describes, the way these components are configured by default depends on the type of connection that was created originally. You can change these settings to suit your needs. If necessary, you can also install additional networking components.

Table 14-2   Default Component Configuration by Connection Type

Dial-Up Component	Description	Broadband	Standard Dial-Up	Dial-Up to Office	VPN
Internet Protocol (TCP/IP)	Required for network communications. By default, Dynamic Host Configuration Protocol (DHCP) is used with connections unless overridden in the property settings.	Y	Y	Y	Y
QoS Packet Scheduler	Manages quality of service for packets and packet scheduling according to priority.	Y	Y	Y	Y
File And Printer Sharing For Microsoft Networks	Enables the sharing of printers and files over the network connection; allows for mapping printers and drives.	N	N	N	Y
Client For Microsoft Networks	Enables Windows Authentication and Windows domain; allows the computer to act as domain client.	N	N	Y	Y

To view or change the networking options for a connection, follow these steps:

1. Double-click the Internet Options tool in the Control Panel and then, in the Internet Properties dialog box, click the Connections tab.

2. Select the connection you want to configure in the Dial-Up And Virtual Private Network Settings list box and then click Settings.

3. In the Settings dialog box, click Properties. This displays a properties dialog box.

4. Click the Networking tab, shown in Figure 14-17. You can now do the following:

   ❑ Configure the protocol used by the connection by using the Type Of Dial-Up Server I Am Calling list, Type of VPN list, or Type Of Broadband Connection To Make list, as appropriate.

   ❑ Enable network components by selecting the related check box in the This Connection Uses The Following Items list.

   ❑ Disable network components by clearing the related check box in the This Connection Uses The Following Items list.

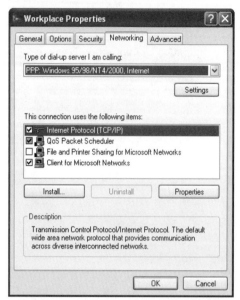

Figure 14-17   Configure networking options to enable or disable protocols and components.

 Tip   If any of the network components shown in Table 14-2 are not available and are necessary for the connection, you can install them by clicking Install. Select the component type, click Add, and then select the component to use in the list provided.

5. By default, connections use DHCP to configure network settings, including the IP address to use, the subnet mask, default gateway, Domain Name System (DNS) servers, and Windows Internet Naming Service (WINS) servers. If you want to assign a static IP address or override other default settings, select Internet Protocol (TCP/IP) and then click Properties. This displays the Internet Protocol (TCP/IP) Properties dialog box, which can be configured as discussed in Chapter 13, "Configuring and Troubleshooting TCP/IP Networking."
6. Click OK three times.

Enabling and Disabling the Windows Firewall for Network Connections

With dial-up, broadband, and VPN connections, you might want to give the computer added protection against attacks by using the Windows Firewall. This built-in firewall protects Windows XP systems by restricting the types of information that can be communicated. By enforcing the appropriate restrictions, you reduce the possibility that malicious individuals can break into a system—and reducing security risks is extremely important when users are accessing the organization's network from outside your protective firewalls and proxy servers.

The Windows Firewall is enabled by default for all connections and can be enabled or disabled on a per-connection basis. To enable or disable Windows Firewall on a per-connection basis, follow these steps:

1. Double-click Windows Firewall in Control Panel. In the Windows Firewall dialog box, select the Advanced tab.

2. Each network connection configured on the computer is listed in the Network Connection Settings panel. Clear the check box for a connection to disable Windows Firewall for that connection. Select the check box for a connection to enable Windows Firewall for that connection.

3. Click OK when you are finished.

Establishing Connections

As discussed in the earlier section of this chapter entitled "Configuring Automatic or Manual Connections," dial-up, broadband, and VPN connections can be established manually or automatically. The manual method lets users choose when to connect. The automatic method connects when users start a program that requires network access, such as Internet Explorer.

Connecting with Dial-Up

Dial-up connections are established between two modems using a telephone line. To establish a dial-up connection, follow these steps:

- You can access dial-up connections you've created in several different ways. With Simple Start Menu, click Start, point to Connect To, and then click the connection you want to use. With Classic Start Menu, click Start, point to Settings, point to Network Connections, and finally click the connection you want to use. The Connect dialog box shown in Figure 14-18 should be displayed.

    Note If you can't access connections using the previously described techniques, someone might have changed the Start Menu properties. Use this technique instead: Click Start, then point to Programs or All Programs as appropriate, then to Accessories, then to Communications, and finally click Network Connections. Afterward, double-click the connection you want to use.

Figure 14-18 Use the Connect dialog box to confirm the settings and then click Dial.

- Confirm that the user name is correct and enter the password for the account if it doesn't already appear.

- To use the user name and password whenever you attempt to establish this connection, select Save This User Name And Password For The Following Users and then select Me Only.

- To use the user name and password when any user attempts to establish this connection, select Save This User Name And Password For The Following Users and then select Anyone Who Uses This Computer. Don't use this option if you plan to distribute this connection through Group Policy because you don't want to give out your connection password.

- The Dial drop-down list shows the number that will be dialed. The primary number is selected by default. To choose an alternate number, click the drop-down list and then select the number you want to use.

- Click Dial. When the modem connects to the ISP or office network, you'll see a connection speed. The connection speed is negotiated on a per-call basis and depends on the maximum speed of the calling modem and the modem being called, the compression algorithms available, and the quality of the connection.

If you have problems connecting with dial-up, use these tips to help you trouble-shoot:

■ *Problem: Modem dials and reaches the other modem but cannot connect. It contin-ues to make connection noises until you cancel the operation.*

Resolution: The phone lines are usually the source of the problem. Static or noise on the line can cause connection failures. Check your connections between the modem and the wall. Check with the phone company to see if they can test the line and resolve the problem.

■ *Problem: Modem dials and seems to connect; then the service provider or office net-work connection is dropped unexpectedly. The connection doesn't seem to complete successfully.*

Resolution: Check your networking protocols and components, as discussed in the earlier section of this chapter entitled "Configuring Networking Proto-cols and Components." If this seems to be okay, determine whether you are passing Windows logon and domain information, as this might be required. See the section earlier in this chapter entitled "Configuring Connection Logon Information."

■ *Problem: Cannot access resources in the Windows domain.*

Resolution: Client For Microsoft Networks might be required to access resources on the office network. Enable this component and ensure that the domain information is being passed as necessary.

■ *Problem: User can never get through. The modem seems to be dialing the number incorrectly. You can hear it dialing too many or too few numbers.*

Resolution: Check the dialing rules for the connection as well as the currently selected dialing location. Make sure these are configured properly for the user's current location.

■ *Problem: A No Dial Tone message is displayed but the modem is installed correctly and seems to be okay.*

Resolution: Check the phone cord and ensure that it is connected properly. Some modems have two line jacks, one labeled Phone/In and one labeled Line/Out. The phone cord from the wall jack should be plugged into the Line/Out jack. Some phone jacks are configured for data only, indicating a plug-in for a high-speed line rather than a phone or modem. Try a different plug.

■ *Problem: The computer freezes when the user tries to use the modem.*

Resolution: This is most likely caused by a device conflict. Follow the tech-niques discussed in Chapter 3, "Configuring Hardware Devices and Drivers," for configuring and troubleshooting devices.

■ *Problem: Some services freeze or don't work.*

Resolution: Check the proxy and firewall settings. These settings can restrict the services that are available.

Connecting with Broadband

Broadband connections are established using a cable modem and a cable line, or a DSL router and a telephone line. To establish a broadband connection, follow these steps:

1. Click Start, then point to Programs or All Programs as appropriate, then to Accessories, then to Communications, and finally click Network Connections.
2. Display the Connect dialog box by double-clicking the connection you want to establish.
3. Confirm that the user name is correct and enter the password for the account if it doesn't already appear.
4. To use the user name and password whenever you attempt to establish this connection, select Save This User Name And Password For The Following Users and then select Me Only.
5. To use the user name and password when any user attempts to establish this connection, select Save This User Name And Password For The Following Users and then select Anyone Who Uses This Computer.
6. Click Connect.

If you have problems connecting with broadband, use these tips to help you troubleshoot:

- *Problem: Cannot connect. Connection doesn't seem to work at all.*

  Resolution: Check your network connections. Ensure that the lines connecting the DSL router or cable modem and the computer are plugged in properly.

- *Problem: Connection is dropped unexpectedly. The connection doesn't seem to complete successfully.*

  Resolution: Check your networking protocols and components as discussed in the earlier section of this chapter entitled "Configuring Networking Protocols and Components." If this seems to be okay, determine whether you are passing Windows logon and domain information, as this might be required. See the section earlier in this chapter entitled "Configuring Connection Logon Information."

- *Problem: Some services freeze or don't work.*

  Resolution: Check the proxy and firewall settings. These settings can restrict the services that are available.

- *Problem: Cannot access resources in the Windows domain.*

  Resolution: Client For Microsoft Networks might be required to access resources on the office network. Enable this component and ensure that the domain information is being passed as necessary.

Connecting with VPN

VPN connections are made over existing connections. These connections can be a local area connection, a dial-up connection, or a broadband connection. To establish a VPN connection, follow these steps:

1. Click Start, then point to Programs or All Programs as appropriate, then to Accessories, then to Communications, and finally click Network Connections.

2. VPN connections are displayed separately from dial-up, broadband, and local area network (LAN) connections. Double-click the connection you want to establish.

3. If the connection is configured to first dial another type of connection, Windows XP tries to establish this connection before attempting the VPN connection. If prompted to establish this connection, click Yes. Then dial the connection as discussed earlier in the section entitled "Connecting with Dial-Up."

4. Once the necessary connection is established, you'll see the Connect dialog box. After you confirm that the user name is correct and enter the password for the account if it doesn't already appear, click Connect.

If you have problems establishing the connection, use these tips to help you troubleshoot:

- *Problem: Cannot connect. Connection doesn't seem to work at all.*

  Resolution: Check your network connections. Ensure that the lines connecting the DSL router or cable modem and the computer are plugged in properly.

- *Problem: Returns error message regarding the host name.*

  Resolution: The host name might be incorrectly specified. Check the settings to ensure the host name is fully expressed, such as *external01.microsoft.com* rather than simply external01. DNS resolutions might not be working properly either. If this is the case, enter the IP address for the host rather than the host name.

- *Problem: Returns error message regarding a bad IP Address.*

  Resolution: Check or reenter the IP address. If the IP address was correct, TCP/IP networking might be improperly configured. Check your networking protocols and components, as discussed in the section of this chapter entitled "Configuring Networking Protocols and Components." You might need to set a static IP address for the connection and a default gateway.

- *Problem: Message stating that the protocol isn't supported is displayed, and the connection doesn't seem to complete successfully.*

  Resolution: Set the protocol to automatic rather than to a specific setting of either PPTP or L2TP. Check the secure logon settings. They might be set to require a secure password instead of smart card or vice versa. If this seems to be OK, determine whether you are passing Windows logon and domain information, as this might be required. See the section earlier in this chapter entitled "Configuring Connection Logon Information."

- *Problem: Cannot map network drives or access printers.*

  Resolution: File And Printer Sharing For Microsoft Networks is required to map drives and printers. Enable this component as discussed in the section of this chapter entitled "Configuring Networking Protocols and Components."

■ *Problem: Some services freeze or don't work.*

Resolution: Check the proxy and firewall settings. These settings can restrict the services that are available

Wireless Networking

To make it easier for users to take their laptops with them to meetings and to other locations in the office, many organizations are implementing wireless networks. Wireless networks can be deployed and used in many different configurations. This section examines the most common configurations.

Wireless Network Devices and Technologies

When you are working with wireless networks, the most common terms you'll run across are *wireless network adapter* and *wireless base station*. Wireless adapters include PCMCIA cards for notebooks, PCI cards for desktops, and universal serial bus (USB) devices (which can be used with notebooks or desktops). A wireless adapter uses a built-in antenna to communicate with a base station. Typically, a base station is directly connected to the organization's physical network and might also function as a network switch or hub itself, meaning it has physical ports that allow direct cable connections as well as wireless connections. Other names for base stations include *wireless access points* and *gateways*.

The most widely used wireless network adapters and access points are based on the Institute of Electrical and Electronics Engineers (IEEE) 802.11 specification. Wireless devices that are based on this specification can be Wi-Fi Certified to show they have been thoroughly tested for performance and compatibility. Table 14-3 provides a feature comparison of the most-used wireless technologies based on IEEE 802.11. As the table describes, there are four standards, and each has its benefits and drawbacks. It should be noted that although 802.11a wireless devices cannot interoperate with 802.11b or 802.11g devices, fewer devices use the 5-GHz range, making it less likely that there will be interference with other types of wireless devices (the majority of which use the 2.4-GHz range). For added security, IEEE has defined the newer 802.11i standard. Unlike the 802.11a, 802.11b and 802.11g standards, the 802.11i standard isn't about transmission speeds and frequencies. 802.11i is a security standard that you can add to the existing standards. More specifically, it adds security functionality to the radio specifications of 802.11a, 802.11b, and 802.11g.This means 802.11a network adapters and access points can include the 802.11i security functionality, as can 802.11b and 802.11g wireless products.

Note   Keep in mind that some computers (particularly laptops) contain integrated chip sets that support multiple wireless networking.

Table 14-3   Wireless Networking Technologies

Wireless Standard	802.11b	802.11a	802.11g
Speed	Up to 11 Mbps	Up to 54 Mbps	Up to 54 Mbps
Transmission Frequency	2.4 GHz	5 GHz	2.4GHz
Effective indoor range	Approximately 100 to 150 feet	Approximately 25 to 75 feet	Approximately 100 to 150 feet
Compatibility	802.11b wireless devices can inter-operate with 802.11g devices (at 11 Mbps). 802.11g wireless adapters can inter-operate with 802.11b access points (at 11 Mbps).	Incompatible with 802.11b and 802.11g.	802.11g wireless devices can inter-operate with 802.11b devices (at 11 Mbps).

Real World   Take a close look at compatibility issues before you deploy wireless devices that aren't IEEE 802.11 based. Increasingly, you'll see devices that achieve speeds higher than 54 Mbps. Some of these devices achieve speed boosts through compression and other similar techniques while staying within the guidelines of the IEEE 802.11 specification. Others might use network technologies that are proprietary, requiring you to use that company's wireless adapters and base stations to achieve the transmission improvements. For more information on wireless standards and certified devices, go to *http://www.wi-fi.com*.

Wireless Security

Securing a wireless network is very different from securing a wired network. With a wired network, a cable is used to connect a computer to the network. A user must physically be connected to the network using a cable and must have access to one of your internal switches or hubs. If an unauthorized person connects a machine to the network, it is fairly easy to determine this and trace the physical cable to the intruder's computer.

When you install wireless networking, anyone within range of one of your wireless access points has access to your network. Not only can they intercept the wireless signals that are being broadcast, they can also try to crack into the network. The bad news is that it is difficult to locate the intruder because there's no physical wire to trace. The really bad news is that if intruders can gain access to a base station, they are usually inside your organization's firewall. To protect the network, you should configure the wireless devices to encode all wireless transmissions and configure its firewall if one is available.

The most basic wireless encryption scheme used is Wireless Equivalency Protection (WEP). With WEP, you encrypt data using 40-bit, 128-bit, 152-bit, or higher private key encryption. With WEP, all data is encrypted using a private key before it is transmitted, and any computer that wants to read the data must be able to decrypt it using the private key. In a typical wired environment, private key encryption alone is sufficient to safeguard your data. In a wireless environment, with a high volume of traffic, there is a possibility that someone would be able to successfully break the private key, and because the private key doesn't change automatically over time, the intruder would then have unlimited access to your organization's internal network.

A newer, more advanced encryption scheme is implemented using Wi-Fi Protected Access (WPA). WPA is able to rotate keys for added security and to change the way keys are derived. By changing the encryption keys over time and ensuring they aren't derived in one specific way, WPA can improve security significantly over WEP. WPA-compatible devices can operate in enterprise mode or in a home/small office configuration.

- In the enterprise mode, wireless devices have two sets of keys: session keys and group keys. Session keys are unique to each association between an access point and a wireless client. They are used to create a private virtual port between the access point and the client. Group keys are shared among all clients connected to the same access point. Both sets of keys are generated dynamically and are rotated to help safeguard the integrity of keys over time.

- In a home/small office configuration, WPA uses a pre-shared encryption key rather than a changing encryption key. Here, the user enters a master key (the group key) into the base station and then configures all the other wireless devices to use this master key. A wireless device uses the master key as a starting point start to mathematically generate the session key. It then regularly changes the session key so that the same session key is never used twice. Because the key rotation is automatic, the key management is handled in the background.

 Note   WPA is officially a part of the 802.11i specification. It is fully compatible with 802.11a, 802.11b, and 802.11g. Many wireless devices shipped before WPA became available (early 2004) can be made fully compatible with WPA through a software upgrade.

Another advanced wireless security technology is Robust Security Network (RSN), which is supported by 802.11i-compatible devices. RSN allows wireless devices to dynamically negotiate their authentication and encryption algorithms. This means the authentication and encryption algorithms used by RSN-compatible devices can be changed. New authentication techniques and algorithms can be added to address security issues. RSN is based on the Extensible Authentication Protocol (EAP) and the Advanced Encryption Standard (AES).

Installing and Configuring a Wireless Adapter

The two main types of wireless adapters you'll use are PCMCIA cards for notebooks and PCI cards for desktops. These adapters are the easiest to configure—and I've found them to be the most reliable. The other type of wireless adapter that you might see is a device that connects to a notebook or desktop computer with a USB cable. When using USB wireless devices, keep in mind there are two USB specifications: USB 1.0, the original specification, and USB 2.0, the faster, newer specification. A wireless device that is USB 2.0–compliant must be connected to a USB 2.0 port to function properly and at the speeds you expect.

Note   Wireless technology is changing so quickly that most wireless devices won't be recognized by Windows XP. This can make installation a bit more difficult because you typically cannot rely on Plug and Play. In fact, with many of the wireless adapters I've worked with, you need to run the installation CD prior to installing the wireless devices. This is particularly true with USB devices. Be sure to read the documentation closely.

As part of the installation process, most installation software will help you configure the wireless device. In the process, you typically will need to specify the name of the wireless network to which you want to connect (the network name) and the mode in which the wireless device will run. Wireless adapters can run in one of two operating modes:

- **Ad Hoc**   In ad hoc mode, you configure the wireless adapter to connect directly to other computers with wireless adapters.
- **Infrastructure**   In infrastructure mode, you configure the wireless adapter for use on a wireless network. In this configuration, the adapter expects to connect to an access point rather than to another computer directly.

After you specify the adapter mode, you might need to specify the encryption key that will be used. If your organization uses WEP security, you will in most cases have to type in the required encryption key, which is usually referred to as the *network key*. With WPA security, you will most likely use a certificate or a smart card to supply the required encryption key.

Checking the Wireless Connection

Once you've completed the installation of the device, you should be able to connect over the wireless network. Much like a wired network card, which has a local area connection, wireless network cards have a wireless network connection. If you right-click this connection and choose Status on the shortcut menu, you'll see a status dialog box similar to the one shown in Figure 14-19.

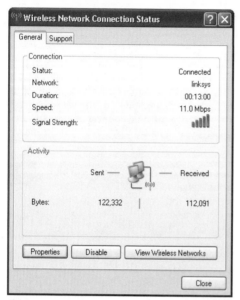

Figure 14-19 Determining the status and signal strength of a wireless network connection.

You can use the Wireless Network Connection Status dialog box to check the status of the connection and to maintain the connection, much as I discussed previously. The network to which you are connected is shown in the Network field. To view available wireless networks, click the View Wireless Networks button. The wireless connection speed and the signal strength are also shown. A signal strength of one bar is poor; a signal strength of five bars is excellent.

In the Status field, you'll see an alert if you have limited or no connectivity to the wireless network. If you have problems establishing a wireless connection, use these tips to help you troubleshoot:

- *Problem: Limited or no connectivity to the wireless network.*

    Resolution: Check the signal strength. If the signal strength is low (poor) you will either need to move closer to the base station or redirect your antenna. For a built-in antenna, you might need to change the position of the laptop relative to the base station. The problem could also be that the network did not assign your computer a network address. To check your IP address assignment, double-click the wireless connection in Network Connections dialog box and then select the Support tab. If the IP address is 0.0.0.0, your computer was not assigned an IP address, and you need to click Repair. If the IP address currently assigned to the computer is in the range 169.254.0.1 to 169.254.255.254, then the computer is using Automatic Private IP Addressing (APIPA). Try clicking Repair to resolve the problem.

■ *Problem: Not connected or unable to connect to the wireless network.*

Resolution: If you are out of the broadcast area, your computer will not be able to connect to the wireless network. Double-click on the connection. The computer will display the Wireless Network Connection dialog box, and in the right pane you will see the message "No wireless networks were found in range." If you think this is an error, click Refresh Network List under Network Tasks. Otherwise, try moving closer to the base station or changing the position of your antenna/computer relative to the base station. The computer also might not be configured properly for establishing a wireless connection on this network.

Tip   You'll have better connection speeds when you have a stronger signal—up to the maximum possible with the wireless technology you are using. If the signal strength is weak, the connection speed might be reduced considerably. To improve the signal strength, try moving the adapter's antenna if one is available or try changing the position of the computer relative to the access point.

Connecting to and Configuring Available and Preferred Wireless Networks

Any wireless access point broadcasting within range should be available to a computer with a wireless adapter. By default, Windows XP is set to allow you to configure the network settings that should be used. This allows you to configure different authentication, encryption, and communication options as necessary. A key property that you can't change is the network name, which serves as the identifier for the network and must match the network name used by the wireless base station.

You can determine which wireless networks are available by completing the following steps:

1. Access Network Connections. Click Start, point to Programs or All Programs as appropriate, then to Accessories, then to Communications, and finally click Network Connections. Or type **control netconnections** at a command prompt.

2. Double-click the wireless connection in Network Connections and then click the View Wireless Networks button.

3. The available networks are shown in the right pane under the Choose A Wireless Network heading. If a network that should be available isn't listed, try clicking Refresh Network List under Network Tasks.

4. To check or change a wireless network's settings, select it in the Choose A Wireless Network list, click Change Advanced Settings under Related Tasks, and then select the Wireless Networks tab, as shown in Figure 14-20.

You can set the preferred network access order or change a wireless network's settings by completing the following steps:

1. In Network Connections, right-click the connection you want to work with and select Properties.

2. Select the Wireless Networks as shown in Figure 14-20. You must select the Use Windows To Configure My Wireless Network Settings check box to be able to set wireless network configuration options. The only time you would want to clear this option is if you are using third-party wireless network software.

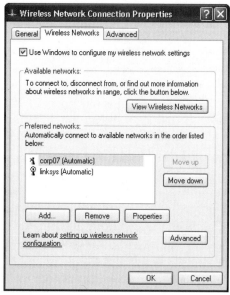

Figure 14-20   A wireless network connection.

3. Use the Preferred Networks panel to set the order in which the computer should try to use the available networks. The network listed at the top of the Preferred Networks list is tried before any others. If the computer fails to establish a connection over this network, the next network in the list is tried, and so on. As necessary, click Add to create a new wireless network that will be added to the Preferred Networks list, or select an existing network and click Remove to delete a listed wireless network.

4. If you want to view or change a network's configuration settings, select the network you want to work with in the Preferred Networks list by clicking it, and then click Properties.

5. Click OK when you are finished.

Controlling Ad Hoc and Infrastructure Networking

By default, a computer can connect to any available wireless network including both ad hoc and infrastructure networks. You can check or change these settings by completing the following steps:

1. Access Network Connections. Click Start, point to Programs or All Programs as appropriate, then to Accessories, then to Communications, and finally click Network Connections. Or type **control netconnections** at a command prompt.

2. Right-click the wireless connection that you want to work with, and choose Properties.

3. On the Wireless Networks tab, click Advanced. You can now configure the networks to access as:

   ❏ **Any available Network (Access Point Preferred)**   The wireless device can make connections to any available wireless network, but any infrastructure networks will always be tried first if available.

   ❏ **Access Point (Infrastructure) Networks Only**   The wireless device can make connections only to infrastructure networks. Connections to ad hoc networks are not permitted.

   ❏ **Computer-To-Computer (Ad Hoc) Networks Only**   The wireless device can make connections only to ad hoc networks. Connections to infrastructure networks are not permitted. Use this option if you are trying to connect computer-to-computer and to avoid connecting to an available infrastructure network.

   Security   In most cases, you will want to configure a computer with a wireless adapter to use only infrastructure networks. This will prevent the computer from communicating directly with other computers and can close some security holes, especially if the user takes the computer out of the office. If you allow ad hoc connections, using the computer in any public location could potentially open the computer to attack.

4. Click Close, and then click OK to complete the configuration change.

Chapter 15

Managing Advanced Internet Options

In this chapter:
Customizing URLs 388
Customizing the Browser User Interface 391
Setting Default Internet Programs 396
Managing Connection and Proxy Settings 398
Managing Browser Cookies and Other Temporary Internet Files 402
Secure Browsing and Local Machine Lockdown. 404
Managing Internet Explorer Security Zones 409
Additional Policies That Might Be Useful for
Managing Internet Options. 417

Microsoft Windows XP includes Microsoft Internet Explorer, a feature-rich Web browser that can be used to access information published on the Internet and corporate networks. (In this book, "Windows XP" refers to Windows XP Professional unless otherwise indicated.) You can customize the configuration of Microsoft Internet Explorer in many areas, including Internet file caching, Internet security zones, Internet privacy preferences, default Internet programs, and other advanced options that control browser features.

Internet Explorer settings can be managed in several ways. When you want to manage Internet Explorer settings for individual users, you'll use the Internet Options tool in the Control Panel. When you want to manage settings for multiple users, you'll use Group Policy. The focus of this chapter is on managing Internet Explorer settings through Group Policy. There are many policies that can be implemented to make your job easier while improving the user experience and getting better control over security and privacy.

Customizing URLs

Internet Explorer is configured with many default Uniform Resource Locators (URLs), which are used for everything from the default home page to favorite lists. Through Group Policy, you can customize the URLs to tailor the browser interface to meet the needs of your organization.

Setting Home Page, Search, and Support URLs

Custom home page, search, and support URLs provide users with quick access to important resources that can make their lives (and yours) a bit easier. To configure these options through Group Policy, follow these steps:

1. Access Group Policy for the system you want to work with. Next, access User Configuration\Windows Settings\Internet Explorer Maintenance\URLs.

2. In the right pane, double-click Important URLs. As shown in Figure 15-1, you can now specify a custom home page, search bar page, and online support page.

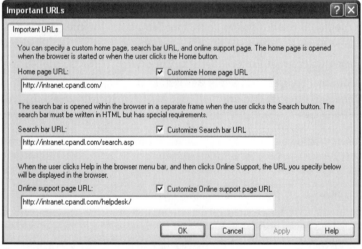

Figure 15-1   Use the Important URLs dialog box to set custom URLs for a home page, search bar page, and online support page.

3. Select Customize Home Page URL, and then in the Home Page URL text box, type the URL of the home page you want to use, such as *http://intranet.microsoft.com/*. The home page URL is opened whenever the browser is started or the user clicks the Home button on the Internet Explorer toolbar.

 Tip   Typically, you'll want to set the home page URL to the home page of your organization's intranet. If you don't have an intranet, you might want to set this to the home page of your company's external Web site.

4. Select Customize Search Bar URL, and then in the Search Bar URL text box, type the URL to the search page you want to use, such as *http://intranet.microsoft.com/search.asp*. The search page is opened in a side frame of the Internet Explorer window whenever a user clicks the Search button.

> **Caution** Getting the search page to work correctly is tricky. Test your implementation locally before rolling it out to multiple users. The search page must be formatted as Hypertext Markup Language (HTML) and should include links targeted at the main frame. Because the search page is opened in a side frame of the browser, you'll need to create a separate version, modified to work as a side frame, of any existing search page on your organization's intranet or external Web site.

5. Select Customize Online Support Page URL, and then in the Online Support Page URL text box, type the URL to the support page you want to use, such as *http://intranet.microsoft.com/helpdesk/*. The support page is opened when a user selects Online Support from the Internet Explorer Help menu.

6. Click OK.

Customizing Favorites and Links

The Favorites and Links lists are designed to provide quick access to commonly used resources. In Internet Explorer, you access Favorites and Links through the Favorites menu. When you click Favorites on the menu bar, you see a list of options that allow you to add, organize, and access favorites. Through Group Policy, you can add favorites and links that make it easier for users to access commonly used online resources, such as expense forms, corporate phone directories, and product specifications. This makes users more efficient and saves time, and it might also increase use of these important resources.

Using Group Policy, you can add favorites and links in two ways. You can add items individually or you can import a folder containing the items you want to use. To create favorites and links one by one, follow these steps:

1. Access Group Policy for the resource you want to work with. Next, access User Configuration\Windows Settings\Internet Explorer Maintenance\URLs.

2. In the right pane, double-click Favorites And Links. This displays the Favorites And Links dialog box shown in Figure 15-2. You can now add submenus and individual options to the Favorites menu in Internet Explorer. These items are available to all users subject to the policy.

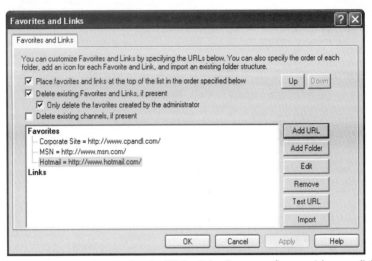

Figure 15-2   Use the Favorites And Links dialog box to configure quick access links to important online resources.

3. When you plan to add several favorites or links, you can create a folder to hold the options. The folder you create appears as a submenu under the Favorites menu in Internet Explorer. To create a submenu, select Favorites and then click Add Folder. This displays the Details dialog box. Enter a name for the submenu in the Name text box and then click OK.

4. To add individual menu options, select Favorites, Links, or a folder entry and then click Add URL. This again displays the Details dialog box. Type the name of the menu option, such as Expense Forms, and then type the URL to the resource, such as *http://intranet.microsoft.com/exp_forms/*. Next, click OK. The entry is then added to the menu or submenu you have chosen.

   Tip   After you add a menu option, you can verify that you've correctly entered the URL by selecting the option and then clicking Test URL. This action loads the selected item in Internet Explorer. If the related page appears in Internet Explorer, you've entered the URL correctly. Otherwise, you've probably made a mistake and should edit the URL.

5. Once you are finished adding submenus and creating menu options, you can specify additional preferences for adding the items to the Favorites menu. These additional preferences include the following:

   ❑ **Place Favorites And Links At The Top Of The List In The Order Specified Below**   Places these items at the top of the menu and in the order in which you entered them in the list box. If you select this option, you can also use the Up and Down buttons to change the order of submenus and menu items in the list box.

❑ **Delete Existing Favorites And Links, If Present**   Removes any existing favorites and links, replacing them with the items you created. Using this option alone removes existing items created by both users and administrators.

❑ **Only Delete The Favorites Created By The Administrator**   Removes previous favorites and links created by the administrator but doesn't remove those created by users. This is a good option to use if you previously configured favorites and links and now want to replace those entries with your current items.

6. Click OK when you are finished.

You can also create favorites and links using a folder and its contents as the basis for a submenu. To do this, follow these steps:

1. Create a folder on a network or local drive that you can easily access. In the folder, add URL shortcuts that point to the locations you want to be able to access. These shortcuts will become the items in the submenu you are creating. Be sure to use descriptive names for the folder and its shortcuts, which will appear in the Internet Explorer Favorites menu.

2. When you are ready to continue, access User Configuration\Windows Settings\Internet Explorer Maintenance\URLs in Group Policy, and double-click Favorites And Links in the right pane.

3. In the Favorites And Links dialog box shown previously in Figure 15-2, select Favorites, Links, or a folder entry and then click Import. This displays the Browse For Folder dialog box. Use this dialog box to select the folder you created in step 1 and then click OK. The folder and its contents are added as a submenu of the selected item.

Note   Only properly formatted URL shortcuts are imported. If the folder contains other types of files or shortcuts, the folder doesn't appear as a submenu and the additional items aren't imported.

4. Follow steps 5 and 6 of the previous procedure to complete the process.

Customizing the Browser User Interface

The Internet Explorer user interface can be customized for your organization using the Browser User Interface policies in Group Policy. These policies allow you to add custom titles to the title bar, custom logos that replace the Internet Explorer logo, and custom toolbars that add to or replace the existing toolbar.

Creating Custom Titles

Using the Browser Title policy you can customize the text that appears in the title bar of Internet Explorer. By default, the title bar displays the title of the current page followed by the text "Microsoft Internet Explorer," such as "My Home Page – Microsoft Internet Explorer." When you add a custom title, the default title is updated so that your string is added to the text "Microsoft Internet Explorer provided by," such as "My Home Page – Microsoft Internet Explorer provided by ABC Publishing."

To add a custom title to Internet Explorer, follow these steps:

1. Access User Configuration\Windows Settings\Internet Explorer Maintenance\Browser User Interface in Group Policy and then double-click Browser Title. This displays the Browser Title dialog box, shown in Figure 15-3.

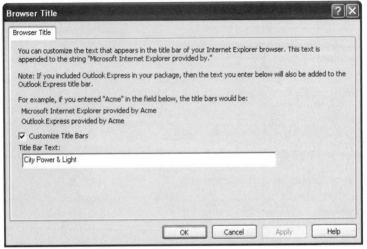

Figure 15-3   Add custom titles to Internet Explorer in the Browser Title dialog box by selecting Customize Title Bars and then entering your custom title.

2. Select Customize Title Bars, and then type the custom title in the Title Bar Text box.
3. Click OK.

 Note   The custom title also appears in Microsoft Outlook Express if this is installed and used on the affected computer or computers.

Creating Custom Logos

Internet Explorer displays two standard logos in the upper right corner of the Internet Explorer window: a static logo and an animated logo. The static logo is displayed when the browser isn't performing an action. The animated logo is displayed when the browser is downloading pages or performing other actions. These logos are produced in one of two sizes, 22 × 22 pixels or 38 × 38 pixels, and they are formatted as bitmap images.

Using the Custom Logo policy, you can replace the standard logos with ones specifically created for your organization. If you want to use custom logos, you should work with your organization's design or art department to create the necessary image files. Images in 256 colors should be indexed to the Windows halftone palette; 15-color images should be indexed to the 15-color Windows palette. The animated bitmap should consist of numbered bitmaps that are vertically stacked into one bitmap. The first bitmap appears static when no action is taking place and the remaining bitmaps appear in sequence when the browser is in use, producing the animation effect. You'll find two tools, the Animated Bitmap Creator (MAKEBMP.EXE) and the Animated Bitmap Previewer (ANIMBMP.EXE), in the Internet Explorer Administration Kit (IEAK), available for download from *http://www.microsoft.com/windows/ieak/downloads/default.mspx*. These tools will help you create and preview animated logos.

Once you finish creating the image files, you should test the files on your local system before using Group Policy to update other computers in the organization. The logo files become part of Group Policy and are stored with the Group Policy files. Because the files are imported before use, they don't need to reside on the local computer initially. In fact, it might be best to put the logos on a network drive so that you can test them locally and then incorporate them into Group Policy using the same file paths.

To add custom logos to Internet Explorer, follow these steps:

1. Access User Configuration\Windows Settings\Internet Explorer Maintenance\Browser User Interface in Group Policy, and then double-click Custom Logo. This displays the Custom Logo dialog box shown in Figure 15-4.

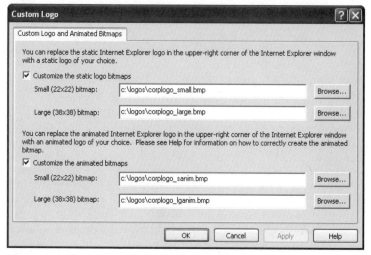

Figure 15-4 Once you create custom logos for Internet Explorer, you can configure them to be used through Group Policy in the Custom Logo dialog box.

2. If you want to set a static logo and have created static logos that are 22 × 22 pixels and 38 × 38 pixels, select Customize The Static Logo Bitmaps. Then perform the following tasks, in any order:

   ❑ In the Small (22 × 22) Bitmap text box, type the path to the small logo that you want to use or click Browse to use the Browse dialog box to find the image that you want to use.

   ❑ In the Large (38 × 38) Bitmap text box, type the path to the large logo that you want to use or click Browse to use the Browse dialog box to find the image that you want to use.

 Note In all cases, the images must be the appropriate size or they won't be imported and set as the default logos. If you see a warning message that says the specified bitmap is too large, you'll need to select a different logo file to continue.

3. If you want to set an animated logo and have created animated bitmap images that are 22 × 22 pixels and 38 × 38 pixels, select Customize The Animated Bitmaps. Then perform the following tasks, in any order:

   ❑ In the Small (22 × 22) Bitmap text box, type the path to the small animated logo that you want to use or click Browse to use the Browse dialog box to find the image that you want to use.

   ❑ In the Large (38 × 38) Bitmap text box, type the path to the large animated logo that you want to use or click Browse to use the Browse dialog box to find the image that you want to use.

4. Click OK. The logo files are then imported and stored in Group Policy.

Creating Custom Buttons for Internet Explorer

Just as you can customize the title bar and logos in Internet Explorer, you can also customize the toolbar. The most common task you'll need to perform is adding a custom button that performs a specific task, such as launching a custom application. Before you can use a custom button, you'll need to do the following:

■ Create a script file containing the commands that you want to run or know the path to an executable file that you want to use. The script file can be a batch file (.cmd or .bat) or a Windows Script Host (WSH) file (.js, .vbs, and so on).

■ Create (or work with the design or art department to create) a color icon file for the button. The color icon file, saved with an .ico extension, contains images for when the toolbar button is active. The icon file must contain three separate bitmaps: one 20 × 20 256-color, one 20 × 20 15-color, and one 15 × 15 15-color. The bitmaps must be indexed to either the 256-color Windows halftone palette or the 15-color Windows palette as appropriate.

■ Create (or work with the design or art department to create) a grayscale icon file for the button. The grayscale icon file, saved with an .ico extension, contains images for when the toolbar button is in the default or inactive state. The icon file must contain three separate bitmaps: one 20 × 20 grayscale image using the 256-color Windows halftone palette, one 20 × 20 grayscale image using the 15-color Windows palette, and one 15 × 15 grayscale image using the 15-color Windows palette.

When you are ready to proceed, you can add a custom button to the Internet Explorer toolbar by following these steps:

1. Access User Configuration\Windows Settings\Internet Explorer Maintenance\ Browser User Interface in Group Policy, and then double-click Browser Toolbar Customizations. This displays the Browser Toolbar Customizations dialog box.

2. On the Buttons panel, click Add to display the Browser Toolbar Button Information dialog box shown in Figure 15-5.

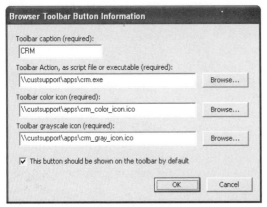

Figure 15-5   Add custom buttons to the toolbar using the Browser Toolbar Button Information dialog box.

3. In the Toolbar Caption (Required) text box, type the button caption, which should be short—no more than one or two words. The button caption appears to the right or below the button when users display both the text and the icon on toolbar buttons.

4. In the Toolbar Action, As Script File Or Executable (Required) text box, type the path to the script or executable file that you want to run when the button is clicked. If you don't know the file path, click Browse and use the Browse dialog box to find the file.

> **Tip**   When setting the toolbar action, think carefully about the file path you use. It should be accessible to all users who will be affected by the policy you are creating. If necessary, you can use environment variables, such as *%SystemDrive%*, to ensure file paths are consistent for different users. You can also use network file paths, provided they are automatically mapped for users.

5. In the Toolbar Color Icon (Required) text box, enter the path to the color icon file that you created for the button or click Browse to locate the file using the Browse dialog box.

6. In the Toolbar Grayscale Icon (Required) text box, enter the path to the grayscale icon file that you created for the button or click Browse to locate the file using the Browse dialog box.

7. If you want the custom button to be displayed on the toolbar by default, select This Button Should Be Shown On the Toolbar By Default. If you don't select this check box, users will need to display the button manually using the Customize Toolbar dialog box. This dialog box is accessed in Internet Explorer by selecting View, pointing to Toolbars, and selecting Customize.

8. Click OK. If you later decide not to use the button, you can remove it by selecting the button on the Buttons list and then clicking Remove.

Setting Default Internet Programs

Each user's profile contains settings for default programs that should be used for the following key Internet Services:

- **HTML Editor**   Specifies the default HTML editor program. On systems on which Microsoft Office is installed, the standard options are Microsoft Office Word and Microsoft Notepad.

- **E-mail**   Specifies the default e-mail program. On systems on which Microsoft Office is installed, the standard options are Microsoft Office Outlook, Outlook Express, and Hotmail.

- **Newsgroups**   Specifies the default Internet newsreader program. On systems on which Microsoft Office is installed, the standard options are Microsoft Office Outlook and Outlook Express.

- **Internet Call**   Specifies the default network meeting program. Typically the only standard option is NetMeeting.

- **Calendar**   Specifies the scheduling program used with Internet Explorer. On systems on which Microsoft Office is installed, the only standard option is Microsoft Office Outlook.

- **Contact List**   Specifies the default address book program. On systems on which Microsoft Office is installed, the standard options are Microsoft Office Outlook and Address Book.

 Note   Additional options might be available if other applications are installed on a system. Furthermore, in some cases (such as with the default HTML editor), you can select a blank value to specify that you don't want to use a default program for this service.

You can set default Internet programs using the Programs tab of the Internet Options tool or through Group Policy. The procedures are very similar. To set default programs through Group Policy, follow these steps:

1. Access User Configuration\Windows Settings\Internet Explorer Maintenance\Programs in Group Policy, and then double-click Programs in the right pane. The Programs dialog box is displayed, as shown in Figure 15-6.

2. If you want to stop using custom program settings, select Do Not Customize Program Settings and then click OK. Skip the remaining steps.

3. If you want to start using custom program settings, select Import The Current Program Settings and then click Modify Settings. This displays the Internet Properties dialog box, shown in Figure 15-7.

4. Use the text boxes provided in the Internet Programs panel to set the default Internet programs.

5. When you install additional browser software, the software might be set as the default Internet browser during installation. To have Internet Explorer check to make sure that it is still registered as the default Internet browser when Internet Explorer is started, select Internet Explorer Should Check To See Whether It Is The Default Browser.

6. Click OK twice when you are finished.

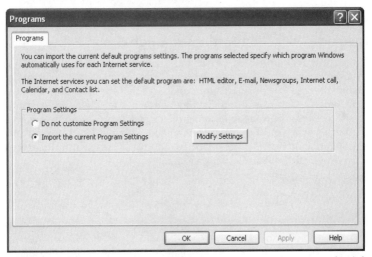

Figure 15-6   Use the Programs policy to customize the program settings for default Internet services.

Figure 15-7   In the Internet Properties dialog box, specify the default programs to use.

Managing Connection and Proxy Settings

Internet connection settings and proxies can be two of the biggest problems for administrators. When you deploy new computers you must configure the connection and proxy settings manually or rely on an image build of a machine that might not be up to date. When you make changes to the network you might need to update the connection settings as well. Performing these procedures manually takes a lot of time—time that can be better spent performing other tasks. Fortunately, Group Policy provides a better way to manage connection and proxy settings, and the related techniques are examined in this section.

Managing Connection Settings through Group Policy

Connection settings for dial-up, broadband, and virtual private network (VPN) access can be managed through Group Policy. You can use Group Policy to deploy new configurations, to update existing configurations when you need to make changes, and to delete existing configurations and replace them with new ones. Local area network (LAN) settings for automatic detection and proxy servers are also imported with the connection configuration settings. The address for automatic configuration scripts is not imported, however. These settings are managed with the Automatic Browser Configuration policy.

To import connection settings into Group Policy, follow these steps:

1. Log on to the system where you created the connection settings that you want to use.

    Real World   Whenever you manage connection settings through Group Policy, you should create the necessary connections on a test system following the techniques discussed in Chapter 14, "Managing Mobile Networking and Remote Access," and then check the connections by dialing in to the network, connecting through broadband, or using VPN as necessary. Then import the settings into the Connection Settings policy from the test system. Be sure to import settings at the appropriate level in Group Policy. In most cases, you won't want to roll these settings out to the entire domain and instead will want to apply these settings only to the appropriate Active Directory organizational units.

2. Access the Group Policy object you want to work with following the techniques discussed in the section of Chapter 9 titled "Group Policy Essentials" and then access User Configuration\Windows Settings\Internet Explorer Maintenance\Connection in Group Policy.

3. Double-click Connection Settings in the right pane. This displays the Connection Settings dialog box, shown in Figure 15-8.

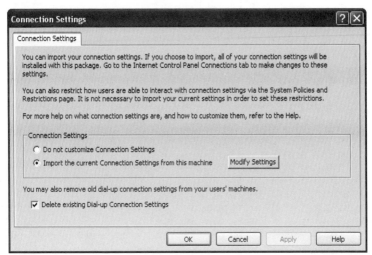

Figure 15-8   Import connection settings from a test computer and deploy the settings to users in the Connection Settings dialog box.

4. Select Import The Current Connection Settings From This Machine. To view or modify the settings that will be imported, click Modify Settings and then use the Connections tab of the Internet Properties dialog box to work with the settings as necessary. The options available are the same as those for the Connections tab of the Internet Options tool.

   Note   Existing connections with the same names as the imported connections are updated with the new settings, so you don't need to delete the existing settings to make these updates. You need to delete existing settings only if you are concerned that users or other administrators have created connections that might no longer be valid and you want to ensure they are removed to prevent connectivity problems.

5. If you are replacing previously configured connections, you might want to specify that existing connections should be deleted. To do this, in the Connection Settings dialog box, select Delete Existing Dial-Up Connection Settings.

   Caution   All previously configured connections are deleted if you elect to delete existing connection settings. This means that previous connections created by both administrators and users are permanently removed.

6. Click OK.

Enabling and Configuring Proxy Settings

When you enable proxy settings, Internet Explorer acts as a Web proxy client. In this configuration, Internet Explorer requests can be directed to a proxy service to determine if access to this protocol is allowed. If the protocol is allowed, the proxy server sends the request on behalf of the client and returns the results to the client securely. Because the proxy server uses network address translation (NAT) or a similar protocol, the actual Internet Protocol (IP) address of the client making the request isn't revealed to the target server. You can configure proxy servers for Hypertext Transfer Protocol (HTTP), Secure Sockets Layer (SSL), File Transfer Protocol (FTP), Gopher, and Socks (the Microsoft proxy service protocol).

You can manage settings for proxy servers in several different ways. One of those ways is to use the Local Area Network (LAN) Settings dialog box, which is accessible in the Internet Options tool. On the Connections tab, click LAN Settings to access the dialog box. When you want to use Group Policy, the preferred technique is to configure standard proxy servers using the Proxy Settings policy. Using this policy, you can configure unique proxy servers for each Web service (HTTP, SSL, FTP, Gopher, and Socks) or you can use one or more proxy servers to handle all types of requests. You can also configure exceptions so that a proxy isn't used for specific servers, IP address ranges, and the local network.

To configure proxy settings through Group Policy, follow these steps:

1. Access User Configuration\Windows Settings\Internet Explorer Maintenance\Connection in Group Policy, and then double-click Proxy Settings in the right pane.

2. In the Proxy Settings dialog box, shown in Figure 15-9, select Enable Proxy Settings.

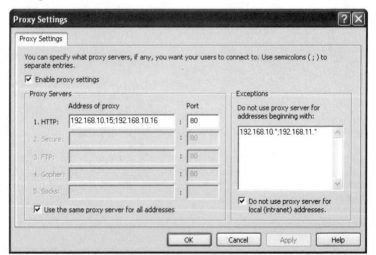

Figure 15-9   If your organization has proxy servers, you can configure Internet Explorer proxy settings using the Proxy Settings policy.

3. Set the IP address for proxies using the text boxes on the Proxy Servers panel. You'll find two columns of text boxes:

   ❏ **Address Of Proxy**   Sets the IP address of the related proxy server or servers. Type the IP address for each service. If multiple proxies are configured for a particular service, type the IP addresses for each proxy server in the order in which you want the Web client to attempt to use them. Each address must be separated by a semicolon. If a proxy isn't configured for a service, don't fill in the related field.

   ❏ **Port**   Sets the port number on which the proxy server responds to requests. Most proxies respond to port 80 for all requests. That said, however, the standard ports are port 80 for HTTP, port 443 for SSL (listed as Secure), port 21 for FTP, port 70 for Gopher, and port 1081 for Socks. Check with your organization's Web administrator for the proper settings.

4. The Use The Same Proxy Server For All Addresses check box is selected by default. This setting allows you to use the same IP address and port settings for the HTTP, SSL, FTP, Gopher, and Socks services. You have two options:

   ❏ If your organization has proxy servers that handle all requests, select Use The Same Proxy Server For All Addresses, type the IP address or addresses that you want to use, and the port number on which the server or servers respond.

   ❏ If you want to use a unique proxy server or servers for each type of service, clear the Use The Same Proxy Server For All Addresses check box and type the necessary IP addresses and port numbers in the text boxes provided.

5. The Do Not Use Proxy Server For Local (Intranet) Addresses check box is selected by default. In most cases you won't want to use a proxy for requests made to servers on the same network segment, so this is a suitable setting. However, this setting doesn't work well when your internal network uses multiple network segments. In this case, you'll need to specify the IP address range for each network segment on the exception list. An example is shown in Figure 15-9. Here you don't want a proxy to be used when accessing servers on the same network segments as the proxy servers, so you configure the IP addresses on these network segments as exceptions.

6. If your network has multiple segments or there are specific address ranges that shouldn't be proxied when accessed, enter the appropriate IP addresses or IP address ranges in the Exceptions list. Each entry must be separated with a semicolon. The asterisk (*) character can be used as a wildcard to specify an address range of 0 through 255, such as 192.*.*.*, 192.158.*.*, or 192.158.10.*.

7. Click OK.

To ensure that proxy settings are applied uniformly to all users of a particular computer, you can set an additional policy that assigns proxy settings per machine rather than per user. When you enable this policy, proxy settings apply to all users of the same computer and users cannot set their own proxy settings. This prevents users from overriding the standard proxy settings for the organization. You can make proxy settings per machine by following these steps:

1. Access Computer Configuration\Administrative Templates\Windows Compo-
   nents\Internet Explorer in Group Policy and then double-click Make Proxy
   Settings Per-Machine (Rather Than Per-User) in the right pane.

2. Select Enabled, and then click OK. The affected computer or computers need
   to be rebooted for this policy to be applied.

 Note   If you disable or do not configure this policy, users of the
same computer can set their own proxy settings. These settings might
override those set through Group Policy.

Managing Browser Cookies and Other Temporary Internet Files

Whenever users browse the Web, many types of temporary Internet files are stored
on their computers. The most misunderstood temporary Internet file is the browser
cookie. Browser cookies are used to store information on client computers so that it
can be retrieved in other pages or in other browser sessions. Cookies are commonly
used to store logon information for protected Web sites, user preferences and shop-
ping cart items. Internet Explorer browsers save cookies in a domain-specific text
file which is stored in the *%UserProfile%*\Cookies folder. Cookies are read from and
written to cookie files as records. Fields in a cookie record detail the domain of the
server that created the cookie, the name of the cookie, the string of data being
stored in the cookie, the expiration date for the cookie, a Boolean value indicating
whether you need a secure HTTP connection to access the cookie, and a path designator indicating the URL path(s) that can access the cookie.

You can manage browser cookies and other types of temporary Internet files using
the Internet Options tool in the Control Panel. If users spend a lot of time on the
Web and you have disk space limitations, you might need to more closely manage
the space used by temporary Internet files. Double-click Internet Options in Control Panel and then use the following procedures as necessary to recover and
restrict disk space usage:

- **Clear out temporary Internet files**
    1. On the General tab, click Delete Cookies and then when prompted, click OK.
    2. Click Delete Files and then when prompted, click OK.
    3. Click Clear History and then when prompted, click Yes.

- **Set disk space usage for temporary Internet files**
    1. On the General tab, click Settings and then use the Amount Of Disk Space
       To Use slider to specify how much disk space can be used by temporary
       Internet files.
    2. By default, temporary Internet files are stored in a folder under *%UserPro-
       file%*. If you want to move this folder to a drive with more space, click
       Move Folder and then use the Browse For Folder dialog box to select the
       new drive to use.

3. Click OK to close the Settings dialog box. Click OK to close the Internet Properties dialog box.

You can configure the way browser cookies are used on the Privacy tab of the Internet Properties dialog box. Double-click Internet Options in Control Panel and then select the Privacy tab. You can then use the Settings slider to specify how cookies should be used. Privacy settings available include: Block All Cookies, High, Medium High, Medium, Low, and Allow All Cookies. When you are using a privacy setting ranging from High to Low, you might want to make an exception for a site rather than raise or lower your privacy setting. To do this, click the Sites button on the Privacy tab. Type the address of the Web site in the field provided and then click Allow or Block as appropriate. If you click Allow, cookies for the site will then be accepted. If you click Block, cookies for the site will then be blocked. Keep in mind that you cannot make exceptions when you use the Block All Cookies or Allow All Cookies setting. With these settings, all cookies are always either blocked or allowed—there is no in between or exception.

The privacy setting options are used as follows:

- **Block All Cookies**   Blocks all new cookies and ensures any existing cookies cannot be read by Web sites. Many Web sites won't function properly if you use a setting of High or Block All Cookies. It is also important to point out that any sites you've configured as Allow exceptions are blocked as well. This means the Allow exception is ignored while this setting is selected.

- **High**   Blocks all cookies from sites that do not have a statement indicating the source, purpose, and lifetime of cookies used by a particular site. It also blocks all cookies that gather any information that could be used to contact you (such as your name, e-mail address, home address, and logon information) unless you give explicit consent.

- **Medium High**   Blocks cookies from sites other than the one you are viewing (such as an advertiser who advertises at the current site) that do not have a statement indicating the source, purpose, and lifetime of cookies used by a particular site. It blocks cookies from other sites (such as advertisers) that could be used to contact you unless you give explicit consent. Further, it blocks cookies from the current site that could be used to contact you unless consent can be implied.

    Note   Implied consent is granted automatically. Basically, it means you haven't opted out or told the site you don't want this information to be collected, so this information can be collected.

- **Medium**   The default privacy setting. Blocks cookies from sites other than the one you are viewing (such as an advertiser at the current site) that do not have a statement indicating the source, purpose, and lifetime of cookies used by a particular site. It restricts cookies from the current site and blocks cookies from other sites (such as advertisers) that could be used to contact you unless consent can be implied.

- **Low**   Blocks cookies from sites other than the one you are viewing (such as an advertiser at the current site) that do not have a statement indicating the source, purpose, and lifetime of cookies used by a particular site. It restricts cookies from other sites (such as advertisers) that could be used to contact you unless consent can be implied.

- **Accept All Cookies**   Accepts all new cookies and allows Web sites to read existing cookies. It is important to point out that any sites you've configured as Block exceptions are allowed as well, meaning the Block doesn't apply while this setting is used.

Secure Browsing and Local Machine Lockdown

To help make the operating system more secure, Internet Explorer security was revised greatly starting with Service Pack 2. These security changes affect many areas of the browser and introduce several new features including:

- Browser Information Bar and general security
- Add-on Manager
- Pop-up Blocker

The sections that follow examine each of these features.

Understanding the Browser Information Bar and Browser Security Enhancements

With Windows XP Service Pack 2 or later, the Browser Information Bar is used in place of many of the common Internet Explorer dialog boxes and prompts. The Information Bar is designed to help users navigate the many security enhancements for pop-up windows, add-ons, and active content. When the Information Bar is displayed, it appears just below the address bar. Anytime this bar is displayed, you can click or right-click the bar to display a shortcut menu with additional options that allow you to enable or disable the related feature and perform other related tasks.

Table 15-1 provides a summary of the most common messages you'll see and the related options in the Internet Options dialog box.

Table 15-1   Understanding Secure Browsing and Lockdown

Information Bar Message	Description	Action/Resolution
Active Content Blocked. To help protect your security, Internet Explorer has restricted this file from showing active content that could access your computer.	This message is displayed for any pages that contain scripts or other types of active content that access information on the local computer. Active Content is blocked by default to ensure malicious files can't be run by accident.	You can configure active content blocking by selecting or clearing Allow Active Content To Run In Files On My Computer on the Advanced tab of the Internet Options dialog box. To allow only this particular page to execute active content, click the Information Bar. Active content on CD AutoRun pages can be controlled using the Allow Active Content From CDs To Run On My Computer.

Table 15-1   Understanding Secure Browsing and Lockdown

Information Bar Message	Description	Action/Resolution
File Download Blocked. To help protect your security, Internet Explorer blocked this site from downloading files to your computer.	This message is displayed to prevent automatic downloading and installation of unwanted programs. Downloads are blocked by default to prevent sites from overwhelming users with download prompts and to help resolve problems with accidentally installing unwanted software.	You can configure automatic prompting through the Web zone security settings. On the Security tab of the Internet Options dialog box, select a Web zone by clicking it and then click Custom Level. In the Security Settings dialog box, select the appropriate option for Automatic Prompting For File Downloads. To allow only this file to download, right-click the Information Bar and select Download Software.
Pop-up Blocked. To see this pop-up or additional options, click here...	This message is displayed any time a page contains a link that opens a new window or a script that calls the *window.open()* method, and the Pop-up Blocker is in effect.	You can configure the blocking of pop-ups by selecting or clearing Block Pop-ups on the Privacy tab of the Internet Options dialog box. To configure pop-up blocking exceptions, click Settings on the Privacy tab and set a specific exception. You can also configure an exception for the current site by right-clicking the Information Bar and selecting Allow Pop-ups For This Site.
Software Install Blocked. To help protect your security, Internet Explorer stopped this site from installing software on your computer.	As with drivers, digital signatures are checked before downloading and installing Active X controls and other executables. This message is displayed anytime you attempt to install an ActiveX control or other executable with a missing or invalid signature. In general, it is a good idea to block these downloads as they are typically from untrusted publishers and might also represent malicious or undesirable types of files, such as adware.	You can configure the blocking of executables by selecting or clearing Allow Software To Run Or Install Even If The Signature Is Invalid on the Advanced tab of the Internet Options dialog box. To allow only this executable to install, right-click the Information Bar and select Install Software.
Software Blocked. Your security settings do not allow ActiveX controls to run on this page. This page might not display correctly.	This message is displayed if running of ActiveX Controls and plug-ins is disabled or blocked by an administrator.	You can configure the way ActiveX controls and plug-ins run by setting Web zone security settings. On the Security tab of the Internet Options dialog box, select a Web zone by clicking it and then click Custom Level. In the Security Settings dialog box, select the appropriate option for Run ActiveX Controls And Plug-ins. To allow ActiveX controls and plug-ins only for the current site, right-click the Information Bar and select Allow This Site To Run ActiveX Controls.

Using the Add-on Manager for Internet Explorer

Internet Explorer functionality can be extended and enhanced through add-ons. Many types of add-ons are available, including the following:

- Browser helper objects that add help dialog boxes and other help information
- Browser extensions that add functionality or enhance browser features
- Toolbar options that add menu items and buttons to the browser toolbar
- ActiveX controls that provide additional functionality, allow execution of additional types of media such as Shockwave Flash files

As Figure 15-10 shows, these and other types of add-ons can be controlled through the Manage Add-ons dialog box on computers running Windows XP Service Pack 2 or later. To access this dialog box, double-click Internet Options in Control Panel and then click Manage Add-ons on the Programs tab. You can then use the following options:

- **Enable add-ons**   To enable an add-on that has been disabled previously, select it and then click Enable. If the option is grayed out (dimmed), the Do Not Allow Users To Enable Or Disable Add-ons policy might be enabled in Group Policy under User Configuration\Administrative Templates\Windows Components\Internet Explorer.

- **Disable add-ons**   To disable an add-on, select it and then click Disable. Internet Explorer Crash Detection allows users to disable add-ons that cause problems with the browser. You can control Crash Detection using the Turn Off Crash Detection policy under User Configuration\Administrative Templates\Windows Components\Internet Explorer.

- **Update add-ons**   If an ActiveX control is known to have an update available (as determined by Automatic Updates), you can select the add-on and click Update ActiveX to update the add-on.

 Real World   Since Windows XP SP2 or later include a built-in pop-up blocker, pay particular attention to any browser add-ons that act as pop-up blockers. In Figure 15-10, you'll see a pop-up blocker provided by Earthlink Inc. is being used. Many Internet Service Providers, Earthlink included, provide pop-up blockers to their customers. Some firewall and anti-virus software includes pop-up blockers as well. Running a third party pop-up blocker in addition to the Windows pop-up blocker can lead to unpredictable results that can be very confusing. Typically, you'll want to use only the Windows pop-up blocker and disable any other pop-up blockers running on the computer. In most cases, you'll find the Windows pop-up blocker is more configurable than other pop-up blockers and easier to work with.

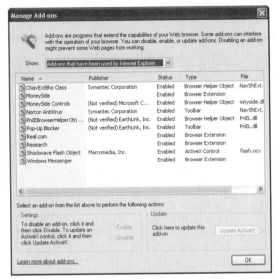

Figure 15-10 ActiveX controls and other browser add-ons can be enabled, disabled, or updated using the Manage Add-ons dialog box.

Configuring the Pop-up Blocker

Many Web pages contain pop-ups, which is a subwindow typically displayed by a call to the *window.open()* method in a script. Some examples of how pop-ups are created include the following:

- A hypertext link contains a command that opens a window when it is clicked.
- A page element contains a command that opens a window when it finishes loading.
- A script in a page opens a window after a function call.

As many pop-ups are ads or are otherwise unwanted, Windows XP with Service Pack 2 or later includes the Pop-up Blocker feature. In the default configuration, Windows XP is configured to block most types of automatic pop-ups and display the Information Bar whenever pop-ups are blocked. A user could then right-click the Information Bar and select Allow Pop-up to display the pop-up or right-click the Information Bar and select Allow All Pop-ups For This Site to configure the site as an Allowed Site automatically which unblocks (or allows) pop-ups from this site.

You can configure pop-up blocking by completing the following steps:

1. Double-click Internet Options in Control Panel and then select the Privacy tab.

2. To disable pop-up blocking, clear Block Pop-ups and then click OK. Skip the remaining steps.

3. To enable pop-up blocking, select Block Pop-ups and then click Settings. This displays the Pop-up Blocker Settings dialog box shown in Figure 15-11.

Figure 15-11 Use the Pop-up Blocker Settings dialog box to configure the way pop-ups are blocked.

4. To allow a site's pop-ups to be displayed, type the address of the site in the field provided, such as *www.msn.com*, and then click Add. This site is then permitted to use pop-ups regardless of Internet Explorer settings.

> **Tip** You might want to configure exceptions for internal sites if these sites call the *window.open()* method in scripts or use similar methods to open windows. In this way, you ensure pop-ups for internal sites aren't blocked, regardless of the browser settings. You can also configure exceptions through the Pop-up Allow List policy under User Configuration\Administrative Templates\Windows Components\Internet Explorer.

5. To stop displaying an information message in the browser when pop-ups are blocked, clear Show Information Bar When A Pop-up Is Blocked.

6. By default, most types of automatic pop-ups are blocked when the Pop-up Blocker is enabled. You can control the types of pop-ups that are blocked using the following options of the Filter Level selection menu:

    ❑ **High: Block All Pop-ups (Ctrl To Override)** Pop-up blocker attempts to block all pop-ups. If you click a link that would normally open a pop-up and you want to see the pop-up, press Ctrl while clicking to open the pop-up.

    ❑ **Medium: Block Most Automatic Pop-ups** Pop-up blocker attempts to block the types of pop-ups most commonly used to display ads or other unwanted content. Some types of new windows are allowed. Again, you can press Ctrl to override blocking while clicking a link.

❑ **Low: Allow Pop-ups From Secure Sites**   With standard (HTTP) connections Pop-up Blocker attempts to block the types of pop-ups most commonly used to display ads or other unwanted content. However, Pop-up Blocker allows pop-ups when you are accessing a site using a secure (HTTPS) connection.

7. Click Close and then click OK.

Managing Internet Explorer Security Zones

Internet Explorer security zones play an important role in ensuring the security of Windows XP systems. You can use security zones to restrict or permit access to specific types of Web content including ActiveX controls and plug-ins, file and font downloads, Java applets, and scripts. You can also use security zones to control the types of actions users can perform while viewing Web content. For example, you can enable launching of programs within an internal browser frame, known as an IFRAME, but disable installation of desktop items.

Group Policy can be used to manage security zones in several ways. You can set policies that control the user actions with regard to security zones and customize the settings for each security zone. Before exploring how these procedures are implemented, let's look at what security zones are and how they are used.

Understanding Security Zones

Security zones are used to control Web content permissions for various content servers based on where they are located and what is known about them. Each security zone is assigned a default security level, which ranges from low to high. Low security means that most actions are permitted and the security restrictions are very relaxed. High security means that most actions are disabled and the security restrictions are very stringent.

You can override the security level by assigning a new security level or setting a custom level. Either way, the security level consists of dozens of parameters that typically are enabled, disabled, or set to prompt a user before the related feature can be invoked.

Table 15-2 provides a list of the security parameters and their configuration for each security level. The security zones these parameters apply to are as follows:

■ **Restricted Sites**   Controls user access to Web content on sites that could potentially damage a computer or its data. Default security level is High.

Security   With Windows XP Service Pack 2 or later, the Binary And Script Behaviors security setting is disabled by default in the Restricted Sites zone. This important security change is designed to prevent the execution of scripts and other components that encapsulate functionality for HTML elements. In other zones, Binary And Script Behaviors is enabled by default, which could allow the execution of malicious scripts.

- **Trusted Sites**   Controls user access to Web content on sites that are explicitly trusted and are considered to be free of content that could damage or harm the computer and its data. Default security level is a slightly modified version of Low, which allows downloading of unsigned ActiveX controls and sets Java permissions to Medium security.

- **Local Intranet**   Controls user access to Web content on the local network, which can include local (intranet) sites, sites bypassed by the proxy server, and all network paths, such as Universal Naming Conventions (UNCs). Default security level is Medium-Low.

- **Internet**   Controls users' access to Web content on all sites not placed in other zones. Default security level is Medium.

Table 15-2   Security Parameters for Each Security Level

Security Parameters	High	Medium	Medium-Low	Low
Automatic Prompting for ActiveX Controls[1]	Disable	Disable	Enable	Enable
Binary And Script Behaviors[1]	Disable	Enable	Enable	Enable
Download Signed ActiveX Controls	Disable	Prompt	Prompt	Enable
Download Unsigned ActiveX Controls	Disable	Disable	Disable	Prompt
Initialize And Script ActiveX Controls Not Marked As Safe	Disable	Disable	Disable	Prompt
Run ActiveX Controls And Plug-ins	Disable	Enable	Enable	Enable
Script ActiveX Controls Marked Safe For Scripting	Disable	Enable	Enable	Enable
Automatic Prompting For File Downloads[1]	Disable	Disable	Enable	Enable
File Download	Disable	Enable	Enable	Enable
Font Download	Prompt	Enable	Enable	Enable
Access Data Sources Across Domains	Disable	Disable	Prompt	Enable
Allow Meta Refresh	Disable	Enable	Enable	Enable
Allow Scripting Of Internet Explorer Webbrowser Control[1]	Disable	Disable	Disable	Disable
Allow Script-initiated Windows Without Size Or Position Constraints[1]	Disable	Disable	Enable	Enable
Allow Web Pages To Use Restricted Protocols For Active Content[1]	Disable	Prompt	Prompt	Prompt
Display Mixed Content	Prompt	Prompt	Prompt	Prompt
Don't Prompt For Client Certificate	Disable	Disable	Enable	Enable
Drag And Drop Or Copy And Paste Files	Prompt	Enable	Enable	Enable
Installation Of Desktop Items	Disable	Prompt	Prompt	Enable
Launching Programs And Files In An IFRAME	Disable	Prompt	Prompt	Enable

Table 15-2   Security Parameters for Each Security Level

Security Parameters	High	Medium	Medium-Low	Low
Navigate Sub-frames Across Different Domains	Disable	Enable	Enable	Enable
Open Files Based On Content, Not File Extension	Disable	Enable	Enable	Enable
Software Channel Permissions	High Safety	Medium Safety	Medium Safety	Low Safety
Submit Nonencrypted Form Data	Prompt	Prompt	Enable	Enable
Use Pop-up Blocker[*]	Enable	Enable	Disable	Disable
Userdata Persistence	Disable	Enable	Enable	Enable
Web Sites In Less Privileged Web Content Zone Can Navigate Into This Zone[1]	Disable	Enable	Enable	Prompt
Active Scripting	Disable	Enable	Enable	Enable
Allow Paste Operations Via Script	Disable	Enable	Enable	Enable
Scripting Of Java Applets	Disable	Enable	Enable	Enable

*   Additional security setting for Windows XP Service Pack 2 and later.

Obvious security risks result from the enabling of ActiveX controls, plug-ins, Java applets, scripts, and downloads. A not-so-obvious risk results from an additional parameter not listed in Table 15-2 named Logon. The Logon parameter determines whether user name and password information is sent automatically to content servers when a logon is needed. Of all the available parameters, Logon is the one that most people overlook. The key risk from the Logon parameter is that computers outside the network can gain access to logon names for your network and unauthorized external users could use the logon names to stage attacks on your system.

With the Logon parameter, all security levels except High present a potential security risk. With High security, content servers prompt for a user name and password when a logon is needed and information is never passed automatically. With Medium or Medium-Low security, the current user name and password are automatically returned for logon requests to resources in the intranet zone, which, as you might recall, can include intranet sites, network paths (UNCs), and sites bypassed by the proxy server. It is these bypassed sites that are easy to forget when you're considering possible security issues. With Low security, logon information is returned for logon requests from content servers in any zone, and this is a dangerous setting when used with external content servers.

Controlling Security Zone Usage through Group Policy

As you set out to manage security zone usage better, you might want to implement restrictions on who can change security zone settings and how settings are applied. Several policies control security zone modification and usage, as follows:

- **Security Zones: Use Only Machine Settings**   Enabling this policy sets security zone settings by machine rather than by user. The policy is intended to ensure that security zones are consistently applied to all users of a computer. Unfortunately, if you enable this policy without also preventing users from changing security zones, any user could make changes to security zones that affect all other users of the computer. This policy is located under Computer Configuration\Administrative Templates\Windows Components\Internet Explorer.

- **Security Zones: Do Not Allow Users To Change Policies**   Enabling this policy prevents users from changing security zone settings. If you enable this policy, the Custom Level and Default Level buttons are disabled on the Security tab of the Internet Properties dialog box. This prevents users from changing the security zone settings established by the administrator. This policy is located under Computer Configuration\Administrative Templates\Windows Components\Internet Explorer.

- **Security Zones: Do Not Allow Users To Add/Delete Sites**   Enabling this policy disables the Sites button on the Security tab of the Internet Properties dialog box. This prevents users from modifying the site management settings for the Local Intranet, Trusted Sites, and Restricted Sites zones, which means users cannot add sites, remove sites, or change the Include settings for the Local Intranet zone. This policy is located under Computer Configuration\Administrative Templates\Windows Components\Internet Explorer.

- **Disable The Security Page**   Enabling this policy removes the Security tab in the Internet Properties dialog box. This prevents users from making any changes to security zones. This policy takes precedence and overrides Security Zones: Do Not Allow Users To Change Policies and Security Zones: Do Not Allow Users To Add/Delete Sites. This policy is located under User Configuration\Administrative Templates\Windows Components\Internet Explorer\Internet Control Panel.

Enable one or more of these policies to enforce restrictions on changing security zone settings. Double-click the policy, select Enabled, and then click OK.

Windows XP Service Pack 2 and later include policies for locking down the local machine security zone. This special security zone applies only to the security of the local computer and is designed to prevent users from making changes that could materially affect the security of their computers. Any policies set under User Configuration\Administrative Templates\Windows Components\Internet Explorer\Internet Control Panel\Security Page\Locked-Down Local Machine Zone are locked out in the local machine zone and set according to their policy configuration. Rather than setting each policy individually, you can use the Locked-Down Local Machine Zone Template policy under User Configuration\Administrative Templates\Windows Components\Internet Explorer\Internet Control Panel\Security Page to set the local machine zone security so that it is consistent with a specific security level.

Configuring Security Zones through Group Policy

Through Group Policy you can implement standard settings for each security zone and deploy these settings to users of one or more computers. Before doing this, you'll need to configure the security settings for each of the four security zones, starting with the Internet security zone. Once you configure the zones, you can import the settings into the Security Zones And Content Ratings policy by following this procedure:

1. Configure each of the four security zones as discussed in this chapter. When you are finished, access User Configuration\Windows Settings\Internet Explorer Maintenance\Security in Group Policy and then double-click Security Zones And Content Ratings.

2. Select Import The Current Security Zone Settings And Privacy Settings and then click Modify Settings. You can now check the security zone settings you defined previously.

3. When you are finished, click OK twice to apply the policy.

Configuring the Internet Security Zone

The Internet security zone sets Web content permissions for all sites not placed in other zones. Follow these steps to configure the Internet security zone:

1. Access the Internet Options tool in the Control Panel and then select the Security tab as shown in Figure 15-12.

2. Select Internet from the zone list.

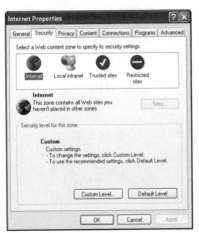

Figure 15-12   Use the Security tab of the Internet Properties dialog box to manage security zone settings.

3. To restore the default level if it was changed, click Default Level. Then click OK and skip the remaining steps.

4. To set a different or custom level, click Custom Level. You can use the Security Settings dialog box shown in Figure 15-13 to set a custom level for individual parameters or reset the zone to a preset security level.

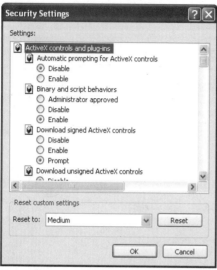

Figure 15-13   Use the Security Settings dialog box to manage individual security parameters or reset the security level completely.

5. If you want to use a custom level, use the buttons provided to set individual parameters and then click OK.

6. If you want to reset the zone to a particular security level, select the level using the Reset To drop-down list, click Reset, and then click OK. The security levels available are Low, Medium-Low, Medium, and High.

Configuring the Local Intranet Zone

The Local Intranet security zone sets Web content permissions on the local network. The default security level is Medium-Low. You can configure this zone by completing these steps:

1. In the Internet Properties dialog box, click the Security tab, then click Local Intranet in the zone list. Set the security level as discussed in the section "Configuring the Internet Security Zone," earlier in this chapter.

2. Next define which sites are included in the Local Intranet zone by clicking Sites. This displays the Local Intranet dialog box shown in Figure 15-14.

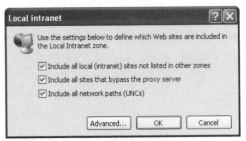

Figure 15-14 Optimize the Local Intranet settings for your environment by including or excluding various options.

3. You can now include or exclude local (intranet) sites not listed in other zones, sites that bypass the proxy server, and network paths (UNCs). To include a resource, select the related check box. To exclude a resource, clear the related check box.

4. If you want to specify additional sites for the Local Intranet zone or require secure verification using Hypertext Transfer Protocol Secure (HTTPS) for all servers in the Local Intranet zone, click Advanced. This displays a new Local Intranet dialog box, in which you can do the following:

    ❑ Add a site by typing its IP address in the Add This Web Site To The Zone text box and then clicking Add.

    ❑ Remove previously defined sites by selecting the site in the Web Sites list box and then clicking Remove.

    ❑ Require secure verification using HTTPS by selecting Require Server Verification (HTTPS:) For All Sites In This Zone.

5. Click OK twice to close the Local Intranet dialog boxes.

Configuring the Trusted Sites Security Zone

The Trusted Sites security zone sets Web content permissions for sites that are explicitly trusted and are considered to be free of potentially offensive or unauthorized content and content that could damage or harm the computer. By default, the security level for this zone is set to Low. You can configure this zone by completing these steps:

1. In the Internet Properties dialog box, click the Security tab, then click Trusted Sites in the zone list. Set the security level as discussed in the section "Configuring the Internet Security Zone," earlier in this chapter.

2. Click Sites to define which sites are included in the Trusted Sites zone. This displays the Trusted Sites dialog box shown in Figure 15-15.

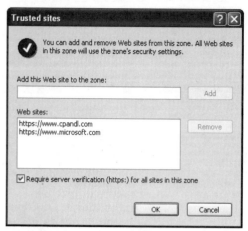

Figure 15-15   Use the Trusted Sites dialog box to select which sites you want to include in the Trusted Sites zone.

3. You can now add and remove trusted sites from this zone. All Web sites in this zone will use the zone's security settings. To add a site, type its IP address in the Add This Web Site To The Zone text box and then click Add. To remove a site, select the site in the Web Sites list box and then click Remove.

4. You can also require secure verification using HTTPS. Select Require Server Verification (HTTPS:) For All Sites In This Zone to enable this feature, or clear the related check box to disable this feature.

5. Click OK.

Configuring the Restricted Sites Security Zone

The Restricted Sites security zone sets permissions for sites with potentially offensive or unauthorized content and content that could damage or harm the computer. By default, the security level for this zone is set to High. You can place sites on the restricted list by completing the following steps:

1. In the Internet Properties dialog box, click the Security tab and then click Restricted Sites in the zone list. Set the security level as discussed in the section "Configuring the Internet Security Zone," earlier in this chapter.

2. Click Sites to define which sites are included in the Restricted Sites zone. This displays the Restricted Sites dialog box, which is similar to the dialog box shown in Figure 15-15.

3. To add a restricted site, type its IP address in the Add This Web Site To The Zone text box and then click Add.

4. To remove a site, select the site in the Web Sites list box and then click Remove.

5. Click OK twice to close the Restricted Sites and Internet Properties dialog boxes.

Note Site restrictions don't prevent users from accessing unauthorized sites; they merely establish a different security level for these sites. To prevent users from accessing restricted sites, you'd need to configure a proxy server or firewall to block access to the sites.

Additional Policies That Might Be Useful for Managing Internet Options

You'll find many policies for managing Internet Options under User Configuration\Administrative Templates\Windows Components\Internet Explorer. Key policies are summarized in Table 15-3. As you'll see when you examine the table, many of these policies are useful in preventing users from performing specific actions in Internet Explorer and for controlling Internet Explorer behavior.

Note An en dash (–) in the policy node column indicates the policy is under User Configuration\Administrative Templates\Windows Components\Internet Explorer. A named entry means the policy is located in a subnode of User Configuration\Administrative Templates\Windows Components\Internet Explorer.

Table 15-3   Additional Policies for Managing Internet Explorer

Policy Node	Policy Name	Description
–	Disable Internet Connection Wizard	Prevents users from running the New Connection Wizard.
–	Disable Changing Connection Settings	Prevents users from changing dial-up settings.
–	Disable Changing Proxy Settings	Prevents users from changing proxy server settings.
–	Turn Off Pop-up Management	Prevents a user from configuring pop-up options and hides related dialog boxes. This means pop-up manager controls, notifications, and dialog boxes do not appear when this option is enabled.
–	Pop-up Allow List	When enabled, permits administrators to specify a list of sites that are permitted to use pop-ups regardless of Internet Explorer settings. Enabling this option and adding internal sites to the list is useful if these sites call the *window.open()* method in JavaScript or use similar methods to open windows.
–	Turn Off Crash Detection	Crash detection allows the browser to track add-ons that cause problems with browser stability. The user can then elect to disable unstable add-ons. By enabling this option, you turn off this browser feature.

Table 15-3   Additional Policies for Managing Internet Explorer

Policy Node	Policy Name	Description
–	Do Not Allow Users To Enable Or Disable Add-ons	Add-on management allows users to control whether browser add-ons are enabled or disabled. By enabling this option, you disable add-on management and prevent users from configuring the related settings.
Browser Menus	Hide Favorites Menu	Removes the Favorites menu from Internet Explorer, preventing users from accessing lists for favorites.
Internet Control Panel	Disable The Connections Page	Removes the Connections tab in the Internet Options dialog box, preventing users from changing connection settings, proxy settings, and automatic configuration settings. Also prevents users from accessing the New Connection Wizard.
Internet Control Panel	Disable The Security Page	Removes the Security tab in the Internet Options dialog box, preventing users from changing security settings.
Internet Control Panel	Disable The Programs Page	Removes the Programs tab in the Internet Options dialog box, preventing users from changing the default Internet programs.
Internet Control Panel	Disable The Advanced Page	Removes the Advanced tab in the Internet Options dialog box, preventing users from enabling advanced features.
Internet Control Panel\ Advanced Page	Allow Software To Run Or Install Even If The Signature Is Invalid	By default, downloaded files and other executables are prevented from running and installing if they have invalid signatures. By enabling this policy, you override the default setting and allow files with invalid signatures to be installed.
Internet Control Panel\ Advanced Page	Allow Active Content From CDs To Run On User Machines	By default, users see a prompt that allows them to continue or cancel the running of the active content from a CD. By enabling this policy, you override the default setting and allow active content from CDs to run without prompting.
Persistence Behavior	File Size Limits For	Allows you to set size limits for cached dynamic files from each of the security zones. You can set per-domain and per-document limits.
Toolbars	Configure Toolbar Buttons	Specifies which buttons are enabled on the standard toolbar in Internet Explorer. If you enable this policy, you can specify whether a particular button is displayed by default or hidden.

You can enable one or more of these policies easily by double-clicking the policy, selecting Enabled, and then clicking OK. In some cases, you'll need to specify additional parameters, such as a file size limit or whether a button is active or inactive.

Chapter 16
Optimizing Windows XP Professional

In this chapter:

Improving Windows XP Performance 419

Optimizing Disk Drives. 422

Enhancing Security 430

Detecting and Resolving Windows XP Errors 437

Scheduling Maintenance Tasks 439

Many different aspects of Microsoft Windows XP can be optimized. To improve system performance, you can optimize settings and remove unnecessary applications and services. To optimize drives and improve their performance, you can clean up temporary files, check for disk errors, and defragment disks. To enhance security, you can encrypt disk contents, use the Security Center, and configure the Windows Firewall. To improve the user's experience, you can resolve problems with applications, services, and processes using the event logs. To make it easier to maintain systems, you can schedule routine maintenance tasks to run automatically.

Improving Windows XP Performance

One of the main areas you should focus on when you want to improve performance is Windows XP itself. You can improve the performance of the operating system by optimizing processor scheduling, appropriately configuring memory management, and removing graphics-intensive features from the menu system. You can also improve Windows XP performance by removing unnecessary startup applications, processes, and services.

Optimizing Processor Scheduling

The processor-scheduling setting controls the amount of processor time given to applications. In most cases, applications run by users should get more processor time than applications, services, and processes run by the operating system. This ensures that user applications have the best response time and share of processor resources possible.

To configure optimal performance for user applications, follow these steps:

1. Double-click System in the Control Panel menu to access the System Properties dialog box. On the Advanced tab, click Settings on the Performance panel to display the Performance Options dialog box.

2. The Performance Options dialog box has three tabs. Click the Advanced tab.

3. In the Processor Scheduling panel, select Programs.

4. Click OK twice.

Optimizing Memory Management

Memory management is another important consideration for optimizing Windows XP performance. Two facets of memory can be optimized: physical memory and virtual memory. Physical memory is the amount of random access memory (RAM) in the computer. Virtual memory is the amount of memory that can be written to disk.

For optimal system performance, each physical disk drive (not each volume) should have a virtual memory paging file. The paging file should have the initial and maximum sizes set equal, which ensures that the paging file is consistent and can be written to a single, contiguous file (if possible). Additionally, the total paging file size for all drives should be set to at least twice the physical memory on the system, meaning a system with 128 megabytes (MB) of RAM would have a paging file of at least 256 MB.

To optimize management of physical and virtual memory, follow these steps:

1. Access the Advanced tab in the System Properties dialog box, and then click Settings on the Performance panel to display the Performance Options dialog box.

2. The Performance Options dialog box has three tabs. Click the Advanced tab.

3. In the Memory Usage panel, select Programs. This ensures that applications are given preference for memory caching over system services.

4. Click Change to display the Virtual Memory dialog box.

5. Select the volume that you want to work with, and then ensure Custom Size is selected. Next, type the paging file size in the Initial Size and Maximum Size text boxes, and click Set. Repeat this step for each volume that you want to configure.

6. Click OK, and if prompted to overwrite an existing PAGEFILE.SYS file, click Yes.

7. Click OK, and then close the System Properties dialog box. Restart the system if prompted.

Optimizing the Menu System

Many graphics enhancements have been added to the Windows XP menu system, including visual effects that are pleasing to the eye but draining on the processor and memory. In many cases, you can improve system performance by reducing the number of visual effects used. To do so, follow these steps:

1. Access the Advanced tab in the System Properties dialog box, and then click Settings on the Performance panel to display the Performance Options dialog box.

2. The Visual Effects tab should be selected by default. Select Custom, and then clear the following options:

   ❏ Animate Windows When Minimizing And Maximizing
   ❏ Fade Or Slide Menus Into View
   ❏ Fade Or Slide Tooltips Into View
   ❏ Fade Out Menu Items After Clicking
   ❏ Show Shadows Under Menus
   ❏ Show Shadows Under Mouse Pointer
   ❏ Show Translucent Selection Rectangle
   ❏ Show Window Contents While Dragging
   ❏ Slide Open Combo Boxes
   ❏ Slide Taskbar Buttons
   ❏ Use Drop Shadows For Icon Labels On The Desktop

3. The remaining options are used to enhance the visual appearance in ways that make the screen easier to read. If you clear some of these options, you'll dramatically change the way that Windows XP works. For example, if you clear Use Visual Styles On Windows And Buttons, you'll cancel out the current theme and revert to the Windows Classic theme. In addition, if you clear Use A Background Image For Each Folder Type and Use Common Tasks In Folders, you are effectively telling Windows XP to use the classic view for Windows Explorer.

4. Click OK twice.

Note If you select Adjust For Best Performance instead of Custom, all the visual effects options are effectively deselected. This causes Windows XP to revert back to the Windows Classic theme.

Optimizing Applications, Processes, and Services

Another way to improve Windows XP performance is to reduce the number of applications, processes, and services running on the computer. You can accomplish this by disabling or uninstalling nonessential services and by removing unneeded operating system components. To check the currently installed applications and components, follow these steps:

1. Start Add Or Remove Programs in Control Panel.

2. Select Change Or Remove Programs to view currently installed programs. Uninstalling applications removes automatic startup settings and cleans up disk space used by the application.

3. Select Add/Remove Windows Components to view a list of the Windows components that are currently installed. Uninstalling unnecessary components reduces the number of background processes and services, which improves performance.

Applications running at startup can also use system resources. Startup applications can be configured on a per user or per machine basis. Follow these steps to prevent startup programs from launching for a specific user:

1. Log on as the user whose startup applications you want to manage. Right-click Start, and then select Explore from the shortcut menu. This opens Windows Explorer with the *%UserProfile%*\Start Menu folder selected.

2. In the left pane, click the Programs folder under Start Menu and then click Startup.

3. To prevent a program from launching on startup, delete its shortcut from the Startup folder.

Follow these steps to prevent startup programs from launching for all users of a computer:

1. Right-click Start, and then select Explore All Users from the shortcut menu. This opens Windows Explorer with the Documents And Settings\All Users\ Start Menu folder selected.

2. In the left pane, click the Programs folder under Start Menu and then click Startup.

3. To prevent a program from launching on startup, delete its shortcut from the Startup folder.

Optimizing Disk Drives

Windows XP makes extensive use of disk drives during startup and normal operations. You can often dramatically improve operating system and application performance by optimizing a computer's disk drives. You should focus on disk space usage, disk errors, and disk fragmentation. You might also want to compress data to reduce the space used by data files and free up space for additional files.

Data security is also an important aspect to consider when optimizing disk drives. The organization's data should be protected and stored in the most secure form possible. With this in mind, you might want to consider converting file allocation table (FAT16 or FAT32) drives to NTFS as discussed in Chapter 10, "Managing Disk Drives and File Systems," in the section "Converting a Volume to NTFS," which allows you to take advantage of the Windows XP user and group security features, and then encrypting drive data once you do this. Data encryption prevents unauthorized users from accessing important files.

Reducing Disk Space Usage

You should closely monitor disk space usage on all system drives. As drives begin to fill up, their performance and the performance of the operating system as a whole can be reduced, particularly if the system runs low on space for storing virtual memory or temporary files. One way to reduce disk space usage is to remove unnecessary files and compress old files by using the Disk Cleanup tool. For details on using this tool, see the section entitled "Working with Disk Cleanup" in Chapter 2, "Configuring the Environment."

Checking for Disk Errors

You should periodically check the integrity of disks using the Check Disk tool. Check Disk examines disks and can correct many types of common errors on FAT16, FAT32, and NTFS drives. One of the ways Check Disk locates errors is by comparing the volume bitmap with the disk sectors assigned to files in the file system. Check Disk can't repair corrupted data within files that appear to be structurally intact, however. You can run Check Disk from the command line or through a graphical interface.

Running Check Disk from the Command Line

You can run Check Disk from the command line or within other tools. At the command prompt you can test the integrity of the C drive by typing the following command:

```
chkdsk C:
```

Check Disk then performs an analysis of the disk and returns a status message regarding any problems it encounters. Without specifying further options, Check Disk won't repair problems, however. To find and repair errors that are found on the C drive, use this command:

```
chkdsk /f C:
```

When you find and repair errors, Check Disk performs an analysis of the disk and then it repairs any errors found, provided that the disk isn't in use. If the disk is in use, Check Disk displays a prompt that asks if you want to schedule the disk to be checked the next time you restart the system. Click Yes to schedule this.

The complete syntax for Check Disk is as follows:

```
CHKDSK [volume[[path]filename]] [/F] [/V] [/R] [/X] [/I] [/C]
    [/L[:size]]
```

The options and switches for Check Disk are used as follows:

- **Volume**   Sets the volume to work with
- **filename (FAT16 and FAT32 only)**   Specifies files to check for fragmentation
- **/F**   Fixes errors on the disk
- **/V**   (FAT16 and FAT32) Displays the full path and name of every file on the disk (NTFS) Displays cleanup messages if any
- **/R**   Locates bad sectors and recovers readable information (implies /F)
- **/L:size (NTFS only)**   Sets the log file size
- **/X**   Forces the volume to dismount first if necessary (implies /F)
- **/I (NTFS only)**   Performs a minimum check of index entries
- **/C (NTFS only)**   Skips checking of cycles within the folder structure

Running Check Disk Interactively

You can also run Check Disk interactively by using either Windows Explorer or Disk Management. Disk Management is preferred because you can use it to access drives on remote systems. To use Disk Management to check disk drives, follow these steps:

1. Start Computer Management from the Administrative Tools menu. Right-click the Computer Management node in the console tree, and then select Connect To Another Computer. Use the Select Computer dialog box to select the computer that you want to work with.

2. In the console tree, expand Storage and then select Disk Management. The current volumes on the system are displayed in the right pane.

3. Right-click a drive, and then select Properties. On the Tools tab, click Check Now. This displays the Check Disk dialog box shown in Figure 16-1.

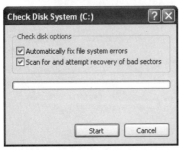

Figure 16-1   Check Disk is available by clicking Check Now in the Properties dialog box. Use it to check a disk for errors and repair them.

4. To check for errors without repairing them, click Start without selecting either of the check boxes in the Check Disk dialog box.

5. To check for errors and attempt to resolve them, select either or both of the following options and then click Start.

   ❏ **Automatically Fix File System Errors**   Determines whether Windows XP repairs file system errors it finds

   ❏ **Scan For And Attempt Recovery Of Bad Sectors**   Determines whether Windows XP checks for bad sectors and attempts to recover readable information from them

6. If the disk is in use, Check Disk displays a prompt that asks if you want to schedule the disk to be checked the next time you restart the system. Click Yes to schedule this.

7. When Check Disk finishes analyzing and repairing the disk, click OK.

Defragmenting Disks

Whenever you add files to or remove files from a drive, the data on the drive can become fragmented. When a drive is fragmented, large files can't be written to a single contiguous area on the disk, and the operating system often must write a single large file to several smaller areas on the disk. This can increase the write time as well as the read time for files. To reduce fragmentation, you should periodically analyze and defragment disks using Disk Defragmenter.

You can analyze a disk to determine the level of fragmentation and defragment a disk by completing the following steps:

1. Start Computer Management. If you want to manage a remote system, right-click Computer Management in the console tree, and then select Connect To Another Computer. Use the Select Computer dialog box to select the computer that you want to work with.
2. Expand Storage, and then select Disk Defragmenter.
3. Select the logical drive or volume that you want to work with by clicking it, as shown in Figure 16-2.

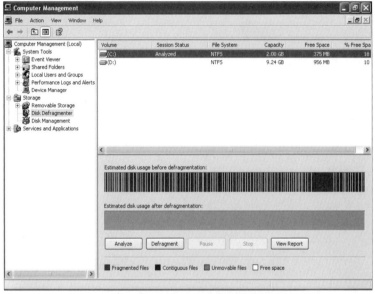

Figure 16-2   Disk Defragmenter analyzes and defragments disks efficiently. The more frequently data is updated on drives, the more often you should run this tool.

4. To analyze the amount of fragmentation on a partition or volume, click Analyze. The progress of the analysis is shown in the analysis display area. Fragmented files, contiguous files, system files, and free space are highlighted using the color codes shown at the bottom of the display area. You can pause or stop the analysis if necessary.
5. When the analysis is complete, Disk Defragmenter recommends a course of action based on the amount of fragmentation. If there is a lot of fragmentation, you'll be prompted to defragment the disk. Otherwise you'll be told the disk doesn't need to be defragmented.
6. To defragment the disk, click Defragment. The progress of the defragment operation is shown in the defragmentation display area. You can pause or stop the operation if necessary.
7. To view a report of the analysis or defragmentation, click View Report.

Compressing Drives and Data

When you format a drive for NTFS, Windows XP allows you to turn on the built-in compression feature. With compression, all files and directories stored on a drive are automatically compressed when created. Because this compression is transparent to users, compressed data can be accessed just like regular data. The difference is that you can store more information on a compressed drive than you can on an uncompressed drive—at a slight cost to performance because compressing and decompressing data requires processing power and memory.

 Note   You cannot compress encrypted data. If you try to do so, Windows XP automatically decrypts the data and then compresses it. Likewise, if you try to encrypt compressed data, Windows XP uncompresses the data and then encrypts it.

Compressing Drives

To compress a drive and all its contents, complete these steps:

1. In Windows Explorer or Disk Management, right-click the drive that you want to compress, and then select Properties.
2. On the General tab, select Compress Drive To Save Disk Space, and then click OK.

Compressing Files and Directories

If you decide not to compress an entire drive, Windows XP lets you selectively compress directories and files. To compress a file or directory, complete these steps:

1. In Windows Explorer, right-click the file or directory that you want to compress, and then select Properties.
2. On the General tab of the related property dialog box, click Advanced. In the Advanced Attributes dialog box, select the Compress Contents To Save Disk Space check box, as shown in Figure 16-3. Click OK twice.

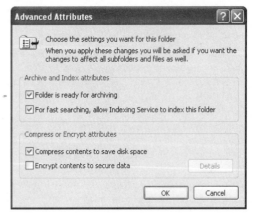

Figure 16-3   With NTFS, you can compress a file or directory by selecting the Compress Contents To Save Disk Space check box in the Advanced Attributes dialog box.

For an individual file, Windows XP marks the file as compressed and then compresses it. For a directory, Windows XP marks the directory as compressed and then compresses all the files in it. If the directory contains subfolders, Windows XP displays the Confirm Attribute Changes dialog box, which allows you to compress all the subfolders associated with the directory. Simply select Apply Changes To This Folder, Subfolders And Files and then click OK. Once you compress a directory, any new files added or copied to the directory are compressed automatically.

Note   If you move an uncompressed file from a different drive to a compressed folder, the file is compressed. However, if you move an uncompressed file to a compressed folder on the same NTFS drive, the file isn't compressed. Remember also that you can't encrypt compressed files.

Expanding Compressed Drives

You can remove compression from a drive as follows:

1. In Windows Explorer or Disk Management, right-click the drive that contains the data that you want to expand, and then select Properties.
2. On the General tab, clear the Compress Drive To Save Disk Space check box, and then click OK.

Tip   Windows always checks the available disk space before expanding compressed data, and you should too. If there is less free space available than used space, you might not be able to successfully complete the expansion. For example, if a compressed drive uses 1 GB of space and has 700 MB of free space available, there might not be enough free space to expand the drive.

Expanding Compressed Files and Directories

If you decide later that you want to expand a compressed file or directory, reverse the process by completing the following steps:

1. Right-click the file or directory in Windows Explorer.
2. On the General tab of the related property dialog box, click Advanced. The Advanced Attributes dialog box appears. Clear the Compress Contents To Save Disk Space check box and click OK twice.

With a file, Windows XP removes compression and expands the file. With a directory, Windows XP expands all the files within the directory. If the directory contains subfolders, you'll also have the opportunity to remove compression from the subfolders. To do this, select Apply Changes To This Folder, Subfolders And Files when prompted and then click OK.

Tip   Windows XP also provides command-line tools for compressing and decompressing your data. The compression tool is called Compact (COMPACT.EXE) and the decompression tool is called Expand (EXPAND.EXE).

Encrypting Drives and Data

Windows XP supports file encryption of data on NTFS volumes. Encryption allows users to store data in encrypted format, which is more secure than standard file access permissions. Files in encrypted format can only be read by the person who encrypted the file. Before other users can read an encrypted file, it must be decrypted by the user. Otherwise, encrypted files can be copied, moved, and renamed just like any other files—and these actions don't affect the encryption of the data.

The process that handles encryption and decryption is called the Encrypting File System (EFS). The default setup for EFS allows users to encrypt files without special permission. Files are encrypted using a public/private key that is automatically generated by EFS on a per user basis.

Tip   By default, the encryption algorithm used is the expanded Data Encryption Standard (DESX), which is enforced using 56-bit encryption. For stricter security, Windows XP supports the Triple DES encryption algorithm (Transport Layer Security [TLS] traffic encryption, RSA public key algorithm for TLS key exchange and authentication, and SHA-1 hashing for any TLS hashing requirements). You can use Triple DES encryption by enabling the System Cryptography: Use the FIPS Compliant Algorithms For Encryption policy in Group Policy. This policy is under Computer Configuration\Windows Settings\Security Settings\Local Policies\Security Options. Regardless of the encryption algorithm you choose, administrators designated as Recovery Agents can decrypt files if necessary.

Encrypting Files and Directories

With NTFS volumes, Windows XP lets you select files and folders for encryption. When you encrypt a file, the file data is converted to an encrypted format that can only be read by the person who encrypted the file. Users can only encrypt files if they have the proper access permissions. When you encrypt folders, they are marked as encrypted, but actually only the files within them are encrypted. All files that are created in or added to a folder marked as encrypted are encrypted automatically.

You can't encrypt compressed files, system files, or read-only files. If you try to encrypt compressed files, they are automatically uncompressed and then encrypted. If you try to encrypt system files, you'll get an error message.

To encrypt a file or directory, complete the following steps:

1. Right-click the file or directory that you want to encrypt, and then select Properties.
2. On the General tab of the related property dialog box, click Advanced. The Advanced Attributes dialog box appears. Select the Encrypt Contents To Secure Data check box, as shown in Figure 16-4.
3. Click OK twice.

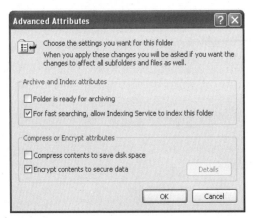

Figure 16-4   Encrypting data makes it more secure.

For an individual file, Windows XP marks the file as encrypted and then encrypts it. For a directory, Windows XP marks the directory as encrypted and then encrypts all the files in it. If the directory contains subfolders, Windows XP displays the Confirm Attribute Changes dialog box, which allows you to encrypt all the subfolders associated with the directory. Simply select Apply Changes To This Folder, Subfolders And Files, and then click OK.

Note   On NTFS volumes, files remain encrypted even when they're moved, copied, and renamed. If you copy or move an encrypted file to a FAT16 or FAT32 drive, the file is automatically decrypted before being copied or moved. Thus, you must have proper permissions to copy or move the file.

Decrypting Files and Directories

If you decide later that you want to decrypt a file or directory, reverse the process by completing the following steps:

1. Right-click the file or directory in Windows Explorer, and then select Properties.

2. On the General tab of the related property dialog box, click Advanced. The Advanced Attributes dialog box appears. Clear the Encrypt Contents To Secure Data check box, and click OK twice.

With a file, Windows XP decrypts the file and restores it to its original format. With a directory, Windows XP decrypts all the files within the directory. If the directory contains subfolders, you'll also have the opportunity to remove encryption from the subfolders. To do this, select Apply Changes To This Folder, Subfolders And Files when prompted and then click OK.

Tip   Windows XP also provides a command-line tool called Cipher (CIPHER.EXE) for encrypting and decrypting your data. Typing **CIPHER** at the command line by itself shows you the encryption status of all folders and files in the current directory.

Enhancing Security

Security settings are critically important for maintaining the integrity of Windows XP computers. Computers with weak or improperly configured security are open to a wide variety of attacks any time they connect to a network. In Windows XP SP2 and later, you can use the Security Center and the Windows Firewall to help enhance system security.

Using Security Center

Security Center, shown in Figure 16-5, is meant to be a central location for checking the most important aspects of system security. Through Security Center you can quickly determine the status of any of these important security features and get recommendations for how these features should be configured.

 Note   Security Center is only available when Windows XP Service Pack 2 or later is installed on a computer. In a domain, the Turn On Security Center policy must be enabled under Computer Configuration\Administrative Templates\Windows Components\Security Center as well. This policy is enabled by default. If you enable this policy and it was previously disabled, you will be able to access Security Center only after you restart the computer. The Turn On Security Center policy does not apply to computers in workgroups. Security Center cannot be turned off for computers in workgroups.

Figure 16-5   Security Center provides a quick overview on the status of essential areas of security.

You can access Security Center by double-clicking Security Center in Control Panel or by clicking the Security Center icon (the red shield with an x) in the system tray. The following are the key areas of security tracked by Security Center:

- **Windows Firewall**   This firewall, an enhanced version of the former Internet Connection Firewall, is installed with Windows XP SP2 and later, and turned on for all connections by default. The firewall helps protect the computer against network-based attacks and other security threats from remote systems.

  ❑ If the firewall is turned off, expand the Firewall entry by clicking the button to the right of the Off designator and then click Recommendations. In the Recommendation dialog box, click Enable Now to turn on the Windows Firewall, click Close and then click OK.

  ❑ If you've installed a firewall that Windows XP doesn't detect, you can tell Security Center that you'll monitor the firewall status yourself. Expand the Firewall entry by clicking the button to the right of the Off designator and then click Recommendations. In the Recommendation dialog box, select I Have A Firewall Solution That I'll Monitor Myself and then click OK. The status of Firewall will change to Not Monitored.

  ❑ If multiple firewalls are enabled and Windows XP detects this, you'll see a warning prompt specifying that to ensure programs operate properly only one firewall should be configured. In this case, you should disable all but one of the firewalls.

- **Automatic Updates**   As discussed in Chapter 1, "Introduction to Windows XP Professional Administration," in the section "Understanding and Using Automatic Updates," you can help protect a computer by keeping the operating system up to date with the latest security patches, hot fixes and service packs. If Automatic Updates are not enabled, you can enable them by clicking Turn On Automatic Updates.

- **Virus Protection**   Antivirus software helps protect a computer from viruses, Trojan horses, and other similar types of attacks. Windows XP doesn't include antivirus software but can detect when it is installed on the system.

  ❑ If antivirus software is installed on the computer, enabled, and running properly, Windows XP should detect this and no further action is necessary.

  ❑ If antivirus software is installed on the computer but isn't enabled or its status is unknown, you'll see a warning. Check the status of this software to ensure that it is enabled and running.

  ❑ If you've installed antivirus software that Windows XP doesn't detect, you can tell Security Center that you'll monitor the software status yourself. Under Virus Protection, click the button to the right of the Not Found designator and then click Recommendations. In the Recommendation dialog box, select I Have An Antivirus Program That I'll Monitor Myself and then click OK. The status of Virus Protection will change to Not Monitored.

Tip   By default, Security Center is configured to alert the currently logged on user if the firewall, virus protection, or Automatic Updates is not properly configured. The alerts are displayed in a balloon message box stating Your Computer Might Be At Risk. To view or configure the alerts, access the Security Center and click Change The Way Security Center Alerts Me under the Resources heading. You can then use the Alert Settings dialog box to enable or disable the alert separately for firewall, virus protection and Automatic Updates.

Configuring the Windows Firewall

Windows Firewall is installed and enabled by default on computers running Windows XP Service Pack 2 or later. Windows Firewall protects the computer by preventing unauthorized users from gaining access. It does this by blocking inbound access to TCP and UDP ports on the computer and disallowing most types of Internet Control Message Protocol (ICMP) requests.

Unlike the Internet Connection Firewall that it replaces, Windows Firewall is enabled for all network connections on a computer automatically. This means all modem, network cable, wireless network, and IEEE 1394 (FireWire) connections are protected by the firewall automatically. The sections that follow discuss techniques for configuring the Windows Firewall, including:

- Enabling and disabling the Windows Firewall
- Configuring exceptions for programs
- Configuring exceptions for TCP and UDP ports as well as services
- Restoring the original Windows Firewall configuration

Real World   For computers that are part of a domain, you'll find several important policies for configuring the Windows Firewall under Computer Configuration\Administrative Templates\Network\Network Connections\Windows Firewall. If Windows Firewall: Allow Authenticated IPSec Bypass is enabled, any authenticated IPSec connection to a computer completely bypasses the Windows Firewall, and you can set specific exemptions (exclusions) for computers, users, and groups. Use the policies under Computer Configuration\Administrative Templates\Network\Network Connections\Windows Firewall\Domain Profile to configure the way Windows Firewall is used when a computer is connected to an Active Directory domain. Use the policies under Computer Configuration\Administrative Templates\Network\Network Connections\Windows Firewall\Standard Profile to configure the way Windows Firewall is used when a computer is disconnected from an Active Directory domain, such as when a laptop user takes his computer home.

Enabling and Disabling the Windows Firewall

You can enable or disable the Windows Firewall in one of two ways: either completely or on a per connection basis. To enable or disable the firewall completely, double-click Windows Firewall in Control Panel. This displays the Windows Firewall dialog box, shown in Figure 16-6. You can now:

- Select On to enable the Windows Firewall and set it to block all outside connections to the computer, with the exception of the exclusions lists on the Exceptions tab and any inbound Internet Control Message Protocol (ICMP) requests allowed on the Advanced tab. In this configuration, Windows Firewall uses Security Alerts to notify you of any programs it is blocking, and you can determine whether to keep blocking the program, unblock the program, or have it prompt you later.

- Select On and choose Don't Allow Exceptions to enable the Windows Firewall, set it to block all outside connections to the computer, and specify that no exceptions from the Exceptions tab should apply. This configuration is best for laptop computers when they are off the corporate network. In this configuration, Windows Firewall will not alert the user when it is blocking programs. Further, it should be noted that any inbound ICMP requests allowed on the Advanced tab are still allowed and are not blocked.

- Select Off to completely disable Windows Firewall. In this configuration, the Windows Firewall is disabled for all connections and the computer is more vulnerable to attack.

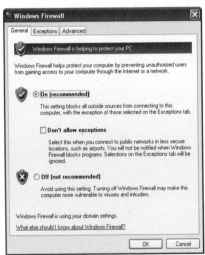

Figure 16-6   Use the General tab to completely enable or disable Windows Firewall.

To enable or disable Windows Firewall on a per connection basis, follow these steps:

1. Double-click Windows Firewall in Control Panel. In the Windows Firewall dialog box, ensure that On is selected on the General tab, and then select the Advanced tab.

2. Each network connection configured on the computer is listed in the Network Connection Settings panel. Clear the check box for a connection to disable Windows Firewall for that connection. Select the check box for a connection to enable Windows Firewall for that connection.

3. Click OK when you are finished.

Configuring Exceptions for Programs

In a domain, Remote Assistance is the only service allowed to remotely connect to a computer by default. In a workgroup, both Remote Assistance and File And Printer Sharing are allowed by default. You can make exceptions for other programs and services as well using the Exceptions tab of the Windows Firewall dialog box. As Figure 16-7 shows, several standard exceptions can be easily allowed or disallowed, including the following:

- **File And Printer Sharing**   If a computer has file shares used by other computers or is acting as a print server and has a printer share, you should allow this exception. Otherwise, enable this exception only temporarily as necessary to remotely access file shares on a computer.

- **Remote Assistance**   Many organizations use the Remote Assistance feature, discussed in Chapter 17 in the section "Using Remote Assistance to Resolve Problems." If your organization allows individuals to provide or receive remote assistance, this exception should be enabled. Otherwise, this exception should not be set.

- **Remote Desktop**   Many organizations allow administrators to make Remote Desktop connections to computers to help maintain and service them. If your organization allows Help Desk or other support staff to make Remote Desktop connections, this exception should be enabled. Otherwise, this exception should not be set.

- **UPnP Framework**   Universal Plug and Play Framework is used with some types of network-attached devices as well as devices connected via USB or FireWire. If a computer has one of these devices connected, enable this exception. Otherwise, this exception should not be set.

You can add programs as exceptions if other computers need to remotely communicate with a program or connect to the computer over a specific port. To configure programs as exceptions, complete the following steps:

1. In the Windows Firewall dialog box, select the Exceptions tab and then click Add Program.

2. In the Add A Program dialog box, select the program in the Programs list or click Browse to find the program using the Browse dialog box.

3. By default, any computer including those on the Internet can access this program remotely. To restrict this further, click Change Scope. You can then select:

   ❑ Any Computer (Including Those On the Internet) to allow any computer to remotely communicate with this program.

   ❑ My Network (Subnet) Only to allow only computers on the same subnet as this computer to remotely communicate with this program.

   ❑ Custom List to enter a comma-separated list of IP addresses that can remotely communicate with this program.

4. Click OK three times to close all open dialog boxes.

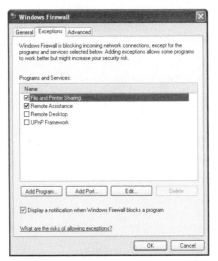

Figure 16-7   Use the Exceptions tab to allow some types of remote connections.

Configuring Exceptions for TCP and UDP Ports

TCP and UDP ports can be opened for remote access to a computer by configuring the appropriate port as an exception. If you know the port that you want to open, complete the following steps to designate it as an exception:

1. In the Windows Firewall dialog box, select the Exceptions tab and then click Add Port.
2. In the Add A Port dialog box, type a descriptive name for the port in the Name field and then type a port number, such as 80, in the Port Number field.
3. Select whether you are making an exception for a TCP or UDP port by choosing the appropriate radio button.
4. By default any computer including those on the Internet can access this program remotely. To restrict this further, click Change Scope, make a different selection, and then click OK.
5. Click OK two times to close all open dialog boxes.

If you are unsure of the port that you want to open, you can open a port based on the name of the service such as for FTP, SMTP, or HTTP. To open a port based on the name of the service, complete these steps:

1. In the Windows Firewall dialog box, select the Advanced tab. Each network connection configured on the computer is listed in the Network Connection Settings panel. Click the connection for which you want to allow remote access to a known service over a TCP or UDP port (taking care not to clear the check mark selecting the connection) and then click Settings.

2. In the Advanced Settings dialog box, shown in Figure 16-8, use the options on the Services tab to enable incoming connections to named services running on the computer, including the following:

   ❑ FTP Server, this opens TCP port 21 for remote connections.

   ❑ Internet Mail Access Protocol Version 3 (IMAP3), this opens TCP port 220 for remote connections.

   ❑ Internet Mail Access Protocol Version 4 (IMAP4), this opens TCP port 143 for remote connections.

   ❑ Internet Mail Server (SMTP), this opens TCP port 25 for remote connections.

   ❑ Post Office Protocol Version 3 (POP3), this opens TCP port 110 for remote connections.

   ❑ Remote Desktop, this opens TCP port 3389 for remote connections.

   ❑ Secure Web Server (HTTPS), this opens TCP port 443 for remote connections.

   ❑ Telnet Server, this opens TCP port 23 for remote connections.

   ❑ Web Server (HTTP), this opens TCP port 80 for remote connections.

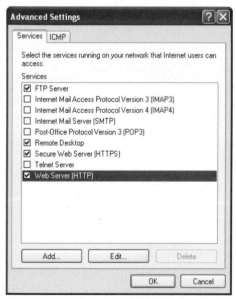

Figure 16-8   Configure exceptions by service name.

3. When you select a service, the Service Settings dialog box is displayed. If remote users connect to the service using an alias (an alternate DNS name) or an alternate IP address, enter this name or IP address in the Name Or IP Address field and then click OK.

4. Click OK two times to close all open dialog boxes.

Restoring the Original Windows Firewall Configuration

If you are unsure of the state of the Windows Firewall and its configuration, it is sometimes better to restore the original Windows Firewall configuration and then modify the configuration as necessary afterward. In this way, you start with a known secure configuration of the firewall and then make changes as necessary for the computer. You can restore the Windows Firewall settings, by completing the following steps:

1. Double-click Windows Firewall in Control Panel. In the Windows Firewall dialog box, select the Advanced tab.

2. Click the Restore Defaults button. When prompted to confirm the action, click Yes.

3. Once the configuration is restored, click OK.

Detecting and Resolving Windows XP Errors

Windows XP stores errors generated by processes, services, and applications in log files. The following three log files are available on Windows XP systems:

- **Application log**   Records events logged by applications.

- **Security log**   Records events you've set for auditing with local or global policies. Note that administrators must be granted access to the security log through user rights assignment.

- **System log**   Records events logged by the operating system or its components, such as the failure of a service to start at bootup.

Entries in a log file are recorded according to the type of activity, which can include errors as well as system events. You'll see the following types of entries:

- **Information**   An informational event, which is generally related to a successful action.

- **Success audit**   An event related to the successful execution of an action.

- **Failure audit**   An event related to the failed execution of an action.

- **Warning**   A warning. Details for warnings are often useful in preventing future system problems.

- **Error**   An error, such as the failure of a service to start.

In addition to type, date, and time, the summary and detailed event entries provide the following information:

- **Source**   The application, service, or component that logged the event.

- **Category**   The category of the event, which is sometimes used to further describe the related action.

- **Event**   An identifier for the specific event.

- **User**   The user account that was logged on when the event occurred. If a system process or service triggered the event, the user name is usually that of the special identity that caused the event, such as Network Service, Local Service, or System.

- **Computer** The name of the computer where the event occurred.
- **Description** In the detailed entries, this provides a text description of the event.
- **Data** In the detailed entries, this provides any data or error code output by the event.

You can access the event logs by completing the following steps:

1. Click Start, point to All Programs, then to Administrative Tools, and finally select Event Viewer. This starts Event Viewer. If you haven't enabled the Administrative Tools menu (by customizing the Start Menu), you can access Administrative Tools from Control Panel.

2. Event Viewer displays logs for the local computer by default. If you want to view logs on a remote computer, right-click the Event Viewer entry in the console tree (left pane) and then select Connect To Another Computer. Then, in the Select Computer dialog box, enter the name of the computer that you want to access and then click OK.

3. Select the log that you want to view, as shown in Figure 16-9.

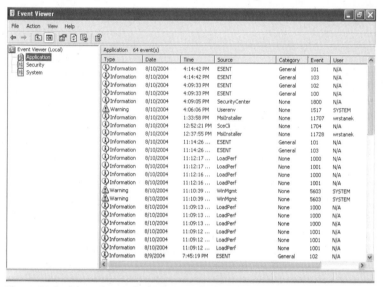

Figure 16-9 Event Viewer displays events for the selected log.

Warnings and errors are the two key types of events you'll want to examine closely. Whenever these types of events occur and you are unsure of the cause, double-click on the entry to view the detailed event description. Note the source of the error and attempt to resolve the problem using the techniques discussed in this book. To learn more about the error and steps you can take to resolve it (if necessary), you can click the link provided in the error description or search the Microsoft Knowledge Base for the event ID or part of the error description.

Scheduling Maintenance Tasks

When you manage desktop and laptop systems, you'll often want to perform routine maintenance tasks on a periodic or recurring basis. To do this, you can use the Task Scheduler service to schedule one-time or recurring tasks to run automatically. You automate tasks by running command-shell scripts, Windows Script Host (WSH) scripts, or applications that execute the necessary commands for you. For example, if you want to defragment disks once a month, you can use the Task Scheduler to run the Disk Defragmenter on a specific day of each month.

Understanding Task Scheduling

Windows XP provides several tools for scheduling tasks, including: the Scheduled Task Wizard and the Schtasks command-line tool. Both can be used for scheduling tasks on local and remote systems. The Scheduled Task Wizard provides a point-and-click interface to task assignment, and Schtasks is its command-line counterpart.

Both scheduling tools use the Task Scheduler service to monitor the system clock and run tasks at specified times. The Task Scheduler service logs on as the Local-System account by default. This account usually doesn't have adequate permissions to perform administrative tasks. To overcome this problem, each task can be set to run as a specific user, and you set the user name and password to use for the task when you create it. Be sure to use an account that has adequate user privileges and access rights to run the tasks that you want to schedule.

The remaining sections of this chapter focus on the Scheduled Task Wizard. This is the primary tool you'll use to schedule tasks on Windows XP systems. To learn more about Schtasks, type **schtasks /?** at the command prompt or refer to Chapter 4, "Scheduling Tasks to Run Automatically," in the *Microsoft Windows Command-Line Pocket Consultant* (Microsoft Press, 2004).

Viewing Tasks on Local and Remote Systems

The current tasks configured on a system are accessible through the Scheduled Tasks folder. This folder can be accessed on a local system by selecting Scheduled Tasks in Control Panel. In a domain, you access the Scheduled Tasks folder on a remote system by completing the following tasks:

1. Start Windows Explorer and then use the My Network Places node to navigate to the computer that you want to work with.
2. Click the computer's icon and then click Scheduled Tasks.
3. Entries in the Scheduled Tasks folder show currently scheduled tasks. Double-click a task entry to view its settings.

For a workgroup computer, you must connect to the computer using a Remote Desktop connection. Once you are remotely connected, you can start Windows Explorer and navigate to the Scheduled Tasks folder.

Creating Tasks with the Scheduled Task Wizard

To schedule a task using the Scheduled Task Wizard, follow these steps:

1. Start the Scheduled Task Wizard by double-clicking Add Scheduled Task in the Scheduled Tasks folder. Read the Welcome dialog box and then click Next.

2. Using the dialog box shown in Figure 16-10, select a program to schedule. The dialog box shows key applications registered on the system, such as Disk Cleanup and Synchronize. The dialog box doesn't show available scripts, however.

3. Click Browse to open the Select Program To Schedule dialog box. Use the dialog box to find the command-shell or WSH script that you want to run.

4. Type a name for the task, as shown in Figure 16-11. The name should be short but descriptive so that you can quickly determine what the task does.

5. Select a run schedule for the task. Tasks can be scheduled to run periodically (daily, weekly, or monthly), or when a specific event occurs, such as when the computer starts or when the task's user logs on.

6. Click Next. The next dialog box you see depends on when the task is scheduled to run.

7. If you've selected a daily running task, set a start time and date. Daily scheduled tasks can be configured to run as follows:

   - **Every Day**   Seven days a week
   - **Weekdays**   Monday through Friday only
   - **Every ... Days**   Every 2, 3, ... N days

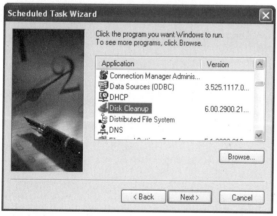

Figure 16-10   Select a program to run. Click Browse to find scripts and other applications.

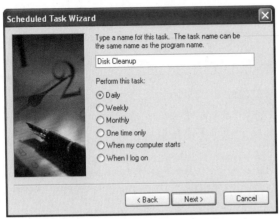

Figure 16-11 Type a name for the task, and then select a run schedule.

8. If you've selected a weekly running task, configure the task using these fields:
   - ❑ **Start Time**   Sets the start time of the task
   - ❑ **Every ... Weeks**   Allows you to run the task every week, every two weeks, or every N weeks
   - ❑ **Select The Day(s) Of The Week Below**   Sets the day(s) of the week when the task runs, such as on Monday, or on Monday and Friday

9. If you've selected a monthly running task, configure the task using these fields:
   - ❑ **Start Time**   Sets the start time of the task
   - ❑ **Day**   Sets the day of the month the task runs; for example, if you select 5, the task runs on the fifth day of the month
   - ❑ **The ...**   Sets task to run on the Nth occurrence of a day in a month, such as the second Monday or the third Tuesday of every month
   - ❑ **Of The Month(s)**   Lets you select during which months the task runs

10. If you've selected One Time Only for running the task, set the start time and start date. The task will then run once only on the date and time you specify.

11. With tasks that run when the computer starts or when the task's user logs on, you don't have to set the start date and time. The task runs automatically when the startup or logon event occurs.

Tip   If you want to configure a startup task for a specific user through the wizard, you'll need to log on as that user and then run the wizard.

12. After you've configured a start date and time, click Next to continue. Then type a user name and password that can be used when running the scheduled task.

 Tip The user name must have appropriate permissions and privileges to run the scheduled task. In Windows domains, you should enter the user name in the form Domain\UserName, such as Adatum\wrstanek, where Adatum is the domain and wrstanek is the user account.

13. The final wizard dialog box provides a summary of the task you're scheduling. Click Finish to complete the scheduling process.

 Tip If an error occurs when you create the task, you'll see an error prompt. Click OK. The task should still be created. You might, however, need to edit the task's properties. In Windows Explorer, double-click the task to open its properties dialog box so that you can correct the specified error. One of the more common errors you'll see is Access Denied. This error can occur if the user credentials provided are incorrect, such as occurs if you enter the wrong password or the user account doesn't exist in the domain. See "Troubleshooting Scheduled Tasks" in this chapter for more help.

Changing Task Properties

To change the settings for a task, follow these steps:

1. Access the Scheduled Tasks folder. On a local system, select or double-click Scheduled Tasks in Control Panel. On a remote system, start Windows Explorer, use the My Network Places node to navigate to the computer that you want to work with, click the computer's icon, and then click Scheduled Tasks.

2. Double-click the task that you want to modify. This displays a properties dialog box similar to the one shown in Figure 16-12. The dialog box has four tabs:

   ❏ **Task** Options on this tab control what the task runs and how the task runs.

   ❏ **Schedule** Options on this tab control when the task runs and also allow you to configure multiple schedules for the same task.

   ❏ **Settings** Options on this tab provide advanced controls that determine whether tasks are started when running on batteries, whether tasks are stopped if they run too long, and how tasks are used when the computer is idle.

   ❏ **Security** Options on this tab determine who has permission to view and modify the scheduled task. By default, Administrators and the special identity System have full control, as does the user who created the task.

3. Click OK when you are finished making changes.

Figure 16-12   You can change task properties at any time.

Enabling and Disabling Tasks

Tasks can be enabled or disabled as needed, depending on your preference. If you temporarily don't want to use a task, you can disable it. When you are ready to use the task again, you can enable it. By enabling and disabling tasks rather than deleting them, you save the time involved in reconfiguring task settings.

To enable or disable a task, follow these steps:

1. Access the Scheduled Tasks folder. On a local system, double-click Scheduled Tasks in Control Panel. On a remote system, start Windows Explorer, use the My Network Places node to navigate to the computer that you want to work with, click the computer's icon, and finally click Scheduled Tasks.

2. Double-click the task that you want to modify. This displays a properties dialog box that is named for the task in question. The Task tab should be selected by default.

3. Select Enabled to enable the task or clear Enabled to disable the task. Click OK.

Running Tasks Immediately

You don't have to wait for the scheduled time to run a task. To run a task at any time, follow these steps:

1. Access the Scheduled Tasks folder.

2. Right-click the task that you want to run, and then select Run.

Copying and Moving Tasks from One System to Another

If you want to take tasks created on one system and use them on another system, you don't have to re-create them manually. Instead, follow this procedure:

1. Use the My Network Places node to navigate to the computer where the tasks that you want to use are currently stored. Click the computer's icon and then click Scheduled Tasks.

2. Right-click one of the tasks that you want to use and then select Copy.

3. Again, use the My Network Places node to navigate through the organization. This time, navigate to the computer on which you want to use the task.

4. With the destination computer's icon selected, right-click Scheduled Tasks and then select Paste.

5. The scheduled task should be copied to the new location. Be sure to check the properties of the task on the destination computer, making sure the settings are suitable.

You can also move tasks from one computer to another. To move tasks, follow these steps:

1. Use the My Network Places node to navigate to the computer where the tasks that you want to use are currently stored. Click the computer's icon and then click Scheduled Tasks.

2. Right-click one of the tasks that you want to use, and then select Cut.

3. Again, use the My Network Places node to navigate through the organization. This time, navigate to the computer to which you want to move the task.

4. With the destination computer's icon selected, right-click Scheduled Tasks and then select Paste.

5. The scheduled task should be copied to the new location. Be sure to check the properties of the task on the destination computer, making sure the settings are suitable.

Deleting Scheduled Tasks

If you no longer need a task, you can permanently delete it by following these steps:

1. Access the Scheduled Tasks folder.

2. Right-click the task that you want to run, and then select Delete.

Troubleshooting Scheduled Tasks

When you configure tasks to run on a computer, you can encounter several types of problems. Some tasks won't run when they are supposed to. Others will start and won't stop. Any task listed as "Could not start" should be examined. Check the task's properties by double-clicking its entry in the Scheduled Tasks folder. If you can't determine what is wrong with the task, you should examine the Task Scheduler log file, Schedlgu.txt, which is stored in the *%SystemRoot%*\Tasks folder. A quick way to access the log is to select View Log from the Advanced menu when the Scheduled Tasks folder is selected in Windows Explorer.

A task that is listed as "Running" might not in fact be running and instead might be a hung process. You can check for hung processes using the Last Run Time, which tells you when the task was started. If the task has been running for more than a day, there is usually a problem. A script might be waiting for input, it might have problems reading or writing files, or it might simply be a runaway task that needs to be stopped. To stop the task, right-click it in the Scheduled Tasks folder, and then select End Task. You can also wait for the system to stop the task. By default, all tasks time out after running for 72 hours.

Chapter 17

Troubleshooting Windows XP Professional

In this chapter:

Using Remote Assistance to Resolve Problems 445

Troubleshooting Startup and Shutdown 453

Using Restore Points 459

Throughout this book, I've discussed troubleshooting techniques that you can use to resolve problems with Microsoft Windows XP. (In this book, "Windows XP" refers to Windows XP Professional unless otherwise indicated.) In this chapter, you'll learn techniques for recovering from specific types of problems, including problems with startup, programs, and Windows XP itself. Let's start with a look at how the Remote Assistance feature can be used to help you troubleshoot problems without your being at the user's keyboard.

Using Remote Assistance to Resolve Problems

Remote Assistance allows support personnel to view a user's desktop and take control temporarily to resolve problems or walk the user through the execution of complex tasks. Once Remote Assistance is configured locally as discussed in Chapter 7, "Managing User Access and Global Settings," or through Group Policy as discussed in Chapter 9, "Configuring User and Computer Policies," you can work with this feature.

Understanding Remote Assistance

Remote Assistance is a feature of Windows XP and Microsoft Windows Server 2003. Only users running these operating systems can initiate and respond to Remote Assistance invitations. Users initiate sessions by creating an invitation request. Support personnel initiate sessions by offering help to users. Once a session is initiated, assistants can chat with users, observe their working screens, and if permitted, control their computers.

Remote Assistance invitations can be created using the following three techniques:

- **E-mail invitation**   E-mail invitations are sent as e-mail messages to a named e-mail address. An attachment provided in the message is used to initiate the Remote Assistance session. You might want to configure a standard e-mail address, such as RemoteAssist@your_company_name.com, to allow users to send invitation requests easily to the support team. If this address is configured in Microsoft Exchange 2000 Server as a distribution list that delivers the invitations to support team members or as an additional mailbox for specific team members, support staff will be able to handle requests more efficiently and users will have a standard way of requesting help.

- **File invitation**   File invitations are saved as Microsoft Remote Control Incident (MsRcIncident) files. Double-clicking the file name initiates the Remote Assistance session. You might want to configure a shared folder that is automatically mapped as a network drive for users and ensure that it is accessible by support personnel. Name the share something that easily identifies it as being used for assistance requests, such as HelpDeskRequest or Assistance-Invitations.

- **MSN buddy list**   MSN invitations are delivered through MSN Messenger Service accounts. To send an invitation through MSN Messenger, the account to which the user wants to send the invitation must already exist and it must be on his buddy list. MSN Messenger invitations are generally used more for user-to-user requests than for official support requests.

Invitations can be created with or without a control password. The control password provides an additional layer of security in the Remote Assistance configuration, ensuring that users must be authorized to provide remote assistance and they must also know the invitation password. You should establish an official guideline that requires the use of invitation passwords. To streamline the invitation process you might want to have predefined passwords that are used with invitations. Passwords should be changed regularly and you might want to assign different passwords to different groups within the organization.

To work properly, Remote Assistance relies on the presence of a network connection between the user's computer and the assistant's computer. Remote Assistance uses Transmission Control Protocol (TCP) as the communications protocol, communicating over port 3389. As most firewalls do not have this port open by default, a firewall between the two computers might prevent the assistance session. Port 3389 must be opened for outbound communications from the assistant's computer to the user's computer.

Creating Remote Assistance Invitations

To create an e-mail or file invitation, follow these steps:

1. Click Start, and then select Help And Support. This displays the Help And Support Center.

2. Under the heading Ask For Assistance, click Invite A Friend To Connect To Your Computer With Remote Assistance.

3. Click Invite Someone To Help You. You can now select the type of invitation to create.

   ❑ To send the invitation to a Windows Messenger contact, click Sign In under Use Windows Messenger. If the .NET Messenger Service dialog box is displayed, enter your .NET e-mail address and password and then click OK. Once you are signed in to your .NET Passport, you will be able to select the contact to which you want to send the invitation. Afterward, click Invite This Person.

   ❑ To send the invitation via e-mail, you must have an e-mail client configured. If a client isn't configured, click Configure ... or click Set Up Outlook Express to configure the default e-mail client. Once the default e-mail client is configured, either type the e-mail address of the assistant in the field provided, or click Address Book to look up an e-mail address. Afterward, click Invite This Person.

Tip You also have the option of saving an invitation as a file. This is useful if you want to save the invitation to a network share or other location that could be accessed by support personnel. When you click Save Invitation As A File (Advanced), the next page you see asks you to enter your name and set the invitation expiration. After you do this, click Continue. Type and confirm a password for the invitation, and then click Save Invitation to display the Save As dialog box. Use this dialog box to specify the save location and name for the invitation. All invitations are saved with the .msrcincident extension. Saving the file using the file name of an existing invitation overwrites the other invitation.

4. As Figure 17-1 shows, you can now enter additional information to send with the invitation. The From text box contains the logon name of the current user. If necessary, you can change this information by typing a new value. The Message text box is for typing additional information regarding the invitation or for providing additional contact information. You should instruct users to provide a brief description of their problem in the Message text box. Click Continue.

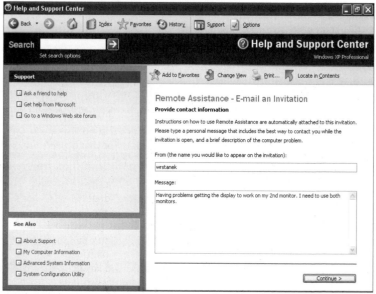

Figure 17-1 Type a message to send with the invitation.

5. As shown in Figure 17-2, invitations are set to expire in 1 hour by default. You can specify another value in minutes, hours, or days up to the maximum limit set for the computer using the Set The Invitation To Expire fields. (If you are creating an invitation file, click Continue to access this password window.)

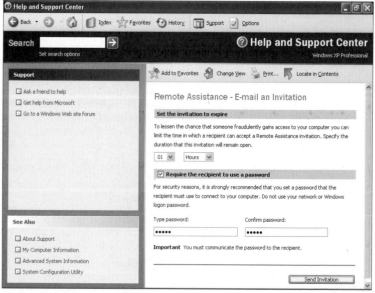

Figure 17-2 Specify when the invitation expires and set a password.

6. To help maintain the security of the system and the enterprise itself, all invitations should have a password. Ensure that Require The Recipient To Use A Password is selected and then enter the password in the Type Password and Confirm Password text boxes.

Caution   Do not use your network or Windows logon password as the invitation password. Use a different password.

7. To submit the invitation, click Send Invitation. If Windows XP is able to submit the message, you'll see a message stating the submission was successful. Otherwise, you'll see a message detailing an error that occurred. Resolve the problem so that Windows XP can submit the message for delivery.

Note   Remote Assistance invitations are generated as files formatted in eXtensible Markup Language (XML) with the .msrcincident file extension. The XML markup identifies the user name specified in the From field, the problem description identified in the Description field, the invitation time limit, the Internet Protocol (IP) address and Domain Name System (DNS) name of the user's computer, and the port used for communications. To protect the file from being modified, the password and key fields have an encrypted hash. Any change to the key fields or the password field invalidates the hash and makes the invitation unusable.

Offering Remote Assistance

If you know that a user is having problems with her computer, you can offer remote assistance rather than waiting for her to send you an invitation. To offer remote assistance, follow these steps:

1. Click Start, and then select Help And Support. This displays the Help And Support Center.
2. Under Pick A Task, click Use Tools.
3. Under Tools, click Offer Remote Assistance.
4. As shown in Figure 17-3, you can now enter the DNS name or IP address of the computer to which you want to connect. This should be the fully qualified domain name or IP address of the user's computer, such as wkstn01.microsoft.com or 192.168.1.101.

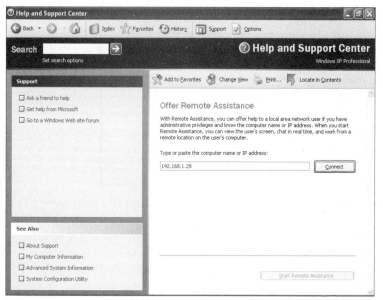

Figure 17-3   Rather than wait for an invitation, you can offer remote assistance.

5. Click Connect to initiate the connection. Windows XP contacts the target computer and attempts to establish a Remote Assistance connection.

6. The user sees a prompt asking her if she'd like to access the connection. If the user accepts the connection, click Start to initialize the session. Once the session is initialized, you'll be able to view her screen and if permitted, control her computer. You can also send chat messages to the user.

Responding To and Accepting Invitations

Remote Assistance invitations sent through e-mail contain an inserted MsRcIncident file. The file format is the same as when you save an invitation to a file.

You can respond to a user's invitation by completing the following steps:

1. Open the e-mail message containing the invitation and then access the attachment, or double-click the invitation if it is a file.

2. The Remote Assistance dialog box shown in Figure 17-4 is displayed.

    Note   Pay particular attention to the Remote Assistance dialog box. You'll be prompted for a password only if one is required. If you don't know the password, the text tells you whom to contact. In this case, it is wrstanek, which is the name entered in the invitation's From field.

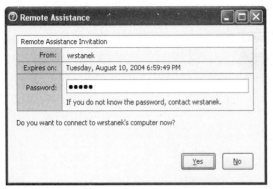

Figure 17-4 Access the invitation file, enter a password if required, and then click Yes to start the Remote Assistance session.

 Caution Watch out for expired invitations. You won't be able to connect to a user's computer using an expired invitation. Expired invitations have the keyword Expired in bold in the Status column.

3. Type the invitation password if prompted and then click Yes to start the session.
4. The operating system attempts to make a connection to the user's computer. Providing you've supplied the correct password and the invitation is still valid, a connection is established.
5. As shown in Figure 17-5, the user sees an Invitation Accepted dialog box and is asked to click Yes to allow the session to be started. If available, the Optimize Performance For Administrator field allows the user to optimize the system by reducing the color quality on the computer and turning off background graphics. Lower resolution screens and fewer graphics mean less screen data is transmitted and allows for smoother screen refreshes.

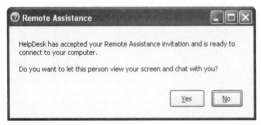

Figure 17-5 The user must accept the invitation request to continue.

6. Once the session is started, you'll be able to view the user's screen and, if permitted, control the user's computer. You can also send chat messages to the user.

Tip   The user has only a few seconds to respond to the request. If he doesn't, a time-out will occur and you'll need to reinitiate the session by double-clicking the file name or opening the e-mail attachment.

Checking Invitation Status

All invitations a user has created can be tracked and managed in a central location. To check the status of existing invitations on a computer, follow these steps:

1. Click Start, and then select Help And Support. This displays the Help And Support Center.

2. Under Ask For Assistance, click Invite A Friend To Connect To Your Computer With Remote Assistance.

3. Click View Invitation Status. As Figure 17-6 shows, invitations are listed with the following details:

   - ❏ **Sent To**   The e-mail address or MSN address used when creating the invitation. If the invitation was saved to a file, the value in this column is listed as Saved.

   - ❏ **Expiration Time**   The expiration date and time for the invitation.

   - ❏ **Status**   The status of the invitation as Open, Closed, or Expired.

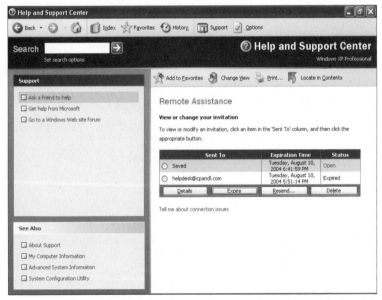

Figure 17-6   Each invitation is listed according to recipient's name, expiration time, and status.

Expiring, Resending, and Deleting Invitations

Invitations can be expired, resent, or deleted at any time. When you expire an invitation, you invalidate it so that it can't be used to establish a connection to the computer. When you resend an invitation, it goes to the original e-mail address set when the invitation was created. When you delete an invitation, it is removed from the invitation status list and canceled so that it cannot be responded to. You can't set a different e-mail address or change the expiration date.

To expire, resend, or delete an invitation, follow these steps:

1. Click Start and then select Help And Support. This displays the Help And Support Center.

2. Under Ask For Assistance, click Invite A Friend To Connect To Your Computer With Remote Assistance.

3. Click View Invitation Status. Each invitation is listed with its current status.

4. Select the option button for the invitation you want to work with and then click Expire, Resend, or Delete as appropriate for the action you want to take.

Troubleshooting Startup and Shutdown

As an administrator you'll often need to troubleshoot problems with startup and shutdown. The sections that follow look at techniques for resolving common problems.

Resolving Startup Issues Using Safe Mode

Most startup problems occur because something on the system has changed; for example, a device might have been incorrectly installed. The system configuration or registry might have been updated improperly, causing a conflict. Often you can resolve startup issues using Safe Mode to recover or troubleshoot system problems. When you are finished using Safe Mode, be sure to restart the computer using a normal startup. You will then be able to use the computer as you normally would.

In Safe Mode, Windows XP loads only basic files, services, and drivers. The drivers loaded include the mouse, monitor, keyboard, mass storage, and base video. The monitor driver sets the basic settings and modes for the computer's monitor; the base video driver sets the basic options for the computer's graphics card. No networking services or drivers are started unless you choose the Safe Mode With Networking option. Because Safe Mode loads a limited set of configuration information, it can help you troubleshoot problems.

You restart a system, in Safe Mode, by completing the following steps:

1. Click Start, and then select Shut Down. In the Shut Down Windows dialog box, select Restart and then click OK.

2. During startup, press F8 several times. If the computer has multiple operating systems or you've installed recovery console, you'll see a prompt labeled Please Select The Operating System To Start and can press F8 at that time.

3. Use the arrow keys to select the Safe Mode you want to use, and then press Enter. The Safe Mode option you use depends on the type of problem you're experiencing. The key options are as follows:

- ❏ **Safe Mode**   Loads only basic files, services, and drivers during the initialization sequence. The drivers loaded include the mouse, monitor, keyboard, mass storage, and base video. No networking services or drivers are started.

- ❏ **Safe Mode With Command Prompt**   Loads basic files, services, and drivers, and then starts a command prompt instead of the Windows XP graphical interface. No networking services or drivers are started.

- ❏ **Safe Mode With Networking**   Loads basic files, services, and drivers, as well as services and drivers needed to start networking.

- ❏ **Enable Boot Logging**   Allows you to create a record of all startup events in a boot log.

- ❏ **Enable VGA Mode**   Allows you to start the system in Video Graphics Adapter (VGA) mode, which is useful if the system display is set to a mode that can't be used with the current monitor.

- ❏ **Last Known Good Configuration**   Starts the computer in Safe Mode using registry information that Windows XP saved at the last shutdown.

4. If a problem doesn't reappear when you start in Safe Mode, you can eliminate the default settings and basic device drivers as possible causes. If a newly added device or updated driver is causing problems, you can use Safe Mode to remove the device or reverse the update.

5. If you are still having a problem starting the system normally and suspect that problems with hardware, software, or settings are to blame, remain in Safe Mode and then try using System Restore to undo previous changes. See the section later in this chapter entitled "Using Restore Points."

6. If System Restore doesn't work, try modifying startup options as discussed in Chapter 2, "Configuring the Environment."

Repairing Missing or Corrupted System Files

Automated System Recovery (ASR) data can often help you recover a system that won't boot. This data includes essential system files, partition boot sector information, and the startup environment for a particular system. You should create recovery data for each computer on the network. Normally, you should update the recovery data when you install service packs, manipulate the boot drive, or modify the startup environment.

Once you create the recovery data, which I'll refer to as a system recovery data snapshot for ease of reference, you can use it to recover the system in most cases. If this fails, you can try to repair and reinstall Windows XP as discussed in the section of this chapter entitled "Repairing and Reinstalling Windows XP."

Creating System Recovery Data

You can create a system recovery data snapshot by completing the following steps:

1. Click Start, point to Programs or All Programs as appropriate, then to Accessories, then to System Tools, and finally click Backup.

2. If wizard mode is enabled, click Advanced Mode (which is hidden in the text one paragraph above the check box). The main interface for the Backup Utility should now be displayed. If you want to start in advanced mode automatically, clear the Always Start In Wizard Mode check box before you click Advanced Mode.

3. Click Automated System Recovery Wizard and then, in the Automated System Recovery Preparation Wizard, click Next.

4. Select the backup media to use, such as a backup tape, and provide a name for the file that will contain the recovery information. In most cases, you'll want this to be a floppy disk location, such as A:\BACKUP.BKF.

5. If using a floppy disk location, insert a blank 3.5-inch, 1.44-MB disk into the floppy drive.

6. Click Next, and then click Finish. When prompted, remove the disk and label it as a system recovery disk.

Using the Recovery Data to Restore a System

When you can't start or recover a system in Safe Mode or using System Restore, your next step is to try to recover the system using the last system recovery data snapshot you made (if available). The recovery data comes in handy in two situations. If the boot sector or essential system files are damaged or if the startup environment is causing problems on a dual or multiboot system, you might be able to recover the system using the recovery data.

You can repair a system using the recovery data by completing the following steps:

1. Insert the Windows XP CD into the appropriate drive, and then restart the computer. In most cases, you can boot from the CD by pressing the spacebar when prompted. If the computer is configured to boot without checking its CD or floppy disk drive, you will need to change the system BIOS so that the CD or floppy disk drive is checked as appropriate when booting the system.

   Tip   If you are booting from a floppy disk, the computer should access the floppy disk automatically (provided BIOS is configured correctly). You'll need to remove and insert floppy disks when prompted.

2. When the Setup program begins, press F2.

   Insert the System Recovery floppy disk when prompted. Files will then be copied from the disk to the computer, and the system configuration will be initialized.

3. The computer will then reboot. When the system restarts, it will reboot and start Windows XP. The graphical Setup will begin, and then the ASR Wizard will start.

4. The ASR Wizard allows you to specify the location of the full system backup to be restored.

5. The computer will reboot again. When it restarts, it should start normally. At this point, the recovery of the system is complete. The system is restored with the configuration and settings it had when the ASR backup was made.

Resolving Restart or Shutdown Issues

Normally, you can shut down or restart Windows XP by clicking Start, selecting Turn Off Computer, and selecting Restart or Turn Off in the Turn Off Computer dialog box. Sometimes, however, Windows XP won't shut down or restart normally and you are forced to take additional actions. In those cases, follow these steps:

1. In a domain, press Ctrl+Alt+Del. The Windows Security dialog box should display. If nothing happens, press Ctrl+Alt+Del twice to force a shutdown, or else click Task Manager.

   In a workgroup, press Ctrl+Alt+Del. The Windows Task Manager dialog box should open. If nothing happens, skip to step 5.

2. On the Application tab, look for an application that is not responding. If all programs appear to be running normally, skip to step 5.

3. Select the application that is not responding, and then click End Task.

4. If the application fails to respond to the request, you'll see a prompt that allows you to end the application immediately or cancel the end-task request. Click End Now.

5. Try shutting down or restarting the computer. Press Ctrl+Alt+Del and then click Shut Down on the menu bar and select Turn Off, or press Ctrl+Alt+Del twice to force a shutdown.

 Real World   As a last resort, you might be forced to perform a hard shutdown by powering down or unplugging the computer. If this is the case, Check Disk will probably run the next time you start the computer. This allows the computer to check for errors and problems that might have been caused by the hard shutdown. If Check Disk doesn't run automatically, you might want to run it manually.

Repairing and Reinstalling Windows XP

When you cannot recover Windows any other way, your final recovery option is to reinstall Windows XP with the repair option. This option tells Windows to reinstall the base operating system over the existing installation. The repair and reinstall shouldn't affect user settings so any programs that were previously installed and any data should remain intact—in most cases.

To reinstall Windows XP with the repair option, follow these steps:

1. Insert the Windows XP CD into the appropriate drive, and then restart the computer.

2. When the Setup program begins, do not select any of the repair options. Instead, press Enter to start Setup normally.

3. Press F8 to accept the license agreement. Windows XP will then search your system for existing Windows installations.

4. On the screen showing your existing Windows installation, press R to start the repair process.

5. The remainder of this procedure follows the same steps as if you were performing a clean install of the operating system. When Setup finishes, the system files will be refreshed, and the existing user settings and data should be available.

Note   Keep in mind that the repair process cannot repair a damaged disk. If the file system is defective, you might need to reformat the disk and then perform a clean install of the operating system. If the disk itself is defective, you will need to replace the disk and then install the operating system.

Making Sense of Stop Errors

The section of Chapter 2 entitled "Configuring System Startup and Recovery" details how to configure Windows XP to write debugging information. If a major error occurs while Windows XP is starting, installing a program, or performing another operation, you'll see a Stop error message across the entire screen. Read this information carefully and write down the following information:

- **Error name**   The error name should be on the third line of the error screen and is listed in all caps, such as KERNEL_STACK_INPAGE_ERROR.

- **Troubleshooting recommendations**   The error name is followed by the troubleshooting recommendations. These recommendations are based on the type of error that occurred and provide general guidelines on resolving the problem.

- **Error number**   The troubleshooting recommendations are followed by technical information. On the next line after the "Technical Information" heading, you'll see the word STOP, an error number, and a list of error parameters. The error number following STOP is what you should write down, such as STOP: 0X00000050.

- **Driver information**   Immediately following the line with the STOP error number is a line that lists the name of the driver associated with the error. This information is only provided if the error can be traced to a specific driver. Write down the driver name.

If the system is configured to write an event to the event logs if a Stop error occurs and it was possible to write the event before the system crashed completely, the error number and error parameters will be written to an event in the System log with an event source of Save Dump. The event will also specify if a dump file was created and where it was saved if applicable.

Real World   Windows XP includes an Online Crash Analysis feature that allows you to send the dump file to Microsoft Product Support Services. If error reporting is enabled as discussed in Chapter 2 in the section "Enabling and Disabling Error Reporting," you will be prompted to send this debugging information to Microsoft when you restart the system. You have the option of sending the debugging information anonymously or using your Microsoft Passport. If you send the debugging information with your name and contact information through Microsoft Passport, a technician might contact you for further information and might also be able to suggest an action to correct the problem. You can check. You can manually upload crash information via the Microsoft Online Crash Analysis Web site (*http://oca.microsoft.com/*). The site also lets you track the status of your issue.

Once you have the Stop error information, you might need to start the system in Safe Mode as discussed earlier in this chapter in the section "Resolving Startup Issues Using Safe Mode." You can then look to resolving the problem:

- **Look up the Stop error on the Microsoft Knowledge Base**   Visit support.microsoft.com and perform a search of the Microsoft Knowledge Base using the error number as the keyword. If there is a known problem related to the error code, you should find a related Knowledge Base article. As appropriate, follow the instructions given to resolve the issue.

- **Check the driver (if driver information was provided)**   When you reboot the system, check the driver to ensure it is digitally signed. If the driver has been updated recently, you might need to consider rolling back to the previous driver version. Just because the driver is listed, it doesn't mean the driver is corrupt and needs replacing, however. The Stop error could have been caused by other factors.

- **Determine what has changed recently**   Stop errors can be caused by both hardware and software. Closely review any programs or hardware that has been installed recently on the computer. If you added new hardware, check to ensure that the hardware is installed correctly and that the latest, signed drivers are installed and that the hardware is properly configured. If you added new software, check to make sure the installation completed successfully. You might also want to check for updates or patches to the software.

- **Check system resources**   Stop errors can occur if the system gets critically low on RAM or disk space. Once you get the system started, check the drives to determine the amount of free space available and, as necessary, free additional disk space using Disk Cleanup or other tools. Also open the Task Manager (in a domain, press Ctrl+Alt+Del and click Task Manager; in a workgroup, simply press Ctrl+Alt+Del) and look at the Performance tab to check the amount of physical and virtual RAM available. If there is very little memory available, determine what programs are using memory and if there are problem programs, such as adware or spyware, running.

- **Repair system files**   Stop errors can be caused by damaged or improper versions of system files. If you suspect a system file as being the cause of the problem and the system won't boot properly, you might need to repair the operating system as discussed earlier in this chapter in the section "Repairing Missing or Corrupted System Files" or reinstall the operating system using the repair options as discussed earlier in the section "Repairing and Reinstalling Windows XP."

- **Check hardware and BIOS**   Stop errors can be caused by faulty hardware. If a computer frequently crashes, you might want to examine the hardware closely. Check the hardware drivers first; a driver might be causing the Stop errors. Check the physical hardware. Look specifically at the hard disks, RAM, CPU, and the graphics card. A hard drive might be going bad, RAM might be defective, the CPU might have overheated, or the graphics card might be incompatible with Windows XP. Also look at the BIOS. Check the settings carefully. You might need to see if an update is available from the motherboard manufacturer.

Using Restore Points

Restore points are created by System Restore, and they can be used to recover systems that are experiencing problems after a system update, software installation, hardware installation, or other change. The following sections provide an overview of how System Restore is used, how restore points can be created manually, and how systems can be recovered using restore points. Restore operations are reversible in most cases.

Understanding System Restore

System Restore monitors the operating system for changes and creates restore points before changes are introduced at regular daily intervals. The feature works by saving a snapshot of a computer's system configuration and writing this to disk so that it can be used to recover the system to a point in time if necessary. It is important to note that System Restore does not affect personal data. You can recover a system to a restore point without affecting a user's application data, cached files, or documents. System Restore doesn't write any information to the My Documents folder either.

System Restore tracks and saves configuration information separately for each drive on a computer. This means each drive has disk space made available to System Restore and you can turn off monitoring of individual drives as needed. If a drive is configured for System Restore monitoring, you can recover from changes if a problem occurs. If a drive isn't configured for System Restore monitoring, configuration changes are not tracked and changes cannot be recovered if a problem occurs. On most systems, you should configure System Restore for the system drive, which stores the operating system files, and for all drives containing critical applications.

The disk space available to System Restore is configurable and determines the number of restore points that can be created. The default configuration is designed so that several weeks of past restore points can be saved to each volume. When System Restore runs out of available space, the operating system overwrites previously created restore points.

Restore points can be restored in one of three ways: by checkpoint, by date, or by event. Individual snapshots scheduled by the operating system are called system checkpoints. When you installed Windows XP, the first snapshot—the initial system checkpoint—was created automatically. Other system checkpoints are made approximately every 24 hours. If a computer is turned off when a daily checkpoint is scheduled, System Restore creates the checkpoint the next time the computer is started.

Some snapshots are created automatically based on events that are triggered by the operating system when you make changes or install applications. For simplicity, I call these snapshots installation restore points, but there's actually a group of them, each with a different purpose. The event-based snapshots are as follows:

- **Program name installation restore points**   Created prior to installing a program that uses a compatible installer. You can use installation restore points to track application installation and to restore a computer to the state it was in before the application was installed. Restoring the computer state means that all file and registry settings for the installed program are removed. It also means that programs and system files altered by the installation are restored to their previous state. Once completed, the program won't work and you'll need to reinstall it if the user wants to use it again.

 Caution   These are called program name installation restore points instead of program uninstall restore points for a very good reason. The restore process doesn't uninstall all the application files. It removes file and registry settings that might affect the operation of the computer. To completely uninstall a program, you'll need to use the Add/ Remove Programs tool in Control Panel.

- **Automatic update restore points**   Created prior to applying an automatic update. If a computer has problems after applying an automatic update, you can use the restore point to recover the computer to its previous state. (You can also use the Add Or Remove Programs dialog box to remove automatic updates.)

- **Restore operation restore points**   Created prior to restoring a computer. If you find that you went back to the wrong restore point or that the restore point doesn't work, you can use these restore points to undo the restore operation and recover the computer to its state before you reversed the previous settings.

- **Unsigned device driver restore points**   Created prior to installation of an unsigned or uncertified driver on a computer. If a computer has problems after installing an unsigned or uncertified driver, you can use these restore points to restore the computer to its state before you installed the driver. For signed and certified drivers, the normal rollback procedure should allow you to go back to the previous driver being used.

■ **Microsoft Backup tool recovery restore points**   Created prior to recovering files or system data using the Backup tool. If the recovery fails or if the computer doesn't work properly after the recovery, you can undo the changes and restore the computer to its previous state.

Users can also create snapshots manually. These snapshots are called manual restore points. You should recommend that users create snapshots prior to performing any operation that could cause problems on the system.

You can restore computers when they are running in Normal or Safe Mode. In Normal Mode, a restore operation restore point is created prior to restoration of the computer. But in Safe Mode, the restore operation restore point is not created because changes you make in Safe Mode aren't tracked and you can't undo them using restore points. However, you can use Safe Mode to restore any previously created restore point.

Creating Manual Restore Points

You can create a manual restore point by following these steps:

1. Click Start, point to Programs or All Programs as appropriate, then to Accessories, then to System Tools, and finally select System Restore to start the System Restore wizard.

2. Select Create A Restore Point, and then click Next.

3. Enter a description for the restore point, such as Prior To Display–Monitor Driver Update And Changes.

4. Click Create. When the create operation completes, click Close.

Recovering from Restore Points

To recover a computer from a restore point, follow these steps:

1. Click Start, point to Programs or All Programs as appropriate, then to Accessories, then to System Tools, and finally select System Restore to start the System Restore wizard.

2. Select Restore My Computer To An Earlier Time, and then click Next.

3. On the calendar, click the date to which you want to restore the computer as shown in Figure 17-7. The current date is selected by default. Dates in boldface have available restore points. If a date is not in boldface, no restore points were saved that day or the restore point was overwritten due to lack of space.

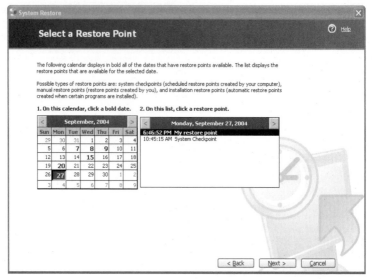

Figure 17-7   Choose a snapshot to restore.

4. In the pane to the right of the calendar, you'll see a list of all snapshots taken on the selected day. Click the snapshot you want to restore, click Next, and then click Next again.

    During the restoration, System Restore shuts down Windows XP. After the restore is complete, Windows XP is restarted using the settings from the date and time of the snapshot.

5. After the system restarts, the System Restore dialog box is displayed again. Click OK. If Windows XP isn't working properly, you can apply a different restore point or reverse the restore operation by repeating this procedure and selecting the restore operation that was created prior to applying the current system state.

Appendix A
Working with Files and Folders

In this appendix:

Windows XP File Structures......................................463

Exploring Files and Folders 466

Managing Files...473

When you think about it, most of your time working with a computer is spent managing files and folders. You create files and folders to store and organize information. You move the files and folders from one location to another. You set file and folder properties, and so on. When you spend so much time working with files and folders, a few simple techniques for effective management can go a long way toward saving you time and effort—and essential techniques for working with files and folders is exactly what this chapter is all about.

Windows XP File Structures

When you work with files and folders on a Microsoft Windows XP system, you'll usually work with FAT or NTFS. FAT (file allocation table) is available in 16-bit and 32-bit versions, which are often referred to as FAT16 and FAT32. The NTFS file system is available in two major versions: NTFS 4 and NTFS 5. What you can or can't do with files and folders in Windows XP depends on the file system type.

Working with FAT and NTFS Volumes

FAT volumes rely on an allocation table to keep track of the status of files and folders. Although FAT is adequate for most file and folder needs, it's rather limited, as Table A-1 shows. FAT16 is the version of FAT widely used prior to Microsoft Windows NT 3. You'll get optimal performance with volumes that are less than 2 GB. FAT32 is the version of FAT introduced with Microsoft Windows 95 release 2 and

Windows 98. FAT32 supports larger volumes—up to 32 GB—and generally allocates space more efficiently than FAT16.

Table A-1   FAT16 and FAT32 Features Comparison

Feature	FAT16	FAT32
File allocation table-entry size	16-bit	32-bit
Maximum volume size	4 GB; best 2 GB or less	2 TB; limited in Windows 2000 to 32 GB
Maximum file size	2 GB	4 GB
Operating systems supported	MS-DOS and all versions of Windows	Windows 95 OS release 2, Windows 98, and all later versions of Windows
Supports small cluster size	Yes	No
Supports NTFS 4 features	No	No
Supports NTFS 5 features	No	No
Use on floppy disks	Yes	Yes
Use on removable disks	Yes	Yes

As Table A-2 shows, NTFS offers a robust environment for working with files and folders. NTFS 4 is the version of NTFS used with Windows NT 4.0. It features full support for local and remote access controls on files and folders as well as support for Windows compression. NTFS 5 is the version of NTFS used with Windows 2000 and later. It features full support for compression, disk quotas, encryption, and other advanced features. Windows NT 4.0 systems with Service Pack 4 or later can access NTFS 5 files and folders, provided they don't use any of the new NTFS features.

Table A-2   NTFS 4 and NTFS 5 Features Comparison

Feature	NTFS 4	NTFS 5
Maximum volume size	32 GB	2 TB in most configurations
Maximum file size	32 GB	Only limited by volume size
Operating systems supported	Windows NT 4.0, Windows 2000, Windows XP, and Windows Server 2003	Windows 2000, Windows XP, and Windows Server 2003; Windows NT 4.0 minimally
Advanced file access permissions	Yes	Yes
Supports Windows compression	Yes	Yes
Supports Windows encryption	No	Yes
Supports the Active Directory directory service structures	No	Yes
Supports sparse files	No	Yes
Supports remote storage	No	Yes
Supports disk quotas	No	Yes
Use on floppy disks	No	No
Use on removable disks	Yes	Yes

File Naming

Windows XP file naming conventions apply to both files and folders. For simplicity, the term "file naming" is often used to refer to both files *and* folders. Although Windows XP file names are case-aware, they aren't case-sensitive. This means that you can save a file named MyBook.doc and the file name will be displayed in the correct case. However, you can't save a file named mybook.doc to the same folder.

Both NTFS and FAT32 support long file names—up to 255 characters. You can name files using just about any of the available characters, including spaces. However, there are some characters you can't use:

? * / \ : " < > |

Tip   Using spaces in file names can cause access problems. Anytime you reference the file name, you might need to enclose the file name within quotation marks. Also, if you plan to publish the file on the Web, you might need to remove the spaces from the file name or convert them to the underscore character (_) to ensure that Web browsers have easy access to the file.

The following file names are all acceptable:

- My Favorite Short Story.doc
- My_Favorite_Short_Story.doc
- My..Favorite..Short..Story.doc
- My Favorite Short Story!!!.doc

Accessing Long File Names under MS-DOS

Under MS-DOS and 16-bit FAT file systems, file and folder names are restricted to eight characters with a three-character file extension, such as chapter4.txt. This naming convention is often referred to as the 8.3 file-naming rule or the standard MS-DOS file-naming rule. Because of this rule, when you work with files at the command prompt you might have problems accessing files and folders.

To support access to long file names, abbreviated file names are created for all files and folders on a system. These file names conform to the standard MS-DOS file-naming rule. You can see the abbreviated file names using the following command:

`dir /X`

A typical abbreviated file name looks like this:

`PROGRA~1.DOC`

How Windows XP Creates an Abbreviated File Name

When Windows XP creates an abbreviated file name from a long file name, it uses the following rules:

- Any spaces in the file name are removed. The file name My Favorite Short Story.doc becomes MyFavoriteShortStory.doc.

- All periods in the file name are removed (with the exception of the period separating the file name from the file extension). The file name My..Favorite..Short..Story.doc becomes MyFavoriteShortStory.doc.

- Invalid characters under the standard MS-DOS naming rule are replaced with the underscore character (_). The file name My[Favorite]ShortStory.doc becomes My_Favorite_ShortStory.doc.

- All remaining characters are converted to uppercase. The file name My Favorite Short Story.doc becomes MYFAVORITESHORTSTORY.DOC.

Afterward, the rules of truncation are applied to create the standard MS-DOS file name.

The Rules of Truncation

To make the file conform to the 8.3 naming convention, the file name and file extension are truncated, if necessary. The rules for truncation are as follows:

- The file extension is truncated to the first three characters of the string that follows the last period in the long file name. The file name Mary.text becomes MARY.TEX.

- The file name is truncated to the first six characters (which is the file's root name), and a unique designator is appended. The unique designator follows the convention ~n, where n is the ordinal number of the file with the six-character file name. Following this, the file name My Favorite Short Story.doc becomes MYFAVO~1.DOC. The second file in this folder that is truncated to MYFAVO becomes MYFAVO~2.DOC.

 Note   The file name truncation rule described here is the one you'll usually see, and you won't often have to worry about anything else. However, if you have a lot of files with similar names, you might see another convention used to create the short file name.

Specifically, if more than four files use the same six-character root, additional file names are created by combining the first two characters of the file name with a four-character hash code and then appending a unique designator. A folder could have files named MYFAVO~1.DOC, MYFAVO~2.DOC, MYFAVO~3.DOC, and MYFAVO~4.DOC. Additional files with this root could be named MY3140~1.DOC, MY40C7~1.DOC, and MYEACC~1.DOC.

Exploring Files and Folders

Windows Explorer is the tool of choice for working with files and folders. You can also use My Computer and My Network Places to perform many file-manipulation tasks. Access My Computer and My Network Places by double-clicking their icons on the Windows XP desktop.

Note   For brevity, this section focuses primarily on using Windows Explorer. However, you can apply similar techniques to My Computer and My Network Places.

Using Windows Explorer

To run Windows Explorer, go to Start, choose Programs, choose Accessories, and then select Windows Explorer. You can now use Windows Explorer to browse local and remote resources.

Windows Explorer Views and Toolbars

Windows Explorer can use multiple viewing panes. These panes include:

- **Explorer Bar**   Shows different views depending on the current action in the left pane of the window. The available views are Folders, Search, History, and Favorites. Folders is the default view.
- **Contents**   Shows the contents of a selected folder or the results of a search.
- **Tip Of The Day**   Displays helpful pointers for working with Windows XP.

As Figure A-1 shows, individual folders can have custom views as well. By default, Windows Explorer displays only the Explorer Bar and the Contents view. To modify the view panes, you can:

- **Display other views on the Explorer Bar**   Select View, choose Explorer Bar, and then select the view you want to use.
- **Display the Tip Of The Day**   Select View, choose Explorer Bar, and then select Tip Of The Day.
- **Remove the Explorer Bar or Tip Of The Day**   Click Close (the X in the upper-left or upper-right corner of the pane).

To change the settings for the Contents view, you use the View menu as well. Selected items are enabled. Cleared items are disabled. The main options are:

- **Toolbars**   Allows you to add, remove, and customize toolbars.
- **Status Bar**   Adds a status bar that displays information about objects that are selected.
- **List**   Displays a list of files and folders instead of the detailed listings or file icons.
- **Details**   Displays detailed listings for files and folders. The detailed view adds file size, file type, and modification date to the Contents panel, as well as several other headings that generally relate to media files.
- **Filmstrip**   Displays large thumbnails for each picture in a folder and allows you to select the picture for preview at a larger size.
- **Icons**   Displays icons that are used to represent files and folders.
- **Arrange Icons By**   Allows you to arrange files and folders by name, type, size, and date. In detailed view, clicking on the column headings has the same effect.
- **Thumbnails**   Allows you to view a miniature version of an image that you can use for quick browsing.

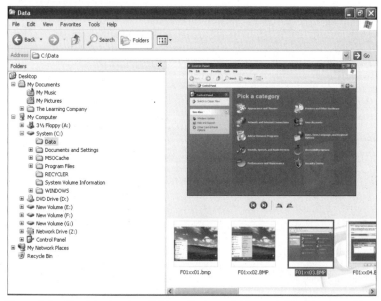

Figure A-1 Filmstrip view is available only when a folder contains pictures, and it provides thumbnails and quick preview.

Understanding Windows Explorer Icons

Each icon displayed in Windows Explorer has a purpose. Key icons displayed in the Folders pane are used as follows:

- **Desktop** A top-level folder that stores files, folders, and shortcuts on the Windows desktop. It is the parent folder of My Computer, My Network Places, My Documents, and Recycle Bin.

- **My Computer** A folder containing all local resources and folders available to the computer.

- **My Network Places** A folder for the network. Click this to browse network resources.

- **Recycle Bin** A folder that stores files and folders that have been deleted. If the system is configured to use the Recycle Bin, you can recover files from this folder before they're permanently removed.

- **My Documents** A folder used to store personal files. In My Documents, you'll find the My Pictures folder, which has special features for previewing images.

- **Drives** Storage devices that are identified with unique icons and drive letters. Windows XP has separate icons for local disks (physical hard disks), floppy disk drives, CD drives (CD and DVD drives), and removable disks (USB/FireWire-attached drives).

- **Network Drives** Remote network resources that are connected to the system.

- **Open Folders**   Folders that have been accessed by clicking them. Open folders show their contents in the Contents pane.
- **Closed Folders**   Folders that have not been accessed. Closed folders don't display their contents.

Tip   To expand a folder without displaying its contents in the Contents pane, click the plus (+) symbol next to the folder. This technique allows you to browse folders on remote systems faster than usual.

You can also use this technique when you're copying files. You display the contents of the folder that you want to copy in the Contents pane and then browse for the destination folder in the Folders pane. When you find the destination folder, you copy the source files to the folder.

Displaying Hidden and Compressed Files in Windows Explorer

As an administrator, you'll often want to see system files, such as DLLs (dynamic-link library files), and files that have or haven't been compressed. By default, however, Windows Explorer doesn't display hidden file types or differentiate between compressed and uncompressed files. To override the initial settings, from the Tools menu select Folder Options and then click the View tab. You can now configure new settings using the dialog box shown in Figure A-2.

- To display hidden files, click Show Hidden Files And Folders.
- To always display file extensions, clear the Hide File Extensions For Known File Types check box.
- To display operating system files, clear the Hide Protected Operating System Files check box.
- To highlight encrypted or compressed files and folders, select the Show Encrypted Or Compressed NTFS File In Color check box.

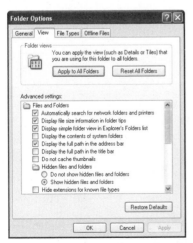

Figure A-2   Set options for Windows Explorer using the Folder Options dialog box.

Customizing Folder Views

Windows XP provides two views for folders: Folder Tasks view and Windows Classic view. When Folder Tasks view is enabled, Windows Explorer supports customizable views for all folders on a Windows XP system. You can change the look and feel of the view on individual folders or on all folders on a system.

Working with Folder Templates

Windows Explorer uses template files to determine what each folder looks like in the Contents pane. It creates these templates as HTML documents. The technologies used to create the templates are Hypertext Markup Language (HTML), cascading style sheets, and scripts. Scripts are used to customize the folders and make them more interactive. The predefined templates include the following:

- **Documents**   A standard view for folders that contain a mix of file types including documents, pictures, and other folders.

- **Music**   A view for folders that contain digital music. When the Explorer Bar is turned off, the Music Tasks pane provides the Play All and Shop For Music Online options.

- **Pictures**   A quick and efficient no-frills view for folders that contain pictures. Each picture is displayed with a thumbnail that you can use for quick browsing. With the Explorer Bar turned off, the Picture Tasks pane provides the View As A Slide Show, Print Pictures, and Copy All Items To CD tasks.

- **Photo Album**   A filmstrip view that provides thumbnails of each picture and a large preview of a selected picture. It also has a Picture Tasks pane.

- **Videos**   A view for folders containing videos. Video Tasks provides the Play All and Copy All Items To CD options, available when the Explorer Bar is turned off.

Folder view settings you use are seen by all users who access the system, either locally or remotely. The default view for most folders is Documents. You can change the view by customizing the folder, provided you have write permissions on the folder. If you like a particular view, you can apply it to all your folders on the system as well. To do this, you must have ownership of the folder.

Enabling Folder Tasks View

Folder templates are used only when Folder Tasks view is enabled. The enabling or disabling of this feature is based on options set in Windows Explorer, which are different for each user who logs on to a computer. To enable or disable Folder Tasks view, complete the following steps:

1. In Windows Explorer, from the Tools menu select Folder Options.
2. To enable Folder Tasks view, select Show Common Tasks In Folders. To disable Folder Tasks view, select Use Windows Classic Folders.
3. Click OK.

Configuring Custom Folder Views

To configure custom views for folders, follow these steps:

1. In Windows Explorer, select the folder you want to customize. If you want to customize all the folders on a system, select any folder and then when you complete this operation, follow the instructions in the next section of this chapter, "Setting Views for Multiple Folders."

2. Choose the Customize This Folder option of the View menu. This displays the folder's Properties dialog box with the Customize tab selected, as shown in Figure A-3.

Figure A-3 Use the Customize tab to choose a folder template to use.

3. Under Use This Folder Type As A Template, choose the template you want to use, such as Photo Album. If you want the view to apply to subfolders of this folder, choose Also Apply This Template To All Subfolders.

4. The folder preview can be customized as well. By default, a folder shows a folder icon with thumbnails for the first few files as a folder preview. If you want, you can set a specific background picture for the folder that will be used instead of the thumbnails. Click Choose Picture, and then use the Browse dialog box to select the picture you want to use as part of the folder's preview.

5. Click OK.

Setting Views for Multiple Folders

Using the Folder Options dialog box, you can apply a custom view to all your folders on a system or restore the default view to all your folders on a system. To do that, complete the following steps:

1. In Windows Explorer, select the folder you want to work with. Use the options of the View menu to configure the folder view that you want to use.

2. From the Tools menu, choose Folder Options and then select the View tab.

3. To apply the current folder view to all your folders on a system, click Apply To All Folders.

4. To restore all your folders to their default view, click Reset All Folders.

Formatting Floppy Disks and Other Removable Disks

Windows Explorer makes it easy to work with floppy and other removable disks. You can format disks by following these steps:

1. Insert the floppy or other removable disk you want to format.

2. Right-click the floppy or other removable disk icon in Windows Explorer's Folders pane.

3. From the shortcut menu select Format, and then use the Format dialog box to set the formatting options. For floppy disks, the only available file system type is the 16-bit FAT. For other removable disks, such as Zip, you can use FAT, FAT32, or NTFS.

 Note If you format removable disks as NTFS volumes, they are formatted as NTFS 5 volumes. Unlike Windows NT 4.0, Windows XP allows you to eject volumes formatted as NTFS at any time. Click Eject on the removable disk drive, or right-click the drive icon in Windows Explorer and then select Eject.

4. Click Start to begin formatting the floppy or other removable disk.

Copying Floppy Disks

To copy a floppy disk, follow these steps:

1. Right-click the floppy disk icon in Windows Explorer's Folders pane, and then from the shortcut menu choose Copy Disk.

2. Use the Copy Disk dialog box to select the source and destination drives. In the Copy From area, select the drive you want to use as the source. In the Copy To area, select the drive you want to use as the destination. If you have only one floppy disk drive, the source and destination drive will be the same (as shown in Figure A-4).

3. Click Start when you're ready to begin copying, and then insert the source and destination disks when prompted. The progress bar in the lower area of the Copy Disk dialog box shows the progress of the copy operation.

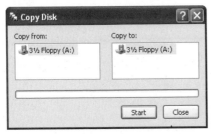

Figure A-4   Use the Copy Disk dialog box to select the source and destination drives.

Managing Files

Windows XP provides many ways to manage files. The most common file operations are *copy* and *move*. You can copy or move files *within* windows—such as within
Windows Explorer—and *between* windows—such as copying a file from Windows
Explorer to the My Network Places window. You can also copy or move files to and
from the desktop.

Selecting Files and Folders

In Windows Explorer you can select individual and multiple files in a variety of
ways. You select individual files by clicking them with the mouse. You select multiple files by:

- Holding down the Ctrl key and then clicking the left mouse button on each file
  or folder you want to select.
- Holding down the Shift key, selecting the first file or folder in a contiguous listing, and then clicking the last file or folder.

Copying Files and Folders by Dragging

To copy or move items to any open window or visible area on the desktop, complete
the following steps:

1. Select the item(s) you want to copy or move.
2. Hold down the mouse button, and drag the item(s) to the new location.
3. If you drag the file or folder to a new location on a different drive, it's copied
   automatically. To move the file instead, hold down the Shift key as you drag the
   file or folder.
4. If you drag the file or folder to a new location on the same drive, Windows XP
   will try to move the item instead. To prevent this, hold down the Ctrl key as
   you drag the file or folder.

Note To copy a file, the source and destination location must be visible. This means you might need to open multiple versions of Windows Explorer or multiple windows and expand the folders within these windows, as necessary.

Copying Files and Folders to Locations That Aren't Displayed

You might also need to copy items to locations that aren't currently displayed. To do this, follow these steps:

1. Select the item(s) you want to copy.
2. Hold down the mouse button, and drag the item(s) into the Folders pane.
3. Slowly drag the items up to the last visible folder at the top of the pane (or down to the last visible folder at the bottom of the pane). You should be able to scroll up or down slowly through the existing tree structure.
4. When you find the destination folder, release the mouse button. If it's on a different drive, the item is copied. Otherwise, it's moved.

Copying and Pasting Files

I prefer to move files around by copying and pasting. When you copy and paste files, you don't have to worry about whether the file will be copied or moved. You simply copy files to the Clipboard and paste them anywhere you like. You can even paste copies of files in the same folder—something you can't do by dragging.

To copy and paste files, follow these steps:

1. Select the item(s) you want to copy.
2. Right-click, and from the shortcut menu select Copy. You could also select Copy from the Edit menu or press Ctrl+C.
3. Access the destination location, then right-click, and from the shortcut menu select Paste. You could also select Paste from the Edit menu or press Ctrl+V.

 Note Windows XP might not let you copy files and folders to special windows. For example, you generally can't copy a file and then paste it into the My Computer window. Similarly, you might not be able to copy items from special folders and paste them into other windows.

Moving Files by Cutting and Pasting

To move files by cutting and pasting, follow these steps:

1. Select the item(s) you want to move.
2. Right-click, and from the shortcut menu select Cut. You could also select Cut from the Edit menu or press Ctrl+X.
3. Access the destination location, then right-click, and from the shortcut menu select Paste. You could also select Paste from the Edit menu or press Ctrl+V.

4. When prompted to move the selected items, click OK.

> **Note** When you use the Cut and Paste commands, Windows XP doesn't delete the item(s) from the original location immediately. The Cut command simply places a copy of the item(s) on the Clipboard. After you use the Paste command to paste the file to the new location, the file is deleted from the old location.

Renaming Files and Folders

To rename a file or folder, follow these steps:

1. Right-click the file or folder name, and then from the shortcut menu select Rename. Or select the file or folder name, and then from the File menu select Rename.
2. The resource name is now editable. Type the new name for the resource.
3. Press Enter, or click the resource's icon.

Deleting Files and Folders

To delete files and folders, follow these steps:

1. Select the items to be deleted.
2. Press the Delete key, or choose Delete from the File menu. Alternatively, you could choose Delete from the shortcut menu.

> **Note** By default, Windows Explorer puts deleted items in the Recycle Bin. To delete the files permanently, you need to empty the Recycle Bin. To delete a file immediately and bypass the Recycle Bin, hold down the Shift key and then press the Delete key, choose Delete from the File menu, or select Delete from the shortcut menu.

Creating Folders

In Windows Explorer you can create a folder by following these steps:

1. In the Folders pane, select the folder that will contain the new folder.
2. In the Contents pane, right-click, and then from the New menu select Folder. A new folder is added to the Contents pane. The folder name is initialized to New Folder and selected for editing.
3. Edit the name of the folder, and press Enter.

Examining Drive Properties

Windows Explorer and My Computer both let you examine the properties of your drives. This includes logical drives, floppy disk drives, removable disk drives, network drives, and CD-ROM drives.

There are two ways you can examine drive properties.

- Right-click the drive's icon. From the shortcut menu, select Properties.
- Select the drive by clicking on it. From the File menu, select Properties.

Figure A-5 shows the Properties dialog box for a local disk. Some of the tabs shown are available only for NTFS. For example, on NTFS you can use the Security tab to set access permissions, auditing, and ownership.

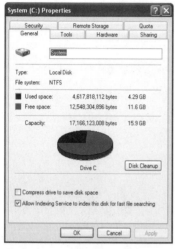

Figure A-5   The Properties dialog box provides a quick overview of the drive. The number of tabs available depends on the type of drive.

The exact number of tabs available depends on the type of drive. Table A-3 provides a quick overview of how the tabs are used and when they're available.

Table A-3   Availability and Description of Drive Property Tabs

Tab	Availability	Description
General	All drive types	Provides an overview of drive configuration and drive space.
Tools	Hard disk drives, floppy disk drives, and removable disk drives, such as USB/FireWire flash drives; not available for CD/DVD drives	Provides access to drive tools for error checking, defragmentation, and backup.
Hardware	Hard disk drives, floppy disk drives, removable disk drives, and CD/DVD drives	Provides access to device properties and troubleshooting features.
Sharing	All local drives	Allows you to share the drive with remote users.
Security	NTFS drives	Sets access permissions, auditing, and ownership.

Table A-3   Availability and Description of Drive Property Tabs

Tab	Availability	Description
Remote Storage	NTFS drives	Manages remote storage.
Quota	NTFS drives	Configures disk usage for users on a per-disk basis.

Examining File and Folder Properties

Windows Explorer, My Computer, and My Network Places all let you examine the properties of files and folders. There are two ways you can do this.

- Right-click the file or folders icon. From the shortcut menu, select Properties.
- Select the file or folder by clicking on it. From the File menu, select Properties.

Figure A-6 shows the Properties dialog box for a folder on NTFS. The General tab provides an overview of the folder and allows you to set its attributes. Folder and file attributes include the following:

- **Read-Only**   Shows whether the file or folder is read-only. You can't modify or accidentally delete read-only files and folders.
- **Hidden**   Determines whether the file is displayed in file listings. You can override this by telling Windows Explorer to display hidden files.
- **Advanced**   Allows you to set compression, encryption, and archiving for the file.

Figure A-6   The file and folder Properties dialog boxes are similar. The availability of tabs depends on the file system type and the file type.

With file and folder properties, the availability of tabs depends on the type of file or folder. Table A-4 provides a quick overview of how the common tabs are used and when they're available.

Table A-4   Availability and Description of Common File and Folder Tabs

Tab	Availability	Description
General	All files and folders	Provides an overview of the item and lets you set its attributes.
Web Sharing	All local folders	Allows you to share the folder with a local Web server (available when the system has Internet Information Services installed).
Sharing	All local folders	Allows you to share the folder with remote users.
Security	NTFS files and folders	Sets access permissions, auditing, and ownership.
Summary	Win32 DLL and executable files	Provides editable summary, authoring, and revision information.
Version	Win32 DLL and executable files	Allows you to check the file version, description, copyright, and other key information.

 Note   When you register a new file type, the file type can create entries that add and remove property tabs or modify the fields of existing tabs. For example, with most image files, you'll see additional fields on the Summary tab. These fields can include Keywords, Description, Caption, Origin, and Credits.

Index

Numbers

16-bit program installation, 147
802.11 wireless specification, 378–379

A

accounts
  domain. *See* domain user accounts
  group. *See* groups
  local. *See* local user accounts
  logon names, 160
  passwords, 161, 169–171
  program installation requirements,
    141–142
  public certificates, 161
  SIDs of, 160
  user. *See* user accounts
  User Account utility, 165–166
  user names, 160
ACLs (access control lists), 268
Active Directory
  Replicators group, 164
  Automatic Updates with, 23
active partitions, 241–243
adapters, 65. *See also* network adapters;
  video adapters
Add Hardware Wizard
  installing drivers, 78–79
  troubleshooting using, 80–82
Add Or Remove Programs
  changes from Service Pack 2, 9
  installing programs, 142–143
  uninstalling programs, 151–152
  viewing installed programs, 150
Address bar keyboard shortcut, 118
Address toolbar
  defined, 113
  purpose, 108
ADMIN$ share, 292
administrative shares, 292–293
Administrative Tools
  accessing, 4
  Computer Management. *See* Computer
    Management Console
  Start menu, adding to, 101, 106–107
Administrator account
  accessing with Run As, 165
  defined, 161
  logging on using, 175
Administrators group
  defined, 163
  ownership of files, 276–277

Advanced System Information
  accessing, 31
  Applications area, 30
  components data, 29
  error logs, viewing, 31
  GPOs, viewing, 31
  hardware resources, 29
  Internet Settings area, 30
  MSINFO32.EXE, 29, 31
  Problem Devices node, 29
  remote computer information, viewing, 31
  services running, viewing, 31
  Software Environment area, 30
  System Summary node, 30
  view options, 31
adware, removing, 155–156
alarms for laptop batteries, 197–200
Allow Automatic Updates Immediate
  Installation policy, 23
Allow Non-Administrators To Receive
  Update Notifications policy, 23
Allow Only Per User Or Approved Shell
  Extensions policy, 296
alternate credentials, 146
alternative IP addressing, 207–208, 328, 330
Always On power scheme, 195
Anonymous Logon identity, 271
antivirus software, 431
APIPA (Automatic Private IP Addressing),
  341
appearance of displays, 131–132. *See also*
  desktops
application framework of help system, 16
Application log, 437–438
applications
  compatibility with XP, 148–149
  firewalls, 434
  frequency of use, viewing, 150
  installing. *See* program installation
  listing installed, 150
  managing, 150
  performance options, 52
  Program menu, 104–105
  publishing, 144
  support links, 151
  uninstalling, 151–156
Applications area, 30
Ask A Friend To Help utility, 15
ASR (Automated System Recovery), 454–456
assigning method of installation, 143–144
audio
  hardware acceleration, 88–89
  multiple devices, configuring, 91

audio, *continued*
quality, 88–89
recording device configuration, 87
sample rate conversion, 88–89
sound effects, configuring, 90
speaker configuration, 87–88
utility for controlling, 85
volume control, 85–87
authentication
Authenticated Users identity, 271
remote access settings, 368–370
smart cards, 369, 370
AUTOEXEC.BAT, 44
automated help system. *See* help system
Automated System Recovery (ASR),
454–456
Automated System Recovery Wizard, 455
automatic connections, 359–360
Automatic Private IP Addressing (APIPA),
341
Automatic Updates
Active Directory with, 23
BITS, 22
configuring, 22–25
details, viewing, 26
Detection Frequency policy, 23
disabling, 22, 25
downloading updates, 25
extended functionality, 21
installing updates, 26
operation, 21
options, 25
options, setting, 64
policies, table of, 23–24
prioritizing by criticality, 21
purpose, 21
removing updates, 26
restarting requirement, 23, 26
restore points, 460
restoring declined updates, 26
Security Center management of, 431
Service Pack 2 changes, 21
uninstalling updates, 23
user notification, 22, 25
AutoPlay command, 140
Autorun, 140

B

Background Intelligent Transfer Service
(BITS), 12, 22
backgrounds, desktop, 122–123
Backup Operators group, 163
Backup tool, 36, 461
base stations, wireless, 378
basic disks
converting dynamic disks, 244–245
defined, 233, 239
disadvantages, 239

drive letter assignment, 249
extended partitions, 239, 247
formatting. *See* formatting drives
logical drive creation, 239, 247–250
partitioning, 233, 239, 247–250
primary partitions, 239, 247
removable disk drives, 240
basic permissions
ACLs, 268
Anonymous Logon identity, 271
assigning to users, 269–270
Authenticated Users identity, 271
Creator Owner identity, 271
denying to users, 269
Dialup identity, 271
Everyone identity, 271
Full Control, 269, 273
groups, 272
inheritance, 271
Interactive identity, 271
List Folder Contents, 269, 272
Modify, 269, 272
Network identity, 271
planning, 271
Read, 269, 272
Read & Execute, 269, 272
recommendations, 271–272
special identities, 271
table of, 269
Users identity, 271
viewing, 268
Write, 269, 272
basic volumes, 233. *See also* volumes
batteries, laptop
alarms, 197–200
Max Battery power scheme, 196
meters, 200–201
batteries, clock, 92
behaviors, power, 193, 202
Binary And Script Behaviors setting, 409
BIOS (Basic Input Output System), 81
BITS (Background Intelligent Transfer
Service)
Automatic Updates using, 22
defined, 12
boot volumes, 241
booting, setting options for, 45–46. *See also*
startups
broadband networking
accessing, 376
connection creation, 357–358
defined, 347
protocol, 370
troubleshooting, 376
VPNs, 348
Browser Information Bar, 404–405
browsers. *See* Internet Explorer
buffer overruns, 8

C

cards, 65
Category Control Panel view, 6
CD drives
    Autorun, 140
    burning features, 297
    lettering, 246
    listing, 234
    preventing automatic play, 118
Change permission, 273, 283
Check Disk tool, 423–424
Cipher, 429
circuit cards, 65
Classic appearance for desktop, 121
Classic Control Panel, 6
classic logon prompt
    benefits, 172
    enabling, 174
    options, 172
    permission for changing options, 174
    policies, 230, 231
Classic Start menu
    Administrative Tools, adding, 101, 106
    changing to simple Start menu, 99–100
    customizing, 100–101
    defined, 4–5
    drag-and-drop with, 101
    hiding unused selections, 101, 107
    icon size options, 101
    icons, default desktop, 123
    options, table of, 101
    Personalized menu options, 107
    scrolling options, 101, 102
CLEANMGR.EXE, 36, 37–39
Client For Microsoft Networks
    purpose, 350
    remote access, 370–371
clock settings, 92–98
closing windows, keyboard shortcut, 118
cluster size, 250, 254
Code Signing For Device Drivers policy, 71
color
    matching, configuring, 137–138
    monitor settings, 135–136
    schemes, desktop, 121, 131
commands, keyboard shortcuts, 118–119
compatibility with XP
    applications, checking, 141
    options, setting directly, 149–150
    overview, 147–148
    Program Compatibility Wizard, 148–149
compressing data
    compress old files option, 39
    enabling, 250, 254
    performance issues, 426–427
Computer Administrator account, 164

Computer Browser service, 340
Computer Management console
    accessing, 13, 67
    configuring devices. *See* Device Manager
    disk quotas, configuring, 312–318
    folders, sharing, 286–289
    Manage command removal, 296
    offline files, making available, 302–303
    remote system management, 68
    Services and Applications tools category, 68
    special shares, viewing, 293
    Storage tools category, 68
    System tools category, 68
    tool categories, 68
computer name, viewing, 49–50
Computers Near Me, 296
CONFIG.SYS, 44
configuration files, system, 44–45
Configure Automatic Updates policy, 24
connections
    Always Dial My Default Connection option, 359
    attempts, limiting, 365
    automatic, configuring, 359–360
    broadband. *See* broadband networking
    Dial Whenever A Network Connection Is Not Present option, 359
    dial-up. *See* dial-up connections
    disconnecting automatically, 365
    domain names, 363
    firewall configuration, 433
    identity validation, 368–370
    logon configuration, 363–364
    manual, configuring, 360
    Never Dial A Connection option, 359
    New Connection Wizard, 349, 354–359, 417
    passwords, 363
    prompting users, 364
    proxy configuration, 361–363
    redialing, automatic, 366
    scripts, 361
    wireless, 381–382
    virtual. *See* VPNs (virtual private networks)
Content Indexer, 39
Control Panel
    Category view, 6
    Computer Management console, accessing, 67
    Display utility, 6–7
    Internet Options tool, 402
    Start menu, options, 101
    User Accounts Wizard, 165
    views, 6
Convert utility, 259
cookies, 402–404

copying
files and folders, 469, 473–474
floppy disks, 472
keyboard shortcut for, 118
Crash Detection option, 417
crash dumps, 40, 41
Create Files/Write Data permission, 273
Create Folders/Append Data permission, 273
creating folders, 475
Creator Owner identity, 271
Critical Battery Alarm, 197, 199
cryptography tools. *See* encryption
currency settings, 91
cursor blink rate option, 83
Cut command, 474
cutting, keyboard shortcut, 118
cycling, keyboard shortcut, 118

D

data compression. *See* compressing data
Data Encryption Standard (DESX), 428
data management policies, 215
date settings, 92–98
decryption, 429. *See also* encryption
default gateways
configuring, 329
diagnostic tools, 346
metrics, 331
multiple, configuring, 331–332
specifying, 208
viewing for connections, 339
Delay Restart For Scheduled Installations policy, 24
deleting
Delete permission, 273
Delete Subfolders and Files permission, 273
Display Confirmation Dialog policy, 296
files and folders, 475
keyboard shortcut, 118
denying permissions to, 269
DEP (Data Execution Prevention), 55–56
deployment. *See* program installation
desktop themes
applying, 120
color schemes, 121, 131
customizing, 121
defined, 120
deleting custom themes, 122
directories for, 122
fonts, 131
mouse pointer options, 121
restoring defaults, 120
screen saver options, 121
sounds for events, 121
windows appearances, 121
Windows Classic, 121

Desktop toolbar, 113
desktops
background selection, 122–123
cleaning up, 126–127
colors for backgrounds, 123
context menus, removing, 297
custom content, adding, 124–126
Customize Desktop, accessing, 124
Desktop Gallery, Microsoft, 125
Desktop icon, 468
display appearance, 131–132
embedded browsers, adding, 124–126
icons, default, 123–124
locking, 126
optimization overview, 122
passwords, screen saver, 128
recreating icons, 124
removing default icons, 124
screen savers. *See* screen savers
themes for. *See* desktop themes
video settings, 132
Web pages, 124–126
DESX (Data Encryption Standard), 428
device drivers
16-bit programs, 147
Code Signing For Device Drivers policy, 71
compatibility with XP, 70
configuring, 72–77
defined, 70
digital signatures, 70, 71–72
disabling, 79
driver cache, 70
enabling, 79
error codes, 80–82
error information, 457, 458
files associated with, 72
Hardware Update Wizard, 69
information, viewing, 72
installing, 73–76, 78–79
keyboard devices, 83
manual installation options, 75
monitors, 134–135
mouse devices, 84
MS-DOS programs, 147
policies for searches, 73–74
removing, 77
restoring system if bad, 460
rolling back, 76–77
Safe Mode for removing, 454
Service Pack 2 changes, 67, 70
Setup Information files, 71
troubleshooting, 80–82
uninstalling, 69, 77, 79
unsigned, 71–72
updating, 67, 69, 73–76
video adapters, 133–134
wireless adapter, 381
XP library, 70

Device Manager
  accessing, 69
  Disable option, 69
  disabling drivers, 79
  driver information, viewing, 72
  Enable option, 69
  enabling drivers, 79
  hidden devices, 70
  installing drivers, 79
  Properties option, 69
  removing drivers, 77
  right-click options, 69
  rolling back drivers, 76–77
  Scan For Hardware Changes option, 69
  Unistall option, 69
  uninstalling drivers, 77
  Update Driver option, 69
  views, 69–70
  Warning symbols, 70
devices
  configuring. *See* Device Manager
  drivers. *See* device drivers
  error codes, 80–82
  external, 66
  keyboards, 83
  legacy, errors from, 82
  mouse. *See* mice
  NICs. *See* network adapters
  Plug and Play compatibility. *See* Plug and
    Play
  sound volume control, 86–87
  troubleshooting, 80–82
  types of, 65–66
  updating drivers, 67, 69
  video adapters, 132–138
DFRG.MSC, 36
DFS tab, 297
DHCP (Dynamic Host Configuration
  Protocol)
  alternate private IP addressing, 207–208
  automatic private addressing, 341
  configuring, 341–343
  diagnostic tools, 346
  DNS configuration, 332
  IP addressing, 206–208, 341
  leases, 339, 341–343
  multiple default gateways, 331
  releasing leases, 342–343
  user movement issues, 342
  WINS configuration, 335, 336
diagnostic startup mode, 43
dialing locations, 350–353
dialing rules, 350–353, 366–367, 375
dialog boxes, keyboard shortcut, 119
dial-up connections
  accessing, 373–374
  account information, setting, 355

  alternate phone numbers, 367–368
  Client For Microsoft Networks, 350
  crashes from, 375
  creating, 350–357
  dial tone missing, 375
  dialing rules, 350–353, 366–367, 375
  digital phones, 356
  domain access failure, 375
  domain-wide, 354, 357
  failed connections, 375
  firewall, 356
  into workplace, creating, 356–357
  ISPs, creating to, 354–356
  locations, 350–353
  logon domains, 357
  networking. *See* dial-up networking
  passwords, 355, 374
  phone numbers for, selecting, 374
  phone numbers for, setting, 354, 357,
    367–368
  protocols, 370
  redialing automatically, 366
  remote access, creating for, 350–357
  troubleshooting, 375
Dialup identity, 271
dial-up networking
  connections. *See* dial-up connections
  defined, 347
  modem pools, 347–348
  typical configuration, 347
  VPNs, 349
directories
  Active Directory, 23, 164
  compressing, 426–427
  encrypting, 428–429
DirectX Diagnostic tool, 37
disconnections, automatic, 365
Disk Cleanup tool, 36, 37–39
Disk Defragmenter tool, 36, 424–425
Disk Management tool
  accessing, 236
  active partitions, marking, 242
  Check Disk from, 423–424
  converting basic to dynamic disks,
    244–245
  deleting volumes, 258–259
  Disk List view, 236
  drive letter assignment, 256–257
  extended partition creation, 247
  extending volumes, 255
  formatting drives, 255–256
  Graphical View, 236
  initializing hard disks, 242
  logical drive creation, 247–250
  moving dynamic disks, 261–262
  partitioning basic disks, 247–250
  primary partition creation, 247

Disk Management tool, *continued*
  Properties view, 237
  purpose, 235
  remote drives, examining, 236
  shadow copies, 319–321
  simple volume creation, 251–254
  status messages, 262–264
  troubleshooting, 262–264
  volume label assignment, 257–258
  Volume List view, 236
disk quotas
  administrators not limited by, 310
  creating entries, 314–315
  deleting entries, 316
  disabling, 318
  enabling, 311–313
  exporting settings, 317–318
  importing settings, 317–318
  local vs. remote volumes, 311
  logging, 313
  modifying entries, 315
  permission required for setting, 311
  policies, 215–217
  purpose, 310
  SIDs, 311
  user view, 311
  viewing entries, 313
  warnings, 310
DiskPart tool
  active partitions, marking, 243
  purpose, 238
display appearance, 131–132. *See also*
    desktops
Display utility, 6–7
distribution groups, 162
DMA (direct memory access), 29
DNS (Domain Name Service)
  browsing test, 340
  configuring, 332–334
  defined, 332
  DHCP for server addresses, 332
  diagnostic tools, 346
  dynamic updates, 334
  multiple servers for, 333
  pinging, 340
  resolver caches, 343–344
  server address configuration, 330
  suffixes, appending, 333
domain group policies, 211
domain user accounts
  changing user access levels, 177–178
  defaults, 176
  defined, 160
  granting access to workstations, 176–177
  logon names, 160
  Other, 176
  overview, 175–176

  password selection, 178–179
  passwords, 161
  public certificates, 161
  removing user access, 179
  resetting passwords, 178–179
  Restricted, 176
  security issues, 176
  SIDs, 160
  Standard, 176
  user names, 160
domains
  GPO updates, 11–12
  Internet time configuration, 98
  service pack policies, 11–12
  user accounts. *See* domain user accounts
  viewing names, 49–50
double-clicking mice
  configuring settings, 84
  defined, 7
  file type associations, 299–300
Dr. Watson, 37, 39–41
driver cache, 70
drivers. *See* device drivers
drives
  basic. *See* basic disks
  CD. *See* CD drives
  defined, 66
  designators, 246, 249, 253
  DVD. *See* DVD drives
  file systems for. *See* file systems
  hard. *See* hard disks
  Hide These Specified Drives In My
    Computer, 296, 298–299
  icons representing, 468
  letter assignment, 256–257, 262
  logical. *See* logical drives
  NTFS. *See* NTFS
  optimization overview, 422
  paths, 246, 256–257
  properties of, viewing from Windows
    Explorer, 475–477
  reducing space usage, 422
  removable storage. *See* removable storage
    devices
DRWTSN32.EXE, 37, 39–41
dump files, 59
DVD drives
  Autorun, 140
  listing, 234
DXDIAG.EXE, 37
dynamic disks
  advantages, 238, 239
  cluster size, 254
  compression option, 254
  converting to basic disks, 244–245
  defined, 234
  drive letter assignment, 253, 262

extending volumes, 254–255
external hard drives as, 240
file system selection, 254
formatting, 253–254
labeling, 254
mounting volumes in NTFS folders, 253
moving to new systems, 261–262
purpose, 239
quick format option, 254
RAID level 0, 239
sector size for conversions to, 244
simple volume creation, 251–254
size of volumes, setting, 252
spanning, 239, 251
striped, 239, 251
volumes. *See* dynamic volumes
Dynamic Host Configuration Protocol. *See*
    DHCP (Dynamic Host Configuration
    Protocol)
dynamic IP addresses, 206, 328, 330. *See also*
    DHCP (Dynamic Host Configuration
    Protocol
dynamic volumes
    advantages, 239
    cluster size, 254
    compression option, 254
    creating, 251–254
    defined, 234
    drive letter assignment, 253
    extending, 254–255
    file system selection, 254
    formatting, 253–254
    labeling, 254
    mounting in NTFS folders, 253
    size, setting, 252

E

EFS (Encrypting File System), 428
e-mail invitations, Remote Assistance, 446,
    447
embedded browsers, adding to desktop,
    124–126
Enable Client-side Targeting policy, 24
encryption
    data files, 428–429
    HTTPS, 415
    Offline File policy, 218
energy settings. *See* power settings
Entire Network, 296
environment variables, 56–57
error reporting
    areas covered by, 19
    configuring, 19–20
    disabling, 21
    purpose, 18
    setting options, 60
    troubleshooting using, 19

errors
    detection, 437–438
    driver information, 457, 458
    hardware based, 80–82, 459
    logging, 31, 457. *See also* logging
    low resource based, 458
    Microsoft Knowledge Base for help with,
        458
    names, 457
    new components, resulting from, 458
    numbering, 457
    Online Crash Analysis feature, 458
    recommendations, 457
    reporting. *See* error reporting
    Stop errors, 457–459
    system file based, 459
Event Viewer, 438
Everyone group, 283
Everyone identity, 271
execution protection, 9
expanding compressed data, 427
extended partitions
    creating, 247
    defined, 233
    deleting, 259
    purpose, 239
external devices, 66

F

fast user switching, 174–175
FAT file system, 246, 249, 254, 265
FAT16, features of, 463–464
FAT32, features of, 463–464
Favorites, Start menu, 101
Favorites, Internet Explorer, 389–391, 418
File And Printer Sharing For Microsoft
    Networks
    defined, 371
    exempting for firewalls, 434
    mapping, required, 377
    remote access, required, 370
file extensions, associations of, 299–300
file invitations, Remote Assistance, 446, 447
file management policies, 215
file naming, 465–466
file security
    FAT vs. NTFS, 265
    file sharing, 267
    ownership, 276–277
    permissions. *See* permissions
file sharing
    $ (dollar sign), 292
    ADMIN$ share, 292
    administration, shares intended for,
        292–293
    Change permission, 283
    Computer Management, 286–289, 293

file sharing, *continued*
connecting to folders, 289–292
creating shared folders, 284–289
defined, 265
FAT vs. NTFS, 265
Full Control permission, 282
group permissions, 283
hidden shares, 284, 292
IPC$ share, 293
model selection, 267
My Network Places, 289–291
names for shares, 284
net share command, 293
network drive creation, 291–292
New Share button, 286
open files, viewing, 293
permissions, 267, 282–289
PRINT$ share, 293
Read permission, 283
security issues, 267, 283
shadow copies, 318–321
simple, 266, 267
special shares, 292–293
standard, 266–267, 282
tools, 284
user sessions, viewing, 293
Windows Explorer for, 284–286, 289
File Signature Verification utility, 37, 42
file systems
FAT, 246, 249, 254, 265
FAT16, 463–464
FAT32, 463–464
NTFS. *See* NTFS
selecting, 249, 254
file type associations, 299–300
files
compressed, displaying, 469
compressing, 426–427
copying, 469, 473–474
cutting, 474
deleting, 475
encrypting, 428–429
hidden, displaying, 469
managing with Windows Explorer,
466–469
naming conventions, 465–466
ownership, 276–277
pasting, 474
properties of, viewing, 477–478
renaming, 475
security options, 478. *See also* file security
selecting, 473
shadow copies, 318–321
sharing, 478. *See also* file sharing
summary information, 478
tab customization, 478
version information, 478
Web Sharing, 478

firewalls
application exemptions, 434
connection configuration, 433
dial-up connections, 356
enabling, 432–433
exceptions configuration, 434–436
File And Printer Sharing, 434
FTP exemptions, 435–436
HTTP port exemptions, 435–436
laptop configuration, 433
mode of action, 432
Plug and Play with, 434
policies, 223, 432
purpose, 432
remote access, 372–373
Remote Assistance, 434, 446
Remote Desktop, 434
Security Center, 431
Service Pack 2 changes, 8
TCP port exemptions, 435–436
UDP port exemptions, 435–436
Windows Firewall. *See* Windows Firewall
floppy disks
copying, 472
formatting, 472
folders
compressed, displaying, 469
connecting to shared, 289–292
copying, 469, 473–474
creating, 475
customizing views, 471
cutting, 474
deleting, 475
Folder Options menus, removing, 297
Folder Tasks view, 470
global view settings, 471–472
hidden, displaying, 469
managing with Windows Explorer,
466–469
MS-DOS names, 465–466
naming conventions, 465–466
ownership, 276–277
pasting, 474
properties of, viewing, 477–478
renaming, 475
security options, 478
selecting, 473
shadow copies, 318–321
sharing, 478. *See also* file sharing
fonts, 131
formatting drives
cluster size, 250
compression, enabling, 250
Disk Management, 255–256
file system creation, 246–247
file system selection, 249
options, 249–250, 253–254
quick format option, 250
volume labels, 250

FSUtil tool, 238
FTP, firewalls with, 435–436
Full Control permission, 269, 273, 282
Full Power scheme, 195

G

gateways
  default. *See* default gateways
  wireless. *See* base stations, wireless
Get Help From Microsoft utility, 15
Go To A Windows Web Site Forum utility, 15
GPOs (Group Policy Objects)
  access to drives, 298–299
  disk quota options, 311–313
  managing. *See* Group Policy Console
  service packs, updating for, 11–12
  viewing, 31
  Windows Explorer policies, 296–298
group policies
  accessing local, 210–211
  application sequence, 210
  Browser User Interface policies, 391–395
  configuring, 214
  connection, settings, 398–399
  console for managing. *See* Group Policy console
  creating, 211
  data management policies, 215
  disabling, 214
  disk quota policies, 215–217
  domain group policies, 211
  editing, 211
  enabling, 214
  file management policies, 215
  importance, 209
  Internet Explorer management, 417–418
  Internet Explorer URL customization, 388–391
  Internet program defaults, setting, 396–397
  legacy run lists, 232
  local. *See* local group policies
  logoff script assignment, 229
  logon policies, 230–232
  logon script assignment, 229
  network access policies, 223–224
  Offline File policies, 218–223
  OU group policies, 211
  policy-based startup programs, 231
  precedence rules, 210
  prioritizing, 211
  proxy settings, IE, 400–402
  purpose, 209
  Remote Assistance policies, 224–226
  run-once lists, 232
  script policies, 226–229
  security zones for IE, 411–413
  shutdown script assignment, 228–229
  site group policies, 211
  startup policies, 230–232
  startup script assignment, 228–229
  startup sequence, 210
  System Restore policies, 217–218
  template management, 214–215
  templates, administrative, 213
Group Policy console
  accessing local group policies, 210
  accessing site, domain, and OU policies, 211
  adding templates, 214–215
  configuring policies, 214
  creating policies, 211
  disk quota policies, 216–217
  editing policies, 211
  logon policies, 231–232
  network policies, 224
  nodes of, main, 212
  Offline File policies, 218–223
  prioritizing policies, 211
  Proxy Settings policy, 400
  Remote Assistance, 225–226
  removing templates, 215
  script policies, 227–229
  startup policies, 231–232
  subnodes, 212
  System Restore policies, 217–218
  viewing templates, 213
Group Policy Objects. *See* GPOs (Group Policy Objects)
groups
  adding local members, 186
  Administrators, 163
  assigning permissions, 269–270
  Backup Operators, 163
  creating local, 185–186
  defined, 159
  deleting, 188
  distribution, 162
  Everyone, 283
  file sharing permissions, 283
  Guests, 163
  local, 162, 185–186
  names, 162
  Network Configuration Operators, 163
  permissions for, 272
  policies. *See* group policies
  Power Users, 163, 165
  purpose, 162
  Remote Desktop Users, 163
  Replicators, 164
  security, 162
  SIDs, 163
  special identity groups, table of, 271
  types of, 162
  Users, 164

Guest account, 161, 187–188
Guests group, 163
GUI (Graphical User Interface). *See* interface
    design

H

hard disks
    active partitions, 241, 242–243
    basic. *See* basic disks
    boot partitions, 241
    Check Disk tool, 423–424
    cluster size, 250
    compressing files, 250, 254, 426–427
    converting basic to dynamic disks,
        244–245
    creating dynamic volumes, 251–254
    defragmenting, 424–425
    deleting partitions, 258–259
    detailed property information on, 237
    Disk Management tool, 235–237
    disk quota policies, 215–217
    disk quotas, enabling on, 311–313
    DiskPart tool, 238
    drive designators, 246, 249, 253
    drive letter assignment, 256–257, 262
    drive paths, 246
    dynamic. *See* dynamic disks
    encrypting, 428–429
    error messages, 261
    errors on, checking for, 423–424
    external, 235, 240
    FAT, 246, 249, 254, 265
    file systems for. *See* FAT file system; file
        systems; NTFS
    file sharing as network drives, 291–292
    formatting, 246–247, 255–256
    fragmentation, 424–425
    FSUtil tool, 238
    graphical view, 236
    Hide These Specified Drives In My
        Computer, 296, 298–299
    icons representing, 468
    initializing, 241–242
    installing, 241–242
    lettering scheme, 246, 256–257, 262
    listing, 234
    logical. *See* logical drives
    low-level meta data, probing, 238
    mixing dynamic and basic, 239
    moving dynamic disks, 261–262
    My Computer, management using,
        234–235
    network, listing, 235
    NTFS. *See* NTFS
    numbering, 233
    optimization overview, 422
    partitioning. *See* partitions

    power conservation mode, 194, 199
    preparing for data, 245
    preventing access from Windows
        Explorer, 296, 298–299
    recovering failed, 261
    reducing space usage, 422
    remote drives, examining, 236
    repairing errors on, 423, 424
    scripted management, 238
    sharing as network drives, 291–292
    sharing files. *See* file sharing
    spanning, 239, 251
    status messages, 262–264
    striped, 239, 251
    summary information view, 236
    system partitions, 241
    troubleshooting, 262–264
    USB-attached, 235
    volume labels, 250, 257–258
    Volume List view, 236
    volumes. *See* volumes
hardware
    configuring. *See* Device Manager
    Conflicts/Sharing node, 29
    disabling, 69
    drivers. *See* device drivers
    enabling, 69
    errors from, 80–82, 459
    external devices, 66
    firmware errors, 81
    keyboards, 83
    legacy, errors from, 82
    memory devices. *See* memory, physical
    mice. *See* mice
    network. *See* network adapters
    Plug and Play compatibility. *See* Plug and
        Play
    profiles. *See* hardware profiles
    properties, viewing, 69
    registry corruption errors, 81
    resource conflict errors, 81
    resources, viewing, 29
    scanning for changes, 69
    sound volume control, 86–87
    troubleshooting, 80–82
    types of devices, 65–66
    uninstalling, 69
    updating drivers, 67. *See also* Hardware
        Update Wizard
    viewing system information, 28
    Windows Explorer Hardware tab,
        removing, 297
hardware profiles
    accessing options, 203
    availability, 203
    copying, 205
    default profile, selecting, 203

deleting, 205
docked and undocked, configuring, 204–205
permissions required to configure, 203
properties, viewing, 205
purpose, 203
renaming, 205
waiting for on startup, 203
Hardware Troubleshooter, 80
Hardware Update Wizard
    accessing, 69
    error codes, 81–82
    manual install options, 75
    policies for searches, 73–74
    updating drivers with, 73–76
headphone configuration, 87–88
help. See help system; Help And Support Center; Help And Support service
Help And Support Center
    Ask A Friend To Help utility, 15
    Backup tool, 36
    DirectX Diagnostic tool, 37
    Disk Cleanup tool, 36, 37–39
    Disk Defragmenter tool, 36
    Dr. Watson, 37, 39–41
    File Signature Verification utility, 37, 42
    Get Help From Microsoft utility, 15
    Go To A Windows Web Site Forum utility, 15
    Network Diagnostics tool, 36, 37, 345
    Offer Remote Assistance tool, 36
    overview, 14–15
    Remote Assistance for. See Remote Assistance
    System Configuration, 36, 42–48
    System Restore utility, 37
    tools, displaying, 36
Help And Support service
    application framework, 16
    defined, 12
    files used by, 16
    Status utility based on, 18
    Support account, 161
    SVCHOST.EXE, 16
help system. See also Help And Support Center; Help And Support service
    application framework, 16
    components, 14
    HelpAssistant account, 161
    keyboard shortcut for displaying, 119
    online support default page, 388–389
    Status utility, 16–18
hibernation, 194, 202
hidden files and folders, displaying, 469
hiding drives in Windows Explorer, 296
High Power scheme, 195
High security level, IE, 410–411

highlighting text, 118
hints for passwords, 170
Home/Office Desk power scheme, 195
homes pages, Internet Explorer, 388–389
HTML editor default, 396
HTTP, firewalls with, 435–436
HTTPS (Hypertext Transfer Protocol Secure), 415

I
icons
    desktop, managing, 123–124
    notification area management, 111–112
    Windows Explorer, 467–469
IEEE 802.11 wireless specification, 378–379
information, system. See system information
inheritance of permissions
    advantages, 278
    basic permissions, 271
    effective, determining, 281
    examples, 278
    overview, 277–278
    parent folders, 277
    propagation, 278
    restoring, 280
    stopping, 279
    troubleshooting, 281
    viewing, 278–279
insertion points, 118
Installation Restore Point snapshots, 61
installing applications. See program installation
installing hardware devices
    Add New Hardware Wizard, 78–79
    non Plug and Play, 78–79
    Plug and Play, 66, 434
    updating drivers, 67
installing Windows XP, 456–457
InstallShield, 140
Interactive identity, 271
interface design
    changes from previous OSs, 4–7
    desktop configuration. See desktops
    Start menu, 4–6. See also Classic Start menu
    themes, 6–7
international settings, 91
Internet Connection Firewall, 223, 431
Internet Connection sharing policies, 223
Internet connections changes, Service Pack 2, 8
Internet Explorer
    Active Content Blocked options, 404
    ActiveX options, 405–406, 410
    add-on options, 406, 418
    Advanced tab policies, 418
    Binary And Script Behaviors, 409

Internet Explorer, *continued*
  blocking sites, 417
  calendar default, 396
  CD content policies, 418
  connection policies, 417, 418
  contact list default, 396
  cookies, 402–404
  Crash Detection option, 417
  default programs policies, 418
  desktop, embedding in, 124–126
  e-mail default, 396
  Favorites, setting with Group Policy, 389–391
  Favorites option, 418
  file download options, 405, 410, 418
  history files, deleting, 402
  homes pages, setting with Group Policy, 388–389
  HTML editor default, 396
  HTTPS specification, 415
  IFRAME options, 410
  Information Bar, 404–405
  Internet phone default, 396
  Internet zone, 410, 413–414
  Local Intranet zone, 410, 414–415
  local machine security zone policy, 412
  Logon parameter, 411
  logos, customizing, 392–394
  newsgroups default, 396
  offline files configuration, 306–308, 309
  online support pages group policy, 388–389
  plug-ins, 405–406
  policies, 417–418
  pop-up blocker options, 405, 407–409, 417
  Privacy settings, 403–404
  program defaults, setting, 396–397
  proxy settings, 400–402
  restricted protocols options, 410
  Restricted Sites zone, 409, 416–417
  scripting options, 411
  search bar pages, setting with Group Policy, 388–389
  security levels, table of, 410–411
  security options, 404–405
  security settings policies, 418
  security zones. *See* security zones, Internet Explorer
  Service Pack 2, 8, 404–409
  Software Blocked options, 405
  Software Channel Permissions, 411
  Software Install Blocked options, 405
  space for temporary files, 402
  temporary files, 402–404, 418
  titles, customizing, 391–392
  toolbar buttons, customizing, 394–395
  toolbar policies, 418

  Trusted Sites zone, 410, 415–416
  URLs, customizing with Group Policy, 388–391
Internet Settings area, 30
Internet time
  configuring, 93–98
  domain configuration, 98
  firewall requirements, 97
  importance, 92
  operation, 92–93
  server, 92
  SNTP, 93
  troubleshooting, 98
  Windows Time service, 92
  Windows Time service settings, table of, 93–96
  workgroup configuration, 97–98
Internet zone, 410, 413–414
intranets
  Local Intranet zone, 410
  proxy servers with, 401
invitations, Remote Assistance
  accepting, 450–451
  buddy list method, 446, 447
  creating, 447–449
  deleting, 453
  e-mail method, 446, 447
  expiring, 453
  file method, 446, 447
  format, 449
  messages in, 447
  MSN method, 446, 447
  passwords, 446, 449, 450
  resending, 453
  status of, checking, 452
  time to live, 448
  types of, 445–446
IP addressing
  alternative DHCP, 207–208, 328, 330
  automatic private (APIPA), 341
  configuration methods, 327–328
  DHCP for. *See* DHCP (Dynamic Host Configuration Protocol)
  duplicate addresses, 341
  dynamic address configuration, 330
  dynamic method, 328
  manual method, 327
  pinging, 328
  private address ranges, 328
  static address configuration, 328–330
  subnet masks, 208
  troubleshooting, 341
  wireless networking, 382
IPC$ share, 293
ipconfig command
  DHCP lease renewal, 343
  DNS resolver cache flushing, 344

multiple connections, selecting from, 343
network adapter settings, 339
IPSec (IP Security), 349
IRQs, 29
ISPs, dial-up connections to, 354–356

K

key rings
    adding, 180–181
    defined, 180
    password field, 181
    removing entries, 182
    server field, 180
    user name field, 181
keyboard shortcuts, 118–119
keyboards, 83

L

L2TP (Layer 2 Tunneling Protocol), 349, 370
LAN connection policies, 224. *See also*
    networks
language settings, 91
laptops
    alarms, 193, 197–200
    alternative IP addresses, 207–208, 330
    Always On scheme, 195
    basic disks, 240
    behavior options, 193
    creating power schemes, 196–197
    default gateway specification, 208
    default schemes, 195–196
    deleting power schemes, 197
    DHCP for IP addresses, 206–208, 330
    energy settings, 129–131, 194–197, 202
    firewall configuration, 433
    Full Power scheme, 195
    hibernation, 194, 202
    High Power scheme, 195
    Home/Office Desk scheme, 195
    IP addresses, 206–208, 330
    Long Life scheme, 195
    Max Battery scheme, 196
    Minimal Power Management scheme, 195
    network configuration, 205–208
    Normal scheme, 195
    Portable Laptop scheme, 195
    power meters, 193, 200–201
    power schemes, 193, 194–197
    power settings, 193–203
    Presentation scheme, 195
    remote access. *See* remote access
    standby mode, 202
    System hibernates mode, 194
    System standby mode, 194
    Turn off hard disks mode, 194
    Turn off monitor mode, 194
Last Known Good Configuration option, 454

Layer 2 Tunneling Protocol (L2TP), 349, 370
legacy run list policy, 230, 232
Limited account, 164–165
Links toolbar, 113
Linux, active partition for, 242
List Folder Contents permission, 269, 272
List Folder/Read Data permission, 273
LMHOSTS file, 334– 336
local area connections
    configuration information, viewing,
        338–339
    creation, 327
    default gateways, viewing, 339
    DHCP leases, 339
    diagnostic tools, 344–346
    disabling, 336
    DNS for. *See* DNS (Domain Name Service)
    duration, viewing, 337
    dynamic IP address configuration, 330
    enabling, 336
    group policies, 398–399
    IP addressing, 327–330, 338
    ipconfig command, 339
    MAC addresses, 338
    packets sent readings, 337
    renaming, 339
    renewing DHCP leases, 342
    speed, viewing, 337
    static IP address configuration, 328–330
    status, viewing, 337
    subnet mask, viewing, 338
    TCP/IP installation, 326
    troubleshooting, 339
    WINS, 334–336
local group policies
    accessing, 210–211
    defined, 209
    Group Policy console, 210
local groups
    adding members, 186
    creating, 185–186
    defined, 162
Local Intranet zone, 410, 414–415
local permissions. *See* NTFS permissions
local user accounts
    Administrator, 161, 165
    creating, 165–166, 183–184
    defaults installed, 161
    defined, 160
    deleting, 188
    denying network access to, 188
    enabling, 187
    Guest, 161, 187–188
    HelpAssistant, 161
    LocalService, 162
    LocalSystem, 162
    logon names, 160

local user accounts, *continued*
   logs, restricting viewing of, 188
   NetworkService, 162
   passwords, 161, 167–171
   public certificates, 161
   renaming, 187–188
   securing Guest accounts, 187–188
   selecting access levels, 166
   Shut Down right, disabling, 188
   SIDs, 160
   Support, 161
   User Account utility, 165–166
   user names, 160
   workstation access, granting, 165–166
Local Users And Groups
   adding members, 186
   creating accounts, 183–184
   creating groups, 185–186
   deleting accounts, 188
   enabling accounts, 187
   renaming accounts, 188
localization settings, 91
LocalService account, 162
LocalSystem account, 162
locations, dialing, 350–353
locking desktops, 126
Log Off command, 101
logging
   accessing logs, 438
   Application log, 437–438
   disk quota warnings, 313
   errors, 457
   Event Viewer, 438
   failure audits, 437
   information events, 437
   information in entries, 437
   offline file events, 218
   paths for, setting, 40
   restricting users from viewing, 188
   Security log, 437–438
   success audits, 437
   System log, 437–438, 457
   types of entries in, 437
   types of logs, 437
   viewing logs, 31
   warnings, 437
   WBEM, 33–34
   WMI settings, 33–35
logging on. *See* logons
logical drives
   basic disks, creating for, 247–250
   conversions to dynamic volumes, 244
   deleting, 258–259
   drive letter assignment, 249
   purpose, 239
logoff script policies, 227, 229

logons
   accounts associated with. *See* accounts
   classic. *See* classic logon prompt
   denying access by removing users, 179
   Internet Explorer Logon parameter risks,
     411
   names, 160
   policies, 230–232
   script policies, 226, 227, 229
   Secure Logon requirement, 179
   Welcome Screen. *See* Welcome Screen
logs. *See* logging
Long Life power scheme, 195
Low Battery Alarm, 197, 197–198
Low security level, IE, 410–411

M

MAC addresses, 338
maintenance, Service Pack 2 changes, 9
managing applications, 150
manual connections, 360
manual IP addressing, 327
manual restore points, 61, 461
mapping network drives, 296
Master File Table (MFT), 246, 260
Max Battery power scheme, 196
Medium security level, IE, 410–411
memory, physical
   16-bit program issues, 147
   defined, 66
   DEP configuration options, 55–56
   management options, 420
   optimization, 420
   Service Pack 2 features, 8
   usage options, 52
menus
   changing Start menu views, 99–100
   Classic Start. *See* Classic Start menu
   optimizations, 420–421
   reasons for optimizing, 99
   simple Start. *See* Simple Start menu
   Start. *See* Start menu
meters, power, 193, 200–201
MFT (Master File Table), 246, 260
mice
   configuring settings, 84
   double-clicking, 7
   Mouse utility, 8
   new features, 7–8
   pointer options, 121
   right-clicking, 7
Microsoft Internet Explorer. *See* Internet
   Explorer
Microsoft Knowledge Base, 458
Microsoft .NET Passport. *See* .NET Passports
Microsoft Office, 38
Microsoft Outlook Express. *See* Outlook
   Express

Microsoft Windows Explorer. *See* Windows Explorer
Microsoft Windows Firewall. *See* Windows Firewall
Microsoft Windows Installer, 140, 144
Microsoft Windows Server 2003, 3
Minimal Power Management power scheme, 195
mobile networking. *See also* remote access
  component configuration, 370–372
  defined, 347–348
  dial-up connections, 350–357
  identity validation, 368–370
  modem pools, 347–348
  proxy servers, configuring, 361–363
  servers, 347
modems pools, 347–348
Modify permission, 269, 272
MOF (Managed Object Format), 33
monitors
  adapter drivers, 133–134
  checking settings, 132
  color matching, 137–138
  color settings, 135–136
  drivers, 134–135
  energy settings, 129–131
  refresh rates, 136–137
  resolution settings, 135–136
  screen savers. *See* screen savers
mouse. *See* mice
moving files and folders, 474–475
.msi files, 144
MS Software Shadow Copy Provider, 12
MSCONFIG.EXE, 36, 42–48
MS-DOS, 147, 465–466
MSINFO32.EXE, 29–31
MSN invitations, Remote Assistance, 446, 447
MsRcIncident files, 446, 450
My Computer, 234–235
My Computer Information
  accessing, 28, 29
  data reported by, 28
  defined, 27
  options, 28
  source of data for, 28
  troubleshooting, 29
My Documents, 101, 468
My Network Places
  browsing service, 340
  Computers Near Me, 296
  Entire Network, 296
  icon for, 468
  shadow copies, viewing, 320
  shared folders, accessing, 289–291
My Pictures, 101
My Recent Documents, 296

N

naming conventions
  files and folders, 465–466
  MS-DOS, 465–466
Net Diagnostics tool. *See* Network Diagnostic tool
.NET Passports, 182–183
net share command, 293
NetBIOS, 334–336
NetMeeting, 396
NetMeeting Remote Desktop Sharing, 12
network access policies, 223–224
network adapters
  alternative IP addresses, 330
  configuration information, viewing, 338–339
  default gateways, viewing, 339
  DHCP leases, 339
  drivers for, 326
  dynamic IP address configuration, 330
  installation, 326
  IP address, viewing, 338
  MAC addresses, 338
  multiple per computer, selecting from, 343
  renaming connections, 339
  static IP address configuration, 329–330
  subnet mask, viewing, 338
  troubleshooting, 339
network bridge policy, 223
Network Configuration Operators group, 163
Network Connections. *See also* connections
  disabling, 336
  DNS configuration, 332–334
  dynamic IP address configuration, 330
  enabling, 336
  Start menu, options for, 101
  static IP address configuration, 329–330
  TCP/IP installation, 326–327
Network Diagnostics tool, 36, 37, 345
network drives
  file sharing with, 291–292
  mapping, 296
  viewing. *See* My Network Places
Network Identification Wizard, 50
Network identity, 271
networks
  adapters. *See* network adapters
  alternative IP addresses, 330
  broadband. *See* broadband networking
  browsing test, 340
  component requirements, 325
  configuring laptops for, 205–208
  connections for. *See* connections
  default gateway specification, 329, 331–332
  diagnostic tools, 344–346
  DNS for. *See* DNS (Domain Name Service)

networks, *continued*
  dynamic IP address configuration, 330
  group policies for, 398–399
  installation overview, 325
  IP addressing, 327–330
  local connections. *See* local area
    connections
  mobile. *See* mobile networking
  My Network Places, 289–291, 296, 320,
    340
  pinging, 328, 340
  protocols for connecting, 370
  security changes with Service Pack 2, 8
  startup policy, 230
  subnet masks, 328, 329
  TCP/IP installation, 326–327
  VPNs. *See* VPNs (virtual private networks)
  WINS, 334–336
  wireless. *See* wireless networking
  wizard for connections. *See* New
    Connection Wizard
NetworkService account, 162
New Connection Wizard
  accessing, 349
  broadband connection creation, 357–358
  ISPs, dial-up connections to, 354–356
  policy, 417
  remote connection creation, 356–357
  VPN connection creation, 358–359
NICs. *See* network adapters
No Auto-restart For Scheduled Automatic
  Updates Installations policy, 24
no execute (NX) feature, 9, 55, 56
Normal power scheme, 195
normal startup mode, 43
notification area
  adding Startup programs, 111
  defined, 110
  hiding inactive icons, 112
  menu display for items, 110
  removing Startup programs, 111
NTBACKUP.EXE, 36
NTFS
  compressing data, 426–427
  converting disks to, 259–260
  defined, 246–247
  encrypting files, 428–429
  permissions. *See* NTFS permissions
  security overview, 265
  selecting during formatting, 249, 254
  versions 4 vs. 5, table of features, 464
NTFS permissions
  basic permissions, 268–272
  effective, determining, 281
  inheritance, 277–280
  key issues, 267
  special permissions, 272–275
NX (no execute) feature, 9, 55, 56

O

Offer Remote Assistance tool, 36
Office, Microsoft, 38
office setup files, 38
Offline File policies
  administratively controlling availability of
    files, 220–221
  allowing, 218
  cache options, 218, 222–223
  configuring, 219–220
  encryption, 218
  event logging, 218
  levels, 218
  locating, 218
  locking down, 219
  logoff policy, 218
  prohibited paths, 219
  redirected folders, 219
  server disconnect polity, 218
  subfolders, 218
  synchronization options, 219, 221–222
  table of, 218–219
offline files
  caching options, 302–303, 309–310
  defined, 39, 301
  disk space usage options, 309–310
  enabling computers for, 304–305
  Exception List, 304
  making folders available as, 301–303
  manually making available, 306
  operation, 301
  policies. *See* Offline File policies
  preventing availability, 303–305
  purpose, 301
  sharing folders step, 302
  synchronization, 301, 305, 307–309
  viewing, 305
  Web pages, 306–308, 309
Online Crash Analysis feature, 458
online support default page, 388–389
optimizations
  application removal, 421–422
  compressing disks, 426–427
  defragmenting disks, 424–425
  memory management options, 420
  menu system performance, 420–421
  process removal, 421–422
  processor scheduling options, 419–420
  services removal, 421–422
Other accounts, 176
OU (organizational unit) group policies, 211
Outlook Express
  changes with Service Pack 2, 8
  titles, customizing, 391–392
ownership of files and folders, 276–277

P

paging files
  configuration options, 53–54
  management options, 420
partitions
  active, 241, 242–243
  basic disks, creating for, 247–250
  boot, 241
  defined, 233
  deleting, 258–259
  drive letter assignment, 249, 256–257
  formatting, 255–256
  mounting in NTFS folders, 249
  primary. *See* primary partitions
  size specification, 248
  system, 241
passports. *See* .NET Passports
passwords
  adding key ring entries, 180–181
  changing for local accounts, 169
  connections, 355, 363
  creating for workgroup user accounts,
    167–168
  dial-up connections, 355
  encrypted data issues, 167, 178
  hints, 170
  invitations, Remote Assistance, 446, 449,
    450
  key rings, 180–182
  management overview, 180
  recovering for local accounts, 169–171
  remote access validation, 369
  removing from local accounts, 169
  reset disks, 170–171, 178
  resetting for domain user accounts,
    178–179
  screen saver configuration 128
  Secure Logon requirement, 179
  secure remote access, 369
  storage, 180–182
  user accounts, 161
  workstation user accounts, 178–179
pasting, 118
PDAs (Personal Digital Assistants), 66
performance
  application removal, 421–422
  compressed disks, 426–427
  defragmenting disks, 424–425
  memory management options, 420
  menu system optimizations, 420–421
  process removal, 421–422
  processor scheduling options, 419–420
  services removal, 421–422
  startup programs, disabling, 422
permissions
  ACLs, 268
  Anonymous Logon identity, 271

  assigning to users, 269–270
  Authenticated Users identity, 271
  basic permissions, 268–273
  Change permission, 273, 283
  Create Files/Write Data, 273
  Create Folders/Append Data, 273
  Creator Owner identity, 271
  Delete, 273
  Delete Subfolders and Files, 273
  denying to users, 269
  Dialup identity, 271
  effective, determining, 281
  Everyone identity, 271
  file ownership, 276–277
  file sharing, 267, 282–289
  Full Control, 269, 273, 282
  groups, 272
  inheritance, 271, 277–281
  Interactive identity, 271
  key issues, 267
  List Folder Contents, 269, 272
  List Folder/Read Data, 273
  local. *See* NTFS permissions
  locating groups, 270
  Modify, 269, 272
  Network identity, 271
  NTFS. *See* NTFS permissions
  planning, 271
  program installation requirements,
    141–142
  Read, 269, 272
  Read & Execute, 269, 272
  Read Attributes, 273
  Read permission, 273, 283
  recommendations, 271–272
  special identities, 271
  special permissions, 272–275
  table of basic, 268–269
  Take Ownership, 273
  Traverse Folder/Execute File, 273
  troubleshooting, 281
  Users identity, 271
  viewing, 268, 274
  Write, 269, 272
  Write Attributes, 273
Personal toolbar creation, 115–116
physical memory. *See* memory, physical
pinging networks, 328, 340
Plug and Play, 66, 434
pointers
  configuring settings, 84
  options, 121
Point-to-Point Protocol (PPP), 370
Point-to-Point Tunneling Protocol (PPTP),
  349, 370

policies
  Automatic Updates, table of, 23–24
  group. *See* GPOs (Group Policy Objects);
    group policies
  service packs, updating for, 11–12
pop-up blocker options, 405, 407–409, 417
Portable Laptop power scheme, 195
power settings
  accessing Power Options, 202
  alarms for, 193, 197–200
  Always On scheme, 195
  Ask Me What To Do option, 202
  behaviors, 193, 202
  creating schemes, 196–197
  default schemes for laptops, 195–196
  deleting schemes, 197
  Full Power scheme, 195
  hibernation, 194, 202
  High Power scheme, 195
  Home/Office Desk scheme, 195
  laptop issues, 193–203
  Long Life scheme, 195
  Max Battery scheme, 196
  meters, 193, 200–201
  Minimal Power Management scheme, 195
  monitors, for, 129–131
  multiple schemes for laptops, 195
  Normal scheme, 195
  passwords, 202
  Portable Laptop scheme, 195
  Presentation scheme, 195
  schemes, 193–197
  sleep button, 202
  standby mode, 194, 202
  System hibernates mode, 194
  System standby mode, 194
  Turn off hard disks mode, 194
  Turn off monitor mode, 194
Power Users group, 163, 165
PPP (Point-to-Point Protocol), 370
PPPoE (Point-to-Point Protocol over
  Ethernet), 370
PPTP (Point-to-Point Tunneling Protocol),
  349, 370
Presentation power scheme, 195
primary partitions
  active, 242
  conversions to dynamic volumes, 244
  creating, 247
  defined, 233, 239
printers
  PRINT$ share, 293
  Start menu, options for, 101
Privacy settings, 403–404
private IP addresses, 207–208, 328
Problem Devices node, 29
processor scheduling options, 52, 419–420
profiles, hardware. *See* hardware profiles

Program Compatibility Wizard, 148–149
program installation
  16-bit programs, 147
  Add Or Remove Programs, 142–143
  alternate credentials, 146
  assignment method, 143, 144
  Autorun, 140
  compatibility check, 141
  Group Policy for, 143–145
  InstallShield, 140
  Microsoft Windows Installer, 140
  MS-DOS programs, 147
  .msi files, 144
  networks, from, 143–145, 297
  permission requirements, 141–142
  process overview, 139
  publishing applications, 144
  registry clean up, 154–155
  reinstalling, 151
  restore point creation, 141
  selectivity of users issues, 145–146, 155
  setup programs, 140
  Setup.exe, 140
  troubleshooting, 142
  uninstalling, 151–156
  Wise Install, 140
programs. *See also* applications
  Compatibility Wizard, 148–149
  installing. *See* program installation
  Program menu, 104–105
  publishing, 144
  startup, managing, 111, 422
properties
  displaying, 118
  file, viewing, 477–478
  system. *See* system properties
proxy servers
  address selection, 363
  automatic configuration for connections,
    361–362
  exceptions list, 363
  Internet Explorer settings, 400–402
  Intranet requests, 401
  manual configuration for connections,
    362–363
  policy, 417
  port settings, 363, 401
  remote access, 361–363
public certificates, 161
publishing applications, 144
purpose of Windows XP Professional, 3

Q

QoS Packet Scheduler, 370, 371
Quick Launch toolbar
  customizing, 113–114
  defined, 113
  Show Desktop button, 114–115

R

RAID level 0, 239
Read & Execute permission, 269, 272
Read Attributes permission, 273
Read permission, 269, 272, 283
Read Permissions permission, 273
recording device configuration, 87
recovery. *See* System Recovery; System
    Restore
Recycle Bin
    deleting by bypassing, 475
    Display Confirmation Dialog policy, 296
    emptying, 38
    icon for, 468
refresh rates, 136–137
refreshing windows, 118
regional settings, 91
registry
    failed installations, cleanup after, 154–155
    InProgress keys, 154
    Welcome Screen account visibility, 172
reinstalling Windows XP, 456–457
remote access
    broadband connections, 357–358
    Client For Microsoft Networks, 370, 371
    component configuration, 370–372
    connecting for, 191–192
    dial-up connections, 350–357
    File And Printer Sharing, 370, 371, 377, 434
    identity validation, 368–370
    modem pools, 347–348
    policies for, 224
    proxy servers, configuring, 361–363
    Remote Assistance. *See* Remote Assistance
    Remote Desktop, 27, 163, 190–192, 434
    smart card validation, 369, 370
    VPNs for. *See* VPNs (virtual private
        networks)
    wireless. *See* wireless networking
Remote Assistance
    acceptance timeouts, 452
    accepting invitations, 450–451
    buddy list invitations, 446, 447
    configuring, 189–190
    connections, 446
    defined, 15, 36
    deleting invitations, 453
    e-mail invitations, 446, 447
    e-mail options, 225
    expiring invitations, 453
    file invitations, 446, 447
    firewalls with, 434, 446
    format of invitations, 449
    HelpAssistant account, 161
    invitation creation, 447–449
    invitation types, 445–446
    level options, 225
    messages in invitations, 447

MSN invitations, 446, 447
MsRcIncident files, 446, 450
offering to users, 449–450
passwords, 446, 449, 450
policies, 224–226
preventing, 226
protocol, 446
purpose, 445
resending invitations, 453
session initiation, 445
status of invitations, checking, 452
time limit options, 225
time to live for invitations, 448
remote computers, viewing system
    information for, 31
Remote Desktop
    configuring, 190–192
    firewalls with, 434
    Interactive identity, 271
    Help Session Manager, 12
    Users group, 163
removable storage devices
    Active status, 241
    disk quota policies, 215
    formatting, 472
    listing, 234
Remove Access To Use All Windows Update
    Features policy, 24
renaming items, 118, 475
repairing Windows XP, 456–457
repeat options, keyboard, 83
Replicators group, 164
Re-prompt for Restart With Scheduled
    Installations policy, 24
Reschedule Automatic Updates Scheduled
    Installations policy, 24
reset disks for passwords, 170–171, 178
resolution of monitor screens, 135–136, 149
restarts, troubleshooting, 456
restore points, 459–462
restoring data, 321
restoring system configurations. *See* System
    Restore
restricted accounts, 176
Restricted Sites zone, 409, 416–417
right-clicking mice, 7
Robust Security Network (RSN), 380
rogue programs, uninstalling, 155–156
rollbacks
    device drivers, 76–77
    shadow copies for, 321
    system. *See* System Restore
RSN (Robust Security Network), 380
RSTRUI.EXE, 37
Run At Once List, 231
Run command, 101
Run These Programs At User Logon policy,
    231

S

Safe Mode, 44, 453–454
scheduling tasks
  accounts, 439
  deleting tasks, 444
  disabling tasks, 443
  enabling tasks, 443
  errors during task creation, 442
  interval selection, 440
  moving tasks between systems, 443–444
  naming tasks, 440
  one time only tasks, 441
  properties of tasks, changing, 442
  running tasks immediately, 443
  Scheduled Task Wizard, 439
  Scheduled Tasks folder, 439
  startup tasks, 441
  task creation, 440–442
  Task Scheduler, 439
  troubleshooting, 444
  viewing tasks, 439
Schtasks tool, 439
screen resolution, 135–136, 149
screen savers
  options in themes, 121
  password configuration, 128
  purpose, 127
  resource usage reduction, 129
script policies
  configuring recommendations, 227–228
  logoff script assignment, 229
  logon script assignment, 229
  recommendations, 227
  shutdown script assignment, 228–229
  startup script assignment, 228–229
  synchronicity, 226
  table of, 226–227
  types of, listed, 226
  visibility, 226–227
  wait times, 226
  writing scripts, 226
searching
  keyboard shortcut, 118
  search bar, customizing, 388–389
Secure Logon, 179
security
  authentication, 271, 368–370
  Event Viewer, 438
  file. *See* file security
  firewalls. *See* firewalls; Windows Firewall
  groups, 162
  Internet Explorer options, 404–405
  levels, Internet Explorer, 410–411
  log, 437–438
  permissions. *See* permissions
  Service Pack 2, 8–9
  tool, 430–432
  wireless issues, 379–380

workgroups vs. domains, 8
zones. *See* security zones, Internet
    Explorer
Security Center, 430–432
Security log
  accessing, 438
  defined, 437
security zones, Internet Explorer
  Binary And Script Behaviors, 409
  Disable The Security Page policy, 412
  Do Not Allow Users To Add/Delete Sites
    policy, 412
  Do Not Allow Users To Change Policies
    policy, 412
  group policies, 411–413
  HTTPS specification, 415
  importance, 409
  Internet zone, 410, 413–414
  Local Intranet zone, 410, 414–415
  local machine policy, 412
  purpose, 409
  Restricted Sites zone, 409, 416–417
  security levels, table of, 410–411
  Trusted Sites zone, 410, 415–416
  Use Only Machine Settings policy, 412
selecting all, 118
selective startup mode, 43
server configuration options, 53
Service Pack 2
  Automatic Updates changes, 21
  device drivers, 70
  drivers, changes for, 67
  firewall changes, 8
  Internet Explorer changes, 404–409
  Internet options changes, 8
  maintenance changes, 8, 9
  memory management changes, 8
  networking changes, 8
  NX feature, 9
  security changes, 8–9
service packs, group policies for, 11–12
services
  disabling for startup, 47–48
  managing, tool for, 13
  Services node, 12–13
Setup.exe, 140
shadow copies
  command line tool, 321
  copying, 321
  defined, 13, 318
  Maximum Size option, 320
  mount points, 321
  number allowed, 319
  placement, 319
  requirements for clients, 319
  restoring, 321
  scheduling options, 320
  servers, configuring on, 319–320

space requirements, 319
viewing, 320–321
VolRest, 321
sharing files. *See* file sharing
shell extensions, 296
shortcuts
  creating, 118
  keyboard, 118–119
  menus, 118
  Unused Desktop Shortcuts, 127
Show Desktop button, 114–115
shutdowns
  powering off, 456
  script policies, 226, 228–229
  Shut Down right, disabling, 188
  troubleshooting, 456
SIDs (security identifiers)
  defined, 160
  disk quota SIDs, 311
  groups assigned to, 163
  user accounts assigned to, 160
signatures, 37, 42
SIGVERIF.EXE, 37, 42
simple file sharing, 266, 267
simple logon policies, 231
Simple Network Time Protocol (SNTP), 93
Simple Start menu
  adding items, 104
  Administrative Tools, adding, 106–107
  Advanced tab, 102–103
  changing to Classic Start menu, 99–100
  command display options, 102
  customizing, 102–103
  defined, 4–6
  frequently used programs options, 102
  General tab, 102
  icon size options, 102
  icons, default desktop, 123
  pinned items, 104
  Recent Documents option, 103
  removing items from, 104
  submenus on mouse hover option, 102
simple volumes
  creating, 251–254
  defined, 234
site group policies, 211
sleep button, 202
sleep mode. *See* standby mode
SLIP (Serial Line Internet Protocol), 370
smart cards, 369, 370
snapshots, system recovery, 455
snapshots, System Restore, 459–462
SNTP (Simple Network Time Protocol), 93
Software Environment area, 30
sound
  effects, configuring, 90
  events, setting in themes, 121

hardware acceleration, 88–89
multiple devices, configuring, 91
quality, 88–89
recording device configuration, 87
sample rate conversion, 88–89
speaker configuration, 87–88
utility for controlling, 85
volume control, 85–87
spanned volumes
  advantages, 239
  conversions to dynamic disks, 244
  creating, 251
  defined, 234
speaker configuration, 87–88
special identities, 271
special permissions, 272–275
special shares, 292–293
Specify Intranet Microsoft Update Service
    Location policy, 24
spyware, removing, 155–156
Standard accounts, 176
standard file sharing
  Change permission, 283
  enabling, 282
  Full Control permission, 282
  group permissions, 283
  permissions, 282–283
  purpose, 266–267
  Read permission, 283
  security issues, 283
standby mode, 194, 202
Start menu
  adding items, 104–106
  Administrative Tools, adding, 101,
      106–107
  arranging items, 104
  changing views, 6, 99–100
  classic version. *See* Classic Start menu
  command display options, 102
  customizing Classic menus, 100–101
  customizing simple, 102–103
  deleting items, 105
  drag-and-drop, 101
  folders, 103–104, 105
  frequently used programs options, 102
  icon size options, 102
  icons, default desktop, 123
  keyboard shortcut for displaying, 118, 119
  pinned items, 104
  Program menu, 104–105
  Recent Documents option, 103
  removing from, 104
  renaming items, 105
  representation of, 103–104, 105
  simple version. *See* Simple Start menu
  Startup folder, 105
  submenus on mouse hover option, 102

Startup folder
  defined, 105
  managing programs in, 111
startups
  applications launched at, disabling, 46–47,
    422
  modes, 43–44
  policies, 210, 230–232
  properties, setting, 57–58
  run-once lists, 232
  Safe Mode, 453–454
  script policies, 226, 228–229
  Stop errors, 457–459
  tasks scheduled at, 441
  troubleshooting, 453–459
static IP addresses, 328–332
Status utility
  Advanced System Information, 27
  defined, 16-17, 27
  troubleshooting using, 18
  viewing statistics, 17
Stop errors, 457–459
striped volumes
  advantages, 239
  conversions to dynamic disks, 244
  creating, 251
subnet masks
  alternate private IP addresses using, 208
  configuring, 329
  disconnected networks, 341
  private network addresses, 328
  viewing, 338
Support account, 161
support services features, 12–13
SVCHOST.EXE, 16
system cache, 52
System Checkpoint snapshots, 61
system configuration
  files, 44–45
  viewing, 28
System Configuration Utility
  boot options, 45–46
  configuration files, changing, 44–45
  defined, 42
  purpose, 36
  services, disabling, 47–48
  startup applications, disabling, 46–47
  startup modes, 43–44
  tasks managed by, list of, 42
system environment variables. *See*
  environment variables
System Health statistics, 28
System hibernates mode, 194
system information
  accessing advanced information, 31
  Advanced System Information, 27, 29–31
  Applications area, 30

  components data, 29
  Conflicts/Sharing node, 29
  general information, viewing, 28
  hardware resources, 28–29
  Internet Settings area, 30
  Microsoft software installed, listing, 28
  MSINFO32.EXE, 29–31
  My Computer Information, 27, 28–29
  Problem Devices node, 29
  property settings. *See* system properties
  Software Environment area, 30
  Status utility, 27
  System Health statistics, 28
  System Information tool, 29–31
  System Summary node, 30
  tools, 27–28, 36–37
System log
  accessing, 438
  defined, 437
  Stop errors, 457
System menus for windows, 118
system properties
  application performance options, 52
  Automatic Updates options, 64
  computer name, 49–50
  DEP options, 55–56
  environment variables, 56–57
  error reporting properties, 60
  general system information, tab for, 49
  memory usage options, 52
  network identification, 50
  performance options, 51–52
  processor scheduling options, 52
  recovery options, 59
  startup properties, 57–58
  system cache options, 52
  System Restore options, 60–64
  tool for managing, 49
  virtual memory options, 53–54
  visual effects options, 51–52
System Recovery, 454–456
System Restore
  defined, 12, 37
  policies, configuring, 217–218
  program installation, creating before, 141
  restore points, 459–462
  setting options, 60–64
  updating drivers, 67
  troubleshooting using, 459–462
System standby mode, 194
System Summary node, 30
system time. *See* Internet time
system tray. *See* notification area
System utility
  Advanced tab, 50–60
  application performance options, 52
  Automatic Updates tab, 64

Computer Name tab, 49–50
DEP options, 55–56
environment variables, 56–57
error reporting properties, 60
General tab, 49
Hardware tab, 50
memory usage options, 52
network identification, 50
performance options, 51–52
processor scheduling options, 52
purpose, 49
recovery options, 59
Remote tab, 64
startup properties, 57–58
system cache options, 52
System Restore tab, 60–64
virtual memory options, 53–54
visual effects options, 51–52
system volumes, 241
SYSTEM.INI, 44
%SystemRoot%, 16

T

tabbing, 119
Take Ownership permission, 273
Task Manager
  resource based errors, 458
  rogue program detection with, 156
  troubleshooting with, 456
Task Scheduler, 439
task scheduling. *See* scheduling tasks
taskbar
  Address toolbar, 108, 113
  Auto Hide feature, 109
  custom toolbars, list of, 113
  default appearance, 108
  Desktop toolbar, 113
  displaying toolbars, 113
  grouping items, 109–110
  hidden, making visible, 109
  importance of, 107–108
  keeping on top, 109
  Links toolbar, 113
  locking, 109
  moving, 108
  name labels for toolbars, 113
  notification area, 110–112
  personal toolbar creation, 115–116
  Quick Launch toolbar, 113–114
  resizing, 108
  Show Desktop button, 114–115
  system tray. *See* notification area
  unlocking, 109
  visibility options, 109
TCP/IP (Transmission Control Protocol/
    Internet Protocol)
  addressing. *See* IP addressing

diagnostic tools, 344–346
dynamic IP address configuration, 330
firewalls, 435–436
installation, 326–327
pinging, 340
policies, 224
remote access, configuring for, 370
static IP address configuration, 329
WINS configuration, 335
temporary files, 38
temporary Internet files, 38, 402–404
themes
  color schemes, 131
  defined, 6
  fonts, 131
  setting with Display utility, 6–7
threads, 41
time
  Internet. *See* Internet time
  settings, 92–98
  Windows Time service, 13, 92–96
toolbars
  Address, 113
  creating Personal, 115–116
  Desktop, 113
  displaying, 113
  Links, 113
  list of, 113
  name labels, 113
  Quick Launch, 113–114
  Show Desktop button, 114–115
tools
  Administrative Tools, 4, 101, 106–107
  Backup tool, 36
  Computer Management. *See* Computer
    Management console
  DirectX Diagnostic, 37
  Disk Cleanup, 36, 37–39
  Disk Defragmenter, 36, 424–425
  Disk Management. *See* Disk Management
    Tool
  DiskPart, 238, 243
  Dr. Watson, 37, 39–41
  File Signature Verification, 37, 42
  Hardware Troubleshooter, 80
  Network Diagnostics, 36, 37, 345
  Remote Assistance. *See* Remote Assistance
  System Configuration, 36, 42–48
  System Restore. *See* System Restore
Traverse Folder/Execute File permission,
    273
Triple DES encryption, 428
troubleshooting
  dial-up connections, 375
  Dr. Watson, 37, 39–41
  hard disks, 262–264
  hardware devices, 80–82
  IP addressing, 341

troubleshooting, *continued*
  Remote Assistance. *See* Remote Assistance
  repairing XP, 456–457
  Safe Mode, 453–454
  services, disabling, 47–48
  startup applications, 46–47
  startup modes, 43–44
  startup problems, 453–459
  Stop errors, 457–459
  system recovery, 454–456
  System Restore, 459–462
truncated file names, 466
Trusted Sites zone, 410, 415–416
Turn Off Hard Disks mode, 194
Turn Off Monitor mode, 194

U

UDP, firewalls with, 435–436
undo, 119
uninstalling drivers, 77, 79
uninstalling programs
  adware, 155–156
  basic process for, 151–152
  clearing all user profiles, 155
  registry clean up, 154–155
  rogue programs, 155–156
  spyware, 155–156
  troubleshooting overview, 152
  Windows Installer Clean Up, 152–153
  Windows Installer Zapper, 153–154
updates, automatic. *See* Automatic Updates
URLs (Uniform Resource Locators)
  Favorites, 389–391
  Group Policy, customizing with, 388–391
  home pages, setting, 388–389
  search bar pages, setting, 388–389
User Account utility, 165–166
user accounts
  Computer Administrator, 164
  creating, 183–184
  defaults installed, 161, 164–165
  defined, 159
  deleting, 188
  domain. *See* domain user accounts
  domain vs. local, 160
  domain vs. workgroup, 164
  enabling, 187
  Limited, 164–165
  local. *See* local user accounts
  logon names, 160
  passwords, 161, 167–171
  public certificates, 161
  renaming, 188
  security issues, 165
  selecting access levels, 166
  SIDs, 160
  user names, 160
  workgroup user access levels, 164–165

User Accounts Wizard
  adding new users, 176–177
  changing access levels, 177–178
  managing passwords with, 180–182
  password assignment with, 167–168
user environment variables. *See* environment
    variables
user experience features, 9–10
user names, 160
user profiles, 51
Users group, 164
Users identity, 271

V

video adapters
  checking settings, 132
  color matching, 137–138
  determining model, 133
  drivers for, 133–134
  installing drivers, 134
  memory, impact of, 135
  refresh rates, 136–137
video settings
  application-specific, setting, 149
  checking, 132
  drivers, 133–134
  Program Compatibility Wizard for, 149
virtual memory
  configuration options, 53–54
  management options, 420
virtual private networks. *See* VPNs (virtual
    private networks)
virus protection, 431
visual effects, performance considerations,
    51–52, 420
VolRest, 321
Volume Shadow Copy. *See* shadow copies
volumes
  active, 241, 242–243
  basic, 233
  boot, 241
  cluster size, 254
  compression option, 254
  creating simple, 251–254
  defined, 234
  deleting, 258–259
  disk quotas, enabling on, 311–313
  drive letter assignment, 253, 256–257
  dynamic. *See* dynamic volumes
  extending dynamic, 254–255
  file system selection, 254
  formatting, 253–254, 255–256
  labeling, 250, 254, 257–258
  mounting in NTFS folders, 253
  NTFS, converting to, 259–260
  quick format option, 254
  shadow copies, 318–321
  simple. *See* simple volumes

size of, setting, 252
spanned. *See* spanned volumes
status messages, 264
striped. *See* striped volumes
system, 241
VPNs (virtual private networks)
accessing, 376–377
broadband, 348
connection creation, 358–359
defined, 347, 348
dial-up connections, 349
file and print sharing issues, 377
host name errors, 377
IP address problems, 377
primary connections, 359
protocol support errors, 377
protocols, 349, 370
security issues, 349
troubleshooting, 377–378

W
wallpaper, desktop, 122
WBEM (Web Based Enterprise
Management) log files, 33–34
Web Client/Publisher temporary files, 38
Web pages, configuring offline files as,
306–309
Welcome Screen
Administrator logons, 175
enabling, 173
fast user switching, 174–175
hidden accounts, 172
logging on with, 172
permission for changing options, 174
policies, 230, 231
purpose, 172
special accounts user list, 172
WEP (Wireless Equivalency Protection), 380
Wi-Fi Protected Access (WPA), 380
Windows Classic theme, 121
Windows Explorer
accessing, 467
advanced option configuration, 295–296
CD burning features, 297
Classic Shell option, 297
compressed file display, 469
Contents pane, 467–468
context menus, removing, 297
copying files and folders, 473–474
copying floppy disks, 472
creating folders, 475
custom folder views, 471
Cut command, 474
deleting files or folders, 475
Desktop icon, 468
Details option, 467
DFS tab, 297

drive properties, viewing, 475–477
expanding folders, 469
Explorer Bar, 467
File menu, removing, 297
file type associations with, 299–300
Filmstrip option, 467
Folder Options menus, removing, 297
Folder Tasks view, 470
folder templates, 470
folder views, global, 471–472
folders, sharing with, 284–286
formatting disks from, 472
Hardware tab, removing, 297
hidden file display, 469
hiding drives in, 296, 298–299
icon options, 467
icons, meanings of, 468–469
List option, 467
Manage command removal, 296
modifying view panes, 467
moving files and folders, 474–475
My Recent Documents, 296
network drives for sharing folders,
291–292
network installations options, 297
offline files, enabling computers for,
304–305
Offline Files folder options, 305
pasting files and folders, 474
policies for, 296–298
Prevent Access To Drives policy, 296,
298–299
properties of files and folders, viewing,
477–478
purpose of, 466
renaming files or folders, 475
Search button, removing, 297
Security tab, removing, 297
selecting files and folders, 473
shadow copies, viewing, 320
shared folders, accessing, 289
Status Bar, 467
Thumbnails option, 467
toolbar options, 467
view panes, 467
Windows Firewall. *See also* firewalls
application exemptions, 434
connection configuration, 433
defaults, 432
enabling, 432–433
exceptions configuration, 434–436
File And Printer Sharing, 434
FTP port exemptions, 435–436
HTTP port exemptions, 435–436
laptop configuration, 433
mode of action, 432
Plug and Play with, 434

Windows Firewall, *continued*
  policies, 432
  purpose, 432
  remote access, 372–373
  Remote Assistance, 434
  Remote Assistance ports, 446
  Remote Desktop, 434
  restoring settings, 437
  Security Center with, 431
  TCP port exemptions, 435–436
  UDP port exemptions, 435–436
Windows Installer
  Clean Up, 152–153
  defined, 13
  Zapper, 153–154
Windows Internet Naming Service. *See*
    WINS (Windows Internet Naming
    Service
WINDOWS key, shortcuts for, 119
Windows Management Instrumentation. *See*
    WMI (Windows Management
    Instrumentation)
Windows Time service, 13, 92–96
Windows Update
  automatic. *See* Automatic Updates
  policies for searches, 73–74
  showing installed updates, 150
WIN.INI, 44
WINS (Windows Internet Naming Service),
    334–336, 340
Wireless Equivalency Protection (WEP), 380
wireless networking
  802.11 specification, 378–379
  access points, 378
  ad hoc mode, 381, 385
  adapters, 378, 381
  availability testing, 383
  base stations, 378
  configuring, 383–384
  connections, 381–382
  defined, 347
  drivers for adapters, 381
  infrastructure mode, 381, 385
  IP address assignment, 382

  keys, 381
  network adapters, 378, 381
  poor connections, 382
  preferred access order, 383–384
  RSN, 380
  security issues, 379–380
  signal strength, 382–383
  technologies, 378–379
  troubleshooting, 382–383
  USB adapters, 381
  WEP, 380
  WPA, 380
Wise Install, 140
WMI (Windows Management
    Instrumentation)
  Advanced tab, 32
  Backup/Restore tab, 32
  Control, accessing, 31–32
  credentials, setting, 33
  defined, 13
  General tab, 32
  log settings, 33–35
  Logging tab, 32
  MOF, 33
  repository, 35–36
  Security tab, 32
  Status utility, gathering data for, 16–18
  storage requirements, 32
  system information dependence on, 28
  tabs of Control, 32
workgroups
  account security issues, 165
  Computer Administrator account, 164
  default user accounts, 164–165
  Internet time configuration, 97–98
  Limited account, 164–165
  passwords, 167–169
  user access levels, 164–165
  user account types, selecting, 166
  User Account utility, 165–166
  user password recovery, 169–171
WPA (Wi-Fi Protected Access), 380
Write Attributes permission, 273
Write permission, 269, 272

About the Author

William R. Stanek (williamstanek@aol.com) has more than 20 years of hands-on experience with advanced programming and development. He is a leading technology expert and an award-winning author. Through the years, his practical advice has helped millions of programmers, developers, and network engineers all over the world. He has written more than 25 computer books. His current or forthcoming books include *Microsoft Windows Command-Line Administrator's Pocket Consultant*, *Microsoft Windows 2000 Administrator's Pocket Consultant, Second Edition*, *Microsoft Windows Server 2003 Administrator's Pocket Consultant*, and *Microsoft IIS 6.0 Administrator's Pocket Consultant*.

Mr. Stanek has been involved in the commercial Internet community since 1991. His core business and technology experience comes from more than 11 years of military service. He has substantial experience in developing server technology, encryption, and Internet solutions. He has written many technical white papers and training courses on a wide variety of topics. He is widely sought after as a subject matter expert.

Mr. Stanek has an M.S. with distinction in information systems and a B.S. magna cum laude in computer science. He is proud to have served in the Persian Gulf War as a combat crewmember on an electronic warfare aircraft. He flew on numerous combat missions into Iraq and was awarded nine medals for his wartime service, including one of the United States' highest flying honors, the Air Force Distinguished Flying Cross. Currently, he resides in the Pacific Northwest with his wife and children.